UNDERSTANDING POLICING

EDITED BY
K.R.E. McCORMICK & L.A. VISANO

CANADIAN SCHOLARS' PRESS   TORONTO   1992

Understanding Policing

First published in 1992 by
Canadian Scholars' Press
180 Bloor St. W., Ste. 402
Toronto, Ontario
M5S 2V6

Canadian Cataloguing in Publication Data

Main entry under title:

Understanding Policing

Includes bibliographical references.
ISBN   1-55130-005-2

1. Police – Canada. 2. Law enforcement – Canada.
I. McCormick, Kevin R.E., 1965-. II. Visano, L.A.

HV8157.U63   1992   363.2'0971   C92-095450-2

Printed in Canada

DEDICATION

To Fulvia,

Remembering with gratitude
the countless lessons of love
that only a twin could impart,

L. A. V.

ACKNOWLEDGEMENTS

This endeavour would never have been possible without the assistance of many people to whom we remain deeply indebted. Firstly we would like to thank the contributors, who representing the leading scholars in the area, bring to the project theoretically and methodologically challenging perspectives. We also would like to thank the many police officers and members of various communities, whose experiences were crucial in informing the contributors and editors as to the dynamic nature of policing. To them we extend our appreciation and gratitude.

Further we are indebted to a number of colleagues and friends for the encouragement afforded the editors during various phases of the book. To Bill Bateman, Robert Doyle, Carol La Prairie, Pam MacDonald, Don MaGee, Wolf Mrusek, Mary Petri, Brenda Presley, Thomas Seager, and Alex Williamson, for their discussions concerning the shape of the text. And to the many students at both York University and University of Toronto, who gave of their time and experience in providing the editors with comments on numerous stages of the book.

We would also like to thank the publisher, Jack Wayne, for undertaking to publish this work and for maintaining the integrity of the theoretical, methodological and substantive concerns of both the editors and contributors.

This work would never have been possible without the expertise of Pamela Hamilton, whose professionalism, diligence and sincerity, served as a constant inspiration to the editors.

Finally and most importantly we would like to thank our families,

Anthony, we thank you for grounding our appreciation of the expansive definitions of policing;

Renee, your compassion and insights continue to provide our work clarity and meaning;

Robynne, we are grateful for your ongoing encouragement and unconditional support during this and other projects;

And to our loving parents Doris, Maria, Gino and Ken, words fail to capture the depths of our love.

TABLE OF CONTENTS

DEDICATION..III

ACKNOWLEDGEMENTS IV

FOREWORD IX
Wesley Crichlow

PREFACE XI
K.R.E.McCormick and L.A.Visano
Policing Understanding: Cultural Controls
and Contesting Contexts

A. OVERVIEW 1

CHAPTER ONE 3
Maureen Cain:
Trends in the Sociology of Police Work

CHAPTER TWO 33
Jerome Skolnick
Democratic Order and The Rule of Law

CHAPTER THREE 57
Allan Silver
The Demand for Civil Order in Civil Society:
A Review of Some Themes in the History of Urban
Crime, Police, and Riot

B. HISTORY 83

CHAPTER FOUR 85
T.A.Critchley
The New Police in London 1750-1830

CHAPTER FIVE 113
J. Daniel Devlin: "Police History"

CHAPTER SIX **129**

Sidney L. Harring and Lorraine M. McMullin:
The Buffalo Police 1872-1900:
Labour Unrest, Political Power
and the Creation of the Police Institution

CHAPTER SEVEN **151**

Leon Radzinowicz
That Strange Word "Police"

C. ROLES, DOMAINS AND POWERS **161**

CHAPTER EIGHT **163**

Richard V. Ericson
The Police as Reproducers of Order

CHAPTER NINE **209**

Clifford D. Shearing and Jeffrey S. Leon
Reconsidering the Police Role:
A Challenge to a Challenge of a Popular Conception

CHAPTER TEN **229**

Kevin R.E. McCormick and Livy A. Visano
Regulating An Urban Order:
Policing Pathologies in the Carceral City (Original Paper)

D. DISCRETION, STYLES AND ENCOUNTERS 247

CHAPTER ELEVEN **249**

David H. Bayley and James Garofalo
The Management of Violence By Police Patrol Officers

CHAPTER TWELVE **277**

Jean-Paul Brodeur
High Policing and Low Policing:
Remarks About the Policing of Political Activities

CHAPTER THIRTEEN **301**

Richard E. Sykes and John P. Clark
A Theory of Deference Exchange
in Police-Civilian Encounters

CHAPTER FOURTEEN 323
Thomas O'Reilly-Fleming
Policing Serial Murder:
The Politics of Negligence (Original Paper)

E. DEVIANCE AND SUBCULTURES 347
CHAPTER FIFTEEN 349
Clifford D. Shearing
Subterranean Processes in the Maintenance of Power:
An Examination of the Mechanisms
Coordinating Police Action

CHAPTER SIXTEEN 371
Gary M. O'Bireck
A Canadian Metropolitan Police Force:
An Exploratory Case Study into Application,
Training and Advancement Procedures:
Subcultural Perspectives (Original Paper)

F. ACCOUNTABILITY AND CONTROL 395
CHAPTER SEVENTEEN 397
Alan Grant
The Control of Police Behaviour

CHAPTER EIGHTEEN 433
Philip C. Stenning
The Role of Police Boards and Commissions
as Institutions of Municipal Police Governance

G. PROTECTING PROFIT 489
CHAPTER NINETEEN 491
Bruce C. Johnson
Taking Care of Labor:
The Police in American Politics

CHAPTER TWENTY 521
Clifford D. Shearing and Philip C. Stenning
Private Security: Implications For Social Control

CHAPTER TWENTY-ONE 545

Steven Spitzer and Andrew T. Scull
Privatization and Capitalist Development:
The Case of the Private Police

CHAPTER TWENTY-TWO 563

Donald W. Scott
Policing Corporate Collusion

CHAPTER TWENTY-THREE 597

Willem DeLint
Inclusionary Strategies (Original Paper)

H. PROSPECTS AND PARADOXES 623

CHAPTER TWENTY-FOUR 625

Jim Harding
Policing and Aboriginal Justice

CHAPTER TWENTY-FIVE 647

Dan McIntyre
Race Relations and Policing

CHAPTER TWENTY-SIX 657

Mimi H. Silbert
Job Stress and Burnout of New Police Officers

CHAPTER TWENTY-SEVEN 665

Robynne S. Neugebauer
Misogyny, Law and the Police:
Policing Violence Against Women (Original Paper)

CHAPTER TWENTY-EIGHT 677

André Normandeau and Barry Leighton
Some Important Challenges

FOREWORD

The examination of policing whether it be from a regional, national or international perspective, requires of the individual an appreciation and comprehension of the multi-facetted system under which policing exists. On numerous occasions a critical scrutiny of these processes is abandoned, in turn adopting a superficial reiteration of the prevailing political rhetoric. Ignoring the diverse constituencies which comprise Canadian society, the study of Policing has neglected to invoke an interdisciplinary approach to the investigation. Issues such as Homophobia, Sexism, Racism and the general misogynistic ideologies of the dominant culture have established themselves as the fundamental canons upon which most criminological investigations have been scripted.

In *Understanding Policing*, McCormick and Visano have compiled a dynamic collection of articles representing diverse disciplines including: History, Sociology, Criminology, Penology and Race Relations. This collection of articles, while acknowledging the contributions of past research, affords the reader with the substantive foundation upon which a critical exploration of current problems facing policing may be engaged. Rather than merely manufacture echoes or sentiments of the past, the contributors individually express diverse accounts of aspects of policing rarely addressed in other texts. Further, collectively the articles present the reader with a dynamic constellation which empowers them with the substantive knowledge and the analytic skills with which to formulate a comprehensive understanding of the complex nature of policing.

While most works in discussing the current state of policing are quite focussed upon a specific audience, McCormick and Visano in *Understanding Policing* challenge diverse constituencies. Students engaging in the discussion of policing for the first time will find the collection highly accessible and a powerfully interrogative introduction. Clearly, those currently involved in the discussion will find the articles both methodologically and theoretically diverse, thereby allowing them to develop for themselves conceptual frameworks with which to conduct their own investigation of various aspects of police processes. Practitioners will find the collection beneficial. For in presenting a myriad of accounts of police forces and practices, those in the field will gain a new appreciation for the unique nuances inherent in policing. Finally, the various communities with whom the police regularly interact will find the text empowering, as it informs them of the often overlooked intricacies of policing from

an introspective approach, establishing the foundation upon which more critical and dynamic discussions of policing may originate.

Throughout my many years of experience as both a community activist
and a former worker within the Criminal Justice System, policing has always
remained a contentious point for a large number of community agencies oriented towards social justice issues. McCormick and Visano provide the reader
with a compilation of powerful articles which respond directly to many of the
concerns currently surrounding the critical discussion of Policing.
Understanding Policing stands as a testament to the concern of the contributors and editors to present the discussion of Policing with engagingly confrontational and challenging insights, which transcend traditional rhetoric and
liberal posturing. Knowledge of the domains, discretion, authority and independence of the police serves as a catalyst for social change. To fully engage
in a dialogue with the police on a number of issues, ranging from racism, sexism, homophobia and classism, is an ambitious and honourable endeavour.

WESLEY CRICHLOW
EXECUTIVE DIRECTOR,
CONSORTIUM ON YOUTH EMPOWERMENT

PREFACE

POLICING UNDERSTANDING: CULTURAL CONTROLS AND CONTESTING CONTEXTS

The subject of policing is a problematic discourse that defies simplistic interpretations. The phenomenon of policing is about exclusion, resistance and accommodations contextualized within the intersections of culture, political economy and history. Moreover, policing, as an exercise of control, fundamentally consists of privilege.

Policing is celebrated quite rhetorically as a forum of public protection inviting the unequivocal support and participation of a consensually oriented society. Images of policing as crime prevention, law enforcement, social service and peace keeping predominate as cultural markers designed to mirror a generic deference to the authority of civil societies. The dominant order, however, scripts policing as a commodity that is marketable and profitable for those who have a stake in conformity. Who, for example, benefits from police discretionary practices? What do police decisions produce and re-produce in terms of existing hegemonic imperatives? What elements of the dominant culture define the appropriateness of policing? Alternatively, how exploitative are policing systems generally of various cultural values. Policing is contextualized culturally, mediated politically and articulated legally.

But, confining discussions of policing to a legal narrative is a meaningless exercise that forecloses any possibility of social justice discourses which presumably must implicate such dynamic features as history and political economy. The ongoing chatter about the police in terms of their juridic roles as rule enforcers within a criminal "justice" system mystifies, trivializes and distracts from a much needed public consciousness and debate.

Policing is far too serious a subject matter to leave in the hands of self-proclaimed police and legal spokespeople. It is also subject matter that moves beyond the dubious celebration of sensational criminal investigations. Rather the study of policing confronts directly the basis of social order, the nature of society and the interpretations of challenges.

Policing is a process of producing the "other," that is the marginalized other who is transformed into a prospective suspect, accused and convict. The nature of the other is determined by the shape of the dominant discourses, legal and cultural. In general, traditional approaches to policing tend to assign primacy to a binary code, artificially bifurcated categories for multi-layered identities or phenomena. For example, policing involves more than either/or decisions about right or wrong, guilt or innocence; rather the police officer is both the *acted subject* and the *subjected actor,* constituting and constituted within the politics of difference and the defiance of deference. Theoretically, the police officer within sites of intervention is an active agent situated within wider constituting contexts. This agent of formal social control, as a cultural subject within discourses of power, is engaged in micro-political (local) struggles shaped by more macro-cultural (global) influences. Likewise, policing is a multiple subject, enjoying a plurality of meanings that are displaced and reconstructed in concert with other hegemonic reproductions of discipline. Policing, therefore, is both a political process and a politicized structure.

This volume of articles is the result of a careful scrutiny and painful appraisal of many studies which were felt to capture more fully the contexts, conditions and consequences of policing on numerous levels of analytic inquiry. This book reflects a commitment to the discipline, to the substantive subject, to undergraduate and graduate students who have for years approached us for providing more challenging directions, and to understanding the difficulties suffered by both the police and the policed.

It is the product of years of learning and teaching from a large number of undergraduate students at York University, University of Toronto and Ryerson who have insisted that a collection of readings from leading scholars in Canada, the U.K. and the U.S.A. is long overdue. Mainstream approaches in encyclopedic textbooks have failed to motivate criminological curiosities. Additionally, extant published empirical research on specific facets of policing remains challenging and focussed but fails to provide an overview based on various vantage points. Readers are urged to suspend, if not escape from prevalent common-sense assumptions about policing until they have, first, journeyed fully through this volume and second, participated actively in interrogating complex problematic relationships. In other words, readers are asked to locate themselves in the debates and struggles which characterize the study of policing, to ground their perceptions, to empower themselves conceptually and to engage in open dialogue. This book challenges the closure of canons within criminological theorizing. Traditional texts obscure more than they reveal, the concept of power remains mysteriously hidden behind the magic of facile reductionism. This book is oppositional, challenging the unitary, polarizing and totalizing view of traditional models which refuse to defy the defining gaze of legal/legitimate authoritative definitions. *Understanding Policing* is a political project that invites readers to position themselves ideologically and historically. Admittedly, this volume is a text typically inscribed in Anglo-centric traditions of privilege in order to demonstrate the origins of current Canadian police values and practices. This volume provides a variety of compelling theoretical formulations that need to be fully appreciated and assessed in order to develop an understanding of policing.

K.R.E.M & L.A.V   July, 1992.

EDITORS' BIOGRAPHIES

KEVIN R. E. MCCORMICK

Kevin McCormick is presently completing his doctoral dissertation in the department of Sociology at York University and is a Fellow of Bethune College. His work is directed at critically examining the corrigibility of traditional sociological theory and method to address the relationships between the offenders and the various law enforcement agents with whom they interact. Further, his research as demonstrated in *Canadian Penology: Advanced Perspectives and Research* co-edited with L. Visano challenges and expands the empirical and conceptual parameters in which contemporary criminological discourse has viewed and responded to the social constructions of the juridic actor within countless social and institutional contexts.

LIVY A. VISANO, ASSOCIATE PROFESSOR, YORK UNIVERSITY.

Professor Visano has taught countless courses, which challenge traditional criminological perspectives, at York University, University of Toronto and Ryerson Polytechnical Institute. He brings to his teaching years of experience in the field of policing, having served as the chair of the Security Advisory Committee of York University, as a consultant to various police forces, and as a volunteer in numerous other programs designed to confront issues concerning corrections within Canada. Further, his work in the area is highlighted by his publications, which partially include: *This Idle Trade, Deviant Designations*, co-edited with T. Fleming, *Beyond The Text* and *Canadian Penology* co-edited with K. McCormick all of which develop and expand the traditional foundations upon which criminological research and theory has been based.

PART
A

OVERVIEW

CHAPTER 1
Trends in the Sociology of Police Work

MAUREEN CAIN

INTRODUCTION

It is strange that, of all the studies of the police produced by sociologists and political scientists, only two (Cain, 1973; Manning, 1977) have attempted a definition of the object of their analysis. For all others, even for those whose purpose is to demonstrate diversity between police organizations and duties, it has been taken for granted that we "know" what the police, as an institution, really is (Bayley, 1976; Mosse, 1975). This unscientific myopia precludes, of course, the raising of questions about what the police might be: the alternatives available to the dissatisfied are titivation of police organization and practices within the prevailing common sense understanding of what policing, in some essential sense, "is"; or, for the more radical, there is the alternative of suggesting that the institution, again as common-sensically understood, should be scrapped. One argument of this paper is that if a theoretically sound definition of policing is constructed a far broader range of alternatives becomes available. More positive changes can be proposed as the transformation of policing is seen to be a real possibility.

Such a definition and such proposals must be based on such concrete knowledge of policing as is available. This involves an analytical and critical appraisal of work which has already been done. This, therefore, is the task to which I address myself first.

Studies of the police reveal both the worst and the best of what sociologists can do. Some specialize in bland banality, garnished occasionally with the pompous platitude (Purcell, 1974; Brown & Howes, 1975); happily the list is much longer of those which evince a genuine theoretical endeavour (Rock, 1973; Muir, 1977), or which use academic skills to illuminate problems of social and political concern (Wintersmith, 1974; Platt & Cooper, 1974). The pity of it is that these last two groups—the theoretically and the politically concerned—should have to be categorized separately. The ensuing discussion should make plain why this is so.

All the exemplars in this introduction have been chosen from works published in the last five years. In order to develop a typology of studies on the police, however, it is necessary to go back 15 years at least. Five types can then be identified. There is a rough chronological sequence in the shift of areas of interest, although some concerns persist throughout, and there is always some chronological overlap between the categories. The studies are organized into the following types: (1) police and civil rights; (2) police organization; (3) police and deviancy; (4) police and community; (5) the politics of policing.

THE POLICE AND CIVIL RIGHTS

The concern with civil rights and police powers is, and should be, continuous. There are, however, waves of interest. In America there was an upsurge of interest at the time of the Civil Rights Movement, and in England when various police atrocities were revealed in the early 1960s, and when middle class nuclear disarmament marchers were arrested in large numbers (Whitaker, 1964). More recently the growing case against the police for the harassment of young black people has been made (Demuth, 1978).

This almost permanent concern provided the starting point for academic research on the police, and it is with studies of this kind, rather than with logical or political debates about police powers, that we are immediately concerned.

Although as early as 1953 Jerome Hall pioneered this area of research rather as he pioneered what came to be known as "emergence studies" in the sociology of law (1952), it was not until the 1960s that scholars in the United States, and lawyers in particular, began seriously to investigate what they described as the exercise of police discretion. Between 1960 and 1965 seven influential papers appeared, plus one collection, and one English paper along similar lines (Donnelly, 1962; Goldstein, 1960, 1963; Kadish, 1962; La Fave, 1962, 1965; Osborough, 1965; Remington, 1962, 1965; Sowle, 1962). Rights to stop, to search, to enter property, to question suspects, and to arrest were all called into question, but the focus of interest was not so much on the rights themselves—although such an interest existed—as on the situations in which and the ways in which these rights were put into practice. And even more than this the concern, whether implicit or explicit, was with police deviancy. The question which these researchers addressed was "do policemen break the law?" Given that the answer was often "yes", the next question became "what can be done to stop it?"

At the same time Newman's work on the courts (1962, 1966) was revealing collaboration between police and court personnel which, if not illegal in itself, was calling into question the idealized image of the legal system. This work too, at least in its early stages, shared the correctional perspective which was fast becoming the dominant tradition in the study of law enforcement. So dangerous are police deviancies in their political repercussions that government commissions (Knapp, 1972; President's Commission, 1967) and sociologists (Chevigny, 1969; Bayley & Mendelsohn, 1969) continued and still continue to seek out evidences of corruption, malpractice, or prejudice.

The reduction of the academic's role to the identification of rule breakers was based on important assumptions and had important consequences.

(i) Nobody questioned what "the police" meant. Thus private police forces, citizen protection groups, and other government policing bodies, were ignored. In a similar way the police task was unquestioned. These were technically competent common-sense studies of a common-sense problem. It could be argued that the academics were policing the police, but since they thought they knew what a policeman was, this did not occur to them.

(ii) The law which defined the police task, and therefore created the boundaries of police deviancy, went largely unquestioned. But this was not yet entirely the case, for the studies were often done by lawyers whose trade is to understand the mutability of the law. It *was* recognized that changing the law could be one "solution" to police deviancy.

(iii) The posing of the problems as "do policemen break the rules" and "are policemen prejudiced" enabled the police to develop their "rotten apple" theory as a defence (Knapp Commission, 1972). According to this view, any large body of people is bound to have a few deviants or "rotten apples" amongst its numbers. This minority gets the whole organization a bad reputation.

(iv) Thus academic attackers and police defenders could agree about what should be done. The rotten apple theory leads to the obvious solution of removing the rotten apples. The reformers could not object to this. Their own suggestions, equally circumscribed by the limited questions posed, were also concerned with improving the quality of individual police men or women. Higher recruiting standards were advocated, and better training.

In sum both the problem of policing and its solution were conceived in a *non-social* way. Relationships and structures were not conceived as problematic in themselves. Bad people caused the trouble, and their improvement or elimination would resolve it.

POLICE ORGANIZATION

The next wave of research took as its focus of concern not the law about policing, but police organization. W.A. Westley's doctoral dissertation of the early 1950's (published as Westley, 1970) and his two seminal articles (Westley 1953, 1956) were the first in this tradition. The most influential work, however, has been that of Skolnick (1966), which admits its debt to Westley. The tradition still flourishes, recent examples being the works of Rubinstein (1973) and Punch (1979).

In retrospect the most important point to note about these works is that *they too regarded police deviancy as the central issue.* Both their methods of investigation and their analyses, however, were dramatically different from the civil rights studies. As a result, their solutions or reform proposals were different too.

First, the method: all these studies have employed the technique of participant observation. That is both their strength and their weakness. It is their strength because this technique does not foreclose the issues before the research begins: it makes possible interpretation and explanation in terms of categories which could not have been thought of before the research began. The weakness is not integral to the technique, but is a temptation to researchers using it. The danger is that the unit of observation—at its largest, the organization—will be used as the unit of analysis. Explanations will be bounded by what the researcher has been able to see or discuss. This is a natural enough tendency: knowledge outside of the unit observed is relatively limited, and inevitably the researcher is hesitant about couching his explanations in terms of that about which he knows less—the government or the wider society. But the technique is elevated to the status of the only valid sociological knowledge. Effectively this precludes the possibility of understanding the ways in which the institutions of society affect one another. Usually it precludes understanding of the upper echelons of organizations since senior people tend to work in individual offices, rather than in units which can economically be observed, and a very great deal of their work is with members of other organizations and has low visibility, being in the form of telephone calls and informal contacts.

The studies of police organization epitomize both these strengths and these weaknesses: the explanation is new, it is bounded by the organization studied, and the senior personnel are not studied.

It is argued, and cogently, that police deviancy is both engendered and condoned by the police organization itself. To require the police to act within legal constraints while at the same time insisting on high productivity involves them in a fundamental contradiction. If a "war on crime" is demanded, and bureaucratic evidence of success in the form of arrest or clear-up rates, then infringements of the rules in order to achieve these objectives become an occupational necessity. Not only is illegality (police primary deviation) engendered, but also secondary deviancy in terms of secretiveness, and the formation of the close knit, self-protective colleague organization which makes secrecy possible. Such an organization renders the police as impervious to explanation from the top of their own hierarchy as to the requirements of courts, lawyers, and concerned members of the public (Cain, 1971, 1972).

A number of other factors have been identified as reinforcing these tendencies. One is the need to break internal rules in order to make the job more congenial, which happens in all occupations; another is the need for mutual defence in the event of possible violence. In this connection it is perhaps worth noting that in England and Wales the rate of injury to police officers on duty has increased rapidly. A report produced in 1975 stated "injuries have more than doubled in the last five years and policing must now be considered as one of the most dangerous occupations in terms of personal injury" (Cain, Hall Williams & Olesen, 1975). Third, there is the peculiar structure of the work itself. Although the police are formally organized as a bureaucratic hierarchy, a high proportion of their work is not delegated to them by management either directly or indirectly as an instruction to respond to certain service demands: much police work comes from neither of these sources but is police initiated, or pro-active work. There is, therefore, no way in which police management can check on whether a man has done everything he might have done. Attempts to institute such a check by demanding reports are typically ineffectual, because a policeman can generate an adequate flow of reports in half a day if he wants to and is prepared to tolerate citizen annoyance, and because reports involve dramaturgical reconstructions of events and the patrol man alone decides in what terms the event should be expressed. Senior officers have no other source of information, even about many of the matters they direct their men to deal with (Wilson, 1968a; Cain, 1971, 1973; Manning, 1977; Chatterton, 1978). Finally, it has been demonstrated by Maurice Punch in England and by Egon Bittner (1974) among others in the

United States, that a great deal of police work is virtually incapable of being made visible to senior officers on a routine basis. Everything is potentially police business if either a citizen or a policeman makes it so. Many of these encounters go unrecorded; others may be recorded in the constable's pocket book. Few will ever find their way to a central information system.

Two answers have been proposed following the analysis of the police organization as itself engendering and condoning police deviancy. One solution is to change the organization. Studies of variations in ideology and practice between departments (Cressey & Elgesem, 1968; Wilson, 1963, 1968b) have encouraged the view that changes in the reward and control structures can be effective in reducing deviancy, although Wilson has pointed out that an increased alienation from the rest of the citizenry results.

A second solution hinted at by Skolnick in his first book and voiced more explicitly in his second (1969), is to change the brief which society gives its policemen. The point is not further developed by the organization theorists. Their problem and their method enable them to do no more than point up the hypocrisy involved in leaving the police to carry the can. What the police are for is plainly a political question, and the dilemma of the organization theorists becomes the starting point for political theorists of the police such as Robinson (1975) and Wolfe (1974). These works are considered in a later section of this paper.

The organization theorists, then,

(1)   still failed to define the police, and therefore examined only police institutions which were "obvious" to common sense;

(2)   still identified police deviancy as the major problem;

(3)   offered a social (rather than an individual) explanation of deviancy, and located these social pressures in the organization of police work;

(4)   offered either technocratic solutions, albeit to do with the organization rather than the individual (Platt & Cooper, 1974), or were vague about solutions which apparently rested with the "wider society".

THE POLICE AND DEVIANCY

After the publication of Becker's *Outsiders* sociological studies of crime took a completely new tack, as is well known. Theoretically, symbolic interactionism and ethnomethodology were called upon to underpin the new approach. For studies of police work too this involved a shift in focus. Now the emphasis was on police encounters with non-police, particularly with youngsters (Werthman & Piliavin, 1967; Piliavin & Briar, 1964) or underprivileged and exposed groups (Stinchcombe, 1963; Bittner, 1967a, 1967b; Chapman, 1970). These studies aimed to show the processes by which a citizen is turned into a deviant. Although they identified some sections of the population as more at risk than others in this process, they were not primarily interested in police prejudice or police deviancy. This mattered to them only in so far as it affected the criminal or deviant in the outside world.

Three developments from this perspective demand mention. First, the part played by the police in the construction of the images or facts of deviance was considered important. Police judgements were seen to be the basis for routine crime statistics (Box, 1974), and also for the creation of crime waves (Young, 1971; Cohen, 1974). More recent work (Chibnall, 1977) has shown in more detail how the police control crime reporting in the press. In a sense, therefore, these students have been able to show how the police create or constitute these groups which they then regard as the objects of their policing efforts.

A much more recent development has been the turning of these analytical techniques back upon the police themselves (Manning, 1977; Chatterton, 1976, 1978). These are really organization studies, and share the weaknesses listed for these. They would not have been possible, however, without the theoretical developments which took place within deviancy theory itself, which is why they are included here. Their merit is that they once again widened the area of interest. The earlier study of *encounters* had been able only to describe, rather than account for, what transpired. Chatterton is able to offer an account, within the limits of an organizational analysis.

The merit of all these studies is that they encouraged a far more detailed ethnography, and the importance of recording and analysing the precise language used in an interaction was realized.

All the early interactionist police studies and the media studies evidence a fierce concern for the underdog (Becker, 1970). So although the identification and explanation of police deviancy is not the object of the analysis, the police are none the less the "baddies". Yet researchers in this tradition have also come to see the police as agents, as proxy baddies, perhaps. The police are seen as agents of the state, which both creates criminal law and the institutions whose task it is to enforce it. By and large these connections between police and state have been asserted (and at one level they are obvious) rather than analysed. An exception here is the contribution of McBarnet (1978) which points out that the sociology of police work in the organization and deviancy traditions particularly, has emphasized unduly the informal organization and turned attention from the enabling legislation which promotes and facilitates the practices for which the police are castigated. The most recent study which makes this connection, and is also plainly within the tradition of studies on the police and the mass media, is that by Stuart Hall of Birmingham, and his collaborators (Hall et al., 1978).

So, from a group of studies which appeared to be going to tell us more and more about less and less: better ethnography of smaller units: the studies generated out of a concern about the police creation of deviancy led finally to the raising of the largest and most fundamental issues of all—questions about the police as agents of the state. Students steeped in the traditions of deviancy theory, however, were not equipped theoretically to tackle the issues to which they had drawn attention. Nor had they a methodology or a theory of knowledge which would enable them to conceptualize and construct evidence about the constitution of the state itself.

How then can one summarize the strengths and weaknesses of scholarly work in this tradition?

(1) The lack of definition, the common sense view of the police, remains. Indeed, the interpretation is more narrow than in the organization studies, for with the focus of attention on interaction between policemen and potential deviants, all the myriad other activities which policemen engage in—and crime has generally been shown to take the smallest part of their time (Martin & Wilson, 1969; Cumming & Cumming, 1965; Bittner, 1974)—were lost to view. This is the more remarkable since by and large it is uniformed departments rather than detective departments which have been investigated. (The exception here is the work of Greenwood & Chaiken (1977), which demonstrates that detectives do very little detecting.)

(2) There was a shift from police deviance as the object to be explained. This was replaced by an examination of the ways in which the police construct deviance.

(3) The analyses and explanations were quite clearly social rather than individual, and dynamic rather than pictorial. All the studies, however, show a tension. In the earlier works the underpinning epistemology does not allow an adequate account of "environing structures" to be presented. Social class, for example, is taken as given in some other order of theoretical reality. Many of these scholars tautologically invoke "the powerful" to explain the residual variables, i.e. everything outside the subjectively con-

structed police world. The invocation of "the powerful" as substitute "baddies" is tautological, because it deals with outcomes. Success is a given, and a theoretical determination of the bases of power is not offered. It is a static and conservative position, which offers no possibility of success in the power stakes to any group which has not at the time of writing achieved such success. This dilemma is in part discussed by Taylor, Walton & Young in their important contribution (1974). The later works in this tradition, however, while liberating the study of the police as creators of criminals from its earlier epistemological base, tend to retain the problem without rooting it in an alternative theory or offering a coherent alternative epistemology.

(4) The solutions offered to this rather differently constructed problem varied. First there were technocratic solutions: the suggestion that the ways in which the police exercise their judgement could be changed by better recruitment and especially by education programmes giving them greater insight into the ways of life and modes of thought of underdogs. As a result simply written and influential training manuals have been produced by academics (Banton, 1973). Secondly, once the problem was conceived as political, with the police being regarded as pre-programmed state agents carrying out the will of "the powerful" or the bourgeoisie, then plainly political solutions were in order. Unfortunately (see 3 above) the theory gave no indication of how political solutions could occur, given the inevitability of domination by "the powerful", etc.

THE POLICE AND THE COMMUNITY

These researches are more closely linked with the organization studies than with those in the deviancy tradition, discussed above. Because the more open technique employed by Westley and the others allowed new problems to emerge, there was a growing realization that organizational factors alone could not account for variations in police practice. These studies, therefore, have in common the use of the *comparative method*. They posited differences in police practice and set out to explain these. The explanations were sought both in the organizations and in their social ambience. Secondly, therefore, it should be noted about these studies that they took as their theme "The policeman in his social setting". Major works in this tradition are those by Banton (1964), Goldman (1963), Wilson (1968a, 1968b), Cain (1973) and later Reiss (1971). In an earlier paper (Cain, 1971) I have attempted to summarize these results.

What these studies demonstrated is that the benign mode of policing variously designated as "peace-keeping" or "service style" is only possible when
the environing community is homogeneous in class terms or, alternatively,
demonstrates an ideological consensus resulting from the existence over a
long time of a stable power structure. Wilson (op. cit.) and Gardiner (1968)
took the matter a stage further, and it was argued that the structure of local
government in the United States, both formal and informal, and the constitutional position of the police, affected the way in which their work was carried
out. A correctionalist stance was adopted by many, but not all of these writers.
By its nature the comparative method raised questions about what kind of
policing one ought to aim for: eliminating brutality and the more dramatic sub-
versions of civil rights no longer seemed enough. Goldman, Wilson, Cain
(1972 esp.) all expressed concern about a "professional" police force which
set and adjudicated its own standards, albeit "high" ones by some (by whose?)
criteria. It was argued that a police force should be responsive to those
policed, while autonomous professionals, even though they may be truthful
and honest and not unduly coercive (this is questionable), have a notorious
tendency to believe that they know what is "really" best for the clients, and
therefore what the clients "ought" to want. In the area of civil liberties such
autonomous standard setting makes no kind of democratic sense. Cain developed the discussion in a slightly different way, arguing that in Britain at least
the professionalization movement masked a growing and covert control by the
central state.

Reiss was more optimistic in his approach, pointing out that much police
work is inevitably a response to very specific and immediate public demands,
and that equally inevitably the man on the spot is vulnerable to public pressure. Muir (1977), in an excellent social psychological study, and Chatterton
(1976) make the same point. A patrol-man will not endear himself to his colleagues if he is constantly requiring assistance with matters which other officers could handle alone. And to handle something alone the mood of the
bystanders and of the participants must be both manipulated and taken positively into account. Reiss, more than the other two and despite the title of
Muir's book, shows an awareness of a political dimension to such on-street
reciprocal manipulations.

Such an argument, however, runs full circle back to the question posed by
Banton, Wilson, et al. For it holds for most policemen in most situations, and
does not account for variation. If the work situation is thus constant, then
accounts of variation must be constructed in terms of other variables.

So these studies led to a political question. As I posed it "whose law do the police enforce and why", more cryptically "whom would a Welsh police-man support if there were a Welsh nationalist secession" (1973, p.26). Not all the studies raised this question explicitly, and certainly none was able to solve it. There were two reasons for this failure. First, most of these authors studied the police and the "community" separately, and then sought to put them together. Thus the exact nature of the pressures was always assumed rather than empirically identified. Yet it is the nature of the links which crucial-ly requires investigation. Cain's work (1971, 1973) however, does delineate more precisely the mediations between police officer and citizen at various lev-els of structure, as well as the organizational mediations. It attempts to explain the direction of loyalties and of compliant behaviour, because it poses these as its initial problem. This work does, however, share the second weakness of these studies of "the policemen in his social setting": it does not examine empirically the work of senior officers and the pressures to which they are sub-ject. Thus decisions about how police should be deployed and trained, about promotion schemes, and about changes in organization are treated as if they are not matter of sociological interest, although lip service may be paid to their importance (Cain, 1971).

Once again I will summarize some of the main points:

(1) These studies started from an Anglo-American common sense understanding of what "the police" are. But because they were comparative they revealed the need for a more adequate defini-tion. Some of the studies met the problem by developing an internal classification of modes of policing (Banton, Goldman, Wilson, 1968a op. cit.) without meeting directly the question of what the prime category (policing) was, within which the sub-classification was being made. Others (Cain, 1973) *ended* by defining the police. But by this time the study was complete, and the definition could not, therefore, do its job of setting bound-aries for the research work.

(2) By using the comparative method the studies exposed the limita-tions of the organization studies, although it must be admitted that they did not all share their strengths. But the treatment by a number of these theorists of "the police" and the "social setting" as separate "variables", often with equal theoretical weight, meant that they, like the organization theorists, were trapped in an institutional level of analysis. it is the merit and the failure of these studies that they drew attention to a problem which by and large they could not cope with. But the problem needed posing: and it had to be stated that one cannot understand the purpose of policing solely by looking at policemen.

(3) New and important political questions were now raised, but often shyly and indirectly, as if they were somehow improper questions for a social scientist to be posing.

(4) Just like the deviancy theorists when they reached this point, the policeman-in-the-community people confronted a dilemma when they asked themselves the question "what next". Those who had kept closest to the institutional level of analyses crept to the shelter of additional technocratic suggestions. The by now familiar battery of organizational changes was proposed. In addition a kind of constitutional technocracy seemed called for in the U.S. After the Chicago riots of 1968 Mayor Daley succumbed to just such a proposal. Nothing fundamental was thereby changed (Robinson, 1975). Those who attempted to pose the issues as political questions provided ammunition for a political response, in the form of a demand for community control. Nothing fundamental was thereby changed either, but the story of these struggles belongs to the next section.

THE POLITICS OF POLICING

Further subdivisions are required in this last category. This is only partly because we are now discussing contemporary writings, so that being in the foreground their diversity and detail is the more apparent, though that indeed is true. There is a sadder reason, which is that the authors within the four categories have not, in the main, taken issue with the literature beyond their boundaries, so that what emerges is four more or less discrete bodies of knowledge. Most of this knowledge has been produced by sociologists. But I am saving the best until the end, and the best has been produced by political scientists and historians.

COMMUNITY CONTROL

Community control of the police emerged as an important political demand in the United States in the 1960's. Following Nelson's (1967) account of how a black community organized successfully to police its own area, and, by providing an alternative standard of order and policing, coerced recognition, "community control" began to seem like a solution in other black communities. But instead of organizing first, and thereby creating an alternative power base which would enable them to influence effectively the existing police force, most citizen groups sought to influence their already existing police force immediately, and to control its operations, or at least, to have a say.

Initially suspicious, the police authorities realized at last that to oppose these movements could help create just such an alternative power base as Nelson's community had achieved. Instead, therefore, the movements were co-opted to already existing police purposes such as crime prevention and transmitting information, and eventually they fizzled out (Washnis, 1976). In large cities white groups, prompted by the fear for their personal safety which Abbott, Gold & Rogowsky have documented (1969), also formed "block associations", with similar consequences.

As Cooper (1975) has rather curtly pointed out, responsiveness to community has not typically been the criterion by which the police have been judged. Such reforms as there have been have been "reformist" rather than structural. Reformist reforms involve community relations programmes, review boards, and efforts to recruit blacks. Structural reform, she claims, involves the decentralization of the power to make decisions, the expansion of popular power, and restructuring the power of the state apparatus. While these three may read very much like the same thing differently expressed, the main thrust of the argument is plain.

But why are community relations programmes reformist? Norris (1973) carried out a study in one locality which makes the reason plain. He distinguished between genuine *interaction,* in which each party influences the other, and public relations, in which the influence is unilateral. His study demonstrates that the police C.R. programme was in fact a P.R. programme, designed to change the police image rather than police behaviour.

In order to render a C.R. programme effective it is necessary for the people of a locality to organize to insist on the matters which they want dealt with and the manner in which they wish these actions to be carried out. Nelson's example cannot be ignored. It is not possible to exert influence without power, and a basis of power must therefore be constructed.

Crucially, the police must be rendered *vulnerable* to community pressure. If they alone can decide which demands to respond to and which to ignore, then one does not have a truly democratic institution, but at best a benign paternalist one, and at worst an authoritarian one. As Richardson (1975) has shown in his discussion of the Weimar police, authoritarianism too can be disguised with the rhetoric of professionalism.

POLICE UNIONISM

Research on the police's own attempts to organize and intervene political-ly is a very recent development. In part this is because the phenomenon itself appeared only recently in the United States (Center for Research on Criminal Justice, 1977); in part it is because, as I have shown, concern with the police has only recently moved away from correctionalism to a position which has greater theoretical economy and concomittantly a wider range of substantive concerns.

According to Skolnick (1969) the mid-1960's police confrontation with demonstrators gave them a heightened sense both of mission and identity, while their often successful struggles against civilian review boards gave them a new sense of political power. Halpern (1974), however, shows on the basis of his three careful and fascinating case studies that the range of "reformist" issues which called reactionary police unions into being is somewhat wider than this, a finding substantiated by Juris & Feuille's (1973) rather more curso-ry study in 22 urban police forces. Halpern argues that the element of reac-tion deriving from a sense not only of mission but also of impotence, decreas-es as the strength of the organizations increases. What these authors docu-ment is a gradual process of co-optation. Once the police organization (they are not always unions in the strict sense) has proved its constituency and made it plain, by various means, that it cannot be ignored, then chiefs of police reluctantly come to accept power sharing. Halpern argues that from this point on the concern for a particular brand of law and order gives place to concern for the traditional union issues of hours, pay, and conditions. Opponents thereafter become partners.

> The routinization of relations impels leaders of both management and labour to oppose a rapid and radical change in the leadership positions of either side (p. 102).

This sounds like a story familiar to students of trades unions everywhere. One thing that is different about police unions is the range of tactics open to them. In the words of Juris & Feuille, bargaining for the police is multi-later-al—involving at least the local authority as well as the chief. Differences between other parties to negotiations can be exploited. City authorities, if they are elected, are directly susceptible to the public opinion which police unions may seek to manipulate, and so on.

Police unions in Weimar, Germany, apparently, never underwent this softening process. According to Kohler (1975) the government's agreement in 1922 that the men could form a union, coupled with the establishment of a review body composed of officers and men within which differences between them were supposed to be thrashed out, led instantly to the officers forming their own counter-union which almost at once claimed 90% support. Kohler is a political scientist, and therefore prepared to take the issue beyond questions of organization, strategy and tactics. He points out that more than half the senior men were former army officers. They "made overtures to be taken over by the military" and were "never very reliable defenders of the Republic".

Perhaps it could be argued that whereas the German police officers were opposed to their government in terms of policy, and denied it legitimacy, the U.S. policemen and women were opposed only to the chosen mode of implementing government policy, and supported its legitimacy.

Be that as it may, the British government made it plain in 1919 that it was fully apprised of the dangers of police unionism. To this day the police are not allowed to form a union, and are denied the right to strike. Their attitudes towards their existing representative body, the Police Federation, are ambivalent (Reiner, 1978b). Reiner's papers (1978a) raise a broader set of questions, shifting concern from the police union as an institution to the position of the police officer in the class structure. All the analyses discussed so far, including that of Reiner himself (1978b) might have been improved if this prior question had been tackled. Thus the issues to which Kohler's work had directed attention are again raised. It is not enough to study the internal structure and workings of a police union, any more than it is enough to study a police organization, if the matter ends there. What is important about a police union is the way it affects police relationships with the other organs of state, and police relationships with the citizenry they are meant to serve. How, precisely, is the power structure changed by the formation of a police union? Does it create more interests in common between police and workers, as being part of one movement? Does it relegate the police to a reactionary island, isolated from both fellow workers and the liberal-democratic agencies of state? Or can they find allies to form an alliance of the right...and so on? These are the questions to which studies of police unionism should lead. It is significant that the study which primarily gives rise to them, that of Kohler, should be an historical investigation.

THE POLICE AND THE STATE

It must be admitted that this is the most eclectic of the four sub-categories in this section on the politics of policing. To impose some kind of order on the diverse writings which have posed questions about the police and the state I will discuss first those which present the relationship between police and state at local level, and then those which consider the relationship at national level.

Brogden (1977) and Robinson (1975) present research findings on local relationships. Brogden demonstrates that in Britain the Police Authority, a strangely constituted body composed of half magistrates (appointed by the Lord Chancellor) and half nominees from among elected local councillors, is powerless. Effectively the Chief Constable sets its agendas and controls the knowledge available to it. As a result it approves his budget and rubber stamps his major decisions, concerning itself only with trivia which are within the everday comprehension of its members. The effective line of authority is thus from Home Office, which supplies the other half of the budget, to Chief Constable. Cain (1972) had argued on other grounds that the powers of this local body were diminishing. In 1977 she argued further that this shift to central control corresponded with a shift in the economy towards international capital. Services for such capital—roads, airports, fuel and power, police, perhaps healthy workers—are typically provided by central rather than by local government, whereas a more local organization of police more adequately met the needs of smaller scale indigenous capitals.

Robinson's study is of the Chicago police, and his purpose is to demonstrate again that an a-political, "professionalized" police force suits the politicians even better than a force they are directly in control of. The influence, he argues, is still there, but city officials and politicians can now disclaim responsibility for police malpractices, while reaping the benefits of their more praiseworthy exploits. As Silver (1967) pointed out for the state as a whole, the police become scapegoats for problems they did not create, mystify and obscure the real culprits, and drain off aggression from the ruling class whose agents they (sometimes unwittingly) are.

There is less research to report on the police and the central state agencies—Bunyan (1976) advances matters by forcing a re-definition. He points out that sociologists have typically ignored not just standard criminal investigation but the whole range of anti-subversion and security activities in which other departments such as MI5 and MI6 are engaged. Studying the friendly beat man because he is available or because deviancy theory defined him as most relevant has blinkered sociologist to the real police task, which is the maintenance of an internal order satisfactory to the state and the ruling class.

Goulden, Pinto, and Webb, all contributing to Platt & Cooper's (1974) collection, seek in different ways to document the financial support which central government in the United States gives, through the Law Enforcement Assistance Administration, to local police forces. Since most of the cash is for hardware, more of it gets spent on anti-demonstration activities than on, say, community relations.

None of these studies attempts to *theorize* the relationship between police and state. They presume homogeneity between various state agencies, and homogeneity of influence upon them by a homogeneous ruling class. While this is plainly a lot better than ignoring the issue, it is plainly not yet good enough. Moreover, it is politically nihilistic, for it confronts the would-be reformer with a monolithic unity in control of everything, in confrontation with which he is impotent. These studies also cast the police in the role of inevitable enemy, doomed to be the agents of the bourgeoisie or ruling elite. Cain (1977) and Woddis (1976) have argued that an alternative position is possible, which recognizes diversity within the state, and appropriately organizes pressure upon it in the interests of greater democracy. The police, as an institution, should be among the first to be democratized in this way.

At this point the analyses of the police and the state meet up with the studies of the police and community control.

Reiner (1978a op. cit.) does attempt to theorize the relationship, by identifying the class position of the police. Thompson (1979) has also noted the nihilistic tendencies of radical attacks on the police, insisting that an accurate and differentiated account of police organization and practices, especially insofar as they impinge on civil rights, is a pre-requisite for democratic political action. Adopting a different tack, Wolfe (1974) argues cogently that "repression is an essential aspect of liberal rule, not something alien to it" (p. 13). The liberal ideal itself, she argues, provides "a rationale for repression". The existence of repression should not be in question, nor should the amount over time. What matters, it is claimed, is the forms which repression takes over time. It is to historical studies that I now turn.

HISTORICAL AND COMPARATIVE WORKS

I said that I would save the best to the end, but this does not mean that these studies are the icing-sugar on the cake. Rather they deal with fundamen-

tal issues, with the chemical processes which make the cake possible at all.
Jeffries (1952) notes that "...The Policeman is, in a sense, a more modern
creation than the police" (p. 7). Comparative and historical works force to our
attention the fact that the police function of maintaining order *as defined by
the group which supports them* has been conceived and institutionalized in
many different ways. Swanson (1975) showed that in the Ottoman Empire the
Head Gardener (Bostanj Bashi) was one of the four most senior police officers, accountable directly to the Grand Vizier, being responsible for all imperial lands and palaces, and in particular for the shores of the Bosporus, he both
controlled and policed (they are different) a large part of imperial trade. Stead
(1957) and Odenkunle (1979) have noted for France and Nigeria respectively
that police carry out a very wide range of jobs, including for example tax gathering and overseeing water supplies and public health. Bayley (1969) notes
that both in the later years of the Raj and since independence, the Indian
policeman has been the only outpost of central government in many remote
regions. He has therefore been called upon to do any central government job
that turned up, from overseeing census enumeration to reporting on the condition of the roads.

Police, then, *must be defined in terms of their key practice.* They are
appointed with the task of maintaining the order which those who sustain
them define as proper. Such a definition makes it possible to raise a much
wider range of questions about police (no longer "the" police) than has hitherto been typical of sociological work. Questions can be posed about the additional jobs they do, about how these affect their relationship with their
employers and those whom they police, about the formal and unofficial ways
in which limits are or are not set to the means they can employ, and about
who sets these limits —the employers or the policed. The structure of the
work situation can now be interpreted differently: its effect on allegiance to
employers must be considered, as must the measures taken to ensure such
allegiance and possible counter measures by those whose definitions of social
order may be different. These last may be sections within the police force, as
well as groups outside it.

Fogelson's (1977) study of the class and institutional struggles which generated police reform movements in the United States documents this point.
While the white upper and middle classes encouraged the first movement to
wean the police from the control of local politicians and the influence, through
them, of working class migrants, the second reform movement was led from
within the police, and took the form of a demand for "professionalization".
Unfortunately, Fogelson does not press his analysis further. Were he to do so

it would probably become clear that, as in England, the demand for a "professional" police, with centrally derived standards, is a function of the changing structure of capital. By the 1930's (where Fogelson first situates this occupational demand) onwards, monopoly capital was replacing local capital. The concomitant was a political demand for a national and international standard of order, carried by a "professional" police, as opposed to local standards borne and effected by local police.

These questions can become more cogent still, as it becomes necessary to identify who—what class, group, or institution—does in fact "sustain" the police. As in the British case, employers and "sustainers" may be different: it is the latter who define the order which the police must maintain.

The dangers of teleological history, which assumes that an internal necessity of the nature of policing caused police forces to rid themselves of "non police" duties and to shape themselves into the present Anglo-American forms of organization, must now become apparent. Such histories—those of Critchley (1967) and Richardson (1970) spring most readily to mind—are not only useless but dangerous, for they have contributed to the social science common sense about what policing "is", and have precluded the raising of these other, more fundamental and more interesting, questions.

Having a definition means that organizations and individuals do not have to call themselves police in order for the sociologist to consider them as such. Hay's gamekeepers (1975), for example, fit neatly into the category. Moreover, this study provides a finely researched example of conflicting definitions of order between the sustainers of the police/gamekeepers, the enclosers of land, and those policed who wanted a return to the old order of common use and other rights. Moreover, the gamekeeper's situation was closely analogous to that, for example, of the Indian policeman described above. He was alone, without immediate protection, surrounded by a populace on whom he was trying to impose a new order, and hated by them. Some accommodation in the way the rules were imposed had to be arrived at. Some accommodation in the way the rules were imposed had to be arrived at. Most of these accommodations, however, were for obvious reasons not recorded and are lost to history.

Problems, from the standpoint of the sustainers, of the allegiance of their police have been a frequent occurrence in history. Bowden (1975b) cites the problems for the British government of the Arab faction within the Palestine police, and his most recent (1978) contribution is organized round the theme of the problematic character of police loyalty in times of crisis. Stead op. cit. discusses the long standing political division within the French police, as institutionalized in the right wing *préfecture* and the left wing *sûreté*. In Palestine, apparently, the government seemed unaware of the nature of the problem, which they tried inadequately to counter by making a whole series of inept organizational changes. But in the main governments have understood the problem only too well, particularly in situations of conquest or colonization.

Most typically, where local people were recruited into the police, as by the British colonial power, the officers were recruited from the colonial power. When provision was made for local people in rare cases to become officers, then elaborate precautions were taken in the form of an extended ideological training (Jeffries, 1952).

Even so, the loyalty of indigenous personnel could not be taken for granted. Jeffries' discussions of Jamaica and Ceylon show that HMG was very well aware of the dangers of local control in an occupied territory. Therefore all colonial police forces, both before and after the establishment of a single service, were part of the *central* administration of the colony. Secondly, they were all para-military in character.

An interesting variation on this theme is presented by Morrison (1975). Discussing the success of the "Mounties", at the time of the Klondike gold rush, he points out that the police had the good fortune to have created a "presence" before this influx occurred. The Canadian government did not welcome the "crucibles of self government" which the small, stable, and unpoliced mining communities were becoming. They therefore sent two officers of the NWMP to "case" the region in 1894, and a force of 20 men and an inspector the following year. At once the force established its authority by supporting a centralized definition of property rights—order—and eliminating the democratic definition of these rights. The issue was some land, originally owned by two men (A and B), who had leased it to a third man (C). C defaulted and failed to pay the miners' wages. The miners' meeting seized the land in lieu of wages, and sold it to D. The police refused to register D's claim, and returned the land to A and B.

In passing it can be noted that these are civil matters. The restriction of policing to criminal matters had occurred neither in fact nor in the popular imagination. What the police were doing was imposing the definition of order of those who sustained them in being.

Chapman (1970) has argued that the style of policing is a function of a Roman Law or a Common law tradition. Tobias (1975) takes issue with this, pointing out that policing in Ulster has always been centralized and para-military in character, despite the Common Law. The discussion of the colonial situation in general shows that Tobias is correct: police "style" is a function of the task they are set, not of their ideological tradition.

On the other hand Jeffries' work does indicate a struggle to accommodate the contradictory rhetorics developed for locally controlled, unarmed policemen in the "mother country", the rhetoric of consent, and that developed in those colonies, in need of "pacification", the rhetoric of conquest. This was achieved in part by insulating the police forces from each other, and in part by the development of a special colonialist language and ideology, to the effect that the conquered peoples were not sufficiently "advanced democratically" to police themselves. Thus lack of democracy became the "obvious" way to promote democracy in these territories!

Welty (1975), on the other hand, considers that the place of the police in the re-productive order, as offering a service which the working classes do not wish to use, determines their bureaucratic structure. His argument, however, leaves insufficient room for the variations which have just been identified. Thorwald's (1966) discussion shows that police style if not the mode of control of the police is affected by ideological developments. The prevailing scientism of the late C19th and early C20th, which still prevails, meant that the police had to equip themselves to appear to produce a new kind of acceptable evidence. This development in forensic science coalesced with a differentiation of the police function in Britain and America, whereby the most visible part of the state police were increasingly to interpret their function as that of dealing with specific and individualized disorders (crimes). Thus the image—always a false one (Pogrebin, 1976)—of "the detective" was created.

Before the question of allegiance is abandoned altogether, there are at least two recorded situations in which police forces were established and sustained by organized groups of citizens, in addition to the two French attempts, in 1848 and 1871, which failed (Stead, 1957). That discussed by Nelson (1967) has already been considered. Bowden (1975a) presents an even more telling example—in 1920 when disorder in Ireland reached one of its many peaks, the General Executive of the IRA agreed to put at the disposal of the Dail "a police force voluntarily recruited from the ranks of the IRA" (p. 60).

So far policing has been considered in a pre-capitalist empire, in nation states, and in colonies. In this sense the practice of policing, and the definition of policing in accordance with it, seems trans-historical, that is, it appears in or applies to more than one mode of production. The argument, in emphasizing the variations in the way policing has been done in different times and places, may have supported this view. It is an important corrective, therefore, to point out that the variations in the way of policing is organized are themselves both a function of a particular mode of production and constitutive of the political level of the formation in which they occur. A trans-historical police-spotting exercise is not being advocated, nor is the police task, however organized, being postulated as a universal one.

It remains to consider studies of policing in the days of international capital. Very little work has been done. Plainly the neo-colonialist powers cannot police directly the territories in which they, often collectively, invest. Yet they have a commitment to maintaining the capitalist concept of order in these places. The risk is that the export of legal and other ideological concepts and constructs may be insufficient to maintain this order. "Modernization" and "development" may be opposed, or may produce new kinds of order problems for the capitalist powers. It therefore becomes necessary *indirectly* to export "good" policing. In Britain scholarships for police officers from colonial and ex-colonial territories to be trained in the colonial country have been available since the 1930's. In the United States the Office of Public Safety finances a police academy, in a building belonging to a major international company (Stork, 1974). According to Klare (1974) the O.P.S. has 90 "public safety advisers" in fifteen countries of Latin America, and 2000 U.S. trained police officers serving there—moreover, additional help, particularly with equipment, is available in crises. While welcoming the adage that "humane" policing is also the most effective technique, one should not be blind to the character of the regimes supported by and for the convenience of international capital.

CONCLUSIONS

This paper has identified five phases in the sociology of police work, culminating in a concern with four aspects of the politics of policing. Thus a dialectical model of the growth of knowledge is encapsulated. Changes in the concrete political situation have in part generated this approach, yet it is also the case that the later studies would not have been possible without the earlier ones. Moreover, the new perspective, involving a definition of policing which is both more scientific and broader in scope, makes possible a fruitful re-interpretation of the earlier data; they can be reconstituted in terms of today's theory. Thus the organization studies, for example, can be re-cast in the new intellectual context, and their value if anything enhanced thereby. In terms of the new set of questions, these studies tell us about the organizational limits on control by sustainers and their more immediate agents; they tell us about the probable effectiveness of training schemes inculcating supposedly authoritative definitions of order and how it should be imposed, and so on. They round out one area of the new puzzle. In a similar way the deviance studies and the civil rights studies can be re-interpreted and newly evaluated.

Civil rights studies, indeed, continue to be carried out. Official limits to the means to be used by the police, and the extent to which they are adhered to, can be informative about the power and the ideology of sustainers, their agents which employ the police; the police themselves with all their internal stratification and variation, and the equally differentiated citizenry. Studies such as those of Humphrey (1972), Witt (1973), and Zander (1972) remain useful.

Within the capitalist world as we now know it two apparently contradictory processes co-exist. One, described in the final section above, is a movement towards greater unity in police practice, both in terms of the range of designated tasks and of style. The other, virtually unreported trend, is the re-growth in private police forces, sustained directly by capitalists. It is a major merit of Bowden's work (1978 op. cit.) that he devotes a chapter to the documentation of this development.

There could be a third trend: those whose definition of order is presently submerged could organize to protect and impose it. To do so, they would need to police it. How can this be done? Local control has been the standard answer, but (a) this no longer matches the pattern of societal organizations: localities are economically and politically interdependent; (b) community control may not be tolerated if it becomes really effective *and* offers an alternative definition of order. What happens, as in the Glasgow example cited by Evans (1974), is that getting on with the community becomes another specialist function. Community relations teams do not do "line" police work. It is therefore an irrelevant group of persons who are getting along so well. If the C.R. men can maintain order inexpensively, sell the police image to more liberal government departments and possibly even to the inhabitants of the favoured localities, *and* bring back information, then they will be encouraged. As then Chief Constable McNee said at the time, it is no good if they become workers on behalf of the community *rather* than policemen (Evans ibid).

Line policemen—some patrol men, CID officers and security police—are not put in positions which would render them easily vulnerable to public pressure. They are structurally capable of disregarding public feeling if necessary without a crisis of conscience. *This is what has to be changed in order to create a democratic police force, in any country.* The ways in which it can be done will vary internationally, but the first step has to be an accurate depiction of the problem, and an accurate sociological identification of the local structure. But I don't want to end with the usual call for more research, because this paper has demonstrated that we have quite a lot already. There is enough, at least, to show that the problem must be tackled both locally, because police work is territorially based, and at the point of sustenance, whether this be the central state or a private company. There is also enough to show that pessimism about the outcome of such efforts would be premature.

> It is, therefore, nothing short of subversion of democracy to turn law and order into code words that stand for their antithesis—repression and acquiescence (New York Times, 1970).

REFERENCES

* This paper was presented, in a slightly different form, to the 8th International Congress of Criminology, Lisbon, September 1978.

This chapter was previously printed in the *International Journal of the Sociology of Law*, Vol 17: 143-167. 1979. Reprinted by permission.

Abbott, D., Gold, L. & Rogowsky, E. (1969) *Police, Race and Politics*. New York and Cambridge, Mass. American Jewish Committee and Harvard University Press.

Banton, M. (1964) *The Policeman in the Community*. London, Tavistock.

_____, (1973) *Police Community Relations*. London, Collins.

Bayley, D. & Mendelsohn, H. (1969) *Minorities and the Police*. New York, Free Press.

_____, (1969) *The Police and Political Development in India*. Princeton University Press.

_____, (1976) *Forces of Order*. Berkeley, University of California Press.

Becker, H. (1962) *Outsiders*. Chicago, Aldine.

_____, (1970) *Sociological Work*. London, Allen Lane.

Bittner, E. (1967a) "The police on skid row". *American Sociological Review* 32.

_____, (1967b) "Police discretion in emergency apprehension of mentally ill persons". *Social Problems* 14.

_____, (1974) "A theory of police". In *The Potential for Reform of Criminal Justice* (Jacob, H., Ed.). London, Sage.

Box, S. (1974) *Deviance, Reality, and Society*. London.

Bowden, T. (1975a) "The Irish underground and the War of Independence 1919-21". In *Police Forces in History* (Mosse, G., Ed.). London, Sage.

_____, (1975b) "Policing Palestine". In *Police Forces in History* (Mosse, G., Ed.). London, Sage.

_____, (1978) *Beyond the Limits of the Law*. Hammondsworth, Penguin.

Brogden, M. (1977) "A police authority—the denial of conflict". *Sociological Review* 25.

Brown, J. & Howes, G. (Eds.) (1975) *The Police and the Community*. Farnborough, Saxon House.

Bunyan, T. (1976) *The Political Police in Britain*. London, Julian Friedman.

Cain, M. (1971) "The changing role of the police in society". Paper presented to the Fourth Cambridge Criminology Conference - mimeo.

————, (1972) "Police professionalism: its meaning and consequences". *Anglo-American Law Review* 1.

————, (1973) *Society and the Policeman's Role.* London, Routledge and Kegan Paul.

————, (1977) "An ironical departure: the dilemma of contemporary policing". In *Yearbook of Social Policy in Britain 1976* (Jones, K. et al., Eds). London, Routledge and Kegan Paul.

————, Hall Williams, J. & Olesen, P. (1975) Paper prepared for the Police Federation, unpublished.

Center for Research on Criminal Justice (1977) *The Iron Fist and the Velvet Glove.* New York, Center Publication.

Chapman, B. (1970) *Police State.* London, Pall Mall.

Chapman, D. (1968) *Sociology and the Stereotype of the Criminal.* London, Tavistock.

Chatterton, M. (1976) "Police in social control". In *Control Without Custody* (King, J., Ed.). Cropwood Papers.

————, (1978) "The supervision of patrol work under the fixed point system". In *The British Police* (Holdaway, S., Ed.). London, Arnold.

Chevigny, P. (1969) *Police Power: Police Abuses in New York City.* New York, Pantheon.

Chibnall, S. (1977) *Law and Order News.* London, Fontana.

Cohen, S. (1974) *Folk Devils and Moral Panics.* London, MacGibbon & K.

Cooper, L. (1975) "Controlling the police". In *The Police in Society* (Viano, E. & Reiman, J., Eds). Mass., Lexington.

Cressey, D. & Elgesem, E. (1968) "The police and the administration of justice". In *Scandinavian Studies in Sociology* (Christie, N., Ed.) Vol. 2. London, Tavistock.

Critchley, T. (1967) *A History of Police in England and Wales 1900-1966.* London, Constable.

Cumming, E. & Cumming, L. (1965) "Policeman as philosopher, guide, and friend". *Social Problems* 12.

Demuth, C. (1978) *SUS: A Report on the Vagrancy Act 1974.* London, Runnymeade Trust.

Donnelly, R. (1962) "Police authority and practises". *Annals of American Academy of Political and Social Science,* January.

Evans, P. (1974) *The Police Revolution.* London, Allen and Unwin.

Fogelson, R. (1977) *Big City Police.* Mass., Harvard University Press.

Gardiner, J. (1968) "Police enforcement of traffic laws". In *City Politics and Public Policy* (Wilson, J., Ed.). London, Wiley.

Goldman, N. (1963) *The Differential Selection of Juvenile Offenders for Court Appearance.* National Research and Information Centre: National Council on Crime and Delinquency.

Goldstein, H. (1960) "Police discretion not to invoke the legal process". *Yale Law Journal* 68.

_____, (1963) "Police discretion: the ideal versus the real". *Public Administration Review* 23.

Goulden, J. (1974) "The cops hit the jackpot". In *Policing America* (Platt, A. & Cooper, L., Eds). Englewood Cliffs, N.J., Prentice Hall.

Greenwood, P. & Chaiken, J. (1977) *The Criminal Investigation Process.* Mass., Lexington.

Hall, J. (1952) *Theft, Law, and Society* (2nd ed.). Indianapolis, Bobbs Merrill.

_____, (1953) "Police and law in a democratic society". *Indiana Law Journal* 28.

_____, et al. (1978) *Policing the Crisis.* London, Macmillan.

Halpern, S. (1974) *Police Association and Department Leaders: the Politics of Co-Optation.* Lexington Books, Lexington: Mass.

Hay, D. (1975) "Poachers and the game laws on Cannock Chase". In *Albion's Fatal Tree* (Hay, D. et al. Eds). London, Allen Lane.

Humphrey, D. (1972) *Police Power and Black People.* London, Pantheon.

Jeffries, Sir Charles (1952) *The Colonial Police.* London, Max Parrish.

Juris, H. & Feuille, P. (1973) *Police Unionism.* Mass., Lexington.

Kadish, S. (1962) "Legal norms and discretion in police and sentencing process". *Harvard Law Review* 75.

Klare, M. (1974) "Policing the empire". In *Policing America* (Platt, A. & Cooper, L., Eds). New Jersey, Prentice Hall.

Kohler, E. (1975) "The crisis in the Prussian Schulzpolizer". In *Police Forces in History* (Mosse, G., Ed.). London, Sage.

Knapp, W. (1972) *The Knapp Report on Police Corruption.* New York, Braziller.

La Fave, W. (1962) "The police and non-enforcement of the law". *Wisconsin Law Review* 179.

_____, (1965) *Arrest: the Decision to take a Suspect into Custody.* Boston, Little Brown.

Manning, P. (1977) *Police Work.* M.I.T., Mass.

Martin, J. & Wilson, G. (1969) *The Police: A Study in Manpower.* London, Heinemann.

McBarnet, D. (1978) "The police and the state: arrest, illegality, and the law". In *Power and the State* (Littlejohn, J. et al., Eds.). London, Croom Helm.

Morrison, W. (1975) "The North West Mounted Police and the Klondike Gold Rush". In *Police Forces in History* (Mosse, G., Ed.). London, Sage.

Mosse, G. (Ed.) (1975) *Police Forces in History*. London, Sage.

Muir, W. K. (1977) *Police: Streetcorner Politicians*. University of Chicago Press.

Nelson, H. (1967) "The defenders: a case study of an informal police organisation". *Social Problems* 15.

Newman, D. (1962) "Pleading guilty for considerations". *Journal of Criminal Law, Criminology, and Police Science* 46.

_____, (1966) *Conviction*. Boston, Little Brown.

New York Times (1970) "Law and order equitably applied". Editorial for 3rd May cited in *Comparative Concepts of Law and Order* (Sutherland, J. & Werthman, M., Eds). Illinois, Scott Foresman, 1971.

Norris, D. (1973) *Police Community Relations*. Mass., Lexington.

Odendunle, F. (1979) "The Nigeria police force: a preliminary assessment of function and performance". *International Journal of the Sociology of Law* 7.

Osborough, N. (1965) "Police discretion not to prosecute juveniles". *Modern Law Review* 28.

Piliavin, I. & Briar, S. (1964) "Police encounters with juveniles". *American Journal of Sociology* 70.

Pinto, V. (1974) "Weapons for the homefront". In *Policing America* (Platt, A. & Cooper, L., Eds). New Jersey, Prentice Hall.

Platt, A. & Cooper, L. (Eds) (1974) *Policing America*. Englewood Cliffs, N.J., Prentice Hall.

Pogrebin, M. (1976) "Some observations on the detective role". *Journal of Police Science and Administration* 4.

President's Commission on Law Enforcement and the Administration of Justice (1967) *The Challenge of Crime in a Free Society*. Washington D.C., U.S. Government Printing Office.

Punch, M. (1979) *Policing the Inner City*. London, Macmillan.

Purcell, W. (1974) *British Police in a Changing Society*. London, Mowbrays.

Reiner, R. (1978a) "The police, class, and politics". *Marxism Today,* March.

_____, (1978b) *The Blue Coated Worker*. Cambridge University Press.

_____, (1978c) "The police in the class structure". *British Journal of Law and Society* 5.

Reiss, A. (1971) *The Police and the Public*. New Haven, Yale University Press.

Remington, F. (1962) "The law relating to 'on the street' detention, questioning and frisking of suspected persons". In *Police Power and Individual Freedom* (Sowle, C., Ed.). Chicago, Aldine, 1962.

_____, (1965) "The role of the police in democratic society". *Journal of Criminal Law, Criminology, and Police Science* 56.

Richardson, J. (1970) *The New York Police.* London, Oxford University Press.

_____, (1975) "Berlin police in the Weimar republic". In *Police Forces in History* (Mosse, G., Ed.). London, Sage.

Robinson, C. (1975) "The mayor and the police". In *Police Forces in History* (Mosse, G., Ed.). London, Sage.

Rock, P. (1973) *Deviant Behaviour.* London, Hutchinson.

Rubinstein, J. (1973) *City Police.* New York, Farrar, Strauss, and Giroux.

Silver, A. (1967) "The demand for order in civil society". In *The Police: Six Sociological Essays* (Bordua, D., Ed.). New York, Wiley.

Skolnick, J. (1966) *Justice Without Trial.* New York, Wiley.

_____, (1969) *The Politics of Protest.* New York, Simon and Schuster.

Sowle, G. (Ed.) (1962) *Police Power and Individual Freedom.* Chicago, Aldine.

Stead, P. (1957) *Police of Paris.* London, Staples Press.

Stinchcombe, A. (1963) "Institutions of privacy in the determination of police administrative practice". *American Journal of Sociology* 69.

Stork, J. (1974) "World cop: how America builds the global police state". In *Policing America* (Platt, A. & Cooper, L., Eds). Englewood Cliffs, N.J., Prentice Hall.

Swanson, G. (1975) "The Ottoman police". In *Police Forces in History* (Mosse, G., Ed.). London, Sage.

Taylor, I., Walton, P. & Young, J. (1974) *The New Criminology.* London, Routledge and Kegan Paul.

Thompson, E.P. (1979) "The secret state". *Race and Class* 20.

Tobias, J. (1975) "Police and public in the United Kingdom". In *Police Forces in History* (Mosse, G., Ed.). London, Sage.

Thorwald, J. (1966) *Dead Men Tell Tales.* London, Thames and Hudson.

Washnis, G. (1976) *Citizen Involvement in Crime Prevention.* Mass., Lexington.

Webb, L. (1974) "Repression—a new 'growth industry'". In *Policing America* (Platt, A. & Cooper, L., Eds). Engelwood Cliffs, N.J. Prentice Hall.

Welty, G. (1975) "The profession, the police, and the future". In *The Police in Society* (Viano, E. & Reiman, J., Eds). Mass., Lexington.

Werthman, G. & Piliavin, I. (1967) "Gang members and the police". In *The Police: Six Sociological Essays* (Bordua, D., Ed.).

Westley, W. (1951) *The Police: A Sociological Study of Law, Custom, and Morality.*

Ph.D. dissertation, University of Chicago.

_____, (1953) "Violence and the police". *American Journal of Sociology* 59.

_____, (1956) "Secrecy and the police". *Social Forces* 34.

_____, (1970) *Violence and the Police.* Cambridge, Mass., M.I.T.

Whitaker, B. (1964) *The Police.* Hammondsworth, Penguin.

Wilson, J. (1963) "The police and their problems: a theory". *Public Policy* 12.

_____, (1968a) *Varieties of Police Behaviour.* Cambridge, Mass., Harvard University Press.

_____, (1968b) "The police and delinquents in two cities". In *Controlling Delinquents* (Wheeler, S., Ed.). New York, Wiley.

Wintersmith, R. (1974) *The Police and the Black Community.* Mass., Lexington.

Witt, J. (1973) "Non-coercive interrogation and the administration of criminal justice". *Journal of Criminal Law, Criminology, Police Science* 64.

Woddis, J. (1976) "The state - some problems". *Marxism Today.* November.

Wolfe, A. (1974) "Political repression and the liberal democratic state". In *Policing America* (Platt, A. & Cooper, L., Eds). Englewood Cliffs, N.J., Prentice Hall.

Young, J. (1971) "The role of the police as amplifiers of deviancy, negotiators of reality, and translators of fantasy". In *Images of Deviance* (Cohen, S., Ed.). Hammondsworth, Penguin.

Zander, M. (1972) "Access to a solicitor in the police station". *Criminal Law Review* 342.

CHAPTER 2
Democratic Order and the Rule of Law

JEROME H. SKOLNICK

For what social purpose do police exist? What values do the police serve in a democratic society? Are the police to be principally an agency of social control, with their chief value the efficient enforcement of the prohibitive norms of substantive criminal law? Or are the police to be an institution falling under the hegemony of the legal system, with a basic commitment to the rule of law, even if this obligation may result in a reduction of social order? How does this dilemma of democratic society hamper the capacity of the police, institutionally and individually, to respond to legal standards of law enforcement?

Such questions have posed a predicament since the introduction of the London metropolitan police in 1829. Charles Reith, in his book *The Police Idea*,[1] describes the hostility of early nineteenth-century England even to the idea of developing a metropolitan police force out of fear that the notorious activities of the pre-Revolutionary French police would be duplicated. He cites a parliamentary report of 1818 which considered the police idea and recommended against the establishment of a police force:

> The police of a free country is to be found in rational and humane laws—in an effective and enlightened magistracy—and in the judicious and proper selection of those officers of justice, in whose hands, as conservators of the peace, executive duties are legally placed, but above all, in the moral habits and opinions of the people; and in proportion as these approximate towards a state of perfection, so that people may rest in security; and thought their property may occasionally be invaded or their lives endangered by the hands of wicked and desperate individuals, yet the institutions of the country being sound, its laws well adjusted, and justice executed against offenders, no greater safeguard can be obtained without sacrificing all those rights which society was instituted to preserve.[2]

Reith, who is pro-police and pro-Peel, may exaggerate somewhat the degree of opposition to the police. Other authors also interpret the period as one of considerable hostility to a formal institutionalization of police. Mather, for example, points out that historians, like Whigs, are fundamentally antipolice.[3] Given such opposition, therefore, before introducing his "Bill for Improving Police in and near the Metropolis" in 1829, Peel laid a formidable groundwork. A. A. W. Ramsay describes it as follows:

> Peel, with his usual caution, brooded for years over the problem before he undertook to solve it. In 1826 he began to collect evidence for the purpose of comparing crime with population. In 1828 he secured the appointment of a Parliamentary Committee to investigate the subject—the last of four successive Committees in the past twenty-five years, but the first to do valuable work. He had at first intended a measure which should create a police force throughout the kingdom: he ended with a modest scheme, whose operation was confined to London, and at first to a limited number of parishes.[4]

To buttress his argument for the necessity of a police force, Peel based his claims on the need for public order. Citing population statistics from London and Middlesex, he argued that crime was dramatically increasing in this early period of industrial revolution, and increasing at a faster rate than population. In the period of 1821 to 1828, population had increased 15 1/2 per cent, while criminal committals had risen by 41 per cent. Deploring the existence of an army of "trained and hardened criminals" in London and Middlesex, Peel announced that "not less than one person in every three hundred and eighty-three had been convicted for some crime or other in 1828,"[5] without mentioning, although he was fully aware of the fact, that the number of acts considered criminal was so large, and the conditions of the working classes so onerous, that the figures he cited were hardly shocking.

In making this appeal for more efficient controls over crime, Peel was quick to add that he was "confident they would be able to dispense with the necessity of a military force in London for the preservation of the tranquility of the metropolis,"[6] an assurance he could hardly dispense with considering the strength of his opposition. The early conception of police accountability to the rule of law is a tradition which has continued to the present day. Maitland reaffirmed it in 1885 when he wrote in a book entitled *Justice and Police*:

> There is a large body of rules defining crimes and the punishment of those who commit them, rights and the remedies of those who are wronged, but there is also a body of rules defining how and by whom, and when and where, rules of the former kind can be put in force....It will little avail us that our law about rights and remedies, crimes and punishments, is as good as many be, if the law of civil and criminal procedure is clumsy and inefficient.[7]

This same tradition of the hegemony of the rule of law is eloquently stated in the 1962 Royal Commission Report in a refutation of the argument that a national police force would lead to the development of a "police state" in Great Britain. The commission argues:

> British liberty does not depend, and never has depended, upon any particular form of police organization. It depends upon the supremacy of Parliament and on the rule of law. We do not accept that the criterion of a police state is whether a country's police force is national rather than local—if that were the test, Belgium, Denmark and Sweden should be described as police states. The proper criterion is whether the police are answerable to the law and, ultimately, to a democratically elected Parliament. It is here, in our view, that the distinction is to be found between a free and a totalitarian state. In the countries to which the term police state is applied opprobriously, police power is controlled by the government; but they are so called not because the police are nationally organized, but because the government acknowledges no accountability to a democratically elected parliament, and the citizen cannot rely on the courts to protect him. Thus in such countries the foundations upon which British liberty rests do not exist.[8]

The theory of the police in the United States mirrors the conflict between order and legality found in English conceptions of the police, but characteristically American features add complexity. In reading about the American police, especially through the period of the 1930s, one feels that constitutional issues of legality have been almost too remote to be of immediate concern. Not that American police conformed to the rule of law. Rather, they seemed so far out of line that a writer summarizing a major American study of police practices entitled his book *Our Lawless Police*. The study, completed in 1931 by the National Committee of Law Observance and Enforcement (the Wickersham Commission), found practices so appalling and sadistic as to pose no intellectual issue for civilized men.[9] It is one thing to talk quietly to a suspect without his counsel and artfully, perhaps by deceit, persuade him to incriminate himself; it is quite another to hang a suspect out of a window by his heels from a great height, or to beat a confession out of him by putting a telephone book on his head and pounding the book with a blackjack so it does not leave marks. Both techniques may be illegal, but responsible police officials would not publicly support blackjack interrogation. On the other hand, interrogation of suspects without the presence of counsel and even deceptive interrogation are standard "professional" police techniques.[10]

For many municipal police forces in the United States, the observer's question is, therefore, not whether police operate under the constraints of due process of law, but whether they operate within bounds of civilized conduct. In the old-fashioned police department, riddled with political appointees and working hand in hand with the rackets, a reformer is not concerned primarily with the niceties of constitutional rights. When the citizenry is facing the arbitrary use of "club, blackjack, and gun,"[11] the police reformer's problem is to reduce gross brutality, which seems traditionally to have been associated with corruption. Given this situation, it is not surprising that the solution to the "police problem" in America has been frequently conceived as changing the quality of people, rather than the philosophies of policing. Fosdick wrote in 1920, in a characteristically American passage on police reform:

> We are concerned with the facts and conditions and not with theories or labels. It is not a matter of democracy, of caste, or birth, or position, or anything else. It is solely a matter of finding the best possible brains to handle a most difficult public task.[12]

Police reform means finding a new source of police, and police control is a matter of having the "right" sort of people in control. "Reform" of police means increasing the efficiency of police personnel. It is rarely recognized that the conduct of police may be related in a fundamental way to the character and goals of the institution itself—the duties police are called upon to perform, associated with the assumptions of the system of legal justice—and that it may not be men who are good or bad, so much as the premises and design of the system in which they find themselves. For example, V. A. Leonard, a specialist in police administration, indicates how the conception of punishment as the basis of order invites objectionable side effects:

> A system of legal justice based upon the thesis of punishment has exerted a tremendously negative effect on the professionalization of police service. As a corollary the low quality of personnel required to exercise the police power under these conditions was not conducive to good public relations, with the result that a negative public opinion had been created. The withdrawal of public interest and support together with public apathy and indifference, has further served to retard the advance toward professionalization. No less important has been the fact that a substandard personnel became easy prey for corrupt political figures and others in the community who profit when the risks associated with vice operations are reduced. The highly lucrative enterprises of prostitution, gambling, and narcotics enjoyed a field day during this period of American police history.[13]

Leonard, however, does not raise the basic issue of the meaning of the "professionalization of police service." Clearly such a notion suggests that police must be honest and capable. But is this enough? The question is what the concept of "professionalization" suggests to police in a society committed to the rule of law.

With the concern for reform of police practices in America, a growing and responsible debate over the theory of the police in America may be anticipated. There are those police officials and other spokesmen for law enforcement who emphasize the importance of social order. They are not unconcerned about the arbitrary use of police authority, but feel that that answer lies in the continued improvement of internal police administration. By raising the standards for admission to the police force and by making efficiency a goal and personal honesty a requisite, the quality of police work will be raised and police work will become akin to a "science."[14]

At the same time, there has always been a considerable body of opinion, usually outside police circles—among defense attorneys, law professors, and judges—demanding that police adhere strictly to the rules governing the legal system, that they ultimately be accountable to the legal order irrespective of their "practical" needs as law enforcement officials. This position was summarized in the landmark case of *Escobedo v. Illinois*,[15] the United States Supreme Court overturning a conviction when the police refused to honor the request of a suspect to have a lawyer present at his interrogation. Justice Goldberg, for the majority, wrote:

> We have...learned the...lesson of history that no system of criminal justice can, or should, survive if it comes to depend for its continued effectiveness on the citizens' abdication through unawareness of their constitutional rights. No system worth preserving should have to fear that if an accused is permitted to consult with a lawyer, he will become aware of, and exercise, these rights. If the exercise of constitutional rights will thwart the effectiveness of a system of law enforcement, then there is something very wrong with that system.[16]

The purpose of this study is to show, through empirical investigation of police, how value conflicts of democratic society create conditions undermining the capacity of police to respond to the rule of law. Its chief conclusion (and orienting hypothesis), elaborated in the closing chapter, may be summarized: *The police in democratic society are required to maintain order and to do so under the rule of law. As functionaries charged with maintaining order, they are part of the bureaucracy. The ideology of democratic bureaucracy emphasizes initiative rather than disciplined adherence to rules and regulations. By contrast, the rule of law emphasizes the rights of individual citizens and constraints upon the initiative of legal officials. This tension between the operational consequences of ideas of order, efficiency, and initiative, on the one hand, and legality, on the other, constitutes the principle problem of police as a democratic legal organization.* The work attempts to analyze, through empirical investigation of police, how conceptions associated with order and interpretations regarding legality develop within a professionalized police department, and to study the processes through which these conceptions and interpretations come to be associated with certain patterns and practices of policing.

LAW AND ORDER: THE SOURCE OF THE DILEMMA

If the police could maintain order without regard to legality, their short-run difficulties would be considerably diminished. However, they are inevitably concerned with interpreting legality because of their use of *law* as an instrument of order. The criminal law contains a set of rules for the maintenance of social order. This arsenal comprises the *substantive* part of the criminal law, that is, the elements of crime, the principles under which the accused is to be held accountable for alleged crime, the principles justifying the enactment of specific prohibitions, and the crimes themselves. Sociologists usually concentrate here, asking how well this control system operates, analyzing the conditions under which it achieves intended goals, and the circumstances rendering it least efficient.[17]

Another part of the criminal law, however, regulates the conduct of state officials charged with processing citizens who are suspected, accused, or found guilty of crime.[18] Involved here are such matters as the law of search, the law of arrest, the elements and degree of proof, the right of counsel, the nature of a lawful accusation of crime, and the fairness of trial. The procedures of the criminal law, therefore, stress protection of individual liberties *within* a system of social order.[19]

This dichotomy suggests that the common juxtaposition of "law and order" is an oversimplification. Law is not merely an instrument of order, but may frequently be its adversary.[20] There are communities that appear disorderly to some (such as bohemian communities valuing diversity), but which nevertheless maintain a substantial degree of legality. The contrary may also be found: a situation where order is well maintained, but where the policy and practice of legality is not evident. The totalitarian social system, whether in a nation or an institution, is a situation of order without rule of law. Such a situation is probably best illustrated by martial rule, where military authority may claim and exercise the power of amnesty and detention without warrant. If, in addition, the writ of habeas corpus, the right to inquire into these acts, is suspended, as it typically is under martial rule, the executive can exercise arbitrary powers.[21] Such a system of social control is efficient, but does not conform to generally held notions about the "rule of law."[22]

Although there is no precise definition of the rule of law, or its synonym, the principle of legality, its essential element is the reduction of arbitrariness by officials—for example, constraints on the activities of the police—and of arbitrariness in positive law by the application of "rational principles of civic order."[23] A statement expressive of the rule of law is found in a report on police arrests for "investigations." The authors, who are lawyers, write, "Anglo-American law has a tradition of antipathy to the imprisonment of a citizen at the will of executive officers."[24] A more explicit definition of the rule of law in the administration of criminal law has been presented as follows:

> The principle of *nulla poena singe lege* imposes formidable restraints upon the definition of criminal conduct. Standards of conduct must meet stringent tests of specificity and clarity, may act only prospectively, and must be strictly construed in favor of the accused. Further, the definition of criminal conduct has largely come to be regarded as a legislative function, thereby precluding the judiciary from devising new crimes. The public-mischief doctrine and the sometimes over-generalized "ends" of criminal conspiracy are usually regarded as anomalous departures from this main stream. The cognate principle of procedural regularity and fairness, in short, due process of law, commands that the legal standard be applied to the individual with scrupulous fairness in order to minimize the chances of convicting the innocent, protect against abuse of official power, and generate an atmosphere of impartial justice. As a consequence, a complex network of procedural requirements embodied variously in constitutional, statutory, or judge-made law is imposed upon the criminal adjudicatory process—public trial, unbiased tribunal, legal representation, open hearing, confrontation, and related concomitants of procedural justice.[25]

Thus, when law is used as the instrument of social order, it necessarily poses a dilemma. The phrase "law and order" is misleading because it draws attention away from the substantial incompatibilities existing between the two ideas. Order under law suggests procedures different from achievement of "social control" through threat of coercion and summary judgment. Order under law is concerned not merely with the achievement of regularized social activity but with the means used to come by peaceable behavior, certainly with procedure, but also with positive law. It would surely be a violation of the rule of law for a legislature to make epilepsy a crime, even though a public "seizure" typically disturbs order in the community. While most law enforcement officials regard drug addicts as menacing to the community, a law making it a crime to *be* an addict has been declared unconstitutional.[26] This example, purposely selected from substantive criminal law, indicates that conceptions of legality apply here as well as in the more traditional realm of criminal procedure. In short, "law" and "order" are frequently found to be in opposition, because law implies rational restraint upon the rules and procedures utilized to achieve order. Order under law, therefore, subordinates the ideal of conformity to the ideal of legality.

CONCEPTIONS AND APPLICATIONS: THE DILEMMA COMPLICATED

The actual requirement of maintaining social order under the principle of legality places an unceasing burden upon the police as a social institution. Indeed, the police is *the* institution best exemplifying the strain between the two ideas. The 1962 Royal Commission on the Police states the law enforcement dilemma as follows:

> The police systems in England, Scotland and Wales are the products of a series of compromises between conflicting principles or ideas. Consequently, in contrast to other public services such as health and education, the rationale of the police service does not rest upon any single and definite concept of the public good. Thus, it is to the public good that the police should be strong and effective in preserving law and order and preventing crime; but is equally to the public good that police power should be controlled and confined so as not to interfere arbitrarily with personal freedom. The result is compromise. The police should be powerful but not oppressive; they should be efficient but not officious; they should form an impartial force in the body politic, and yet be subject to a degree of control by persons who are not required to be impartial and who are themselves liable to police supervision.[27]

The law enforcement dilemma, however, is more complex than suggested by the Royal Commission. Not only are the police in a democracy the product of a series of compromises between conflicting principles or ideas, but the ideas themselves are not as clear as they (and we) have so far suggested. If "law and order" is a misleading cliche, then a gross conception of order may be even more misleading. Depending on the institution or community, there may be quite different conceptions of order, some more permissive, others less. A traditional martial conception of order, for example, abhors individual differences. The soldier whose bearing or uniform sets him off from his comrades in arms is an abomination to his commanding officer. Even the slightest deviation, such as wearing gloves on a cold day, is forbidden as an expression of differences in individual feelings. In any given military unit, either all the soldiers wear gloves, or none do. The hands of some soldiers will perspire, others will be numb with cold, but all soldiers *will* act alike.

Other institutions or portions of society are traditionally more yielding. The area surrounding the University of Paris is noted for its emphasis upon individuality. Students, artists, writers may be dressed elegantly or poorly, raffishly or provocatively, the mode being considered an extension of the ego, an expression of personality, or perhaps merely an attempt to experiment with novelty. The idea of order in this setting is surely a more permissive conception than the standard military notion. Our conclusion is that conceptions of order seem to be variable and tend to correspond to the requirements of different communities or institutions.

Conceptions of order also seem to be associated with conceptions of appropriate modes of achieving it. The response of a soldier needs to be quick and unquestioning, since failure to respond instantaneously may result in severe damage to himself and to his comrades-in-arms. The socialization of the soldier therefore emphasizes unquestioning *obedience*. A trained soldier is a man who responds unthinkingly to command, and the norm of command is *sharp* command. Failure to respond is met with punishment, seemingly severe to those who receive it. Its justification, however, is located not in the precipitating act itself, but in the implications of nonobedience for the combat situation. The basic trainee whose inspected boot has been found to have a relatively low gloss may lose a weekend's liberty not because a less than sparkling boot is intrinsically important, but because it presumably signifies future sloth.

By contrast, an institution expressive of liberal and humanistic values, such as a university, will usually emphasize persuasion through reason as the instrument for the achievement of order. Since its institutional goal is scholarship, it is traditionally tolerant of behavioral and attitudinal variations, stressing contemplation and dialogue over obedience to rules, and persuasion rather than force as the instrument of an order predicated upon diversity. University police, for example, are far more permissive than local urban police forces. Later on, some of the reasons for such a difference are discussed, notably the relative absence of danger within the university community. Here it is enough to state as an hypothesis of the study that varying social conditions—the nature of the criminal law, the presence of danger in the community, the political complexion of the community, the social dissimilarity of the population being policed—all contribute to the conception of order held by the police.

The organizational model of the police also influences their conception of order. To the degree that police are organized on a military model, there is also likely to be generated a martial conception of order. Internal regulations based on martial principles suggest external cognitions based on similar principles. The presence of an explicit hierarchy, with an associated chain of command and a strong sense of obedience, is therefore likely to induce an attachment to social uniformity and routine and a somewhat rigid conception of order. Such a conception of order is probably increasingly at variance with segments of the community where police, perceiving themselves as "workers" who should exercise initiative, are coming to be concentrated. As this process occurs, police are more likely to lean toward the arbitrary invocation of authority to achieve what they perceive to be the aims of substantive criminal law. Along with these effects is an elevation of crime control to a position where it is valued more than the principle of accountability to the rule of law.

Aiding this process is ambiguity about the application of the rule of law. In the abstract, the rule of law embodies rational restraints upon authority as it defines criminal conduct. There must be specificity, clarity, prospectivity, and strict construction in favor of the accused. There must be procedural regularity and fairness, and so forth. In practice, however, such standards may not be clear. The principle of procedural regularity and fairness commanding that the legal standards be applied so as to "minimize the chances of convicting the innocent, protect against the abuse of official power, and generate an atmosphere of impartial justice"[28] is, for example, subject to varying interpretation by the police and the courts. One year illegally seized evidence may be admitted into evidence under a legal system subscribing to the rule of law, and the next year it may not. A confession may be admitted into evidence at one point in time whether or not the suspect was informed of his right to counsel; at a slightly later point in time such a confession is found to violate constitutional protections. Thus, although certain fundamental and relatively changeless principles of the rule of law are specifiable, the practical constraints on official conduct derived from these principles are always in a degree of flux. A legal order is never a fixed body of rules, but, as Fuller suggests, and "enterprise" of governance by rule.

It may also be suggested, as some of the following materials will show, that whenever rules of constraint are ambiguous, they strengthen the very conduct they intended to restrain. Thus the policeman already committed to a conception of law as an instrument of order rather than as an end in itself is likely to utilize the ambiguity of the rules of restraint as a justification for testing or even violating them. By such a process, the practical ambiguity of the rule of law may serve to undermine its salience as a value. In sum, the actual enterprise of maintaining order by rule of law serves to complicate the conflict of these principles inherent in a democratic society.

THE SECLUSION OF ADMINISTRATION: THE DILEMMA'S SETTING

Perhaps if the administration of criminal law conformed to its popular image, study of the police would be less important. Popularly, even though the police are an object of much romanticized attention, the trial is perceived as the *culmination* of the process of administering criminal law.[29] Trials are dramatic spectacles, and folklore surrounding prominent criminal trial attorneys has had a profound impact on the general public. In fact, the typical method of conviction is by the accused's plea of guilty, with no trial required. In the federal courts, the guilty plea receives the heaviest use, 86 per cent in the fiscal years 1960 through 1963, while in the state courts, the use of the plea trails by 5 to 10 per cent.[30] (The county under study in this report was about average, with 82 per cent of convictions obtained by plea of guilty in 1961.) Mostly, therefore, the system of administering criminal justice in the United States is a system of justice *without* trial.[31]

The plea of guilty is often seen by criminal law personnel as a means of coping with the problem of limited court facilities. In partial justification for a heavier sentence on the one of five defendants who refused to plead guilty, a federal judge opined: "...if in one year, 248 judges are to deal with 35,517 defendants, the district courts must encourage pleas of guilty. One way to encourage pleas of guilty is to establish or announce a policy that, in the ordinary case, leniency will not be granted to a defendant who stands trial."[32] Not only is the plea of guilty recognized as playing an integral role in the criminal process, it is also evident that the necessity for frequent invocation of the plea is a key institutional factor in shaping the position of the defendant vis-à-vis the State.

The statistical pattern of guilty pleas and the reasons for this pattern are interesting themselves, but not so interesting as their implication that routine decision-making in the administration of criminal justice is hidden from public view. When a plea of guilty is entered, encounters between prosecutor and defense attorney, defense attorney and client, prosecutor and policeman, policeman and suspect, are never brought to public attention, and in the nature of the situation cannot be. The case is often "tried" in an informal setting, perhaps over a cup of coffee or in the corridor behind the courtroom.

The frequency and seclusion of the plea of guilty raise far-reaching questions in legal theory: (1) To the extent that courts seek to control the behavior of police in such areas as searches and seizures, eavesdropping, and confessions, does the frequent invocation of the plea of guilty serve to shield from public view the patterned occurrence of violations of criminal law by police? (2) At every other level of the system are there systematic practices which rarely or never come to light because the guilty plea "covers up" whatever took place before it occurred? (3) What factors influence agreement to a plea of guilty, and what is the relationship of these factors to what would be countenanced in the formal system of appellate decisions? (4) Finally, how does heavy dependence on the plea of guilty affect the accomplishment of the goals of the legal system?[33]

Police work constitutes the most secluded part of an already secluded system and therefore offers the greatest opportunity for arbitrary behavior. As invokers of the criminal law, the police frequently act in practice as its chief interpreter. Thus, they are necessarily called upon to test the limits of their legal authority. In so doing, they also define the operative legality of the system of administering criminal law. That is, if the criminal law is especially salient to a population which has more or less recurrent interactions with the police, it is the police who define the system of order to this population. This work of interpretation, this "notice-giving" function of police, is a crucial consideration in assessing the degree to which legality penetrates a system of criminal justice.

Whenever a system of justice takes on an *insular* character, a question is raised as to the degree of *justice* such a system is capable of generating. Lon L. Fuller, a legal philosopher, has suggested the broadest significance of the seclusion of criminal law administration when he discusses the affinity between legality and justice. He asserts that both share a common quality, since they act by known rule. Fuller discusses the significance of public scrutiny as follows:

The internal morality of the law demands that there be rules, that they be made known, and that they be observed in practice by those charged with their administration. These demands may seem ethically neutral so far as the external aims of law are concerned. Yet, just as law is a precondition for good law, so acting by known rule is a precondition for any meaningful appraisal of the justice of law. "A lawless unlimited power" expressing itself solely in unpredictable and patternless interventions in human affairs could be said to be unjust only in the sense that it does not act by known rule. *It would be hard to call it unjust in any more specific sense until one discovered what hidden principle, if any, guided its interventions.* It is the virtue of a legal order conscientiously constructed and administered that it exposes to public scrutiny the rules by which it acts.[34]

The system of justice without trial is not a system of "unpredictable and patternless interventions." Rather, it is one which operates against a background of known rules, but which also, especially in the instance of the police, develops a set of informal norms or "hidden principles" in response to the formal rules. These, in turn, are influential in determining how the formal rules actually operate.

LAW AS AN ENTERPRISE

That law is an enterprise summons us to its empirical study. It reminds us that highly general propositions about law may be either circular or premature. Consider the following propositions: the economic structure of the society affects law; the power structure affects law; public opinion affects law; the Protestant ethic affects law; and so on. All such statements are but a beginning, as is a statement that law is "integrative," or that law affects the economy. Whether law is seen as an independent or dependent variable, the important work is the specification of those processes intervening between the two. Thus, from the perspective of law as an enterprise, what needs to be specified is how economy affects law, politics affects law, and the kind of legal order enhancing types of social integration. The development of a sociology of law depends upon detailed analysis of the social foundations of legality and of empirical elaborations of processes through which relations among variables result in determinate outcomes.[35]

It may be instructive to draw an analogy to the sociology of bureaucracy, where scholars have taken a similar view. They have not tried to spell out the "functions" of bureaucracy in society, but rather have concentrated on case studies investigating problems associated with certain forms of organized cooperation. Neither have they primarily attempted to be managerial experts who would improve the efficiency of this system. They have been concerned, to be sure, with the effects of different forms of organized cooperation on the satisfactions of human existence; but as scholars, they have sought first of all to understand the conditions under which these forms result in varying outcomes. Their approach has been to consider what Crozier has termed "the bureaucratic phenomenon."[36]

Crozier sees this as the indispensable "exploratory" phase of scientific development, a phase which elaborates the problem by the generation of descriptive hypotheses. Such hypotheses serve only as examples, to be sure, and are valid only for the case at hand. Crozier adds, however, that, limited as such examples may seem initially, they are capable of yielding more information about the functioning of social systems of the same order, and even of larger systems, than studies insisting upon a "premature rigor." He concludes:

> To resolve upon a clinical approach may seem regressive after certain earlier ambitions of the social sciences. However, this seems to us indispensable for all those problems which touch upon the sociology of institutions and the sociology of action. There are no shortcuts possible. General statistical relations, which can be perceived at the opinion level, are fragmentary and undifferentiated; they can testify to accomplished changes, but not to the process of change, nor to the laws of action, nor even to the general direction of the evolution. Only models of functioning at an operational level can help us progress. This is what a clinical approach can offer us.[37]

Crozier's examination of French bureaucracy also indicated to him that understanding the dynamics of bureaucracy is not possible unless its operations is examined within the setting of a culture. Although there are similarities, under close empirical examination the dynamics of bureaucracy in France and in Germany are distinguishable. Crozier asserts that the "study of the bureaucratic phenomenon permits a new breakthrough at this more 'operational' level."[38] Similarly, Blau found that certain features of the bureaucratic model were not equally applicable in different cultures. He argues that in the Germany of Max Weber strict hierarchical control may have constituted the most efficient method of management, but that in an American culture valuing social equality "permitting junior officials considerable discretion in discharging their responsibilities may be a more efficient system of administration."[39] Such findings, and others as well,[40] suggest that the operation of social organizations will always reflect the cultural, political, social, and economic contexts in which they are located. The important task is to *specify* the role of culture and ideology in determining the conduct of men and their social organizations.

LAW ENFORCEMENT IN DEMOCRATIC SOCIETY

The police in this study are considered as a class of authorities facing the problem of managing divergent expectations of conduct. Democracy's ideological conflict between the norms governing the work of maintaining order and the principle of accountability to the rule of law provides the justification for various demands upon the policeman. He may be expected to be rule enforcer, father, friend, social servant, moralist, streetfighter, marksman, and officer of the law. The problem of organizing and defining such demands furnishes the basis for the institutional analysis of police. The problem itself suggests the situational difficulties affecting the policeman's capacity to be a responsible law enforcement official who enforces order under the rule of law.

The dilemma of the police is further complicated. It is possible in practice for applications of the rule of law as well as conceptions of order to vary. Standards for applying the rule of law are developed by the courts in the setting of specific police practices. Standards governing search and seizure practices, for example, are usually developed in narcotics cases, while standards of the legality of procedures for obtaining confessions typically arise in cases where there is an element of assault. Similarly, conceptions of order are subject to varying interpretations and tend to influence and be influenced by conditions prevailing in police work. General statements about the police conception of order and its sources can be made, but it is also possible to show how the generalized conception is modified by the perceived requirements of various police assignments. When the informer system is discussed, for example, it becomes clear that the meaning of criminal conduct is differently evaluated depending on how the perceived criminality fits in with procedures characteristically used to enforce specific categories of the law.

The division of labor within the police department (burglary, vice control, traffic control, patrol) supplies a methodological framework for observing and comparing the assumptions and outcomes of police practices in democratic society. Policing specialties generate distinctive patterns for the invocation and enforcement of the law of crimes: who first sees a criminal act, how it is reported, how apprehension takes place. In gathering participant-observational data, then, the division of police labor set the background for the working hypothesis of the study: *the characteristic pattern of enforcement, with its special arrangements for gathering information, processing offenders, and evaluating the competence of personnel, all under rule of law, determines operational law enforcement.* The idea of operational law enforcement should suggest both the attitudes and behavior of policemen responding to judicial rulings, and interpersonal relations with the accused, the prosecutor, defense attorney, judge, and whenever applicable, with the general public.

Underlying this working question is a more general and fundamental issue growing out of the concept of law enforcement. This issue is the meaning and purpose of law in democratic society. The idea of law enforcement in such a society, taken seriously, suggests that legally constituted institutions such as the police exist not only to preserve order, but to serve the rule of law as an end in itself. On the other hand, the circumstances of the occupational environment, with its associated requirements that the police maintain order, might develop a very different conception of law in police, a conception without articulation or explicit philosophical justification, but existing nevertheless. Such a conception might perceive law not primarily as an instrument for guaranteeing individual freedom, but, as in the Soviet Union, an instrument of education, as a father is a teacher of children. Harold Berman describes the paternalistic character of Soviet legality and its consequences as follows:

> Soviet law cannot be understood unless it is recognized that the whole Soviet society is itself conceived to be a single great family, a gigantic school, a church, a labor union, a business enterprise. The state stands at its head, as the parent, the teacher, the priest, the chairman, the director. As the state, it acts officially through the legal system, but its purpose in so acting is to make its citizens into obedient children, good students, ardent believers, hard workers, successful managers.
>
> This, indeed, is the essential characteristic of the law of a total state.
>
> We have seen that legal consequences follow from this conception of the role of law. Court procedure is informal and speedy; the judge protects the litigants against the consequences of their ignorance, and clarifies to them the nature of their rights and duties; there is elaborate pre-trial procedure directed toward uncovering the whole history of the situation. The rule: "Let the punishment fit the crime" is supplemented (though not supplanted) by the rule: "Let the punishment fit the man."[41]

The conception of law as a teacher is closely connected with the idea that law is primarily an instrument for achieving social order. Thus, the Soviet regime (and the Chinese Communist as well) adopted a secret police almost immediately on coming into existence. The Soviet secret police, the Cheka, was given broad powers, although it was not until 1924 that even a document was published explaining its existence and purposes. Under this statutory authorization, the main task of the secret police was to act as the investigative and punitive arm of the dictatorship, hunting out and liquidating "counterrevo-lutionary...attempts and actions throughout Russia, no matter what their origin."[42] The Cheka was answerable only to the top leadership of the Party and government, although experience was to demonstrate that whatever actions the Cheka considered necessary to defend the dictatorship (of the proletariat), including arrest, imprisonment, and even execution, would he approved by the Party leadership, notwithstanding any formal or legal limitations on its power.

As a system based upon law as the instrument for imposing a "necessary" social order, the Cheka became the object of wide-ranging criticism, not only among its opponents, but within the ranks of the Party itself. Its own *Weekly* acknowledged these complaints, noting that "reports are coming in from all sides that not only unworthy but outright criminal individuals are trying to penetrate the...Chekas."[43] But in reply to such criticisms, Lenin defended the secret police on grounds that the arbitrary use of authority was permissible in the cause of achieving a society ordered on proletarian principles. He said to a conference of Cheka representatives in November, 1918 that despite the presence of "strange elements" in its ranks, the Cheka was "putting into practice the dictatorship of the proletariat, and in this respect its role is invaluable; there is no other path to the freeing of the masses than the suppression of the exploiters by force. The Cheka is engaged in this, and in this consists its service to the proletariat."[44]

The meaning of law in a society is ultimately dependent upon its political and social philosophy. When law is viewed primarily as an instrument of education or as an instrument of order, rather than as a goal in itself, the society no longer conceives of punishment as a last resort, to be used only reluctantly. Lipson describes Soviet law as the instrument of state morality as follows:

> Coercion to virtue is esteemed not only for virtue's sake but also as a means of reducing the incidence of lawbreaking. The number of violations of public order is swollen by the difficulties of the society and by the broadly inclusive notion of what *amounts* to a violation. The more precarious the equilibrium of the state, the greater

perceived danger of subversion; the narrower the line, the harder it is not to deviate from it. Even short of disorder, subversion, and deviation, the failure to do one's part in raising the wealth of the state is an offence against the presuppositions of the leaders and thus against the laws of the realm. If *homo oeconomicus* is not yet respectable enough to be allowed on the stage, let his lines be given to *homo juridicus*: Soviet morality permits the government to threaten pain in order to push the citizen to many acts which it cannot yet pull him by hope of reward.[45]

It is not only that the law of a total state has as its essential condition that the society conceive of itself as a single great family. Single great families where the question of values is open to discussion are imaginable. There needs to be also a conception of the inevitability of events, a sense of place in the interpretation of the grand sweep of history, a logical connection, and, ultimately, a belief in the righteousness of killing for the sake of logic. This sort of certainty as to what is right, and the willingness to adopt the most extreme punitive measures in defense of it, is the essence of the conception of law in a total state. Father knows all in such a family, and he may, if he thinks it necessary, rule by the rod. This conception of law necessarily contemplates minimal restraint on authority.

By contrast, a democratic society envisions constraint upon those who are granted the right to invoke the processes of punishment in the name of the law. They must draw their rules clearly, state them prospectively. The rules themselves must be rational, not whimsically constructed, and carried out with procedural regularity and fairness. Most important of all, rule is from below, not above. Authorities are servants of the people, not a "vanguard" of elites instructing the masses. The overriding value is consent of the governed. From it derives the principle of the accountability of authority, accountability primarily to courts of law and ultimately to a democratically constituted legislature based upon universal suffrage.

It is interesting that while Lenin justified the excesses of the Cheka on ideological grounds, namely, that they were necessary to establish the sort of social order envisioned by the conception of the dictatorship of the proletariat, a more sociological analysis of the excesses was made by a high-ranking Chekist, Martin Latsis, who saw the occupational environment as creating the conditions for Chekist brutality. Latsis asserted that "work in the Cheka, conducted in an atmosphere of physical coercion, attracts corrupt and outright criminal elements which, profiting from their position as Cheka agents, blackmail and extort, filling their own pockets.... However honest a man is, however crystal-clear his heart, work in the Cheka, which is carried on with almost unlimited rights and under conditions greatly affecting the nervous system, begins to tell. Few escape the effect of the conditions under which they work."[46]

The Soviet secret police may be taken as an example of law enforcement which, while having administrative accountability, is without serious dilemmas regarding the rule of law.[47] The philosophy of the society does not see legality as an end in itself but as the instrument for the achievement of a political order in which law will ultimately disappear. The theory is that "legal rules will undergo a qualitative transformation into non-juridical moral standards. This in turn will lead to a concomitant expansion of the sphere of behavioral norms and habits identified...as 'rules of socialist community life.'"[48] What happens during the period of transformation is, however, open to some question. Latsis' observation that unconstrained authority corrupts suggests one consequence. His conclusion is by no means new, but a sociologist wishes for the opportunity to study the process by which even the honest and well-meaning policeman in a totalitarian society may become corrupted. From the point of view of the social scientist, not only the outcome is important, but also the analytic exploration among variables in the system accounting for the outcome. The nature of a totalitarian society, however, precludes such investigation.

One of the virtues of a society with democratic values is the obligation police themselves may feel for self-analysis and improvement, including even a willingness to have themselves examined on the job by a potentially critical professor. In return, they are entitled to factual accuracy and tenable interpretation in the description and analysis of their work. The emphasis upon the work of police should in this study not be understood as an investigation such as the police themselves might conduct. That much is assumed. The interest here is analytic description, the understanding of conditions under which rules may be violated with greater or lesser intensity. There is an emphasis on the "action perspective" (elaborated in the next chapter) and on the meaning of his work to the policeman himself, especially as it is derived from and reflects back upon societal ideal regarding worker autonomy, the need for order, and the rule of law. Such an emphasis should provide the basis for conclusions on how the working environment of police influences *law* enforcement, that is, the capacity of police to respond and contribute to the rule of law as a master ideal of governance. Such conclusions should hopefully contribute to the development of a theory of law enforcement in democratic society, and to the role of police within such a system.

ENDNOTES

* Reproduced with the permission of Macmillan Publishing Company an imprint of Macmillan Publishing Company, Inc. from *Justice Without Trial: Law Enforcement in Democratic Society* by Jerome Skolnick. Copyright © 1978 by Macmillan Publishing Company.

1. Charles Reith, *The Police Idea: Its History and Evolution in England in the Eighteenth Century and After* (London: Oxford University Press, 1938).

2. *Ibid.*, p. 188.

3. F. C. Mather, *Public Order in the Age of the Chartists* (Manchester: The University Press, 1959), p. v.

4. A. A. W. Ramsay, *Sir Robert Peel* (New York: Dodd, Mead and Company, 1938), p. 88.

5. *Op. cit.*, p. 250.

6. *Ibid.*

7. F. W. Maitland, *Justice and Police* (London: Macmillan and Company, 1885), pp. 1-2.

8. Royal Commission on the Police Cmnd. 1728. (London: Her Majesty's Stationary Office, 1962), p. 45.

9. National Commission on Law Observance and Enforcement (Washington, D.C.: U. S. Government Printing Office, 1930-1931), Publications, No. 1-14.

10. See Fred E. Inbau and John E. Reid, *Criminal Interrogation and Confessions* (Baltimore: The Williams and Wilkins Company, 1962), pp. 20-115; Charles E. O'Hara, *Fundamentals of Criminal Investigation* (Springfield, Illinois: Charles C. Thomas, 1956), pp. 95-114; and Worth R. Kidd, *Police Interrogation* (New York: R. V. Basuino, 1940), pp. 124-125, pp. 133-186.

11. For a summarization of the Wickersham Commission Report, see Ernest Jerome Hopkins, *Our Lawless Police* (New York: The Viking Press, 1931), index reference to "National Commission on Law Observance and Enforcement."

12. Raymond Fosdick, *American Police Systems* (New York: The Century Company, 1920), p. 221. (Fosdick's italics.)

13. V. A. Leonard, *Police Organization and Management* (Brooklyn: The Foundation Press, 1951), p. 6.

14. Cf. William H. Parker, *Parker on Police,* ed. O. W. Wilson (Springfield, Illinois: Charles C. Thomas, 1957); O. W. Wilson, *Police Planning* (Springfield, Illinois: Charles C. Thomas 1962); also see two police journals, *The Police Chief* (pub. Chicago) and *Police* (pub. Springfield, Illinois).

15. 378 U.S. 478 (1964).

16. 378 U.S. 478, 490.

17. See, for example: Harry Elmer Barnes and Negley K. Teeters, *New Horizons in Criminology* (New York: Prentice-Hall, 1951); *Sheldon Glueck, Crime and Correction: Selected Papers* (Cambridge: Addison-Wesley Press, 1952); Richard R. Korn and Lloyd W. McCorkle, *Criminology and Penology* (New York: Holt, 1959); Norval Morris, *The Habitual Criminal* (Cambridge: Harvard University Press, 1951); Joseph Slabey Roucek, *Sociology of Crime* (New York: Philosophical Library, 1961); Walter Cade Reckless, *The Crime Problem* (New York: Appleton-Century-Crofts, 1961); and Edwin Hardin Sutherland and Donald R. Cressey, *Principles of Criminology,* 6th ed. (Philadelphia: Lippincott, 1960).
     One exception is the text of Paul W. Tappan, which emphasizes criminal procedure in great detail. Tappan, it should be noted, however, was also trained as a lawyer. See *Crime, Justice and Correction* (New York: McGraw-Hill, 1960).

18. Thus, a current leading casebook in criminal law devotes its final sections to problems in the administration of criminal law. See Monrad G. Paulsen and Sanford H. Kadish, *Criminal Law and Its Processes* (Boston: Little, Brown and Company, 1962).

19. See Sol Rubin, Henry Wiehofen, George Edwards, and Simon Rosenzweig, *The Law of Criminal Correction* (St. Paul: West Publishing Co., 1963); Paul W. Tappan, *op. cit.*; and Lester B. Orfield, *Criminal Procedure from Arrest To Appeal* (New York: New York University Press, 1947). An excellent discussion of problems of criminal procedure is found in Abraham S. Goldstein, "The State and the Accused: Balance of Advantage in Criminal Procedure," *Yale Law Journal, 69* (June, 1960), 1149-1199.

20. See Alan Barth, *Law Enforcement Versus the Law* (New York: Collier Books, 1963).

21. See Charles Fairman, *The Law of Martial Rule* (Chicago: Callaghan and Company, 1943), especially Chapter 3, "The Nature of Martial Rule," pp. 28-49.

22. See Notes 23, 24, and 33, *infra.*

23. Philip Selznick, "Sociology and Natural Law," *Natural Law Forum, 6* (1961), 95.

24. *Report and Recommendations of the Commissioners' Committee on Police Arrests for Investigation* (District of Columbia, July, 1962), 42.

25. Sanford H. Kadish, "Legal Norm and Discretion in the Police and Sentencing Processes," *Harvard Law Review, 75* (1962), 904-905.

26. *United States v. Robinson,* 361 U. S. 220 (1959). Lon Fuller criticizes the grounds of the decision. The court held in this case that the statute violated the Eighth Amendment by imposing a "cruel and unusual punishment" for an "ill-

ness." Professor Fuller argues that the statute should have been overturned on grounds that it is both *ex post facto* and vague in *The Morality of Law* (New Haven: Yale University Press, 1964), pp. 105-106. My own position is in between, since I do not conceive of an addict as one who necessarily had the intent of becoming one when he began using drugs. Therefore, I find the *ex post facto* objection less than compelling. On whatever grounds, however, the case stands as a good example of positive law in violation of the rule of law.

27. Royal Commission on the Police, *op. cit.*, p. 9.

28. Kadish, *op. cit.*

29. Thus, a recent television program called "Arrest and Trial" implied by its title that the latter inevitably follows upon the former. The tendency to make the implication is understandable.

30. United States, Administrative Office of United States Courts, Annual Report of the Director, 1963, p. 132.

31. Some important work on the plea of guilty has been conducted by Donald J. Newman. See his "Pleading Guilty for Considerations: A Study of Bargain Justice," in Norman Johnston, Leonard Savitz, and Marvin E. Wolfgang (eds.), *The Sociology of Punishment and Correction* (New York: John Wiley and Sons, Inc., 1962), pp. 24-32; and his *The Decision as to Guilt or Innocence* (Chicago: American Bar Foundation, 1962). An able review of the subject is to be found in a paper prepared by Dominick R. Vetri, "Note: Guilty Plea Bargaining: Compromises by Prosecutors to Secure Guilty Pleas," *University of Pennsylvania Law Review*, 112 (April, 1964), 865-895. Also, some interesting materials on the guilty plea are to be found in Arnold S. Trebach, *The Rationing of Justice: Constitutional Rights and the Criminal Process* (New Brunswick: Rutgers University Press, 1964).

32. *United States v. Wiley*, 184 F. Supp. 679 (N.D. Ill., 1960). See also, Vetri, *ibid.*

33. Donald J. Newman points out that the effect of informal conviction methods ("bargain justice") on selection for probation is to make placement on probation dependent on the skill of the defendant or his lawyer rather than on factors thought to have relevance for rehabilitation through probationary treatment. See his "Pleading Guilty for Considerations...," *op. cit.*

34. Fuller, *op. cit.*, pp. 157-158. (Italics added.)

35. Although the subjects of this research are primarily policemen, and police mirror the conflict between legality and order, the theoretical concern is with the phenomenon of law and its enforcement, rather than with the police as an occupational category. It is, therefore, to be interpreted as a study in the sociology of law, rather than as one concerned with issues found in the sociology of work. The fundamental concern of the sociology of work is with the division of labor in society and how the nature and conditions of work affect society and are affected by it. The sociologist of work is, for example, interested in such

issues as the sources of recruitment into an occupation, the conditions under which occupations rise and fall or achieve a status in society and how working conditions influence men's feelings regarding the meaningfulness of labor. These important concerns may be more or less related to the issues of the sociology of law. In studying law enforcement, for example, the question of the social status of police work is significant to the extent that it affects the policeman's working manner. Analysis of the latter is the distinctive concern of the legal sociologist.

36. Michel Crozier, *The Bureaucratic Phenomenon* (Chicago: University of Chicago Press, 1964).

37. *Ibid.*, pp. 4-5.

38. *Ibid.*, p. 8.

39. Peter Blau, *The Dynamics of Bureaucracy* (Chicago: University of Chicago Press, 1955), pp. 202-203.

40. Reinhard Bendix, *Work and Authority in Industry* (New York: Harper and Row, 1963); Burton R. Clark, *The Open Door College* (New York: McGraw-Hill, 1960); Alvin Gouldner, *Patterns of Industrial Bureaucracy* (Glencoe, Ill.: The Free Press, 1954); and Philip Selznick, *TVA and the Grass Roots* (Berkeley: University of California Press, 1949).

41. Harold J. Berman, *Justice in the U.S.S.R.* (New York; Random House, 1963), p. 366.

42. *Pravda*, Dec. 18, 1927, p. 2, quoted in Simon Wolin and Robert M. Slusser (eds.), *The Soviet Secret Police* (New York: Frederick A. Praeger, 1957), p. 4.

43. *Yezhenedel'nik* [Cheka Weekly], No. 2, September 29, 1918, p. 11, quoted in Wolin and Slusser (eds.), *op. cit.*, p. 6.

44. V. I. Lenin, *Sochineniya* [Works] (Moscow-Leningrad, 1926-1932, 2nd ed.), 23, pp. 273-274, quoted in Wolin and Slusser (eds.), *op. cit.*, p. 6.

45. Leon Lipson, "Host and Pests: The Fight against Parasites," *Problems of Communism*, 14, 2 (March-April, 1965), 72-73.

46. M. Ya. Latsis, *Chrezvychainye komissii po bor'be s kontrrevolyutsiyei* [The Extraordinary Commissions for Combating Counterrevolution] (Moscow, 1921), p. 11, quoted in Wolin and Slusser (eds.)., *op. cit.*, p. 6.

47. In the United States, by contrast, the Federal Bureau of Investigation, corresponding roughly to the Cheka as a "national" law enforcement agency, is greatly concerned about responsibilities to obey the rule of law. Most restrictions on police have originated on the federal level, and the states usually have had to be brought into conformity with the more stringent constraints upon authority imposed upon federal law enforcement bodies.

48. Albert Boiter, "Comradely Justice: How Durable Is It?" *Problems of Communism*, 14, 2 (March-April, 1965), 90.

CHAPTER 3
The Demand for Order in Civil Society: A Review of Some Themes in the History of Urban Crime, Police and Riot

ALLAN SILVER

CRIMINALS AND THE "DANGEROUS CLASSES"

Crime and violence in the life of city dwellers have long evoked complaints which have a quite contemporary tone. Peaceful and propertied people in eighteenth-century London, for example, confronted a level of daily danger to which they and their spokesmen reacted indignantly. It was in such terms that Daniel Defoe dedicated a pamphlet on crime to the Lord Mayor of London:

> The Whole City, My Lord, is alarm'd and uneasy; Wickedness has got such a Head, and the Robbers and Insolence of the Night are such, that the Citizens are no longer secure within their own Walls, or safe even in passing their Streets, but are robbed, insulted and abused, even at their own Doors....The Citizens...are oppressed by Rapin and Violence; Hell seems to have let loose Troops of human D—ls upon them; and such Mischiefs are done within the Bounds of your Government as never were practised here before (at least not to such a degree) and which, if suffered to go on, will call Armies, not Magistrates, to suppress.[1]

In the body of his pamphlet, Defoe describes a situation of pervasive insecurity, stressing the mounting and unprecedented extent of criminal attack. The idea of crime wave is already quite explicit:

> Violence and Plunder is no longer confin'd to the Highways....The
> Streets of the City are now the Places of Danger; men are knock'd
> down and robb'd, nay, sometimes murther'd at their own Doors,
> and in passing and repassing but from House to House, or from
> Shop to Shop. Stagecoaches are robb'd in High-Holbourn, White-
> Chappel, Pall-Mall, Soho and at almost all the Avenues of the City.
> Hackney-Coaches and Gentlemen's Coaches are stopt in
> Cheapside, St. Paul's Church-yard, the Strand, and other the most
> crowded streets, and that even while the People in Throngs are
> passing and repassing... 'Tis hard that in a well-govern'd City...it
> should be said that her Inhabitants are not now safe...[2]

We may note in passing that equally contemporary themes richly abound
in magazines that urban Americans read six decades ago. To cite but two
examples:

> Individual crimes have increased in number and malignity. In addi-
> tion to this...a wave of general criminality has spread over the whole
> nation....The times are far from hard, and prosperity for several
> years has been wide-spread in all classes. Large sums are in unac-
> customed hands, bar-rooms are swarming, pool-rooms, policy shops
> and gambling houses are full, the races are played, licentiousness
> increases, the classes who "roll in wealth" set intoxicating examples
> of luxury and recklessness, and crime has become rampant.[3]

In that period, it was, of course, commonplace also to ascribe the fundamental causes of mass criminality to large-scale immigration:

> In the poorer quarters of our great cities may be found huddled
> together the Italian bandit and the bloodthirsty Spaniard, the bad
> man from Sicily, the Hungarian, the Croatian and the Pole, and the
> Chinaman and the Negro, the cockney Englishman, the Russian and
> the Jew, with all the centuries of hereditary hate back of them. They
> continually cross each others' path. It is no wonder that altercations
> occur and blood is shed....
>
> We claim to be a rich and prosperous city and yet we cannot afford
> to employ enough policemen to keep thieves and burglars out of our
> houses and thugs and robbers from knocking us on the head as we
> walk along our own streets....The bald, bare, horrible fact is that the
> conditions existing in Chicago today are the most criminal and
> damnable of any large city on the face of the earth.[4]

Thus the current rhetoric of concern about crime and violence draws on
established motifs of both older and newer vintage: an indignant sense of per-

vasive insecurity; a mounting current of crime and violence as a result of both unaccustomed prosperity and prolonged poverty; the bad example of the self-indulgent wealthy; the violent proclivities of immigrants and other newcomers; and the ironic contrast between the greatness of the metropolis and the continued spread of crime.

But at times there was a somewhat different attitude toward urban crime and violence. In the London and Paris of the late eighteenth and the early nineteenth centuries, people often saw themselves as threatened by agglomerations of the criminal, vicious, and violent—the rapidly multiplying poor of cities whose size had no precedent in Western history. It was much more than a question of annoyance, indignation, or personal insecurity; the social order itself was threatened by an entity whose characteristic name reflects the fears of the time—the "dangerous classes." The phrase occurs repeatedly. Thus, an anonymous essayist of 1844 writes of the situation in urban England, where "destitution, profligacy, sensuality and crime, advance with unheard-of-rapidity in the manufacturing districts, and the dangerous classes there massed together combine every three or four years in some general strike or alarming insurrection which, while it lasts, excites universal terrors...."[5] But even where the term is not explicitly invoked, the image persists—one of an unmanageable, volatile, and convulsively criminal class at the base of society.[6]

This imagery is only in part the product of class antagonisms in early industrial society; rather, the working classes were included in an older and continuing concern with criminality.[7] Urban administrators regarded the swelling numbers of the poor as unmanageable. Indeed, the image of the "dangerous classes," as distinct from that of pervasive criminality, seems to have flourished especially during periods of very rapid population growth, reflecting the migration of the numerous poor, without employment skills or a history of urban life. During this period, the labor force of the metropolis was still not primarily industrial.[8] Thus, the events and the antagonisms of early industrialism inflamed but did not create the image of the "dangerous classes." It referred primarily to the unattached and unemployed. An advocate of police reform in London, writing in 1821, defined the problem in these terms:

> The most superficial observer of the external and visible appearance of this town, must soon be convinced, that there is a large mass of unproductive population living upon it, without occupation or ostensible means of subsistence; and, it is notorious that hundreds and thousands go forth from day to day trusting alone to charity or rapine; and differing little from the barbarous hordes which traverse an uncivilized land....The principle of [their] action is the same; their life

is predatory; it is equally a war against society, and the object is alike to gratify desire by stratagem or force.[9]

As class tensions involving the threat of riot and revolutionary violence subsided in London, the older concern with diffuse criminality rather than the "dangerous classes" reemerged. Thus, Henry Mayhew's immense reportage on London's criminals, vagabonds, and casually employed, published in 1861, was suffused variously by moralism, indignation, pity, compassion, horror, and mere curiosity—but not by the sense of dread that had earlier afflicted those confronted by the dangerous classes.[10] Indeed, contemporary writing in mid-century London exhibits a sense of relief and victory over the forces of mass violence. Contrasting the present with the past, a writer in 1856 observed that "the only quarter in which any formidable riot could take place would be eastward, in the neighborhood of the docks, where there are at least twelve thousand sailors in the river or on shore, ready for a spree, fearless and powerful, and acting with an undoubted *esprit de corps*. These, if associated with the seven or eight thousand dock labourers and lightermen, would certainly produce a force difficult to cope with."[11] Such a prospect clearly was judged as a great improvement.

To judge from contemporary accounts, New York did not experience a comparable sense of relief or improvement. Indeed, it appears that by 1872 New York was already being compared unfavorably to London with respect to crime and violence:

> ...If the vice and pauperism of New York are not so steeped in the blood of the populace [as in London and other European cities] they are even more dangerous....They rob a bank, when English thieves pick pockets; they murder, where European prolétaires cudgel or fight with fists; in a riot they begin what seems about to be the sacking of a city, where English rioters merely batter policemen or smash lamps....[12]

For this observer, whose book is largely concerned with relief and other remedial programs among New York's poor, the dangerous classes are very much a part of the city—which, after all, had only a decade earlier suffered the great Draft Riot of 1863:

> There are thousands upon thousands in New York who have no assignable home, and "flit" from attic to attic, and cellar to cellar; there are other thousands more or less connected with criminal enterprises; and still other tens of thousands, poor, hard-

pressed....Let but Law lift its hand from them for a season, or let the civilizing influences of American life fail to reach them, and, if the opportunity afforded, we should see an explosion from this class which might leave the city in ashes and blood.[13]

Such rhetoric is not, as we have seen, an inevitable expression of concern with criminality, riot, and violence—even when these were of an order unthinkable in daily urban life today.[14]

What are some of the factors that underlie relationships between urban criminality and disorder and the significance ascribed to them by the peaceful and properties classes? An adequate answer to this question would need to consider important aspects of economic, political, and urban history, the labor movement, and demography. For our purposes, however, we will focus on two aspects of the situation that until recently have been neglected: the significance of the police and the culture of riotous protest.

THE POLICED SOCIETY

Some modern nations have been police states; all, however, are policed societies. Practical men have never underestimated, though they have often distorted, the importance of the police. Sociological theory in the "social control" tradition, however, has usually slighted the police in favor of normative or voluntary processes.[15] The significance of the police, for our purposes, can best be understood as they appeared to a generation for whom modern police were an unprecedented innovation—Englishmen in the middle third of the nineteenth century.

The London police, created in 1829, were from the beginning a bureaucratic organization of professionals.[16] One of their tasks was to prevent crime by regularly patrolling beats, operating under strict rules which permitted individual discretion. The police also had a mission against the "dangerous classes" and political agitation in the form of mobs or riots. On all fronts they were so successful that initial and strong objections to them rapidly diminished; from being a considerable novelty, they quickly became a part of "British tradition."

The policed society is unique in that central power exercises potentially violent supervision over the population by bureaucratic means widely diffused throughout civil society in small and discretionary operations that are capable of rapid concentration. All of these characteristics struck contemporary observers as remarkable. Fear of mob or riot diminished when early police showed that fluid organization can overcome numbers:

> There seems to be no fear a London mob will ever prove a serious
> thing in the face of our present corps of policemen. A repetition of
> the Lord George Gordon riots would be an impossibility. Those who
> shudder at the idea of an outbreak in the metropolis containing two
> millions and a half of people and at least fifty thousand of the "dan-
> gerous classes" forget that the capital is so wide that its different sec-
> tions are totally unknown to each other. A mob in London is wholly
> without cohesion, and the individuals composing it have but few
> feelings, thoughts or pursuits in common. They would immediately
> break up before the determined attack of a band of well-trained men
> who know and have confidence in each other.[17]

Another writer put the same point in more impersonal terms:

> As each police constable being alone might easily be over-powered,
> and as the men of each section, or even division, might be inferior
> in numbers to some aggregation of roughs or criminals collected in a
> given spot, it is arranged that...reserves of force can be
> gathered...and concentrated upon the disquieted area, and as the
> commissioners command the whole district, and the force is orga-
> nized and united, while roughs act in small areas, and have diverse
> and selfish interests, the peace of London may be held secure
> against violence.[18]

The peaceful and propertied classes appreciated two other advantages of
the modern police: they relieved ordinary respectable citizens of the obligation
or necessity to discharge police functions, especially during emergencies; and
they also made less likely a resort to the military for the purposes of internal
peace-keeping. Both involved changes in the relationship of these classes to
the criminal or disorderly.

In unpoliced society, police functions were often carried out—if at all—by
citizens rotating in local offices (sheriffs, constables, magistrates) or acting as
members of militia, posses, Yeomanry corps, or watch and ward committees.[19] Not only was this system inefficient but it also directly exposed the
propertied classes to attack. Agrarian men of property were frequently willing
to undertake these tasks. Thus the Yeomanry, a cavalry force whose characteristic tactic was the sabre charge, was largely composed of small
landowners[20] who were especially zealous in police duty against mobs and
riots and especially disliked by working people.[21] For these reasons, the
Yeomanry were particularly popular among the landowning classes as a

means of defense. Praising them in the course of a parliamentary debate in 1817, for example, a member observed that "the people would in many instances be debarred from violence by seeing those arrayed against them to whom they were accustomed to look up to as their masters."[22]

But this machinery exposed the Yeomanry, once an emergency had passed, to direct attack in the course of daily life.[23] It also enabled private persons sometimes to modify police missions to suit their own proclivities and convenience. Thus, during the extensive agricultural uprisings of 1830 in southern England, fifty men of the village of Holt enrolled as special constables and "declared their willingness to turn out to protect all property except threshing machines; they did not wish to show disrespect to their poorer neighbors."[24] Yet threshing machines were the very form of property then under attack.

The urban and industrial properties classes, however, were much less eager to take up the tasks of self-defense as volunteer or co-opted police. Landowning military officers attempting to encourage self-defense among commercial or industrial capitalists met with much reluctance. Replying in 1819 to advice from Wellington, the army commander in the newly industrializing north of England replied in exasperated terms:

> I have always fought against the dispersal of my force in trivial detachments; it is quite impossible to defeat the disaffected if they rise, and at the same time to protect any town from plunder; that resistance should be made by the inhabitants....But I am sorry to say the general remark from the manufacturers is that government is bound to protect them and their property.[25]

We are dealing here not merely with the classic confrontation of an agrarian military tradition and a pacific commercial and industrial one; what also emerges is a specific demand for the bureaucratization of police functions. Not only did the manufacturing classes wish to avoid personal danger and inconvenience while protecting their property, but they also saw that—contrary to the social rationale underlying the yeomanry—the use of social and economic superiors as police exacerbated rather than mollified class violence.[26] This emerges clearly in the testimony of one Thomas Ashton, "the owner of considerable property in manufactures, and the employer of about 1500 persons," before the Royal Commission of 1839 concerned with extending the professional police from London to the provinces.[27] Among other reforms, Ashton favored the use of personnel from outside a locality affected by violence and for a reason other than the reluctance of local personnel to act against their neighbors:

> On such urgent occasions, I think it extremely desirable that a stipendiary magistrate should be sent into the district and entrusted with the administration of the law. A great majority of the more serious disturbances originate in disputes between master and servant. The local magistracy is chiefly composed of the resident landowners and manufacturers, and the irritation of the workmen against their employers is greatly increased when they find the person, with whom the disputes have arisen openly supported by, and giving directions to, the military, and subsequently punishing them for breaches of the peace, which would never have been committed unless such disputes had occurred. Ought the employer to be placed in such a situation? Is it likely that animosities would be allayed or peace maintained by it? What safety has the proprietor of machinery?

This reasoning was accepted by the commissioners in their report, which was largely written by the Benthamite reformer Edwin Chadwick:

> In several instances where there was an effective resistance given to the rioters, we have been informed that the animosities created or increased, and rendered permanent by arming master against servant, neighbour against neighbour, by triumph on one side and failure on the other, were even more deplorable than the outrages actually committed....The necessity for such painful and demoralizing conflicts between connected persons should be avoided by providing a trained and independent force for action in such emergencies....The constitutional authority of the supreme executive is then emphatically asserted. In reply to recent inquiries made of local authorities in the manufacturing districts, why they took no steps for the repression of riotous or alleged treasonable proceedings within their districts, why so long a career of criminal incitements was permitted, the prevalent answer has been, that such proceedings were understood to be exclusively within the province of government.[28]

Thus, at a time when the agrarian rich often sought to multiply and reconstruct the traditional means of self-defense against violent uprising and attack, those who sprang from the newer sources of wealth turned toward a bureaucratic police system that insulated them from popular violence, drew attack and animosity upon itself, and seemed to separate the assertion of "constitutional" authority from that of social and economic dominance.[29]

Other means than a bureaucratic police—especially the army itself—were available for this purpose. But although the army played a crucial role during crises or situations with revolutionary potential, it was ill-equipped to meet the enduring needs of a policed society.[30] It was largely officered by an agrarian class which sometimes did not distinguish itself for zeal in protecting the property of manufacturers.[31] More fundamentally, however, it was difficult for the army to act continuously in small dispersed units in civilian society, although it might do so on an emergency basis. More characteristic of the army was an alternation between no intervention and the most drastic procedures—the latter representing a declaration of internal war with lingering consequences of hate and resentment.[32] The police were designed to penetrate civil society in a way impossible for military formations and by doing so to prevent crime and violence and to detect and apprehend criminals.[33] Early descriptions by contemporaries describe both sorts of police action, taken today as routine, as novel and startling.[34]

The police penetration of civil society, however, lay not only in its narrow application to crime and violence. In a broader sense, it represented the penetration and continual presence of central political authority throughout daily life. In an important defense of characteristically modern social arrangements, Edward Shils has argued that close integration of the social and geographic periphery is a unique achievement of "mass society." In his view,

> mass society is not the most peaceful or "orderly" society that has ever existed; but it is the most consensual. The maintenance of public peace through apathy and coercion in a structure of extremely discontinuous interaction is a rather different thing from its maintenance through consensus in a structure of more continuous interaction between center and periphery....[35]

But in Shils' account the integration of the periphery emerges entirely as a moral normative process:

> The mass of the population is no longer merely an object which the elite takes into account as a reservoir of military and labor power or as a possible or actual source of public disorder....Most of the population...stand in closer moral affinity and in a more frequent, even though mediated, interaction with the center than has ever been the case....The greater proximity to the center—to the institutions which constitute it and the views which are embodied in it. There is, accordingly, a greater feeling within the mass of being a part of the same substance of which one is oneself formed.

That the modern nation represents an unprecedented extension of the organizational and moral community is undoubted. But the wholly normative language in which this account is cast risks eliding the simultaneous extension of the police throughout the "periphery" both as the agent of legitimate coercion and as a personification of the values of the "center." Far from being a latter-day consequence of organizing the police for purely coercive tasks, this was explicit in early police doctrine and much remarked upon by early observers. Their accounts stress the capacity of bureaucratic organization to make the values of the "center" palpable in daily life by means of detached persons operating on organizationally defined missions.

> Amid the bustle of Piccadilly or the roar of Oxford Street, P.C.X. 59 stalks along, an institution rather than a man. We seem to have no more hold of his personality than we could possibly get of his coat buttoned up to the throttling-point. Go, however, to the section-house...and you no longer see policemen, but men....They are positively laughing with each other![36]

And they also stress the power of the police over mass disorder, which stems not only from superior organization and the rational application of force but also from its presence as the official representative of the moral order in daily life:

> The baton may be a very ineffective weapon of offence, but it is backed by the combined power of the Crown, the Government, and the Constituencies. Armed with it alone, the constable will usually be found ready, in obediance to orders, to face any mob, or brave any danger. The mob quails before the simple baton of the police officer, and flies before it, well knowing the moral as well as physical force of the Nation whose will, as embodied in law, it represents. And take any man from that mob, place a baton in his hand and a blue coat on his back, put him forward as the representative of the law, and he too will be found equally ready to face the mob from which he was taken, and exhibit the same steadfastness and courage in defense of constituted order.[37]

In this setting, early police doctrine and observers agreed from the beginning that it was necessary to rely on the moral assent of the general population; even the earliest policemen were elaborately instructed in the demeanor and behavior required to evoke, establish, and sustain that assent.[38] This was more than a mere technical convenience. The replacement of intermittant military intervention in a largely unpoliced society by continuous professional bureaucratic policing meant that the benefits of police organization—continual pervasive moral display and lower long-term costs of official coercion for the state and propertied classes—absolutely required the moral cooperation of civil society.

Thus, the extension of moral consensus and of the police as an instrument of legitimate coercion go hand in hand. Along with other ramifying bureaucratic agencies of the center, the police link daily life to central authority. The police, however, rely not only on a technique of graduated, discretionary, and ubiquitous coercion but also on a new and unprecedentedly extensive form of moral consensus. The center is able to supervise daily life more closely and continuously than ever before; but police organization also requires pervasive moral assent if it is to achieve the goals peculiar to its technique. In earlier times, as we have seen, voluntaristic and nonbureaucratic police permitted the sabotage of official coercion by allowing participating classes to make their services conditional. In a police society (as distinct from a police state), a hostage is also given to fortune: the fundamental assent, not of the classes who comprise volunteer or nonprofessional quasi-police, but of the general population. Without at least a minimal level of such assent, coercive functions become costly in exactly the ways that those who created the policed society in England sought to avoid. In this sense, then, the extension of the moral community and of the police are aspects of the same historical development.

CULTURES OF RIOTOUS PROTEST

The themes of mass criminality and of political riot and mob protest have long been intertwined. In a notable and recent contribution George Rudé has been especially concerned to refute the classic view—associated with such nineteenth-century conservatives as Burke, Taine, and Le Bon—that political crowds, mobs, and riots are essentially criminal in character.[39] According to Rudé's analysis, demonstrating crowds and mobs in the latter half of the eighteenth and the first half of the nineteenth century were characteristically composed not of pauperized, unemployed and disorganized "rabble" but of locally resident, respectable, and employed people.[40] It is not surprising that privileged classes attempt to define popular protest as criminal—that is, fundamentally and unconditionally illegitimate. But this rhetoric and the very real fears of privileged and propertied people facing recurrent popular agitation in an unpoliced age, must not lead us to overlook the evidence for another aspect of this older relationship between elite and agitational population: riots and mobs, however much they were feared and detested, were also often means of protest that articulately communicated the desires of the population to a responsive, if not sympathetic, elite.[41]

This is a major feature of Eric Hobsbawm's analysis of the pre-industrial "city mob."[42] While stressing that such mobs were a "pre-political phenomenon" and often reacted directly to fluctuations in wages and food prices, Hobsbawm also emphasizes, in effect, the normative character of such riots:

> ...There was the claim to be considered. The classical mob did not merely riot as a protest, but because it expected to achieve something by its riot. It assumed that the authorities would be sensitive to its movements, and probably also that they would make some immediate concession; for the "mob" was not simply a casual collection of people united for some *ad hoc* purpose, but in a recognized sense, a permanent entity, even though rarely permanently organized as such.[43]

Insisting with Rudé on the essentially noncriminal character of such riotous protests, Hobsbawm summarizes the system as a whole:

> Provided that the ruler did his duty, the populace was prepared to defend him with enthusiasm. But if he did not, it rioted until he did. This mechanism was perfectly understood by both sides, and caused no political problems beyond a little occasional destruction of property....The threat of perennial rioting kept rulers ready to control prices and distribute work or largesses, or indeed to listen to their faithful commons on other matters. Since the riots were not directed against the social system, public order could remain surprisingly lax by modern standards.[44]

We will briefly illustrate the system as described by Hobsbawm and Rudé with an example from rather late in this period—London in 1831.[45] "Illuminations" were occasions on which those favoring a given cause or person placed lights in their windows; and it often happened that demonstrating crowds went from house to house demanding that those within "illuminate" and smashing their windows or sacking their houses if they did not. The residences thus besieged were usually selected with precision—the ruling class in eighteenth- and early nineteenth-century cities was not anonymous, physically inaccessible, or effectively insulated by a professional and preventive police force. Such a crowd, pressing for electoral reform of the Commons, gathered in April 1831. The following is a contemporary account of its doings, clearly written from an unfriendly point of view:

...The reformers of London, endeavoured to get up an illumination on Monday, the 25th; but that having been a failure, they prevailed on the Lord Mayor to announce another for the evening of Wednesday the 27th. On that evening, the illumination was pretty general....The mobs did a great deal of mischief. A numerous rabble proceeded along the Strand, destroying all windows that were not lighted....In St. James' Square they broke the windows in the houses of the Bishop of London, the Marquis of Cleveland and Lord Grantham. The Bishop of Winchester and Mr. W. W. Wynn, seeing the mob approach, placed candles in their windows, which thus escaped. The mob then proceeded to St. James' street where they broke the windows of Crockford's, Jordan's, the Guards, and other Club houses. They next went to the Duke of Wellington's residence in Piccadilly, and discharged a shower of stones which broke several windows. The Duke's servants fired out of the windows over their heads to frighten them, but without effect. The policemen then informed the mob that the corpse of the Duchess of Wellington was on the premises, which arrested further violence against Apsley House....[46] After the action just described the mob marched off to attack other residences, including that of Robert Peel, the political founder of the police.

At every point the normative character of the mob is clear. In this case their cause was generally popular, and they had the support of the Lord Mayor and many other worthies favoring reform, whereas many mob actions, of course, lacked such sanctions. But "antagonistic cooperation" between the mob and parts of the elite had a long history.[47] Indeed, even prereform electoral politics sometimes required parts of the elite not only to compete for the favor of the people but to expose themselves to rough treatment by electors and nonelectors alike. Thus, a French observer of 1819, watching the customary postelection procession of successful parliamentary candidates, described a scene which Halevy calls "one long familiar to the English public":

[They] were immediately pelted with filth, greeted with a shower of black mud....I saw Lord Nugent with one side all black....Lord John Russell attempted with difficulty to wipe off the stinking patches of dirt which continually bespattered his cheeks....Some had their windows broken and their furniture damaged. The houses of Lord Castlereagh and several others met with the same fate. The constables were insufficient to restore order, and the troops had to be called out.[48]

The English elite, then, sometimes lived on rather casual terms with popular volatility so long as the latter did not—as for a time the "dangerous classes" and early working class movements seemed to—challenge the fundamentals of the current system. They did not do so willingly, to be sure, but in a kind of symbiosis in which "consideration" was exchanged for "support." Thus, to see everyday, nonrevolutionary violence or unruliness solely or even largely as an impediment to the emergence of stable democracy is to blur important distinctions between kinds of popular violence and ways in which it may be integrated into a political system. Popular violence which forms part of an articulate system of demands and responses, in which needs and obligations are reasonably clear to each party, may not be at all necessarily "irrational," "criminal," or "pointless"—to use words often applied to riotous protest in contemporary democracies. Indeed, the English case suggests that—granted the many other conditions that lie outside our present scope—such a system may well conduce to the establishment of stable democracy. For although Hobsbawm calls the system "pre-political," it is one in which ordinary people express their will and elites have learned to listen.[49] The existence of the normative culture of mob and riot in many places other than England is enough to show—if the disclaimer need be made at all—that the mere existence of normative riot and violence is not a sufficient condition for the emergence of institutionalized democracy.[50] Yet in an age when institutions did not organize, represent, or press the claims of ordinary people, and in which the streets were therefore a political arena, it is important to distinguish between kinds of popular violence, rather than consider it wholly as an anachronism.

THE DEMAND FOR ORDER IN CONTEMPORARY DEMOCRACY

Such a protodemocratic system of riotous demand and elite response, however, is confined to unpoliced, hierarchical, pre-industrial society. It is not found where entrepreneurs or managers, career bureaucrats, or professional politicians have displaced former ruling groups; where popular volatility may disrupt tightly woven political and market ecologies; and where the state makes its presence felt ubiquitously in the form of police. In the latter situation, the demand for "law and order" becomes what it was not before—a constitutional imperative stemming from an unprecedentedly pervasive consensus and personified and enforced by police. Simultaneously, the standards of daily decorum increasingly restrict occasions for normative violence; thus Georg Sorel observed at the start of this century how marked had been the decline of daily and casual violence during the last, and how crucial a role these new standards played in the emerging policy of the liberal democratic state toward both the working and dangerous classes.[51]

With rising standards of public order has come an increasing intolerance of criminality, violence, and riotous protest. Daniel Bell has suggested that a breakdown of spatial barriers between the daily round of urban propertied classes and the criminal or unruly poor has made the former more aware of violence in daily life.[52] We may perhaps envisage three stages in such a sequence: one in which the prosperous or respectable often lived in unimagineable closeness to crime and the threat of riot or mob; a second in which these groups succeeded in insulating themselves—spatially, by regroupment in and outside the centers of cities and organizationally, by the police;[53] and a third in which penetrations of these barriers evoke a response which would be considered exorbitant by the standards of earlier years.

The character of the police as a public bureaucracy may also raise expectations about the level of public peace it is possible to attain. As the instrument of public policy they are easily seen in terms of a naive social instrumentalism—as technicians applying efficient means that are in principle capable of fully realizing their ends. Have not public bureaucracies eliminated plague, solved the enduring problems of urban sanitation, and prevented gross impurities in purchased foods? Why cannot the police similarly "clean up" crime and control violence?"[54] In short, the historic and strategic success of the police raises expectations and exposes them to pressures engendered by the idea of a uniformly peaceful civil society.[55]

Not only are expectations of public order higher than before, but the arena to which these expectations refer has expanded. It has done so not only because of the continuing, though obviously very incomplete, extension of a single moral order throughout the national community—a process which takes territoriality rather than the divisions of class, locality, or group as its ideal boundaries. The arena of expectation widens as smaller formations—regions, states, local communities—find it harder to control or influence the moral climate in which they live. The "nationalization" of civil rights, federal involvement in municipal programs like housing, the erosion of the power of localities to control the content of mass media, pressure from judiciaries on informal and quasilegal police practices—all mean that smaller formations come to see themselves as less able to control or influence their moral destiny.[56] Thinking themselves more vulnerable to incursion from the larger society, they extend moral demand and expectations to a wider environment than in the past was thought relevant to daily life.

These trends mesh with others. The imagery of the "dangerous classes" is being reborn in contemporary America. The nascent demand for a pervasively benign environment arises as the urban poor, disorganized, and unemployed—especially Negroes—bear more heavily upon the awareness and daily life of an urban society in which proportionately more people are "respectable" than ever before.[57] Violence, criminality, and riot become defined not only as undesirable but as threatening the very fabric of social life. Police forces come to be seen as they were in the time of their creation—as a sophisticated and convenient form of garrison force against an internal enemy.[58] Lacking a strong tradition of urban violence as a form of articulate protest, it is all the easier to define such events as merely irrational.[59] Such definitions work not only on the respectable but also on the riotous poor. Like American society as a whole, the American poor lack a traditional past: on neither side of the boundaries of class and race do the conditions for "articulate riot" exist in generous measure. "Criminal" acts like looting and violent assault are likely to dominate riotous protest, rather than explicitly political gestures. Similarly, the propertied and respectable are ill-prepared to react in terms other than a confrontation with uncontained and shapeless criminality. Articulate riot, however, requires that both rioters and their target or audience jointly define the meaning of riotous acts. The frequency with which recent riots by Negroes in American cities are interpreted officially as "meaningless" contrasts with the ability of the English elite, especially before it was severely threatened from the late eighteenth century on, to interpret the meaning of riotous behavior.

Current concern over violence and riot, then, involves a problem of the political language in which these events are described and interpreted. The problem is likely to sharpen as the official stance, relying in part upon the rhetoric of diagnostic sociology, becomes strained by the urgent pressure of events. The gap between the official diagnostic style and a cultural response that makes little provision for "normative"—is likely to widen as the urban situation grows even more aggravated. It therefore remains to be seen whether American elites—creative, professional, and political—can or will sustain a diagnostic posture that seeks and interprets the meaning of these events.

It is not to idealize even the optimal "traditional" political society—that of England—with its brutalities, squalidness, and hardness of—, to point out that it often provided the unorganized poor with a language by which, in the absence of representative institutions or the ability to participate in them, they might articulately address the propertied classes through riot and disorder. And it is not to derogate the American adventure in modernity to suggest that, however richly endowed with representative and responsive institutions, it has not provided such a language for those in its cities who have long been outside their compass—a language whose grammar is shared by speaker and listener, rioter and pillaged, violent and frightened.

ENDNOTES

* I want to thank Daniel Bell, Burton Fisher, Robert Fogelson, Morris Janowitz, and Jack Ladinsky for their comments on an earlier version. I am indebted to the Russell Sage Foundation's Program in Law and Sociology at the University of Wisconsin for the leisure and stimulus to consider, among other matters, the issues discussed in this paper.

This chapter, "The Demand for Order in Civil Society" by Allan Silver was originally published in *The Police: Six Sociological Essays*, David Bordua (ed.), 1967. Pp. 1-24. Copyright © 1967 John Wiley and Sons, Inc. Reprinted by permission of John Wiley and Sons, Inc.

1.   An *Effectual Scheme for the Immediate Prevention of Street Robberies and Suppressing of all other Disorders of the Night; with a Brief History of the Night-houses and an Appendix Relating to those Sons of Hell call'd Incendiaries* (London, 1730).

2.   *Ibid.*, pp. 10-11.

3.   James M. Buckley, "The Present Epidemic of Crime," *The Century Magazine*, (November 1903), p. 150.

4.   James Edgar Brown, "The Increase of Crime in the United States," *The Independent* (April 11, 1907), pp. 832-33.

5.   "Causes of the Increase of Crime", *Blackwood's Magazine* (July 1844) p. 2. The phrase appears in another work published four years later, *The Communist Manifesto*—where, however, it is instantly interpreted in terms of the 'lumpen-proletariat" idea.

6.   Honoré Antoine Frégier, *Les Classes Dangereuses de la Population dans les Crondes Villes* (Paris, 1840) is a work often cited by contemporaries. A relevant modern work on Paris is Louis Chevalier's *Classes Laborieuses et Classes Dangereuses à Paris pendant la Première Moitié du XIX Siècle* (Paris, 1958). In Paris of that time, he writes, "le proliferation des classes dangereuses etait...l'un des faits majeurs de l'existence quotienne de la capitale, l'un des grands problèmes de l'administration urbaine, l'une des principales préoccupations des tous, l'une des formes les plus incontestables de l'angoisse sociale." The city was one "où le crime a une importance et une signification que nous ne comprenons guère..." (pp. iii-iv).

7.   Influential books expressing this concern were Henry Fielding's *Enquiry into the Causes of the Late Increase of Robbers* (1751) and Patrick Colquhoun's *Treatise on the Police of the Metropolis* (1796). According to Chevalier (*op. cit.*, pp. 451-68), the Parisian bourgeoisie made little distinction between the

"industrious" and the "dangerous" poor.

8. According to the census, the population of London tripled in the first half of the nineteenth century. On its occupational composition, see the *Census of Great Britain in 1851* (London, 1854), p. 182, *passim*.

9. George Mainwaring, *Observations on the Present State of the Police of the Metropolis* (London, 1821), pp. 4-5. The anonymous essayist of 1844, quoted above on the connection between the dangerous classes and the "manufacturing districts," went on to write: "In examining the classes of society from which the greater part of the crime comes, it will be found that at least three-fourths, probably nine-tenths, comes from the very lowest and most destitute....If we examine who it is that compose this dismal substratum, this hideous *black band of society*, we shall find that it is not made up of any one class more than another— not of factory workers more than labourers, carters or miners—but it is formed by an aggregate of the most unfortunate or improvident of *all classes....*" *Blackwood's Magazine* (July 1844), p. 12 (italics in original).

10. This was the fourth and final volume of *London Labour and the London Poor*, separately titled *Those That Will Not Work*.

11. *London Quarterly Review* (July 1856), p. 94. Many observers, though still concerned with criminality, acknowledge a change for the better at this time. Remarking that accounts of the earlier situation in London "seem like tales of another country," a writer in 1852 went on to detail improvements: "No member of Parliament would now venture to say that it was dangerous to walk in the streets of London by day or night...Bad as the dens of infamy in London still are, they are not to be compared with those older places of hideous profligacy....In the most disorderly part of the town, such as St. Giles, Covent Garden, and Holborn, the streets every Sunday morning exhibit the most outrageous scenes of fighting, drunkenness and depravity....Crimes, too, are greatly diminished in atrocity. The large gangs of desperate robbers, thirteen or fourteen in number, now no longer exist..." *Edinburgh Review* (July 1858), p. 12-3.

12. Charles L. Brace, *The Dangerous Classes of New York* (New York, 1872), p. 26.

13. *Ibid.*, p. 29.

14. Thus, Defoe saw the intolerable conditions of his time as a result of the arrogance and bad influence of a rapidly increasing group of prostitutes and their "bullies"; and his solution was to disperse them by raids (*op. cit.*, pp. 26-32)

15. In the book which more than six decades ago named and founded this tradition, E. A. Ross was crisply aware of the expanding role of police: "In the field of physical coercion, there is an increase in the number of lictors, bailiffs, police, and soldiers told off to catch, prod, beat, and hold fast recalcitrants, and they are brought under a stricter discipline. They are more specialized for their work and an *esprit de corps* is carefully cultivated among them." *Social Control* (New York, 1901), pp. 398-9. Furthermore, Ross was quite tough-minded about the cause of this development: "All this does not happen by simple fiat of

the social will. Certain groups of persons—the executive, cabinet, the central government, the party machine, the higher clergy, the educational hierarchy, 'authorities' of every kind in short—are always striving for more power. When the need of a more stringent control makes itself felt, they find the barriers to their self-aggrandizement unexpectedly giving way before them. Formerly they were held in check, while now they find encroachment strangely easy" (*Ibid.*). Neither kind of emphasis survived the subsequent failure of works in social control to treat the characteristics of the policed society in a comprehensive way or to see organized and legitimate coercion as intrinsic to social control. (Representative treatises are L.L. Bernard, *Social Control*, New York, 1939, and Richard T. LaPiere, *A Theory of Social Control*, New York, 1954). Ross himself distinguished between the normative processes of "public opinion"— uniquely flexible, preventive, and ubiquitous—and the coercive effects of "law"—which were clumsy, retrospective, and remote (*op. cit.*, pp. 89-105). Important and influential as this distinction is, it tends to obscure—as we shall see—some of the distinctive features of policed society. Recent attempts to incorporate civil violence in the framework of social theory are included in *Internal War*, Harry Eckstein, ed. (New York, 1964), especially the essays by Eckstein, Parsons, and Feldman.

16.   Useful accounts of British police history are the writings of Charles Reith, especially *The Police Idea* (1938), *British Police and the Democratic Ideal* (1943), *The Blind Eye of History*, (1952), and *A New Study of Police History (1956). See also F. C. Mather, Public Order in the Age of the Chartists (Manchester, 1959). Like most contributors to the English literature on "public order," these writers—especially Reith—work from palpably conservative assumptions.*

17.   "The Police and the Thieves", *London Quarterly Review* (July 1856), p. 93.

18.   "The Metropolitan Police System", *Westminister Review* (January 1873), p. 16. An early historian of the New York Draft Riot of 1863 was similarly impressed by the decisive contribution of the telegraphic system in linking police stations within the city to each other and to those in Brooklyn. He devoted considerable space to the mob's attacks on the telegraphic system, citing the defense of its equipment and personnel as a key phase in the struggle for control of the streets. See J. T. Headley, *The Great Riots of New York* (New York, 1873).

19.   A good summary is in F. C. Mather, *Public Order in the Age of the Chartists*, pp. 75-95.

20.   John Fortesque, *A History of the British Army* (London, 1923) Vol. XI, p. 43). Since the yeomanry were required to supply their own horses and equipment, their status as agrarian men of property was largely assured. See K. Chorley, *Armies and the Art of Revolution* (London, 1943), p. 167.

21.   J. L. and B. Hammond, *The Town Labourer* (London, 1928), p. 89. Also, F. C. Mather, *op. cit.*, p. 148. Yeomanry, for example, precipitated the

"Peterloo" massacre.

22.   Quoted in Reith, *The Police Idea*, p. 191.

23.   For example, many resigned when they received threatening letters after Peterloo. See Ione Leigh, *Castlereagh*, (London, 1951), p. 127.

24.   J. R. M. Butler, *The Passing of the Great Reform Bill* (London, 1914), p. 132.

25.   Despatch of General Byng quoted in Reith, *The Police Idea*, p. 202.

26.   "Respectable tradesmen cannot, without detriment to themselves, be so engaged as constables..." (George Mainwaring, *Observations on the Police...*, p. 46).

27.   *First Report of the Commissioners Appointed as to the Best Means of Establishing an Efficient Constabulary Force in the Counties of England and Wales* (London, 1839), pp. 158-9.

28.   *Ibid.*, p. 205.

29.   "I hope to get up a troop of Yeomanry at Cheltenham," wrote Lord Ellenborough during the critical year of 1832, "but this requires delicate management....Yeomanry however we must have, or we shall be beaten." A. Aspinall, *Three Early Nineteenth Century Diaries* (London, 1952), p. 275.

30.   See the accounts in F. C. Mather, *Public Order in the Age of the Chartists*, pp. 153-81, and Joseph Hamburger, *James Mill and the Art of Revolution* (New Haven, 1963), pp. 203-14.

31.   See, for example, Frank Darvell, *Popular Disturbances and Public Order in Regency England* (Oxford, 1934), pp. 80-1, 267-8.

32.   All these points of superiority of police over army were explicit among those who advocated or created the early professional police. See for example, the *First Report of the Commissioners...*, *op. cit.*, pp.159-61; George Mainwaring, *Observations on the Present State of the Police...*, p. 69; Charles Reith, *British Police and the Democratic Ideal*, pp. 9-30; and *Edinburgh Review* (July 1852), p. 6.

33.   Great stress was initially laid on the "preventive principle," at the time a new principle in internal peace-keeping. See Reith. *ibid.*, pp. 18-23, and the same author's *A New Study of Police History.*, pp. 221-4. For the view of a contemporary advocate of police, see Mainwaring, *op. cit.*, pp. 9-10.

34.   Note, for example, the obvious astonishment that underlies an account of the tracing of a burglar, who had robbed a house in central London, to an obscure hiding place in the East End ("The Police System of London," *Edinburgh Review*, July 1852, pp. 8-10).

35.   "The Theory of Mass Society," *Diogenes* (1962) pp. 53-4 (for this and succeeding quotations).

36.   "The Police and the Thieves," *London Quarterly Review* (July 1856), p. 93.

37. "The Police of London," *London Quarterly Review* (July 1870), p. 48.

38. Charles Reith, *A New Study of Police History*, pp. 140-2.

39. *The Crowd in History, 1730-1848* (New York, 1964), pp. 7-8, 199-204.

40. *Ibid.*, p. 47-65.

41. Expressions of this fear are vivid and aboundingly frequent. "At this time," wrote the Tory poet Southey in 1812, "nothing but the Army preserves us from the most dreadful of all calamities, an insurrection of the poor against the rich, and how long the Army may be depended upon is a question which I scarcely dare ask myself" (Elie Halevy, *A History of the English People*, New York, 1912, Vol. I p. 292). Seven years later a peer discussing the political situation observed: "We are daily assailed with undisguised menace, and are little removed from the expectation of open violence..." (*Substance of the Speech of the Rt. Hon. Lord Grenville in the House of Lords, November 19, 1820*, London, p. 23). A year later in a memorandum to Liverpool, Wellington, then Prime Minister—urging the creation of a police force—wrote: "I feel the greatest anxiety respecting the state of the military in London...Very recently strong symptoms of discontent appeared in one battalion of the guards....There are reports without number in circulation respecting all the Guards....Thus, in one of the most critical moments that ever occurred in this country, we and the public have reason to doubt the fidelity of the troops, the only security we have, not only against revolution but for the lives and property of every individual in this country who has anything to lose..." (Quoted in Reith, *The Police Idea*, p. 213). Robert Peel, fearing for his family's safety at their country estate, left London during the crisis of 1831 and asked a friend to send weapons. "I have this day got you fourteen carbines, bayonets, and accoutrements," the friend replied. "How will you have them sent to you? I have only desired a cask of ball cartridges to be put in the case" (Tresham Lever, *The Life and Times of Sir Robert Peel*, New York, 1942, p. 144). A general description of the situation is given in Reith, *Police Principles and the Problem of War*, pp. 46-8. In his revisionist account, *James Mill and the Art of Revolution*, Joseph Hamburger maintains that this standard portrait of elite mentality is exaggerated and that it does not apply to the Whig reformers in the period before 1832, who were more concerned with long-range than with imminent crises (see pp. 33-47).

42. *Primitive Rebels: Studies in Archaic Forms of Social Movements* (Manchester, 1959).

43. *Ibid.*, p. 111.

44. *Ibid.*, p. 116.

45. See the summary of this theme in *The Crowd in History*, pp. 254-7. See also the interesting article by R. B. Rose, "Eighteenth Century Price Riots and Public Policy in England," *International Review of Social History* (1961), pp. 277-92, and the more general remarks in this connection by Joseph Hamburger,

op. cit., pp. 199-202.

46.   *Annual Register*, 1831, p. 68. Quoted by Reith in *British Police and the Democratic Ideal*, pp. 90-1. Hamburger places this incident squarely in the "tradition of riot" (see *James Mill....*, pp. 139-42).

47.   It is Hamburger's thesis that in the case of the Reform Crisis of 1830-1832, proreform leaders manipulated the threat of the mob, rather than wielding a substantial revolutionary threat. But this sort of manipulation was itself a tradition—for a case that succeeded before the mob ever took to the streets, see Thomas Perry, *Public Opinion, Propaganda and Politics in Eighteenth Century England: a study of the Jew Bill of 1753* (Cambridge, Massachusetts, 1962). So strong was this tradition that Lady Holland, the wife of the great Whig aristocrat prominent in the struggle for reform, could remark disapprovingly on Wellington's reaction to the prospect of mob attack on his house: "Is it not strange that the Duke of Wellington has boarded with very thick planks *all* his windows upstairs to Piccadilly and the Park?...The work of *darkness* began on Coronation Day and is now completed. He says, I hear, that it is to protect his plate glass windows from the mob, who will assail him on the Reform Bill! As it cannot be for thrift, it looks like defiance; and the mob will be irritated when they discover his intentions." Earl of Ilchester, ed., *Elizabeth, Lady Holland to Her Son*, (London, 1946), p. 118. (Italics in original.)

48.   Halevy, *op. cit.*, p. 118.

49.   It is suggestive to compare Hobsbawm's perceptive comment on the situation in parts of Europe which did not experience a comparably gradual development of democratic institutions. Speaking of popular riot and enthusiasm in support of the *status quo,* he remarks: "Legitimate monarchs or institutions like churches may not welcome this. The Emperor Francis I of Austria took a poor view of the revolutionary legitism of his people, observing correctly: 'Now they are patriots for me; but one day they may be patriots against me!' From the point of view of the genuinely conservative institution, the ideal is obediance, not enthusiasm, whatever the nature of the enthusiasm. Not for nothing was "Ruhe ist die Erste Burgerpflicht' (Tranquility is the first duty of every citizen) the slogan of every German princeling" (*Primitive Rebels....*p. 119).

50.   See Hobsbawm, *passim.* See also the comprehensive discussion by Charles Tilly, "Reflections on the Revolution of Paris," *Social Problems* (Summer 1964), pp. 99-121, which, among other matters, deals with the literature on these themes in the case of France.

51.   See Chapter 6 of *Reflections on Violence.* On the special sensitivity of modern society to public disorder, see Karl Polyani, *The Great Transformation* (New York, 1944), pp. 186-7: "The market system was more allergic to rioting than any other economic system we know....In the nineteenth century breaches of the peace, if committed by armed crowds, were deemed an incipient rebellion and an acute danger to the state; stocks collapsed and there was no bottom to prices. A shooting affray in the streets of the metropolis might destroy a sub-

stantial part of the nominal national capital."

52. "The Myth of Crime Waves: the actual decline of crime in the United States," in *The End of Ideology* (New York, 1962), pp. 151-74.

53. "The beats vary considerably in size; in those parts of the town which are open and inhabited by the wealthier classes, an occasional visit from a policeman is sufficient, and he traverses a wide district. But the limits of the beat are diminished, and of course the frequency of the visits increased, in proportion to the character and the density of the population, and throng and pressure of traffic, and concentration of property, and the intricacy of the streets....Nor must it be supposed that this system places the wealthier localities at a disadvantage, for it is an axiom in police that you guard St. James' by watching St. Giles'" ("The Police System of London," *Edinburgh Review*, July 1852, p. 5). St. Giles was one of the most notorious of London's "rookeries."

54. It is more than accidental that Edwin Chadwick (see p. 26, above) was also a prime mover in the reform of urban sanitation. See his report, *Sanitary Conditions of the Labouring Population in England, 1842* (London, 1843).

55. See Bell, *op. cit.*, p. 152 on the relationship between better policing and a "higher" crime rate. The artifactual character of this relationship, sometimes hard for contemporaries for whom the police are taken for granted to grasp, was obvious to an observer witnessing the transition to a policed society. See "Causes of the Increase of Crime," *Blackwood's Magazine* (July 1844), p. 5.

56. Attempting to account for respectable people's greater awareness of violence in daily life, Bell has also suggested that the emergence of heterogeneous audiences for the mass media, which include groups previously less exposed to violent themes, has heightened awareness of violence even as its occurrence in daily life has declined (*ibid.*, pp. 170-4). Simultaneously, local communities and states are losing their formal powers to control such materials and are relying more often on informal control. (See Richard Randall, *Some Political Theories in Motion Picture Censorship Decisions: Prior Restraint Reconsidered*. Paper delivered at the Midwest Conference of Political Science, Bloomington, Indiana, April 1965).

57. Here we follow Shils' argument, *op. cit.*, p. 56.

58. For the American police this situation may render a chronic problem acute. At the time when the police are more urgently charged than ever before to do society's "dirty work" but also are more stringently supervised by the public, various interest groups and the judiciary, their morale and operating problems are further exacerbated by their failure to embody moral consensus in the eyes of the general community, their "clientele," and themselves as thoroughly as do the British police. For detailed observations about some of these matters, especially the last, see Michael Banton, *The Policemen in The Community* (London, 1964), a comparative account of Scottish and American police forces. Obviously, the rural South would require special treatment. See W. J. Cash,

The Mind of the South (New York, 1941), *passim*, and H. C. Brearly, "The Pattern of Violence", in W. T. Couch, ed., *Culture in the South* (Chapel Hill 1934). Our focus, however, is on urban situations. Thus, for example, there was a suggestion in that the few food riots of nineteenth-century New York, those in 1837 and 1857, were carried out largely by foreign-born, rather than native, poor. See the chapters on these episodes in J. F. Headley, *The Great Riots* (New York, 1873).

59.   I am indebted to Robert Fogelson's analysis (as yet unpublished) of these riots and of the official responses to them—notably the McCone Commission's report on the Watts riot of August 1985.

PART B

HISTORY

CHAPTER 4
The New Police in London 1750-1830

T.A. CRITCHLEY

The history of the first 1,000 years of police in England, up to, say, 1729, is mainly the story of how the tythingman changed into the parish constable, and latterly of the constable's slow decline; that of the next 100 years, in London at least, is the story of the way in which a medley of local parish officers and watchmen came to be replaced by a single body of constables embodied into a police *force*, the governing principles of which were unity of control and professional excellence.

Enough has been said in the previous chapter about the frightening breakdown of law and order in London during the first half of the eighteenth century. Some saw a remedy in increasing the severity of the penal code; societies for the reformation of manners proliferated; all who could afford to do so formed mutual protection societies, paying annual subscriptions towards the cost of capturing and prosecuting thieves; and the commonplace offer of rewards and free pardons for information leading to the capture of felons seemed to practical men a more worthwhile form of insurance than pinning their faith to the discredited system of justices, parish constables, and nightwatchmen. Even so, the need to put fresh life into the well-tried principles of the Statute of Winchester was constantly reiterated, and for many years it does not seem to have occurred to Parliament that these principles might have grown obsolete. The old idea of collective responsibility was reaffirmed by the Riot Act of 1715, which made the inhabitants of a hundred liable to make amends for certain offences committed within their boundaries; and an Act of 1735 likewise attempted to revive the institution of hue and cry by providing that a constable who neglected to raise it, or failed to join in the pursuit, should be liable to a fine of £5, and any person who apprehended the offender within forty days should receive a reward of £10, levied on the hundred responsible. In keeping faith with the ancient principles, however, the various Metropolitan authorities attempted from early times to remedy their limitations by increasing the number of paid night-watchmen.

Of these authorities, the City of London was pre-eminent in importance and in having the most highly developed form of government, based on a series of ancient charters and enactments. When the Statute of Winchester became law in 1285, the City received its own separate statute, as a result of which the area was divided into twenty-four wards, each containing six watchmen supervised by an alderman. In addition to this 'standing watch', there was also a 'marching watch', which was called out on special occasions.[1] The curfew one hour after sunset and the nightly closing of the City gates and taverns completed the arrangements for keeping the peace, the whole of which were under the authority of the Mayor and City aldermen. In 1963, an Act passed by the Court of Common Council provided for the employment of 1,000 watchmen, or bellmen, to be on duty from sunset to sunrise. The effectiveness of these 'Charlies' (so called in memory of King Charles II, in whose reign they were instituted) was improved by an Act of 1737, which also established a system of day police. But the wages paid to Charlies were derisively low: for the most part they were contemptible, dissolute, and drunken buffoons who shuffled along the darkened streets after sunset with their long staves and dim lanterns, calling out the time and the state of the weather, and thus warned the criminal of their approach, while attracting to themselves the attention of ruffians and practical jokers. Even so, the City was probably better policed than any other part of the country during the eighteenth century, and a Parliamentary committee of 1812 considered that it afforded 'an example of that unity, and of that dependence of parts on each other, without which no well-constructed and efficient system of police can ever be expected': a similar system, they concluded, would bring great benefit to Westminster and its adjacent parishes.

For conditions in the remainder of the Metropolitan area were, by comparison, chaotic. The agglomeration of houses and shops and streets, comprising some 152 separate parishes with an aggregate population, towards the end of the eighteenth century, of upwards of a million, lacked any unitary control or corporate being. Westminster itself was until 1584 under the control of the Abbey authorities, and stretching out in every direction was a diverse and growing collection of townships, manors, parishes and villages without coherence of any kind. During Elizabeth's reign an Act of Parliament provided a form of government under which the city was divided into twelve wards, but for policing reliance was still placed on the ubiquitous system of parish constables. A medieval hierarchy of Lord High Steward, High Bailiff, Burgesses, Court of Burgesses, Court Leet, Annoyance Jury, and others survived until the

nineteenth century, so that it is not surprising to find that, staggering under
this confusion, Westminster was the first authority in the whole of England to
promote, in 1662, a local Improvement Act. This established a new local
authority with powers in both the City of London and Westminster itself, and,
as the commissioners who comprised it (one of whom was the diarist Evelyn)
had their office in Scotland Yard, they were known as the 'Commissioners of
Scotland Yard'—although curiously enough, it seems that they exercised no
police functions. Most of the 152 parishes outside Westminster followed suit
during the eighteenth century, and under the authority of their own local
Improvement Acts employed small bodies of watchmen. These watchmen
confined their activities, such as they were when they were not dozing in their
watch-boxes, to their own small parish; co-operation between parishes was
virtually non-existent; local jealousies were intense; and there was, naturally,
no pooling of information. Such were the arrangements for policing London
which challenged the ingenuity of the straggling line of police reformers that
started with Henry Fielding and ended, three-quarters of a century later, with
Peel. Midway through the period, 1797, they were well summed up by Patrick
Colquhoun, the first man ever to carry out a systematic survey of London's
policing: 'The watchmen destined to guard the lives and properties of the
inhabitants residing in near eight thousand streets, lanes, courts, and alleys,
and about 162,000 houses...are under the direction of no less than above seventy different Trusts; regulated by perhaps double the number of local acts of
Parliament (varying in many particulars from one another), under which the
directors, guardians, governors, trustees, or vestries, according to the title they
assume, are authorised to act, each attending only to their own particular
Ward, Parish, Hamlet, Liberty, or Precinct.'

THE INFLUENCE OF THE FIELDING BROTHERS

The manner in which Henry Fielding succeeded to the office of Chief
Magistrate of Bow Street in 1748, and set about rescuing the administration
of justice from the corrupt state into which it had fallen. But Fielding was not
content merely to challenge the judicial processes. From his vantage-point at
Bow Street, he soon turned the abundant genius, compassion, and understanding of human nature that had filled his novels to no less a task than the
reformation of a whole society whose sense of security had been shaken by
the rebellion of 1745, and whose morals were being corroded by alcoholism
aided by cheap gin. Within three years of taking office he published a pam-

phlet, *An Enquiry into the Causes of the Late Increase of Robbers,* with the declared intention 'to rouse the civil power from its present lethargic state'. At the outset he defined the delicate poise whose attainment was to baffle thinkers on the subject of police reform for three-quarters of a century: his was a design which 'alike opposes those wild notions of liberty that are inconsistent with all government, and those pernicious schemes of government which are destructive of true liberty'. Four more pamphlets followed, in which Fielding established himself as a pioneer thinker on questions of penal policy and criminology, resourceful in remedies to deal with what he conceived to be the social causes of crime—drunkenness, gambling, obscene literature, sexual laxity, vagrancy, and others—and with the over-severity of the criminal law and the administration of justice.

As a police reformer, however, Fielding was less radical. He influenced the first of a long series of Parliamentary committees, set up in 1750, to recommend a strengthening of the nightly watch in Westminster, but he sought no change in the traditional system of parish constables. He did, however, embark on two cautious initiatives which showed his awareness of the police problem, and established a slender foundation on which others were to build. The first was to publish *The Covent Garden Journal,* which appeared twice a week during the course of 1752. Fielding wrote the greater part of it himself, giving account of cases that had come before him as a magistrate, with the object of educating public opinion to a greater sensitivity to penal problems; he also used the journal to advertise descriptions of robbers. His other main initiative resulted in the formation, in 1750, of a small body of 'thief-takers' attached to his office at Bow Street. For this purpose he recruited six or seven householders 'actuated by a truly public spirit against thieves', who undertook to continue as constables after their year of office had expired. This nucleus, drawn from the area of Bow Street, he placed under the joint leadership of himself and the High Constable of Holborn, a man named Saunders-Welch, who became a friend of Dr. Johnson. They had several early successes in breaking up gangs of criminals, and the men received the rewards, (or 'blood money', as they were known) offered for the apprehension of criminals. They had no uniform other than the distinctive staff of a parish constable. The enterprise was continued temporarily with the aid of a Government grant of £600. It evolved, many years later, into the Bow Street Runners; but the scheme marked no major departure from the past, and Fielding seems to have intended none.

Henry Fielding died at the early age of forty-seven, and was succeeded, in 1754, by his blind half-brother John who, in the course of twenty-five years as

Chief Magistrate at Bow Street, carried Henry's ideas forward. John, like Henry, received £200 a year (later increased to £400) from secret Government funds; and after his retirement in 1779 the payment of a salary to the Chief Magistrate was openly acknowledged. As Professor Radzinowicz puts it, the greatness of the brothers 'as educators of public opinion, lies in the single-minded determination with which, over a period of nearly thirty years, they strove to demonstrate to their contemporaries how serious were the dangers which threatened to engulf the nation and how pressing was the need for discarding fragmentary remedies in favour of a larger plan'. John Fielding published several pamphlets, the most notable of which was *A Plan for Preventing Robberies within Twenty Miles of London,* containing the suggestion that householders should combine in bands of twenty for the purpose of supplying Bow Street with information about criminals. He also described the work of his brother's band of 'thief-takers', and elaborated the idea of disseminating quick and accurate information about known criminals among magistrates and constables throughout the country. Under his guidance Bow Street became a clearing-house of crime information, and he published regular broadsheets entitled *The Quarterly Pursuit of Criminals* and *The Weekly Pursuit,* with an occasional supplement, *The Extraordinary Pursuit,* which were the forerunners of the *Police Gazette.* These sheets were widely distributed, and the detailed descriptions of offenders which they contained were fixed to church doors, inns and other public places. Meantime, John Fielding was extending the corps of Bow Street semi-regulars started by his brother, and he obtained a grant of £400 a year from the Treasury to enable him to pay four 'pursuers' who were available to act anywhere in the country, together with ancillary staff at Bow Street. The grant also covered the cost of printing his handbills and broadsheets, and the maintenance of two horse patrols. By these steps what had started as 'Mr. Fielding's men' had, by about 1785, become the Bow Street Runners. A further temporary Treasury grant in 1763 enabled Fielding to establish a night horse patrol of eight men to guard the roads leading into London against highwaymen, but the Government had little enthusiasm for the plan: in the following year the grant was withdrawn, and the horse patrol was not revived for another forty years.

Thus the actual achievements of the Fielding brothers after thirty years of sustained effort were meagre: for the last sixteen years of his life John Fielding was able to maintain only the four 'pursuers' and two horsemen of the original scheme. But their influence was out of all proportion to their achievements. In 1761 John Fielding was knighted, and in 1770 he was the principal witness before the first of a long series of Parliamentary committees set up to consider the policing of London after a particularly serious breakdown in law and order caused by Wilkes. Fielding pleaded that, in the interests of unity of command and co-ordination, the Bow Street magistrates should be entrusted with 'the whole direction' of all Westminster constables and watchmen. The committee, however, faithful to the old principles, contented itself with a series of recommendations designed to enforce more rigorously the obligation of householders to serve as constables, to encourage parishes to recruit better men as night-watchmen, to transfer control of watchmen from the parish vestry to the magistrates, and to establish closer supervision over pawnbrokers, public houses, prostitutes, and other encitements to crime. This committee is of permanent interest, however, in recording the discovery that the parishes which formed part of the Metropolis were 'under no particular Act of Parliament, but exercised their authority under the Statute of Winchester [which], being very obsolete, is a very improper regulation'. They did not, however, seek to correct its impropriety or to replace it by something more attuned to the times. The only outcome of the inquiry was an Act of 1774 designed to regulate the nightly watch in Westminster, which, however, had little effect.

The outlook of this committee, and of others which succeeded it, is typical of the apathy towards any radical reform of the police which marked the end of the Fieldings' early initiatives. Everywhere enthusiasm ebbed; for, to quote Professor Radzinowicz again, 'During this long period of more than three-quarters of a century, from 1750 to 1828, there was no section of public opinion, no group in Parliament or outside, no leading newspaper or periodical which would advocate a reform in the traditional machinery for keeping the peace'. The partnership of the justice and parish constable 'had acquired an almost constitutional validity'. For many years the English people had no desire for a police institution; 'indeed, with few exceptions, they regarded its non-existence as one of their major blessings'. The reasons for this hostility to the police idea must now be examined.

PITT'S ABORTIVE BILL OF 1785

At about the time when the Fieldings were initiating their cautious reforms in the face of a largely apathetic or hostile public opinion, the term 'police' was coming into common usage, and to most people it had a sinister ring. John Fielding was complaining in 1761 that the term had been 'greatly misunderstood and misrepresented', but distrust of the police idea in no way abated as the century advanced. Dr. Johnson recognised the French origin of the word, and defined it in his dictionary as 'The regulation and government of a city or country, so far as regards the inhabitants'. To most people the French origin was enough to damn the idea of something like a *gendarmerie* from the start, and the more the reformers argued for its acceptance as a means of maintaining law and order, the more the emotive power of the term 'police' darkened men's minds to any advantage its introduction might bring to this country. In France, it was popularly held—and with some justification—there were spies and informers everywhere; once admit a police force into England, and the long-cherished liberties of Englishmen would be swept away in a regime of terror and oppression.

So persistent was this attitude that it survived the shock of the Gordon Riots, when for nearly a week, in the summer of 1780 London was abandoned to mob violence, from which it was rescued only by the Army, following the personal intervention of the King. Ironically, John Fielding lay dying as London blazed and the rioters sacked Bow Street and made a bonfire of his papers and Henry's manuscripts. The state of impotence to which parish constables and watchmen had been reduced was ludicrous. At one time, near the spot where fires were burning fiercest, a watchmen was seen passing with a lantern in his hand' calling the hour as in a time of profound tranquility'. Shelburne, who two years later became the first Home Secretary, spoke up boldly on the second day of the riots in praise of the French police system, which was 'wise to the last degree' in its construction, and only abominable in 'its use and direction'. A similar organisation ought, he urged, to be adopted in England. His, however, was virtually a lone voice. The riots shocked public opinion into questioning the evident weakness of the forces of law and order, and a welter of suggestions poured into the Home Office, some well-considered, many silly. The most favoured were for a further strengthening of the already savage criminal law, reliance on mobilisation of the ancient *posse comitatus* with the hue and cry, and the creation of voluntary associations of armed citizens who would act, in effect, as a 'people's police'.

Pitt's Government, however, took the lesson of the Gordon Riots to heart, and in 1785 Sir Archibald Macdonald, his Solicitor-General, introduced into Parliament a radical Bill, prepared with the help of the Bow Street magistrates. The Bill, owed much to the influence of the Fieldings, but went a great deal further. They, in common with everyone who had ever concerned themselves with the police problem since the fourteenth century, had held that the proper authority to control the police were the justices. Pitt's Bill proposed to sever this ancient link. It embodied all the major proposals of the last thirty years and, presenting them in an imaginative sweep, anticipated Peel's

Metropolitan Police Act by nearly half a century. The Bill provided for the establishment of a strong police force to act throughout the whole of the Metropolitan area (including the City), which, for police purposes, was to be a unified 'District of the Metropolis'. The Crown was to be empowered to appoint a board of three salaried commissioners of police, who would be deemed to be justices of the peace. The Metropolitan area was to be divided into nine divisions, in each of which was to be a force of 'petty constables' under the command of a chief constable and, ultimately, of the police commissioners. The constables, who were to be regarded as 'ministerial officers of the peace', were to patrol on foot and on horseback, and to be armed with powers of search and arrest. The existing parish constables and watchmen were to be retained, but their duties were to be co-ordinated with those of the regular police. Existing Metropolitan justices were to be stripped of their executive police duties and confined to the exercise of judicial functions only.

This advanced measure was greeted with widespread dismay by the Press and in the City of London, and it was bitterly opposed by the justices. Predictably, the City saw it as a violation of their corporate dignity and right to self-government—'if a torch had been applied to the buildings there it could not have created greater alarm', according to one City alderman whose memory of the Gordon Riots was short. The benches of the Middlesex and Surrey justices regarded it as 'a dangerous innovation and an encroachment on the rights and security of the people'.

Pitt bowed before the storm. Perhaps, like Peel, he should have had the political sagacity not to interfere with the City. Admitting that he was not 'perfectly master of the subject', he allowed the Bill to be withdrawn, and the opportunity to establish a Metropolitan police force was lost for over forty years. Thereafter what little enthusiasm there had been for police reform disappeared, and the establishment of the tyranny in France, three years after the outbreak of the Revolution in 1789, served further to alienate most Englishmen from an institution which, always regarded with suspicion, was now plainly exposed to the world as an instrument of terror. When, therefore, a private Member introduced a modes reforming measure into Parliament in 1792 (three months before the September massacres), the proposals it embodied were timid in comparison with Pitt's abortive plans. They were accordingly acceptable to Parliament.

The Middlesex Justices Act, 1792, as this measure is entitled, was primarily an attempt to reform and purify the London magistracy, and as such it was of far-reaching importance; it was only secondarily concerned with providing a more effective means of policing. The Act created seven magistrates' offices in the Metropolitan area, additional to the Bow Street office, to each of which three stipendiary magistrates were appointed at salaries originally fixed at £400; each of the seven offices was to employ six full-time constables at a weekly wage of 12s. A controversial clause subsequently added to the Bill authorised the constables to arrest on suspicion. Originally enacted only for a period of three years, the Act was subsequently made permanent in 1812. Admittedly a step forward in the recognition of the need for a paid constabulary force in London, it was of little long-term significance, for its tendency was reactionary—reverting to the principle of placing separate groups of constables under the control of justices—and it was conceived on too paltry a scale to have much effect. Including the Bow Street Runners, which by 1797 had been expanded to a force some seventy strong, London at the turn of the century had a total of about 120 full-time police officers, and the main burden of maintaining law and order still rested on the elderly, ailing, or indifferent shoulders of isolated pockets of parish constables and watchmen, whose attitude to the newcomers was one of deep suspicion and hostility.

But Pitt's Bill of 1785 had not been entirely lost. The bold plans that England rejected, Ireland was quick to seize. The abortive Bill was enacted, substantially in its original form, by the Dublin Parliament in the following year, 1786, and thus laid the first slender foundations for the Royal Irish Constabulary. As a result, Robert Peel, who was Chief Secretary for Ireland between 1812 and 1818, introduced police reforms in that country, but it was not until 1838 that a Metropolitan force was established in Dublin on the lines of Peel's London police. Nevertheless, Maitland makes an interesting point in suggesting that 'A full history of the new police would probably lay its first scene in Ireland, and begin the Dublin Police Act passed by the Irish Parliament in 1786'.

POLICING AS A NEW SCIENCE

One of the successful applicants for a post as magistrate in the new offices established by the Middlesex Justices Act 1972 was a Glasgow merchant named Patrick Colquhoun. A self-made man who had been appointed Lord Provost of Glasgow at the early age of thirty-seven, he turned his immense energy selectively to a wide variety of social problems; but his dominating interest, throughout twenty-five years as a Metropolitan magistrate, was in the reform of the police. In 1797 he published *A Treatise on the Police of the Metropolis,* which was widely acclaimed and went through no fewer than seven editions in the course of ten years. Its language was revolutionary: 'Police is an improved state of Society....Next to the blessings which a Nation derives from an excellent Constitution and System of general Laws, are those advantages which result from a well-regulated and energetic plan of Police, conducted and enforced with purity, activity, vigilance, and discretion.'

The treatise broke new ground. In the painstaking manner in which he marshalled statistics relating to crime and criminals, and in relying on this systematic evidence as a basis for drawing up wide-ranging plans, Colquhoun adopted a technique which is commonplace in our times, but was then virtually unknown. He threw down a challenge to the traditionalists in declaring that a well-regulated police, whose primary aim should be the prevention of crime, was 'perfectly congenial to the principle of the British constitution', and proceeded to develop sweeping proposals embracing the reform of the criminal law and the magistracy, projects for the moral reformation of society, and a system of preventive police which owed much to an acknowledged admiration of the French—which had reached 'the greatest degree of perfection'—a fact which so delighted our enemies that at the height of the Napoleonic War Colquhoun's treatise was translated and published in France. Fascinated by the novelty of this subject, Colquhoun wrote in the Preface to the sixth edition of his *Treatise* (published in 1800) that 'police in this country may be considered as a new science; the properties of which consist not in the judicial powers which lead to punishment and which belong to the magistrates alone; but in the prevention and detection of crimes; and in those other functions which relate to internal regulations for the well order and comfort of civil society'. This science 'was not yet perfectly understood'.

Colquhoun followed the abortive proposals of 1785 in insisting on the complete separation of judicial and police powers. He proposed the creation of a central police board, consisting of five commissioners, who were to be 'able, intelligent, prudent and indefatigable' men. The Home Office itself had too many other tasks to enable it to give the 'strength, vigour, and energy' to a police system, but the board should be under the general control of the Home Secretary. A nucleus of professional police should be established in every parish, at the head of which should be a 'high constable of the division', who would be assisted by a parochial chief constable. These officers would be paid and controlled by the central police board, and they would take charge of the local constables elected by the court leet or the magistrates without the option of employing deputies. To reap the full benefit of centralisation, Colquhoun carried forward three ideas borrowed from the Fieldings, to whose pioneer work he justly paid tribute: the central police board should organise an intelligence service; it should maintain a register of known offenders, with classified information about particular groups; and it should publish a *Police Gazette,* not only for the purpose of aiding in the detection of crime, but also as a vehicle of moral education—'with commentaries suited to the comprehension of the vulgar, tending to operate as warnings, and to excite a dread of crimes', with 'occasional observations on the horrors of a gaol; on punishments—whipping, the pillory, the hulks, transportation and public executions'.

Colquhoun's proposals thus represent an important link between the old and the new ideas. In essence, his plan was put forward as a means of revitalising the parish constabulary and superimposing over it a meed of professional direction and co-ordination deriving authority from the Home Secretary. This balance was nicely adjusted to the spirit of the times. Colquhoun's ideas were enthusiastically receive by the Press and in Parliament, but not in the City, where the proposed police board was seen as 'a new Engine of Power and Authority so enormous and extensive as to threaten a species of despotism and inquisition hitherto without a parallel in this country'. In the same year that he published his treatise, Colquhoun was one of only three witnesses (another of whom was his close friend and associate, Jeremy Bentham) to be called before a Select Committee on Finance, etc., appointed by Pitt to consider particularly police, including convict establishments. For a time Colquhoun carried all before him. In a closely reasoned and well-documented report, this committee, in its *Twenty-eighth Report,* published in 1798, substantially endorsed his plans. The Government prepared a Bill, and the moment seemed ripe at last for the establishment of a modern police system in London. Then, for reasons which remain a mystery, the whole project was abandoned. For the next ten years interest in general police reform died away, until a shock to public confidence even greater than that caused by the Gordon Riots allowed the voice of reform to be heard once again.

In December, 1811, two whole families in the East End of London were silently exterminated in macabre circumstances which created a wave of public panic. One, consisting of a linen-draper named Marr, his wife, child and shop assistant, were savagely butchered with a ripping chisel and maul. The sense of horror had not abated when, a week later, a man named Williamson and his wife and servant were found with their skulls fractured and their throats cut; a bloodstained iron crowbar and maul lay beside the bodies. De Quincey later treated the 'Wapping murders' with light irony in his essay, *Murder Considered as One of the Fine Arts,* but no one treated them lightly at the time. Complacency about the need for reforming the police vanished overnight. The watchmen in the area were instantly discharged. Special armed patrols were appointed, and several neighbouring parishes volunteered to supply additional men for night-patrolling. Public concern mounted throughout the whole country, and just as after the Gordon Riots, so again a welter of suggestions poured into the Home Office from all over the country. Some even favoured radical reform of the parish constable system, but most seem to have looked no further than an improvement in the quality of the parish police and the nightly watch. Even Colquhoun now contented himself with a series of minor suggestions designed to improve the quality of watchmen.

The Home Secretary acted in two ways. The suspect, a man named Williams, was at length caught; but he evaded justice by hanging himself from a beam so low that, as the *Morning Post* commented, he must have been obliged 'to sit down as it were to accomplish his purpose'. The Home Secretary accordingly satisfied public opinion by authorising the body to be displayed, along with the ripping chisel and maul, in a high, open cart which, driven slowly along the crowded streets, at length paused outside the Marrs' house and then drove on to where a hole had been dug in the ground. The body was flung in and a stake driven through it, the instruments of murder being consigned to Bow Street. Secondly, the Home Secretary moved Parliament to set up a committee of enquiry into the state of the nightly watch and the effectiveness of the various local Acts within the Metropolitan area, but made it clear that he did not expect or desire any radical recommendations from the committee. Pitt's abortive Bill of 1785 seems to have been entirely forgotten, although the report of 1798 embodying Colquhoun's proposals was specially reprinted for the use of the new enquiry. The committee, however, disregarded it. They produced a hasty, ill-informed, and disappointing report, the principal recommendation of which was to introduce arrangements by which the state of the watch should be regularly inspected by officers paid to make rounds during the night. By these means it was thought that elderly and unfit watchmen could be weeded out. The committee proposed better arrangements for supplying information to the eight 'police offices', as the magistrates' offices were now generally called, and Bow Street was to be recognised as a clearing-house for crime under the direct authority of the Home Secretary. A Bill embodying these recommendations was introduced into Parliament in July, 1812, but by then the shock of the Wapping murders had faded. The Bill was quietly dropped. In the calm light of reason, men argued that no police system, however perfect, could ever prevent murders from being committed. The most that could be hoped for was to prevent a murderer's escape or to detect him more speedily, and these considerations pointed to the need to strengthen the nightly watch. With such agreeable and stoical reflections, rate-payers were relieved at being spared the burden of a costly police system which nobody wanted, and the zealots for personal liberty achieved further triumph. Colquhoun's 'new science of police' was not merely imperfectly understood. Nobody wanted to understand it.

RIVER POLICE AND BOW STREET RUNNERS

In the meantime, the stagnancy of the long debate about the theory of policing had not held up some useful reforms that were gradually providing London with a nucleus of professional police—offensive to constitutional principles as they might be.

In two chapters of his *Treatise,* Colquhoun called attention to the extent to which the vast wealth which poured into the Port of London was a prey to thieves, and he later dilated on this in a *Treatise on the Commerce and Police of the River Thames,* published in 1800. With characteristic precision, he estimated that there were no fewer than 10,000 thieves, footpads, prostitutes, and pilferers at work on the jetties and quays that lined the riverside, and that the plunder and pillage represented an annual loss of over half a million pounds. This argument for the establishment of a preventive police for the river appealed instantly to the shipping interests, and a Marine Police Establishment was set up in June, 1798 (four-fifths of the cost being borne by West Indian merchants), consisting of some sixty salaried officers—considerably more full-time men than in all the police offices put together. The men were given careful instructions to 'spurn with indignation' any attempt to corrupt them, and at all times to display 'the utmost zeal, vigilance, prudence, discretion, and sobriety'. Colquhoun had associated himself with a man of buccaneering propensities named John Harriot in recommending the scheme to the Government, and the new force was placed under Harriot's immediate command, with Colquhoun as its superintending magistrate. The experiment met with striking success; and two years later, in July, 1800, the Thames River Police Act, which owed much to the joint efforts of Colquhoun and Bentham, converted the private venture into a public concern. A ninth police office was created on the lines of that of Bow Street and the seven set up by the Middlesex Justices Act, 1792, and the justices of the new Thames Police Office were empowered to appoint and dismiss constables. The Thames magistrates acted directly on the detailed instructions of the Home Secretary; and the Thames river police thus became the first regular professional police force in London.

It was followed, before long, by a rapid expansion of the Bow Street foot and horse patrols founded half a century earlier by the Fielding brothers. The seven police offices created by the Middlesex Justices Act had been authorised to employ not more than six constables each, but this limit was increased in 1811 to twelve. The magistrates office at Bow Street, however, which had existed from much earlier times, enjoyed a prestige and a freedom from statutory regulation which provided the Chief Magistrate, with the Home Secretary's support, unlimited scope for experiment. The holder of the office in the early years of the nineteenth century, Sir Richard Ford, was an enterprising man. Dividing his time equally between the Home Office and Bow Street, he was ever ready to act on the Home Secretary's directions in appointing his constables as spies and informers to deal with enemy aliens during the Napoleonic Wars. He also took vigorous steps to combat crime. In 1805 he revived John Fielding's idea of a horse patrol and stationed some sixty men on the principal roads within twenty miles of London. They were carefully selected, preference being given to applicants who had served in a cavalry regiment. This roisterous body of men, some of whom made substantial fortunes out of their shady business in trafficking in crime, undoubtedly formed something of a *corps d'elite,* creating in their own lifetime the myth of the Bow Street Runners, a body well summed up by Professor Radzinowicz, taking a cue from Sir John Moylan, as 'a closely knit caste of speculators in the detection of crime, self-seeking and unscrupulous, but also daring and efficient when daring and efficiency coincided with their private interest'. They undertook missions all over the country and even abroad, but also contrived to clear such notorious places as Hounslow Heath of highwaymen. Their routine duty was to patrol the main roads as far out as Enfield, Epsom, Windsor and Romford, giving confidence to travellers with their greeting, 'Bow Street Patrol'.

In 1821 a second echelon, 100 strong, was established. This, curiously known as the 'Unmounted Horse Patrol', served to train men for promotion to the mounted branch, and operated in the suburban areas within a radius of five or six miles from London. Elaborate arrangements for conference points between the two branches of the horse patrol were worked out. The men were sworn in by the Chief Magistrate of Bow Street to act as constables throughout Middlesex, Surrey, Essex, and Kent and they acted under the direct authority of the Home Secretary: both branches of the Horse Patrol were commanded by a Home Office official named William Day, who, as Keeper of the Criminal Registers in the Department, had helped to organise the first patrol in 1805; he later set up office in Cannon Row. These patrols became the first uniformed police force in the country (the river police had no distinguishing uniform). They wore blue coats with yellow metal buttons, a scarlet waistcoat, blue trousers, Wellington boots, and black hats. To the scarlet waistcoats they owed the nickname 'Robin Redbreasts'.

The foot patrol, in the meantime, had been considerably strengthened. Like the horse patrol, it also split into two branches. The first in point of time was a night patrol, about 100 strong, which came to be organised in an increasingly sophisticated manner. By 1818 one body, known as the 'country party', would start their beats between four and five miles from London, patrolling inwards along the main roads leading into the capital, while a 'town party' would set out from the centre to meet them. In 1821, however, the increase of crime in central London led to the withdrawal of the 'country party' into the inner area, their place in the outer suburbs being taken by the unmounted horse patrol mentioned above. The foot patrols were given a measure of local discretion, generally starting off at about dusk and remaining out until one o'clock in the morning. They wore no uniform, but carried a truncheon, a cutlass, and occasionally a pistol. They were heartily detested by watchmen, who regarded them as spies set on themselves, but they co-operated with the horse patrols.

The fourth and last of these special Bow Street patrols was an outcome of a recommendation by a Parliamentary committee of 1822 under Peel's chairmanship. This was a special foot patrol by day, consisting of twenty-seven men, designed as a preventive force against daylight robbery, and instructed to watch for suspicious activities which might suggest plans for night burglaries. The men, mostly old soldiers, appeared in the streets for the first time in August, 1822, wearing a uniform (in contrast to the plain-clothes night-patrol) which consisted of a blue coat and trousers and a red waistcoat, which, Peel thought, would make them 'proud of their establishment'.

Hence by 1828, on the eve of the formation of the Metropolitan Police, a substantial corps of professional full-time officers already existed in London: the constables employed by the seven police offices, the various Bow Street patrols, and the Thames river police totalled some 450 men directly under the control of the Home Secretary. It was a meagre force to serve a population of nearly one and a half million, and at best it could do little more than attempt to catch a few criminals and bring them to justice. As a preventive force it was negligible. In addition, there were upwards of 4,500 watchmen employed by the City of London or, in the Metropolitan district, by various parishes, often under Improvement Act powers. The total cost to London of the old police during its last years amounted to the not inconsiderable sum of about a quarter of a million pounds.

THE UTILITARIANS

By the 1820s the agonising struggle to avoid introducing a police system into London was entering its concluding stages, though few could have suspected it, for the currents of fresh thinking that helped to bring matters to a head flowed deeply below the surface of public affairs.

Sixty years earlier, when the Fieldings were striving to educate public opinion, they had ranged indiscriminately over the whole field of criminal law reform and police reform; but as the century advanced the two movements followed divergent paths, each attracting its own, largely separate, protagonists. Professor Radzinowicz has pointed out that most of the early thinkers in this field—Blackstone (1723-80), Adam (1723-90), and Paley (1743-1805)—were hostile to the idea of a preventive police, holding, to put it in Utilitarian terms, that the greatest happiness for the greatest number was unlikely to be advanced by an elaborate system calculated to interfere with individual liberty: an admittedly imperfect police system was part of the price of freedom. Thus they assumed a position directly contrary to that of the police reformers, who held that without an efficient police the happiness of both State and individual was constantly at risk. The argument, therefore, involved one of the greatest of all human issues—namely, the responsibility of the State in relation to the rights of the individual. To this argument there could (and can) be no finality, but an escape from the logical dilemma was available to those who saw in the reform of the criminal law a preferable alternative to the creation of a civil force of police. Hence the cause of penal reform drew support from that of police reform, for it faced none of the obstacles that stood in the way of the latter: its objects were attainable without significant public expense, and it offered no threat to personal liberty. It thus became possible to argue that the more dangerous ideas should be shelved until the effect on society of such humanitarian measures as the abolition of public executions and the amelioration of prison life had been evaluated. While, therefore, for many years the police reformers supported the reform of the criminal code, the law reformers were generally hostile to the cause of police reform.

After the turn of the eighteenth century, however, under the influence of Jeremy Bentham (1748-1832), the two movements began to draw together once more. A man of catholic learning, liberal principles and incalculable influence in many branches of public affairs, Bentham had early been impressed by the work of the Italian Marquis Beccaria, whose *Essay on Crime and Punishments,* with a commentary by Voltaire, had been published in an English translation in 1767. Beccaria, in a passage which, in Professor

Radzinowicz's words, had all the force of a new concept, wrote: 'It is better to prevent crimes than to punish them. This is the chief aim of every good system of legislation, which is the art of leading men to the greatest possible happiness or to the least possible misery, according to calculation of all the goods and evils of life'. Beccaria pleaded for the revision of traditional attitudes towards crime and punishment, but was himself lukewarm towards the French idea of policing. Bentham, working out his vast and labyrinthine philosophies of Utilitarianism over a period of many years, espoused both causes and attracted disciples to further each—Romilly, the criminal law reformer, whose influence did much to purify the criminal code from its medieval barbarity; and Colquhoun, the pioneer police reformer, whose work has already been mentioned. And then, towards the end of his long life, Bentham proposed in his *Constitutional Code* the creation of a completely centralised preventive police system under the control of the Government. These views came to the attention of a young lawyer, Edwin Chadwick, who was to play a notable part in gathering up the thinking of three-quarters of a century and complete the Utilitarians' theoretical study of the 'science of police', without which Peel's political skill could have achieved little.

But these powerful currents of thinking caused few surface ripples. Parliament continued to regard the police idea with disfavour. Three more Parliamentary committees, in 1816, 1818, and 1822, rejected it as incompatible with British liberty. The first published copious evidence, but made no proposals. The second at last recognised the weakness of a system of parish constables and watchmen, and proposed to rescue the office of high constable from oblivion by attaching a salary to it and giving the high constable effective control over the parish constables, who themselves should be more carefully selected; a reliable certificate of character should be required from the deputies, and a limit put to their period of service. On one point, however, this committee was emphatic: a system of police on the Continental model would be 'odious and repulsive, and one which no government could be able to carry into execution...it would be a plan which would make every servant of every house a spy on the actions of his master, and all classes of society spies on each other'. The third committee, of 1822, set up on the motion of the newly appointed Home Secretary, Peel, similarly contented itself with proposals for minor reform designed to strengthen the traditional system, recommended the formation of the Bow Street day patrol, and took the conventional line (warmly endorsed by *The Times*) about the dangers of any new-fangled system of police. In a much-quoted passage they declared:

It is difficult to reconcile an effective system of police, with that perfect freedom of action and exemption from interference, which are
the great privileges and blessings of society in this country; and Your
Committee think that the forfeiture or curtailment of such advantages would be too great a sacrifice for improvements in police, or
facilities in detection of crime, however desirable in themselves if
abstractedly considered.

THE METROPOLITAN POLICE ACT, 1829

The Chairman of this thoroughly reactionary committee was, of all men,
the Home Secretary, Robert Peel, who nevertheless in the same year was
speaking in Parliament of a project for 'a vigorous preventive police, consistent with the free principles of our free constitution'. A politician of exceptional genius, Peel was clearly not prepared to commit his reputation too swiftly or
too deeply to so controversial a public issue as police reform, although there is
no doubt that he had set his heart upon it from the beginning of his term at
the Home Office. Instead, he devoted his early years as Home Secretary to
the cause of the reform of criminal law. So passed several years, during which
Peel seems to have been preparing himself, by discussion with authorities
abroad as well as at home, to re-enter the struggle for police reform when he
judged the moment ripe. By 1826 he had drawn up a plan for setting up a
single police system within a radius of ten miles of St. Paul's with the exception of the City, 'with which', he told a correspondent, 'I should be afraid to
meddle'. Then in the following year, 1827, he found himself a fellow member
with Lord John Russell of yet another Parliamentary committee on criminal
matters. The second report of this committee, published in July, 1828, struck
a modern note in asserting that 'the art of crime, if it may be so called, has
increased faster than the art of detection.' For the counties, the committee
rather lamely saw a means of salvation once again in the office of high constable, but significantly commented that there was ground 'for instituting inquiry
into the management of the Police of all our great towns'.

The recommendation came too late, for six months earlier the stage had
been set for the last of this wearisome procession of Parliamentary inquiries.
In February, 1828, Peel moved for the appointment of an inquiry with disarm-
ing terms of reference: 'to enquire into the cause of the increase of the number of commitments and convictions in London and Middlesex for the year
1827; and into the state of the police of the Metropolis and the district adjoining thereto'. Having thus adjusted priorities to a realistic assessment of the

state of public opinion, he proceeded in all that followed to display consum-
mate Parliamentary skill. His latest biographer has suggested that he was deliberately dull and unemotional. He delivered some unexciting statistics about
crime and, playing the whole matter down, declared, 'I must confess that I am
not very sanguine with respect to the benefits to be derived from this committee'. He despaired of persuading the City of London to co-operate in any general system of policing. He described the defects of the existing arrangements,
but did not 'believe that any effectual remedy can be devised by which the evil
can be cured'. Nevertheless, he did not wish to disguise the fact that 'the time
is come, when, from the increase in its population, the enlargement of its
resources, and the multiplying development of its energies, we may fairly pronounce that the country has outgrown her police institutions and that the
cheapest and safest course will be found to be the introduction of a new mode
of protection'. Addressing himself now to 'those who live in agricultural districts', he demanded: 'Why, I ask, should we entrust a grocer, or any other
tradesman, however respectable, with the direction and management of a
police for 5,000 or 6,000 inhabitants? Why should such a person, unpaid and
unrewarded, be taken from his usual avocations and called upon to perform
the laborious duties of a night constable?' He apologised for speaking for so
long, observing that, although the select committee would be concerned only
with London, 'the subject matter of the inquiry is connected with objects of
such deep importance, not merely as they regard the security of individual
property, but also as they regard the morals and habits of the entire population'. There is little doubt that Peel saw as his ultimate objective the creation of
a police system throughout the country.

The committee reported within six months, in July, 1828. Among the witnesses was Edwin Chadwick, who, with Bentham and Colquhoun made up the
trinity of Utilitarians whose school of thought finally reconciled the English
ideal of liberty with the French idea of police. Chadwick, 'the heir of
Bentham's doctrine of police', and his devoted friend and admirer during the
last years of the philosopher's life, played a valuable part in representing to
the committee the Utilitarians' insistence on the primary importance of the
preventive nature of police work. The report of the committee gave Peel all he
wanted. It noted that the existing policy system in London had been almost
uniformly condemned by all previous inquiries, and recommended the creation
of an Office of Police under the direction of the Home Secretary, who should
have unified control over the whole police in the Metropolitan area, including
the nightly watch. Specially appointed justices should be in charge of the
Police Office, but the committee abstained from advising on the detailed man-

agement of the force. The cost should be met partly from public funds and partly by a special rate levied on the Metropolitan parishes. Probably in fulfilment of a bargain struck behind the scenes, the committee recommended that the City should be excluded from the arrangement, but refrained from offering convincing reasons for doing so.

In April of the following year, 1829, Peel introduced his 'Bill for Improving the Police in and near the Metropolis'. The circumstances could not have been more favourable. In the Duke of Wellington he now had a Prime Minister who, ever since the shock of Peterloo, had preferred to entrust the maintenance of law and order to professional police rather than soldiers; influential public opinion had been educated by the work of Bentham and Colquhoun; confidence in parish constables and watchmen had largely disappeared; and political opposition had been bought off or conciliated. The Bill largely followed the recommendations of the committee, defining the area for which the new Police Office was to be responsible as the 'Metropolitan police district', a district extending over roughly a seven-mile radius from central London. The 'two fit persons' who as justices were to take charge of the Police Office were authorised to create and administer a police force composed of 'a sufficient number of fit and able men'. The men were to be sworn in by one of the justices as constables, and to have the powers and privileges of a constable at common law. The justices (or commissioners, as they were called later) were to exercise their powers to direct and control the force under the authority of the Home Secretary, and their power to frame orders for the government of the force was likewise subject to his approbation. A Receiver was to be appointed by the Crown with a duty to control the revenue required for the force and manage its property and legal business, and power was given to levy a police rate, not exceeding 8d., throughout the Metropolitan police district. Thus the Bill provided for a complete separation of police administration in London from its centuries-old link with the magistracy and the parishes. In introducing the Bill, Peel declared that 'the chief perquisites of an efficient police were unity of design and responsibility of its agents'. He intended to proceed slowly in establishing a police force, with a 'cautious feeling of his way and deriving aid from experience, essential to the ultimate success of all reforms'. He would apply the Bill to a few districts in the vicinity of the Metropolis at first and then gradually extend it to the others as 'its advantages unfolded themselves'.

It is one of the most remarkable facts about the history of police in England that, after three-quarters of a century of wrangling, suspicion, and hostility towards the whole idea of professional police, the Metropolitan Police

Act, 1829, was passed without opposition and with scarcely any debate. Part of the explanation no doubt lies in the adroitness Peel showed in excluding the City from his plans, in return for which it seems probable that the Whigs undertook to give the Bill an easy passage. 'Pray pass the bill through this session', Peel wrote to the Duke of Wellington when it was to go up to the House of Lords, 'for you cannot think what trouble it has given me.' Another remarkable fact is that Peel's Act remains the governing statute of the Metropolitan Police to this day. Recognition of Peel's genius ought not, however, to obscure his own want of originality of thinking about police reform. Regrettably, in harvesting the corn he failed to acknowledge his debt to those who had long prepared the way: Henry and John Fielding, who sowed the seed three-quarters of a century earlier, Patrick Colquhoun, who raised the crop, and Bentham, who tilled the soil in which it grew.

THE FIRST POLICEMEN

The story has too often been told to need retelling here, even if space allowed, of the events which followed. A brief outline must suffice.

The Metropolitan Police Act became law on July 19th, 1829, and Peel at once set about appointing the first commissioners of police (as the two justices soon came to be called). For one he sought an ex-soldier able to enforce discipline, and for the other he hoped to find a practical and efficient lawyer. His appointments could not have been more successful. Colonel Charles Rowan was a retired officer of forty-six who had fought with the Light Brigade under Wellington at Waterloo; his colleague, Richard Mayne, to whom he was introduced in a room at the Home Office within a fortnight of the Act receiving the Royal Assent, was a young Irish barrister thirteen years Rowan's junior. The partnership was a famous one. The newly appointed commissioners found accommodation at 4 Whitehall Place, which backed on to a narrow lane to the east of Whitehall known as Scotland Yard. This rear entry gave a name to the new office which has been inherited by successive buildings.

Planning proceeded apace. While alterations were going on in the Scotland Yard building, the new commissioners occupied a room at the Home Office, and were given a small staff of civilians. The Act was largely an enabling measure, which sensibly left the details of the organisation to be worked out in the light of experience. It was decided to divide the Metropolitan district into seventeen police divisions, each containing 165 men, making a grand total of nearly 3,000. The limits were roughly those of the Bow Street foot patrols, with a radius up to seven miles from Charing Cross. Each division was to be put in the charge of an officer entitled 'superintendent', under whom were to be four inspectors and sixteen sergeants. The title 'inspector' was borrowed from the Bow Street patrols, and that of 'sergeant' was taken from the Army. Each sergeant had control of nine constables. After some hesitation, the decision was taken to clothe the men in a non-military uniform consisting of a blue tailed coat, blue trousers (white trousers being optional in summer) and a glazed black top-hat strengthened with a thick leather crown, which, in Melville Lee's happy phrase, 'was just just homely enough to save the situation'. A rattle was to be carried, together with a short truncheon concealed beneath the long tails of the coat. The Receiver embarked on the prodigious task of finding accommodation all over London for housing the men and providing the first station houses—the term 'police station' came later.

During August the commissioners set about the task of recruiting nearly 3,000 men. A ready-made source of volunteers was the Bow Street foot patrol (the unit continued an independent existence until 1839), and parish vestries were invited to supply lists of parish constables or watchmen who might wish to be considered for appointment. Few were found to be qualified. The regulations demanded that men should be under thirty-five, of good physique, at least five feet seven in height, literate, and of good character. From the outset it was a deliberate policy to recruit men 'who had not the rank, habit or station of gentlemen'. There was to be no caste system as in the Navy or Army, and ranks up to that of superintendent were to be drawn, typically, from ex-warrant officers and N.C.O.s. When vacancies occurred, promotion to higher rank was to be given to men from within the force. The wage of a constable, at a guinea a week, was deliberately fixed at a level to deter ex-officers, and at the same time to keep down the cost of the force. Among the flood of applications which poured into Scotland yard, those from military men of senior rank and from people with influence in the Government were generally turned down. From the start, the police was to be a homogeneous and democratic body, in tune with the people, understanding the people, belonging to the people, and drawing its strength from the people. A former sergeant-major named John May was appointed superintendent of 'A' Division at Scotland Yard, and he undertook the preliminary interviewing of applicants, passing the more promising on for final selection by the two commissioners.

Next came the important task of framing the instructions for the new force. Peel knew only too well how unpopular had been the decision to establish it; if it were to succeed, it must rely on public co-operation and goodwill. Hence the principles embodied in the first enlightened instructions (which remain valid to this day) exactly reflect the circumstances of 1829:

> It should be understood at the outset, that the[2] object to be attained is the prevention of crime.
>
> To this great end every effort of the police is to be directed. The security of person and property and the preservation of a police establishment will thus be better effected than by the detection and punishment of the offender after he has succeeded in committing crime...
>
> He [the constable] will be civil and obliging to all people of every rank and class.
>
> He must be particularly cautious not to interfere idly or unnecessarily in order to make a display of his authority; when required to act, he will do so with decision and boldness; on all occasions he may expect to receive the fullest support in the proper exercise of his authority. He must remember that there is no qualification so indispensable to a police-officer as a perfect command of temper, never suffering himself to be moved in the slightest degree by any language or threats that may be used; if he do his duty in a quiet and determined manner, such conduct will probably excite the well-disposed of the bystanders to assist him, if he requires them.
>
> In the novelty of the present establishment, particular care is to be taken that the constables of the police do not form false notions of their duties and powers.

By Saturday, September 26th, 1829, the planning was virtually completed. Substantial numbers of men had been enrolled and recruits were flowing in daily. That day the men paraded in the grounds of the Foundling Hospital in Holborn to be sworn in by Rowan and Mayne. They formed ranks, their conditions of service and instructions were read out, and each man was given a parcel of uniform. On the Monday they were told where they were to be lodged and fed, and that evening they were shown their beats. And then, at 6 p.m. on Tuesday, September 29th, the first parties of the 'new police' marched out from a still only partly converted 'station house' at Scotland Yard and five of the old watch houses. Londoners regarded them with hostility or derision, and coined nicknames—'peeler' or 'bobby'. Considering the novelty of the experiment, and the astonishing speed with which the whole unprecedented operation had been conducted, all went smoothly; and on October 10th Peel was able to report to his wife: 'I have been again busy all the morning about my Police. I think it is going very well. The men look very smart and a strong contrast to the old Watchmen.' He had, he said, been laughing at a cartoon 'called "Peeling a Charlie", in which I am represented stripping one of the old watchmen of his great-coat, etc.'. Next month the Duke of Wellington told Peel, 'I congratulate you upon the entire success of the police in London. It is impossible to see anything more respectable than they are'; to which Peel replied in the memorable sentence: 'I want to teach people that liberty does not consist in having your house robbed by organised gangs of thieves, and in leaving the principal streets of London in the nightly possession of drunken women and vagabonds.'

By May, 1830, the Metropolitan Police was a force about 3,300 strong, with many names on a waiting list—who did not, however, have to wait long, for the turnover in manpower, mainly on account of dismissals for drunkenness, was extremely high. The force's testing time was about to come.

The early 1830s saw the Reform Bill Riots in London, and the growth of subversive activities which provided endless opportunities for the police to perfect techniques of crowd-control and practise the newly acquired art of baton charges. The London parishes, on whose shoulders the whole cost of the force was to be borne, were not so easily mesmerised by Peel as Parliament had been, and during 1830 meetings of vestries all over London passed resolutions denouncing the new police as an 'outrage and an insult' to the people. A typical pamphlet (preserved in the Public Record Office) came to the attention of Peel. Insisting on the restoration of parish policing, it concluded with the brave exordium, 'Join your Brother Londoners in one heart, one hand, for the Abolition Of The New Police'. Peel minuted: 'Here is another proof of the necessity of a clear, detailed, and authorised explanation in the public Papers of the Metropolitan Police, and in so far as Rates are concerned. We are run down by the Press when we have truth completely on our side.' But the parishes, Press, and public continued to fulminate against the new police. Wild rumours circulated. It was said that the police were being drilled in order to put the Duke of Wellington on the throne, and placards appeared in the London streets carrying inflammatory exhortations to Englishmen to get rid of 'Peel's bloody gang', who were alleged to be arming themselves with cutlasses. Policemen attempting to control traffic were ridden down and lashed with whips. In August, 1830, the first Metropolitan policeman to be killed on duty, John Long, was stabbed in Gray's Inn Road. Complaints about police poured into Scotland Yard, and Rowan and Mayne, carefully investigating each personally, were accordingly accused of constituting a sinister 'police court'; outrage and insult could go no further.

Peel worked loyally with the commissioners in riding out these storms, but he was succeeded in November, 1830, by Melbourne. The new police had lost their creator and mentor; and their worst months were still to come when, in the summer of 1833, a conjunction of events led to the setting up of two Parliamentary committees of inquiry into their conduct. The first concerned a sergeant named Popay, who had been a schoolmaster before joining the police. Popay was discovered to have insinuated himself in the guise of a poor artist into a subversive movement, where for some months he acted as a double agent. In the sensitive state of public opinion about the new police, the discovery fed renewed outcries against tyranny, for now there was triumphant evidence that at least one policeman had been used, or had chosen to caste himself, as a spy. A Parliamentary committee exonerated the authorities from connivance in Popay's conduct, which they condemned as 'a practice most abhorrent to the feeling of the people and most alien to the spirit of the constitution'. Popay was dismissed, but the damage had been done. Later in the same year came the first major clash between the Metropolitan Police and the London mob. This was a public meeting organised by the National Political Union in Cold-Bath Fields. Melbourne instructed the police commissioners to have the ringleaders arrested if, despite warning, the meeting were held. Rowan himself directed operations, in the course of which the police were stoned, baton charges ensued, and three policemen were stabbed, one of whom was killed outright. Such was the public feeling against the police that at the inquest on the dead man the jury, against all the evidence, brought in a verdict of 'justifiable homicide'. The Government indignantly and successfully applied to the Court of Kings Bench for the verdict to be quashed. A Parliamentary committee heard some 'buck passing' between Melbourne and the commissioners about what instructions had been given to whom, but in the result upheld authority. Public opinion, fickle as ever, veered in favour of the police.

Such were the intolerable conditions in which the Metropolitan Police forged the reputation which, within a few years, was to make this force world-famous. Their imperturbability, courage, good humour, and sense of fair-play won first the admiration of Londoners and then their affection. Henry Fielding, nearly a century earlier, had set out to reconcile order with freedom in the streets of London. The sensible principles which governed the force in the early testing years effected the reconciliation in characteristically British fashion. It may well be that the long public debate over the theory of policing, and the instinctive obstinacy with which the police idea had time and time again been repudiated, paid dividends in the 1830s in the way in which 3,000 unarmed policemen, cautiously feeling their way against a hostile public, brought peace and security to London in place of the turmoil and lawlessness of centuries. The process of settling down was also no doubt aided by the fact of the Home Secretary's accountability for the force, which must have provided a valuable Parliamentary check during the formative years. Above all, however, credit for the successful transition from the era of parish constables and watchmen to that of professional policing belongs to Rowan and Mayne. London was admirably served by its first commissioners of police. Praising the conduct of the police, a Parliamentary committee which sat in 1833 and 1834 declared: 'Much, in the opinion of Your Committee, is due to the judgement and discrimination which was exercised in the selection of the individuals, Colonel Rowan and Mr. Mayne, who were originally appointed, and still continue to fill the arduous office of Commissioners of Police. On many critical occasions and in very difficult circumstances, the sound discretion they have exercised, the straightforward, open, and honourable course they have pursued—whenever their conduct has been questioned by the Public—calls for the strongest expression of approbation on the part of Your Committee.' The committee reported that complaints against the police 'have not been well founded'. And now at last the old bogy that had haunted man's imagination for so long was laid: 'It appears to your committee that the Metropolitan police has imposed no restraint, either upon public bodies or individuals, which is not entirely consistent with the fullest practical exercise of every civil privilege, and with the most unrestrained intercourse of private society.' English liberty had survived.

It remained to mop up. Peel's Act isolated the decrepitude of the City's Charlies, Colquhoun's old-established Thames river police, the scattered groups of constables employed in the police offices set up by the Middlesex Justices Act, 1792, and the legendary Bow Street Runners, who for several years yet were able to pursue their profitable line of business in undertaking missions on behalf of wealthy and influential clients. In 1832, and again in 1838, the City police system was reorganised; and in the following year, threatened by Lord John Russell, the Whig Home Secretary, with a Bill to amalgamate the City and Metropolitan police districts—which caused the Corporation to address an urgent petition to Queen Victoria—the Corporation promoted a City of London Police Bill which established a force, some 500 strong, under the command of a commissioner appointed by the Corporation. In the same year a second Metropolitan Police Act converted the River Thames force into the Thames Division of the Metropolitan Police, put an end to the anachronism of the constables employed in magistrates' offices, and

absorbed the Bow Street foot patrol. (The horse patrol had already been amalgamated with the Metropolitan Police by an Act of 1836, and thus formed the
nucleus of the mounted branch.) Finally, the Act of 1839 enlarged the boundaries of the Metropolitan police district to cover an area, encompassing a
radius some fifteen miles from Charing Cross, which remained unaltered until
minor adjustments were made by the Police Act, 1946. Thus Lord John
Russell, who had early been associated with Peel in the series of Parliamentary
committees of the 1820s which paved the way to reform, set the seal on his
political opponent's work, while at the same time, carrying it into the
provinces.

From this point onwards the history of the Metropolitan Police—the formation of the Detective Department (forerunner of the C.I.D.) in 1842, the
sad last years of Richard Mayne, who reigned too long alone after Rowan's
retirement in 1850, (a successor to Rowan was appointed, but by an Act of
1856 the force was placed under a single Commissioner) the quarrel between
a high-handed commissioner, Sir Charles Warren, and the Home Secretary in
1888 which led to the former's resignation, the Battle of Sidney Street, fingerprinting, and an endless succession of notorious murders—all belongs properly
to the story of Scotland Yard; and developments in the Metropolitan Police
can be mentioned only where they have a bearing on the more general history
of police in England.

ENDNOTES

* This chapter, "The New Police in London 1750-1830" was originally published in *History of the Police in England and Wales* by T.A. Chrichley. Copyright © 1978 Constable Publishers, London. Pp. 29-57. Reprinted by permission of Constable Publishers, London.

1   A picturesque description of the watches garlanded and in 'bright harness' marching for 'three thousand two hundred tailor's yards' is contained in Stow's *Survey of London* (1598), Everyman edn. (1912), pp.92-3.

2.   In a second draft of the instructions, Peel inserted the word 'principal'.

CHAPTER 5
Police History

J. DANIEL DEVLIN

The modern professional police forces seem to bear as little resemblance to the old high and petty constables of the 18th century as they bear to the systems of mutual pledging and hue and cry of a thousand years ago. And yet the differences in all three systems, considerable as they are, are not so important as their two most notable common features: that all three systems have their origin in the common law and ensure that those charged with the duties of policing are in the same legal position as other citizens; and secondly, that all three are essentially local in character. That these features should be possessed by all three systems is not surprising, for the earliest developed, through the next, into the present.

Historically, the first feature is the reason why, today, constables have few powers not possessed by ordinary citizens, a characteristic which, more than any other, distinguishes the police service of this country and those countries whose legal systems are based on the common law of England, from police systems of other lands. It has been well said that,

> The police of this country have never been recognized, either in law or by tradition, as a force distinct from the general body of citizens. Despite the imposition of many extraneous duties on the police by legislation or administrative action, the principle remains that a policeman, in the view of the common law, is only "a person paid to perform, as a matter of duty, acts which if he were so minded he might have done voluntarily".[1]

The second feature explains why our modern police service is organized in a number of separate police forces, rather than in one centrally-controlled body as is so often the case in other countries.

It is often said that the history of the police service may be divided into the three stages mentioned in the opening words of this chapter, but it would be wrong to believe that these stages are well defined or that they began and ended at particular moments of time. On the contrary the service has a more or less continuous history of well over a thousand years and each stage developed gradually into the next.

First the responsibility of maintaining law and order was in the hands of local associations of the citizens themselves, every person ensuring that his neighbour kept the peace. Later it became the practice to appoint constables who with the Justices of the Peace enforced the law. Finally paid professional police forces of the modern type were created.

MUTUAL PLEDGING

When the Saxons settled in England they introduced their tribal system of police under which the head man and the members of each settlement were answerable for each other's conduct and for the internal peace of their locality. Later on, when the country had become one kingdom, the King, in return for the allegiance and mutual good conduct of his subjects, guaranteed them a state of peace and security which was and still is, known as the "King's peace".

In the reign of Alfred the Great (870-901) there was an effective system for preserving order. The earls of the provinces were responsible for the keeping of the King's peace. The country was divided into shires or counties, and a shire reeve or sheriff was appointed in each county to be responsible to his earl for the peace of his county. Each shire contained many tithings or groups of about ten families, and every freeman over twelve years of age had to be enrolled in his tithing and give his pledge or surety (or *borh*) for the good behaviour of the other members of his group. The chief man was known as the tithingman, headborough, or borsholder, and he was responsible to the sheriff for the peace and order which should be maintained by this pledged union of freemen. Once a year the sheriff visited each tithing and reviewed the system of the mutual pledging of the freemen, which was known as frank pledge.

This system was a personal and local system; the freemen were banded together on oath to see that the peace was kept in their locality, and as the inhabitants were responsible for the district, they were particularly careful about strangers, who were looked on with suspicion until they satisfied the residents that they were not dangerous to the local peace. The tithings were joined into unions of ten and this larger group comprising about 100 families was known as a hundred.

Thus, the Anglo-Saxon police system was primarily a preventive system. Every man was made responsible for his own actions and for the actions of his neighbours, and if a man broke the law he had to reckon with the members of his community. Every freeman was in effect a police officer, bound by oath to assist in the preservation of the peace and in the detection and punishment of an offender. The tithingman was in command of the men of his group and it was his duty to raise the hue and cry, to collect his neighbours, and pursue any criminal who had fled from the district. If a tithing could not catch its criminal and so clear itself all the pledged members were liable to a fine. This system of mutual policing was, to some extent, submerged by the introduction of the feudal system after the Norman conquest in 1066.

William I increased the power of the sheriff but regarded him as his representative whose duty was to look after the King's rights and interests in the county. The sheriff continued to deal with offences and the frank pledging of the residents, but his main duty was to procure money for the King by exacting heavy fines. In addition, the feudal baron from his castle ruled absolutely over his retainers and serfs so that law and order usually depended on the power and will of the local lord. By degrees the lords procured the King's consent to have their own local courts which were known as Courts Leet and were conducted by Stewards appointed by the Lords of the Manor. Thus, for a time, the control of police work passed from the freemen to the baronial nobility.

In the reign of Henry I (1100-1135), who maintained the King's peace with such success that he was known as the "Lion of Justice", the old Saxon courts of the hundred and of the shire were revived, and he sent out itinerant justices or judges to decide cases in the counties, thereby bringing the Crown into close contact with local police.

During these Norman days the towns and boroughs kept alive the Saxon idea of local and personal guarantees for mutual protection against crime and violence. The word "borough" is derived from an Anglo-Saxon word meaning defence and safety. It now means an incorporated town, but in those early days it indicated an association of men pledged to preserve order such as a tithing or a town in which the residents combined for their own protection and policing.

The anarchy and bloodshed of Stephen's reign (1135-1154) made the country ripe for the restoration of law and order, and Henry II (1154-1189) had the support of the nation in his successful fight to end the feudal independence of the barons and to enforce the rule of law. His Assize of Clarendon (1166) restored the system of frank pledge, and the sheriffs were ordered to see that this system of mutual responsibility for the prevention of crime was everywhere maintained. He also sent out itinerant justices to supervise the administration of justice and the main tenance of the peace. His Assize of

Arms (1181) directed that every freeman should bear arms for the purpose, when necessary, of preserving the peace and securing criminals. When a criminal or suspected person was discovered in any district it was the duty of the residents to arrest him, and if he fled it was the duty of the principal inhabitant (then called the headborough), to raise the hue and cry with horn and voice. Every adult in the locality was then bound to arm himself and take up the chase; the hue and cry being passed on to other districts traversed until the wanted person was caught or reached sanctuary.

The absence of Richard Coeur de Lion (1189-1199), the misdeeds of John (1199-1216), and the weak rule of the third Henry (1216-1272) left the country again in a state of confusion which was soon remedied by the ability of Edward I (1272-1307), one of the greatest of our Kings. His Statute of Winchester (1285) was founded on Henry's Assize of Arms and provided a definite system for keeping the peace of the country. It is well to note three points from this statute:

1.   The hundred was to be answerable for all offences committed in it. Every man between 15 and 60 was to have arms in his house prescribed in accordance with his rank and property, ready for use in keeping the peace.

2.   The hue and cry was to be revived. The sheriffs were to follow law breakers with the whole countryside and the pursuit was to follow everywhere and anywhere until the offender was caught or reached sanctuary. If the hue and cry was not levied at once the residents were to be fined.

3.   Watch and ward was to be kept in towns. The gates of walled towns were to be shut between sunset and daybreak and a watch of six men was to guard each gate. Every borough was to have a watch of twelve persons, and small towns were to have watchmen according to their population.

Edward, in the same year, also provided for the needs of the capital, enacting that the gates of London were to be shut at night and that the city should be divided into twenty-four wards each with six watchmen controlled by an alderman. A "marching" watch was also to move about and assist the watchmen in the wards, all the watchmen being authorised to arrest offenders and bring them before the Mayor.

In this manner Edward I made practical and long lasting arrangements for policing the country, going back to the Anglo-Saxon system of making the people themselves responsible for the preservation of law and order.

THE CONSTABLE AND THE JUSTICE OF THE PEACE

The office of Justice of the Peace was created after that of constable, although they are both of ancient origin. The office of Justice was (and is) local in nature and in jurisdiction, but holders were (and are) appointed by the Crown, originally to perform police functions and later also with judicial authority.

In 1195 Richard I appointed knights to see that all males over 15 took the oath to maintain the peace. After about fifty years these knights became conservators or wardens of the peace, co-operating with the sheriff in the policing of his county. Their duties were of an executive nature, and in 1344 Edward III directed that they should examine and punish law breakers. He took a great interest in these officers and was careful to appoint only good and moral men who had landed property in their county, and finally in 1360 he authorised them to hear and determine all manner of crimes and to order persons who were not of good fame to give surety that they would keep the peace.

These justices were men of good position and authority. They were respected by the local people and were appointed and favoured by the Crown as a check on the power of the nobles, particularly during the Yorkist and Tudor periods (c.1460-1600). For several centuries the Justice of the Peace was in fact in charge of public affairs in the counties.

The term constable or petty constable, meaning a man whose business it was to take actual part in enforcing the law, comes under notice in the reign of Henry III (1252) in connection with the keeping of watch and ward.

The word "constable" is of Norman origin, coming from the Latin *comesstabuli*, meaning master of the horse, and in England the title has been applied to various officers appointed by the Crown. Where the Anglo-Saxons used the terms tithingman or headborough the Normans would use the word constable. The names became interchangeable, and in the end the tithingman who kept the peace was called the constable. He acted for and in his parish, and a place was not regarded as a parish unless it had a constable. These officers became the hands and eyes of the justices. They supervised the watchmen, inquired into offences, served summonses, executed warrants, organised the hue and cry, took charge of prisoners and prosecuted them, and in general obeyed the orders of the justices. They were appointed to their office by the Court Leet or Manorial Court, but they were sworn in by the justices and acted under their direction.

Thus we find at the close of the Tudor period that the tithing and its free men bound by oath to maintain order had disappeared, being replaced by the justice and the parish constable. The hue and cry still existed as the method for the pursuit of offenders, and localities were still liable to fine if they did not catch and prosecute their criminals.

It is very noteworthy that in these early days the duty of keeping the peace and suppressing crime was regarded as a public duty, inherent in every free man both on his own behalf and in respect to his neighbours. This duty is still obligatory on every citizen. Under the common law of the realm any person who is present when a felony or serious crime is committed is bound to arrest the offender. Every citizen is bound to assist a police officer who demands his aid in the lawful taking of a felon or in the suppression of an affray, and any person who refuses without good excuse is liable to punishment. A citizen may arrest for the purpose of stopping a breach of the peace or preventing the commission of a felony.

However, in time what was everybody's business became nobody's duty and the citizens who were bound by law to take their turn at police work gradually evaded personal police service by paying others to do the work for them. In theory constables were appointed annually, but in fact their work was done by deputies or substitutes who so acted year after year, being paid to do so by the constables. These early paid police officers did not rank high in popular estimation as indicated in contemporary references. They were usually ill-paid and ignorant men, often too old to be in any sense efficient.

The Civil War left the country in a lawless state. Cromwell would not depend on the justices, who were mainly county gentry and loyalists, so he had to fall back on military rule. He divided England and Wales into 12 districts, each in charge of a Major-General, and these officers had at their disposal a mounted force of over 6,000 soldiers, available for "the preservation of the peace, the suppression of vice and the encouragement of virtue". The Major-Generals acted as police and sat as judges. This military police system lasted for two years (1655-1657), and the removal of its stern control was followed by the licence and disorder of the Restoration of 1660.

As it was found that the lords of manors did not regularly hold their Courts Leet and appoint constables to preserve order, Charles II (1673) empowered the justices to appoint constables every year. From this time it was usual for justices to appoint one or more constables in rural parishes, and where the Courts Leet continued to function (particularly in the smaller towns) this Court annually appointed two constables with a headborough to assist them. These persons were usually men of position in the town, and they had paid watchmen and other assistants sometimes called "thief takers", to carry out the active duties of police officers.

In cities and large towns there were also paid watchmen controlled by the civil authorities, and any city or town could also have, in an emergency, a force of constables specially appointed by the justices. London had its parish night watchmen and constables. It also had the Bow Street Foot and Horse Patrol, a force of paid men originated by Henry Fielding the novelist (who was a London Police Magistrate from 1748 to 1754), to police the streets and the highways leading out of London. There were also about a dozen Bow Street "runners", paid men attached to the Chief Magistrate's office at Bow Street, who were engaged in the detection of crime. In 1792 the Middlesex Justices Act established seven new police offices, each of which had three paid Magistrates with six paid constables under their orders. In effect this was the first officially organised paid English Police Force. Already in 1786 the City of Dublin had been provided by Act of Parliament with a paid and organised police force, and it is interesting to note that in this Dublin Police Act the word "police" was officially used.

The word "police" comes from the Greek _polis_, a city, through the Latin _politia_, which means the condition of a state or government. "Police" connotes a system of administration or regulation, but it is now generally used to indicate the organised body of civil officers in a place, whose particular duties are the preservation of good order, the prevention and detection of crime, and the enforcement of the laws.

At the beginning of the nineteenth century there were, therefore, many types of police officers, controlled by entirely unconnected local authorities. There were the parish constable, the deputy or petty constable who was paid by the constable to do his work; the constable and the headborough appointed annually by the Court Leet; the constable appointed by the justices; the special constable sworn in during an emergency; the paid night watchman; the paid street keeper; the paid night constable, and so forth.

In London there were watchmen, Bow Street patrols and runners, constables attached to the police offices, and water police. The severe penal laws of the age did not deter criminals. The system of paying rewards for the arrest of offenders had but little effect and was much abused. Crime and disorder were prevalent and the law was almost powerless, and remained so until the professional police forces of the modern type had gained the respect and trust of the public, a process which is traced in the next section.

THE MODERN POLICE SERVICE

Today, when we look back at the appalling prevalence of crime and public disorder of the eighteenth and nineteenth centuries it is difficult to understand why such a state of affairs was tolerated when the creation of a modern type police service would have brought a measure of peace and tranquillity and reduced the crime to manageable proportions. The fact was that Parliament and public alike distrusted the idea of a strong, efficient, professional force and, except for a few humanitarians and reformers, believed that the cure would be worse than the malady. As was said in 1822,[2]

> ...It is difficult to reconcile an effective system of police, with that perfect freedom of action and exemption from interference, which are the great privileges and blessings of society in this country; and Your Committee think that the forfeiture or curtailment of such advantages would be too great a sacrifice for improvements in police or facilities in detection of crime, however desirable in themselves if abstractedly considered.

A great many attempts were made to set up an effective police system during the half-century before 1829 but they all failed because no scheme could reconcile the freedom of action of individuals with the security of person and property.

The problem was eventually solved by effecting a compromise between two irreconcilable aims—the creation of a force, impartial and immune from outside influence, and the provision of a system of external, democratic control. This was achieved by the use of four principles:

1.   the members of the "New Police", as the service was called, were constables, whose common law powers and duties were preserved;

2.   the form of control of constables which had existed for five centuries, the justice of the peace, was continued;

3.   the authorities responsible for appointing, equipping, paying and maintaining, which were also given a degree of supervision over the forces, were more or less democratically elected bodies; and

4.   the members of the forces were independent in enforcing the law, subject only to the internal discipline of the forces and the lawful commands of the justices.

The first of the modern police forces, the Metropolitan Police, was created by Act of Parliament in 1829 as a result of the initiative of Sir Robert Peel, the then Home Secretary. He is regarded as the creator of the modern police system, and the names "Bobby" and "Peeler" still remain as memorials of his work.

His Act was designed "for improving the police in and near the Metropolis", and it established a police office at Scotland Yard from which the new force of paid efficient policemen was to be supervised by two Commissioners. 1,000 men commenced duty on 29th September, 1829, and in the following year the Force was over 3,000 strong.

It was the first police force provided with a definite uniform, consisting of a blue swallow-tailed coat and blue trousers strapped over the boots, a leather top-hat and a leather stock, and white duck trousers were worn in summer. The helmet and tunic came into use in 1863.

The success of this new force was followed by legislation providing for the improvement of the police system throughout the country.

Some of these new Acts of Parliament recognised the existing system and were designed to improve its working, but others finally established the modern system of county and borough police forces. In the first category were the Special Constables Act 1831 and the Parish Constables Act 1842 which though amended by later Acts, were in existence, but inoperative in practice, until repealed and replaced by the Police Act 1964.

The Special Constables Act empowered justices to order citizens to serve as special constables in a time of emergency, and this Act, in effect, enunciated the early English principle that it is the duty of every citizen to assist in preserving the peace.

The modern police system was established throughout England and Wales by the Municipal Corporations Act and by the County and Borough Police Acts. Under the former Acts of 1835 and 1882 the Council of every corporate town had to appoint a Watch Committee which was bound to establish and maintain a police force adequate for the town. Thus, a local police authority was created, responsible for the policing of cities and boroughs.

The County Police Acts of 1839 and 1840 allowed the justices in Quarter Sessions to establish a paid police force for their county. These new forces, commanded by Chief Constables, were to supersede the existing police forces in the county, except those borough forces established under the Municipal Corporations Act.

However, some counties failed to make use of these Acts, and finally the County and Borough Police Act of 1856 directed that in every county in which a police force had not been established for the whole of the county, the justices in Quarter Sessions should establish a sufficient police force for the whole county.

This Act also introduced two new principles of far-reaching importance. It provided for the appointment of H.M. Inspectors of Constabulary who were to visit the county and borough forces and report on their efficiency to the Home Secretary, but also directed that the State should pay one quarter of the cost of the pay and clothing of every police force which was certified by an inspector of constabulary to be efficient as regards it numbers and discipline.[3] Thus since 1856 the whole of England and Wales has been policed by county and borough police forces which are regulated by statute, are subject to government inspection, and receive part of their expenses (now one-half) from the State, but which are under the control partly of the local authorities, partly of the Home Secretary, and partly of the Chief Constables.

These forces are independent of each other. Each has its own police authority and Chief Constable and is in charge of a definite area. Up to the end of the First World War the rates of pay and other conditions of service of these forces materially differed. The larger towns paid higher wages than the counties and smaller towns, and the many wide differences between one force and the other called for investigation and improvement. In the year 1919 a committee, presided over by Lord Desborough, made a searching enquiry into the conditions of service, and the "Desborough Report" forms a landmark in police history.[4] As a result of the recommendations of this committee the pay and conditions of service of the police were standardized and the police service became in fact a "service". Now police work is a profession with responsibilities and obligations of a particular nature attached, a profession to which a man devotes the best years of his life, and which, having regard to the amount of knowledge a policeman ought to possess, seems to be growing into a learned profession.

In the second quarter of this century, and especially in the post-war years a change could be detected in police-public relations. A greater number of citizens were coming into contact with the police, due in great measure to the wider use of the motor car, and a great many more real or supposed grievances against the police were made public. Whether this undoubted change in attitudes amounted to a worsening in police-public relations may be doubted;[5] but certainly a large part of the public felt concern. Some sections of the public entertained misgiving that the police forces in the provinces were not subject to adequate accountability[6] and that complaints by members of the public were ineffective.[7]

Accordingly in, January 1960, a Royal Commission[8] was appointed which recommended measures which would secure three objectives:[9]

(i) A system of control over the police, and a basic organisation which, while enabling them to perform their duties impartially, would achieve the maximum efficiency and the best use of manpower.

(ii) Adequate means within this system of bringing the police to account, and so of keeping a constitutionally proper check upon mistakes and errors of judgment.

(iii) Arrangements for ensuring that complaints against the police by the public are effectively dealt with.

The Commission did not recommend the creation of a nationalised police service[10] and took the view that the above objectives could be achieved on the basis of the present system of separate local police forces.

A great many of the Commission's recommendations were either adopted at the suggestion of the Home Secretary or embodied in the Police Act 1964, which consolidated and amended the principal statutory provisions relating to the police, reconstituted the police authorities, re-defined the functions and duties of chief constables, police authorities and the Home Secretary, and preserved the local affiliations and loyalites of the police. As the Commission said,

> ...the recommendations contained in this report are based on a continuance of the idea of partnership between central and local government in the administration of the police service, but with a shifting of the emphasis, rendered inevitable by developments within the police service and by broad changes in our civilisation and ways of life, towards firmer control by the central government.[11]

As already mentioned, the county police originated in 1839 and after 1856 a county police force had to be established in every county; the borough police derived their origin from an act of 1835; the Metropolitan Police Force was created in 1829; and the City of London Police exists as a separate force, partly from powers derived from ancient charters and partly from special statutes especially one in 1839.

Since the earliest days of the modern police service there has been a process of consolidation and amalgamation of forces whereby small units joined with their larger neighbours in the interests of economy and efficiency.[12] The result is that by 1st January, 1965 the number of separate police forces[13] in England and Wales had been reduced to 126: 51 county and combined forces; 73 city and borough forces; the Metropolitan Police; and the City of London Police; and the number is likely to decrease.

Although there are so many separate police forces in England and Wales, their members serve under similar conditions, and since 1919 the rates of pay and pension have been identical.[14] The forces are separate but their members are linked together by common duties and interests in which they co-operate freely and cordially. Chief officers, detectives, training officers, traffic officers, and others meet regularly in conferences held throughout the country and members of forces meet frequently on duty. It can now be said that there is but one police service, growing more and more uniform in organization, training and practice, and in their discipline, *esprit de corps* and conduct, which every police service should display.

Writing in 1796, in a treatise on the Police of the Metropolis, Dr. Colquhoun, in recommending the establishment of a proper police force, made the following noteworthy comments:

> Next to the blessings which a nation derives from an excellent constitution and system of general laws, are those advantages which result from a well regulated and energetic plan of police conducted and enforced with purity, activity, vigilance and discretion. The police have a fair claim, while they act properly, to be esteemed as the civil defenders of the lives and properties of the people. Everything that can heighten in any degree the respectability of the office of constable adds to the security of the State and to the safety of the life and property of every individual.

In the words of the Desborough Report, the police officer acts as a citizen representing the rest of the community and exercising powers which, at any rate in their elements, are possessed by all citizens alike, and his whole power rests on the support both moral and physical, of his fellow citizens. As Captain Melville Lee observes in his "History of English Police", the police occupy a position of vital importance in the Commonwealth being the primary constitutional force for the protection of individuals in the enjoyment of their legal rights. They are designed to stand between the powerful and the weak, to prevent oppression, disaster and crime, and to represent the cause of law and order at all times and in all places. In every court and alley the policeman stands for good citizenship; he is a reality that the most ignorant can comprehend, and upon his impartiality, efficiency and intelligence depends the estimation in which the law is held by the masses.

The following are the principal dates and events in the history of the Police Service of England and Wales:

870-901	The reign of Alfred the Great, during which an effective system of mutual pledging existed.
1066	The Norman conquest, after which the Anglo-Saxon system fell into disuse.
1166	The Assize of Clarendon whereby Henry II restored Frank Pledge.
1181	The Assize of Arms. Every freeman to bear arms for preserving the peace and securing criminals, and when necessary to raise the hue and cry.
1195	Richard I appointed knights to assist in the maintenance of law and order. These were later known as conservators of the peace and, later still, Justices of the Peace.
1252	The term "constable" was used.
1285	The Statute of Winchester. The police system of Edward I based on the Hundred and the use of the hue and cry, and watch and ward.
1344	Conservators of the peace given judicial functions.
1360	The title "Justice of the Peace" first used. Their powers, duties and functions were enlarged.
c.1600	The tithing system had disappeared and had been replaced by justices and constables.
1655-57	Cromwell's military police system in being.
1673	Justices empowered to appoint constables.
1748	Henry Fielding became a London police magistrate.
1786	The City of Dublin police force created.
1792	The Middlesex Justices Act established new police magistrates' offices.
1829	The Metropolitan Police created.
1831	Special Constables Act.
1833	The Lighting and Watching Act. Parishes empowered to elect inspectors and appoint watchmen.
1835	The Municipal Corporations Act. Every borough required to appoint a watch committee with a duty of maintaining a police force.
1839	Justices in quarter sessions empowered to establish police forces in counties.

1856   The County and Borough Police Act. The estab-
          lishment of a police force in every borough and
          county made compulsary. The appointment of
          Her Majesty's Inspectors of Constabulary and
          payment of an Exchequer grant sanctioned.

1882   The Municipal Corporations Act. Repealed and
          replaced Act of 1835.

1888   The Local Government Act. Standing Joint
          Committees created. Exchequer grant increased
          from one quarter to one half.

1919   The Desborough Committee appointed. The
          Police Act. Standardization of pay and conditions
          of service.

1948   The Oaksey Committee appointed.

1960   The Royal Commission on the Police ("Willink"
          Commission) appointed.

1964   The Police Act. Much of the nineteenth-century
          police legislation repealed. Functions and duties of
          police authorities, Home Secretary, and chief
          constables defined.

ENDNOTES

* This chapter was previously published in *Police Procedure, Administration and Organization*, by Daniel Devlin. Copyright © 1966 Butterworths. Pp. 1-17.

1. Report of the Royal Commission on Police Powers and Procedure, 1929 (Cmd. 3297), para. 15.

2. Report of the Select Committee on the Police of the Metropolis, 1822, quoted in the final report of the Royal Commission on the Police, 1962, Cmnd. 1728, (The "Willink" Report), para. 38.

3. And see further, as to Government grants, L.D. Devlin, Chap. 42, in *Police Procedure, Administration and Organization*, p.606, post; and as to inspectors of constabulary, Chap. 9, p. 98, post.

4. See L.D. Devlin, in *Police Procedure, Administration and Organization*, Chap. 13, p. 150, below.

5. The Willink Commission found that there was no reason to suppose that relations were anything but good: op. cit. paras. 338-340. And see Chap. 21, p. 268, below.

6. The Home Secretary, before the passing of the Police Act, 1964 was answerable in Parliament for the actions of the Metropolitan Police but not for the actions of the provincial forces. See also L.D. Devlin, in *Police Procedure, Administration and Organization*, Chap. 39, p. 554, below.

7. The Willink Commission found that this charge was not supported by the evidence: op. cit. para. 428. As to the present procedure in relation to complaints, see L.D. Devlin, in *Police Procedure, Administration and Organization*, Chap. 16, p. 188, below.

8. Royal Commission on the Police, Interim Report, 1960, Cmnd. 1222; Final Report, 1962, Cmnd. 1728. The Reports are examined in detail in Chap. 13, p. 156, below.

9. Final Report, op. cit. para. 19.

10. In a Memorandum of Dissent, however, Dr. A.L. Goodhart proposes a national police service, administered regionally.

11. Op. cit., para. 23.

12. And see further, as to amalgamation, L.D. Devlin, in *Police Procedure, Administration and Organization*, Chap. 4, p. 42, below.

13. This figure does not include the River Tyne Police Force.

CHAPTER 6
The Buffalo Police 1872-1900: Labor Unrest, Political Power and the Creation of the Police Institution

SIDNEY L. HARRING
LORRAINE M. MCMULLIN

INTRODUCTION

There are only a few systematic analyses of the development of the police institution in the United States. Yet this work is by no means irrelevant. The current demand for "law and order" cannot be adequately understood without reference to the social processes which originally constructed both the "problem" of "law and order" and its solution: the police, prisons, and the rest of the criminal justice system.

Historians of the police, like most criminologists, have tended to see the police institution and its development from a "value-free" perspective that emphasizes the idea that the institution emerged as a rational response to patterns of disorder—crime, riot, drunkenness—which occurred as the society became more heterogeneous, industrialized, and urban. Studies of Boston (Lane, 1967) and New York City (Richardson, 1970) are the best examples of this perspective.

This kind of analysis, however, fails to adequately account for the important political and economic conflict occurring during this period of intense industrial and urban development as manufacturers struggled to establish control over workers and the work process, and workers countered with strikes and other forms of resistance. The police institution often served the narrow class interests of these manufacturers, and its development was structured along channels emphasizing the control of strikes and working-class organiza-

tions, the control of working class communities, and the control and re-social-
ization of immigrants imported to serve the demands of industry.

The purpose of this paper is to offer a preliminary analysis of the development of the police institution in a particular urban, industrial location—Buffalo,
New York—in the context of the political and economic struggles that
occurred there as the city grew and industrialized during the last three decades
of the nineteenth century.

BUFFALO: 1872-1900

In the years after the Civil War, Buffalo experienced an economic boom
that led to its development as a thriving industrial center. While maintaining its
earlier pre-eminence as a water transportation and grain trading center,
Buffalo also became a center for manufacturing, railroading, and steel and iron
making. Its central location situated where the Erie Canal and manufactured
products from the East met the Great Lakes and raw materials from the West,
and easy access to the coal-fields of Pennsylvania, combined with the promotion and developmental skills of local businessmen and manufacturers, created
this transformation. In 1873 when railroad lines connected Buffalo with the
coal fields the trend moved increasingly from trade to manufacturing. In all sixteen railroads built tracks to Buffalo creating one of the nation's largest rail
centers. Additional opportunities were created in construction, real estate
speculation, and supporting services (Dunn, 1972; Powell, 1962; McLaughlin,
1970).

These changes fundamentally altered the nature of the city. From a population of 117,714 in 1870 its population grew to 352,387 in 1900. Most of
this growth occurred in the twenty years between 1880 and 1900. In 1870
most of the population was composed of Americans of New England or
Eastern New York stock who moved West with the development of the Erie
Canal. German was the predominant immigrant group, although there was
also a substantial Irish community. Rapid industrial development brought in a
large Polish immigration beginning in the 1880's who from the beginning
made up the largest pool of unskilled factory laborers. These new immigrants
were crowded into a small section of the East Side and scattered in other
undesirable living areas along the waterfront, around factories and near stock
yards where they lived with little income in generally deplorable conditions as
seen in a slightly later account:

Forty to sixty people crowded into ten room houses and sometimes
boarders could not rent homes but only spaces on beds for a night
or day turn. Ninety-four percent of the Poles in Buffalo had an
income of less than $635, the living wage for that time....(Buffalo
Express, March 15, 1910)

While these workers were necessary for the development of industry, their
influx necessarily had an impact on the community far more significant than
merely an increase in size. The creation of a large, immigrant, unskilled work
force housed in isolated areas around factories created totally different communities within Buffalo which had no social relationship with other segments
of the population outside of their work role. This makes the city a much more
complex social unit, and introduces an uncertainty and volatility to the life of
the city which must be taken into account by the power structure in organizing
the city to perform new industrial functions.

Chart I—Social Backgrounds of Buffalo Mayors, 1870-1900 *

Date	Mayor	Occupation/Business
1870-71	Alexander Brush (R)	Partner with brother in most extensive brickmaking
1872-73		business in Western New York. (Earning between
1880-81		18 and 20 million dollars per year).
1874-75	Dr. Louis P. Dayton (D)	Health Physician with City Health Department
1876-77	Phillip Becker (R)	Founded Phillip Becker and Co. in 1854. It grew
1886-87		to most important wholesale grocery and glass house
1888-89		in New York State.
1878-79	Solomon Scheu (D)	Grocery supplier of provisions to lake and canal forwarders. Owned a restaurant, cafe and billiards room and built up a large and very lucrative busi-ness. He was a wealthy man and a recognized power in poli-tics.

Chart I—(continued)

Nov. 1881- Nov. 1882	Grover Cleveland (D)	In 1869 member of firm of Lansing, Cleveland, and Folsom. In 1870 became Sheriff of Erie County. Then joined firm of Bass, Cleveland and Bissell which had a large and lucrative practice. It later became Cleveland and Bissell.
Nov. 1882- Dec. 1882	Marcus M. Drake (R)	A captain of the Erie Railway's line of steamers. In 1869 superintendent of building and repairs for Erie Railways line. Finally superintendent of Union Dry Dock Company.
Dec. 1882- Jan. 1883	Harmon S. Cutting (D)	Attorney and police commissioner. In 1882 attorney and also mayor's clerk. He "had, as Mayor Cleveland's clerk, practically been mayor for the twelve-months."
1883	John B. Manning (D)	Owned the largest malt house in the United States and probably one of the largest in the world. One of the largest individual maltsters in the United States. In 1880 was president of the National Malster's Association and president of the Buffalo Board of Trade.
1884-85	Jonathan Scoville (D)	In 1860 established a foundry for the manufacture of car wheels. It became a concern doing $4,000,000 per annum yielding an income of $500,000. He established brand works in Toronto and also conducted an extensive blast furnace in Chenango County, New York.

Chart I—(continued)

1889-1895	Charles F. Bishop (D)	In 1869 established a whole-sale coffee and spice store which became one of the largest in Buffalo.
1895-97	Gen. Edgar B. Jewett (R)	In 1865 admitted to father's firm of John C. Jewett and Son. In 1885 elected president and general manager. The company operated with stove foundries across the United States. His family had interests in the Marine and Columbia Banks, and the New York Central Railway.
1898-1901	Dr. Conrad Diehl (D)	A prosperous medical doctor.

* *Source: Biographical data throughout comes from a number of contemporary sources, including the Buffalo City Directors; the Buffalo Evening News; and numerous biographical accounts in Hubbell (1893).*

Buffalo was administered during this period by a remarkably homogeneous line of businessmen of German and New England stock for whom participation in city government was both civic duty and good business sense. Political control shifted between Republicans and Democrats regularly but power was always held by substantial businessmen. Mayor Alexander Brush (1870-73, 1880-81) and his brother owned the most extensive brick manufacturing business in Buffalo doing 18-20 million dollars a year in business. Mayor Philip Becker (1876-77, 1886-87, 1888-89) was a former steamship captain who had served as superintendent of building and repairs of the Erie Railroad; Superintendent of the Union Dry Dock Company; and Manager of the Lackawanna Transportation Company; John B. Manning (1883) was one of the largest individual malsters in the United States, and President of the Board of Trade. He had four malting plants, including the largest in the United States. Mayor Jonathan Scoville owned a foundry for the manufacture of railroad car wheels which did a business of $4,000,000 per year yielding an income of $500,000.

The effect of this direct control of city government by the richest and most successful businessmen is summarized by Mayor and former Police Commissioner Edgar Jewett (1895-97), President of the Jewett Refrigerator Company with interests in Columbia Bank and the New York Central and Hudson Railway: "Enterprises are attracted by wise, conservative, and businesslike government....To me the city of Buffalo appears to be not a political hive, but a vast business corporation" (Annual Message of the Mayor, 1895).

Buffalo was not immune from the general municipal mismanagement common to the period however—in no small part due to the business priorities of its leadership. Day to day administration was frequently inept and corruption occurred necessitating periodic "reform administrations" like that of Grover Cleveland (1881-82), a successful lawyer.

THE BUFFALO POLICE: ORGANIZATION AND CHANGE

As in other cities the organization of a permanent police came late in the development of Buffalo. In April 1871, a law was drafted creating the first Buffalo police department. The population of Buffalo at that time was in excess of 120,000.

There had been earlier police organizations in the area. The Buffalo Police Department superceded the Niagara Frontier Police Force, which had four captains and 100 patrolmen covering the City of Buffalo and which had been created in 1866 when the population of Buffalo alone was over 95,000.

Up until 1834 there had not been one watchman in Buffalo. In that year the mayor was given power to appoint "as many constables as he deemed necessary" who were to be paid fees according to arrests. This "experiment" proved of little value and became something of a political football until the common council established a set of rules and limited the number of constables to ten. Until 1845 when the population exceeded 30,000 people the force consisted of a captain and eight watchmen. In that year it was increased by six additional watchmen. Proposals for further increases in the force were repeatedly turned down. Even the 15 man force was felt unnecessary for in 1858 Chief of Police Robert H. Best led a force of only eleven police constables. The population in 1860 was 81,129 (Hubbell, 1893:76).

During this period of rapid growth Buffalo was primarily a commercial center, most important as the western terminus of the Erie Canal. Even with a large waterfront area, and hundreds of thousands of transients passing through to the West, Buffalo had no pressing problems in social control, and the power structure felt no need for any more than a token watch force. The force was virtually unchanged in size for twenty-five years while the population rose from just over 10,000 to over 80,000.

By 1866, when the Niagara Frontier Police Force was organized, substantial changes had occurred. Not only had the population increased to 95,000, but the Civil War had laid the base in Buffalo as elsewhere for a new economic order based on accumulated wealth, expansion and consolidation of enterprises, and a more industrial and less commercial base. Still the necessity of the new force was not universally accepted. In order to enact a new police law a group of Republican businessmen circumvented the Democratic controlled city council and went directly to the State legislature. The driving force behind the new police force, and the author of the legislative bill which created it was Jonathan S. Buell, a leader of the Buffalo Building and Loan Association, and Secretary of the Petroleum Oil Company, the first oil company in America. Besides authoring the bill, Buell was one of the three original police commissioners and is given credit for efficiently organizing and administering the force. In 1870 Buell, O.J. Green and James Adams, the three Republican commissioners, were removed and three Democratic ones appointed. The next year the Niagara Frontier Police Force was disbanded and the City of Buffalo given authority to create its own force (Hubbell, 1893:91).

The original force consisted of 204 men organized into precincts. Direct control was under Police Superintendent John Byrne who in turn was under a board consisting of the mayor and two police commissioners. Each precinct was under the direction of a captain and two or three sergeants. These appointments were political and the force was poorly trained. Dismissals, resignations, and demotions occurred at a high rate until the 1890's.

The growth of the Buffalo force had no direct relationship to either the growth of the population or to an increase in crime. Between 1873 and 1880 the force remained roughly the same size while population increased by about 25 percent; between 1880 and 1890 the force increased by about 100 percent while the population increased by about 67 percent. Between 1890 and 1900 the population increased by about 40 percent while the police increased by about 80 percent.

Chart II—Changes In Arrest Rates in Buffalo, 1873-1900

Year	Population	Size of Force	Total Arrests	Public Order Offenses	Crimes of Violence
1873	117,714*	204	12,535	8,278	84
1875	134,557	205	9,991	5,885	88
1880	155,134	193	9,012	5,587	97
1885	205,400	304	10,998	7,702	65
1890	255,664	401	17,628	12,979	140
1895	304,025	636	24,889	17,668	154
1900	352,387	732	28,347	20,505	219

*1870
Source: Population data from United States Census (1870, 1880, 1890, 1900), and New York State Census (1875, 1885, 1895); arrest and other police data from Annual Report of the Board of Police.

A comparison of the size of the police force and the crime rate is more complex. Between 1870 and 1900 the amount of serious crimes declined generally relative to the population. Population growth then did not result in any crime wave in Buffalo. This result is consistent with findings for other places studied during the same period (Ferdinand, 1972:574). The misdemeanor rate however fluctuates much more uncertainly from year to year but generally declines from 1870 to 1880, rises from 1880 to 1895 and then declines. For these misdemeanors, particularly such offenses as drunkenness, disorderly conduct, vagrancy, and tramps, fluctuations need to be analyzed carefully because arrests for these offenses can be used to control large, lower class segments of the population (Faler, 1974:381).

It seems clear that the increase in the size of the police force cannot be attributed to an increase in the level of serious crimes. The police reports themselves say as much:

> Your honorable body (the police commissioners) are of course familiar with the fact that the size of the force is insufficient to meet the

wants of the city. At present it consists of 220 men....This leaves
about 150 men for actual patrol duty, and as only one-half of this
number, or about 75 men, are on duty at one time, they are
required to patrol 350 miles of streets. It is indeed a very small force
of men to guard the lives and property of 200,000 people, yet, not
withstanding this fact, no crimes of any magnitude were committed
during the year (Annual Report, 1883:5).

Misdemeanor arrests are in a different category and the meaning of fluctuations in those rates will be discussed in a later section. In any case the growth
of the Buffalo Police Department outstripped the growth of both the population and the crime rate.

THE CONTROL OF THE BUFFALO POLICE

Between 1870 and 1900 the Buffalo Police force was under the tight
control of the most powerful business interests in the city. Buffalo was administered by businessmen with the purpose of making the city a favorable place
to conduct business. The business interests of the mayors were the most
important business ventures in Buffalo. The mayors were not small businessmen—they were the owners of the largest factories in Buffalo. These mayors,
together with two police commissioners that they appointed one Republican
and one Democratic, directed the police department. The police commission
set general policies, made rules, and hired and fired the Superintendent and
other officers.

The police commissioners also represented business interests although
generally less important ones than the mayor. The first two commissioners
selected in 1872 were John Pierce (1872-1877), the owner of a prosperous
livery business and an alderman, and Jacob Buyer, a dry goods merchant.
Succeeding commissioners included Robert Mills (1880-1883), the owner of a
large shipyard and dry dock, and holder of a string of Republican political
appointments including marine inspector and canal collector for the Port of
Buffalo; Frank Sears (1878-79) was a partner in a malting firm; Edward
Shafer (1887-89) was General Manager and Treasurer of the Buffalo School
Furniture Company.

During the period under consideration virtually every major business interest in Buffalo was represented among the Police Commissioners at one time
or another. These positions were not honorary ones: the board met from one
hundred to one hundred fifty times each year, and the Commissioners were

paid three times the annual salary of a patrolman. All major and many extremely minor decisions affecting the police were made by the two commissioners. When Buffalo considered adopting the patrol wagon and signal box communication system the Commissioners made two lengthy trips to observe the system in operation in Philadelphia, Brooklyn, New York City, and Boston, and submitted a detailed report to the City Council (Annual Report, 1886). The importance of Buffalo's businessmen attached to the control of the police institution is indicated by the fact that some of the city's most successful entrepreneurs took time off from their businesses to serve in the capacity of Police Commissioner.

Control of the police by business interests was not done solely through the commissioners. It was not uncommon for the police superintendents themselves to be businessmen. Daniel J. Morganstern, police superintendent (1890-93) had served as a detective from 1866 to 1871 with the Niagara Frontier Police but then spent 19 years as a proprietor of a "lucrative dry goods business" before being elected a colonel in a civil war regiment; George Chambers (1893-94) was division superintendent of the Erie Canal; William S. Bull (1894-99) was the "agent" of a paper manufacturer. Even though some men served as police superintendent who were promoted through the ranks, the fact that the commissioners repeatedly felt free to put the direct day to day operation of the department under a fellow businessman rather than a professional policeman demonstrates the firmness of their grip on the office. The Buffalo police were directly controlled by upper class business interests without even resorting to control by "middle men."

Chart III—Social Backgrounds Of Police Commissioners In Buffalo, N.Y., 1872-1900

Date	Comissioner	Occupation/Business
1872-77	John Pierce	For a time in the service of the New York Central Railroad. After that, he went into the livery business with J.F. Tyler and that became his permanent vocation.
1872-77	Jacob Beyer	Owner of a dry goods store.
1878-79	Elijah Ambrose	In 1866, he was city auditor. From 1868-71 was Receiver of Taxes, and in 1878, Deputy City Treasurer.

Chart III—(continued)

Date	Comissioner	Occupation/Business
1878-79	Frank A. Sears	In 1871, with the firm of Sears and Davis, a malting firm.
1880-83	Robert Mills	At age 21, captain of one of the largest schooners on the lake and soon became owner and commander. In 1855, established a floating dry dock and general ship repairing business. In 1866, bought shipyard and dry dock of F. W. Jones.
1880-82	William J. Wolf	In 1866, appointed patrolman by Niagara Frontier Police. In 1868, appointed Special Detective and in 1872, promoted to rank of detective. Six months later, became captain of precinct, a job he held for eight years.
1882-83	James M. Shepard	Started as a patrolman, was a captain of the 1st precinct in 1882 and a detective for the 1st precinct in 1883.
1883-87	Isaac O. Crissy	In 1878, he was editor on the Buffalo Express. In 1879, was a school book salesman for Harper and Bros. In 1880, was office manager of the commercial Line of Steamers.
1883-85	Michael Newell	In 1883, he was a Commissioner of Travel Agents for Risley and Company, with a salary of $4,250 per annum.
1887-89	Edward C. Shafer	In 1877, became a partner in the Buffalo Hardware Co. In 1883, became a cashier of the big Buffalo School Furniture Company. In 1886, he was General Manager with a substantial interest of the business.
1889-94	Frank Illig	Proprietor of successful hardware and stove business. Appointed Civil Service Commissioner in 1888.
1890-91	William Churchyard	Owned the Buffalo Planning Mill and Bellows Factory. Chairman of the Republican City Committee.
1892-94	James Ryan	Grocer, saloon-keeper, and Water Commissioner.

Chart III—(continued)

Date	Comissioner	Occupation/Business
1894	Edgar Jewett	One of Buffalo's most substantial business-men. President of Jewett Refrigeration Company. Family had extensive railroad, banking, and foundry interests. Elected mayor in 1895.
1895-1902	Charles A. Rupp	Firm of Rumrill and Rupp, Buffalo's largest building contractors.
1895-99	James E. Curtis	Firm of Burch and Curtis, grain brokers.
1899-1901	John H. Cooper	Secretary and Treasurer of Red Jacket Distillery Company.

Judging from the chaotic career patterns of the captains in 1892 there had been a very direct exercise of control by the commissioners. Fully six of the twelve captains in 1892 had substantial "irregularities" in their career patterns. John Kraft, captain in 1880, demoted to patrolman for "political" reasons in 1883, then reappointed captain three years later in 1886. Captain John Martin of the 10th precinct had resigned as sergeant in 1887 and been detailed to the New York Central station as a patrolman for five years. In 1892 he was promoted all the way to captain. Captain Edward Forrestal was made a captain in 1883 without ever having served a day on any police force. He was demoted four years later to patrolman; then four year later in 1891 re-promoted to captain (Hubbell, 1893:318-54).

Thus even with a stable political situation and after several reforms (1880 and 1883) the job of a police captain in Buffalo was very unstable and subject to all kinds of direct political control. Since the "politics of Buffalo was business" according to Mayor Jewett, and this fact is reflected in a simple look at who exercised control; the meaning of this is that the police forces were in a position to be directly responsive to the business interest's needs.

Chart IV—Social Backgrounds Of Police Superintendents in Buffalo, N.Y., 1872-1900

Date	Superintendent	Occupation/Business
1872-79	John Byrne	Before war was a carriage maker. A colonel during the war. In 1866, became captain of the Niagara Frontier Police Force. In 1869, was a detective with the Albra and Byrne Detective Agency.
1879-80	William A. Phillip	Detective, then Assistant Superintendent of Police.
1880-82	William J. Wolf	In 1866, appointed patrolman by Niagara Frontier Police. In 1868, appointed Special Detective and in 1872 promoted to rank of detective. Six months later, became captain of precinct, as job he held for eight years.
1882-83	James M. Shepard	Started as a patrolman, was a captain of the 1st precinct in 1882 and a detective for the 1st precinct in 1883.
1883-84	Thomas Curtin	In 1872 he was appointed a patrolman. In 1877, was a detective. In 1879, organized the private detective agency of Watts and Curtin.
1887-1890	Martin Moran	Detective.
1890-93	Daniel J. Morganstern	Owned lucrative dry goods business.
1893-94	George Chambers	From 1883-85, and from 1890-92, division superintendent for Erie Canal. In 1889 assistant superintendent of police.
1894-99	William S. Bull	In 1878, with the firm of Sanford and Company, a paper manufacturer. From 1889-1893 he was with the Courier Company.

THE POLICE AND LABOR UNREST

It is not sufficient to show that the wealthiest business interests in Buffalo exercised direct control over the police department. The important factor is determining the uses to which this power was put. If the model that the police institution emerged to deal with a rising urban crime rate is not borne out of crime statistics, and the development of the police outstripped population growth, then police power was created for still other purposes.

We have seen that historians have reviewed the police institution as having been created to deal with the danger of riot and civil disorder. In essence this is just half of the story. Riots and civil disorders describe a wide variety of phenomena common on the urban scene of the time. As cities became more complex, larger and more stratified, there came to be an increasing danger of large scale disorder. In Buffalo (1872-1900) this "disorder" was based almost entirely on disputes between business owners and workers over wages and working conditions. Behind these disputes are political questions dealing with fundamental relationships of power and wealth, ownership and control. The problem became the major impetus to the development of the Buffalo police force during the years Buffalo was developing its industry.

The annual reports of the Buffalo Police Department were primarily an opportunity for the force to account for its actions and request additional resources of the city council. In these reports are detailed one side of the official struggle against labor organization in Buffalo. Labor problems are repeatedly cited as a basis for additional police appropriations and for more men. While there were some mass strikes which involved some crowd violence, the primary effort was to stop and diffuse the "labor problem" before any such activities took place. Peaceful and legal labor activities were seen as requiring police intervention because it was assumed they would lead to "trouble."

It seems that in fact "trouble" was relatively rare in labor strikes in Buffalo, unless the strike itself and the accompanying threat to existing power relationships is so defined. The normal procedure was a large police reaction at the first "reports" of possible strike. It was not unusual for the entire force to be ordered on duty at the moment the strike was declared and to remain on duty continuously until the strike ended—even if it was a period of over a month and no violence occurred.

This process can be seen quite clearly from a police report in 1893:

> The quiet and orderly condition of the city has not been disturbed during the past year. The strike of the employees of the Lehigh

Valley Railroad being the most serious. The strike was declared at midnight November 19th. Immediately on being notified of the fact I took prompt measures to preserve law and order and to protect property. On my recommendation to your Honorable Board the entire force was ordered on duty and remained so until the strike was declared off after a period of nearly three weeks. The principal scene of the strike being the Eleventh Police Precinct, a large detail officers from the other precincts were detailed there and placed under the efficient command of Captain Killeen, the regular force in the Seventh and Ninth wards reinforced by officers from other precincts.

To the prompt action and untiring vigilance of the police is due the fact that no serious breach of the peace occurred during the strike, and their efficiency was highly commended by the officers of the company (Annual Report, 1893:13).

A 1900 strike report describes a remarkably similar control process:

On April 29th, in anticipation of a strike among the freight handlers at the New York Central car shops, the Lehigh Valley and other railroads, the entire force was ordered on duty.

April 30th Company F was detailed to No. 2 and instructed to be placed on picket duty on the streets leading to the freight house to protect the men who should report for work.

On May 1st the following details were made: Company B to No. 1, Company K to No. 7, Company C to No. 8, Companies H and M to No. 11. Captain Killeen was ordered to No. 11 with Company M and placed in charge of the detail, he being the senior officer.

On May 6th the companies ordered on duty May 1st were relieved by the following companies: Companies E and L to No. 11, Company G to No. 1, Company A to No. 7 and Company I to No. 1. These details were continued until June 7th, when the strike was declared off, when all details were relieved and ordered back to their respective precincts. The force returned to three-men platoon system except a detail left at Nos. 7 and 11 (Annual Report, 1900:15).

If these strikes had been violent confrontations such a massive police response might have been justified, but the evidence is that this was not the case. The 1893 railroad strike was peaceful throughout. On the first day a newspaper account reported that:

The men uttered nothing but pacific words and one of the leaders said after the meeting that just because they were on strike was no reason they should mediate any destruction of the companies' property. We are all American citizens and we shall maintain order to the end (Buffalo Evening News, November 19, 1893).

Remarkably similar sentiments come from the Lehigh Valley superintendent in Buffalo:

> The men in the Northern division are as good a lot of men as any railroad in the country can boast of. They are naturally peaceable, sober, and orderly, and I do not think that they will use any but legitimate means to gain their ends (Buffalo Evening News, November 20, 1893).

No pickets were mounted at the railroad yards, the strikers assuming that simply withdrawing their skilled labor would be sufficient to stop the trains. Non-union workers (scabs) were hired to replace the regular workers beginning two days after the commencement of the strike. These workers were permitted to leave the yards without opposition (Buffalo Evening News, November 19 - December 6, 1893).

There is no mention in any contemporary source of the police taking any action during the strike after the entire force had been ordered out on the first day. For three weeks they remained on duty although no threat of violence existed. When the strike was finally settled with the strikers taking pay cuts of 50 cents a day (from wages of $2.70 to $3.00 a day) but regaining their jobs and establishing the power of the union, the force was finally taken off 24-hour duty.

Labor problems are clearly seen as the most pressing social problem of the era. The major threat to the "peace and good order" of Buffalo during the 1872-1900 period was labor unrest. Crime frequently got much less mention in police reports than labor problems did. Furthermore, the force was organized to more effectively deal with strikes at the expense of effectively controlling crime. Emphasis was on a platoon system with a strong reserve for occasions "when a number of officers are immediately needed" rather than one emphasizing more men on the streets for patrol duty (Annual Report, 1893:13). Clearly the former is based on a riot control strategy while the latter is based on a crime control strategy. Finally the 1875 report states that "the force is being drilled regularly in U.S. Infantry tactics." Such tactics, of course, are related only to riot control (Annual Report, 1875:6). Detective Patrick Kilroy, also detailed as drillmaster, spent most of his time during the Winter months drilling the entire uniformed force. In strike situations Drillmaster Kilroy was frequently put on special duty in command of the units called up for strike service (Hubbell, 1893:365-66). Captain Killeen, as we have seen, also frequently performed similar duties, thus developing "specialists" in anti-labor activity.

The use of substantial force was readily and proudly resorted to when officials decided upon such a course. An 1884 report describes in glowing terms "An impetuous charge and free use of the locust (club) soon cleared the street and numerous arrests were made..." (Annual Report, 1884:9). In a later incident "an officer drove his horsedrawn patrol car zig zag through the crowd, which quieted and dispersed them temporarily" (Annual Report, 1893:12).

The singularly one-sided nature of the police institution during strikes clearly emerges in a letter to the Police Superintendent from a railroad official:

> The Captain and officer of No. 11 Station on the morning following the strike of the machinists on the 24th at this shop, without any request the officers were sent from No.11 Station early on the morning of the 25th, informing me that they understood that there was a strike at this shop and they were sent to render any assistance they could to protect the companies' property, and would furnish as many officers as it was deemed necessary to protect the companies' property and employees...Also thanks for letting me have just what men I thought was best to cope with this kind of work, and I trust they will be able to handle the situation in the future as they have in the past (Annual Report, 1904).

The Buffalo Police Department in voluntarily offering the railroad "just what men the railroad thought best" is essentially functioning as a private army.

It is clear that there were acts of violence committed by workers in pursuit of class interests. "Scabs" were beaten up and attempts were made to block entrances to factories and docks. Police response to "labor trouble" generally came before any such activity had the chance to occur—usually beginning at the moment the strikers went off the job. Strikers were kept away from plants and frequently not even permitted to picket. Where violence did occur we have no way of knowing whether it was due to the strike, to attempts by the police or company employees to suppress it, or to company paid provocateurs.

The police did more than control strikes. Workers' meetings were also broken up. One of the more famous of these incidents was the Broadway Market Riot in the heart of the Police community. This broke out after a police charge disrupted a labor meeting and workers scattered through the community attacking property. Large numbers of police reinforcements had to be called to quiet the disturbance (MacTeggart, 1940:128-29). Radical working class meetings fared even worse as the police prevented meetings scheduled in hired halls by blocking entrances, and by arresting street-corner speakers (Kager, 1951:78-81).

Efforts to control workers were not limited to patrol, police charges, and efforts to disperse the crowd. Arrests were freely made in an effort to control labor problems. Offenses such as disorderly conduct, vagrancy, tramp, drunkenness can be freely used to control any group of working class people if the police are so inclined.

The years 1884 and 1893-94, years of high strike activity, produce increases in proportion of laborers arrested as opposed to those of other occupations. After the strike activity declines the proportion of laborers arrested drops back to a "normal" level. Since the backbone of Buffalo's industrial labor force was composed of laborers it seems clear that a great increase of arrests of laborers during a strike year results from police control of strike activity.

For example, the proportion of laborers arrested increased from 40 percent of the total arrested in 1892 to 48 percent in 1893 to 74 percent in 1894, then drops to 37 percent in 1895. The year 1894 is most noted in labor history for the Pullman Strike, one of the nation's most widespread strikes involving the railroad unions. Buffalo, a major railroad center, also saw a great deal of strike activity. The arrest rate that year rose by 35 percent, almost entirely in arrests for vagrancy, tramps, and disorderly conduct.

Arrests of Poles, Buffalo's largest ethnic group and composed almost entirely of factory laborers increased from 5 percent of total arrests in 1892 to 7 percent in 1893 to 13 percent in 1894, the year of peak strike activity. In 1895 it dropped back to 7 percent. Put another way, twice as many Poles were arrested during the strike year of 1894 as in 1893, and only half as many were arrested in 1895, a phenomenon which can only be attributed to police control of strike activity.

Control of workers communities is another important part of the discipline of the labor force. The Polish community was a matter of particular importance to the power structure beyond the context of strike activity. As the largest, most distinguishable and most heavily working class ethnic group the control of Polish workers was critical. The existence of this large pool of unskilled workers was essential to the industrial development of Buffalo. Furthermore, the Polish community was more threatening to business interests because it was both the most recently immigrated, and the most radical politically. Socialist organizers were very active on the Polish East Side in the 1880's and 1890's (Kager, 1951; MacTeggart, 1940: Chap. 5).

The business community relied heavily on the police to "socialize" this new immigrant group! Special "Polish" precincts emerged with special functions: "In this precinct are located a large number of people of Polish nationality, a great many of whom not being acquainted with the laws of the State are a constant watch and care of the police" (Hubbell, 1893:342). This 1892 description, typical of many others illustrates the concerns of police in the 8th precinct, the heart of the Polish East Side, and also reflects the thought of the business interests of the period on the "problem" of ignorant immigrants.

This "watch and care" was entrusted to a "special" type of police force. Four of Buffalo's twelve police captains were of German origin. They, together with Buffalo's few German Sergeants, manned four contiguous East Side precincts, leaving the entire remainder of the city to the Irish. Considering the existence of considerable antipathy between the German and Polish people in Buffalo since many Poles emigrated because of Prussian depredations in Poland, and the higher status of the German community in relation to the Irish, this seems too much for coincidence (Obidinski, 1968:33). Captain Kraft of the 9th precinct was reputed to be a "thorough disciplinarian"; Captain Zacher of the 8th precinct described above "succeeded in preserving order among so turbulent an element." Between 1885 and 1895 the arrest rate in Buffalo nearly doubled from 75.5 arrests per 1,000 males to 131 arrests per 1,000 males, perhaps the most clear reflection of the major difficulties in controlling the new urban underclass. Almost all of this increase was for "public order" crimes rather than serious offenses.

During succeeding years the police fought a number of "skirmishes" with the East Side Polish community. The Polish press complained repeatedly of police harassment while the city press generally kept referring to Polish "riots" and "attacks." The Polish arrest rate exceeded their proportions of the population in Buffalo continuously from the earliest time it is possible to measure it. Given the existence of widespread poverty this might be expected but this cannot be separated from the function they performed in the community and the insecurities the prevailing powers felt about the rise of this large ethnic community. Control of this, the largest working class community, was essential to controlling labor activity.

CONCLUSIONS

Buffalo during the years 1872-1900 grew from a small commercial and trading center to a large industrial center. During the period the crime rate declined but the police force grew much more rapidly than the population. Central to the concern for additional police services was a growing problem of labor organization and demands for economic concessions from the owners of the businesses. The owners of these businesses throughout this period maintained direct control of the mayor's office, the offices of the police commissioners, and much of the time, the police superintendent's office itself. Through indirect controls such as appointments and promotions control of the rest of the force was maintained.

This police force was used at the earliest indication of a strike to patrol the area, to keep the workers from assembling, and from maintaining an effective picket line, which necessarily impedes the effectiveness of the strike. Many assemblies were broken up by violent police action, thousands of workers were arrested for strike activity. Through this activity the police force was repeatedly improved in terms of its organization and increased in size essentially becoming the department the city has today. This image of the development of the American Police Institution requires further examination of the role of power elites in the development of the police institution and of the function the police served in building capitalist industrial societies.

REFERENCES

* This chapter was previously published by *Criminal and Social Justice* Vol.4 Pp. 5-14. Copyright © *Crime and Social Justice*. Reprinted by permission of *Social Justice*.

Bacon, Shelton, 1939. *The Early Development of American Municipal Police: A Study of the Evolution of Formal Controls in a Changing Society.* Yale University, Ph.D. Dissertation.

Buffalo Police Department, 1873-1900. Annual Reports.

Dunn, Walter, 1972. *History of Erie County, 1870-1970.* Buffalo: The Buffalo and Erie County Historical Society.

Faler Paul, 1974. "Cultural Aspects of the Industrial Revolution: Lynn, Massachusetts Shoemakers and Industrial Morality 1826-1860". *Labor History* (Summer).

Ferdinand, Theodore N., 1967. "The Criminal Patterns of Boston Since 1849". *American Journal of Sociology* 73 (1) (July).

_____, 1972. "Politics, Police and Arresting Policies in Salem, Massachusetts Since the Civil War". *Social Problems* 19 (4) (Spring).

Hubbell, Mark, 1893, *Our Police and Our City: A Study of the Official History of the Buffalo Police Department.* Buffalo: Bensler and Wesley.

Kager, James, 1951. *History of Socialism in Buffalo, New York.* Canisius College, M.A. Thesis.

Lane, Roger, 1967. *Policing the City: Boston 1822-1885.* Boston: Harvard University Press.

_____, 1968. "Urbanization and Criminal Violence in the Nineteenth Century". *The Journal of Social History* II (2) (December).

Levine, Jerald Elliot, 1971. *Police, Parties and Polity: The Bureaucratization of the New York City Police 1870-1917.* The University of Wisconsin, Ph.D. Dissertation.

Liazos, Alexander, 1974. "Class Oppression: The Function of Juvenile Justice". *Insurgent Sociologist* (Winter).

McLaughlin, Virginia Yans, 1970. *Like the Fingers on the Hand: The Family and Community Life of First Generation Italian-Americans in Buffalo, New York*, SUNY at Buffalo, Ph.D. Dissertation.

MacTeggart, R.E., 1940. *A Labor History of Buffalo, 1846-1917.* Canisius College, M.A. Thesis.

Obidinski, Eugene Edward, 1968. *Ethnic to Status Group: A Study of Polish Assimilation in Buffalo*, SUNY at Buffalo, Ph.D. Dissertation.

Parks, Evelyn L., 1970. "From Constabulary to Police Society: Implications for Social Control". *Catalyst* (Summer).

Powell, Elwin H., 1962. "The Evolution of the American City and the Emergence of Anomie: A Culture Case Study of Buffalo, New York 1810-1910". *British Journal of Sociology* V (13) (June).

_____, 1966. "Crime as a Function of Anomie". *The Journal of Criminal Law, Criminology and Police Science* (57) (2).

Richardson, James, 1970. *The New York Police: Colonial Times to 1901*. New York: Oxford University Press.

CHAPTER 7
That Strange Word "Police"

LEON RADZINOWICZ

Severe laws were held to be essential for the internal safety of the nation. Often, as in the case of the Riot Act, they were also a much needed weapon in the hand of the Justice of the Peace who alone with the soldier barred the way of a riotous mob: for 'to these two it is entirely owing that they [the mob] have not long since rooted all the other orders out of the commonwealth'.[1] The diligent and impartial execution of these laws was the honourable mission of the English police, 'which Word', wrote John Fielding in 1761, had 'been greatly misunderstood and misrepresented'.[2]

When the word 'police' was first introduced into England in the early part of the eighteenth century it was regarded with the utmost suspicion as a portent of the sinister force which held France in its grip. In the early twenties the word was still almost unknown. About 1720 Edward Burt wrote from Scotland to a friend in London:[3]

> But here are no idle young Fellows and Wenches begging about the Streets, as with you in *London*, to the Disgrace of all Order, and, as the *French* call it, *Police*. By the Way, this Police is still a great Office in *Scotland*, but as they phrase it, is grown into *Desuetude* though the Salleries remain. Having mentioned this *French Word* more by Accident than Choice, I am tempted (by way of Chat) to make Mention likewise of a *Frenchman*, who understood a little *English*. Soon after his Arrival in *London*, he had observed a good deal of Dirt and Disorder in the Streets, and asking about the *Police*, but finding none that understood the Term, he cried out, Good Lord! how can one expect Order among these People, who have not such a Word as *Police* in their Language.

In 1732 Dean Swift defined 'what the French call the police' as the government of great cities to prevent the disorders occasioned by great numbers of people and carriages, especially in narrow streets.[4] The French origin of the word was also emphasised by Dr. Johnson:[5] 'Police. *s.* [French] The regulation and government of a city or country, so far as regards the inhabitants'.

The threat to liberty, which so greatly alarmed many Englishmen of the day, lay not so much in any of these definitions as in the origin of the word and in the associations it evoked. It was thought preferable to have no word for it in the English language than to have the thing itself: 'Let us rather bear this insult than buy its remedy at too dear a rate'.[6] This attitude which made itself apparent almost as soon as the word itself became known was remarked with envy by many French visitors. Travelling in England in the late thirties Le Blanc, although surprised to find that the English, who otherwise took such care to preserve their wealth, should have done so little to secure it against robbers, observed that evidently they preferred to be robbed by 'wretches of desperate fortune' than to be persecuted by the executive.[7]

In John Fielding's time the word 'police' began to gain greater currency, largely no doubt owing to his efforts. It would seem that Henry Fielding had never used it;[8] but John included it in the title of a pamphlet which he published in 1758,[9] and again in that of a draft proposal for the organisation of a police force which he submitted to Charles Jenkinson, probably in 1761.[10] He used it in the introduction to his *Extracts from...The Penal Laws*, and frequently in subsequent years in circulars to magistrates. By the middle of the eighteenth century the word had acquired a significance which was described with some sarcasm by the anonymous writer of a letter to the *Public Advertizer*:[11]

> The Word *Police* has made many bold Attempts to get a Footing...but an neither the Word nor the Thing itself are much understood in London, I fancy it will require a considerable Time to bring it into Fashion; perhaps, from an Aversion to the French, from whom this Word is borrowed; and something under the Name of Police being already established in Scotland, English Prejudices will not soon be reconciled to it. Not long ago, at a Bagnio in Covent Garden, on my complaining of some Imposition, I was told by a fair North Briton, that it was the regular established *Police* of the House. This, I own, is the only Time...I have heard it used in any *polite company*; nor do I believe it has yet made any considerable progress (except in the News Papers), beyond the Purlieus of *Covent Garden*.

But though the word itself was growing more familiar, it was used somewhat loosely to denote a variety of activities. Burke, for instance, meant by it something akin to a civilised government or else, on another occasion, a 'policy': 'There must be', he said, 'a peace police and a war police'. Pitt's emergency legislation was to him the preventive measure of a war police.[12] Even in Scotland, where the term had been known much earlier than in England,[13] its usage was somewhat inconsistent. There was thus 'a police in employing of the poor',[14] and a 'public police' which might require a highway to be carried through a private estate, or enforce the laws calculated to provide the community 'with a sufficient quantity of the necessaries of life at reasonable rates, and for preventing of dearth'.[15] Lord Kames included under the heading 'police', regulations for the prevention of fires, the sale of bread and the closing of taverns.[16] And Adam Smith defined it as 'the second general division of jurisprudence, ...which properly signified the policy of civil government, but now it only means the regulation of the inferior parts of government, viz:—cleanliness, security and cheapness or plenty'.[17]

In the seventies and eighties of the century, largely due to Fielding's lead, the term began to acquire more of its modern significance, being taken to mean 'such part of social organisation as is concerned immediately with the maintenance of good order, or the prevention or detection of offences'.[18] It was included in the titles of a considerable number of books and tracts.[19] In Parliament it was used in 1780, during a debate on the Gordon Riots, when the Earl of Shelburne repeatedly referred to the police of Westminster— 'imperfect, inadequate and wretched'—and to the police of France—'wise to the last degree in its institution, but being perverted in its use'.[20] In 1781 when the defective state of the police of Westminster was under discussion Sheridan said: 'Gentlemen would understand what he meant by the term police; it was not an expression of our law, or of our language, but was perfectly understood'.[21] The word was again used in Parliament four years later during a debate on a Bill referred to as 'The London and Westminster Police Bill'.[22]

Eighteen years after John Fielding's death, and three years after Patrick Colquhoun had published his *Treatise on the Police of the Metropolis*,[23] a Committee was appointed to inquire among other things into the state of the 'police'.[24] But even then the word was still suggestive of terror and oppression.[25] In his time, John Fielding had obviously been aware of its sinister ring. The police, he explained, must always be suited to 'the Nature of the Government and Constitution of the Country where it is exercised. The Police of an arbitrary Government differs from that used in a Republic; and a Police proper for *England*, must differ from them both; as it must always be agreeable to the just Notion of the Liberty of the Subject, as well as to the Laws and Constitution of this Country'.[26] And elsewhere he wrote:[27]

The Police of Foreigners is chiefly employed, and at an immense Expence, to enquire into and discover the common and indifferent Transactions of innocent Inhabitants and of harmless Travellers, which regard themselves only, and but faintly relate to the Peace of Society; this Police may be useful in arbitrary Governments, but here it would be contemptible, therefore both useless and impracticable. The manly Police of England, which is the Civil Power, considered either in its private or collective Capacity, cannot affect the Liberty of the meanest of his Majesty's Subjects, until he has been charged on Oath with some criminal Offence, or a violent and reasonable Suspicion of the same, unless by Virtue of some particular Act of Parliament for that Purpose.

This traditional approach was wholly characteristic of both the Fieldings. Although they were so anxious to endow the Metropolis with a new and professional police, they still clung to the idea of the old parochial forces. Indeed they considered it expedient to produce still another treatise for the use of parish constables.[28] At that time such publications were already numerous, 'yet', wrote John Fielding, peace officers 'cannot have too many guides'.[29] There is evidence of this attachment to the ancient forms of civil power in Henry Fielding's *Enquiry into the Late Increase of Robbers*, which contains a nostalgic evocation of the system for the maintenance of public order as it had existed in the later Middle Ages.[30] It was a system based on the division of counties and shires into hundreds, tithings or decenaries, where peace was preserved by close bonds of individual and collective responsibility; where the sheriff could call the whole county to arms in an instant; and where the civil power was centred in the hands of the Justices of the Peace.

But it was also Henry Fielding's great merit to have been the first seriously to question the continued efficacy of these arrangements when applied to the more complex society of his day, particularly in towns where personal ties and ancient allegiances had become tenuous or ceased to exist.[31] 'Is that civil power, which was adapted to the government of this order of people, in that state in which they were at the conquest', he asked, 'capable of ruling them in their present situation? Hath this civil power kept equal pace with them in the increase of its force, or hath it not rather, by the remissness of the magistrate lost much of its sprawling suburbs, tangled lanes, alleys and withdrawn courts, where 'a thief may harbour with as great security as wild beasts do in the deserts of Africa or Arabia', was in itself a challenge to the old order. The underworld of London had become highly organised. Theft and robbery had been reduced to 'a regular system' and, armed with every method of evading the law, the criminal could easily defy those rare officers of the peace whom he might encounter. There were enough 'rotten members of the law' to forge his defence, enough false witnesses ready to support him. It was, said Fielding, 'a melancholy truth that, at this very day, a rogue no sooner gives the alarm, within certain purlieus, than twenty or thirty armed villains are found ready to come to his assistance.'[32]

Nevertheless in the remedies advocated by himself and his brother the primary aim was not to supersede the existing institutions, but to strengthen and improve them. Nowhere did they suggest that the parish police should be abolished or that the power to enlist and direct constables should be withdrawn from the Justices of the Peace and vested in government officials. The reformed police of the Metropolis which they envisaged was still to be under the authority of the magistrates, whose dual judicial and administrative function should remain unimpaired. They admitted that the existing night watch in Westminster and the adjoining counties was totally inadequate; constables and watchmen neglected their duty; many were too old or drunken or corrupt. The need for reform was urgent. But given vigilance and good-will these defects could be remedied. The united efforts of high and petty constables, supported by the magistracy, would be sufficient to reveal the civil power 'in its true and proper Light' and would 'ever be capable of suppressing Evils of the most Dangerous Nature'.[33]

ENDNOTES

* This chapter was originally published in *A History of English Criminal Law and Its Administration from 1750, Vol. 3.* Pp. 1-8. Copyright © 1956 Sweet and Maxwell, London. Reprinted by permission of Sweet and Maxwell, London.

1. Henry Fielding, Covent Garden Journal, No. 49, June 20, 1752, 'I hate the mob'; Works (ed. by Leslie Stephen, 1882), Vol. 6, p. 133. The first article appeared in No. 47, June 13, 1752.

2. Sir John Fielding, *Extracts from...the Penal Laws,* etc. (new ed., 1768), p. 3.

3. *Letters from a Gentleman in the North of Scotland to his Friend in London,* etc. (ed. of 1754), Vol. 1, pp. 166-167.

4. 'An Examination of Certain Abuses, Corruptions,...in the City of Dublin' *The Prose Works* (ed. by Temple Scott, 1905), Vol. 7, p. 267.

5. *Dictionary* (8th ed., 1799), Vol. 2 (no pagination). The first edition was published in 1755.

6. See *An Apology for the Life of Mr. Colley Cibber* (ed. 1756), Vol. 1, p. 232 (often ascribed to H. Fielding); and Essay 189, by Adam Fitz-Adam (Lord Chesterfield) in *The World* (1756), Vol. 6, p. 136.

7. J. B. Le Blanc, *Letters on the English and French Nations* (written in 1737, transl. in 1747), Vol. 2, p. 191.

8. Though in the Introduction to 'The Journal of a Voyage to Lisbon', *Works* (ed. by Leslie Stephen, 1882), Vol. 7, p. 14, he refers to the plan which he drew up at the request of the Duke of Newcastle 'to demolish the then reigning gangs, and to put *the civil policy* into such order that no such gangs should ever be able for the future to form themselves into bodies...formidable to the public' (my italics).

9. *An Account of the Origin and Effects of a Police set on foot by his Grace the Duke of Newcastle in the year 1753 upon a Plan presented to his Grace by the late Henry Fielding* (1758).

10. 'Abstract of Sir John Fielding's Plan of Police', *Liverpool Papers*, Vol. 145, Add. MSS. 38, 334, f. 75.

11. 'A Letter to the Printer', signed Tom Tipsey, the *Public Advertizer*, October 21, 1763. The letter is also reproduced in the *British Magazine* (October, 1763, p. 542.

12. Referring to Turkey he wrote: '...this is done in favour of a barbarous nation,

with a barbarous neglect of police, fatal to the human race...'; 'A Letter to a Member of the National Assembly, etc.' (1791), *Works* (Bohn's ed., 1855), Vol. 2, p. 530. And *Parl. Hist.* (1792-1794), Vol. 30, 'Traitorous Correspondence Bill, March 15-April 9, 1793', cols. 581-647 at col. 642.

13. Chamberlayne, *Magnœ Britanniœ Notitia: Or The Present State of Great Britain* (ed. of 1737), Part 2, Book III, p. 60: [Scotland]. 'A list of the Lords and others, Commissioners of Police'. The commissioners being seven noblemen and three gentlemen, were first appointed by Queen Anne on December 13, 1714, for the purposes of the general administration of the country: the occasion is regarded as the first on which the word 'police' had been used in any official communication in Great Britain.

14. P. Lindsay, *The Interest of Scotland Considered with Regard to its Police in employing of the Poor, its Agriculture, its Trade,* etc. (1733).

15. John Erskine, *An Institute of the Law of Scotland* (1828), Vol. 2, Book 4, Tit. 4, p. 1037; first publ. in 1773.

16. Lord Kames (Henry Home), *Statute Law of Scotland, abridged with Historical Notes* (1st ed., 1757), pp. 269-277.

17. *Lectures on Justice, Police, Revenue and Arms delivered in the University of Glasgow* (first publ. in 1776; edited by Edwin Cannan, 1896), p. 154. For Adam Smith's views on this subject, see below. p. 422 *et seq.* In *A Tour in Scotland and Voyage to the Hebrides in 1772*, Thomas Pennant writes: 'The police of *Glasgow* consists of three bodies; the magistrates with the town council, the merchants house, and the trades house'; (ed. of 1790), p. 146.

18. F. W. Maitland's definition; see his *Justice and Police* (1885), note 1 at p. 105.

19. Sir William Mildmay, *The Police of France; Or, An Account of the Laws and Regulations established in that Kingdom* (1763); *Westminster Police Bill. Reasons why the Bill entitled 'A Bill for the more effectual Administration of the Office of a Justice of Peace...'*, should not pass into a Law, by a Friend to Justice and English Constitution (1774). The tract refers to the officers of police, 'or by whatever other new-fangled name they may be called' (p.2); on this Bill see below p. 129. See further Jonas Hanway, *The Defects of Police: the Cause of Immorality, and the continual Robberies committed, particularly in and about the Metropolis* (1775), his *The Citizen's Monitor; Shewing the Necessity of a salutary Police* (1780); and his *A New Year's Gift...pleading for...a more vigorous and consistent Police* (1784); Sir William Blizard, *Desultory Reflections on Police* (1785); Josiah Dornford, *Seven Letters...on the Police* (1785); H. Zouch, *Hints on the Public Police* (1786); and W.M. Godschall, *A General Plan of Parochial...Police,* etc. (1787).

20. *Parl. Hist.* (1780-1781), Vol. 21 'Proceedings in the Lords relating to The Riots, June 2-3, 1780', cols. 664-686, at col. 680. On this debate, see also below, p. 91 *et seq.*

21. *Ibid.,* 'Debate on Mr. Sheridan's Motion respecting the defective State of the

Police of Westminster, March 5, 1781', cols. 1305-1325 at col. 1305. In fact even then its meaning was not uniformly understood. One writer, for instance, included the following offences under the heading: Felonies 'against the police': (3) Bankruptcy, breaking prison, returning from transportation, rescuing bodies after execution, destroying granaries, smuggling, breaking quarantine laws, treason—including coining and uttering false money, concealing the death of a bastard, witchcraft; John Webb, *Thoughts on the Construction and Policy of Prisons...To Which is added An Abstract of Felonies Created by Statute, And other Articles Relative to the Penal System* (1786), pp. 73-81.

22.   *Parl. Hist.* (1785-1786); Vol. 25, 'The London and Westminster Police Bill, June 23-June 29, 1785', cols. 888-913. On this important Bill, see below, p. 108 *et seq.*; its full title is 'A Bill for the Fuller Prevention of Crimes, and for the more speedy Detection and Punishment of Offenders against the Peace, in the Cities of *London* and *Westminster*, the Borough of *Southwark*, and certain Parts adjacent to them'.

23.   See below, pp. 220-222 *et seq.*

24.   'Twenty-Eighth Report from the Select Committee on Finance, etc., Police, Including Convict Establishments', 348 (1798), repr. in *Parl. Papers* (1810), Vol. 4, p. 375.

25.   See below, p. 311 *et seq.*

26.   *Extracts from...the Penal Laws*, etc (new ed., 1768), p. 3.

27.   Circular, 'To the Acting Magistrates', Oct. 19, 1772, in S.P. 37/9; reproduced in Appendix 1(2), below, p. 483.

28.   'A Treatise on the Office of Constable' appended to John Fielding's *Extracts from...the Penal Laws*; written by Henry, it was published by John in 1761.

29.   *Extracts from...the Penal Laws*, etc. (new ed., 1768), Appendix, Treatise on Office of Constable, p. 322. The best known among the treatises on the offices of Justice of the Peace and of constable which were first published in the eighteenth century are: Sir Thomas De Veil, *Observations on the Practice of a Justice of the Peace*, etc. (1747); Saunders Welch, *Observations on the Office of Constable with Cautions for the more safe Execution of that Duty*, etc. (1754) (a new ed., publ. in 1758, was entitled *An Essay on the Office of Constable*, etc.); Richard Burn, *Justice of the Peace and Parish Officer* (1755, and subs. editions); John Paul, *The Parish Officer's Complete Guide; containing the duty of the Churchwarden, Overseer, Constable*, etc. (1776, and subs. editions), and his *Complete Constable* (1785); J. Hewitt, *A Guide for Constables and all Peace Officers*, etc., By an Acting Justice (1799); [Spencer Perceval], *The Duties and Powers of Public Officers and Private Persons with respect to Violations of the Public Peace* (1785); *The Duty of Constables, containing Instructions*, etc. (1790); J. Ritson, *Office of Constable, being an entirely new compendium of the Law concerning that ancient Minister for the conservation of the Peace* (1791, and subs. editions); Thom. Walter Williams, *The Whole Law relative to the Duty and Office of a Justice of the*

Peace, comprising also the Authority of Parish Officers (1793); [B. Bird], The Laws respecting Parish matters, Containing the Several Offices and Duties of Churchwardens, Overseers...Constables, Watchmen, etc. (1795).

30. 'An Enquiry into the Causes of the late Increases of Robbers' etc. (1751); Fielding, Works (ed. by Leslie Stephen, 1882), Vol. 7, pp. 225-233.

31. Ibid., p. 158.

32. Ibid., p. 241

33. See Sir John Fielding, Extracts from...the Penal Laws, etc. (new ed., 1768), Appendix, 'Treatise on Office of Constable', p. 323; and his evidence before the Committee of the House of Commons of 1770, Parl. Hist. (1765-1771)', Vol. 16, Report on Sir John Fielding's Plan for preventing Burglaries and Robberies, April 10, 1770, cols. 929-943, particularly cols. 932-933. On this Committee see below, p. 64 et seq.

PART
C

ROLES,
DOMAINS
AND POWERS

CHAPTER 8
The Police as Reproducers of Order

RICHARD V. ERICSON

POLICING: EXPANSIVE AND EXPENSIVE

Police forces funded by government are a fact of life. The acceleration of their growth and the dispersal of their activities are now so widespread we tend to forget that the modern policing system has been in existence only 150 years. Before that, policing and crime control were mainly in the hands of the 'private' sector (cf Beattie, 1981).

The new police system was not introduced and accepted overnight. At least in Britain, the new police had to work constantly at establishing their legitimacy. There was a general cultural resistance to plainclothes detectives of any type (Moylan, 1929; Miller, 1979; Ericson, 1981: chapter 1), and uniformed officers only gained acceptance via 'tacit contracts' with local populations whereby they used their discretion in law enforcement in exchange for the co-operation of citizens in matters that served the interests of the police and the state (Cohen, 1979; Ignatieff, 1979). As front-line agents in the 'reproduction of social order,' the police eventually gained acceptance and established systematic patterns of operation on this micro-level of everyday transactions with the citizenry. Indeed, they set out to do this from the beginning, after repeated governmental failures in using military force to handle disorder (Silver, 1967).

The legitimacy of modern policing, and its success at keeping intact the glass menagerie of social order, continue to rely first and foremost on this micro-level. However, as policing has evolved it has also entered into other arenas of 'legitimation work.' In keeping with the general trend in modern organizations, police forces have been made professional and bureaucratic. Criteria of efficiency and effectiveness have evolved, particularly in 'crime' work, and these criteria are used in 'selling' the organization to the community.

As we will consider in more detail, the police have been assigned, and have taken on, an impossible responsibility for controlling crime as the key indicator of their success at reproducing order (Manning, 1971, 1977). Regardless of their success in other respects, they have been successful in using their crime work to increase their resources and the dispersal of their activities. Their 'product' of crime control is conveniently elastic, carries a virtuous ring, and cannot be easily assailed: who can deny a people's desire for peace and security, or at least for *a feeling* of security?

There can be no doubt that recent decades have witnessed a major transformation in police organizations in terms of size and resources. In the past three decades in Ontario, for example, the trend has been toward fewer, but larger, more bureaucractic, and more centrally controlled, police forces. In the Toronto area each municipality previously had a separate police force, but these were amalgamated to form the Metropolitan Toronto Police Force in 1957. In the 1970s, several regional municipalities were formed in Ontario, and with them came the amalgamation of many small municipal forces into large, bureaucratic regional forces. Furthermore, many small rural municipalities disbanded their own police forces in favour of using the large, centralized Ontario Provincial Police force. In Ontario in 1962 there were 278 municipal police forces. By 1975 there were only 128.

This trend has been duplicated in other Canadian provinces, and in Britain. Always the argument is that bigger is better (and maybe cheaper). Moreover, whenever a small municipality clings to at least the feeling of autonomy that comes with maintaining its own police force, it is subject to continuing and various pressures to conform with the trend to larger units (Murphy, 1981). If police officers in these small forces are caught by allegations of wrongdoing, the central authorities argue that such things are almost inevitable in forces of this type and that the obvious cure is to take them over as part of a larger regional or provincial policing unit (e.g. 'Tillsonburg Police Probe Ordered,' *Toronto Star,* September 30, 1980). The authorities apparently do not stop to think about the fact that large regional, metropolitan, and national police forces have also experienced continuing, sometimes systematic, wrongdoings by their officers.[1]

At the same time that police forces have expanded through amalgamation, they have also multiplied their manpower and technological resources. Spending on the police in Canada increased at a level far outstripping the rate of inflation (Solicitor General of Canada, 1979). This increase is greater than that in other segments of the system of crime control, and the recent rate of growth is also greater than in other areas of government 'welfare' spending (Chan and Ericson, 1981). Between 1962 and 1977 the number of police personnel per 1,000 population increased 65 per cent from 1.7 to 2.8

(Statistics Canada, *Police Administration Statistics,* 1962 to 1977). While this enormous expansion has been accompanied by greater degrees of specialization in police services, most of this growth has been in patrol policing.[2]

Given this expansion of the police, one would expect to find some basic research on obvious questions: How do the police spend their time? What do they concentrate on and what do they ignore? How do they accomplish their results in dealings with the public? Whose interests are served by these outcomes? What does all of this tell us about the role of the police? What wider functions of the police can be theorized from this?

There is an evolving research tradition that focuses upon these general questions. However, this research is largely American, with a few British studies and virtually no Canadian studies. This book, and the research upon which it is based, are aimed at addressing these questions in the Canadian context. The main vehicle for doing this is the use of data collected on the basis of systematic observation in a large Canadian municipal police force. These data are compared with the existing research literature on the police, and related to wider theoretical issues of concern to 'socio-legal' scholars. Before outlining the research design and presenting the results, I shall raise the theoretical issues and define the concepts which inform them.

THE POLICE, CRIME, AND REPRODUCING ORDER

Conventional wisdom—fuelled by the police themselves along with the media, some academics, and other instruments of social reproduction— equates police work with crime work. In television 'cop shows,' in news reports on individual criminal cases, in police annual reports listing levels of crime and clearance rates, and in the research literature dealing with the effectiveness of police as crime fighters, the image is constantly reinforced that crime is, after all, almost everything the police are about.[3] Of course there is talk about the police as a social-service agency—usually including the well-worn assertion that the police are the only 24 hour-a-day, 7-days-a-week social-service agency—but in the minds of police officers, in keeping with the thinking of the public, real police work is crime work.

This view has remarkable currency, given that the police, especially the patrol police, actually spend only a tiny fraction of their time dealing with crime or something that could potentially be made into crime. For example, research by the British Home Office included a survey of 12 urban policing areas and found that on average only 6 per cent of a patrol policeman's time was spent on incidents finally defined as 'criminal' (cited by McCabe and Sutcliffe, 1978). Similarly, Reiss (1971:96) employs data from the Chicago police department to document 'the low productivity of preventive patrol for criminal matters alone, since only about two-tenths of 1 per cent of the time spent on preventive patrol is occupied in handling criminal matters. What is more, only 3 percent of all time spent on patrol involves handling what is officially regarded as a criminal matter.' Various ethnographic studies also document the fact that most patrol-officer contacts with the public do not involve criminal matters (e.g. Cumming et al., 1970; Punch and Naylor, 1973; Cain, 1973; Payne, 1973; Comrie and Kings, 1975; Punch, 1979). Reiss (1971: 73) reports from his Chicago study that 58 per cent of complaints were regarded by the complainants as criminal matters, but only 17 per cent of patrol dispatches to complainants resulted in official processing as criminal incidents.

It is clear that the patrol police do not often have the occasion to designate something as a criminal matter. Indeed, the vast majority of their time is spent alone in their patrol cars without any direct contact with citizens. For example, Pepinsky (1975:4) reports that more than 85 per cent of police patrol time is spent not dealing with citizens.

If, in light of this evidence, one is still committed to a view of the patrol police as crime fighters, one could argue that by their visible presence on the street the patrol police are preventing crime. However, this argument is difficult to sustain. In the Kansas City study by Kelling and associates (1974), it was found that increasing preventive patrol by a factor of two or more over a one-year period had no significant impact upon the incidence of crime (for reviews of this type of research, see Clarke and Heal, 1979; Kelling et al, 1974). Even the most optimistic researchers (Wilson and Boland, 1979) produce results which question the advantage of flooding the streets with large numbers of patrol officers, and of aggressive, proactive—i.e., police-initiated— patrol. In their survey of 35 American cities, Wilson and Boland present data to argue that police resources (patrol units on the street), and on-the-street-activity,[4] independently affect the robbery rate after controlling various socio-economic factors. However, the same analysis demonstrates no similar effect for rates of burglary and auto theft.

Furthermore, there is no apparent value in having more patrol cars available for quick response (Pate et al., 1976), except perhaps in a tiny minority of incidents with elements of violence, and as a means of reassuring the citizen with a *feeling* of security. In a recent critique of their own research, Kelling et al. (1979) conclude that the introduction and subsequent technological 'refinements' of mobile patrol operations have had no appreciable effect on the incidence of crime (for similar critiques of the role of police technology, see Skolnick, 1966; Rubinstein, 1973; Manning, 1977).

Another factor to consider in deciding whether flooding the streets with patrol officers can stem the tide of crime waves is police recording practices. Given the propensity of bureaucratic police forces to measure the productivity of officers, increasing manpower may increase recording, especially of minor matters (McDonald, 1969, 1976; Chan and Ericson, 1981).

Of course, the primary function of the uniformed police has always been to patrol the petty. Thus in the 1830s, following the establishment of the new police in London, 85 per cent of arrests were for non-indictable offences such as public drunkenness and disturbing the peace (Ignatieff, 1978). Apparently, the more police one has the more petty matters will be pursued, especially if organizational procedures are in place to measure and reward that pursuit.

Evidence from these various sources leads one to conclude that patrol police work is not primarily or essentially about crime prevention or law enforcement. It leads one to question what is the place of the criminal law in the work of patrol officers, and to ask what else is going on as they go about their work. Several researchers on the police, along with other 'socio-legal' scholars and social theorists, have provided some answers to these questions. We shall summarize their views—an apparently shared understanding that the patrol police are essentially a vehicle in the 'reproduction of order.'

'Order' is a multi-faceted word that has at least seven meanings pertinent to our concerns *(Oxford Paperback Dictionary,* 1979:445): 'a condition in which every part or unit is in its right place or in a normal or efficient state, *in good working order: out of order;* the condition brought about by good and firm government and obedience to the laws, law and order; a system of rules or procedure; a command, an instruction given with authority; a written direction...giving authority to do something; a rank or class in society, the lower orders; a kind or sort or quality, *showed courage of the highest order.'*

The mandate of police patrol officers is to employ a system of rules and authoritative commands to transform troublesome, fragile situations back into a normal or efficient state whereby the ranks in society are preserved. This is to be done according to means which appear to be of the highest quality and is directed at the appearance of good and firm government.

Of course, it is not the mandate of the police to produce a new order. On the contrary, their everyday actions are directed at reproducing the existing order (the 'normal or efficient state') and the order (system of rules) by which this is accomplished. They are one tool of 'policing' in the wider sense of all governmental efforts aimed at disciplining, refining, and improving the population. As such, most of what they do is part of the social machinery of verifying and reproducing what is routinely assumed to be the case (cf Berger and Luckmann, 1966: chapter 2). Their sense of order and the order they seek to reproduce are that of the status quo.[5]

The order arising out of their action is a reproduction because it is made with reference to the existing order and designed to keep it in its original form. However, the 'seed of change' is contained in every 'interactional sequence' (Giddens, 1976) and the outcome may not quite duplicate what was there before the interaction. Moreover, the term 'reproduction' implies that order is not simply transmitted in an unproblematic manner but is worked at through processes of conflict, negotiation, and subjection.

The police are the most visible front-line agents for ordering the population. They represent the extreme end of the 'carceral continuum' (Foucault, 1977), serving as a model of judicial-legal ideology. To the extent that they are successful in portraying their work as professional according to the principles of formal legal rationality (cf Balbus, 1973) and bureaucratic rationality, the police accomplish legitimacy as agents of the state. They can convince the citizenry that they are being policed as legal subjects instead of 'class' subjects (cf Cohen, 1979: 129-30).

The police have always had an ideological function as well as a repressive function. They have been repeatedly employed as an 'advance guard' of municipal reform, especially for altered uses of social space and time (public order) and protection of property, to ensure free circulation of commodities (including labour power) (ibid:120). Yet part of their success has been to present their problems as technical, related to the control of crime, rather than as ideological: they have difficulty controlling crime because the laws are inadequate; they do not have the communications system necessary to reduce response time; they do not have sufficient manpower to have a deterrent effect, and so on.

The police actively campaign to have the community believe that things will be more orderly if the police are supplied with better cars, better crime laboratories, better-trained police officers, more enabling laws, and so on. The effort is reflected in extensive public relations, including follow-up interviews with victims of crime to make it appear that something is being done (Greenwood et al., 1975; Sanders, 1977; Ericson, 1981), displays at shopping plazas, lectures to students and to other selected groups in the community, and using press officers who generate contacts with the media and 'feed' them (cf Fishman, 1978, 1980). In these efforts the police are concerned not with the dangerous 'symbolic assailant' as conceived by Skolnick (1966), but rather with the symbolic support of 'respectable' citizens who encourage police efforts directed at anyone but themselves.

In addition to reproducing legal and bureaucratic ideology, the police also impose social discipline in the name of public propriety (Cohen, 1979). They are responsible for establishing a fixed presence in the community for systematic surveillance. They patrol with a suspicious eye for the wrong people in the wrong places at the wrong times, reproducing a 'social penality of time and place' (Foucault, 1977). Far from being unsystematic and arbitrary, this work is based on established rules and produces regular results. The patrol officer is more likely to watch closely and stop on suspicion a young man in his 'shag-wagon'[6] than a granny in her stationwagon, because the former is more likely to have contraband and is deemed more in need of being kept in his proper place.

The police have a sense of the order they are there to reproduce. This is reflected in the activities they are taught to pursue, in the techniques they are taught to use in pursuit, and in their own identification with the values of middle-class respectability. In keeping with the entire reproductive apparatus of the state, they are there to ensure that everyone possible appears to be the middle Canadian in theory and the working Canadian in practice. Their sense of order is reflexive: they think that they are doing what the powerful and respectable want at the same time as they see this as something they themselves support, but in a way that sustains their own sense of autonomy and purpose.

As Bittner (e.g. 1967, 1967a, 1970) and Manning (e.g. 1977, 1979, 1980) have argued, this sense of order frames the resources needed to maintain it. That is, in dealing with any particular situation the patrol officer decides what, if anything, is out of order and then employs the various tools at his disposal to reconstruct order. If he is seeking compliance from a citizen, he can rely upon the aura of the general authority of his office; his procedural legal powers to detain, search, and use physical force; his substantive legal powers to charge; and various manipulative strategies that form part of the 'recipe' knowledge of his craft. In short, he 'negotiates order,' variously employing strategies of coercion, manipulation, and negotiation (Strauss, 1978).[7] This work is always carried out with respect to rules, including legal rules, administrative rules, and 'recipe' rules of the occupational culture of line officers. In other words, it is the work of producing and controlling deviance, of using social rules in the construction of social order (cf Douglas, 1971).

This view of how order is constituted is neither 'high sociology' (Rock,

1979) nor empiricist sociology of the 'phenomenological' variety. Rather, it is a 'search...for a joining of social structural and social interactional considerations but with [an] antideterministic stance still intact' (Strauss, 1978: 16; see also Ranson et al., 1980). Attention is focused upon the strategies of coercion, manipulation, and negotiation, and the patterns these indicate, which allow particular parties to secure their interests and sustain advantages over others. These strategies are conceived as deriving from social structure, and their use in interaction serves to reproduce dialectically social structure. The task of the sociologist using this model is primarily empirical: to examine at close hand the strategic interaction as it is used by one's subjects in the reproduction of social order.[8]

Within this 'transactional' view, the police are conceived as 'enacting' their environment as well as reacting to it (Weick, 1969:63-4; Manning, 1979:29). While they are responsive to the community and operate within particular elements of social organization (Black, 1968), they also carve out part of their mandate based on properties of their own organization. On the macro-level, this interplay is indicated by such things as public-relations campaigns, setting up special units (e.g. community-relations officer units; ethnic relations units), and 'selling' the organization in terms of the community's 'crime problem.' On the micro-level the mutual influences of the community organization and police organization are seen in the level and nature of reactive (citizen-initiated) mobilization and proactive (police-initiated) mobilization and in the specific approach taken by police officers and citizens in various types of troubles they come together to deal with.

In studying the reciprocal influences between community forces and police forces, there is no point in trying to weigh up the forces on each side and making a final decision as to who controls. Apart from the inevitable looseness of any such measurement, by the time such an exercise was completed new forces would come into play requiring remeasurement or, more probably, a new system of measurement. However, one thing is clear. In the past few decades the police, along with other forms of governmental policing, have become a force to be reckoned with. As Banton (1964:6) has observed, the police have changed their role from being 'professional citizens' who carry out 'obligations which fall upon all citizens,' to 'an official exercising authority and power over citizens.' Much of this authority and power comes from within the bureaucratic organization of policing rather than from the law or other community sources.

Something not so clear is the complex ways the police, and political powers in the community, maintain their legitimacy while going about their everyday work. People do not like to be interfered with, lectured, badgered, and harassed, yet the patrol officer must do these things every day. Perhaps they are able to do this routinely because of the macro-level 'selling job' done by the administration, associations of chiefs of police, police associations, politicians, and the media. 'The more resources allocated to increasing the efficiency of repressive policing, the more manpower has to be poured into "community" relations' to restabilize the public image of the force' (Cohen, 1979: 1 33).

As stated earlier, a major part of this 'image work' is carried out in terms of the police mandate to control crime. A lot of work is done via the media, and official statistics of crime rates and clearance rates, to support the view that the police are struggling to keep the lid on the massive amounts of deviance in the community. The police are held responsible for crime control, even though the causes of crime (social, economic, cultural, and political) are clearly beyond their control (cf Manning, 1971, 1977, 1980).

This situation is ripe for contradiction. The police have to show that they can keep the lid on crime and generally keep the streets clean, yet not so successfully as to suggest that they do not need more resources to fight crime and other filthy activity. Thus there has to be a lot of the disorder they are selling themselves as being able to reduce in order to justify more resources. More generally, the police are agents of the status quo, of consensus, yet each incident they deal with belies the consensus they symbolize. Some researchers (e.g. Wilson, 1968) have observed that in more heterogeneous communities where conflict is great there is likely to be a trend toward policing that is oriented to law enforcement. The irony is that the less the consensus the more the police are used as symbols to produce the appearance that there is consensus.

The very existence of crime control in a community indicates that other means of control have failed and is testimony to the degree of conflict in the community. Moreover, high levels of crime control mean that the symbolic aspects of the wider institutions of law itself are failing. The more repressive the reaction becomes, the more visible are the main contours of conflict and contradiction. In these circumstances the police are most able to increase their own power, even to the point of having some effect on the legislative process itself (Chambliss and Seidman, 1971: especially 68; see also Hall et al., 1978; Cohen, 1979; Taylor, 1980).

This process has the characteristics of 'deviance amplification' as discussed by 'labelling' theorists (Wilkins, 1964; Schur, 1971; Ericson, 1975; Ditton, 1979). The typical reaction to *indicators* of conflict such as crime is to expand the apparatus of control. This occurs not only in more visible forms such as increased resources for the police, but also in expansion of the welfare state (Chan and Ericson, 1981). One effect is an amplifying spiral of official reactions, including an increased rate of officially designated crime (McDonald, 1976: especially chapter 6).

All of this leads one to suspect that the police and other agencies in the reproductive apparatus are not out to eradicate the phenomena they deal with, but to classify, record, contain, and use them in perpetuity (Foucault, 1977). One must suspect that their mandate to constitute and deal with crime distorts more fundamental processes and that the popular conception of the police as crime fighters must itself be treated as creating a problem for both the police and the community. Crime control is an impossible task for the police alone. They are expected to handle a phenomenon caused by social, political, economic, and cultural forces beyond their control and have to give the *appearance* that things are (more or less) under control. Thus there is bound to be a gulf between the structured rhetoric about the police and crime and the everyday reality of policing. One part of the order the police reproduce is the mystical one of crime control, of 'lawandorder,' but their everyday work is of a different order.[9]

The empirical focus of the research reported in this book is the everyday work of the patrol police and the structures reproduced by their work. These structures have systems of rules which control, guide, and justify their actions. We now turn to a discussion of those rules as they relate to the more general question of police powers (discretion) and how these powers are used in the reproduction of order.

POLICE DISCRETION AND USES OF RULES

Discretion is the power to decide which rules apply to a given situation and whether or not to apply them. Legal scholars traditionally view discretion in terms of what *official* rules can be held to govern the actions of policemen. These rules include laws and administrative instructions. For example, Pound (1960) sees discretion as an authority conferred by law to make considered judgments under specified conditions; it belongs 'to the twilight zone between law and morals' where the official has the autonomy to make judgments within a framework provided by the law.

Some lawyers and sociologists have defined discretion in terms of whether decisions are, or can be, reviewed according to official rules. Thus Goldstein

(1960) is concerned with decisions of 'low visibility' in which the police of ficer takes no official action—he does not write an official report and does not invoke the criminal process via arrest and charge. Goldstein sees these actions as discretionary because there is no routine opportunity for administrative or judicial review. This is similar to Reiss's (1974:67) definition of discretionary justice existing 'whenever decisions made in criminal cases are not legally or practically open to re-examination.'

'Low visibility' is just one resource available to police officers to maintain control over their decisions. Moreover, while a specific decision may not be reviewed, or may not even be practically reviewable, legal and administrative rules are nevertheless taken into account in making the decision. These rules remain 'invisible,' but they do have an effect.[10]

The question of effects brings us to the essential aspects of the concept of discretion. Davis (1969:4) refers to discretion as existing 'whenever the *effective* limits on [the official's] power leave him free to make a choice among possible courses of action or inaction' (emphasis added). The limits are not only the formal expectations of the criminal law and administrative rules, but also expectations from other sources such as the occupational culture of police officers and specific groups in the community. Black (1968:25) provides a complementary definition of police discretion 'as the autonomy of decision-making that an officer has.'

Obviously the definition of discretion in terms of effective limits and autonomy incorporates a conception of *power*. Power involves the probability that one party in an encounter can effect a course of action and outcome he desires in spite of the contrary wishes and/or actions of the other parties. As such power is a *potential* element in any interaction but it is not necessarily exercised. It is therefore difficult to gauge power empirically, except via an analysis of the power resources of the parties being studied, and through observing instances and rates of compliance. As a potential element power mediates between actors' intentions and the realization of outcomes. In use, power involves the mobilization of resources to effect outcomes which serve particular interests.

Another way of formulating the definitions of discretion provided by Davis and by Black is to say that in situations where others do not have the power to circumscribe the person's action, he himself has power because he can choose a course of action and effect an outcome that reflects that choice. Any analysis of decisions made during a sequence of interactions must take into account the relative power advantages of the participants. Who has the advantage is heavily dependent upon access to and control over resources that can be mobilized to influence others to one's own advantage (Turk, 1976). Thus, a focal point for the analysis of power is the resources available to effect it. 'The use of power in interaction can be understood in terms of resources or facilities which participants bring to and mobilize as elements of its production, thus directing its course' (Giddens, 1976:112).

One group's acquisition of autonomy may involve another group's loss of autonomy. In what area does a group have the ability to coerce, manipulate, or negotiate the establishment of its own rules which others conform to? Those who have control over the law-making process, other agencies of crime control, police supervisors, and various groups of citizens are all able to use rules limiting the choices of patrol officers, while these officers can in turn use rules from these sources and their own 'recipe' rules to control their working environment.

The use of rules in organizational contexts has been a key topic of enquiry among sociologists studying police work. Part of this enquiry has focused on the discovery of the framework of rules used by police officers to constitute their 'sense of order.'[11] This is necessarily an empirical task. For the sociologist, as for the actors he studies, 'to know a rule is not to be able to provide an abstract formulation of it, but to know how to apply it to novel circumstances, which includes knowing about the *context* of its application' (Giddens, 1976:124). Rules as stated formally have a fictional character; this can only be understood, and the operating rules gleaned, by examining rules in action (Chambliss and Seidman, 1971). As Manning (1977a:44) emphasizes, 'since the context of rules, not the rules themselves, nor the rules about the rules (so characteristic of formal organizations), determine the consequential (i.e., actionable) meanings of acts, situated interactions, accounts and shared understandings should be examined.'

Rules serve as tools of power and as justifiers of actions taken. In the case of criminal-law rules, the police have an enabling resource to control what and whom are proceeded against and to legitimate actions taken. The law provides 'cover' in two senses. It provides 'blanket' cover through the wide range of substantive offences available to handle any troublesome situation the officer is likely to confront (Bittner, 1967, 1967a, 1970; Chatterton, 1976). Also, the legal procedures for police actions are so enabling that there are very few instances when what the officer wishes to do cannot be legitimated legally (McBarnet, 1979, 1981).

Beyond this, the police officer has control over the production of 'facts' about a case, and this control of knowledge becomes a very potent form of power. The rules are not only taken into account, but they also form part of the account to legitimate the action taken (Kadish and Kadish, 1973; Sanders, 1977; Ericson, 1981, 1981a). In sum, the normative order of rules made applicable and the meanings applied to a situation are closely related (Giddens, 1976:109, 110). The powerful nature of rules is not to be gleaned from 'perceptible determination of behaviour,' but rather in how rules 'constrain people to *account* for their rule-invocations, rule violations, and rule applications' (Carlen, 1976, referring to Durkheim, 1964).

The motive for patrol officers' actions comes from particular interests defined within their occupational culture. This includes an array of 'recipe' rules which guide him on how to get the job done in ways that will appear acceptable to the organization, which persons in what situations should be dealt with in particular ways (e.g. who should be 'targeted' for stops on suspicion, who should be charged for specific offence-types, etc.), how to avoid supervisors and various organizational control checks, when it is necessary to produce 'paper' regarding an incident or complaint, and so on. No matter what interests provide the motive, the law can provide the *opportunity* to achieve an outcome reflecting those interests (McBarnet, 1976, 1979, 1981).

The criminal law becomes a 'residual resource' used when other methods of resolving a situation are unavailable or have been tried and are unsuccessful. Similar to the way citizens use the police (cf Black, 1968; Reiss, 1971), police use the law according to what other forms of social control are available and can be used effectively. For the patrol police, this is particularly the case in interpersonal disputes and problems of public order and decorum. When all else fails or is deemed likely to fail, the officer decides he must remove one party in the conflict from the situation, and consequently he arrests someone. A specific infraction with a clearly applicable law does not determine the arrest, but rather the law is used to make the arrest to handle the situation. As Chatterton (1973, 1976) found, charges are sometimes used 'as the legal vehicle for conveying someone to the police station and ... the grounds for the *decision to use it* [are] to be found elsewhere than in the reasons provided to justify its use to the courts.'[12]

The patrol officer's concern for the law as an 'all purpose control device' (Bittner, 1970:108) bears on how he can make it applicable across a range of situations. From his viewpoint, the broader the applicability the better the law, which may explain why the police resist legal changes which decrease their repertoire (cf Goldstein, 1970:152). When the law is changed, other laws have to be used to serve the same purpose. For example, Ramsay (1972:65) refers to liquor-law changes in Saskatchewan which prevented police officers from continuing to charge for intoxication in public places; RCMP members continued to arrest and charge persons intoxicated in public places, substituting the 'causing a disturbance' provision of the Criminal Code.

The procedural criminal law is also enabling for the patrol police.[13] As McBarnet (1976, 1979, 1981) has argued, Packer's (1968) dichotomy between a due-process model of procedural protections for the accused and a crime control model of expedient law enforcement turns out to be not a dichotomy at all, especially in countries such as England, Scotland, and Canada where the suspect and accused do not have entrenched rights. In the law as written, and the law in action, 'due process if *for* crime control.' That is, the rules of procedure as written and used explicitly serve the expedient ends of law enforcement. Even in the United States, where rights are entrenched, there is frequently no empirical referent in law for ideals such as the rule of law or due process (Black, 1972). Furthermore, empirical studies on the implementation of due-process rules such as *Miranda v Arizona* (1966) 384 *US* 436 US Sup Ct indicate that the rules are routinely side-stepped or incorporated into existing police practices (e.g. Wald et al., 1967; Medalie et al., 1968; Ayres, 1970). As Thurman Arnold (1962), cited by Carlen (1976: 95), states, 'When a great government treats the lowliest of criminals as an equal antagonist...we have a gesture of recognition to the dignity of the individual which has an extraordinary dramatic appeal. Its claim is to our emotions, rather than on our common sense.' As pragmatic actors whose 'recipe' rules for practice are based on common sense, the police can use the procedural law to achieve the outcomes they deem appropriate.

Criminal-law rules, along with administrative rules and rules within the occupational culture, are also useful to patrol officers in formulating accounts that will justify their actions. Thus, rules are used prospectively in taking action, and retrospectively in showing to interested others (especially supervisory officers and the courts) that the action taken was justifiable and appropriate. Prospectively, one rule of the occupational culture is 'Unless you have a good story, don't do it' (Chatterton, 1979:94). Justice becomes a matter of justifications, as patrol officers set out to do what they believe is necessary to put things in order. They seek the 'cover' of legitimate justifications and take their decisions with a view to 'covering their ass' vis-à-vis any possible source of objection. Indeed, this is the only form of 'under-cover' work patrol officers routinely undertake! In addition to other forms of patrol work, they patrol the facts of 'what happened,' transforming a conflict with a colourful kaleidoscope of complexities into a black-and-white 'still' of factual-legal discourse.

Manuals provide instruction on how to write reports to impress favourably other actors in the crime-control network (e.g. Inbau and Reid, 1967:129).

Socio-legal research also informs us about techniques of this nature. Sanders (1977) examines the process of report construction, showing how the same facts can be used to legitimate a range of offence types, or no offence at all. Wald and associates (1967:1554) suggest that the police often take statements from accused persons simply as a basis for convincing the prosecutor that a case exists at all. Skolnick (1966:133) notes how the rules of criminal discovery in the jurisdiction he studied require the prosecutor to allow the defence lawyer to examine arrest reports, producing a situation where 'the police do not report as the significant events leading to arrest what an unbiased observer viewing the situation would report. Instead they compose a description that satisfies legal requirements without interfering with their own organizational requirements.'

In saying the police officer is able to construct the facts of the case, we are not saying that it is a fabrication, although there are many accounts of police fabrication and perjury (see Buckner, 1970:especially 99-100; Morand, 1976; Morris, 1978). Our point is that the rules become embedded in the formulations used to make the case, so that it is difficult to distinguish between the generation of fact, its provision to senior officers and the court, and the use of rules for its accomplishment (see Sanders, 1977:especially 98-99; and generally, Ditton, 1979). Thus, the way in which factual accounts and rules are intertwined makes it difficult to establish what is a fabrication and what is

In summary, rules are a power resource of the patrol officer in accomplishing whatever seems appropriate to the situation. Discretion takes rules into account; it is not necessarily a deviation from or outside legal rules. As we shall see in the next section, these rules have many sources and can serve varied functions. Ours is not a government of law; it is a government of men who use law.[14]

THE ORGANIZATIONAL FORUMS OF POLICE WORK

Patrol officers go about their work sensitive to expectations from the organizations within which they operate, including the community, the law and court organizations, and the police organization. The literature on the police deals with influences from each of these sources, but individual studies tend to emphasize one source to the virtual, and sometimes complete, exclusion of others.

One tradition of enquiry explores the influence of the community. These studies consider the influence on police decisions of citizens dealing with the

police (informant, victim, complainant, suspect, accused) and of the circumstances in which they encounter the police (who mobilizes the police, where
the encounter takes place, the nature of the matter in dispute). These studies
are similar to the multiple-factor approaches used in asking why people commit crimes, but here the question has shifted to why a policeman charges people, records an occurrence, and so on.

Patrol officers typically have little information besides the appearance of
an individual and of a situation. They can perhaps learn more from accounts
and from documents shown them (e.g. driver's licence), and the CPIC
(Canadian Police Information Centre) system. Many encounters involve a
'negotiation of status claims' (Hudson, 1970:190)—officers look for and
employ status 'cues' to determine what action they should take; in this sense,
'police activity is as much directed to who a person is as to what he does'
(Bittner, 1970:10).[15] The more that other types of information are lacking,
the more the officer is likely to forge a stereotypical response based on a 'second code' (MacNaughton-Smith, 1968) of these criteria, which may ultimately
be used to define the situation as a legal problem.

The studies of this type are centred upon two central variables of
American sociological inquiry, race and socio-economic standing, as these are
influenced by and influence other variables, especially demeanour, the nature
of the incident (seriousness, evidence available, dispute type), and whether the
person is 'out of place.' Some researchers have argued that variables of citizen
input make spurious simple relationships between status and role characteristics and police decision-making; to the extent members of racial minorities and
those of low socio-economic standing tend to be 'unstable,' less deferential,
and to request particular forms of police action, police activity towards them is
different from that towards other types of citizens.

Black (1968) demonstrates that in reactively mobilized encounters, the
most important determinants (in addition to seriousness of the alleged offence
and evidence questions) of police action to record an occurrence or arrest are
the preference of the complainant, the social distance between complainant
and suspect, and the degree of deference shown by both complainant and suspect. When the complainant's preference for action is unclear the degree of
deference shown by the suspect becomes a significant influence. In these situations, blacks tend to be more disrespectful towards the police, thereby increasing the probability of arrest (Black, 1971:1101). 'Negroes, it is clear, have a
disproportionate vulnerability to arrest mainly because they are disproportionately disrespectful toward police officers' (Black, 1968:231).

Sykes and Clark (1975) attempt to show that it is because lower-status people have less ability to express deference that they more often end up being officially processed. They confirm Black's findings concerning non-white lower-status citizens, who are more likely to be unilaterally disrespectful to the police than whites and those of higher status. They show also that the police are reciprocally more disrespectful to young, male suspects in order mainte-nance situations and least likely to be disrespectful in service calls involving women, senior citizens, and the middle class.

Several other researchers, using a variety of methods, have considered the influence of the offender's deference and demeanour on police action. Sullivan and Siegel (1974:253), in a decision-game study, found that the 'attitude of the offender' was the most important item selected by police-officer subjects in reaching a final decision about whether or not to arrest. Research on police handling of juvenile offenders has also emphasized this aspect (Werthman and Piliavin, 1967; Chan and Doob, 1977). Similarly, it has been shown that traf-fic-law offenders are more likely to be ticketed if they are 'offensive' than if they are 'respectful' (Gardiner, 1969:151; Pepinsky, 1975:41).

There is no consensus among researchers on all facets of police response to citizens' preference and suspects' deference. In the research by Reiss and Black, in 14 per cent of reactive encounters the complainant requested unoffi-cial handling of a felony or misdemeanour, and the police invariably complied (Reiss, 1971: 83). Moreover, Black (1968: 216-17) concludes that 'the police are more likely to arrest a misdemeanor suspect who is disrespectful toward them than a felony suspect who is civil.' In their research, Clark and Sykes (1974: 483n) found that the police almost invariably record, and arrest where possible, in felonies regardless of complainant preference or suspect defer-ence.

Other explanations claim that the poor and blacks are particularly vulnera-ble when 'out of place,' i.e. in social or geographical contexts in which they do not normally participate (Bayley and Mendelsohn, 1969:93; Werthman and Piliavin, 1967:78; Rubinstein, 1973:part ii). Others have attempted to demonstrate that the important influences are the occupational and domestic stability of the suspect. For example, Skolnick (1966:84-5) argues that blacks are more likely to be arrested by warrant officers because they are less likely 'to possess the middle-class virtues of occupational and residential stability' that would lead the officers to believe that fine payments could be met. Green (1970) presents data to demonstrate that blacks are more likely to possess such lower-class characteristics as residential mobility and working at marginal jobs or being unemployed, and that these characteristics rather than race per se account for higher arrest rates. Werthman and Piliavin (1967:84) point out that citizens with these characteristics are aware of how the police assess them and manipulate their appearances accordingly. For example, some of their subjects who were unmarried wore wedding rings 'in order to bolster their moral status in the eyes of the police.'

The influence of personal characteristics, especially socio-economic status, has also been shown to vary by how the police are mobilized and the nature of the matter in dispute. Black (1968) and Reiss (1971) introduced the distinction between proactive (police-initiated) and reactive (citizen-initiated) mobilizations. Proactive policing is directed at lower-status citizens who present problems of public order, or who are out of place. As John Stuart Mill remarked, one of the benchmarks of civilization is the extent to which the unpleasant or uncivilized aspects of existence are kept away from those who most enjoy the benefits of civilization. Patrol officers have a mandate to reproduce civilization in this form, maintaining the boundaries of deviant ghettos and keeping the streets clean of those who are, at the most, offensive rather than offenders (Scull, 1977; Cohen, 1979).

Proactive policing also occurs in traffic regulation, and here higher status people have frequent contact with the police. Proactive traffic work has been identified as a major area of conflict between the police and the public, e.g. Royal Commission on the Police, 1962:114; Willett, 1964; Black, 1968:14. Higher-status citizens view the police largely as reactive agents responding to their complaints, not as proactive pursuers of minor technical violations (Cressey, 1974:219). Furthermore, they know patrol officers frequently do not charge for traffic offences. Several writers (ibid: 227; LaFave, 1965:131-2; Grosman, 1975:2) have stressed that when the police are known to ignore violations systematically this becomes a public expectation; a hostile reaction can occur when someone is selected out and issued a summons. Enforcement of traffic laws is the one area where technically based full enforcement of observed violations is possible, and yet discretion is very frequently used there. Order is reproduced through *selective* use of the law.

According to Reiss and Black, the vast majority of patrol police mobilizations are reactive (87 per cent in their study). They use this finding in support of their argument that the patrol police are dependent on citizens and operate mainly as servants responsive to public demands.

Citizens mobilize the police ('the law') as a power resource to assist in handling their own troubles and conflicts: 'The empirical reality of law is that it is a set of resources for which people contend and with which they are better able to promote their own ideas and interests against others' (Turk, 1976:

abstract of article). Mobilizing the police as the first step in using the law is usually done 'less for a sense of civic duty than from an expectation of personal gain' (Reiss, 1971:173). The 'middle orders' do not typically initiate direct contact with the police except when they are victims of property crime (Black, 1968:185). The 'lower orders' frequently use the police for this purpose and also mobilize them to handle interpersonal conflicts because other forms of social control have failed, are unavailable, or are absent. There may be conflict over the rules of a relationship, with at least one party trying to establish order by the threat of using the external formal rules which the police have at their disposal (ibid:108,181). Research shows that this type of demand is especially frequent at particular times and in particular places (Cumming et al., 1970:187) and among the 'lower orders' (Black, 1971, 1972, 1976; Meyer, 1974:81-2; Bottomley, 1973:45).

Obviously mobilization, type of dispute, citizen characteristics, and citizen input influence decision-making by patrol officers and I examine these elements in later chapters. However, we must also consider the internal dynamics of the police organization and the legal organization within which the police operate. There are major limitations in studies which concentrate on characteristics of the community.

These studies, following the work of Reiss and Black, tend to overemphasize the reactive role of the police and their apparent dependence on the public. Reiss and Black's findings on reactive policing probably reflect their sampling methods (see chapters 2 and 4), and their model is generally one of 'stimulus-response.' Many encounters, however, are long-lasting and complex, with both sides trying to coerce, manipulate, and/or negotiate an outcome that serves particular interests.

'Crime is, above all, a function of the resources available to know it' (Manning, 1972:234). The citizen can choose not to inform the police about a particular instance of trouble. If he reports it, he can formulate the trouble in ways he believes will influence police actions in the direction he himself wants. He also has choices about giving police access to information (e.g. school, employment, credit records); the police are dependent upon 'those socially structured features of everyday life which render persons findable' (Bittner, 1967a:706). He can also influence the patrol officer by appealing police actions through the citizen complaint bureau of the police department or through legal action.[16]

The police officer in turn has several resources at his disposal. These include the law, the 'low visibility' of his actions, and the general aura of his office. Manning (1979:24-6) suggests the significance of calls for service has been exaggerated in previous research. The officer has discretionary power outside the control of his supervisors to transform the encounter. He can use his organizational resources to convince the citizen that the action he is taking is the most appropriate and legitimate one (for examples, see Ericson, 1981: chapter 5). The officer's efforts are eased by the public-relations work of the force as a whole. 'One of the first explanations for police investment in provision of services only peripherally related to law enforcement is that this gives them knowledge and control in situations that have been previously associated with disruption of law and order' (Clark and Sykes, 1974:462). If the force in general, or a specific policy, is sold properly it can help to further citizen cooperation in providing information and can ultimately generate more crime and other products for the police to commit to their records.[17]

In sum, the more appropriate model is a transactional one of stimulus interpretation-response. General patterns may be revealed in quantifying status-role and dispute characteristics, but one must also examine how these patterns, and indeed the decisions themselves, are produced. A blend of quantitative and qualitative analysis is called for, and this is the approach we have taken.

A qualitative analysis allows for a better account of the role of legal and police organizational elements. For example, even a cursory examination of the law reveals that many citizen characteristics treated by researchers as 'extra-legal' are an integral part of the written law. This is clearly the case in police handling of juveniles; showing that charging and cautioning are significantly related to status, stability, and respectability should therefore come as no surprise (e.g. Chan and Doob, 1977). Similarly, specific statutes, such as the Bail Reform Act in Canada, for handling adult offenders, rely explicitly on criteria of stability and respectability such as place of residence and previous criminal record. Furthermore, what happens inside a police organization influences the initiation of encounters with citizens and what happens during those encounters. Available manpower, organizational priorities, production expectations, 'recipe' rules for 'targeting' segments of the population, and many other elements influence transactions and the production of case outcomes. In sum, the patrol officer's sense of order in the community is inextricably bound up with his sense of legal order and police organizational order, and these must be taken into consideration in a full account of police work.

Another aspect of legal organization which patrol officers incorporate into their actions is the organization of the court system, including the roles and rules used by judges, justices of the peace, defence lawyers, and crown attorneys. While the historic constitutional position of the constable is that he is answerable to the law alone, in practice he must justify his actions to other actors whose job it is to use the law. He must establish relationships with the various actors in court and respond to their expectations and rules (some of which may have the force of law), in order to achieve outcomes that serve organizational interests.

The constitutional position of the police has meant that the judiciary has not generally interfered with police discretion to investigate or to invoke the criminal process. For example, in the well-known *Blackburn* cases in Britain—*R. v Metropolitan Police Commissioner ex parte Blackburn* (1968) 1 All ER *763; R. v Metropolitan Police Commissioner ex parte Blackburn (1973) 1* All ER 324—the court of appeals stated the opinion that the courts will only intercede regarding a chief officer's discretion where there is an abdication of responsibility for law enforcement in a particular area of criminal law. For example, if a police force had a policy not to charge for housebreaking or theft where the loss was relatively small, the courts would step in; but there would be no intervention in individual cases, or where the policy covers types of crime such as statutory rape involving couples close in age. In everyday law enforcement it is up to the police themselves to decide what action to take.

In spite of this general distance, there are obviously many ways in which judges can and do influence police actions. They can alter the administrative organization of the court in a way that leads to a change in police practice. For example, Gardiner (1969:132) describes a situation where night-shift police officers were reluctant to issue traffic summonses because they would have to work irregular hours by appearing in court on the next day shift; a traffic-court judge began to allow deferred appearances in court, and the night-shift officers began to write more traffic tickets. Judges also have considerable control *within* some areas of the law. The law of confessions in Canada is made by judges, and decision-making on the admissibility of confessions in each individual case is largely subjective.

Judicial practices in sentencing can influence police practices in charging. Some researchers (e.g. Grosman, 1969; Klein, 1976) have pointed out that the tendency of Canadian judges to give concurrent sentences for multiple convictions gives the police less bargaining power in laying multiple charges with the intention of later withdrawing some in exchange for a guilty plea. British research indicates that in jurisdictions where police are reluctant to caution rather than charge people for minor offences, the courts tend to give a relatively large number of nominal sentences such as discharges; conversely, where police cautioning rates are high nominal sentencing rates are low

(Bottomley, 1973:72; Steer, 1970:20). The unwillingness of the courts to grant sentences other than discharges for certain types of offences and offenders may encourage the police to handle them without charge. The court can support the local police in the way it deals with certain types of charges that arise out of conflicts between police and citizens, such as 'assault police' or 'causing a disturbance' (see Williams, 1974:186-7). The degree to which the court upholds these charges, which usually rely solely on police testimony, may affect the degree to which the police will use formal charges in these situations as opposed to more summary actions.

Similar to their use of rules coming from other sources, police officers incorporate the rules of judicial practice into their own practices. They are very successful at doing this, in some cases continuing or even strengthening their existing practices while managing a show of conformity with the new rules. Of course, this is a typical result of attempts to introduce new rules in any organizational setting.[18]

The police are able to sustain control over the criminal process because of their 'positional advantage' (Cook, 1977) vis-à-vis the other agents of criminal control. The police have 'low visibility' to these other agents and produce the information required by these others. The latter are thus heavily dependent and must act on trust without any routine independent checks on how the police have made their case.

The research literature abounds with examples of these relationships and speculation on their effects. Blumberg (1970:especially 281) describes how the police develop exchange relationships with prosecutors and defense counsel, who are co-opted as 'agent mediators' to encourage the accused to enter guilty pleas. Prosecutors are heavily dependent on the police for evidence and they reciprocate by accepting police recommendations and practices in a way that allows the police to influence the decision-making authority of the prosecutor (Skolnick, 1966:especially 179, 191; Ericson, 1981:chapter 6). Applications for warrants from justices are routinely granted, usually without question (LaFave, 1965:34; Ericson, 1981:chapter 6). Similarly, police information and recommendations are crucial in decisions to grant release from custody and bail conditions (Bottomley, 1973:especially 101-3).

Undoubtedly, the police officer must keep in mind the rules of these others as he goes about preparing his case, operating with a set of 'prefigured justifications' (Dalton, 1959) in the event his actions are challenged. However, because of his skill at doing this and because of the organizational arrangements in court, he is rarely challenged. In the vast majority of cases the accused pleads guilty, and the judge knows little if anything as to why that decision was made, including police influences on it. While there is a formal judicial power to enquire into whether or not the plea of guilty was in order— *Adgey v The Queen* (1973) 23 CRNS 278—this is rarely done (cf Grosman, 1969:30). In this sense most criminal cases result in a determination of guilt without judicial review and control, and the process takes on many of the features of an inquisitorial system (Heydebrand, 1977). Only those cases going to trial have a public adversarial nature,[19] and this includes *possible* counter-accusations that call police judgments into question. In the small minority of cases that go to trial, the trial can be viewed as an appeal from police decisions about an individual (cf Law Reform Commission of Canada, 1973:9-10).

Typically, when the police officer decides to invoke the criminal process, he 'not only satisfies probable cause but also concludes after his careful evaluation that *the suspect is guilty and an arrest is therefore just*, (Reiss, 1971:135; see also Wilson, 1968:52). In proceeding to court, he is primarily seeking routine confirmation of what he assumes to be the case. If this confirmation is not routinely forthcoming, he may see that the other agents are calling into question his judgmental processes, his legitimacy, and their trust. It may be seen as an attack on his competence and, by implication, on police competence. The possible effects are many, ranging from rethinking the desirability of charging in similar situations to an alteration in strategies of presentation in court while otherwise continuing to do the same thing. As Newman (1966:196) states, 'Efforts at control are resisted by the police, who do not rethink the propriety of the enforcement program but rather adopt alternative methods of achieving their objectives.'

Overall, the legal organization within the court structure is enabling for the police. 'Social order depends upon the co-operative acts of men in sustaining a particular version of the truth' (Silverman, 1970:134). The ordering of the criminal process is very much under the influence of the police because their versions of the truth are routinely accepted by the other criminal-control agents, who usually have neither the time nor the resources to consider competing truths. In the vast majority of cases, the effective decision is made by the police, with the co-operation of the prosecutor, free from direct judicial constraint. The message from the literature seems to be that when additional formal rules and opportunities for judicial review are created, the police are still able to construct truth in a way that allows their version and their desired outcome to be accepted. This has led one commentator to conclude that a system of judicial control of the police is not practically possible. 'The absence of sufficient information is one reason why it would be unrealistic to expect the courts to investigate and control the discretionary powers of the police in law enforcement, especially those concerned with prosecutions, through the familiar process of judicial review of administrative action' (Williams, 1974:164).

One must look *within* the police organization to see how legal rules are placed in the context of other organizational rules. Additionally, it is necessary to examine dynamics within the police organization because most police decisions are not directly related to criminal law anyway. As we saw earlier, very little of the patrol officer's time is spent doing criminal-law investigation or enforcement. Most of the time is spent waiting or looking for trouble. When trouble is reported or discovered, the possibility of defining the matter as criminal may be taken into account, but this is only one among a range of justifiable choices. A host of decisions about mobilizations and information gathering form the bulk of all decisions by patrol officers, and they are subject to few if any formal rules from outside the police organization. In sum, a full view of police decision-making requires a look inside the police organization to see how internal expectations articulate with those from the outside.

The research record suggests that increasing bureaucratization and professionalization have brought the police organization increased autonomy from the community (Reith, 1943; Silver, 1967; Bordua, 1968; Fogelson, 1977; Miller, 1977; Ignatieff, 1979). Studies of attempts at organized community control of the police and of dealings between police administrations and police commissions show that the police are able to co-opt community efforts at control to serve their own organizational interests (e.g. Norris, 1973; Evans, 1974; Washnis, 1976; Brogden, 1977). In Britain, several researchers are arguing that the police have become a fundamental force in shaping community structure, using the media and other sources of power (e.g. Bunyan, 1976; Hall et al., 1978; Cohen, 1979; Taylor, 1980).

At the level of the individual patrol officer, bureaucratization has meant distancing from the community. Encounters between citizens and officers involve *a* policeman, not *the* policeman, with less personalized contact and the displacement of responsibility to a more anonymous entity. Bureaucratization and professionalization also foster a greater orientation to law enforcement (Wilson, 1968; Murphy, 1981).

In addition to insulating the patrol officer from the community, bureaucratization and professionalization can militate against internal control of the line officer while giving the appearance of greater control. In an ironic and contradictory fashion, bureaucratization and professionalization can have a strong

debureaucratizing effect, shifting power into the hands of line officers as a collective force (Clark and Sykes, 1974:473). As the size and degree of specialization within the police organization increase, the line officers come to rely
on their immediate colleagues, rather than distant superiors, for co-operation
(Cain, 1973:222). Moreover, expansion and specialization lead to increased
conflict, with sub-units establishing their own interests, often in direct conflict
with those of other sub-units (Banton, 1964: especially 263; Skolnick, 1966).
Various means are used to create and perpetuate internal power resources,
such as not communicating, or selectively communicating, essential information (Bittner, 1970:65).

The police organization differs from most other organizations in the
extent to which essential decisions and the input of knowledge occur among
the lowest-ranking members and filter upwards. In most industrial concerns
policies are set by the board and senior executives and are then passed on to
managers who oversee its implementation by those working on the line. The
line member's task is to carry out what has been delegated to him, although
he can of course object that the demands are too stringent or develop other
ways of accomplishing the task. In the police organization, the administration
can establish general production guidelines, but it is much more heavily dependent on the decisions taken and information produced by line members.

Wilson (1968:7) points out, 'The police department has the special property...that within it discretion increases as one moves *down* the hierarchy."
This is owing to both the 'low visibility' of these decisions and their 'situated'
nature. As Wilson (p 66) goes on to state, due to the fact the administrator
'cannot in advance predict what the circumstances are likely to be or what
courses of action are most appropriate)—because, in short, he cannot be
there himself—he cannot in advance formulate a policy that will 'guide' the
patrolman's discretion by, in effect, eliminating it' (see also Bittner, 1974;
Punch, 1979). Given the variety of human beings and troubles the patrol officer deals with, it is unlikely that rules could be written short of a compendium
on the manners of society (Laurie, 1970:111).

The police officer's rules for action are the 'recipe' rules learned on the
job. Of course, these rules take into account rules from other sources—the
community, the criminal law, and the police administration—especially as they
are useful in the formulation of accounts for justifying actions taken. However,
these 'recipe' rules also cover a range of circumstances and practices not
directly addressed within other rule systems. They 'are not the administrative
rules, which derive substantially from the criminal code or municipal regulations, but are those "rules of thumb" that mediate between the departmental

regulations, legal codes, and the actual events he witnesses on the street' (Manning, 1977:162-3). They cover a wide range of matters, such as whom to stop on suspicion in what circumstances; when official paper is necessary as opposed to a notebook record or nothing at all; how to prepare official paper; when and how to charge, including charging-up and multiple-charge possibilities; how to deal with lawyers and crown attorneys in the construction of case outcomes; and so on.

Many of the 'recipe' rules are known only among line officers. The rules of the 'law in action' are fully known and thus predictable only to them, and not to police administrators, other criminal control agents, and the public. Patrol officers control the creation of these rules, their use, and knowledge about them in ways that fundamentally secure their power within the organizational 'order of things.'

The administration attempts to compensate for lack of control by emphasizing bureaucratic and professional standards. As mentioned earlier, this accomplishes the appearance of control, but also strengthens tendencies it was designed to oppose, especially 'occupational individualism and defensive fraternal solidarity' (Bittner, 1970:67). Administrative control systems provide cover for the control systems within the occupational environment of patrol officers. They '(a) protect against the claim that something was not done; (b) punish persons after the fact; (c) maintain the appearance of evaluation, if not evaluational capacity; (d) maintain autonomy among and between units within the system by leaving the principal integrative bases tacit and unspecified' (Manning, 1979:26; see also Manning, 1977:chapter 6).

The police administration's efforts at control are multifaceted and include a disciplinary code, direct supervision, measurement of production, and a division of labour in terms of resources.

The appearance of a disciplined and cohesive unit, the embodiment of consensus, is created through the use of military-style dress and procedures. This gives a police patrol operation *some* of the characteristics of 'total institutions' as described by Goffman (1961). Definitions of reality constructed within the organization are intended to exclude conflicting meanings and thereby solidify particular orientations to the range of problems the patrol officer has to deal with. This is accomplished by techniques such as 'identity stripping' in the initial training and socialization phase for new members of the organization, and by an appearances code that includes such things as military-style uniforms and 'parades' before each shift. The result is an image of strict control over symbolically important matters even if they have little to do with the essential work of patrol officers. Unlike in total institutions, however, members are not cut off from routine contact with those outside. On the contrary, the central task of patrol officers is to confront outsiders and to engage directly in conflicts over competing definitions of reality.

The disciplinary code provides an enabling framework for the administration in its efforts to create an appearance of organizational order (for an analysis, see Ericson, 1981a). As Rubinstein (1973:41) observes, 'The Duty Manual offers almost unlimited opportunities to bring charges against a man.' The rules, subsumed under provincial police acts (e.g. Ontario Police Act RSO 1970) and departmental orders, are written in such broad and general form that they resemble rules for maintaining 'good order and discipline' within prisons (Ericson, 1981a). Every police officer violates them. Some have even noted that rules are contradictory, so that following one necessarily entails violation of others (Ramsay, 1972). The rules place the patrol officer in a state of 'dependent uncertainty' (Cain, 1973:especially 181) because he knows the administration can always 'get' him if he falls from official grace in other matters of importance. Just as patrol officers use enabling criminal-law rules to deal selectively with troublesome citizens, the police administration is able to use Police Act and departmental rules to deal selectively with troublesome officers.

The appearances code has another control function for the administration: to the extent that petty complaints regarding dress, coffee breaks, cheap meals at restaurants, etc., become the focal point of occupational grievances, the administration can play out concessions in these areas and deflect the more fundamental labour-management problems which characterize any bureaucratic working environment. Concerted effort at control from line officers—even in the apparently strong police-union movement in the United States (Juris and Feuille, 1973; Halpern, 1974)—is deflected into these areas of petty grievance, deflating the opposition of line officers and ultimately co-opting them.

The administration also employs line supervisors (patrol sergeants) to patrol and enforce its conception of internal order (see especially Rubinstein, 1973:chapter 2; Muir, 1977). These supervisors develop procedures covering a variety of matters, from office routine to handling prisoners. They give daily briefings which include directions about what areas of enforcement to concentrate on or ease up on. They spend considerable time patrolling in a platoon area. Their ability to listen in on messages from dispatchers to patrol officers means they can respond to any dispatched call, and this possibility is constantly kept in mind by patrol officers. The patrol sergeant and other higher-ranking officers review any official written reports submitted by patrol officers, and this is also kept in mind in deciding whether and how to construct reports (Reiss, 1971:124-5).

Part of the 'recipe' knowledge the patrol officer learns is directed at controlling supervisors. This takes the form of an exchange, whereby the officer follows the appearances code and formulates official reports in the appropriate bureaucratic framework in return for leniency in areas which ease the humdrum nature of patrol work. A lot of time and energy is spent on 'easing' work (Cain, 1973; Chatterton, 1979), but the first requirement is to gain the co-operation of the patrol sergeant. This is relatively easy given the importance of the appearances code within large bureaucratic police forces.[20]

Productive appearances are of considerable significance. Measures of productivity serve to inform supervisors what a patrol officer is up to, and they also provide data with which the organization as a whole can 'sell' itself. One obvious form of control is the development of quota requirements for enforcement activity. For example, researchers have documented how patrol-officer involvement in traffic-law enforcement can be influenced by a quota system. Wilson (1968: 97) reports that in Oakland a quota of 2 tickets per traffic division officer per hour was met with an actual rate of 1.97 tickets per traffic division officer per hour over a six-week period selected at random (see also Gardiner, 1969).

Another form of influence is the establishment of policy and attendant rules concerning charging. Senior administrators have attempted to articulate criteria concerning the decision to charge or caution. The rate of cautioning has been shown to be significantly influenced by the preferences, ideological or otherwise, of particular police chiefs (Steer, 1970:17).

Research has shown that adoption of production criteria fundamentally affects decision-making about arrest and charging. One consequence of measurement in any organization is overproduction in the areas that can be measured and underproduction in the areas more difficult to measure. For example, detectives concentrate on cases that can be cleared rather than on those which require considerable investigative attention and are unlikely to result in a measureable payoff (Greenwood, 1975; Ericson, 1981). Similarly, patrol officers are more likely to concentrate on measureable areas of proactive enforcement, such as traffic, liquor, and narcotics, rather than on more abstract areas of reproducing order, if they are explicitly rewarded for doing so (cf Fisk, 1974:25).

The emphasis upon 'clearances' of all sorts rather than just charges can lead to a number of other practices. In his research, Steer (1970:especially 21, 38) found that when adults are formally cautioned, the caution is typically employed as an alternative to no formal action, because of a lack of evidence, rather than as an alternative to prosecution. Indeed, Steer found that many cautions are given for activities that do not legally constitute a crime and could be more suitably written off as unfounded. Cautioning procedures thus help to swell clearance rates and make suspects arrested and investigated with no substantial grounds believe that there were grounds but that the police are exercising leniency.

Police officers with a high volume of cases to work on and perceiving administrative expectations to clear as many as possible may try to obtain a greater number of clearances for each arrest and reduce the overall number of investigations and arrests (Chaiken, 1975:chapter 9). This is frequently accomplished by having the suspect admit to a large number of offences on the promise that he will not be charged for them. Lambert (1970) reports that in a sample of 2,000 recorded property offences in Birmingham, 43 per cent of those cleared were done so by this method. LaFave (1965:374) records that in Detroit, when talking with an accused, 'the interrogating detectives stress the fact that any additional offences admitted are "free offences" in that there will be no prosecution for them.' Skolnick (1966:78) cites the case of two accused persons who received lenient sentences in exchange for admitting to over 500 burglaries.

Where police officers perceive extreme organizational pressure for production they may turn to more extreme methods, including excessive use of physical force (cf Whitaker, 1964). However, the research literature shows that such measures are relatively rare because they are not necessary (cf Skolnick, 1966:especially 174; Reiss, 1968:12; Wald et al., 1967:1549). The other tactics enumerated above provide enough resources to allow the line officer to proceed by way of the carrot rather than the stick. These procedures become bureaucratically accepted and routinized, allowing predictability and control in a way that other approaches, such as excessive physical force, cannot accomplish.

These practices have important ramifications for the productive efforts of police organizations as a whole. They lead to the production of crime rates in a way that seriously affects their validity as measures of crime control, although they serve the organization's 'crime-fighting' image. Several writers have pointed out that similar processes operate in other organizational contexts (see generally, Ditton, 1977, 1979). For example, Bensman and Gerver's (1963) study of an airplane factory revealed that line workers used an illegal tool that caused long-term hazards to airplane safety. They did so because it helped to meet production quotas; moreover, its use was condoned sub rosa by superiors. There are also many similarities in the work of bailiffs (McMullan, 1980). In sum, members of occupational cultures, in response to bureaucratic demands, can be adaptive and creative in producing their own rules to achieve their own needs. Those in the police organization can circumvent expectations from the wider organization of crime control and indeed alter the nature of both organizations.

Administrative influence affects resource allocation and the division of labour. For example, various types of dispatch systems regarding calls for service have control implications for patrol officers (Cordner, 1979; Manning, 1979; Jorgensen, 1979). In most police organizations, dispatched calls are tape-recorded and also recorded on a card system by the communications officer and dispatch officer. The officer is required to report back to the dispatcher on what happened, although if he is not filing official paper this may be only a brief coded message. Pepinsky (1975, 1976) found that in dispatches where the dispatcher named an offence, especially other than traffic, sex, or assault, the officer filed an official report on the offence as dispatched subject only to routine collaboration by the complainant (see also Jorgensen, 1979). Some police forces have attempted to control further through the instalment of vehicle-locator systems. Moreover, some forces may circumvent collusion among dispatchers and patrol officers by having civilian dispatchers, who do not have the experience of, and affinity with, the occupational culture of patrol officers.

While there appears to be substantial control via the dispatch system, ethnographers (e.g. Rubinstein, 1973; Manning, 1977, 1979) have documented the many means by which patrol officers collectively resist this form of control. Those who book off on a call can remain booked off while they go about their personal business after handling the call. Dispatchers can 'cover' for patrol officers who are 'missing' and the subject of inquiry from supervisors. The majority of calls do not result in official paper, and these can be accounted for in ways the dispatcher is unable to check. Even when official paper is submitted, there is usually no systematic linking of the paper with the original dispatch; moreover, most supervisors know that events become transformed and there is no meaning in a correlation between dispatcher labels and the officer's final accounting. There are strategies for circumventing vehicle-locator systems, e.g. finding spots where the signals are distorted.

Specialized division of labour characterizes urban police forces. An obvious division is between uniformed patrol officers and detectives. For example, in the Metropolitan Toronto Police Department there is an administrative regulation stipulating that uniformed personnel must turn over all arrested suspects to the detective branch for further investigation and charging, except in provincial-statute cases and areas of the Criminal Code dealing with driving and public order. This type of bureaucratic ordering significantly influences what the respective units work at (see Ericson, 1981: especially chapter 3).

Obviously, it is essential to examine the internal order of police organizations because it is there that the sense of order from community and legal organizations is translated into action. A fully social account of patrol-officer discretion must inquire into the sense of order derived from each of the organizational forums within which he operates, and ascertain how this sense of order frames what he does on the job. In this way we shall learn something about the reproduction of order within organizations (cf Ranson et al., 1980) and how this articulates with the reproduction of social order.

REPRODUCING ORDER: SOME RESEARCH QUESTIONS

In this chapter we have described and scrutinized the socio-legal literature on the police in order to derive a conception of their work. The position advanced is that the patrol police operate within a framework of rules emanating from the community and legal and police organizations. These rules collectively provide patrol officers with their sense of order, as they work to reproduce this order by taking these rules into account and using them as part of their accounts.

In light of the expansion and expense of police in Canada, it is surprising that there has been little attention by researchers to the police. Moreover, the police are an excellent vehicle for studying topics of significance to social science, including most generally how forms of social control are related to the reproduction of social order. Questions of importance to both academics and public administrators are involved in this area of research.

Some basic questions need to be addressed. As the editor of a recent collection of articles on the British police states, the most basic question is, who controls the police and how is this accomplished? (Holdaway, 1979). How do police officers spend their time? What do exercises of discretion look like? What does this tell us about the role of the police in constituting crime and other objects of their environment? What does it suggest about their wider social, cultural, economic, and political functions? Ultimately, does the view of policing portrayed in research lead us to question the massive build-up of policing and its dispersal as an everyday fact of community life?

Tentative answers to these questions require major research on a continuing basis. In this book I study patrol officers in a large Canadian municipal police force. We used systematic observation, official records, and unstructured interview data to study police patrol work from the viewpoint of the line officers whose work it is. We utilized both quantitative and qualitative data, emphasizing the strengths and limitations of each in providing a rounded view of patrol officers at work.

Accepting the portrayal of previous researchers including Bittner, Chatterton, and Manning, we do not view criminal-law enforcement as the primary work or goal of patrol work, but rather see it as one of many tools used by the patrol officer to order the population. In consequence this is not a study in the tradition of police effectiveness as crime fighters.[21]

Our research is concerned with patrol officers as *actors* who actively shape, and are shaped by, the nature of the work they undertake. We are interested in their use of rules, of the citizens they confront, and of each other. This work is largely within the 'social action' tradition in sociology (cf Blumer, 1969; Strauss, 1978; Rock, 1979a). Man is given the ontological status of producer. The locus of inquiry is interaction, which reveals both the nature of the structures produced by actors and the influence of these structures upon them. As Giddens (1976:122) points out, 'The proper locus for the study of social reproduction is in the immediate process of the constituting of interaction. On the other hand, just as every sentence in English expresses within itself the totality which is the "language" as a whole, so every interaction bears the imprint of global society; that is why there is a definite point to the analysis of "everyday life" as a phenomenon of the totality.'

ENDNOTES

1.   For example, allegations of brutality and other wrongdoings by members of the Waterloo Regional Police Force (Ontario Police Commission, 1978) and by members of the Metropolitan Toronto Police Force (Morand, 1976) and allegations of various illegalities and wrongdoings by members of the Royal Canadian Mounted Police (Mann and Lee, 1979; McDonald Commission, 1981).

2.   The figures on police personnel per 1,000 population include full-time employees other than sworn police officers. Police-officer strength in 1977 was 2.3 per 1,000 population. The vast majority are uniformed patrol of ficers. In the police force we studied as part of the research for this book, less than 20 per cent of police-officer personnel were assigned to detective units (Ericson, 1981). In a survey of American municipal and county police departments, Chaiken (1975:vii) discovered that on average 17.3 per cent of police officer personnel are assigned to detective units.

3.   This view is the dominant one in criminology and contributes more than anything else to making that subject less than respectable academically. As Hay (1975: 24n) notes, 'Historians have accepted the assumptions of reformers, which are also those of modern criminology: that the criminal law and the police are no more and no less than a set of instruments to manage something called crime. Effective detection, certain prosecution and enlightened rehabilitation will accomplish this practical task. Criminology has been disinfested of grand theory and class purpose. Much of it has thereby become ideology.'

4.   Wilson and Boland categorized 'police activity' as 'aggressive' if a city had a high volume of traffic citations, on the assumption that those highly proactive in this area are also highly aggressive in making proactive stops on suspicion. This assumption may be correct to the extent that traffic stops are also used to check out suspicions about the vehicle's occupants. However, the assumption requires confirmation from first-hand observation rather than solely from police records as employed by Wilson and Boland. A higher proactive-stop rate may be characteristic of police forces that have a lack of better things to do, including a lack of serious crime, which may be explained by factors independent of the police operation. For a critique of the work by Wilson and Boland, see Jacob and Rich (1980).

5.   Of course, changing the status quo will not change the structural position of the police. As E.P. Thompson (1979: 325) remarks: 'The police, as defenders of "law and order," have a vested interest in the status quo, whether the *status* be capitalist or communist, and whether the *quo* be that of Somoza's Nicaragua or Rokosi's Hungary: that is, the occupation is one which is supportive of statist and authoritarian ideologies. And, more simply, in whatever kind of society, the police will always have good reasons for pressing for more resources, more

powers, and more pay. There is nothing sinister about this, in an alert and democractic society, since, once these things are understood, proper measures will be taken to ensure that the police have adequate resources for their legitimate functions, and to curtail in the strictest way those functions which are not. This is not a new problem. It is a problem we have lived with ... for centuries.'

6.   'Shagwagon' is a slang term for a van or truck that has been customized with a finished interior and is used for driving adventures as well as amorous adventures. It was a term in currency among patrol officers and youths at the time the research for this book was undertaken.

7.   This perspective is within the 'social action' tradition in sociology. 'Social action' theorists emphasize the 'situated,' 'negotiated,' 'tenuous,' 'shifting' nature of social order: 'Order is something at which members of any society, any organization, must work. For the shared agreements, the binding contracts—what constitute the grounds for an expectable, non-surprising, taken-for-granted, even ruled orderliness—are not binding and shared for all time.... In short, the bases of concerted action (social order) must be reconstituted continually' (Strauss et al., 1963:129).

8.   Mennel (1974: 116-17) counsels: 'Social order is the result of some people being able to coerce others into obedience; or it rests on general agreement among the members of society; or it stems from their striking bargains with each other which are to everyone's individual advantage as well as the collective advantage. But it is unhelpful to see these viewpoints as mutually exclusive. For the sociologist, social order must be a matter for empirical investigation.'

9.   Friedenberg (1975: 90-1) suggests in a different context why social problems such as crime are perpetuated through mystification instead of being potentially subject to eradication: 'Public figures in quest of power have always found it useful to exploit prevailing myths, for it is the nature of myths both to dramatize conflict—psychic and social—and to conceal that conflict's real dynamism, thus ensuring that policies based on myth will not actually remedy the situation they dramatize. The day the boulder stays at the top of the hill, Sisyphus is out of office.... The very fact that politicians must accept and promote a formulation of social problems that so distorts the underlying dynamics as to make any real assessment of it impossible simply means that the popular conception itself becomes the problem, and usually a more serious problem than the one to which it refers.'

10.   As Bittner (1970: 24) observes on the effect of established court rules upon police decision-making: 'The norms observable in open court reach down and govern even the process of its evasion. In the criminal process, like in chess, the game is rarely played to the end, but it is the rare chess player who concedes defeat merely to save time. Instead, he concedes because he knows or can reasonably guess what would happen if he persisted to play to the end. And thus the rules of the end-game are valid determinants of chess-playing even though they are relatively rarely seen in action.'

11. Manning (1977, 1977a, 1980) is the leading student of this link between rules and the sense of order used by the officer to place police work in context: 'The sense of order that emerges from and is displayed in organizationally bounded encounters is in part dependent upon the rules that are called upon or invoked by participants to order the interaction. Rules, although *tacitly* understood, make salient the set of assigned features of events that interactants take into account as members-in-role. Rules are thus resources to be used tacitly by participants, and by doing so participants negotiate the limits upon organizationally sanctionable activities' (1977a: 57).

12. This point has been repeatedly stressed by Bittner (1967, 1967a, 1970). Based on his observations of patrol policing in a skid-row area, Bittner (1967a:710) concludes: 'Patrolmen do not really enforce the law, even when they do invoke it, but merely use it as a resource to solve certain pressing practical problems in keeping the peace.... The problem patrolmen confront is not which drunks, beggars or disturbers of the peace should be arrested and which can be let go as exceptions to the rule. Rather, the problem is whether, when someone 'needs' to be arrested, he should be charged with drunkenness, begging, or disturbing the peace.'

As Bittner (1970:109) states elsewhere, the substantive law in these circumstances is simply employed as a convenient tool without regard to abstract principles such as legality: 'In discretionary law enforcement involving minor offences, policemen use existing law largely as a pretext for making arrests.... Because persons who in the judgment of the police should be detained must be charged with something the law recognizes as valid grounds for detention, many arrests have the outward aspects of adhering to principles of legality. In point of fact, however, the real reasons for invoking the law are wholly independent of the law that is being invoked. The point to be emphasized is not that this procedure is illegal, though it often enough is, but that it has nothing to do with considerations of illegality.'

13. For a detailed analysis of the procedural criminal law in Scotland and England as it supports police practices, see McBarnet (1976, 1979, 1981). For a similar analysis in the Canadian context, see Freedman and Stenning (1977) and Ericson (1981a). See also Ratushny (1979).

14. The ideal of full enforcement and the rule of law has been particularly emphasized by some American legal scholars (e.g. Goldstein, 1960; Packer, 1968). Goldstein states that it is the duty of the police to carry out the dictates of the law by investigating every situation in which a criminal-law violation is suspected, to attempt to ascertain who violated the law, and to present the relevant information to the prosecutor for his further action. He documents that many American police acts specifically state this duty of full enforcement. The related ideal of the rule of law or principle of legality means that the police as agents of the criminal law should be restricted in their power to judge and punish by explicit rules which provide a justificatory framework for action or inaction. The aim is to reduce arbitrariness in police action, allowing assessment in review of

the 'justice' of their action.

As stated earlier, in Canada there are no entrenched rights which might curtail a procedural law that is enabling for the police. Moreover, there is no provincial or federal statute explicitly imposing the duty of full enforcement, and the police officer's broad duties and responsibility for following directives from both police and political superiors are emphasized (Cameron, 1974: 40). There is some contradiction between the constable's constitutional position as having an original authority in law, and his organizational position as a subordinate who must follow orders on penalty of possible legal proceedings under the Police Act, but this has apparently caused little conflict (see Williams, 1974; Gillance and Khan, 1975; Oliver, 1975; Ericson, 1981a). In Canada, there is a recognition that ours is a government of both laws and men.

15.   Reviews of this literature are provided by Box (1971) and Hagan (1979). Of course, the police are only one of many occupational groups employing moral judgments about status claims as a means of assessing what actions to take. For example, the medical profession makes moral judgments in discriminating among clients seeking the use of hospital emergency services (Roth, 1972).

16.   The empirical record indicates that while citizens have these resources of resistance, manipulation, and coercion, they do not often use them. Citizens routinely turn over documents to the police and provide other information without question (Ericson, 1981), and the channel of formal complaint is not often used, especially by the 'lower orders,' who have recurrent dealings with the police (Russell, 1976). This is particularly important regarding the previously mentioned 'low visibility' of the police. The patrol officer operates with 'high visibility' to those with whom he has regular contact, but these people typically have relatively little power. They therefore have no recourse or, except in an isolated and sporadic manner, cannot mobilize resources to take action if they do have recourse .

17.   For example, Steer (1970:10) reports that the development of juvenile liaison schemes in the United Kingdom resulted in more people reporting offences to the police because they believed the police would not prosecute and might even assist the offender. The net result was an overall increase in the number of offences known to the police. Skolnick and Woodworth (1967) report on differential enforcement of statutory rape by two police forces in California; the force which gained routine access to sources in welfare agencies for family support had a dramatically higher enforcement rate than the force which did not.

18.   In the case of the police, this has been particularly well documented with respect to the law of confessions and the accused's right to silence (e.g. Wald et al., 1967; Medalie et al., 1968; Chambliss and Seidman, 1971; Greenawalt, 1974; Zander, 1978). It has also been shown to happen in relation to policies and attendant rules emanating from the police administration (e.g. Chatterton, 1979; James, 1979). Examples from other organizational settings include the way in which prison guards have dealt with apparent due-process protections for inmates (Harvard Center for Criminal Justice, 1972), and the way in which

school principals have circumvented attempts to control their disciplinary actions against troublesome students (Gaylin et al., 1978:136ff).

19. The arguement can be made that while not publicly visible in the courtroom, pre-trial 'plea bargaining' sessions between counsel for the defence, police, and prosecutor take on an adversarial character (e.g. Utz, 1978).

20. Bittner (1970:55) summarizes the matter: 'Because the real work of the police-man is not set forth in the regulations, it does not furnish his superior a basis for judging him. At the same time, there are no strongly compelling reasons for the policeman to do well in ways that do not count in terms of official occupa-tional criteria of value. The greater the weight placed on compliance with inter-nal departmental regulations, the less free is the superior in censoring unregu-lated work practices he disapproves of, and in rewarding those he admires, for fear that he might jeopardize the loyalty of officers who do well on all scores that officially count—that is, those who present a neat appearance, who con-form punctually to bureaucratic routine, who are visibly on the place of their assignment, and so on. In short, those who make life easier for the superior, who in turn is restricted to supervising just those things. In fact, the practical economy of supervisory control requires that the proliferation of intradepart-mental restriction be accompanied by increases in license in areas of behaviour in unregulated areas. Thus, one who is judged to be a good officer in terms of internal, military-bureaucratic codes will not even be questioned about his con-duct outside of it.'

21. Some of the leading 'effectiveness' researchers have come to appreciate the lim-itations of their approach and the need to address more general issues with a theoretical focus. Kelling et al. (1979) stress that the effectiveness research which they and others have engaged in 'focuses on where police officers are, how fast they get there, how many of them there are, and how they are orga-nized. For all practical purposes, none deal with what police of ficers do in han-dling incidents and what effects their actions have. It is almost as if policing were an automated vending machine of service, with officer performance dis-counted as a "human factor," a mere electrical noise in an otherwise perfect system.'

REFERENCES

Ayres, R. 1970. 'Confessions and the Court,' in A. Niederhoffer and A. Blumberg, eds. *The Ambivalent Force*. Waltham, Mass.: Ginn, pp 2748.

Balbus, I. 1973. *The Dialectics of Legal Repression*. New York: Sage.

Banton, M. 1964. *The Policeman in the Community*. London: Tavistock.

Bayley, D. and Mendelsohn, H. 1969. *Minorities and the Police: Confrontation in America*. New York: Free Press.

Beattie, J. 1981. 'Administering Justice without Police: Criminal Trial Procedure in Eighteenth Century England,' in *Proceedings of A Symposium on the Maintenance of Order in Society*. Ottawa: Canadian Police College.

Bensman, J.and Gerver, I. 1963. 'Crime and Punishment in the Factory: The Function of Deviancy in Maintaining the Social System,' *American Sociological Review* 28: 588-98.

Berger, P. and Luckmann, T. 1966. *The Social Construction of Reality: A Treatise in the Sociology of Knowledge*. Harmondsworth: Penguin.

Bittner, E. 1967. 'Police Discretion in Emergency Apprehension of Mentally Ill Persons,' *Social Problems* 14: 278-92.

⸺, 1967a. 'The Police on Skid Row: A Study of Peace Keeping,' *American Sociological Review 32*: 699-715.

⸺, 1970. *The Functions of the Police in Modern Society*. Rockville, Md.: NIMH.

Black, D. 1968. 'Police Encounters and Social Organization: An Observation Study,' PhD dissertation, University of Michigan.

⸺, 1971. 'The Social Organization of Arrest,' *Stanford Law Review 23*: 1087-1111.

⸺, 1972. 'The Boundaries of Legal Sociology,' *Yale Law Journal* 81(6): 1086-1110.

Blumberg, A. 1970. 'The Practice of Law as a Confidence Game: Organizational Cooptation of a Profession,' in A. Niederhoffer and A. Blumberg, eds. *The Ambivalent Force*. Waltham, Mass.: Ginn, pp 279-92.

Blumer, H. 1969. *Symbolic Interactionism*. Englewood Cliffs, N: Prentice-Hall.

Bordua, D. 1968. 'The Police,' in D. Sills (ed.), *International Encyclopedia of Social Science*. New York: Free Press, pp 17481.

Bottomley, A. 1973. *Decisions in the Penal Process*. London: Martin Robertson.

Bottomley, A. and Coleman, C. *1979*. 'Police Effectiveness and the Public: The Limitations of Official Crime Rates.' Paper presented to the Cambridge Conference on Police Effectiveness, Cambridge, England, 11-13 July.

Box, S. 1971. *Deviance, Reality and Society.* New York: Holt, Rinehart and Winston.

Brogden, M. 1977. 'A Police Authority—the Denial of Conflict,' *Sociological Review* 25: 325-49.

Buckner, H. 1970. 'Transformations of Reality in the Legal Process,' *Social Research* 37: 88-101.

Bunyan, T. 1976. *The Political Police in Britain.* London: Julian Friedman.

Cain, M. 1973. *Society and the Policeman's Role.* London: Routledge and Kegan Paul.

Cameron, N. 1974. 'The Control of Police Discretion,' Draft manuscript, Centre of Criminology, University of Toronto. 91 pp.

Carlen, P. 1976. *Magistrates' Justice.* London: Martin Robertson.

Chaiken, J. 1975. *The Criminal Investigation Process. Vol. 11: Survey of Municipal and County Police Departments.* Santa Monica: Rand Corp.

Chambliss, W. and Seidman, R. 1971. *Law, Order and Power.* Reading, Mass.: Addison-Wesley.

Chan, J. and Doob, A. 1977. *The Exercise of Discretion with Juveniles.* Toronto: Centre of Criminology, University of Toronto.

Chan, J. and Ericson, R. 1981. *Decarceration and the Economy of Penal Reform .* Toronto: Centre of Criminology, University of Toronto.

Chatterton, M. 1973. 'A Working Paper on the Use of Resources—Charges and Practical Decision-Making in Peace-Keeping.' Paper presented to seminar on the sociology of police, Bristol University.

————, 1976. 'Police in Social Control,' in *Control without Custody.* Cropwood Papers, Institute of Criminology, University of Cambridge.

————, 1979. 'The Supervision of Patrol Work under the Fixed Points System,' in S. Holdaway (ed.) *The British Police.* London: Edward Arnold.

Clark, J. and Sykes, R. 1974. 'Some Determinants of Police Organization and Practice in Modern Industrial Democracy,' in D. Glaser, *Handbook of Criminology.* Chicago: Rand-McNally, pp 455-94.

Clarke, R. and Heal, K. 1979. 'Police Effectiveness in Dealing with Crime: Some Current British Research,' *The Police Journal* 52(1): 24-41.

Cohen, P. 1979. 'Policing the Working-Class City,' in B. Fine et al. *Capitalism and the Rule of Law.* London: Hutchinson.

Cohen, S. 1979. 'Guilt, Justice and Tolerance: Some Old Concepts for a New Criminology,' in D. Downes and P. Rock (eds.), *Deviant Interpretations.* Oxford: Martin Robertson.

Comrie, M.D. and Kings, E.J. 1975. 'Study of Urban Workloads: Final Report.' Home Office Police Research Services Unit (unpublished).

Cook, K. 1977. 'Exchange and Power in Networks of Interorganizational Relations,' *The Sociological Quarterly* 18: 62-82.

Cordner, G. 1979. 'Police Patrol Work Load Studies: A Review and Critique.' Unpublished paper, Michigan State University.

Cressey, D. 1974. 'Law, Order and the Motorist,' in R. Hood (ed.), *Crime, Criminology and Public Policy*. London: Heinemann, pp 213-34.

Cumming, E. et al. 1970. 'Policeman as Philosopher, Guide and Friend,' in A. Niederhoffer and A. Blumberg (eds.), *The Ambivalent Force*. Waltham, Mass.: Ginn, pp 184-92.

Dalton, M. 1959. *Men Who Manage*. New York: Wiley.

Davis, K. 1969. *Discretionary Justice*. Baton Rouge: Louisiana State University Press.

Ditton, J. 1977. *Part-Time Crime*. London: Macmillan.

_____, 1979. *Controlology: Beyond the New Criminology*. London: Macmillan.

Douglas, J. 1971. *American Social Order*. New York: Free Press.

Durkheim, E. 1964. *Rules of Sociological Method*. Trans. S.A. Solovay and John H. Mueller. New York: Free Press.

Ericson, R. 1975. *Criminal Reactions: The Labelling Perspective*. Farnborough: Saxon House.

_____, 1981. *Making Crime: A Study of Detective Work*. Toronto: Butterworths.

_____, 1981a. 'Rules for Police Deviance,' in C. Shearing (ed.), *Organizational Police Deviance*. Toronto: Butterworths.

Evans, P. 1974. *The Police Revolution*. London: Allen and Unwin.

Fishman, M. 1978. 'Crime Waves as Ideology,' *Social Problems* 25: 531-43.

_____, 1980. *Manufacturing the News*. Austin: University of Texas Press.

Fisk, J. 1974. *The Police Officer's Exercise of Discretion in the Decision to Arrest: Relationship to Organizational Goals and Societal Values*. Los Angeles: UCLA Institute of Government and Public Affairs.

Fogelson, R. 1977. *Big City Police*. Cambridge, Mass.: Harvard University Press.

Foucault, M. 1977. *Discipline and Punish: The Birth of the Prison*. Trans. Alan Sheridan. New York: Pantheon.

Freedman, D. and Stenning, P. 1977. *Private Security, Police and the Law in Canada*. Toronto: Centre of Criminology, University of Toronto.

Friedenberg, E. 1975. *The Disposal of Liberty and Other Industrial Wastes*. New York: Doubleday.

Gardiner, J. 1969. *Traffic and the Police: Variations in Law Enforcement Policy*. Cambridge, Mass.: Harvard University Press.

Gaylin, W. et al. 1978. *Doing Good: The Limits of Benevolence*. New York: Pantheon.

Giddens, A. 1976. *New Rules of Sociological Method*. London: Hutchinson.

Gilliance, K. and Khan, A. 1975. 'The Constitutional Independence of a Police Constable in the Exercise of the Powers of His Office,' *Police Journal* 48(1): 55-62.

J Goffman, E. 1961. *Asylums*. New York: Doubleday.

Goldstein, H. 1970. 'Police Discretion: The Ideal versus the Real,' in A. Niederhoffer and A. Blumberg, (eds.), *The Ambivalent Force*. Waltham, Mass.: Ginn, pp 148-56.

Goldstein, J. 1960. 'Police Discretion Not to Invoke the Criminal Process: Low Visibility Decisions in the Administration of Justice,' *Yale Law Journal* 69: 543-94.

Green, B. 1970. 'Race, Social Status and Criminal Arrest,' *American Sociological Review* 35: 476-90.

Greenawalt, K. 1974. 'Perspectives on the Right to Silence,' in R. Hood (ed.), *Crime, Criminology and Public Policy*. London: Heinemann.

Greenwood, P. et al. 1975. *The Criminal Investigation Process. Volume III: Observations and Analysis*. Santa Monica: Rand Corp.

Grosman, B. 1969. *The Prosecutor*. Toronto: University of Toronto Press.

————, 1975. *Police Command Decisions and Discretion* . Toronto: MacMillan.

Hagan, J. 1979. 'The Police Response to Delinquency: Some Observations on a Labelling Process,' in E. Vaz and A. Lodhi (eds.), *Crime and Delinquency in Canada*. Scarborough: Prentice-Hall.

Hall, S. et al. 1978. *Policing the Crisis* . London: Macmillan.

Halpern, S. 1974. *Police Association and Department Leaders: The Politics of Co-Optation*. Lexington, Mass.: Lexington Books.

Harvard Center for Criminal Justice 1972. 'Judicial Intervention in Prison Discipline,' *Journal of Criminal Law and Criminology* 63: 200-28.

Hay, D. 1975. 'Property, Authority and the Criminal Law,' in D. Hay et al. *Albion's Fatal Tree*. Harmondsworth: Penguin.

Holdaway, S. 1979. 'Introduction,' in S. Holdaway (ed.), *The British Police*. London: Edward Arnold.

Hudson, J. 1970. 'Police-Citizen Encounters that Lead to Citizen Complaints,' *Social Problems* 18: 179-93.

Hydebrand, W. 1977. 'Organizational Contradictions in Public Bureaucracies: Toward a Marxian Theory of Organizations,' *Sociological Quarterly* 18: 83-107.

Ignatieff, M. 1978. *A Just Measure of Pain*. London: Macmillan.

————, 1979. 'Police and People: The Birth of Mr. Peel's "Blue Locusts,"' *New Society* (30 August): 443-5.

Inbau, F. and Reid, J. 1967. *Criminal Interrogation and Confessions.* Baltimore: Williams and Wilkins.

James, D. 1979. 'Police-Black Relations: The Professional Solution,' in S. Holdaway (ed.), *The British Police.* London: Edward Arnold, pp 66-82.

Jorgensen, B. 1979. *Transferring Trouble: The Initiation of Reactive Policing.* Unpublished research report, Centre of Criminology, University of Toronto.

Juris, H. and Feuille, P. 1973. *Police Unionism.* Lexington, Mass.: Lexington Books.

Kadish, M. and Kadish, S. 1973. *Discretion to Disobey: A Study of Lawful Departuresfrom Legal Rules.* Stanford: Stanford University Press.

Kelling, G. et al. 1974. *The Kansas City Preventive Patrol Experiment.* Washington, DC: Police Foundation.

————, 1979. 'Policing: A Research Agenda for Rational Policy Making,' Paper presented to the Cambridge Conference on Police Effectiveness, Cambridge, England, 11-13 July.

Klein, J. 1976. *Let's Make a Deal.* Lexington, Mass.: Lexington Books.

LaFave, W. 1965. *Arrest: The Decision to Take a Suspect into Custody.* Boston: Little, Brown.

Laurie, P. 1970. *Scotland Yard.* London: Bodley Head.

Law Reform Commission of Canada. 1973. *Evidence: Compellability of the Accused and the Admissibility of His Statements.* Study Paper. 42 pp.

McBarnet, D. 1976. 'Pre-Trial Procedures and the Construction of Conviction,' in P. Carlen ed *The Sociology of Law.* Keele: Department of Sociology, University of Keele.

————, 1979. 'Arrest: The Legal Context of Policing,' in S. Holdaway (ed. *The British Police.* London: Edward Arnold.

————, 1981. *Conviction: Law, the State and the Construction of Justice.* London: MacMillan.

McCabe, S. and Sutcliffe, F. 1978. *Defining Crime: A Study of Police Decisions.* Oxford: Basil Blackwell.

McDonald Commission. 1981. *Final Report.* Ottawa: Ministry of Supply and Services.

McDonald, L. 1969. 'Crime and Punishment in Canada: A Statistical Test of the "Conventional Wisdom", *Canadian Review of Sociology and Anthropology* 6: 212-36.

————, 1976. *The Sociology of Law and Order.* London: Faber and Faber.

McMullan, J. 1980. 'Maudit Voleurs: Racketeering and the Collection of Private Debts in Montreal,' *Canadian Journal of Sociology* 5: 121-43.

MacNaughton-Smith, P. 1968. 'The Second Code: Toward (or away from) an Empiric Theory of Crime and Delinquency," *Journal of Research in Crime and Delinquency* 5: 189-97.

Mann, E. and Lee, J. 1979. *R.C.M.P. vs. The People*. Don Mills: General Publishing.

Manning, P. 1971. 'The Police: Mandate, Strategy and Appearances" in J. Douglas (ed.), *Crime and Justice in American Society*. Indianapolis: Bobbs-Merrill, pp. 149-94.

_____, 1972. 'Observing the Police: Deviants, Respectables and the Law,' in J. Douglas (ed.), *Research on Deviance*. New York: Random House, pp 213-68.

_____,1977. *Police Work*. Cambridge, Mass.: MIT Press.

_____, 1977a. 'Rules in Organizational Context: Narcotics Law Enforcement in Two Settings,' *Sociological Quarterly* 18: 44-61.

_____, 1979. 'Organization and Environment: Influences on Police Work.' Paper presented to the Cambridge Conference on Police Effectiveness, Cambridge, England, 11-13 July.

_____, 1980. *The Narcs' Game: Organizational and Informational Limits on Drug Law Enforcement*. Cambridge, Mass: MIT Press.

Medalie, R. et al. 1968. 'Custodial Police Interrogation in Our Nation's Capital: The Attempt to Implement Miranda,' *Michigan Law Review* 66: 1347-1422.

Mennel, S. 1974. *Sociological Theory*. New York: Praeger.

Meyer, J. 1974. 'Patterns of Reporting Non-Criminal Incidents to the Police,' *Criminology* 12: 70-83.

Miller, W. 1977. *Cops and Bobbies*. Chicago: University of Chicago Press.

_____, 1979. 'London's Police Tradition in a Changing Society,' in S. Holdaway (ed.), *The British Police*. London: Edward Arnold.

Morand, Mr Justice. 1976. *Royal Commission into Metropolitan Toronto Police Practices*. Toronto: Queen's Printer.

Morris P. 1978. 'Police Interrogation in England and Wales.' A critical review of the literature prepared for the UK Royal Commission on Criminal Procedure.

Moylan, J.F. 1929. *Scotland Yard*. London: Putnam.

Muir, W. 1977. *Police: Street Corner Politicians*. Chicago: University of Chicago Press.

Murphy, C. 1981. 'Community and Organizational Influences on Small Town Policing.' Forthcoming PhD dissertation, Department of Sociology, University of Toronto.

Newman, D. 1966. *Conviction: The Determination of Guilt or Innocence Without Trial*. Boston: Little, Brown.

Norris, D. 1973. *Police Community Relations*. Lexington, Mass.: Lexington Books.

Oliver, 1. 1975. 'The Office of Constable, 1975' *Criminal Law Review* 313-22.

Ontario Police Commission. 1978. *Inquiry into Police Practices in the Waterloo Regional Police Force*. Toronto: Ontario Police Commission.

Packer, H. 1968. *The Limits of the Criminal Sanction.* London: Oxford University Press.

Pate, T. et al. 1976. *Police Response Time: Its Determinants and Effects.* Washington, DC: Police Foundation.

Payne, C. 1973. 'A Study of Rural Beats,' *Police Research Services Bulletin* 12: 23-9.

Pepinsky, H. 1975. 'Police Decision-Making,' in D. Gottfredson (ed.), *Decision Making in the Criminal Justice System: Reviews and Essays.* Rockville, Md.: NIMH, pp 21-52.

_____, 1976. 'Police Patrolmen's Offense-Reporting Behavior,' *Journal of Research and Crime and Delinquency* 13(1): 33-47.

Punch, M. 1979. *Policing the Inner City.* London: Macmillan.

Punch, M. and Naylor, T. 1973. 'The Police: A Social Service,' *New Society* 24(554): 358-61.

Quebec Police Commission. 1977. *The Fight Against Organized Crime in Quebec.* Quebec City.

Ramsay, J. 1972. 'My Case Against the R.C.M.P.,' *MacLean's* (July): 19.

Ranson, S. et al. 1980. 'The Structuring of Organizational *Structures.*' *Administrative Science Quarterly* 25: 1-17.

Ratushny, E. 1979. *Self-Incrimination in the Criminal Process.* Toronto: Carswell.

Reiss, A. 1968. 'Police Brutality—Answers to Key Questions,' *Trans-Action* (July-August): 10-19.

_____, 1971. *The Police and the Public.* New Haven: Yale University Press.

_____, 1974. 'Discretionary Justice,' in D. Glaser (ed.), *Handbook of Criminology.* Chicago: Rand McNally, pp 679-99.

Reith, C. 1943. *The Police and the Democratic Ideal.* London: Oxford University Press.

Rock, P. 1979. 'The Sociology of Crime, Symbolic Interactionism and Some Problematic Qualities of Radical Criminology,' in D. Downes and P. Rock (eds.), *Deviant Interpretations.* Oxford: Martin Robertson, pp 52-84.

_____, 1979a. *The Making of Symbolic Interactionism.* London: Macmillan.

Roth, J. 1972. 'Some Contingencies of the Moral Evaluation and Control of Clientele: The Case of the Hospital Emergency Service,' *American Journal of Sociology* 77: 839-56.

Royal Commission on the Police (United Kingdom). 1962. *Final Report.* London: HMSO.

Rubinstein, J. 1973. *City Police.* New York: Farrer, Strauss and Giroux.

Russell, K. 1976. *Complaints Against the Police: A Sociological View.* Leicester, UK: Milltak Ltd.

Sanders, W. 1977. *Detective Work.* New York: Free Press.

Schur, E. 1971. *Labeling Deviant Behavior.* New York: Harper and Row.

Scull, A. 1977. *Decarceration.* Englewood Cliffs, NJ: Prentice-Hall.

Silver, A. 1967. 'The Demand for Order in Civil Society: A Review of Some Themes in the History of Urban Crime, Police, and Riot,' in D. Bordua (ed.), *The Police: Six Sociological Essays.* New York: Wiley, pp 1-24.

Silverman, D. 1970. *The Theory of Organizations.* London: Heinemann.

Skolnick, J. 1966. *Justice without Trial.* New York: Wiley.

Skolnick, J. and Woodworth, J. 1967. 'Bureaucracy, Information and Social Control: A Study of a Morals Detail,' in D. Bordua (ed.), *The Police: Six Sociological Essays.* New York: Wiley, pp 99-136.

Solicitor General of Canada. 1979. *Selected Trends in Canadian Criminal Justice.* Ottawa: Communication Division, Ministry of the Solicitor General of Canada.

Steer, D. 1970. *Police Cautions—A Study in the Exercise of Police Discretion.* Oxford: Basil Blackwell.

Strauss, A. 1978. *Negotiations.* San Francisco: Jossey-Bass.

Strauss, A. et al. 1963. 'The Hospital and Its Negotiated Order,' in E. Friedson (ed.), *The Hospital in Modern Society.* New York: Free Press.

Sullivan, D. and Siegel, L. 1974. 'How Police Use Information to Make Decisions,' *Crime and Delinquency* 18: 253-62.

Sykes, R. and Clark, J. 1975. 'A Theory of Deference Exchange in Police Civilian Encounters,' *American Journal of Sociology* 81(3): 584-600.

Taylor, I. 1980. 'The Law and Order Issue in the British and Canadian General Elections of 1979: Crime, Populism and State,' *Canadian Journal of Sociology* 5: 285-311.

Thompson, E.P. 1979. 'On the New Issue of Postal Stamps,' *New Society* 50: 324-26.

Turk, A. 1976. 'Law as a Weapon in Social Conflict,' *Social Problems* 23: 276-92.

Utz, P. 1978. *Settling the Facts: Discretion and Negotiation in the Criminal Courts.* Lexington, Mass.: Lexington Books.

Wald, M. et al. 1967. 'Interrogations in New Haven: The Impact of Miranda,' *Yale Law Journal* 76: 1521-1648.

Washnis, G. 1976. *Citizen Involvement in Crime Prevention.* Lexington, Mass.: Lexington Books.

Weick, K. 1969. *The Social Psychology of Organizing.* Reading, Mass.: Addison Wesley.

Werthman, C. and Piliavin, I. 1967. 'Gang Members and the Police,' in D. Bordua (ed.), *The Police: Six Sociological Essays.* New York: Wiley, pp 56-98.

Whitaker, B . 1964. *The Police.* Harmondsworth: Penguin.

Wilkins, L. 1964. *Social Deviance.* London: Tavistock.

Willett, T. 1964. *Criminal on the Road.* London: Tavistock.

Williams, D. 1974. 'Prosecution, Discretion and the Accountability of the Police,' in R. Hood (ed.), *Crime, Criminology and Public Policy.* London: Heinemann, pp 161-95.

Wilson, J. 1968. *Varieties of Police Pehavior.* Cambridge, Mass.: Harvard University Press.

Wilson, J. and Boland, B. 1979. 'The Effect of the Police on Crime,' *Law and Society Review* 12: 367-90.

Zander, M. 1978. 'The Right of Silence in the Police Station and the Caution' in P. Glazebrook (ed.), *Reshaping the Criminal Law.* London: Stevens, pp 108-19.

CHAPTER 9
Reconsidering the Police Role: A Challenge to a Challenge of a Popular Conception*

CLIFFORD D. SHEARING
JEFFREY S. LEON

INTRODUCTION

For some time now a debate has been taking place both within academic and police circles with respect to the role of the police. This debate has taken the form of a challenge to the popular conception of the police officer's role as principally a crime-fighter and law-enforcer. Social scientists and police administrators have argued that in fact policemen, at least at patrol level spend relatively little of their time fighting crime or enforcing the law; rather, they spend the vast majority of their time doing social service type work.

One of the earliest studies to consider how policemen in fact spend their time was reported in a paper by Cumming et al. (1964). These authors suggested that the roles of social agencies could be viewed as involving two components: a controlling element and a supporting element. They argued further that it was probably impossible for a role to accord equal emphasis to each of these two components. However, it was equally unlikely that a role could emphasize one of these components to the exclusion of the other. Accordingly, within any particular role one was likely to find that one component was overt while the other was latent. In applying this general conceptual

Reproduced by permission of the *Canadian Journal of Criminology*, Vol. 19(4), pages 331-345. Copyright by the Canadian Criminal Justice Association.

framework to the police, the authors write:

> The policeman's role in an integrative system is, by definition and by
> law, explicitly concerned with control—keeping the law from being
> broken and apprehending those who break it — and only latently
> with support...besides latent support, the policeman often gives
> direct help to people in certain kinds of trouble. When he does this,
> the balance between support and control has shifted, and he is act-
> ing overtly as a supportive agent and only latently in his controlling
> role. He has, at the same time, changed from a professional to an
> amateur. (1964: 277)

This statement clearly gives predominance to the control function in the
police role and draws attention to an aspect of the police role that, because of
its latent character, had previously tended to be ignored. In their essay the
authors proceed via consideration of citizen requests for help to examine this
latent aspect of the police role. Following an analysis of the nature of the calls
for service and the police response to them, the authors summarize and reflect
on their findings:

> More than one-half of the calls coming routinely to the police com-
> plaint desk, and perhaps to detectives, appear to involve calls for
> help and some form of support for personal and interpersonal prob-
> lems. To about three-quarters of these appeals, a car is sent. When
> the policeman reaches the scene, the data suggest that he either
> guides the complainant to someone who can solve his problem or
> tries to solve it himself. To do this, he must often provide support,
> either by friendly sympathy, by feeding authoritative information into
> the troubled situation, or by helping consensual resolution to take
> place. We started with the assumption that these activities belonged
> to the latent aspect of his role, and he is certainly an amateur—these
> policemen have no training for this kind of service. (1964: 285-6)

Further, after discussing a number of reasons why the police are called upon
so frequently to exercise their amateur talents, the authors conclude that:

> Some modern advocates of 'professionalization' of police work rec-
> ognize that the policeman on the beat spends about half his time as
> an amateur social worker and they hope, instead of improving the
> referral process, to equip him with the skills of a professional. The
> policeman will then have a role containing both overtly supportive
> and overtly controlling elements. If our assumption that these are
> incompatible activities is correct, this development would lead to a

division of labor within police work that would tend once more to segregate these elements. This, in turn, would result in a basic shift in the relationship of the police to the rest of the integrative system. (1964: 286)

Michael Banton, (1964) in a book published at about the same time as the paper by Cumming et al., develops this distinction between types of policemen based on the nature of the activities in which they engage. Banton writes:

> Some years ago the Home Secretary observed: 'The British policeman is a civilian discharging civilian duties and merely put into uniform so that those who need his help know exactly where to look for assistance.' Today, especially in connection with the traffic laws, this description is not accurate: the policeman is increasingly seen as an official exercising authority and power over citizens. A division is becoming apparent between specialist departments within police forces (detectives, traffic officers, vice and fraud squads, etc.) and the ordinary patrolman. The former are 'law officers' whose contacts with the public tend to be of a punitive or inquisitory character, whereas the patrolmen...are principally 'peace officers' operating within the moral consensus of the community. Whereas the former have occasion to speak chiefly to offenders or to persons who can supply information about an offence, the patrolmen interact with all sorts of people and more of these contacts centre upon assisting citizens than upon offences. (1964: 6-7)

In a subsequent chapter Banton expands this statement as follows:

> ...the policeman on patrol is primarily a 'peace officer' rather than a 'law officer'. Relatively little of his time is pent enforcing the law in the sense of arresting offenders; far more is spent 'keeping the peace' by supervising the beat and responding to requests for assistance....
>
> My argument that the patrolman is primarily a peace officer is, however, based less upon any calculation of how he spends his time than upon a consideration of how he responds when he has to deal with offences. In my experiences, the most striking thing about patrol work is the high proportion of the cases in which policemen do not enforce the law. (1964: 127)

As a result of these and similar writings, the notion that policemen on patrol spend the majority of their time (both in terms of the type of incidents responded to and the nature of their response) as "amateur social workers"

rather than as "law officers" has become increasingly wide spread among academics, police administrators and policy makers, and has formed the focal
point for an on-going debate over the what the police *should* be doing. The
debate has crystallized essentially around two polar positions along the lines
predicted by Cumming et al. On the one hand, there are those who argue that
the time police spend as amateur social workers detracts from what should be
their primary function, namely crime-fighting and law enforcement. On the
other hand, there are those who argue that this emphasis on the "control"
function is misplaced: that is, the police should be responsive to the nature of
the demands made on them by the public and accordingly should define their
role so that the "supportive" functions are recognized as equally legitimate and
essential parts of the police role as the "control" functions. This latter position
has come to be regarded as the "progressive" position and is a position that
tends to be endorsed in "progressive" policy statements about the future role
of the police.

For example, in 1967, the President's Commission on Law Enforcement
and the Administration of Justice wrote:

> While each person has a somewhat different impression of the
> nature of the police function, based primarily upon his personal
> experiences and contacts with police officers, there is a widespread
> popular conception of the police, supported by the news and enter-
> tainment media. Through these, the police have come to be viewed
> as a body of men continually engaged in the exciting, dangerous,
> and competitive enterprise of apprehending and prosecuting crimi-
> nals. Emphasis upon this one aspect of police functioning has led to
> a tendency on the part of both the public and the police to underes-
> timate the range and complexity of the total police task.
>
> A police officer assigned to patrol duties in a large city is typically
> confronted with at most a few serious crimes in the course of a sin-
> gle tour of duty. He tends to view such involvement, particularly if
> there is some degree of danger, as constituting real police work. But
> it is apparent that he spends considerably more time keeping order,
> settling disputes, finding missing children, and helping drunks than
> he does in responding to criminal conduct which is serious enough
> to call for arrest, prosecution, and conviction. This does not mean
> that serious crime is unimportant to the policeman. Quite the con-
> trary is true. But is does mean that he performs a wide range of
> other functions which are of a highly complex nature and which
> often involve difficult social, behavioural and political problems.
> (1967: 13)

This view was recently echoed in Canada by the Task Force on Policing in Ontario:

> Within the context of the overall objectives [namely, crime control, protection of life and property, and the maintenance of peace and order], police have six principal functions: response, referral, prevention, public education, crime solving, and law enforcement. Popularly, the latter two have been seen to be the main components of the police role. To a large degree, this perspective is shared by the police tradition, and the other functions are seen to be largely peripheral to 'real police work'. We are of the view, however, that a far better balance among the six functions must be sought if the province's needs for crime control, protection of life and property, and peace and security are to be met. (1974: 17)

This debate, in our view, is based on a partial and, therefore, inadequate conception of the police role. When a more adequate conception of the role is adopted, the research finding that police spend relatively little time actually enforcing the law may be viewed in an entirely different light and need not give rise to a controversy which distinguishes and then contrasts the "control" and "support" functions of the police. Our purpose in this paper is first to reveal the inadequacy of the present conception of the police role by showing that it is based on inadequate theoretical framework, and then to present a more accurate conception of this role.

THE PREMISES OF THE DEBATE

The misconceptions implicit in the debate we have just summarized can be explicated by considering the theoretical framework underlying this debate. The debate over the police role considers police actively within a theoretical framework comprised of two major elements, expectations concerning what policemen should do and a description of what police actually do.

The debate over the police role takes as its point of departure three claims which are not at issue in the debate. The first is that the police in western societies have traditionally been expected to fight crime and enforce the law. Second, empirical research shows that, in fact, policemen, especially patrolmen, spend only a relatively small proportion of their time (the estimates vary between fifty per cent and twenty per cent) fighting crime and enforcing the law and that the rest of their time is spent in a more general social service function. Finally, it is argued that the activities performed by the police should be consistent with the expectations about what police should do. The controversy arises over a difference of opinion as to how the consistency between expectations and concern for objectives and activities is to be achieved. The difficulty with this debate is that the two elements of objectives and activities do not constitute an adequate theoretical foundation for an analysis of roles, whether the police role or any other role. The concept of role (based on the twin elements of objectives and activities) that underlies the debate on the police role does not meet the generally accepted minimum requirements of a theoretical framework for the analysis of social action.

Talcott Parsons (1968) has argued, in our view convincingly, that the most fundamental framework for the analysis of social action is what he has termed the "action frame of reference".[1] The action frame of reference developed by Parsons is based on the means/end schema as a theoretical framework for the analysis of human action. Within the means/end schema human beings are viewed as being oriented towards the achievement of ends and to selecting from among the available means in order to achieve these ends. The availability of means is a function of the circumstances or conditions outside of the control of the actor, within which action takes place. Parsons has further suggested that the three elements of means, ends and conditions are not sufficient for an understanding of human action. In order to provide a schema that is adequate as a fundamental framework for an understanding of human action, a normative element, concerned with the choice of means, must be included within the means/end schema. Parsons discusses this idea of a minimally acceptable theoretical framework for action as follows:

> It takes a certain number of...concrete elements to make up a complete unit act, a concrete end, concrete conditions, concrete means, and one or more norms governing the choice of means to the end...

> It is essential to distinguish from the concrete use of the theory of action, in this sense, the analytical. An end, in the latter sense, is not the concrete anticipated future state of affairs but only the difference from what it would be, if the actor should refrain from acting. The ultimate conditions are not all those concrete features of the situation of a given concrete actor which are outside his control but are those abstracted elements of the situation which cannot be imputed to action in general. Means are not concrete tools or instruments but the aspects or properties of things which actors by virtue of their knowledge of them and their control are able to alter as desired.

> ...This frame of reference [namely, the action frame of reference] consists essentially in the irreducible framework of relations between

these elements and is implied in the conception of them, which is common to both levels, and without which talk about action fails to make sense. It is well to outline what the main features of this frame of reference are.

First, there is the minimum differentiation of structural elements, ends, means, conditions and norms. *It is impossible to have a meaningful description of an act without specifying all four,* just as there are certain minimum properties of a particle, *omission of any one of which leaves the description indeterminate.* Second, there is implied in the relations of these elements a normative orientation of action, a teleological character. Action must always be thought of as involving a state of tension between two different orders of elements, the normative and the conditional. As process, action is, in fact, the process of alteration of the conditional elements in the direction of conformity with norms. Elimination of the normative aspect altogether eliminates the concept of action itself and leads to the radical positivistic position. Elimination of conditions, of the tension from that side, equally eliminates action and results in idealistic emanationism. Thus conditions may be conceived at one pole, ends and normative rules at the other, means and effort as the connecting links between them. (1968: 731-2, our emphasis)[2]

Hence, the debate on the role of the police summarized above is inadequate and misleading precisely because it does not encompass the four elements central to a consideration of human action. Consequently, it "fails to make sense" of police action. The two elements ignored in the debate on the police role are the elements of means, and norms relating to the use of these means in attaining ends.[3] The debate has been based exclusively upon an analysis of what police *should* do and what they *actually* do, and has overlooked what the police *can* do and have the *authority* to do. The means available constitute a horizon of possibilities that must be considered if the significance of any particular police activity is to be appreciated. A particular police activity can only be properly understood if it is viewed from within the context of possible action, (that is, possible actions the policeman has both a right to take and is capable of taking) from which the action in question is *selected.* Failure to take this horizon of possibilities into account leads to the crude empiricism[4] that underlies this debate.

REDISCOVERING THE POLICE ROLE

In the remainder of the paper we will present a conception of the police role that meets the minimum requirements of theoretical adequacy as outlined by Parsons. However, as our task is to consider the *police* role, our strategy will be to explicate those elements of this role that differentiate the police from other occupational roles and from citizens in general. That is, our focus will be on identifying those aspects of the police role that set the police apart from others. We will argue that while all four elements identified by Parsons in his action frame of reference must be taken into consideration in providing an adequate account of the police role it is the elements of means and the norms relating thereto, that define the essential and unique character of the police role and set it apart from other roles.

Let us begin by considering the objective of the police. There is little argument within the literature that the function of the police in western societies is the maintenance of order. Hobbes has provided for western society the theoretical framework and the political justification for social control as a responsibility of the State. The police are the agents employed by the State to fulfil, at least in part, this social control function.[5] This concept of the police as being responsible for the maintenance of order is as old as the police themselves. It appears in Peel's principles published in 1829 and is to be found embodied in most documents setting out the duties of police today. For example, in Canada, the RCMP Act[6] clearly indicates that it is the duty of members of the police force to preserve the peace. However, while this may be the principal objective of the police, it cannot be used to differentiate the police from others. For every citizen may be viewed as being charged with the responsibility to maintain order.[7]

If the objective of the police does not provide a basis for differentiating the police role from that of others, neither do the conditions of action. The conditions which limit the police in striving to preserve order are essentially the same as those that any other citizen faces in seeking to achieve this end.

However, as we turn to the elements of the means available to the police, and the norms concerning them, we find an important distinction between the police and others, and consequently, the nub of the police role—that which sets the police apart from others. While the policeman shares with other citizens a wide range of skills and resources that can be used in responding and in maintaining order, he also has access to resources which are unique to him and differentiate him sharply from others. Our task, therefore, in considering what is essential about the police role, is to articulate these differences.

In specifying what it is that differentiates the police from others, it has often been suggested that the central difference is simply that the police are accessible to the public as an emergency service, twenty-four hours a day (c.f. The President's Commission on Law Enforcement and Administration of Justice, 1967: 14). We will argue that this is in fact a consequence of a more fundamental difference between the policeman and other citizens, and is not itself the basis for this difference.

In order to isolate those elements of means and norms that are definitive of the police role it is essential to distinguish between what it is that police can do that others cannot (that is, what they are able to do because of the unique resources available to them), and what they as policemen, in contradistinction from others, have the authority or right to do. This distinction will assist us in identifying what it is that sets the police apart from others at both a *de facto* and a *de jure* level. What is unique about the police at a *de jure* level we will, following Hughes' general usage of the term licence, (1958) call the *police licence,* and what is unique to them at a *de facto* level we will call the *police capability.* The police licence and capability refer to the normative and factual elements of the means that are unique to the police.

The means that are uniquely available to the police, and that, therefore, provide for the substantive content of the police licence and the police capability, are: (a) unique access to the law as a means to be used in maintaining order; (b) unique access to legitimized physical force as a means of maintaining order.

THE LAW AS A MEANS OF MAINTAINING ORDER

The law is both a body of statements (primarily rules) that defines what is to be considered a breach of the peace, and a body of statements (once again primarily rules) providing authorization for instructions about how to deal with such breaches of peace. The process of dealing with problems under the authority and direction of the law is what is referred to as law enforcement. From the police point of view, law enforcement involves essentially two possible actions, arrest and charge/summons.[8]

Furthermore, from the police point of view, the law is, in most cases, much more relevant as a means for *dealing* with problems than as a means of *defining* problems. Policemen for the most part face situations which have been pre-defined as problems by one or more citizens (cf. Black, 1968; Reiss,

1971; Shearing, 1974) in which they are asked to do something. Policemen faced with such situations review the resources available to them (both those resources that are specific to their office and those that are more general in nature) as means which might be used to deal with the problem. This problem-solving orientation, and the notion that policemen review a wide variety of resources in considering how to respond to problems, has been discussed by Wilson as follows:

> To the patrolman, the law is one resource among many that he may use to deal with disorder, but it is not the only one or even the most important; beyond that, the law is a constraint that tells him what he must *not* do but that is peculiarly unhelpful in telling him what he *should* do. Thus, he approaches incidents that threaten order *not in terms of enforcing the law but in terms of 'handling the situation'.* The officer is expected, by colleagues as well as superiors, to 'handle his beat'. This means keeping things under control so that there are no complaints that he is doing nothing or that he is doing too much. To handle his beat, the law provides one resource, the possibility of arrest, and a set of constraints, *but it does not supply to the patrolman a set of legal rules to be applied.* (1968: 31)

Wilson, in this passage, is correct in arguing that: (a) the policeman's *task* is one of order maintenance rather than of law enforcement; (b) law enforcement provides only one means among others available to policemen in maintaining order; (c) the law limits the policeman's choice of the means he can legally use in responding to a problem; and (d) the law, while providing the limits of what a policeman can do, does not provide positive instruction as to what he should do in any particular situation.

There are, however, difficulties with Wilson's argument given his position that the law enforcement resource the policeman has at his disposal in responding to problems is not important. If by this Wilson simply means that policemen in fact do not often arrest and charge people in the course of maintaining order, then we have no quarrel with him. If, however, he intends that, as compared to other means at the policeman's disposal, law enforcement does not have a very special status, or that the possibility that the policeman may choose to use law enforcement as a means for dealing with the problem is not one of the things that all parties to the situation are alive to, then Wilson is quite simply wrong and his stress on order maintenance as opposed to law enforcement as the principle responsibility of policemen is very misleading.

The policeman shares with others a wide variety of resources that can be used in dealing with a problem. However, these resources exist within the context of those resources (law enforcement and force) which he does not share with others and that are, in effect, unique characteristics of his role. This context completely permeates, and thereby changes the meaning and significance of all the other resources at his disposal.

This general point can be illustrated with reference to the specific resource of law enforcement. The law provides the police with greater powers of law enforcement, particularly with respect to arrest, than the average citizen. Furthermore, the organization of the police, and more generally the criminal justice process, provides the police with greater practical access to law enforcement as a means of handling breaches of order both in terms of what they can actually "get away with" (as opposed to their legal powers), and in terms of their organizational access to knowledge of their powers, justices of the peace, prosecutors, jails, etc.

As a result of this *special* access to law enforcement, law enforcement becomes more than simply one resource among others which the policeman has at his disposal. It is a resource which is, in reality, unique to the police. This special status has two consequences: (a) it becomes definitive of the police role (that is, the police are not simply seen as problem solvers, but as problem-solvers-who-have-a-special-access-to-law enforcement as a means of dealing with problems); and (b) the special status of law enforcement means that it provides a context in which other problem solving resources are perceived. For example, given the special significance of law enforcement as a means for dealing with problems, a policeman's decision to use some other means of dealing with a problem is seen not merely as a decision to do such-and-such but as a decision not to enforce the law. Thus, for instance, a motorist who is stopped for speeding and told to drive more carefully regards himself as fortunate because he received a warning rather than the ticket that the policeman was able and entitled to give him. More generally, citizens regard the police as persons whose status as policemen is intrinsically bound up with their special access to law enforcement as a means for maintaining order.

This character of the police access to law enforcement, while particularly clear in relation to traffic problems, applies equally to other problems. It is difficult to conceive of a problem situation where the policeman could not, if he chose, argue that some law had been breached and, therefore, could not, if he chose, enforce the law. This is something that both the police and the public are continually aware of and take into account in dealing with each other.[9]

PHYSICAL FORCE AS A MEANS OF MAINTAINING ORDER

There is, in addition to law enforcement, a second resource to which the police have special access that is definitive of the police role, namely, physical force. As in the case of law enforcement, the police are differentiated from others both in terms of their right to and ability to use force as a means of dealing with problems.[10] This special status of force with respect to the police role has been recognized by Bittner. He writes that:

> ...police intervention means above all making use of the capacity and authority to overpower resistance to an attempted solution in the native habitat of the problem. There can be no doubt that this feature of police work is uppermost in the minds of people who solicit police aid or direct the attention of the police to problems, that persons against whom the police proceed have this feature in mind and conduct themselves accordingly, and that every conceivable police interaction projects the message that force may be, and may have to be, used to achieve a desired objective. It does not matter whether the person who seeks police help is a private citizen or other government official, nor does it matter whether the problem at hand involves some aspect of law enforcement or is totally unconnected with it.... What matters is that police procedure is defined by the feature that it may not be opposed in its course, and that force can be used if it is opposed. This is what the existence of the police makes available to society. Accordingly, the question, 'What are policemen supposed to do?' is almost completely identical with the question, 'What kinds of situations require remedies that are non-negotiably coercible?' (1970: 40-41)

Bittner summarizes his argument as follows:

> In sum, the role of the police is to address all sorts of human problems when and insofar as their solutions do or may possibly require the use of force at the point of their occurrence. This lends homogeneity to such diverse procedures as catching a criminal, driving the mayor to the airport, evicting a drunken person from a bar, directing traffic, crowd control, taking care of lost children, administering medical first aid, and separating fighting relatives.
>
> There is no exaggeration in saying that there is topical unity in this very incomplete list of lines of police work. Perhaps it is true that the common practice of assigning policemen to chauffeur mayors is based on the desire to give the appearance of thrift in the urban fisc. But note, if one wanted to make as far as possible certain

that nothing would impede His Honor's freedom of movement, he
would certainly put someone into the driver's seat of the auto who
has the authority and the capacity to overcome all unforeseeable
human obstacles. Similarly, it is perhaps not too farfetched to
assume that desk sergeants feed ice cream to lost children because
they like children. But if the treat does not achieve the purpose of
keeping the youngster in the station house until his parents arrive to
redeem him, the sergeant would have to resort to other means of
keeping him there. (1970: 44)

Bittner makes clear that he does not intend to imply that policemen spend
all or even much of their time using physical force but simply that this possibility is central to the police role:

It must be emphasized...that the conception of the centrality of the
capacity to use force in the police role does not entail the conclusion
that the ordinary occupational routines consist of the actual exercise
of this capacity. It is very likely, though we lack information on this
point, that the actual use of physical coercion and restraint is rare
for all policemen and that many policemen are virtually never in the
position of having to resort to it. (Bittner, 1970: 41)

We agree in the main with Bittner's arguments as to the centrality of the
police authority and capacity to use physical force for the police role, but we
dispute his claim that this is the *only* factor that needs to be considered in
specifying what is unique about the police role. In our view, both law enforcement *and* physical force are essential features of the police licence and capability, and, therefore, of the police role. While these two factors are clearly
related to one another, to attempt to reduce one to the other (for example, by
arguing that law enforcement is ultimately a matter of coercion or that the
police authority to use physical force is ultimately founded in law) tends to
muddy rather than clarify one's understanding of the police role.

SUMMARY AND CONCLUSIONS

In sum, we view the police licence and capability as being definitive of the
police role in the sense that they refer to those elements in the police role that
differentiate the police from others. The police capability is defined by their
special access to physical force and law enforcement as resources in dealing
with the problems that confront them. The police licence is their authority to
use these two resources.

Everything a policeman does takes place within the context of the police licence and capability. This context, while not an objective feature of the situation in which the policeman is acting, is an ever-present symbolic backdrop to all his activities that is recognized and taken into account by the participants involved in the situation with the policeman. This symbolic backdrop is of critical importance in understanding the policeman's role and the interactions he is involved in, and has an enormous influence on the character of the interaction that takes place between the police and the public.[11] For instance, when a policeman is called in to deal with a domestic dispute, his *access* to law enforcement and physical force as a possible means of dealing with the problem plays a very important part in his responses, and the responses of the other participants involved, even in those situations where neither of these two means is used and where no overt reference is made by the police or the public to either. For example, if a policeman in dealing with a domestic dispute politely asks one of the parties to the dispute to leave or to put down the weapon they are holding, there is not doubt in anyone's mind that if the policeman's request is not acceded to, the policeman may choose to resort to either law enforcement or physical force to ensure that his request is met.

In terms of this analysis of the police role any suggestion, on the basis of the fact that policemen seldom actually enforce the law or use physical force, that the police in reality serve a "social service" rather than a "law enforcement" function is clearly unfounded. Equally unfounded is any attempt to classify police activity into two classes, "social service" or "law enforcement". To suggest that a policeman is a "law-officer" only when he is actually enforcing the law is as misleading as to suggest that a surgeon is only a surgeon when he is actually performing surgery.

Within the conception of the police role we have developed, the empirical finding that the police spend at least fifty per cent of their time maintaining order without enforcing the law does not suggest that the police are "amateur social workers" or "peace officers" rather than "law officers", but that the symbolic presence of the police licence and capability has in most cases enabled the police to deal with the problems facing them without having to resort to law enforcement as a concrete course of action. As the symbolic backdrop of the police licence and capability is always present whenever a policeman responds to a problem, he is always responding as a policeman and not as a social worker, whether amateur or professional. Indeed the continual presence of the police licence and capability mitigates against him *ever* being able to play the role of a social worker as everyone (including the policeman) will know the ultimately he has access to the means uniquely accessible to policemen.

Following Bittner, we regard the police licence and capability as providing a "topical unity" to all the policeman's actions. Further, this unity does not occur regardless of the fact that the police are reactively organized (Black, 1968) and, therefore, do not control the problems that come to their attention, but to a considerable degree because of it. The public do not call the police, as those who emphasize the 24-hour availability of the police would argue, simply because they have no one else to whom to turn. In the vast majority of cases to which the police respond, it is clear that the police are *not* the only people who could have been called upon for help, but rather that they are, as Bittner has argued, viewed by those asking for assistance as the most appropriate people to call in terms of the resources available to them. For example, if one is involved in a quarrel with a relative and fears that serious personal injury is imminent, one does not want the services of a social worker and would not call for the assistance of a social worker even if one could be found instantly and would respond immediately. One wants a policeman, namely, someone with the authority and ability to restore order as quickly as possible. The social worker may be much better equipped to isolate the cause of the problem and work towards a long term solution, but he is not likely to be as effective as the policeman in resolving the present crisis of the moment. The 24-hour availability of the police, far from being the source of the distinctive character of the police role, is, it seems, a consequence of it. It is because the police licence and capability place the police in a unique position to handle a wide variety of crisis situations (cf. Bittner, 1967) that the police have evolved into a 24-hour emergency trouble-shooting service.

The common sense view of the police as law enforcers and crime fighters contains an important element of truth that has recently been obscured as a result of the interpretations that have been made of the findings of studies analyzing police activity. Our concerns in this paper has been an attempt to rediscover it.

ENDNOTES

*   An earlier version of this paper was presented at the Annual Meeting of the Canadian Sociology and Anthropology Association, August 1974, in Toronto, under the title "The Police Image".

1.   While Parsons' theoretical developments have been subjected to considerable and very telling criticism, the elements of the action frame of reference itself have generally been accepted without modification by most critics, with the exception of those who advocate a *strictly* behaviourist approach to human action.

2.   For purposes of this paper, it is not necessary to consider the other two features of an action frame of reference considered by Parsons.

3.   While the element of conditions is not specifically mentioned in the debate, it is clearly implied.

4.   What Parsons in the passage cited above refers to as the "radical positivistic position".

5.   The notion of State agents is used here in the sense in which Weber uses the concept "administrative staff". (1964: 324-5)

6.   The *Royal Canadian Mounted Police Act*, Revised Statutues of Canada, 1970, Chapter R-9, Section 18.

7.   A legal responsibility or duty to take *positive* action has generally not been inposed via the criminal law power. In Canada, for example, the *Criminal Code* (Revised Statutes of Canada: 1970, chapter C-34) does not deal with the duty of the police officer to maintain order; rather, this duty is imposed, as noted above, by the various police acts. (The *Code* generally refers to the powers of peace officers, which includes certain officials other than police officers. For present purposes, however, the term police officer will be used.) As regards non-police officers, the *Code* does specify a positive obligation to assist a police officer in the execution of his duty when one is called upon to do so (section 118, para. (b)) as well as a duty to prevent the commission of treason (subsection 50(1), para. (b)) but there is no general legal duty imposed with regard to the maintenance of order. It is significant to note, however, that at common law, misprison of felony (an omission to report a felony to the police) was a misdemeanour. This offence was abolished in England by the Criminal Law Act 1967 (Smith and Hagan, 1973:597). At common law, the powers of the police were similar to those of the ordinary citizen.

8.   In Canada, for example, under the *Criminal Code*, a police officer may issue an appearance notice (section 451 and subsection 452(1), para. (e)) or may, along with any person, lay an information before a justice of the police (section 455;

cf. subsection 452(1), para. (d)) who may in turn issue a summons (section 455.3). The procedure for the issuance of a warrant for the arrest of an accused is set out in section 455.3, with the warranr to be exercised by the police officer to whom it is directed (subsection 456.3(2)). The legal powers of a police officer to arrest without a warrant (section 450) are much broader than those of persons who are not police officers (section 449).

9. This orientation and ability to find a law that has been breached is particularly evident in detective work.

10. In Canada, for example, the *Criminal Code* provides for the justifiable use of force by persons acting under legal authority, including (but not exclusively) police officers (section 25). Other provisions in the *Code* deal with the *limited* rights of all persons to use force in order to prevent the commission of certain offences (section 27) and to prevent a breach of the peace (section 30).

11. One of the more visible aspects of this symbolic backdrop is the police uniform (cf. Bickman, 1974: Toch, 1965).

REFERENCES

Banton, M., 1964. *The Policeman in the Community*. London: Tavistock Publications.

Bickman, L., 1974. "The Social Power of a Uniform." *Journal of Applied Social Psychology, 4*, 47-61.

Bittner, E., 1967. "The Police on Skid-Row: A Study of Peace Keeping." *American Sociological Review, 32*, 699-715.

_____, 1970. *The Functions of the Police in Modern Society: A Review of Background Factors, Current Practices, and Possible Role Models*. Chevy Chase, Md.: National Institute of Mental Health, Centre for Studies of Crime and Delinquency.

Black, D. J., 1968. *Police Encounters and Social Organization: An Observational Study*. Unpublished Ph.D. Dissertation, University of California, Berkeley.

Critchley, T. A., 1967. *A History of the Police in England and Wales 900-1966*. London: Constable and Co.

Cumming, E., Cumming, I. and Edell, L., 1964. "Policeman as Philosopher, Guide and Friend." *Social Problems, 12*, 276-286.

Hobbes, T., 1968. *Leviathan*. Aylesbury, Bucks: Penguin Books.

Hughes, E. C., 1958. *Men and Their Work*, New York: Free Press of Glencoe.

Parsons, T., 1968. *The Structure of Social Action*. New York: Free Press of Glencoe.

The Presiden's Commission on Law Enforcement and Administration of Justice, 1967. *Task Force Report: The Police*, Washington, D.C.: U.S. Government Printing Office.

Reiss, A. J., Jr., 1971. *The Police and the Public*. New Haven, Conn: Yale University Press.

Shearing, C. D., 1974. "Dial-a-Cop: A Study of Police Mobilization" in *Crime Prevention and Social Defence*. (R. L. Akers and E. Sagarin, eds.). New York: Praeger.

Smith, J.D. and HOGAN, B., 1973. *Criminal Law*. (3rd ed.). London: Butterworth's.

The Task Force on Policing in Ontario: Report to the Solicitor General, 1974. Toronto: Queen's Printer.

Toch, H. 1965. "Psychological Consequences of the Police Role." *Police, 10* (Sept.-Oct.), 22-25.

Weber, M. 1964. *The Theory of Social and Economic Organization*. (A. M. Henderson and T. Parsons, trans.) New York: Free Press of Glencoe.

Wilson, J. Q. 1968. *Varieties of Police Behaviour: The Management of Law and Order in Eight Communities*. Cambridge, Mass: Harvard University Press.

CHAPTER 10
Regulating An Urban Order: Policing Pathologies in the Carceral City

K.R.E. McCormick
L.A. Visano

THE URBAN ORDER: CONSTRUCTING THE PATHOGENIC CITY

The relationship between urbanization and control continues to be a major focus of criminological inquiry. A study of urban processes is basic to an understanding of social order. Clearly, cities are special communities that organize, allocate and integrate tasks necessary for the maintenance of a normative social order.

Urban sociology reflects a diverse appreciation of the phenomena of social order. An overview of the early sociological understanding and current police practices will yield some interesting conceptual insights into the problematic relationship between control and the city. Sociological and criminological contributions are reflective of long-held biases about the nature of the city, assumptions that frame common-sense notions which have been conveniently exploited by norm enforcers like child savers, crusaders, politicians, police officials, urban planners, etc. As will be argued in this paper, the so-called urban malaise that plagues large cities and their inner-city districts is a mythology that fits well within the calculus of policing strategies. Throughout history various campaigns have been launched to sanitize the inner city of its imputed criminogenic features—the social disorganization, anonymity, segmented social relationships, traffic of large numbers of suspicious or, more euphemistically, "different" people; to name only a few characteristics which theorists and practitioners alike tend to delineate.

Despite their differences, classical theorists of the nineteenth century were in no doubt as to the crucial impact of urbanization in transforming the structure of social relations. In analysing the qualitative experiences of new urban populations, the early writers were fundamentally concerned with the distinctions between traditional (rural) and modern (urban) communities. For example, simplicity and complexity, field and factory, *Gemeinschaft* and the more impersonal *Gesselschaft* were contrasted; Durkheimian notions of mechanical and organic solidarities were related to the division of labour. Typically, urbanization introduced forced forms of social cohesion based on exchange relationships.

For Marx and Engels, the structure of social relations attendant with urbanization was a blessing of dubious value. On the one hand, urbanization provided an indispensable environment—necessary stage for the generation of a revolutionary force and consciousness. On the other hand, these same historical processes transformed workers into appendages of the machine; pushing working class families into dense and squalid districts. The new industrial urban order with its contradictions, alienation and powerlessness was seen to be a fertile site for deviance, that is, for "criminogenic" proclivities.

Likewise, Weberian analyses noted the dissolution of the feudal order; new rational and bureaucratic forces had produced a retrograde urban environment. The negative effects of increasing bureaucratization were also expressed in terms of alienation. In exploring the development of legal authority, Weber commented on the emerging impersonal and legalistic norms that constituted the institutional structures of authority. Central to this discussion of the impersonal order is the coercive apparatus of the state. Weber observed that the "city often represents a locality and a dense settlement of dwellings forming a colony so extensive that personal reciprocal acquaintance of inhabitants is lacking" (1958:65). But, the city, according to Weber, encourages individuality, innovation and diverse life-styles (Sennett, 1969:6).

Similarly, modern city life for Simmel consisted of a rapid flow of events, dense living conditions and constant interactions which result in an overwhelming intensification of nervous stimulation. This in turn produces a blasé attitude (Simmel, 1969: 51), an impoverishment of creative drives, frustration and powerlessness. Too many demands are placed on the urbanite. Accordingly, personal relationships emerge which are rational, functional, segmented, specialized and exchange-oriented. Underlying the social order of the city lies the ceaseless conflict and hostility of each person against every other. Simmel attributed these traits to products of an urban condition that are essentially social psychological in nature. Despite these onerous constraints which produce estrangement, urban life for Simmel remained liberating. Formal controls such as the division of labour are more bearable than the coercive power of tradition with its overwhelming informal controls.

It is precisely within the Chicago School perspective within the sociology of crime, with its blending of insights derived from Durkheim, Weber and Simmel, as well as white male middle class value systems, that the problem of urban landscape assumed exaggerated significance.

The early Chicago School sought to examine the social processes which create trouble. The first large-scale research into deviance/crime developed within the Department of Sociology at the University of Chicago in the 1920s. Researchers at the University of Chicago shifted the perception of pathology from the personal to the social. Adverse economic and social conditions, broken families, poverty, inadequate housing, and increased immigration contributed to disorganization which ultimately led to deviance/crime. This social disorganization, the result of urbanization, was an immoral order and an expression of personal dislocation. As cities grew in size and density, impersonality, social distance and social disharmony increased. Adopting a monolithic conception of order, scholars at the Chicago School maintained that population increases were followed by competition and differentiation. The assumption that social disorganization gave rise to deviance/crime was related to a view of the actor as a passive recipient of basic drives and adverse social conditions.

In fact, Robert Park asserted that "social control was the central fact and central problem of society" (Turner, 1967:xi). The basis of social order—consensus, solidarity or cohesion (Park, 1955:72, 74)—is greatly altered by transformations of society, notably the rapid rise of cities and immigration. Social order, therefore, is severely threatened by the dispossessed, rootless and "discordant medley of hundreds of thousands of individuals without any personal relations" (North, 1926: 233-237).

As envisaged by Durkheim and Park, Louis Wirth argued:

> The bonds of kinship, of neighbourliness, and the sentiments arising out of living together for generations under a common folk tradition are likely to be absent, or at best, relatively weak in an aggregate, the members of which have such diverse origins and backgrounds. Under such circumstances, competition and formal control mechanisms furnish the substitutes for the bonds of solidarity that are relied upon to hold a folk society together (1964:70).

The city as "a relatively large, dense and permanent settlement of socially heterogeneous individuals" (ibid:66) could not provide the much needed single normative order (Park, 1955; Wirth, 1964:71; Suttles, 1972:29-30). Consequently, the attenuation of primary ties and consensus necessitated the reliance on formal controls to combat disturbances (Park et al., 1925:107), "irresponsibility and potential disorder" (Wirth, 1964:74). For Wirth, new integrative and consensual mechanisms such as law, bureaucracy, segregation of land use, professional norms, organized interest groups and the criminal justice system became the inevitable imperatives of urbanism.

For both Park and Wirth, the ascendancy of divisions of labour affected the structure of ties. Specifically, "impersonal, superficial transitory and segmental" secondary relations (ibid, 1964:79) were based on simple specialized, functional or utilitarian roles (Suttles, 1972:31). The operations of the pecuniary nexus led to predatory relationships and a greater dependency on formal organizations (Wellman and Leighton, 1978:6). Punctuality of services and material goods replaced personal relations as the basis for association (Wirth, 1964:76). Also, greater differentiation and specialization (ibid:74), and greater interactions with varied roles and personalities tend to break down simple class distinctions (ibid:75).

For Park and his contemporaries, urbanization spelled a loss of community. However, Park also foresaw its progressive and liberative consequences. That is, the breakdown of tradition mapped ways for releasing new energies and ambitions of a new social order (Park, 1955:121, 128-141). The city, despite its many challenges, was paradoxically quite attractive (ibid, 1955:201).

A concern for social order was coupled with a relentless and romantic search for the pre-urban community. Alluding to the central notion of the *pathogenic city,* the early Chicago School maintained that the disintegrating relationships between "individual" and "environment" contributed to trouble, disorder and unrest. Moreover, the popular culture in literature, the mass media oral traditions communicated messages of disease, sin and crime which were firmly entrenched in the stench of the city. Remarkably similar to Foucault's analysis of the politics of health, this renewed pathological orientation served to inspire a whole mythology, give rise to medical discourses of urban morbidity and to place under surveillance a whole range of urban development, constructions and institutions (Foucault, 1980:175).

For decades, systemic indictments of city life have proliferated regarding the physical growth and expansions of cities, as well as concomitant social and personality disorders. These new Sodoms and Gomorrahs were credited with debilitating moral orders; loss or decline of community; and lack of attachments. In contrast to rural areas, modern cities were perceived to be high risk settings as expressed in higher rates of crime, greater mental illness, sexual deviation, incorrigibility, concealment, and stimuli overload. Within an essentially structural functionalist causation model, the theme of social disorganization prevailed. The inner city, conditions of density, deteriorating old houses, diversity of population and lack of social services were causally related to degrees of social, moral and physical deterioration, that is, psychic disturbances and deviance. There is then a clear, albeit biased and simplistic image of the inner city as an area where misfits, dregs, the sediment of society live. The behaviours of these unruly, predatory and unprincipled individuals were "never socially regulated; no life organization worthy of the name is ever imposed on them" (Thomas, and Znaniecki, 1958 [1920]:295). They were beyond society, free from middle-class values, alienated, without satisfying contacts and forever producing disequilibrium (Yablonsky, 1962). The inner cities as bailiwicks of disease, criminality, poverty, and physical deterioration were perceived as contagious and hazardous to its inhabitants and passers-by alike.

Essentially, the work of the early Chicago School represented a renewed interest in ecology, the relationship between organisms and their environments. In this context, the term ecology specifically referred to the spatial and temporal distribution of crime within a given city or neighbourhood. Robert Park and Ernest Burgess were the first sociologists to systematically apply plant and animal ecology to societal analysis. In their analysis of Chicago in the 1920s and 1930s, Park and Burgess employ the concepts of natural areas, symbiotic balances, and deviance configurations within certain zones of the city. They focussed attention on the community and its effect on the individual. Using an anthropological methodology of description, Park studied the ecology of neighbourhoods, isolated pockets of poverty and social problems. He was convinced that factors in the environment produced deviance. The urban environment promoted crime by disorganizing the well respected notion of the family. Park further noted that socio-economic status varies with distance from the city centre. As migrants settle in old housing at the city centre, other groups move outward as status increases. Poverty combined with the exodus of the middle class from the city to the suburbs intensified deviance. Deviance—i.e., suicide, vice, crime and illegitimate pursuits—accompany congestion. Accordingly, areas in which populations are unstable and composed of a variety of racial and ethnic groups have higher percentages of immigration and weaker neighbourhood controls. To demonstrate that deviance/crime varies with physical and geographic spacing, Park, Burgess and McKenzie (1925), in their seminal text, *The City,* distinguish five major zones which they believed were characteristic of any city. They envisaged a scheme of concentric zones to analyse urban growth and its inherent social deviations. They include:

Zone 1: "The Loop" which is the central business district, the economic centre.

Zone 2: "The Zone of Transition," containing the rooming house district, underworld dens, brothels, Chinatown, Little Sicily and the Ghetto. This zone of deterioration was originally residential but business moved in and housing was cheap. It was interstitial—neither business nor residential.

Zone 3: "The Zone of Working Class Homes."

Zone 4: The residential zone of apartment buildings, flats, residential hotels on the fringe, and single family dwellings.

Zone 5: "The Commuter's Zone"—respectable suburbs.

These zones were believed to be the result of ecological processes, urbanization and migration. Deviance for Burgess and Park was located within geographic and social areas, that is delinquency areas. The inner areas of the city reflected economic uncertainties and pressures of urban processes.

Likewise Henry McKay and Clifford Shaw demonstrated that official rates of delinquency varied in Chicago and elsewhere. Rates of delinquency varied inversely in proportion to the centre of the city. High rate areas such as the "Loop" persisted over time, and even higher rates of delinquency were located in neighbourhoods experiencing rapid population changes, poverty and substandard housing. They lacked social stability, cohesion and effective social controls.

These areas near the centre of the city and near industrial subcentres were natural sites for gangs. Here truancy and delinquency predominated and more youths were arrested. Despite the changes in ethnic and racial compositions of these areas over time, they continued to be high delinquency areas. The persistence of high rates of crime and delinquency is attributable to the process through which deviance was "learned." Specifically, in some neighbourhoods pre-existing cultural patterns were transmitted to newcomers through their interactions with local residents.

In sum, central to the work of Shaw and McKay (1931) was the notion that deviance/crime emerges within the context of changing urban environments. Crime, manifested in social disorganization, was viewed as a product of decaying transitional neighbourhoods populated by alien cultures and diffuse cultural standards.

The social ecological perspective emerging out of the early Chicago school revealed a behavioural diversity which was linked to a generalized social pathology. It was argued that the city produces an anonymous milieu which facilitates deviant behaviour primarily because informal social controls are relatively weak. Areas of social disorganization were associated with values and cultural patterns supportive of delinquency.

Ecological studies indicated that illegal acts were most prevalent in areas characterized by low social cohesion, weak family ties, low socio-economic levels and high mobility rates. Subsequent cross-cultural studies have supported this thesis.

Lamentably, the above normative images of the city, held by both academics and supported by the dominant culture, have also informed police ideologies and framed their central conceptions guiding control gestures. Currently these images of the city frame the everyday experiences and cognitive maps of police officers and administrators. While performing their duties, officers apply common-sensical impressions regarding the constitution of order in the city. The city is recast as a socially constructed fact with discernible crime patterns.

THE CARCERAL CITY: FROM THE "DISEASED" TO THE CRIMINAL

The orthodoxy of pathologizing the city documents a tight congruence between urbanism and disorder. For criminology the physical and social environments had become identical, necessitating the same processes of control— the police. Historically, the city has always been carved according to "catchment" areas that are susceptible to considerable police attention. Within certain districts of the city, for example, the police equate territory with criminal typologies. Under the guise of a seductively simple and seemingly innocuous ideology of benevolent communal security, the police keep watch and are wary of "strangers" or "outsiders." Policing institutions in all social systems and in all times have deviantized, if not criminalized so called "unauthorized" personnel. A rather extensive literature exists to demonstrate that "suspiciousness" for the police incorporates such attributes as class, race, age, sexual orientation, gender, homelessness and transience—to name only a few of the features leading to increased vulnerability. Figure one highlights a few interrelated dimensions of police-citizen contacts on a number of analytic levels of inquiry.

Order in the city is maintained by armies of specialized functionaries who have easy and immediate access to resources of control such as a legal and legitimate monopoly over physical force. The regulation of public space has been appropriated by the police. That is, it has become the central responsibility of the modern police to keep the peace and sanction activities within "public" arteries. A particular order, however, is maintained and certain movements are monitored. The police role of keeping the peace requires a visible occupation of space and an attendant preoccupation with individuals and communities designated as "publicly" troublesome.

Figure 1
Interactional, Institutional and Structural Elements

THE PHYSICAL ENVIRONMENT	<<<>>>	POLICE ORGANIZATIONAL PRIORITIES
NEIGHBOURHOOD	v	
BUSINESS/COMMERCE	v	
TECHNOLOGY	v	
	v	
THE LAW	>>>>>>>>>	
	THE SITUATED ENCOUNTER	
^	WITNESSES, ROLES, VISIBILITY	
^		
^		
^		
THE SOCIAL ENVIRONMENT	<<<<<<< >>>>>>>>	OFFICER/CITIZEN CHARACTERISTICS
	^	KNOWLEDGE
	^	DEFINITIONS
	^	DEFERENCE
	^	CLASS, GENDER, RACE,
	^	SEXUAL ORIENTATION,
	^	AGE
	^	SUSPICIOUSNESS
IDEOLOGY OF PUBLIC AND PRIVATE TROUBLES	>>>>>>>>>>	CONSENT

The relationship between the public policing and the urban order is complex and interwoven. The same forces which created the modern city have also shaped processes of policing in western liberal societies. As a result of the twin forces of industrialization and mass migration, societal institutions of discipline have been transformed. Historically, modern policing is rooted deeply in the development of ideas about the city. According to Bellam (1971:245), the term "police" stems from the Greek word, "polis"—the "city." Essentially, the emergence of the police, that is, the creation of a central authority was a response of the privileged classes to perceived problems of unrest in urban settings.

As a result of the series of industrial revolutions in science, technology and agriculture, the Napoleonic Wars, the agrarian law reforms, etc. the cities in England during the seventeenth and eighteenth centuries experienced burgeoning dense populations, massive dislocations and migrations from rural areas, violent riots, and widespread popular discontent. As Mayhew (1967:34) describes, during the 1830s there were approximately 30,000 persons of "bad character infesting five of the principle [sic] towns in England." Consequently, civic associations like the Bow Street Horse and Foot Patrols, parish constables, and designated watchmen could not cope with this unprecedented social disorder (Amos, 1957:11-12). In 1829, a single police force for the Metropolitan London area was established, consisting of one thousand well- trained uniformed constables under the authority of Parliament (McDonnell, 1975:8)—the first modern police force. Parenthetically, this is not to suggest that elaborate systems of order maintenance did not previously exist; the ancient cities of Athens and Rome had substantial policing systems usually composed of slaves who kept "watch by day and night, alert for the menace of fire as well as malefactors" (Bellam, 1971:246).

The provisions of an effective control system required considerable investments and unified structures of administration. Policing the city had become a routine service after 1829. Much of the work of the police involved the supervision of public space primarily because there was virtually no other form of control over the source, destination and route of traffic. The related goals of control and safety were associated with urban policing. The enforcement role was conspicuous in regulating the movement of people, in delineating "appropriate" belongingness to the city and in compelling compliance to extant hegemonic standards. The physical presence of the police in the public domain played a major role in uniting as well as in separating different communities. As Sharp (1984:94) notes, the dangerous classes were associated with urbanism:

as the product of rapid industrialization and urbanization which, it was felt, had concentrated the lower orders in desperately poor and intrinsically dangerous masses. In the lowest quarters of every major city, it was thought, there existed a geographical area whose inhabitants lived mainly on the proceeds of crime, who enjoyed a lifestyle different from the bourgeoisie and the respectable poor....

Encounters with the police, for example, generated considerable hostility. The police mandate as constituted in case law and various police statutes over the century inexorably legitimated police intrusions in the main thoroughfares of cities. Policing the public streets was not simply a residual function, something officers do when they are not doing something else (Gardiner, 1969:51). Rather, patrolling the streets, according to police authorities serves to reduce major "street crimes" (Wilson, 1977:94). This city army, therefore, fortified a much needed order to protect the perceived threatened interests of powerful stakeholders in the city.

The police typically occupy long periods of their shifts concerned with activities on the street in order to control public space. It is imperative to note that the police are not mere passive pawns in an unfolding urban evolution, but rather remain active forces in shaping the politics of a seige mentality so characteristic of large urban centres. Interestingly, excessive territorial policing stimulates not only a convenient moral panic replete with mythologies that invites hysteria on the one hand and relentless deference to authority on the other.

The police have developed strategies and techniques of enforcing laws in the public sphere. A "fit" or correspondence between social behaviour and the socio-physical setting is first established. Judgments are made regarding the visibility, accessibility and stability of neighbourhoods. To what extent has the discourse on the physical environment been manipulated to facilitate further detection and control? Since the inception of the modern police, officers have been attending to features of the physical environment during the course of their routine work. On the basis of their collective wisdom and organizational priorities, the police have imposed sanctions on entire neighbourhoods located in areas designated as limited, "out of place"—such as gay and lesbian neighbourhoods, areas heavily travelled by various ethno/racial communities, youth-oriented sites like arcades, billiard halls, community centres and shopping malls, doughnut shops, public parks frequented by street transients, striking workers on picket lines, and subsidized housing projects. Organized police territorial surveillance satisfies both intelligence operations as well as the more highly publicized and distracting community relations efforts. Continued observations tend to alert the police to "strange" intrusions into the community. Since the public, according to police logic, fails to act as the eyes and the ears of the police, this more proactive police initiative is legitimated.

The street continues to be "an impersonal domain" (Suttles, 1968) controlled only occasionally by its residents and users. Instead, a centralized and highly bureaucratized para-military organization has over the decades claimed ownership over these concerns. Spatial arrangements are manipulated to constrain movements ostensibly in the interests of crime prevention and law enforcement. The physical space has always been controlled by the "occupiers" rather than the occupants of an area.

Surveillance and territoriality have been pivotal phenomena in maintaining an "urban order," that is, in creating the "carceral city." The former incorporates techniques of keeping "offensive" elements under observation; the latter connotes the processes of marking, protecting and eventually possessing the space under scrutiny. In other words, the parts of the city are "colonized" often by foreign interests disciplined according to the seductive and seemingly innocuous ideologies of benevolence and security. By keeping watch over "strangers" or "outsiders," policing institutions have always deviantized if not criminalized unauthorized personnel. In the area of police-informant exchanges, it is recognized by street transients who report regularly to the police, that police officers expect to be treated like landlords on public street-corners—extorting information as part of the rent to be collected. As brokers of information, the police permit certain individuals and groups to engage in illicit hustling activities provided that they share information (Visano, 1990, forthcoming). Technology, as an element of the physical space, also influences police decisions. Technological innovations have redefined the environment—providing it with new and expansive implications for social control (McCormick, 1991). The increased access to information has enhanced the brokerage of information, reduced response time, computerized records of local interactants, etc. In the city, familiarity with and access to local residents are mediated by technology.

Police technology permits greater intrusions into the lives of the more "publicly" visible while ignoring swindlers hiding behind more private corporate castles. Crimes by the latter seem undetectable especially since corporations are invisible, untouchable and very well protected by law and in the culture of private property.

Police activities tend to be concentrated in "central most" behaviour settings. These milieux include places of greater mobility — usually commercial and business districts. Within these focal points street crimes are dealt with swiftly in an effort to avoid the interruption of trade or commerce. Control over these public spaces becomes crucial to the police in maintaining the smooth flow and circulation of capital, that is, in protecting the private property of the powerful.

On the other hand, economically depressed neighbourhoods are treated as semi-public. Traditionally, privacy for the disadvantaged was never respected by the police. Contrast, for example, the obvious difference in the treatment of street transients and corporate suite executives by the police. In fact, areas replete with housing projects are considered to be sociofugal — inhibiting or discouraging contacts with the police; the privileged areas remain sociopetal—fostering healthy contacts. These different locations contextualize police—public encounters. It is certainly interesting to witness not only the contradictions related to enforcement practices, but to listen to the arguments bifurcating space into public and private. Correspondingly, crime is also dichotomized respectively according to well enshrined liberal protections of peace, privacy or property. To elaborate, domestic violence, on the one hand, is often trivialized as a private matter just as is gay bashing by a group of thugs in a public park or even wholesale corporate corruption. On the other hand, such examples of public order troubles including the violation of traffic laws, especially the failure to stop when requested by the police, have recently resulted in the fatal shootings of people of colour in Toronto and Montreal; the beatings of Aboriginal people charged with public intoxication; or the co-ordinated campaign of torture as experienced by Rodney King in Los Angeles. The urban disturbances in Los Angeles in 1992 like the riots of the 1960s clearly are responses to the structural conditions of inequality. These police-sparked riots are then used by authorities to further justify oppression by appealing to convenient claims of threats to public order. These disturbances are symbolically reproduced and tragically articulated by the conduct of the police, often acting like an occupying foreign force of "public" custodians determined to find trouble in the public domain while legally impotent, culturally silenced and organizationally incompetent to investigate crimes protected by institutions of private property.

As Wenninger and Clark (1967:162) note, the character of the relationship between police forces and the communities in which they operate determines sanctions. Since police officers routinely interact with the public, any explanation of police behaviour must take into account their "mutual interpositional organizations" (Goffman, 1961), their respective social environments. Banton (1964) and Wilson (1977) equally argue that the adoption of a police role or style is largely contingent upon the nature of the community with reference to the degree of imputed moral consensus. Quinney (1970) and Buckner (1967) point out that the social cohesion of the community and the gradual habituation of the police to the needs of the local population facilitate order maintenance without resorting to the law enforcement option. Conflicts, however, emerge whenever the concentration of police presence is not fully clarified to a local community. Public suspicion of police-discriminatory behaviour surfaces; symbols of legitimate authority are replaced with images of coercion. The failure of the police to respond to local community expectations has led to the mobilization of citizen participation in trying to re-claim their respective public "turf." Despite the large quantity of police-public contacts on a daily basis, the quality of these encounters remains segmented, uni-dimensional and often catering to police investigative purposes. A diversification of contacts is long overdue in order to restore a modicum of public confidence in policing. Informal measures are often overshadowed by organizational criteria which set a rigid agenda for police-public contacts.

Police strategies consist of various mechanisms to control the openness and closedness of an area. Spatial norms conducive to surveillance are adopted. The patrolled area is an "interactional territory" with unambiguous boundaries and rules regarding entry and egress. Access is selectively controlled in the cruiser and its extension—the controlled neighbourhood. In his erudite study, Foucault (1977) details interesting conceptual links between "proxemics" and order/ "discipline." For Foucault, discipline proceeds from the distribution of individuals in space by employing a number of integrated techniques. To elucidate, techniques which organize and distribute space include "enclosures" and "partitions" (ibid:141-142) which aim to effect ultimate order, and

> to establish presences and absences, to know where and how to locate individuals, to set up useful communications, to interrupt others, to be able at each moment to supervise the conduct of each individual, to assess it, to judge it, to calculate its qualities or merits. (ibid: 143)

The modern urban police, as a disciplinary tool, operates within enclosed and segmented spaces supervising movements, recording events and locating individuals (ibid: 197). Although patrol work is an activity which is frequently perceived by the public to be relatively harmless and trivial, police patrols assure "the ordering of multiplicities" (ibid: 218). Order demands that the police be concerned with everything that happens including "unimportant events" (ibid: 213) in areas defined as suspicious within the public domain. Historically,

Palmer (1988:9) argues that the great majority of arrests in the public domain are for drunks, vagrants, and disorderly characters, not serious criminals. In fact Palmer suggests that the new police with their uncompromising vigilance over public behaviour were never interested in reducing crime nor preventing disorder, but rather according to the logic of E.P.Thompson, in "making of the English working class." Although the police claim to represent the interests of a law abiding citizenry, it is as Bunyon (1976:289) points out, that the police have always been opposed to the interests of the working class as a whole.

The relationship between urbanization and social order cannot be disputed. But, as argued by the classical writers, the conditions of urban life certainly do not necessarily follow from linking disorganization with urbanism. Much of the disorganization thesis involves a tendency towards tautological reasoning in that the forms of behaviour explained by the urban conditions are used, at the same time, to demonstrate the behaviour's existence. In other words, social relations in the community are explained by the conditions of living in that community .

Recently, more sophisticated analyses of urbanism have endowed the concept with wider meanings to include the existence of non-ecological factors, such as socio-economic level, ethnicity, stages in life cycle, gender, values, age, etc. Rapid migration has not, for example, directly produced alienation, anomie or other symptoms of social disorganization. Urbanism may thus be a contributing factor, not a major cause, of certain social conditions to which systems of order and control respond. Attempts ought to be directed towards the examination of the relevance of the problems of the city, not merely the city as a locus of the problems, and towards considerations of the city as a constituent and dominant part of a complex society .

The links between crime and the urban order are conceptually threadbare and often reduced to normative orientations. The notion that urban life is composed of pluralities of different worlds is blurred, understated, or covered up. Order is far too frequently decontextualized and too readily extricated from the larger processes of urbanization, industrialization, the attendant divisions of labour, changing property relations or the transformation of space, etc., which loom large in structures of social relations. Moreover, given the ceaseless conflicts over scarce resources, social order as a general, vague and all-embracing frame of reference for identifying, arranging and interpreting remains relatively problematic. Simply stated, social order emerges within "a nexus of multiple involvements" of networks promoting their own interests and concerns. What warrants further empirical investigation, therefore, is not only social order and its often neglected structural embeddedness but, more precisely, the nature of competing orders, inevitable intersections and structural linkages of communities in conflict or those simply different. Towards this end, we ought to consider network analysis.

CONCLUSION: CARCERAL CONNECTIONS

The above overview suggests that social order and its attendant controls exist within certain relational environments—notably the community. But the concept of community has been subject to endless and confusing debates. Urbanization, therefore, is characterized neither by the withering away of primary relationships and the triumph of secondary relationships, nor only by the persistence of localized, autonomous kinship, friendship or neighbourhood associations. More appropriately, urbanization is accompanied by a growth of specialized networks of social relations extending across wide areas which intersect, overlap or interact in various complicated ways. That is, the lowering of spatial barriers and the increased freedom to choose social relations have led to a proliferation of personal and informational communities consisting of networks of complicated ties.

Many of the assumptions about deviance, crime and control persist within a dominant normative paradigm which alludes unyieldingly to integration and consensus. The problematic nature of order within the urban context has not been fully explored. Instead, studies proceed to accept the prevailing white male middle-class heterosexualist conception of conformity while devaluing differences.

Great efforts have been directed towards modifying and, at times, refuting some of the above observations. For many, the much celebrated and nostalgically reconstructed images of normative social order of rural communities have been over-estimated (Pearson, 1979:200). In fact, this sense of solidarity was perhaps never available to the mass of men and women, but only to a small elite of landowners and the propertied. Class stratification, status rivalry and intense social conflict were equally capable of developing in pre-urban, rural peasant environments. Moreover, this contrast of social orders may simply remain a heuristic device exercised for political purposes especially since some people are of the city, but not in it; and others are in the city, but not of it. The mosaics of subcultures in the city fractionate a community-wide normative order into parochial varieties of segmented units.

This paper problematizes the relationship between the need for order in the city and the inherent pathogenic character of the city. Pathologies are created, in effect, to cause trouble that invariably invites intervention and control. For the powerful the law is a convenient tool to pre-empt the spread of urban unrest. Law localizes conflict and distracts attention from more structured conditions of injustice. The law disguises contradictions within the economic order and the history of the state's political economy. The city today is more than the laboratory of the Chicago School or a playground to be visited by the privileged. The city is part of the cultural capital that is exploited metaphorically and condemned publicly in order to support strategies of confinement, dispersal and accommodation. The city has become part of the rhetoric of law and the polemic of politicians. Fear of the city is manipulated by those who have become experts only in the public domain—the police. Crimes against class, gender and race, for example remain well hidden in the private domain, conveniently well beyond the vigilance let alone the reach of the police.

As Reiner (1985:2) suggests:

> In a society which is divided on class, ethnic, gender and other dimensions of inequality, the impact of the laws even if they are formulated and enforced quite impartially and universally will produce those divisions. This is the point encapsulated in Anatole France's celebrated aphorism: "The law in its majesty equally forbids the rich, as well as the poor, to sleep under bridges, to beg in the streets, and to steal bread."

REFERENCES

Amos, M. 1957. *British Criminal Justice*. London: Longman's.

Banton, M. 1964. *The Policeman in the Community*. London: Tavistock.

Bellam, R. 1971. *The Evolving City*. Toronto: Copp Clark.

Buckner, H. 1967. *The Police: The Culture of A Social Control Agency*. Unpublished doctoral dissertation, University of California at Berkeley.

Bunyon, T. 1976. *The Political Police in Britain*. London: Julian Friedmann.

Foucault,M. 1980. *Power and Knowledge: Selected Interviews and Other Writings 1972-1977*. Edited by C. Gordon. N.Y.: Vintage.

_____, 1977. *Discipline and Punish*. N.Y.: Pantheon.

Gardiner, J. 1969. *Traffic and the Police*. Cambridge: Harvard University Press.

Goffman. E. 1961. *Encounters: Two Studies in the Sociology of Interaction*. Indianapolis: Bobbs-Merrill.

Mayhew, H. 1967. *London Labour and the London Poor*. London: Frank Cass.

McCormick, K. 1991. *Technological Intrusions: A Critical Examination of Computer Applications in Qualitative Sociology*. Research Review Paper, York University.

McDowell, C. 1975. *Police in the Community*. Cincinnati: W.H.Anderson.

North,C. 1926. "The City as a Community: An Introduction to a Research Project." In E. Burgess (ed.) *Urban Community*. Chicago: University of Chicago.

Palmer, S. 1988. *Police and Protest in England and Ireland:1780-1850*. N.Y.: Cambridge University Press.

Park, R. 1955. *Human Communities*. N.Y.: Free Press.

_____, E. Burgess and R. McKenzie. 1925. *The City*. Chicago: University of Chicago.

Pearson, G. 1979. *The Deviant Imagination*. London: Macmillan.

Quinney, R. 1970. *The Social Reality of Crime*. Boston: Brown, Little and Company.

Reiner, R. 1985. *The Politics of the Police*. Brighton, Sussex: Wheatsheaf.

Sennett, R. 1969. *Classic Essays on the Culture of Cities*. N.Y.: Appleton-Century-Crofts.

Sharpe, J. 1984. *Crime in Early Modern England: 1550-1750*. N.Y.: Longman.

Shaw, C. and H. McKay, 1931. *Social Factors in Juvenile Delinquency*. Washington, D.C.: U.S. Government Printing House.

Simmel, G. 1969. *The Sociology of Georg Simmel*. Edited by K.Wolff. N.Y.: Free Press.

Suttles, G. 1968. *The Social Order of the Slum*. Chicago: University of Chicago.

———— 1972. *The Social Construction of Communities*. Chicago: University of Chicago.

Thomas, W. and F. Znaniecki. [1920],1958. *The Polish Peasant in Europe and America* Boston: Badger.

Turner, R. 1967. *Robert Park: Selected Papers*. Chicago: University of Chicago.

Visano, L. 1990. "Crime as a Negotiable Commodity: The Police Use of Informers." *Journal of Human Justice*. v.2, no.1 (Autumn).

———— (forthcoming) *Beyond the Text*. Toronto: Butterworth.

Weber, M. 1958. *The City*. (Translated and edited by D. Martindale and G.Neuwirth). N.Y.: Free Press.

Wellman, B. and B. Leighton. 1978. " Networks, Neighbourhoods and Communities" Research Paper #97, Centre for Urban and Community Studies, University of Toronto.

Wenninger, E. and J. Clark. 1967. "A Theoretical Orientation for Police Studies." In *Juvenile Gangs in Context*. M.W. Klein (ed.). Englewood Cliffs: Prentice-Hall.

Wilson, J. 1977. *Thinking About Crime*. N.Y.: Random House.

Wirth, L. 1964. "Urbanism as a Way of Life." In *Louis Wirth: On Cities and Social Life* by A. Reiss (ed.). Chicago: University of Chicago.

Yablonsky, L. 1962. *The Violent Gang*. N.Y.: Macmillan.

DISCRETION, STYLES AND ENCOUNTERS

CHAPTER 11
The Management of Violence by Police Patrol Officers

DAVID H. BAYLEY
JAMES GAROFALO

This study examines the dynamics of potentially violent encounters between police and public. It is based on systematic observation of about 350 eight-hour tours of duty by patrol officers in three precincts of New York City during the summer of 1986. It compares the tactics and resulting outcomes found in encounters handled, respectively, by patrol officers believed by their peers to be especially skilled at minimizing violence and a cross section of all other patrol offcers. Its major conclusions are (1) violence, even verbal aggression, is relatively rare in police work; (2) most conflict is dampened by the arrival of the police, leaving little scope for the use of defusing tactics; and (3) the behavior of officers judged by colleagues to be skilled in minimizing violence is measurably different from the behavior of "average" patrol officers, and in ways that suggest that colleagues may be good judges of on-street performance.

American police are running scared. They are afraid that routine patrol encounters with the public, the mainstay of policing, will explode unpredictably into violence, causing injury to police and citizens and polarizing community sentiment about the propriety of police action. The effects are especially serious and unsettling when the citizens involved are minorities. Latent hostilities between police and community may be rekindled in an instant, and years of patient bridge-building lost.

Police, too, can be caught up and changed. They become wary of individual contacts with the public, preferring to act in groups; they become defensive, resenting any commentary by "outsiders" about their actions; they become preemptive and adversarial in approach on the street. Violent encounters may also have catastrophic financial effects on individual police officers as well as entire police departments as a result of criminal and civil liability actions.

With so much at stake, it is not surprising that police departments across the country are profoundly concerned with minimizing the potential for violence in patrol encounters with the public. They would especially like to know whether there are tactics that officers can adopt to avoid violence, perhaps even defuse it when it cannot be avoided. The research we report here was meant to provide this sort of information.

We set out to determine the frequency of violent encounters in patrol work, the determinants of police use of force, and whether particular tactics employed by patrol officers are more likely than others to reduce (or increase) violence during encounters with citizens. To answer these questions, we observed a large number of police-citizen encounters. Unlike most observational studies of patrol work, we were concerned not only with the determinants of police action but also with the effectiveness of that action (Friedrich, 1977, 1980; Geller, 1985; Lundman, 1974; Reiss, 1971; Sherman, 1980; Sykes and Brent, 1983). That is, we tried to describe as accurately as possible the actions police officers took and the outcomes that resulted (McIver and Parks, 1983; Teplin, 1984).

Police officers themselves believe that tactics can make a great difference. They claim repeatedly that experience teaches important lessons about how to handle the varied and unpredictable work of patrol (Bayley and Bittner, 1985). Often this is illustrated with anecdotes about colleagues who defused situations with clever retorts, humorous asides, or unexpected approaches. Indeed, it is almost an article of faith in police circles that the skills of policing, especially encounter tactics, are learned exclusively on the job and that formal training, as in police academies, is largely irrelevant.

Police officers also believe that they know who the really skilled officers are (Geller, 1985; Rubinstein, 1973; Scharf and Binder, 1983; Wambaugh, 1970). Patrol-officers live in a very judgmental world. Their actions are continually observed by other officers—partners, colleagues, backup teams, support personnel—and performance is continually commented on, sometimes pointedly and cruelly. The good as well as the bad performers are thought to be well known in the squad rooms of American police stations.

If police can truly discern the skilled from the unskilled officer in handling potentially violent encounters, the exciting possibility emerges that the seeds of improved performance are already planted within the police community.

Strategies for change can utilize role models who are already accepted by the rank and file. The tactical effectiveness of patrol personnel can be raised, if this is true, using the resources of the institution itself.

Accordingly, our research also sought to determine whether patrol officers recognize differences in performance among their peers. To do this, we added a new wrinkle to standard observational methodology. We compared the performance of patrol officers who had been designated by their peers as being especially skilled at handling potentially violent situations with the performance of a cross section of all others. In this way we hoped to uncover the "trade secrets," if any, of effective patrol officers.

Imbedded in this approach is an interesting methodological question: Are patrol officers willing to identify colleagues with respect to quality of performance? If so, we can answer another interesting question: Do peer evaluations of skill agree with more general and impersonal assessments made by police supervisors? Police officers complain endlessly that their street skills are not appreciated by supervisors. Their work, so they claim, is judged by vague criteria unrelated to the exigencies of their workaday world (Brown, 1981; Ianni and Reuss-Ianni, 1984). Although we asked patrol officers to identify colleagues who were particularly adept at handling conflict situations, rather than being "good" patrol officers in general, we think it is fair to compare their evaluations with more broadly based departmental ones because the ability to handle such situations is considered among police to be the gravest test of skill, the very "art of policing." There is likely to be a coincidence of judgments about this specific skill and more general ones, and judgments about this skill might often be made by officers on the basis of inferences from general performance, since opportunities to observe colleagues in conflict situations are probably limited.

METHODOLOGY

The research was carried out in New York City during the summer of 1986. Observations of patrol work were made in three precincts. Generalizations about the behavior of patrol officers in New York City cannot be made from these data because no attempt was made to choose precincts that were representative of New York City policing. Rather, we tried to maximize opportunities for observing problematic patrol encounters. Consequently, we selected three precincts that were busy, mixed in ethnicity, and characterized by a diverse mixture of crime and calls for police service.[2] For the same reason, we observed patrolling almost exclusively during the busiest shift, 4 p.m. to midnight.

Because we wanted to observe not only a large number of potentially violent encounters but encounters handled, respectively, by officers who were considered especially skilled and by officers who were not, the key step was drawing the sample of the presumptively skilled. To do this, we solicited the help of patrol officers at roll calls for all shifts in each of the three precincts. Because New York patrol officers rotate through three shifts over several weeks, virtually all patrol personnel were candidates for evening-shift observation.

After being introduced, we explained the purpose and design of the research. We emphasized that this was not a study of "good" versus "bad" officers; we wanted to know the names of only superior performers. We promised that the names of the designated officers would be known only to the two principal investigators.

After answering questions, we asked each officer to write down the names of three persons, other than herself or himself, assigned to radio cars in the precinct who the officer considered to be particularly skilled at handling conflict situations. Three names were requested to guard against partners being named exclusively. Officers were asked to make their selections on the spot.

The answer to our methodological question can now be given: Patrol officers were willing to name colleagues they considered superior performers. Specifically, they identified fellow officers, on a confidential basis, who they believed were especially skilled at handling conflict in encounters with citizens. Out of approximately 165 officers solicited, only a dozen refused to respond or returned invalid ballots.

Although a group of superior performers stood out in the tally, opinions were scattered. In shifts of approximately 25 officers, the maximum votes anyone received was rarely more than 8. We considered as more skilled those officers who received four or more votes. We chose 10 in each precinct plus 3 or 4 alternates. We refer to this group as experimental subject officers (ESOs). The comparison group, also numbering 10 per precinct (but with a larger number of alternates), was selected from all other patrol officers in the precinct who had not received more than one vote as being especially skilled. Those officers are referred to as comparison subject officers (CSOs).

Because New York City radio cars are staffed by two officers, it was important for observers to code whether actions were taken by subject officers, who could be either experimental or comparison, or by partners. Altogether, we observed 24 ESOs and 38 CSOs, including 5 alternates among the ESOs and 11 among the CSOs. Alternates substituted for originally designated officers who were not available due to transfer, leave, sickness, training, and so forth. We were less stringent about using alternates for CSOs than for ESOs because the CSOs and their alternates were both basically drawn from a cross section of all officers who had not been designated as especially skilled.

Most of the observations were conducted by six mature students in criminal justice programs in the Albany and New York City areas. After being trained on procedures and instruments, the observers rode with officers for several practice shifts and were given individual feedback on this practice work. They were then supplied with rosters of assignments for successive two-week periods specifying precinct, shift, subject officer, and up to five alternates. They were not told whether a subject officer was in the experimental or comparison group.

Observations were recorded on detailed schedules that had been field-tested in previous research by Bayley (1986). Adapted from the schedule used by Reiss for the President's Commission on Law Enforcement and Administration of Justice in the mid-1960s (see Black and Reiss, 1967), the instrument enabled observers to distinguish actions taken by patrol officers at different stages during an encounter.

Police officers do not act only once in an encounter, they act several times according to the changing requirements of involvement. In all except the briefest of encounters, it is possible to distinguish actions of officers at initial contact, in the middle as they search for an appropriate resolution, and at leaving. We call these stages, respectively, contact, processing, and exit. Although the importance of this point has been recognized by others, it has rarely been incorporated into observational research (Goldstein, 1977; Scharf and Binder, 1983; Sykes and Brent, 1983). Bayley's (1986) mapping of police tactics using this instrument had shown that patrol officers chose from among a far larger array of actions than all but a handful of researchers had considered (McIver and Parks, 1983; Whitaker, 1982).

Observers were instructed to record information about all police-citizen encounters involving disputes, intervention by the police to apply the law against specific individuals, and all police attempts to question suspicious persons. Wanting to err on the side of inclusiveness, we instructed observers to record the details of any encounter about which they were uncertain. In addition, the observers kept shift summaries in which they noted the full range of officer actions (excepting only meal breaks, informal conversations with others, and the like).

Thus, the events described in detail in our data set do not cover all the work that the patrol officers performed. In fact, only about one-third of the events noted on the shift summaries were coded for our study. The other events represent a diversity of police actions, most involving no police-citizen contact: running checks on suspicious unoccupied vehicles, radio calls that were cancelled while the officers were enroute, and false burglar alarms, for example. Other excluded events did involve police-citizen contact, but in contexts in which the potential for conflict was virtually nonexistent: assisting emergency medical services with a sick person, taking an incident report for a "cold" crime, giving directions, and so forth.

The data set used in our analyses consists of 467 police-citizen encounters that had at least some possibility of resulting in violence. We refer to these as *potentially violent mobilizations, or PVMs.*[3]

The research findings are presented in four sections. First, we estimate the prevalence of violence in patrol work. Second, we analyze the factors associated with the use of force in police-citizen encounters. Third, we compare the performance of patrol officers designated as especially skilled with the performance of a cross section of all others. Fourth, we examine the extent of agreement between the performance evaluations made by peers and supervisors. After presenting the findings, we discuss their implications for improving officer performance in police-citizen encounters.

VIOLENCE IN PATROL WORK

The unambiguous fact is that patrol officers rarely face violence in encounters with the public. They are only occasionally called to situations where it has occurred; it is seldom directed against them; and it produces few serious injuries either to police or the public. This does not mean, of course, that attention should not be given to such events, nor that precautions should not be taken against them. Even a single act of violence may have catastrophic consequences. But it does mean that the dangers of patrolling occur very episodically.[4]

In three-quarters of the 467 potentially violent incidents to which police responded, whether initiated proactively or through radio dispatch, there were no indications of violence, such as fighting, weapons, or criminal injuries. Since we studied only potentially violent mobilizations (PVMs), the proportion of mobilizations with indications of violence among all patrol jobs is even lower.

The other side of the coin is that in one-quarter of PVMs, officers had solid reasons for expecting violence. In addition, among the 255 PVMs initiated by radio dispatch, about half were deemed urgent or important by responding officers. They reacted with speed, though not necessarily with lights and sirens. Excitement, heightened readiness, and a surge of adrenalin are a part of the workaday life of patrol officers, even if subsequent events do not live up to expectations.

Among the 120 PVMs in which clear indications of violence existed at mobilization, 27% involved reports or observations of fighting in progress, 22% involved weapons, 3% involved injuries, and the remainder involved a variety of things, such as an emotionally disturbed person or a threatening crowd.

Thirty-six percent of the PVMs were initiated proactively by officers. As one might expect, police response to violent personal crimes, disputes, and disturbances occurs largely as the result of radio dispatch. Traffic stops, on the other hand, are mostly proactive.

On arrival at an incident, officers encountered visible conflict in 17% of the PVMs (n = 78). By and large, conflict discovered on arrival was between citizens. In only 4 of the 78 cases was the conflict between citizens and officials, including police already on the scene. In absolute numbers, out of 467 potentially violent mobilizations observed in New York City during approximately 350 eight-hour tours of duty, only 78 started with visible conflict.[5] Moreover, the conflict in most cases hardly qualified as violence. In 90% of the cases it was verbal or demonstrative, meaning threatening gestures at most. In only 8 of the 78 cases was the conflict physical. Contrary to radio-dispatch reports, weapons were rarely found on arrival (reported in 8% of all PVMs, found in 2%).

Forceful conflict occurred even more rarely between police and citizens during the course of an encounter. In only 42 encounters was force used by police against citizens or by citizens against police—37 and 11 cases, respectively (both kinds of force occurred in 6 cases).[6] The force used by police consisted almost exclusively of grabbing and restraining. Firearms were never used.

Correspondingly, injuries growing out of conflict between police and the public were also extremely rare; they occurred in only 5 of the 467 PVMs and involved 14 persons. All but two were minor—bruising rather than cuts or broken bones. Only three police officers were injured, all in minor ways.

Most of the PVMs involved traffic enforcement (33%) or intervention in interpersonal disputes (30%); another 8% were minor disturbances. Even though we observed high-crime precincts, violent crime accounted for only 6%

of all PVMs. Most of the violent crimes were domestic assaults (17 of 21). Major property crimes accounted for only 3% of the PVMs, and minor property crimes accounted for just 4%. These findings support the conclusions of other research that the most common judgmental situations facing patrol officers in American cities are disputes and traffic regulation (Bayley, 1986; McIver and Parks, 1983; Parks, 1980; Reiss, 1971; Vera Institute, 1977; Whitaker, 1982).

Among the 78 encounters in which conflict was occurring on police arrival, the distribution of types of incidents is markedly different from that for the total group encounters. Most conflict grew out of interpersonal disputes (38%), violent crimes (17%), and minor disturbances (10%). None of these incidents was a traffic stop.

In summary, on the basis of research designed to increase the amount of conflict observed, we found that patrol officers arrived at the scene of ongoing conflict about once every four and one-half working days, and most of that conflict was verbal only. Officers became involved in incidents in which either they or members of the public used physical force against each other about once every eight and one-third working days, and that force consisted mostly of grabbing, shoving, pushing, or restraining. The fact is that the opportunity to display superior skill in defusing conflicts occurs relatively rarely in patrol work.

EXPLAINING POLICE USE OF FORCE

The rareness of violence in patrol encounters limits our ability to determine whether particular tactics used by patrol officers raise or lower the likelihood of physical conflict. Thirty-seven encounters in which police used force is too small a number to permit analysis of tactical efficacy while controlling for factors that prior research has found to affect the outcome of police encounters, such as the substantive nature of the incident and the demeanor, age, and sex of the citizens involved (Black, 1980; Friedrich, 1980; Sherman, 1980). With only 37 cases, one cannot statistically hold these potentially influential factors constant and search for patterns of association with specific tactics at the contact, processing, and exit stages. In effect, the number of relevant independent variables overwhelms the number of events we had hoped to explain.

On the other hand, our data show clearly that the nature of the situation when the officers arrive has a major effect on the likelihood of force being used in the encounter. Police used force in 8% of the 467 encounters. When there was no overt conflict occurring at arrival, the police used force in 6% of the encounters, but when overt conflict was occurring, the figure reached 15% (chi-square = 7.15, p < .01, phi = .12).

Although the use of force by citizens against officers was even rarer than the use of force by police (11 cases versus 37), the initial situation also affected citizen use of force. Among encounters in which overt conflict was not occurring when the officers arrived, only 1% resulted in citizens using force against officers; when conflict was occurring, the rate was 9% (chi-square = 17.84, p <.01, phi = .20).

It is not surprising that police intervention in situations in which conflict is active has a greater likelihood of leading to the use of force, by police and by citizens. Citizens' tempers are flaring, and the participants in the conflict are often not receptive to calm reasoning. Officers are trained to establish their authority quickly in such situations, and they are also wary that the conflict could be redirected toward them. It is exactly in these types of situations that the kinds of police force most often found in our research (grabbing and restraining) are used by officers to restore order.

Despite the apparently strong effect of the nature of the initial situation that officers come upon, two caveats should be noted. First, while the existence of overt conflict at arrival raises the probability that officers will use force, the use of force even in these situations is not common. In 85% of such cases, the officers did not find it necessary to use force, which suggests that simply the arrival of the police is usually sufficient to quell conflict. Second, despite the higher probability of officers using force when conflict is occurring, most of the instances in which police did use force were not characterized by overt conflict at arrival (25 out of 37).

What we have is the common analytic problem of low base rates. Not only does the behavior that we seek to explain—police use of force—occur infrequently, but an apparently important explanatory variable—conflict occurring when police arrive—is also relatively uncommon.

The problem becomes very evident in multivariate analyses. We tried, for example, to conduct multiple regression analyses with police use of force as a dichotomized dependent variable and a group of dichotomized explanatory variables: existence of conflict when police arrived, whether the encounter took place in a public area, weapon possession by a citizen, drug or alcohol use by a citizen, whether a citizen directed obscene or insulting remarks or gestures at officers, presence of bystanders, use of various tactics (such as verbal ploys) by officers, and so forth. Results using three of the strongest predictors are shown in Table 1.

All three of the predictor variables in Table I (existence of conflict on arrival, possession of a weapon by a citizen, use of obscene or insulting remarks or gestures by a citizen) have statistically significant coefficients. The total R^2, however, is only .04. When we examine the numbers of cases affected by the predictor variables, these results are not surprising.

When none of the three predictor variables was "positive," only 6% of the encounters resulted in police use of force (Table 2). When any one factor was "positive," the proportion rises to 16%. With two or three factors "positive," the use-of-force rate is 23%. This illustrates that the explanatory factors have sizable effects when they are present. But they are rarely present. Only 12 of the 467 cases have "positive" values on two of the factors, and only 1 case has three "positive" values. Thus, the three explanatory factors used in Tables 1 and 2 have substantial effects on the rate of police force, but the factors occur so infrequently that they cannot account for the majority of incidents in which police did use force.

Table 1—Multiple Regression of Police Use of Force with Three Predictor Variables

Variable	Coefficient	Standardized Coefficient	P
Conflict at Arrival	.073	.100	.03
Citizen Weapon Possession	.137	.095	.04
Obscene/Insulting Remarks or Gestures by Citizen	.156	.119	.01
Constant	.055		

NOTE: The dependent variable and the three predictor variables are dichotomies, with Yes = 1 and No = 0.

Multiple R = .196, R^2 = .038, F-ratio = 6.15, p = .00.

Table 2—Police Use of Force, by Number of "Positive" Scores on Three Predictor Variables

Number of Predictor Variables With "Positive" Scores	Police Use of Force		
	Yes	No	Total
None	5.5% (20)	94.5% (345)	100% (365)
One	15.7% (14)	84.3% (75)	100% (89)
Two or Three	23.1% (3)	76.9% (10)	100% (13)

NOTE: The predictor variables are all dichotomized. A "positive" value means: overt conflict was occurring when the officers arrived, or at least one citizen was found to be in possession of a weapon, or at least one citizen directed obscene or insulting remarks or gestures toward the officers.

Chi square = 14.52, p = .001; Phi = .176.

It can be argued that our data set does not adequately reflect some features of the events that can help to explain the use of force: "mood" of an encounter or subtle physical movements, for example. Although it should be possible to refine future research to record some of the more subtle situational and behavioral factors associated with the use of force in patrol encounters, the relative rarity of forceful encounters remains a problem—at least for researchers. An enormous number of routine patrol shifts would have to be observed to accumulate a respectable number of use-of-force cases for thorough analysis. For better or worse, then, empirical knowledge about the effectiveness of different police tactics in dealing with potential violence is imperfect and, in our judgment, likely to remain so.

From a policy perspective, police managers interested in minimizing violent encounters between police and citizens are justified in giving special attention to situations involving overt conflict, but they should recognize that most of these will deflate on arrival and that patrol officers will choose to use mild force in a variety of other circumstances. Most of the time, regardless of the situation, police will easily take charge. Training for the avoidance of violent encounters is difficult because they are very rare events.

THE "SKILLED" PATROL OFFICER

Patrol officers were asked to identify colleagues they served with who were especially skilled at handling situations with a potential for violence. Unexpectedly, the patrol teams containing presumptively more skilled officers (the ESOs) turned out to use force more often than the teams with CSOs—9% versus 6% of all PVMs. The difference in police use of force was evident only in encounters in which overt conflict was occurring when the officers arrived. In the absence of initial conflict, there was no difference between ESO and CSO teams in officers' use of force. (See Table 3.)

Unfortunately, we cannot determine with any certainty whether ESO teams actually took a different approach to encounters in which conflict was occurring at arrival. As we saw earlier, other factors (such a weapon possession by a citizen) affect police use of force. Given the small numbers of conflict-on-arrival encounters in Table 3, especially for CSO units, it is not feasible to check the possibility that these types of encounters were qualitatively different for ESO and CSO units. This possibility cannot be dismissed because the overall characteristics of the encounters in which ESO teams became involved differed from the characteristics of encounters involving CSO teams.

Compared with CSO teams, the ESO teams were more likely to handle violent crimes, disputes, and disturbances (47% of their encounters vs. 37% for CSOs) and less likely to handle traffic cases (31% vs. 38%). With traffic cases eliminated, a somewhat greater proportion of encounters involving ESOs than CSOs involved overt conflict at arrival (26% vs. 19%).

At the same time, the patrol officers selected as superior performers displayed real differences in behaviors on the street. Peers may or may not have successfully spotted higher skill in handling potential violence, but they did know which officers performed differently in general and, it seems fair to infer, in ways they thought were praiseworthy.

Table 3—Police Use of Force among Units with ESOs and CSOs, Controlling for Occurrence of Overt Conflict When Police Arrived

Police Use of Force

	Yes	No	Total
Conflict			
Occurring			
Team Contains:			
ESO	20.0%	80.0%	100%
	(11)	(44)	(55)
CSO	4.4%	95.6%	100%
	(1)	(22)	(23)
Conflict			
Not Occurring			
Team Contains:			
ESO	6.6%	93.4%	100%
	(16)	(228)	(244)
CSO	6.2%	93.8%	100%
	(9)	(136)	(145)

Conflict occurring: Chi-square = 3.05, p = .081; Phi = .198.
Conflict not occurring: Chi-square = 0.02, p = .892; Phi = .007.

ESOs were more active than CSOs. Patrol teams with ESOs, for example, averaged 1.62 PVMs per shift as opposed to 1.02 for teams with CSOs. ESOs also displayed much more initiative: they had twice the proportion of proactive—that is, on-view—mobilizations as CSOs. The difference was even greater for nontraffic incidents, for which ESOs were 3.5 times more active.

In the following sections, we compare the tactical responses of ESOs and CSOs at the contact, processing, and exit stages of encounters. We partially control for the nature of situations by eliminating all traffic incidents. Traffic stops never sparked the use of force by either officers or citizens. In effect, the comparisons presented below pertain to the more serious and forcefully problematic encounters between police and the public.

CONTACT

At the contact and processing stages of an encounter, our observers noted which officer in the team played the lead role—the subject officer (ESO or CSO), his or her partner, or neither. The observers also recorded up to five actions for each officer in the team at each of the three stages in the encounters.

ESOs were more likely than CSOs to take the lead role during contact and processing, and they engaged in a greater number of actions than CSOs during all three stages. At contact, ESOs took the lead in 57% of the nontraffic encounters in which they were involved, compared with 34% for CSOs. They engaged in an average of 2.2 actions during the contact stage, compared with 1.7 for CSOs. More striking than the average number of actions is the difference between ESOs and CSOs in the proportion of nontraffic encounters in which they took a single course of action during contact: 30% for ESOs and 55% for CSOs.

On initial contact with citizens in 311 nontraffic encounters, the primary line of action for both ESOs and CSOs was to try to find out what was going on (Table 4)—by asking about identities and relationships, the nature of the problem, and accounts of citizen behaviors (62% of ESO actions and 57% of CSO actions). ESOs, however, tended to be more authoritative and confrontational than CSOs. They were not as likely as CSOs to simply stand by and take notes, to be passive partners (ESOs 4%, CSOs 15%). They were more likely than CSOs to challenge citizens to "explain themselves" (16% vs. 7%) rather than simply ask questions about the nature of the problem (31% for both groups). Similarly, they were slightly more likely (11% vs. 8%) to take verbally or physically forceful actions (give controlling orders, order dispersal, threaten force, physically separate or restrain).

Contrary to the popular "war stories" in policing, few officers used clever verbal comments to manage potential conflict. ESOs were much more likely to do this than CSOs (11% vs. 4%), however.

PROCESSING

After officers had intervened, establishing their presence and control, they searched for a course of action appropriate to the situation. As at the contact stage, ESOs were more likely than CSOs to play the lead role on their teams during processing (58% vs. 30%) and to engage in a greater number of specific actions (average of 2.7 vs. 1.8 actions).

The most common approach used by all officers was to continue to ask questions in order to understand better what the incident was about (Table 5). Differences in specific actions between ESOs and CSOs were very small. At best, ESOs tended to be slightly more responsive to complainants. They were less likely to reject the complainant's definition of the problem or to indicate that there was little the police could do. They were a little more likely than CSOs to give advice, make a referral, or provide information. Take-charge actions—restraining, interrogating, warning, and so forth—were used almost equally by ESOs and CSOs during the processing stage of the nontraffic encounters.

Table 4—Specific Actions Taken during Contact Stage by ESOs and CSOs; 311 Nontraffic Encounters

Action	ESOs		CSOs	
	%	N	%	N
Observed, Stood by, Took Notes	4.4	20	14.6	26
Sought Identity, Relationships of Parties	15.4	70	19.1	34
Questioned to Elicit Nature of Problem	30.8	140	30.9	55
Asked Citizens to "Explain Themselves"	16.0	73	7.3	13
Stated Problem as Police Saw It	3.5	16	3.4	6
Verbally Tried to Defuse, "Cool Out" Situation	11.0	50	4.5	8
Verbally Restrained Citizens (gave controlling orders)	5.9	27	2.8	5
Physically Restrained Citizens	2.2	10	0.6	1
Threatened Physical Force	1.1	5	2.2	4
Separated Disputants in a Nonphysical Manner	2.9	13	4.5	8
Physically Separated Disputants	1.1	5	0.0	0
Requested Dispersal of Citizens	1.1	5	0.6	1
Ordered Dispersal of Citizens	0.7	3	2.8	5
Other	3.9	18	6.8	11
Total	100%	455	100%	177

NOTE: Up to five actions were coded for each officer.

EXIT

At the exit stage, ESOs were once again more likely than CSOs to take multiple actions (1.9 vs. 1.4 per encounter) and were less likely to engage in a single line of action (44% vs. 73%).

In terms of specific actions, CSOs were much more likely to be passive at exit than ESOs, either standing by while their partners acted (15% vs. 2%) or essentially just leaving without taking concluding action (18% vs. 5%). (See Table 6). ESOs more frequently offered sympathy, gave friendly advice, and provided advice about legal remedies (24% vs. 13%). ESOs, however, were also more likely to give pointed advice, disperse or separate citizens, issue citations or desk appearance tickets, and take someone into custody (32% vs. 15%).

In sum, the data on actions at contact, processing, and exit indicate that ESOs were more willing than other officers to take a lead role in resolving the encounters in which they became involved. They showed more versatility than CSOs, drawing on a greater range of tactical actions throughout encounters.

Since ESOs became involved in conflict situations more often than CSOs, an interesting question arises. Does versatility grow out of handling a greater variety of situations or does willingness to become involved stem from confidence in one's versatility? Surely the latter. If so, it follows that the more versatile, deft, or skilled officers will not be the ones who become involved less in conflict situations in which forceful responses are often appropriate. On the contrary, their more active approach to their work should be expected to bring them into problematic situations more frequently than their peers.[7] One hopes, however, that they are the officers who are best able to handle such situations.

Table 5—Specific Actions Taken during Processing Stage by ESOs and CSOs; 311 Nontraffic Encounters

	ESOs		CSOs	
Action	%	N	%	N
Observed, Stood by, Took Notes	3.1	17	8.4	16
Controlled Discussion; Gave Each Person Chance to Speak in Turn	10.1	56	8.9	17
Probed with Questions	19.4	107	15.7	30
Accepted Complainant's Definition of the Situation	3.8	21	3.1	6
Rejected Complainant's Definition	1.4	8	3.1	6
Urged Signing of a Complaint	1.1	6	1.0	2
Tried to Talk Someone out of Signing a Complaint	1.3	7	1.0	2
Indicated That There Was Little the Police Could Do	2.7	15	4.2	8
Gave Advice on Legal Actions	7.6	42	6.8	13
Gave Advice on Informal Actions	4.9	27	4.7	9
Referred to a Third Party	1.6	9	0.5	1
Provided Information	4.0	22	3.1	6
Searched Persons or Premises	7.6	42	8.4	16
Interrogated Suspect	4.9	27	4.2	8
Warned Citizens	5.2	29	4.7	9
Admonished Disputants to Make Truce	2.7	15	3.1	6
Lectured about Proper Behavior	4.5	25	4.7	9
Physically Restrained Someone	2.2	12	1.0	2
Assisted Someone	1.4	8	2.1	4
Collected Information	2.7	15	4.2	8
Other	7.6	42	6.8	13
Total	100%	552	100%	191

NOTE: UP to five actions were coded for each officer.

Table 6—Specific Actions Taken during Exit Stage by ESOs and CSOs; 311 Nontraffic Encounters

Action	ESOs %	ESOs N	CSOs %	CSOs N
Observed, Stood by, Took Notes	2.3	9	14.6	21
Gave Advice About Legal Remedies	10.6	41	4.9	7
Offered Friendly Advice	11.1	43	6.9	10
Gave Pointed Advice	9.6	37	4.2	6
Offered Comfort, Sympathy	2.8	11	1.4	2
Referred to Third Party	1.6	6	2.1	3
Promised Future Police Assistance	1.6	6	2.1	3
Arranged for Transport of Injured/ Disabled Person	4.2	16	3.5	5
Got Disputants to Agree on a Settlement	2.8	11	2.8	4
Dispersed "Troublemakers"	7.0	27	4.2	6
Separated Disputants	4.7	18	2.1	3
Warned about Future Trouble	7.5	29	6.9	10
Lectured, Admonished Citizens	7.5	29	8.3	12
Escorted Someone from Premises	2.6	10	2.1	3
Issued Citation, Summons, Desk Appearance Ticket	3.1	12	0.0	0
Took Someone into Custody	7.5	29	4.9	7
Essentially Just Left	5.2	20	18.1	26
Other	8.3	32	11.1	16
Total	100%	386	100%	144

NOTE: UP to five actions were coded for each officer.

RESULTS OF ENCOUNTERS

There were no noteworthy differences between the outcomes of encounters handled by police units containing ESOs and units containing CSOs. Arrests and issuance of citations, summonses, and desk appearance tickets occurred with similar frequency. Injuries to police or citizens were equally rare for both types of units. When there was a complainant who made a specific request, ESO and CSO units were equally likely to comply with the request.

The attitudes of citizens at the end of encounters were usually neutral to positive. Moreover, the proportions of positive and negative attitudes among citizens at the conclusion of encounters were almost exactly the same for ESO and CSO units.

As for the police themselves, in most incidents both ESOs and CSOs had no particular reaction to what had occurred; more than half the time, they considered the encounter to be routine and unremarkable. When they did react, they were more likely to be upbeat than downbeat about how things had worked out.

SUMMARY

Even though we could not determine whether officers identified by their colleagues as being more skilled in handling conflict were in fact so, we did find that they performed differently on the job. Specifically, they handled more jobs per shift, were more proactive, and were more likely to become involved in serious law enforcement situations. They were more inclined to take charge, and they exhibited greater versatility in their tactical behaviors. They were less willing to wash their hands of matters by simply leaving or saying there was nothing the police could do.

EVALUATING PATROL WORK

The fact that there are important differences in performance between ESOs and CSOs would seem to lead to a heartening conclusion. Police rank and file respect colleagues who exhibit behavior that police departments want to encourage—activity, high motivation, versatility, concern, inventiveness. The peer culture of policing does not seem to admire unsympathetic, unmotivated officers who simply put in time on the job. It respects qualities that the public respects and would intuitively associate with the ability to minimize violence, even though our data cannot demonstrate that such qualities do actually minimize violence.

In short, police would seem to be reliable observers of qualitative differences in the street performance of other officers. They discriminate fairly accurately among colleagues on the basis of what they do.

The problem with this line of reasoning is that the officers designated by their peers as being more skilled in handling conflict were also older and more experienced. On average, ESOs were about 3 years older than CSOs and had 18 more months of experience on the job. It is possible that the ESOs were selected by their peers on the basis of age and experience rather than on a solid knowledge of their street behavior. Even though this possibility seems remote considering the slight magnitude of the differences in age and experience between the two groups, we checked for it by comparing the tactics of ESOs and CSOs after stratifying by age and experience. This was done by conducting a separate analysis of encounters in which the subject officers were less than 30 years old and had less than 36 months of experience in the police department.

Among the incidents handled by the younger, less experienced officers, differences between ESOs and CSOs with respect to numbers and types of tactical actions continued to be evident. Moreover, the numbers and types of actions taken by the younger, less experienced ESOs were virtually the same as those taken by older, more experienced ESOs.[8]

An implication of this finding is that police officers do not automatically equate age and experience with street skills. Although older, more experienced officers were more likely to be chosen as especially skilled by their peers, younger, less experienced officers were similarly chosen. And these younger, less experienced ESOs displayed the same patterns of on-street performance as the older, more experienced ESOs.

It is important to note that the ESOs were not chosen by their peers on the basis of race/ethnicity or gender. Although the ESOs were predominantly white males, minority officers and women showed up in equal proportions among the ESOs and the CSOs.

The New York City Police Department, like most large urban departments, regularly assesses the performance of its personnel. Departmental evaluations are more broadly based than those we asked patrol officers to make about their colleagues (i.e., their skill at handling conflict). Nevertheless, we can address, in a rough way, the interesting question of whether peer opinions agree or disagree with departmental appraisals.

As it turns out, they do agree. As shown in Table 7, the average overall rating on departmental evaluations for ESOs was 3.75 as opposed to 3.38 for CSOs. The overall rating as well as the more specific ratings of job performance are made on 5-point scales, with 5 being the highest rating.

Table 7—Departmental Performance Rating Scores
of ESOs and CSOs

Rating Item[a]	Mean Score[b]	
	ESOs	CSOs
Overall Rating	3.75	3.38 *
Appearance	3.88	3.77
Communication Skills	3.46	3.47
Community Relations	3.50	3.32
Human Relations-Impartiality	3.75	3.62
Judgment-Decision Making	3.75	3.29 *
Police Ethics	3.79	3.47 **
Self-image	3.67	3.38
Service-oriented	3.79	3.44 **
Stability-Flexibility	3.62	3.44
Street Knowledge	3.71	3.29 *
Work Analysis	3.83	3.29 *
Number of Subjects[c]	24	34

a See descriptions of the rating items in the appendix.
b Rating scales ranged from 1 (lowest) to 5 (highest).
c Performance ratings were not available for four CSOs.

* T-test significant at the .01 level. ** T-test significant at the .05 level.

Among the specific items, differences between ESOs and CSOs were statistically significant for judgment/decision making, ethics, service orientation, street knowledge, and work analysis. (See descriptions of the contents of these items in the appendix.) These are some of the qualities one would expect in officers judged by their peers to be especially skilled, and found on the street to be active, involved, and diverse in their actions. There were no significant differences in departmental ratings between ESOs and CSOs with respect to personal appearance, communication skills, community relations, impartiality, self-image, or stability/flexibility.

Contrary, then, to the claim often made by rank-and-file officers about the arbitrariness of departmental evaluations, our findings show that the supervisors and the frontline personnel agree about who the outstanding performers are. It would seem that the department and its frontline officers are on the same wavelength when it comes to judging patrol performance.

POLICY IMPLICATIONS

What are the implications of this research for the way in which police departments may minimize violent confrontations between police and public growing out of routine patrol operations? We think there are six.

First, the employment of clever defusing tactics once contact has been made is probably not the key to minimizing force. Most conflict stops as soon as the police arrive, attacks on police are rare, and the force used by police is usually slight. Officers need to be trained to avoid obvious provocations, such as using insulting language and acting without listening. But fine-tuning of tactics during encounters is probably not needed. We doubt that training in "defusing" will diminish the kind of low-level force that occasionally occurs in patrol work.

At the same time, more extensive and elaborate tactical training may be justified for other reasons. Our analysis shows that activity and tactical range are qualities admired by colleagues, and they would seem to be intuitively related to preferred tactical outcomes, even if our data cannot demonstrate this. Our analysis also shows that activity and versatility are concomitants of achieving success in a police career according to departmental criteria. Two devices might be used to encourage valued qualities. One, more extensive role-playing of street encounters. This is done in many police departments but might be increased; there is no substitute for practice. Two, more systematic sharing of information about tactical approaches and outcomes. Departments can help all officers, not just recruits, learn to use knowledge about valued tactical responses. This might be done through in-service seminars or discussion groups, scheduled routinely rather than in the aftermath of crises.

Second, anticipating problems before they arise is probably more important in avoiding unnecessary and injurious use of force then being clever after encounters begin. The problem is that incidents that seem to require caution—such as dispatch reports of violence and weapons or the discovery of conflict on arrival—so often prove easy to handle without force. Although force is more likely to be used when conflict is present upon arrival, even more use of force will occur during the larger number of wholly routine encounters. The point is that patrol officers need to be alert even when "the boy isn't crying wolf."

Police training must focus on the fact that physical conflict is a rare event. Despite the emphasis placed during training on the dangers of policing and the consequences of thoughtless action, officers soon learn that every tour is not a war and every call for service not a crisis. There is a paradox here. Police officers must be trained for war but prepared for peace. Inattention may be more serious than not being able to shoot straight.

Third, training in the use of force in patrol encounters should concentrate on techniques of effective restraint rather than hitting, striking, or shooting. The most common use of force by police officers in our study was grabbing and holding. And it would be worth studying whether greater facility in the use of low-level force by officers might reduce the number of occasions in which serious and lethal force are employed.

Fourth, police departments can confidently rely on "the troops" to help select appropriate role models for use as field-training officers, resource persons for in-service training, and perhaps even as academy instructors.

Fifth, police departments should find ways to encourage experienced officers to remain in patrol work. Although our research found that valued patrol skills were not restricted to seasoned officers, the officers chosen as superior performers by their peers (and by departmental evaluations) tended to be somewhat older and more experienced.

Sixth, the climate of opinion among frontline personnel, at least with respect to street tactics, appears to be more of a help than a hindrance in reinforcing approved norms of policing. Officers who are active and who employ a wide range of actions in seeking resolutions to the problems they encounter on patrol are recognized as superior by their peers and their supervisors. Patrol officers, at least in New York City, are not out of step with qualities that would, presumably, elicit public approval.

APPENDIX
INSTRUCTIONS FOR RATING CRITERIA
IN NEW YORK CITY POLICE DEPARTMENT
PERFORMANCE EVALUATIONS

Appearance: Consider the impression this officer makes on people by his/ her personal neatness, hygiene, weight, dress, and bearing. Is this officer physically fit?

Communication Skill: Consider the officer's effectiveness in discussion and expression in person-to-person or group interactions. Is this officer an attentive listener? Does he/she express ideas in writing with facility?

Community Relations: Consider the extent of this police officer's involvement with the community. Is this officer knowledgeable of the cultural aspects of the community and sensitive to its needs? Does this officer try to integrate police and community goals?

Human Relations—Impartiality: Consider if this individual is friendly, tactful, and empathetic to people regardless of their ethnic, religious, racial or cultural background. Does this officer evoke a positive response from people by offering equal service to all?

Judgment—Decision Making: Are all available factors weighed before judgments are made? Are decisions based on a correct assessment of available facts?

Police Ethics: Consider the extent to which this individual can be relied upon to adhere to the department's policy on ethics. Is this officer's attitude toward such policy professionally oriented?

Self-image: Does this individual consider himself/herself a professional by demonstrating a positive attitude toward work and placing a special value on it? Does this officer possess professional self-confidence in dealing with others?

Service-oriented: Is this individual concerned with giving service to the victim and complainant and is this officer respectful and responsive to them? Does this officer derive job satisfaction from public service by going out of his/her way to be helpful and extending efforts beyond procedural boundaries? Is this individual person-oriented?

Stability-Flexibility: Consider the way this individual acts in times of crises. Is this officer able to control the situation? Does this officer adapt to different circumstances or is this individual rigid in his/her approach? The rater is required to comment as to the individual's overall behavior in enforcement and regulatory situations as well as his/her use of appropriate and justifiable force.

Street Knowledge: Does this officer possess adequate street knowledge to perform as a service-oriented police officer? Is this individual adept at quickly sizing up situations and taking appropriate action? Is this officer able to recognize police problems in their incipiency and to take corrective action before they become major problems?

Work Analysis: Consider this individual's interactions and interventions with people on service calls. Assess this officer's investigative skill and analyze the quality of his/her arrest activity. Consider this individual's punctuality, attendance record, and overall job activity.

Overall Rating: Should be consistent with the pattern of rating on the criteria above. A member's overall rating should not be affected by his/her relative standing in the group.

NOTE: All items are rated on a 5-point scale, ranging from "well above standards" to "well below standards."

REFERENCES

Bayley, David H., 1986. "The tactical choices of police patrol officers." *Journal of Criminal Justice* 14: 329-348.

Bayley, David H. and Egon Bittner, 1985. Learning the skills of policing. *Law and Contemporary Problems* 47: 35-39.

Black, Donald, 1980. *The Manners and Customs of the Police.* New York: Academic Press.

Black, Donald and Albert J. Reiss, Jr., 1967. *Field Surveys III. Studies in Crime and Law Enforcement in Major Metropolitan Areas.* Vol. 2. Washington, D.C.: President's Commission on Law Enforcement and Administration of Justice.

Brown, Michael K., 1981. *Working the Street: Police Discretion and the Dilemmas of Reform.* New York: Russell Sage Foundation.

Friedrich, Robert J., 1977. "The impact of organizational, individual, and situational factors in police behavior." Ph.D. dissertation. University of Michigan, Ann Arbor.

_____, 1980. "Police use of force: Individuals, situations, and organizations." *Annals of the American Academy of Political and Social Science* Nov.: 82-97.

Fyfe, James J., 1988. *The Metro-Dade Police-Citizen Violence Reduction Project: Final Report,* Executive Summary. Washington, D.C.: Police Foundation.

Geller, William A., 1985. Officer restraint in the use of force: The next frontier in the police shooting research. *Journal of Police Science and Administration* 13: 153-171.

Goldstein, Herman, 1977. *Policing a Free Society.* Cambridge, Mass.: Ballinger.

Ianni, Francis and Elizabeth Reuss-Ianni, 1984. "Street cops vs. management cops: The two cultures of policing." In Maurice Punch (ed.), *Control in the Police Organization.* Cambridge, Mass.: MIT Press.

Lundman, Richard J., 1974. "Domestic police-citizen encounters." *Journal of Police Science and Administration* 2: 22-27.

McIver, J.P. and Roger B. Parks, 1983. "Identification of effective and ineffective police actions." In Richard R. Bennett (ed.), *Police at Work.* Beverly Hills, Calif.: Sage.

Parks, Roger B., 1980. "Using sample surveys to compare police performance." *Workshop in Political Theory and Policy Analysis,* Bloomington, Ind.

Reiss, Albert J., Jr., 1971. *The Police and the Public.* New Haven, Conn.: Yale University Press.

Rubenstein, Jonathan, 1973. *City Police.* New York: Ballantine Books.

Scharf, Peter and Arnold Binder, 1983. *The Badge and the Bullet.* New York: Praeger.

Sherman, Lawrence, 1980. "Causes of police behavior: An inventory of research findings." *Journal of Research in Crime and Delinquency* 17: 69-100.

Smith, Douglas A., 1987. "Police response to interpersonal violence: Defining the parameters of legal control." *Social Forces* 65: 767-782.

Sykes, R.E. and E.E. Brent, 1983. *Policing: A Social Behaviorist Perspective.* New Brunswick, N.J.: Rutgers University Press.

Teplin, Linda, 1984. "Managing disorder: Police handling of the mentally ill." *Mental Health and Criminal Justice* 20: 157-175.

Vera Institute of Justice, 1977. *Women on Patrol: A Pilot Study of Police Performance in New York City.* New York: Vera Institute of Justice.

Wambaugh, Joseph, 1970. *The New Centurions.* Boston: Little, Brown.

Whitaker, Gordon P., 1982. "What is patrol work?" *Police Studies* 4: 13-22.

CHAPTER 12
High Policing and Low Policing: Remarks About the Policing of Political Activities

JEAN-PAUL BRODEUR

Policing political activities is usually regarded as deviant police action. The deviance approach focuses on police abuse, which is deemed to be secretive and to confuse legitimate dissent with political delinquency, such as terrorism. I take issue with the deviance approach and attempt to replace it by distinguishing between high policing and low policing models of police action. Political policing is then seen as a core of feature high policing instead of merely being a suspicious peripheral aspect of the police apparatus. I also argue that mainly through technological change, western police forces are increasingly operating under the high policing model.

To write on the subject of policing political activities is from the outset difficult, because one can bog down in problems of semantics. The very meaning of the phrase "policing political activities" is fraught with ambiguities. The phrase can be narrowly interpreted to mean "keeping elected politicians honest"; more broadly, it can refer to police interventions in the struggles taking place inside society over the possession and exercise of state power. Compounding this difficulty, policing political activities is deemed to be not even a real topic in Canada and in the United States; the target of such policing—political deviance—has no official status outside the criminal law. Hence, many people claim that there are no political prisoners in North America. Others, such as Platt and Cooper (1974), take an opposite stand and argue that notions such as "deviance" or "social reaction" can only be understood as political processes. Any form of policing thus becomes political.

To escape this all or nothing dichotomy, I first examine the implicit definitions of political policing which are shared by Canadian and U.S. government inquiries into alleged police wrongdoing: aggressive operations performed under the blanket mandate of protecting "national security." Then I look at what I call the "deviance approach" to the policing of political activities and, noting its shortcomings, I distinguish between low and high policing and apply the latter to modern policing.

GOVERNMENT INVESTIGATIONS

Several Congressional committees scrutinized the U.S. intelligence community in the wake of the Watergate scandal of the early 1970s. The most thorough investigation was conducted by the Senate Select Committee on Intelligence Activities, chaired by Idaho Senator Frank Church. The committee's report (U.S. Congress: Senate, 1976) contained detailed accounts of domestic operations performed against political dissenters by the Federal Bureau of Investigation (FBI), under its infamous Counter Intelligence Program (COINTELPRO).

In Canada, investigations into the propriety of security service operations got off to a bad start. In 1966, the federal government appointed Judge Dalton C. Wells to investigate charges that the Royal Canadian Mounted Police (RCMP) had exerted undue pressure on the post office to fire Victor Herbert Spencer on the alleged grounds that he had spied for the Soviet Union. Spencer was found dead in his house a week before the inquiry was scheduled to begin. Later in 1966, the government appointed a royal commission to examine the protection of national security in Canada. It released an expurgated report (Canada, 1969).

The two major commissions of inquiry into political policing in Canada were established in 1977. They examined events surrounding the "October crisis" of 1970, during which the federal government imposed the equivalent of martial law in Québec and sent in the army in response to political kidnappings and unrest. The common object of these commissions was to investigate the RCMP security service and its Disruptive Tactics program, the Canadian counterpart of the FBI's COINTELPRO. The Québec government created its commission first, headed by lawyer Jean F. Keable (Québec, 1981). A second commission was quickly appointed by the federal government. Chaired by Judge D.C. McDonald, its mandate paralleled closely the provincial inquiry (Canada, 1981a,b).

FOCUSSING ON POLICE DEVIANCE

Both the above-mentioned commissions of inquiry and the media's discussion of their findings use what I call a deviance approach to political policing. This approach, which is also used in academic literature on political policing,[1] focuses primarily on active police tactics of intervention and stresses those operations which appear to be illegal or at least reprehensible. A model case for this approach would be the FBI's attempts to blackmail Martin Luther King. (The FBI had intercepted what they claimed were compromising telephone conversations between the black civil rights leader and his alleged mistresses.)

The deviance approach distinguishes between active intervention tactics, which explicitly purport to disrupt and neutralize groups and individuals, and mere intelligence-gathering operations, or general surveillance. Though distinct, these two kinds of activities frequently overlap: disruption and neutralization are frequently achieved through the release of damaging information on groups and persons perceived as security threats. The deviance approach also distinguishes between lawful activities, such as analyzing the contents of extremist publications, and illegal operations such as criminal libel, blackmail, and theft of property. But here again, though the distinction is easy to formulate in theory, it is fraught with difficulty in practice, as recent court decisions have show in Québec. After the Québec government released the Keable report in 1981, 17 RCMP officers were indicted for crimes ranging from arson and theft of dynamite to stealing the membership list of the Parti Québécois, which, at the time of the theft, was the official opposition party in the Québec National Assembly (Parliament). So far not one conviction has been obtained before the courts.

The main flaw of this deviance approach is that it views the policing of political activities as a suspicious increment to criminal policing. I argue that political policing is not a belated and anomalous accretion to the police system. Rather, it forms the pervasive core of a whole model of policing, which I call "high policing." North American police agencies, traditionally thought to be engaged in "low policing," are evolving toward the "high policing" model, in which political policing permeates the whole structure of police action.

However, before taking issue with the deviance approach on its main flaw, I first criticize two of its less theoretical tenets. My criticism arises from a personal involvement for more than two years with the Keable inquiry into police wrongdoing in Québec. From 1979 to 1981 I was the commission's official spokesman and main consultant for its report. During these two years,

I experienced growing reservations about two features of the deviance approach, which have dire consequences on the practical level. These are: (1) its assumptions about the secrecy of political activities: and (2) what seems to me to be a futile attempt to distinguish between lawful dissent and political delinquency, such as terrorism. Because my personal exposure to the deviance approach has been in Québec, I use mainly Canadian events to illustrate my argument. However, I believe the features of the deviance approach which I criticize are common in the United States as well.

CONVENIENT SECRECY

I argue two points about the secrecy which surrounds the policing of political activities:

> 1) The secrecy of deviant political policing is, to a significant extent, the product of a deliberate illusion.

Once the notion of secrecy is adequately qualified, it is found to have a much more restricted application to the policing of political activities than we are led to believe. Indeed, the Royal Commission on Security in Canada stated:

> A security service will inevitably be involved in actions that may contravene the spirit if not the letter of the law, and with clandestine and other activities which may sometimes seem to infringe on individual's rights (Canada, 1969:21).

Anyone familiar with public government documents produced by or about security agencies is aware that they use "laundered language."[2] The above quotation from the royal commission's report comes as close as any document revised for publication to stating in plain English that the RCMP security service took liberties with the law. Indeed, the royal commission recommended that the security service be separated from the RCMP because the former's activities were bound to damage the latter's reputation for abiding by the law. Obviously, this is not the kind of proposal that a commission makes without standing on firm ground. However, not having a specific mandate to inquire into RCMP wrongdoing and, furthermore, not being under pressure from public opinion, the royal commission did not disclose a particular incident which the media might have dramatized, thus raising a public outcry for reforms and sanctions. Its report was quickly forgotten and failed to produce any perceptible reform.

In 1977, following public allegations of wrongdoing by the RCMP security service and by other security squads operating in Québec, the Keable and the McDonald commissions were created. (These allegations were made by an ex-member of the RCMP security service, who was then on trial for having placed a bomb on the back doorstep of a prominent Montreal businessman.) Part of their task was to see if there were any grounds for prosecuting police officers who were alleged to have violated the law. Predictably, what the commissions produced were detailed illustrations of the general statement that had been made, to no avail, by the royal commission 12 years before. Moreover, the McDonald report made exactly the same recommendations as the royal commission: that the security service be withdrawn from the RCMP and be made into a separate civilian agency.[3]

Thus, the overwhelming difficulty of gathering legal evidence against individual policemen who may have undertaken or authorized illegal operations should not be confused with plain ignorance about the nature and ways of political policing as such. As any police officer can bear witness to, knowledge and legal proof are very different things; the first notion concerns the substance of the facts, whereas the second is largely a question of formal procedure. The Keable and the McDonald reports confirmed in 1981 what had been clearly said in 1969. To confuse a lack of compelling evidence against persons with a lack of reliable information about political policing only strengthens the tendency to repress knowledge which threatens cherished illusions about institutions, namely that they abide by the law. It also provides governments with a welcome alibi for idleness in curbing abuses.

In other words, I strongly object to a line of reasoning that would unfold thus: (1) If you can't make a legal case, then you don't have a point. (2) But you can't get any proof, because operations are cloaked in secrecy. (3) Hence, little can be done against the infringement of civil rights by political policing. This line of reasoning only protects police interests and precludes significant reform.

> 2) The secretive aspects of political policing, whether real or fabricated, stem from a partnership among the police, politicians, the courts, and, ironically, the victims of aggressive political policing themselves. The press is an important investor in this secrecy corporation.

Members of government have neither the interest nor the inclinations to seek confirmations of what they suspect, or have been "confidentially" told. In theory, they too could be indicted for actions that took place with their knowledge. The more knowledgeable they are about illegal activity, the more vulnerable and accountable they might be. Thus they insulate themselves from detailed knowledge of police wrongdoing. The third report of the McDonald commission documents in striking detail the Canadian government's reluctance to follow explicit leads to RCMP lawlessness (Canada, 1981b).

The attitude of the courts provides no encouragement to politicians. The best-kept secret about the most abusive forms of political policing is whether Canadian judges believe it to be illegal. One cannot help but be struck by the court's resistance to pronounce clearly on this matter. Up to March 1983, not one of the six prosecutions undertaken after extended investigation of police wrongdoing in Québec during the early 1970s succeeded in eliciting a substantial ruling from the courts; procedural irregularities were cited in each case.

Few political organizations which have been the victims of police disruption are willing to take official action which might disclose the extent to which they have been infiltrated by the police: such revelations are liable to drastically reduce their credibility in the eyes of other movements and their membership.[4] (One exception is the U.S. Socialist Workers Party, which has launched a civil suit against the Attorney General of the United States.) The police are well aware of this reluctance and deliberately spread rumors of infiltration to destabilize political groups.

The attitude of investigative journalism toward the exposure of deviant political policing is somewhat akin to the behavior of the tabloids toward sex scandals. The scandal sheets try to hide their pornographic character by pretending to denounce what they prey upon, thus partaking in what they affect to repudiate. Similarly, investigative journalism presents as sensational feats of intelligence the numerous cases of police delinquency which it succeeds in unearthing, thereby suggesting that these wrongdoings are occurring behind a leaden veil of secrecy which only the "free press" can lift. The growing banality of these so-called "revelations" bears witness to the fact that political policing has become a reservoir for fishing out deviance, in order to increase plummeting circulation rates.

Public disclosure of police deviance has no intrinsic value in itself, except perhaps for securing some political advantage or for selling more newspapers. It is goes no further than providing a lively stage for a play on police agencies to infringe upon civil liberties by demoralizing the potential victims of these violations.

REPRESSIONS OF DISSENT AS A REQUIREMENT OF POLICING

Critics of political policing, whether writing in the press, in official reports or in academic literature, repeatedly stress its failure to distinguish between lawful dissent, on the one hand, and political violence and its advocacy, on the other hand. Police deviance is then defined as illegitimate and wrongful intervention into law-abiding radical (or alternative) politics.

I do not want to dispute the accuracy of this criticism. The list of persons arrested during the October Crisis of 1970, as well as the types of movements which were the target of police disruption in the United States and Canada during the early 1970s, show that the police were not, to say the least, sensitive to the distinction between dissent and deviance. Such insensitivity is not, however, a specific feature of a particular type of policing, namely policing political activities. In my opinion, it is a general feature of policing itself.

One striking aspect of research on the police is its demystifying character. After having undermined certain widely held beliefs about patrol work and, more generally, about the amount of activity that a police force devotes to fighting crime, research has recently focussed on detective work, undertaken by both general investigation teams and by more specialized units, such as narcotics squads. Greenwood et al. (1975), Sanders (1977), Manning (1980), and Ericson (1981) have emphasized the inability of detectives to identify offenders not already identified by victims or other informants. Detective work is aptly characterized, in the words of Ericson (1981:136), as "the processing of readily available suspects." I believe this statement also applies to the policing of political activities.

Counter-intelligence and security work is to a large extent prone to the same difficulties as criminal detective work, and is performed mainly by persons with a background in criminal detection. The problem of identifying political offenders is even more complicated because the intended victim of political deviance is the state itself. Since the identification of offenders depends greatly upon information provided by victims or informants, the following paradox emerges: the state, as law-enforcer, has to rely on itself, as a victim or informant, to identify its enemies. There are three practical ways to break out of this circle. The first is for the police to transform into criminal enemies those who publicly criticize the state. Such persons are precisely those we refer to as "dissenters": they believe they can lawfully advocate radical change through the spoken word and achieve it through public persuasion. However, by so doing they identify themselves as suspects for police processing. The second solution is to rely on intelligence provided by paid informers.[5]

Professional informers, however, have an interest in selling, as prized offenders, members of the groups that they infiltrate and literally prey upon. A third strategy is to act upon the belief that dissenters and violent political delinquents form a tightly knit web, the latter occupying its center; one then tries to use as unwilling informants those dissenters thought to operate on the outer fringe of the web. In all three cases the law-abiding dissenter becomes a law-enforcement target through what I believe to be a permanent operational constraint of policing: producing suspects.

The tendency to confuse lawful dissent with illegal behavior is, in my opinion, an insuperable feature of policing political activities; no amount of legal safeguards can do away with this tendency. Striving to prevent political policing from hampering the right to dissent is as hopeless as trying to keep a stake from casting it shadow.

HIGH POLICING AND LOW POLICING

So far, I have deliberately used the expressions *policing political activities* and *political policing* as loose synonyms. This way of speaking might create a wrong impression: that policing can be said to be political only if it interferes with the political activities of citizens, whether lawful or unlawful. This seems to me to be too narrow a perspective, for it implies that if all counter-subversive and counter-intelligence divisions presently existing in police forces were suppressed, we would be left with non-political law-enforcement. I believe that political policing not only refers to a certain number of programs and operations undertaken by specialized units inside a police force. Rather, it constitutes a general paradigm for policing or, in other words, a definite pattern of relations between a set of goals and the means to achieve them. I now briefly describe some of the main features of this paradigm and suggest that uncontrolled changes presently taking place in information technology are increasingly leading police forces to operate under this model.

It is unfortunate that most books on the police trace its modern origins[6] to Sir Robert Peel's preventive police.[7] This is but one of the paradigms for policing, which I call, in accordance with historical terminology, "low policing." Following Bordua (1968), Chapman (1970), and Tobias (1972), Manning (1977:106) equates low policing with criminal policing. I elaborate further on the difference between high and low policing, tentatively describing the latter as forceful reaction to conspicuous signs of disorder, whether or not of a criminal nature. A few examples from the history of policing make the difference between high and low policing more perceptible.

It is easy to overlook the first police organization comparable to modern forces, the one created in France in 1667, under Louis XIV. Its explicit aim was to strengthen royal authority in all fields of activity. According to Clement (1978) and Chassaigne (1975), this force rapidly grew into an apparatus devoted to high policing (*haute police*), under the Lieutenancy of René d'Argenson, who headed the French police between 1697 and 1715. A concrete insight into the nature of high policing is provided by Fontenelle's eulogy for d'Argenson, read before the French *Académie des Sciences*. One of the luminaries of the reign of Louis XIV, Fontenelle was then secretary of the prestigious *Académie*. His eulogy describes in striking fashion the duties of the police, as they came to be perceived:

> To perpetually feed in a city like Paris an immense consumption,[8] of which some of the sources can be dried up by an infinite number of accidents; to repress the tyranny of the merchants against the public, while at the same time stirring up their trade; to draw from an infinite crowd all of those who can so easily hide within it their pernicious industry; either to purge society of them or to tolerate their being insofar as they can be useful in performing tasks which nobody would assume or carry out as well; to hold necessary abuses within the precise bounds of necessity which they are always prone to violate; to reduce these abuses to such obscurity as they must be condemned, and not even to retrieve them from it by too glaring a punishment; to ignore what it is better to ignore than to punish, and to punish only rarely and usefully; to penetrate inside families through underground passages and to keep the secrets that they never imparted for as long as it is unnecessary to use them; to be everywhere without being seen; finally, to move or to check at will a vast and tempestuous multitude and to be the ever active and nearly unknown soul of this great body; these are the duties of the police magistrate. (Quoted in Clement, 1978:334; translated here by the author).

This description stands in sharp contrast to Peel's principles of policing (Reith, 1975). High policing is actually the paradigm for political policing: it reaches out for potential threats in a systematic attempt to preserve the distribution of power in a given society.

High policing has four basic features, the first of which is the most important:

1) High policing is first of all absorbent policing.[9] This feature itself has two traits: (1) It aims to control by storing intelligence. (2) This intelligence

gathering is all-encompassing: it extends to any domain that may further the implementation of state policies.[10] This description is as valid today as it was at the beginning of French high policing. In an interview that the director of *Renseignements Généraux* (General Intelligence, a division of the French *Police Judiciaire*) granted me in December 1982, he described his service in 1982 as performing "police journalism on behalf of the state." In using the word "journalism" he meant that no field of activity in France was alien to police reporting. However, gathering intelligence is accomplished not only through the accumulation of data; it is also greatly enhanced by exhaustively charting the physical and social space into definite coordinates in order to increase the scope and precision of surveillance. Thus, in his 1749 memoir on the reform of the French police, Guillaute, (1974), an officer of the *Maréchaussée* (provincial police), not only outlined the first automated system of police records but also made elaborate proposals for numbering houses, apartments, and stairways; for identifying all vehicles; and for listing occupations, travels, hotel occupancy, and so forth. Intelligence gathering in this paradigm was not restricted to physical behavior (actual deeds). Words, whether spoken aloud or whispered in private, and whether written for publication or in a personal correspondence, were a primary focus of surveillance; mail opening was melodramatically said to be performed in a *"cabinet noir"*—a black cabinet.

2) High policing is not uniquely bound to enforce the law and regulations as they are made by an independent legislator.[11] The head of the French police was originally a ruling magistrate; he had wide powers of regulation and was often directly commissioned by the executive branch of the government to perform special duties. The extent of his power can be gauged from the fact that he could, in certain cases, officially pronounce the death penalty. The French police apparatus had a double structure: its higher personnel was divided between *commissaires* (commissioners), who had judicial powers and *inspecteurs* (inspectors), who had executive powers. Together, the head of the French police and his personnel of commissioners and inspectors possessed the three forms of power (legislative, judicial, and executive) that are traditionally separated.

3) Protecting the community from law violators is not an end in itself for high policing; crime control may also serve as a tool to generate information which can be used to maximize state coercion of any group or individual perceived as threatening the established order. Crime is thus conceived as something which lends itself to manifold exploitation. The use of common criminals to crush political deviance is a regular tactic of high policing. This type of

policing is, therefore, more deeply involved in crime management than in crime repression. This third feature of high policing has been aptly formulated by Hans von Henting in his book on Fouché, one of the main originators of high policing: "A political police is not so much an instrument for the protection of society as a form of political activity through the medium of the police" (Quoted in Radzinowicz, 1956:572).

4) High policing not only makes extensive use of undercover agents and paid informers, but it also acknowledges its willingness to do so. It strives in this way both to maintain a low operational visibility and to amplify the fear of denunciation. Madelin (1930) and Williams (1979) have shown that, between 1700 and 1815, the dread instilled in the French population over its alleged penetration by police informers was in no way proportionate to their actual number. But whatever the real number of informers actually used by a high police apparatus, this apparatus always pursues a double strategy of actual infiltration (which can become quite extensive) and of maximization of insecurity among the target groups by deliberately spreading rumors about the pervasive character of its deployment.

THE COMING OF AGE OF HIGH POLICING

Limitations of space of prevent me from offering detailed arguments here to support my belief that North American police forces are already operating under the high policing paradigm—or that they will increasingly be doing so, the long arm of the law being, so to speak, curtailed in favor of the wide eyes of the police. I suggest, however, that this hypothesis deserves careful consideration. In linking the features of high policing to present aspects of policing, I first briefly deal with its last three features and then concentrate on the most important feature, absorbent policing.

The police as legislator is nowhere more active than in spelling out the details of its alleged mandate to monitor domestic political activities. Earlier quotes from reports on the RCMP security service show that its mandate is not given by Canadian statutes. Instead, the commissions of inquiry showed that the mandate was pieced together from a motley array of legal, executive, and police internal policy documents (Brodeur: 1981). Indeed, when questioned about its mandate by the Keable commission in 1978, the RCMP security service commissioned its lawyers to introduce as legal exhibits a few pages of the long-forgotten 1969 royal commission report. With regard to the United States, Donner (1980) provides a compelling demonstration that the

FBI's domestic intelligence activities were performed under a slack interpretation of a pseudo-directive by President Franklin D. Roosevelt.

Exploiting crime for political purposes is a particularly blatant police practice in the law enforcement field of "morality" (prostitution, gambling, and drug and alcohol control). Brothels have traditionally been protected for intelligence gathering and blackmail. A more vivid example of crime management is provided by Epstein (1977), who makes a convincing case that the Nixon administration planned to use the Drug Enforcement Agency (DEA) as a political tool and was succeeding in its plan when the Watergate scandal broke. An extreme form of crime exploitation is the use of *agents provocateurs* to "stimulate" criminal behavior, a practice which has been a focus of concern both in the United States (Marx, 1974, 1980, 1981) and in Canada.

Police recourse to regularly paid informants (informers) integrates and is based on all features of high policing. The increasing reliance of the police on low-visibility informers is well documented; a wealth of material has recently been released on this issue, both in the United States and Canada.[12] Most noteworthy on this matter is the report of Judge Charles D. Breitel (1980) in a civil suit brought by the U.S. Socialist Workers Party against the U.S. Attorney General. Not only does the report show that this party was literally ridden with FBI informers, but it also documents the fact that, to all practical purposes, the FBI's Manual of Instructions filled a legal vacuum regarding questions related to the infiltration and control of informers. (This subject is closer to a legal "black hole" than to the proverbial "grey area" within the law.) Wrote Breitel:

> From approximately 1961 to 1971, the FBI maintained a counterintelligence program (Cointelpro) against the SWP [Socialist Workers Party] and YSA [Young Socialist Alliance] entitled the "SWP Disruption Program," which consisted in part of the dissemination of information by the FBI designed to impair the ability of the SWP and YSA to function....The tactics utilized in these programs included disclosing to the press the criminal records of SWP candidates, and sending anonymous letters to SWP members, supporters, spouses, and employers. Informant [informer] involvement in the counterintelligence programs consisted in part of providing the FBI with information it utilized in anonymous letters and of reporting to the FBI on the effects of counterintelligence programs. The FBI's investigation of the SWP and YSA was conducted pursuant to the instructions contained in Section 87 of the FBI Manual of Instructions ("the Manual").... From at least 1960 until1976, Section 87 of the Manual instructed FBI field offices to develop informants on all levels of organizations, such as SWP and YSA, which were the subjects of

domestic security investigations.... Approximately 55 FBI informants held offices or committee positions in the SWP and YSA between 1960 and 1976. (Breitel, 1980:4-5).

Finally, it is an avowed fact that informers are recruited by the police among persons facing criminal charges, which are provisionally dropped in return for information. All three features of high policing under discussion— supplementing the law, exploiting crime, and recruiting informers—are thus involved in the question of infiltration.[13]

Though substantial, the connections I have made so far do not point decisively to a drift towards high policing. However, all western countries now have computerized criminal information centers, and this seems to me to be the hub of the issue.

Bunyan (1976) predicted that by 1979 there would be over 36 million names and entries on file in the British Police National Computer Unit—most of them concerning motor vehicles. In the United States in 1982, the criminal records of over 36 million people were stored in computers (Slade and Biddle, 1982). The FBI manages the National Crime Information Center (NCIC). The experimental System for Electronic Analysis and Retrieval of Criminal Histories (Project SEARCH) is a permanent appendix of the NCIC (NCIC-Computerized Criminal Histories, or NCIC-CCH) and stores 1.3 million criminal records. One could multiply the acronyms: for instance, the U.S. National Security Agency (NSA) had its MINARET watch-list of protestors during the Vietnam War. In Canada, the RCMP operates the Canadian Police Information Center (CPIC) and several provinces have their own computerized criminal information center, such as Québec's *Bureau de renseignements criminels du Québec* (BRCQ).

The establishment of such information centers is legitimized by the alleged needs of crime control. The point that I wish to stress is that the uncontrolled profligacy in storing crime and crime-related information is liable to transform the nature of policing. By its sheer weight, criminal intelligence gathering, whose scope is very loosely, if at all, regulated by law, can progressively give birth to a general surveillance—the equivalent of high or political policing.

Some authors play down these concerns. Colton (1978) suggests that the efficiency of computers in policing has been overrated. Similarly, the September 1982 issue of *Police Magazine* is titled "Police and the computer: Still working out the glitches."[14] Others defend the emerging system. I will respond to four main lines of defense.

1) Morgan (1980:164) says there is agreement among the police that

information should not be collected randomly on political dissenters and that all intelligence gathering must be linked to preventing a specific crime. Unfortunately, making files out of unbridled criminal suspicions is a free police exercise. But more generally, I would say that crime prevention is such an open category that it allows almost any kind of information to be stored. RCMP Commissioner Robert Simmonds told the McDonald commission that *any* information stored in government data banks might prove crucial in an emergency: for example, police might seek the medical record of a highjacker for clues to his or her psychological profile (Vastel, 1981). In a newspaper interview, Simmonds requested that the police be legally granted freedom of access to all federal data banks, adding that the police *would manage anyhow to get the information it wanted*: legalizing the process would only make it less costly and more effective (Préfontaine, 1980). Our problem thus concerns much more than the police's own computers.

2) Like other contributors to Hoffman (1980), Westin (1980:173) claims that the use of computers has "not yet" led the police "to collect more intrusive or sensitive personal information" than before (Colton's observations, like the *Police Magazine* issue, boil down to a "not yet" type of impatience). However, as the U.S. Privacy Protection Study Commission (1977) emphasized, computers are not mere data repositories; their real potential lies in interconnecting already available data. Intrusiveness is more than the depth of penetration into personal intimacy; it is also measured by the breadth of information processed. Computers do not, of course, intrude by themselves; however, they can transform into a system of pseudo-knowledge intrusive gossip by police informers and input mistakes by unskilled clerks.[15]

3) Daunt (1980:191) an FBI officer, argues that police computers store only what is public record (the "rap sheet"). Indeed, in *Paul v. Davis* (1976) the U.S. Supreme Court refused to extend federal privacy protection to the dissemination of criminal justice information (on the dubious grounds that an arrest by the police is hardly a private affair). Does this imply that someone arrested on a false charge will forever have this fact on their public record and possibly be trapped in a "data-prison of denied credit and foreclosed job opportunities?" (Katzenbach and Tomc, 1973:65). Moreover, the objection assumes that what is computerized is only a matter of public record. This may be true for certain NCIC computer programs, but it is less true of local police force data banks which are reputed to be more prolific, listing *suspects*[16] (Kansas City's ALERT: Automated Law Enforcement Response Team) and alleged narcotic addicts, (New York State's Identification and Intelligence System). Many such local systems exist both in the United States and Canada.

Whether stored in computers or not, medical records are not a matter of public record, yet the police are requesting legal access to them. The Ontario Commission of Inquiry into the Confidentiality of Health Information (1980) has shown that the police were given wide access to medical files by informer-doctors, who were thus violating their medical oath.

4) One might invoke legislation such as the U.S. Privacy Act of 1974 to argue that the legal protection is provided against invasions of privacy. However, the U.S. Privacy Protection Study Commission (1977:53) has stressed that "the Act's failure to attend to the impact of technological advances on individual liberties and personal privacy" has significantly weakened its guarantees. The same criticism holds against Canadian legislation on the protection of privacy. Bill C 43, which consists in part of a privacy act, was passed by the Canadian Parliament in June 1982. It is more protective of state prerogatives than of the citizen's right to privacy.

Thus, it is a genuine concern that instead of protecting and serving the community, the police may bring about a state monopoly over a computerized ghost citizenry readily available for manipulation and control. Doubtless, this process is no more deliberate than was the transformation for all practical purposes, of drivers' licences into identity cards. I must agree with Pyle (1972:103) that "once born, political data banks appear to grow through the normal processes of bureaucratic accretion." Seemingly innocuous things sometimes beget unforeseen and unwanted results. High policing is, in itself, less an evil than a threat. After all, France has harbored it for more than three centuries and is still a living democracy. High policing is none the less bound to cause a significant (if not grievous) erosion of freedom if it is left unchecked.

CONCLUSION AND IMPLICATIONS

Government inquiries and public controversies over the policing of political activities have adopted a deviance approach, which assumes that unwarranted police activities consist only of aggressive, illegal intrusions of individual policemen or programs into the lives of private citizens. It adopts a "low policing" view of the problem. In so doing, it unknowingly rejects another, more appropriate model of police work in general, and political policing in particular. This alternate view stresses the similarities and overlap between political policing and police work in general. Contemporary developments, especially in computer technology, make the high police model much more compelling. These two models suggest different approaches to the problem of controlling the police and to containing unacceptable intrusions of the police into political life.

While unwilling to surrender to what might derisively be called the "big computer scare," I do wish to underline that the traditional legal distinction between private and public is becoming socially obsolete. It should be replaced by a three-fold distinction among (1) what is public; (2) what is recorded for the benefit of some agency or some organization; and (3) what is still private. The scope of what is on file in that uncertain middle ground between the public and the private seems to be expanding over the years, and the intermediate zone is spreading over both sides of its boundaries. I believe it should be a matter of concern not to let that middle ground become a colony of the police.

How can this be achieved? The standard answer is that it should be done by establishing controls on policing, thus creating some form of police accountability. Quite so. However, controlling is an exercise very much akin to policing. Just as there are two models of policing, might there not also be two paradigms for controlling the police, namely high and low control? I believe that the misguided reliance of the deviance approach on the prosecution of individual violations of law by police officers exemplifies a self-defeating attempt to check the abuses of high policing through the inadequate means of low control. Consequently, what should be done is to inquire whether there are any features of high policing which could be useful in articulating a strategy of high control. There are at least two such features. First, high policing is not a piece-meal endeavour; it is relentless and implies systematic *continuity*. Second, it focusses on the processing of information, from which future events can be foreseen and, if need be, averted (through subsequent policy-making).

Thus, high control needs, first, a *permanent* institutional base from which it can be independently exercised. An example can be found in the French National Commission on Computer Technology and Freedoms, appointed by law in 1978 with an explicit mandate to see that no application of computer technology infringes on civil liberties. Second, the wealth of information on high policing must be transformed into a cogent body of knowledge from which we can act on decisively to preclude what is intolerable in an open society.

But again, what will prompt us to act in such a way? Perhaps nothing short of an ideological conversion that will make us feel how vulnerable we have become. It is dismaying to find how our notion of the human mind is influenced by psychology which, with few exceptions, conceives it as some sort of inner data bank. This sunken computeroid is deemed so private that only a psychologist can retrieve some of its most emotional secrets. This ideology of inwardness appears to me completely outdated by changes that are now wantonly occurring in society. As human subjects, we are becoming objectified as a set of external traces. Hence, the time has passed to salvage what little has remained inside us; the task now is to protect what we are daily emptied of.

ENDNOTES

* This is a revised and slightly expanded version of a paper presented at the 34th annual meeting of the American Society of Criminology in Toronto, November 1982. Correspondence to: Ecole de Criminologie, Université de Montreal, C.P. 6128, Succursale A, Montréal, Québec H3C 3J7, Canada.

This chapter was previously published by the University of California Press. Copyright ©1983 by the Society for the Study of *Social Problems*. Reprinted from *Social Problems*, Vol. 30 (5), pp. 507-520, by permission.

1.   In the United States, the deviance approach is exemplified in academic literature by Blackstock (1976), Donner (1980), Halperin et al., (1979), Morgan (1980), Rowan (1978), Theoharis (1978), and Wise (1979). It is also illustrated by most of the contributors to Berman and Halperin (1975), Borosage and Marks (1976), Fain (1977), Frazier (1978), and *Columbia Human Rights Law Review* (1973). For Canada, see Brown and Brown (1978), Dion (1979), Mann and Lee (1979), Sawatsky (1980), Shearing (1981), and Fournier et al., (1978). This survey is by no means exhaustive and I have quoted only recent literature.

2.   For detailed descriptions of police laundering of language, see Mann and Lee (1979) and Brodeur (1981). Mann and Lee have coined the expression "laundered language." Perhaps the most famous example of such laundering is the Central Intelligence Agency's replacement of "assassination" by "termination with extreme prejudice."

3.   There is some irony in the fact that, though identical in content, the recommendations of the Mackenzie royal commission and the McDonald commission stem from opposite grounds. Commissioner Mackenzie wanted the security service out of the RCMP because he believed that the former's lawlessness was incompatible with the untarnished image that had to be projected by the latter. Volume 2 of the McDonald report (Canada, 1981a: part 6, chapter 3) argues that the weight of bad habits inside the RCMP would preclude any significant reforming of the security service if it was left under the RCMP's control.

4.   It was revealed during the hearings of the commission of inquiry of which I was a staff member that a *bona fide* member of one of the main Québec leftist organizations, *En Lutte*, was in fact a police informer. In the months following the publication of the commission's report, this organization dissolved itself.

5.   An informer provides the police with information on a regular basis, in return for gratifications which may widely vary. An informant might be, for instance, an indignant witness to a crime.

6.   The words "modern origins" need to be stressed here. Policing functions have been performed since early antiquity. According to Jacob (1979), public slaves owned by the state were used as a police force in ancient Greece.

7. The qualification "preventive" does not purport here to contrast one distinctive type of policing with another. For the English reformers of the 19th century, policing was seen in itself as an alternative to sentencing by the judiciary, the harshness of punishment being notoriously inefficient in England. Thus *any* kind of policing (even of the most repressive kind) would still have been called preventive. Put another way, Peel's preventive police was essentially thought of as a *deterrent* police.

8. One of the original tasks of the French police was to ensure that Paris was adequately provided with food supplies, in order to prevent riots.

9. Mathiesen (1980:277) uses the expression "the absorbent State" in a sense akin to my own meaning.

10. The letters of Joseph Fouché, Napoleon's minister of police, are particularly illuminating on the nature of high policing. "The police," wrote Fouché to Wellington in 1816, "is a political magistracy, which, apart from its special functions, should co-operate by methods, irregular perhaps, but just, legitimate and benevolent, in augmenting the *effectiveness of every measure of government.*" (Quoted in Radzinowicz, 1956:555, emphasis added).

11. Again, Fouché shows that there was continuity in French high policing before and after the Revolution of 1789. In a letter to Napoleon, he wrote, "the police, as I conceive it, should be established in order to forestall and prevent offences and to check and arrest *such as have not been foreseen by the law*" (Quoted in Radzinowicz, 1956:566, emphasis added).

12. Donner (1980:137) claims that some 37,000 paid informers were used by the FBI between 1940 and 1978. This is given as a "conservative" figure. The Keable report presents detailed descriptions of the police use of informers (Quebéc, 1981).

13. Maximizing insecurity by spreading rumors is also a prominent feature of the use of informers by the police. The Keable report cites an RCMP document on anti-subversive tactics which reads: "We prevented the much-mooted FLQ *[Front de libération du Québec]* renaissance of 1971 by a simple reversal of our earlier policies—a reversal inspired by the theories of Dr. Gustav Morf and others about the group dynamics of secret associations. Instead of hoarding our intelligence, we gave it away to individuals identified as particularly susceptible, by our psychologist, among members of emerging cells. The cells in question, exaggerating the extent of our knowledge of them, dispersed as if by magic" (Quoted in Québec, 1981:250).

14. An article by Rosen (1982) in this issue of *Police Magazine* is entitled "Police and the computer: The revolution that never happened."

15. Slade and Biddle (1982) mention that almost half a sample of FBI computerized criminal records were found by the Office of Technology Assessment to be incomplete or inaccurate.

16. According to Funk and Werkentin (1978), the German police collects data on persons who are "close to being suspects" (*verdachtnäh*).

REFERENCES

Berman, Jerry J., and Morton H. Halperin. 1975. *The Abuses of the Intelligence Agencies.* Washington, D.C.: Center for National Security Studies.

Blackstock, Nelson. 1976. *Cointelpro: The FBI's Secret War on Political Freedom.* New York: Vintage.

Bordua, David J. 1968. "The police." Pp. 174-181 in *International Encyclopedia of Social Science.* New York: Free Press.

Borosage, Robert L., and John Marks. 1976. *The CIA File.* New York: Grossman Publishers.

Breitel, Charles D. 1980. *Final Report of Special Master.* New York: Political Rights Defence Fund.

Brodeur, Jean-Paul. 1981. "Legitimizing police deviance." Pp. 127-160 in Clifford Shearing (ed.), *Organizational Police Devianc.*, Toronto: Butterworths.

Brown, Lorne, and Caroline Brown. 1978. *An Unauthorized History of the RCMP.* Toronto: James Lorimer.

Bunyan, Tony. 1976. *The History and Practice of the Political Police in Britain.* London: J. Friedman.

Canada 1966. *Report of the Commission of Inquiry into Complaints Formulated by George Victor Spencer* (The D.C. Wells Report). Ottawa: Queen's Printer.

_____, 1969. *Abridged Report of the Royal Commission on Security* (The Mackenzie Report). Ottawa: Queen's Printer.

_____, 1981a. *Second Report of the Commission of Inquiry Concerning Certain Activities of the Royal Canadian Mounted Police: Freedom and Security Under the Law* (The McDonald Report, 2 volumes). Ottawa: Minister of Supplies and Services.

_____, 1981b. *Third Report of the Commission of Inquiry Concerning Certain Activities of the Royal Canadian Mounted Police: Certain RCMP Activities and the Question of Governmental Knowledge* (The McDonald Report). Ottawa: Minister of Supplies and Services.

Chapman, Brian. 1970. *Police State.* London: Pall Mall.

Chassaigne, Marc. 1975. *La lieutenance générale de police de Paris.* Genève: [1906] Slatkine, Megoriatis.

Clément, Pierre 1978 *La police sous Louis XIV.* Genève: Slatkine, Megoriatis. [1866]

Colton, Kent W. 1978. "A decade of experience since the crime commission: Conclusion and recommendations." Pp. 281-293 in Kent W. Colton (ed.), *Police Computer Technology.* Lexington, Mass. Lexington Books.

Columbia Human Rights Law Review (ed.) 1973. "Surveillance, Dataveillance, and Personal Freedoms." Fair Lawn, N.J.: R.E. Burdick.

Daunt, Jerome J. 1980. "Comment." Pp. 186-192 in Lance J. Hoffman (ed.), Computers and Privacy in the Next Decade. New York: Academic Press.

Dion, Robert. 1979. Les crimes de la Police Montée. Montréal: Editions coopératives Albert Saint-Martin.

Donner, Frank J. 1980. The Age of Surveillance: The Aims and Methods of America's Political Intelligence System. New York: Alfred A. Knopf.

Epstein, Edward Jay. 1977. Agency of Fear. New York: G.P. Putnam's Sons.

Ericson, Richard V. 1981. Making Crime. Toronto: Butterworths.

Fain, Tyrus G. 1977. The Intelligence Community. New York: R.R. Bowker Co.

Fournier, Louis. 1978. La police secrète au Québec. Montréal: Editions Québec/Amérique.

Frazier, Howard. 1978. Uncloaking the CIA. New York: The Free Press.

Funk, A., and Falco Werkentin. 1978. "Pour une nouvelle analyse du développment de la police en Europe occidentales." Déviance et Société 2(2): 97-129.

Greenwood, Peter W., Jan Chaiken, Joan Petersilia, and Linda Prusoff 1975. The Criminal Investigation Process. Volume 3: Observations and Analysis. Santa Monica, Calif.: Rand Corporation.

Guillaute, M. 1974. Mémoire sur la réformation de la Police de France. Paris: Hermann. [1749]

Halperin, Morton, Jerry Berman, Robert Borosage, and Christine Marwick. 1979. The Lawless State. New York: Penguin Books.

Hoffman, Lance J. 1980. Computers and Privacy in the Next Decade. New York: Academic Press.

Jacob, Oscar. 1979. Les esclaves publics à Athènes. New York: Arno Press. [1928]

Katzenbach, Nicholas de B., and Richard W. Tomc. 1973. "Crime data centers: The use of computers in crime detection and prevention." Pp. 59-67 in Columbia Human Rights Review (ed.), Surveillance, Dataveillance, and Personal Freedoms. Fair Lawn, N.J.: R.E. Burdick Publisher.

Madelin, Louis. 1930. Fouché. Paris: Plon.

Mann, Edward and John A. Lee. 1979. RCMP vs. The People. Don Mills, Ontario: General Publishing Co.

Manning, Peter K. 1977. Police Work. Cambridge, Mass.: The MIT Press.

————, 1980. The Narc's Game. Cambridge, Mass.: The MIT Press.

Mathiesen, Thomas. 1980. Law, Society, and Political Action. London: Academic Press.

Marx, Gary T., 1974. "Thoughts on a neglected category of social movement participants: Agents provocateurs and informants." *American Journal of
Sociology* 80(2): 402-442.

_____, 1980. "The new police undercover work." *Journal of Urban Life* 8(4):
400-446.

_____, 1981. "Ironies of social control: Authorities as contributors to deviance
through escalation, non-enforcement, and covert facilitation." *Social
Problems* 28(3): 221-246.

Morgan, Richard E., 1980. *Domestic Intelligence: Monitoring Dissent in America.*
Austin: University of Texas Press.

Ontario 1980. *Report of the Commission of Inquiry into the Confidentiality of
Health Information* (The Krever Report). Toronto: Queen's Printer for
Ontario.

Platt, Anthony, and Lynn Cooper. 1974. *Policing America.* Englewood Cliffs, N.J.:
Prentice-Hall.

Préfontaine, André. 1980. "Le policier devrait avoir accès à tout ce qui lui est utile,
selon le commissaire de la GRC." *Le Devoir* (Montréal), February 10: 1.

Pyle, Christopher H. 1972. "Political data banks and civil liberties." Pp. 103-119 in
Richard H. Blum (ed.), *Surveillance and Espionage in a Free Society.* New
York: Praeger.

Quebec 1981. *Rapport de la commission de'enquête sur des opérations policières
en territoire quebecois* (The Keable Report). Québec: Ministere des
Communications.

Radzinowicz, Leon. 1956. *A History of English Criminal Law and its
Administration from 1750.* Volume 3: *Cross-Currents in the Movement
for the Reform of the Police.* London: Stevens and Sons Limited.

Reith, Charles. 1975. *The Blind Eye of History: A Study of the Origins of the
Present Police Era.* Montclair, N.J.: Patterson Smith.

Rosen, Daniel M. 1982. "Police and the computer: The revolution that never happened." *Police Magazine* 5(5): 8-21.

Rowan, Ford. 1978. *Technospies.* New York: G.P.Putnam's Sons.

Sanders, William. 1977. *Detective Work.* New York: The Free Press.

Sawatsky, John. 1980. *Men in the Shadows.* Toronto: Doubleday.

Shearing, Clifford. 1981. *Organizational Police Deviance.* Toronto: Butterworths.

Slade, Margot and Wayne Biddle. 1982. "Police and public in the United Kingdom."
Journal of Contemporary History 7(1-2): 201-219.

U.S. Congress: Senate 1976. *Intelligence Activities and the Rights of Americans* (The Church Report). Select Committee to Study Governmental Operations With Respect to Intelligence Activities. 94th Congress, 2nd session. Washington, D.C.: U.S. Government Printing Office.

U.S. Privacy Protection Study Commission 1977. Personal Privacy in an Information Society. *The Report of the Privacy Protection Study Commission.* Washington, D.C.: U.S. Government Printing Office.

Vastel, Michel. 1981. "La Gendarmerie des années 80: Plus francophone, plus puissante, et mieux contrôlée." *Le Devoir* (Montréal), March 13: 2.

Westin, Alan F. 1980. "The long-term implications of computers for privacy and the protection of public order." Pp. 167-181 in Lance J. Hoffman (ed.), *Computers and Privacy in the Next Decade.* New York: Academic Press.

Williams, Alan 1979. *The Police of Paris: 1718-1789.* Baton Rouge: Louisiana State University Press.

Wise, David 1979. *The American Police State.* New York: Random.

Case Cited.
Paul v. Davis 424 U.S. 693, 1976.

CHAPTER 13
A Theory of Deference Exchange in Police-Civilian Encounters

RICHARD E. SYKES
JOHN P. CLARK

The authors suggest an explanation of police-civilian behavior based
on a normative and interpersonal construct rather than on a psychological construct. Police behavior must be explained in terms of the
rules which order their relations with civilians and which are usually
mutually acknowledged by both. Among these rules the authors
[posit] that in a typical encounter relations are governed by an asymmetrical status norm when deference exchange is involved. This
norm effects various statuses in different ways. Data from an extensive study of police-civilian encounters in which the process of interaction was coded using a special interaction process analysis category system are used to test hypotheses derived from the theory.

Since the pioneering studies of Westley (1953, 1956) police behavior has
been explained as a function of attitudes possessed by police as an occupational group. Westley was originally concerned with the practice of secrecy among
police as well as their apparent tendency to use and rationalize extralegal violence. A decade later Skolnick (1966) proposed that a construct developed by
sociologists of work—that of "working personality"—be extended to police.
Skolnick argued that certain "outstanding elements in the police milieu, danger, authority, and efficiency...combine to generate distinctive cognitive and
behavioral responses" (p. 42). Subsequent scholars have sought to extend this
theory of police behavior. Tauber (1967), for example, emphasized the influence of danger and argued that "out of the multitude of demands and expectations of their role a working police personality develops" (p. 69). Hartjen
(1972) again re-asserted the important occupational concerns of police for

danger, authority, efficiency, hostility, and suspicion. One writer (Dodd 1967) went so far as to assert that the chief components of police culture are violence, graft, and secrecy. More moderate in their assessment, Bordua and Reiss (1967) concluded that police tend to become overauthoritative in socially ambiguous situations—securing compliance at the cost of unnecessary levels of hostility.

Personality or attitudinal constructs have also been used to explain tensions between police and minority groups. Authoritarianism and prejudice are commonly utilized to explain differential arrest rates, brutality, and poor service. Yet, evidence indicates that, while many police dislike minority groups, there is considerable doubt whether they differ in this regard from civilians of similar socioeconomic status or whether they normally treat minority civilians differently from others (Black and Reiss 1970; Rafsky 1973).

We do not wish to deny the occasional excesses of police, but several objections may be raised to the working personality explanation of police behavior. First, rather extensive personality testing of police has not confirmed that police are in any way different from the average citizen. Most officers are within the normal range insofar as personality traits are concerned (Trojanowicz 1971; Balch 1972; Niederhoffer 1967). Second, studies of police behavior have shown convincingly that violence is very infrequent in police work, and that the incidents of danger are less than in other occupations, for example, mining and construction (Clark and Sykes 1974; Reiss 1971). These same studies have also shown that most police work is routine, often bureaucratic, and in response to citizen rather than police initiative. Third, and perhaps the most serious objection, is that uniformed police typically do most of their work in interaction with civilians, and any explanation of their behavior must take their mutual relations into account.

The issue remains whether police behavior is to be explained utilizing hypothetical constructs of traits attributed to individual officers (because of selective recruitment or common experience shared by them) who interact with civilians characterized by some other set of traits. Such an explanation seems to reduce itself ultimately to one of actors driven by internal forces and behaving in each other's presence, but without taking each other into account. Their behavior together is a kind of epiphenomenon. The traits of the actors, generated by occupational experiences, childhood deprivation, or a variety of other factors, are decisive.

Our perspective, however, is that such an explanation neglects the propensity or, in fact, the necessity of actors to organize their activities toward one another not solely on the basis of personality predispositions, but by virtue of the positions they occupy. Positions have neither motives, traits, nor personal histories in the sense that persons do. Furthermore, the theoretical construct of position always implies location relative to another position. There exists a domain of phenomena which might be described as the process of relations between positions which cannot be explained by hypothetical psychological constructs because (a) positions are not persons, and (b) the set of relations between positions is a phenomenon entirely distinct from psychological phenomena. For example, one may study the personality traits, occupational or otherwise, of football players, but never, even remotely, approach and adequate explanation either of the game of football or of the typical behavior of the left tackle by such a construct.

The literature on police is very nearly devoid of theoretical work recognizing the importance of this domain of mutual interpositional organization. Even such writers as Tauber and Hartjen, who seem to begin with such a perspective, in the final analysis abandon it. In their preoccupation with police, they forget the role of civilians, except as objects of police perceptions, instead of viewing them as actors who, with police, must organize their relations. We would suggest the domain of sociological explanation is entered only when the *mutual* relations or organization between two or more positions are taken into account.

We wish to propose an explanation of police behavior based on a sociological (normative) and interpersonal construct rather than on what is more essentially a psychological (working personality or prejudice) construct. Police behavior must be explained in terms of the rules which order their relations with civilians and which are usually mutually acknowledged by both officers and civilians. Among these rules we posit the influence of an interpersonal norm governing police-civilian relations which we shall term an "asymmetrical status norm" (after Brown 1965) and which is evident in many relationships between those of unequal status in addition to police and civilians. Police are of higher status than many citizens with whom they interact by virtue of their occupational role and, in many instances, by virtue of their general socioeconomic condition. We hypothesize then that this difference in status influences the flow of deference so that it is expected that it will be expressed differently downward or upward. This difference in the flow of deference also explains many otherwise anomalous facets of the police-civilian relationship.

The failure of scholars to perceive these rules governing the flow of deference has led to the treatment of police in an often unsympathetic and stereotypical manner. There has also been a tendency to confuse the rules ordering interpersonal behavior (including the sanctioning of violations of these rules)

with the law because of the special association between this particular occupational group and law enforcement. Yet it would be strange indeed if police and
civilians did not order their relations by the same rules of interpersonal conduct as others, despite their special status vis-à-vis the law.

THEORETICAL ORIENTATION

ENCOUNTERS AS UNITS OF ANALYSIS

In recent years sociologists have taken an increased interest in natural
instances of focused interactions which Goffman (1961) terms "encounters,"
as distinguished from "small groups." In an encounter persons come together
to give their attention to a particular activity and then disperse; they do not
attribute an enduring identity to their joint endeavors. A small group, on the
other hand, has an identity separate from any particular gathering of its members; an encounter does not. A family or standing committee, for example, is
a small group; a noontime bridge game or autumn hunting party is an
encounter. If we accept this distinction, then the coming together of police
and citizens is more akin to the latter. It is ephemeral, requires the participants, maintenance of continuous engrossment in the official focus of activity,
and ceases to exist when the participants disperse (Goffman 1961, p. 11).

Yet on reflection, if a police-civilian meeting is an encounter, then it is of
a special kind. Unlike most encounters, there is a peculiar contrast in the
nature of the roles. On the one hand, some actors enter into the encounter as
part of their job and are cloaked with special authority and obvious power. In
Goffman's terms, officers often display role "embracement," for they are fully
seen in terms of its image and confirm expressively their acceptance of it
(Goffman, 1961, p. 106). On the other hand, citizens often will not embrace
their roles, not only because they are irregular performers, but because they
are commonly reluctant performers; this is true even when the encounter is
civilian initiated. In fact, every civilian participant displays some of those very
properties which are important not to display in focused interaction: embarrassment, lack of poise, distraction, failure to take proper turns at speaking,
and disregard of spacing rules. Civilians fail to be properly demeaned
(Goffman 1956, p. 489); they are not just citizens altercast as violators, but
include accident victims, householders who have locked themselves out, spouses assaulted by husbands who have since hastily departed, or tavern keepers
who have been robbed at gunpoint. Even if the actors are composed, the
occasion of the meeting is often such as to embarrass the citizen, for, in a cer-

tain sense, to be a victim is to have been made a fool, and to broadcast it publicly is to disclose one's foolishness.

Participation in the encounter is even more problematic for an alleged violator. Not only may he lose his freedom by being so defined, but his new status is often created by the reactions of fellow citizens as much as by the police. He has not violated the law as much as some established set of relational rules. For example, by beating his wife too severely or too frequently he may have caused her to complain, thus violating the rules of the family. Or, by displaying intemperate behavior in an encounter with tavern patrons, he may have caused the bartender to call for assistance. While the law may be invoked in these examples, it is often as a kind of pretext, an external means utilized because he had not displayed the proper deference toward his civilian fellows. Indeed, the resolution accomplished by police is normally in response to the desires of the citizens present (Black and Reiss 1970).

ORDERING RULES OF ENCOUNTERS

Even if these encounters are somewhat unusual, it still seems likely that they are, or, from the perspective of participants, should be rule governed, but that the rules should "fit" the situation. In police-citizen encounters, as in others, this order revolves around exchange of deference and maintenance of proper demeanor. Goffman defines deference as that "component of activity which functions as a symbolic means by which appreciation is regularly conveyed *to* a recipient *of* this recipient, or something of which this recipient is taken as a symbol, extension, or agent" (Goffman 1956, p. 477; italics in the original). It is our thesis that, in a typical encounter, relations between officers and citizens are governed by an asymmetrical status norm when deference exchange is involved (Brown 1965, p. 55). Such a norm symbolizes some special evaluation of actor, in this case one in which the officer generally has greater social value and influence than the citizen. Brown writes that such a norm may be operative in a relation of direct but temporary subordination (p. 69), and that in contemporary America it is manifested with intonation, vocal quality, and vocabulary selection rather than with the pronouns of address (p. 66).

That an officer should expect the encounter to be governed by such a norm should not be surprising. [Note that Goffman speaks of a recipient of deference as being "taken as a symbol, extension, or agent" (p. 477).] Certainly the officer is symbolic of the law, the ultimate Weberian rational legal basis of social authority in modern societies. In this sense he may be said to symbolize the sacred in the Durkheimean sense. On the occasions when he is called upon by citizens (Reiss 1971), those citizens who invited him to be present are obligated at least to express deference in return for his presence (Weinstein, DeVaughn, and Wiley 1969). In addition, when someone alleged to be a violator is present, his very status as violator implies not only to the officer, but to others, that in some sense he is already guilty, if not of a crime, then of failure to display deference toward his fellow citizens. He then is twice obligated; not just to the citizens, but, by showing deference to the officer, he reestablishes himself as someone willing to fulfill his interpersonal obligations and membership in the moral community. For if he refuses deference to the officer, the symbol of that community's authority, he may be suspected of openly announcing his secession from it: "to be pointedly refused an expected act of deference is often a way of being told that open insurrection has begun" (Goffman 1956, p. 480). The obligation is proportionate to the offense; the greater the violation, the more he must defer in order to establish that he really respects the basic social obligations. Finally, it should be noted that since most contacts by police are with working- or lower-class citizens, citizens of no more than equal status of the officer, the asymmetrical status norm may extend to broader dimensions of the actors' identities than those peculiar to the legal focus of the encounter.

If the norm is asymmetrical, deference will be expressed differently downward than upward. The higher-status actor is not expected to show the same regard as the lower. We would, in fact, expect him to show an amount of regard precisely related to the status of his fellow actor. If the citizen is not a violator but his normal demeanor is absent due to the special circumstances of his embarrassment, the proper response of the officer might well be the "rational bureaucratic framework of civility" (Bordua and Reiss 1967, p. 297) which citizens are said to regard sometimes as disrespect. If the citizen is alleged to be a violator, the asymmetry will be even greater. And if the citizen chooses to behave like a violator, that is, like someone deliberately disregarding the social conventions, he will purposely fail to display deference, with consequent effect on the officer's asymmetrical response. "There are situations where an actor conveys ritual profanation of a recipient while officially engaged in talk with him or in such a way that the affront cannot be easily over-looked" (Goffman 1956, p. 495).

Such a theoretical perspective does not invalidate the past emphasis upon the consequences of personality characteristics to events of an encounter, but it does suggest that the more fundamental and pervasive force of a norm may be operating simultaneously.

SPECIAL COMPLICATIONS
OF POLICE-MINORITY CIVILIAN ENCOUNTERS

If these rules do order all such encounters, they apply to encounters by police with minority as well as with majority participants. But if this is true from the officer's perspective, from the point of view of a minority citizen it may be difficult to discriminate subjectively between the general operation of the asymmetrical status norm and the special asymmetrical norm governing relations based on ethnic stratification. Orans (1971) suggests that when a group is subordinated by another, and this subordination is internalized, subordination takes the form of a rank concession syndrome: acceptance of oneself as socially inferior and of the attributes of rank of the superior society (p. 90). This syndrome is manifested through special deference, but in a time when upward mobility is arduously pursued and subordination is sharply denied as an aspect of identity, display of such deference is rejected decisively. "Pride, self-help, and militance," says Orans (p. 121), become especially salient values.

Under such circumstances it is not surprising that neither police nor minorities desire contact with one another unless absolutely necessary, for they possess conflicting expectations and obligations. An entirely unprejudiced officer, in expecting general deference, may be interpreted by a minority civilian as indicating the officer's own ethnic group's superordination. On the other hand, the minority citizen's refusal to express deference may be viewed by the officer as refusal to acknowledge normal social obligations of all citizens and the officer's symbolic status. Thus, it is in encounters between the formerly subordinate and the symbolic representatives of the authority which subordinated them that both tend unintentionally to discredit each other. Even with the best intentions, an officer may become a "racist pig" and the citizen a "wise-ass" if they misunderstand one another's indications. Each may impose on the other his definition of reality. Thus, we agree with Hartjen (1972), but only with the provision that stereotyping is mutual. Not just stereotyping is involved, however, for to each actor the indicators which express the asymmetrical status norm convey a double meaning and place both in a double bind (Watzlawick, Beavin, and Jackson 1967). The asymmetrical status norm, operative in most police-citizen encounters, is difficult to distinguish from the special asymmetrical status norm operative when ethnic subordinates interact with superordinates.

COMPLEXITIES CONFOUNDED BY SEX AND AGE

These asymmetrical normative expectations may be confounded by two other status factors: sex and age. Police readily admit that they find it difficult to handle a female suspect who "bad mouths" or aggressively resists them. Norms against publicly using the same language or physical means against a woman that one would with a man "cramp their style." Insofar as public interaction is concerned, the asymmetrical status norm operates in reverse. Men, including police officers are expected to be as deferent as or more deferent than women.

Age is also a complicating factor; obedience and deference are expected from young civilians. On the other hand, an adult officer is expected to treat a senior citizen with due respect for the citizen's age. The aged many also be correspondingly less deferent toward the officer. An old woman is free to say what she likes, but the asymmetrical norm prevents the officer from responding in kind.

THE RESOURCES OF STATUS

We assume a kind of common "coin" of exchange is used to bestow social value, and the tokens of such coin are the niceties of ceremony. Within any particular universe of social evaluation such tokens are distributed unequally, so that lower-status persons have fewer resources with which to express deference and to maintain demeanor. For this reason, the actual level of deference expressed within any particular social status will vary. The deferential quality of interaction is less within a lower social rank. If the asymmetrical norm is operative, then the officer is obligated to display much less deference toward those of lower status than toward those of higher; since the actual level is lower, he will always be expected to display relatively less. It is as if a regressive tax were levied on the coin of ceremonial exchange.

DATA

COLLECTION

During a 15-month period beginning in June 1970, we conducted a quantitative observational study of police in a city of more than 500,000 and in two suburbs, of which about 5% were either black or Indian American. A group of observers, trained over three months, travelled with police on a random-time sample basis, using portable electronic coding equipment and an interaction process code.

The date base consists of 1,466 encounters involving about 9,000 citizens. When such calls involved verbal or nonverbal behavior toward citizens, the interaction was simultaneously and sequentially content analyzed. Among the situational factors coded were whether the encounter was an on-scene or radio call, the purpose of the call, the kind of space in which the activity occurred (if indoors, how the police entered), and whether there was conflict between citizens when the officers arrived. The exchange of deference was measured by a wide variety of action and interaction codes pertaining to civility and incivility, giving and following orders, display of anger, and codes relating to specific kinds of violence, aggressive threats, or acts. The specific outcome of the encounter was also encoded. Demographic data were collected from visual and audial observation and coded for complainant, victim, alleged violator, participants, and bystanders. Interobserver reliability was calculated utilizing Scott's II (Scott 1955; Krippendorff 1970), and the coefficient for codes reported herein ranged between .70 and .80.

MEASURES OF NORMATIVE BEHAVIOR

Each statement throughout the encounter was rated by the observers as being either deferring (respectful) or disrespectful. Signs of respect included police language, neutral or positive tone, and acknowledgment of the legitimacy of the self presented by the other. Signs of disrespect included impolite language, negative tone, and statements of the kind that tended to discredit the self of the other. Existence of an asymmetrical status norm was inferred whenever interaction by officers toward a particular status was consistently less respectful over many encounters.

These indices of the respect/disrespect dimension were calculated: (a) absolute deference level (ADL); (b) index of discrediting mutuality (IDM); and (c) index of unilaterality (IU). The ADL measures the absolute amount of deference by either citizens or police; IDM measures the tendency of police and citizens to be mutually disrespectful of one another; and IU measures the extent to which a relationship between police and citizens is asymmetrical.

In addition, the X^2 statistic is utilized to test for significant differences in the state of the encounter (mutually deferent, unilaterally disrespectful by citizen or by officer, mutually disrespectful) when distinguished by the status variables. Tests are also made for interaction effects between two or more status variables (Goodman 1971).

Measures of status are dichotomized. Citizens who are young, lower class, nonwhite, or alleged to be violators are assumed to be of lower status. Women and senior citizens are assumed to occupy a "protected," if not higher status.

Contacts pertaining to crimes against persons or property are assumed to be more serious than those pertaining to violations of public decorum or which result from needs for police service.

ANALYSIS AND RESULTS

HYPOTHESIS 1

As citizen status declines, the level of deference also declines. Status is a function of role and seriousness of violation as well as of class and ethnicity.

An examination of Table 1 shows that chances of citizens being entirely deferent are less in the direction predicted above. When any three of the four status variables are held constant, the fourth varies in the direction predicted as well. As expected, the highest percent (96.7) of civilian-deferent encounters is characterized as including no violator, in which the civilian is white and middle class and where no violation of person or property is involved.

Table 1
Absolute Deference Level (ADL) of Encounters with Police
(N = 1,466)

Status	Encounters (N)	Deferent (N)	ADL (%)
Middle class	498	456	91.5
Lower class	968	821	84.8
Complainant	946	879	92.0
Violator	520	407	78.3
White	1,293	1,137	87.9
Nonwhite	173	140	80.9
Decorum/service	584	537	92.0
Person/property	882	740	83.9

Note — ADL with police is the percentage of encounters for any particular category which were mutually deferent in their entirety, plus those in which the citizens were unilaterally entirely deferent. ADL with citizens in the percentage of encounters for any particular category which were mutually deferent in their entirely, plus those in which the police were unilaterally entirely deferent.

The lowest percent (67.3) of civilian deference occurs in encounters involving a violator who is lower class and nonwhite and is alleged to have committed a violation of person or property.

HYPOTHESIS 2

The amount of deference displayed by officers will be less than that displayed by citizens. We infer the existence of an asymmetrical status norm from such ordered, asymmetrical reciprocity.

Table 2
Differences Between Civilian and Police ADL Indices
By Lower and Higher Statuses
(N=1,466)

Status	Difference (%)
Higher:	
Decorum/service	-3.0
Complainant	-1.5
Middle class	-4.4
White	-6.5
Average difference	-3.85
Lower:	
Person/property	-8.5
Violator	-14.7
Lower class	-7.3
Nonwhite	-4.6
Average difference	-8.77

Note — See the footnote to Table 1 for the bases of the indices. In each case the ADL with police has been subtracted from the ADL with citizens. The differences are negative because in all instances the ADL with police was larger, that is, in all cases the ADL by police with citizens was less than the ADL by citizens with police.

Table 2 shows that in every case officers were entirely deferent in a lower percentage of encounters than citizens. After grouping higher-status categories and lower-status categories separately and calculating the mean differences, it is evident that not only are police in every case entirely deferent in a lower percentage of encounters, but that the average difference is twice as great in the lower group (-3.85% for higher; -8.77% for lower). The only unexpected finding is that the difference between the white and nonwhite groups is not in the expected direction, a matter which will be analyzed more fully below. The ADL index confirms that (1) there tends to be a lower absolute level of citizen deference where citizens are of lower status; and (2) police deference tends in every case to be lower than citizen deference. In addition, it appears that the difference increases as the status of the citizen declines.

Table 3

Index of Unilaterality (IU)

Status	Index
Middle class	46
Lower class	38
Complainant	71
Violator	26
White	38
Nonwhite	58
Decorum/service	47
Person/property	38

Note — *The IU was calculated by dividing the number of encounters which contained unilateral citizen disrespect by the number of encounters which contained unilateral officer disrespect. The closer the dividend to zero the greater the tendency toward unilateral officer disrespect. Generally, an asymmetrical relationship may be inferred when one status is deferent or disrespectful in a unilateral manner, that is, when one is consistently disrespectful and the other deferent or vice versa.*

Further evidence of behavior from which an asymmetrical status norm may be inferred is found in Table 3. In every instance the IU index shows that police are more apt to be unilaterally disrespectful to citizens than citizens to police. But it also shows that with the exception of nonwhite citizens those of lower status are *less* likely to be unilaterally disrespectful than those of higher status. As civilian status increases, the IU may be hypothesized to approach equity or exceed it. In fact, evidence indicates that senior citizens and women in certain categories may be unilaterally disrespectful to officers without any case of unilateral disrespect occurring by officers, which is a reversal of the data shown in Table 3.

Finally, the IDM index in Table 4 demonstrates that in relations with those of high status mutual disrespect is less likely to occur. Police and high-status civilians are most likely to defer to each other. Most likely to indulge in mutual insult are police and alleged violators and police and nonwhites.

Table 4
Index of Discrediting Mutuality (IDM)

Status	Index
Middle class	6
Lower class	15
Complainant	5
Violator	28
White	10
Nonwhite	18
Decorum/service	6
Person/property	16

$\overline{X}$	(higher status)	6.75
$\overline{X}$	(lower status)	18.75

Note — The IDM was calculated by dividing the number of encounters which contained mutual disrespect by the number of encounters which contained only mutual deference. The higher the number the greater the tendency toward mutual disrespect. Generally, a symmetrical relationship may be inferred when either deference or disrespect by one status tends toward a one to one ratio to a similar quality of the other. Deferent mutuality tends to mutual acceptance of selves; disrespect, to mutual discreditation.

HYPOTHESIS 3

Since police and minority citizens misunderstand the respective indications of the other, their interaction will display much less mutual deference and much more mutual disrespect.

An examination of the ADL, IU, and IDM indices in regard to nonwhites shows a pattern somewhat different from that of the other variables. There is not much difference between the ADL index of police and nonwhites and police and middle-class civilians (see Table 2). Similarly, nonwhites are more apt to be unilaterally disrespectful to police than any group other than complainants (see Table 3). From these two indices, nonwhites appear more like high-status civilians, but they are also more likely to indulge in mutual insults with police than any group except alleged violators. We interpret these data as suggesting that in refusing to display special deference minority citizens are interpreted by police as refusing to display general deference and, therefore, as willfully disregarding their obligations. From the officer's point of view they deserve to be treated harshly. By acting as if they expected the special deference due an ethnic superordinate, the police, from the minority citizen's viewpoint, deserve to receive indications that the minority is not subordinate, that is, deference is withheld. This explains why on two indices nonwhites are similar to higher-status civilians, while on the third index they are similar to lower-status civilians. On the one hand, nonwhites respond as if they were of equal or superior status to officers. Sometimes officers accept this relationship; but often they do not, and then mutual disrespect occurs. An uneasy relation, therefore, exists in which the normative flow of deference remains problematic.

STATISTICAL TESTS

Examination of Figures 1-6 shows that all the variables have significant effects on the operation of the norm. Thus, there are increases in unilateral officer disrespect when there is an activity related to maintenance of law and order, with suspects, younger and male citizens. Mutual disrespect tends to increase as officer and citizen reach a similar age. Generally, any kind of disrespect is unlikely with service activities, females, senior citizens, and the middle class. Ethnicity has the least effect. An examination of the contribution made by individual cells to the X^2 ratio shows that despite the large N in the first cell of each row, less than a quarter of the ratio is attributable to those cells.

Contrary to expectations, there were no significant interactions between the variables when combined in three or more dimensions.

Figure 1
Type of Activity

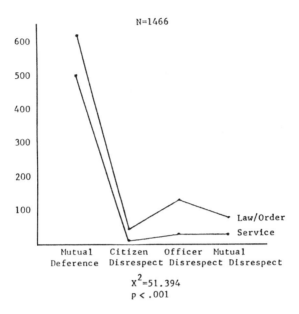

N=1466

x^2=51.394
p < .001

Figure 2
Suspect Presence

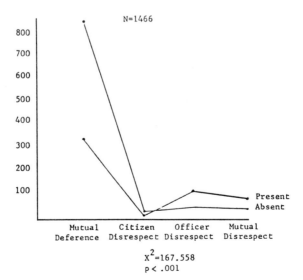

N=1466

x^2=167.558
p < .001

Figure 3
Age

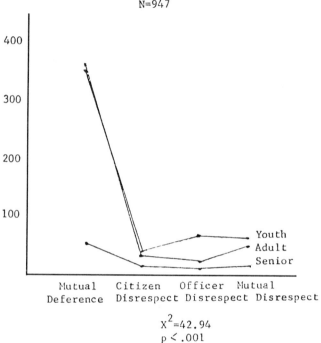

N=947

400
300
200
100

Youth
Adult
Senior

Mutual   Citizen   Officer   Mutual
Deference   Disrespect Disrespect Disrespect

$$x^2 = 42.94$$
$$p < .001$$

SUMMARY

We have hypothesized that the flow of deference between police and civilians is governed by an asymmetrical status norm. Officers expect to be deferred to by citizens occupying a lower or damaged status. Officers are consistently less deferent than citizens, although their actual level is relative to that of the citizens.

When the status of a grouping is in the process of change, as is the case with American blacks, the norms controlling the flow of interpersonal deference also gradually change, but in the interim the uncertainties disturb the inertia of asymmetrical civility and temporarily result in the breakdown of mutually deferent, if asymmetrical relations.

Figure 4
Social Status

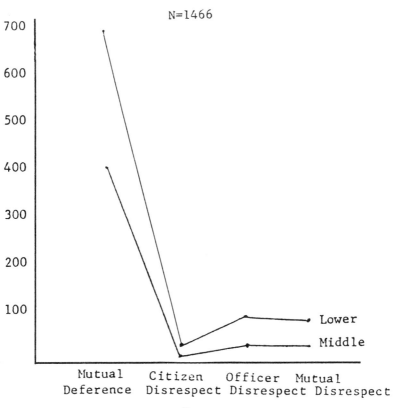

$X^2=22.713$
$p < .001$

Figure 5
Ethnicity

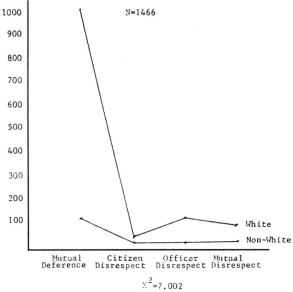

$$X^2 = 7.002$$
$$p = .07$$

Figure 6
Sex

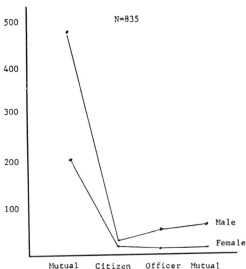

$$X^2 = 15.35$$
$$.01 > p > .001$$

ENDNOTES

* This chapter was originally published by *The American Journal of Sociology*, Vol. 81 (3), pages 584-600. Copyright © 1975 University of Chicago Press. Reprinted by permission.

1.   This research was supported by grant RO1 MH17917-02, "Quantitative Studies of Police Encounters," from the United States Public Health Service, National Institute of Mental Health, Center for Studies of Crime and Delinquency.

REFERENCES

Balch, Robert W. 1972. "Police Personality: Fact or Fiction?" *Journal of Criminal Law, Criminology and Police Science* 63 (1): 106-19.

Black, D.J., and A.J. Reiss, Jr. 1970. "Police Control of Juveniles" *American Sociological Review* 35 (February): 63-77.

Bordua, David J., and Albert J. Reiss, Jr. 1967. "Law Enforcement." Pp. 275-303 in *Uses of Sociology,* edited by Paul Lazarsfeld, William H. Sewell, and Harold L. Wilensky. New York: Basic.

Brown, Roger. 1965. *Social Psychology.* New York: Free Press.

Clark, John P., and Richard E. Sykes. 1974. "Some Determinants of Police Organization and Practice in a Modern Industrial Democracy." Pp. 455-94 in *Handbook of Criminology,* edited by Daniel Glaser. Chicago: Rand-McNally.

Dodd, D.J. 1967. "Police Mentality and Behavior." *Issues in Criminology* 3 (summer): 47-67.

Goffman, Erving. 1956. "The Nature of Deference and Demeanor." *American Anthropologist* 58 (3): 473-502.

_____, 1961. *Encounters: Two Studies in the Sociology of Interaction.* Indianapolis: Bobbs-Merrill.

Goodman, Leo A. 1971. "Partitioning of Chi-Square, Analysis of Marginal Contingency Tables, and Estimation of Expected Frequencies in Multidimensional Contingency Tables." *Journal of the American Statistical Association* 66 (June): 339-44.

Hartjen, Clayton A. 1972. "Police-Citizen Encounters: Social Order in Interpersonal Interaction." *Criminology* 10 (May): 61-84.

Krippendorff, Klaus. 1970. "Bivariate Agreement Coefficients for Reliability of Data." Pp. 139-50 in *Sociological Methodology,* edited by Ernest Borgotta and George Bohrnstedt. San Francisco: Jossey Bass.

Niederhoffer, Arthur. 1967. *Behind the Shield: The Police in Urban Society.* Garden City, N.Y.: Doubleday.

Orans, Martin. 1971. "Caste and Race Conflict in Cross-cultural Perspective." Pp. 83-150 in *Race, Change, and Urban Society,* edited by Peter Orleans and William Ellis. Beverly Hills, Calif.: Sage.

Rafsky, David M. 1973. "Police Race Attitudes and Labelling." *Journal of Police Science and Administration* 1 (1): 65-86.

Reiss, Albert J., Jr. 1971. *The Police and the Public.* New Haven, Conn.: Yale University Press.

Scott, William A. 1955. "Reliability of Content Analysis: The Case of Nominal Scale Coding." *Public Opinion Quarterly* 19 (Fall): 321-25.

Skolnick, Jerome. 1966. *Justice without Trial.* New York: Wiley.

_____, 1969. *The Politics of Protest.* New York: Clarion.

Tauber, Ronald K. 1967. "Danger and the Police: A Theoretical Analysis." *Issues in Criminology* 3 (1): 69-81.

Trojanowicz, Robert C. 1971. "The Policeman's Occupational Personality." *Journal of Criminal Law, Criminology and Police Science* 62 (4): 551-59.

Watzlawick, Paul, Janet H. Beavin, and Donald D. Jackson. 1967. *The Pragmatics of Human Communication.* New York: Norton.

Weinstein, Eugene, William L. DeVaughn, and Mary Glenn Wiley. 1969. "Obligation and the Flow of Deference in Exchange." *Sociometry* 32 (1): 1-12.

Westley, W.A. 1953. "Violence and the Police." *American Journal of Sociology* 59 (July): 34-41.

_____, 1956. "Secrecy and the Police." *Social Forces* 34 (March): 254-57.

CHAPTER 14
Policing Serial Murder: The Politics of Negligence

THOMAS O'REILLY-FLEMING

INTRODUCTION

Ericson et al. (1991:7) have argued that law and news police the major institutions of our society and that this fosters "a perpetual public conversation about what institutional arrangements are most appropriate." This chapter is concerned with a form of crime that has generated considerable public dialogue, particularly in the 1990s, and that is the policing of serial murder. Studies of policing have traditionally concentrated, and understandably so, on a diversity of topics related to the day-to-day functioning of police organizations (Ericson, 1982; Manning, 1988); the practices of detectives (Ericson, 1981); police deviance and more recently police accountability (McMahon and Ericson, 1987; McMahon, 1989). The majority of police work in North America is reactive, that is, comprised of responding to citizen-initiated calls rather than proactive (or police-initiated) in nature. While researchers in the above studies have demonstrated a remarkable capacity for entering into and reconstructing the world of policing there have been no studies which have examined the politics of policing in the area of serial murder investigation. So, there is a dysjuncture between the considerable public conversation on serial murder which has become an almost daily topic of discussion on television talk shows, radio, and in newspapers and our lack of knowledge of policing practices in this area. This disjuncture is worthy of our attention I will argue in this chapter since serial murder is a crime which generates a considerable number of victims other than the deceased.

In the wake of the movie *Silence of the Lambs* public interest has accelerated along with concomitant academic focus on this form of criminality. The exploits of Jeffrey Dahmer in Milwaukee who lured young men to his apartment to drug, dismember, cannibalize, and exhibit in a kind of personalized chamber of horrors added to this public concern. The Dahmer case heightened public fears, particularly amongst the most frequent victims of serial killers, women, concerning the number of serial murderers who might be operating in North America. More often than not, public interest is in understanding what appears to be the seemingly unbelievable acts of those who kill serially. The random nature of serial killing involving the selection of victims who are either unknown or only slight acquaintances of the perpetrator has also had the effect of fuelling fears about potential victimization.

This chapter will develop a critical analysis of policing in serial murder cases. First, a discussion of the phenomenon of serial murder will be presented to provide a groundwork for analysis of police investigative and networking problems. It is argued that the politics of policing have functioned to severely handicap the investigation and apprehension of serial murderers on the investigative level, in terms of inter-agency networking and co-operation, and finally vis-à-vis police interaction with the public and secondary victims of serial killers. This is accomplished through a case analysis of several major serial murder investigations and a review of exisiting literature. Finally, suggestions for the future of police efforts in this area are developed which attempt to address current deficiencies.

SERIAL MURDER : A MODERN PHENOMENON?

DEFINITIONAL ISSUES

Although serial murder has assumed a significant place in academic research over the past decade, it is not correct to assume that the phenomenon is either new or limited strictly to the modern North American context. Research by Jenkins (1988) into serial homicide in historical context has resoundingly demonstrated the existence of the phenomenon in both Britain and the United States over the past century. Before 1983, when it is contended that Robert Ressler, an F.B.I. agent associated with the Behavioral Sciences Unit at Quantico, Virginia the term serial murder was not used to define these forms of sequential killing. For the general public certain cases in both these countries aroused widespread anger directed towards those who committed 'multiple' murders (Leyton, 1986) but it was not thought that this form of murder was frequently committed. In fact, our state of historical knowledge on this topic would suggest that it was the very atypical nature of this form of crime that excited public attention.

Serial murder may be simply defined (Egger, 1990) as a series of three or more murders committed over a period of days, weeks, months or years with a resting period in between murderous events.

This is distinguished from several other forms of murder with which readers will be familiar:

1. **Spree killing**—in which the killer murders one victim after another with no period of rest and contemplation between acts.

2. **Family murders**—in which the killer disposes of their family often followed by suicide. In cases where teenagers murder their entire families the tendency to suicide is less pronounced (See Leyton, 1990).

3. **Mass murder**—This form of multiple homicide involves the killing of a large number of victims at one time. The "Montreal Massacre" of 13 female engineering students at L'Ecole Polytechnique in Montreal by Marc Lepine; the "MacDonald Massacre" perpetrated by James Huberty and the murder of victims in Killeen, Texas.

   Fox and Levin (1993) in reviewing criminal statistics for the United States estimate that there are three mass murders committed per month in the United States. Further, they have suggested that this form of homicide has become so commonplace that murderers must kill ten or more victims in order to be featured on national news broadcasts.

4. **Murders committed as secondary to another criminal act**—These are cases in which the murderer(s) kill individuals to eliminate witnesses (Dietz, 1986) while committing another crime.

5. **Multiple murders committed by assassins**—Although there is some academic debate concerning the boundaries of definitions regarding serial murder (Dietz, 1993) the hired assassin kills neither randomly nor without motive.

Serial murder certainly, by definition, includes those murders of boarders in rooming houses by their 'guardians,' so-called "angels of death" who are anxious to relieve them of their worldly possessions. The case of Dorothea Montalvo Puente graphically demonstrates the phenomenon of multiple murder by poisoning as well as female serial killing. In 1986 Puente made arrangements with California social work authorities in Sacramento to send her elderly clients to room at her boarding house. During the next few years some of them dropped out of sight, their disappearances explained by them having wandered off or returned to live with distant relatives. It was not until neighbours complained of the smell emanating from Puente's backyard. She explained the odour away as being the result of fish emulsion. In November of 1988 police attended at her boarding house after a social worker reported one of her clients missing. Police suspecting foul play began to excavate her yard on November 11 and unearthed seven bodies. In all 25 persons were reported missing by relatives although, as is common in serial murder cases, only a few of the bodies were recovered. Puente's motive had been greed. She killed her charges to obtain their social security cheques to which she forged their signatures.

The term has also come to include serial murderers who operate in "teams." Eric Hickey (1991:174-200) devoted an entire chapter of his recent book to the subject of team killers. He identified 32 cases involving 76 offenders for his analysis of this new, and as he notes "rapidly" growing phenomenon. Interestingly, despite cultural and media myths to the contrary, full thirty-eight percent of these cases involved one or more female offenders. Eleven percent of the known offenders were black and an additional 2% were drawn from other racial minorities. Why has there been such an increase in this and other forms of serial killing in North America? Hickey cites four key factors which have contributed to this increase:

1.   Law enforcement officials benefitting from educational and increasingly sophisticated crime detection technologies are able to identify and apprehend more serial killers than in previous time periods. Computerized fingerprinting programs can now sort through hundreds of thousands of known fingerprints in minutes, thus assisting in the apprehension of suspects.

2.   Hickey (1991:176) argues that some individuals commit serial killings as a response to downturns in the American economy either venting anger at being displaced by the system or as a psychological response to depressive states.

3.   Increasingly, certain segments of our community, innundated by violence in the media, in movies, on television, in videos, place little value on human life and also upon violence as a solution to their problems. Killing is often followed by celebration, joking, and both a charge of adrenalin and a discharge of unwanted feelings for the killer.

4.   The growing number of senior citizens in our society provides an increasing population of potential victims for serial killers.

Perhaps the most well known serial murder "team" has been that of

Kenneth Bianchi and his cousin Angelo Buono collectively known as "The Hillside Strangler." During 1977 and 1978 the two murderers sexually assaulted and strangled at least ten victims in the Los Angeles area leaving their nude bodies strewn on the hills of the city. Bianchi was 26 years old, Buono 44, and in common with the team killers Leopold and Loeb of an earlier era, they "decided to kill someone just to see what it would feel like" (Hickey, 1991:177). The majority of victims were bound, gagged, sodomized, tortured, and beaten before they were finally strangled. The killings generally took place in Buono's home and the young women were later transported to be disposed of. It was not until Bianchi relocated to Bellingham, a small town in the state of Washington where he murdered two young women on his own, that he was finally apprehended. The youngest known victims of the killers had been two 12 and 14-year-old schoolgirls who disappeared from a suburban mall.

Bianchi originally constructed an elaborate defence based upon multiple personality disorder. He claimed that an alter ego Thomas Walker had taken over his body and murdered the young women. At the times of the murders, he "Ken," was actually not aware of what had happened and had no memory of the events. Although Bianchi was an experienced and skilful liar, who specialized in fabricating anything and everything about his life, he was not able to convince noted psychiatrist Martin Orne that he was mentally disordered. Bianchi was, in fact, malingering, and *was* able to get several world authorities in psychiatry to believe his story. Bianchi eventually abandoned his insane self, and pleaded guilty to the murders in Bellingham. He was spared the death penalty when he agreed to testify against his cousin Angelo, who in contrast to Bianchi uttered not a single word during the trial. The trial itself was one of the longest and most expensive in California history lasting over one year. Buono was sentenced to life imprisonment without parole. He married a 36-year-old woman in a prison ceremony in 1986 when he was 52 years of age despite his conviction in nine murder cases. Bianchi received a life sentence in Washington which will make him technically eligible for parole in the year 2110.

Another case with which Canadian readers will have some familiarity is that of Leonard Lake and Charles Ng. In June of 1985 Lake was arrested in San Francisco and charged with the possession of an illegal weapon and a silencer. While in his jail cell Lake ingested cyanide in tablet form and died four days later. He produced the driver's licence of Robin Stapley upon arrest, the founder of the San Diego Guardian Angel's chapter who was missing. Lake was a 39-year-old Vietnam veteran who lived in Wilseyville outside of the San Francisco city area. Police soon obtained a search warrant for the premises and there found a bizarre encampment. There investigators discovered torture devices and a number of diaries produced by Lake documenting the humiliation, and vicious cruelties inflicted on their female victims. Male victims were hunted down like wild game on the property while women were forced to act as slaves performing sexual acts while being videotaped. After they had finished with their victims they were either strangled or summarily shot and their bodies cut up with power saws and put into large metal drums for incineration. Police found over 45 pounds of bone fragments at the site. Their torturers, Lake and Ng were prominently featured in these videos. In common with many serial murderers who make elaborate preparations for a private place to torture and kill their victims, Lake and Ng had built a bunker on the property which doubled as a torture chamber.

Ng, a 24-year-old fled from authorities to Canada where he was finally arrested trying to shoplift food in a Calgary Hudson's Bay store on July 6, 1985. The store security guard was shot in the hand by Ng who was subdued by the guard and customers. Ng's case was the subject of intense public scrutiny since he resisted deportation to stand trial for the charges laid against him in California in relation to the murders at Lake's encampment. Some four years later on November 29, 1988, following numerous judicial appeals at both the provincial level in Alberta, and the federal level, the Minister of Justice ruled that although Canada's criminal code strictly forbids extradition to a country or state which still has the death penalty, that in the case of Ng, the protection of the community and the broader interests of justice required his extradition. Ng's final appeal of the extradition order was refused on August 31, 1989. It is estimated by police that Lake and Ng disposed of 25 human beings.

CHARACTERISTICS OF SERIAL KILLERS

After almost a decade of research our academic knowledge of serial murder has been best characterized by criminologist Steven Egger (1990) as "an elusive phenomenon." Some of the most important work has emanated from the Federal Bureau of Investigation's Behavioral Sciences Unit which has concentrated its efforts largely in the area of criminal profiling. Robert Ressler et al. (1986) studied a group of serial murderers in order to attempt to construct a typology which would assist police in ongoing inquiries with the identification of strong possible suspects. Their research involved extensive interviews with 36 serial killers and recorded 119 offense variables, 57 victim (on offence) variables and 47 crime scene variables. Their work identified two quite distinct forms of serial killer with quite remarkably different characteristics.

The first group of serial killers the researchers referred to as organized offenders. The twenty-four organized subjects had accounted for 97 victims. From the research, patterns of behaviour emerged that marked off this form of serial killer. Organized offenders were found to have planned their acts. The abduction and subsequent confinement of victims involved the use of restraints. These men reported that they committed sexual acts with the live victims. They were able to show or display control when with the victim in the form of manipulation, threats, and their verbalized desire to have the victim show fear. Finally, they were mobile, using a car to transport their victims.

Disorganized killers on the other hand were found to represent a very different form of serial offender. First, their crimes were marked by the fact that they would leave a weapon at the scene of the crime. Secondly, they took time to position the dead body. In a recent case involving eleven murders in the Highland Park area of Detroit, Michigan the victims have all been black females, who worked as prostitutes, were addicted to crack cocaine, and were found in abandoned buildings or motels. In each of the cases, the victims have been killed quickly by the murderer using a strangle hold from behind, and the bodies then have been positioned purposefully in specific locations, often against the back of shower stalls. This type of serial killer wishes to establish control quickly and kill quickly as they are often quite nervous of being discovered. They tend to perform sexual acts on the dead body, and also to keep the dead body. They may try to depersonalize the victim by mutilation, especially of identifying facial features. They do not use vehicles, often living within walking distance of each of the crime scenes.

Organized offenders displayed the following significant variables; they were intelligent, skilled in occupation, and likely to think out and plan the crime. At the time of the crime they are often depressed or angry about some event in their life and to have suffered a precipitating stress that has acted as a catalyst to their murderous acts. This can take the form of a marital problem, loss of a job or financial woes. They tend to have a vehicle that is in good working order, often a 'power' car. Investigators are often faced with another dead end in investigation as the offender is likely to change his employment or leave town after the crime or when the public outcry becomes too great. Most disturbingly, he will be likely to follow events in the media, relishing the infamy that he must enjoy in anonymity. Psychopaths enjoy and seek out the spotlight. Clifford Olson, the Canadian serial murderer who brutally killed whose case will be analyzed in some detailed later in this paper commented that

Disorganized offenders on the other hand are more likely to be low birth order children in a family where the father does not enjoy steady employment.

Their treatment as a child is marked by hostility. In terms of sexuality they are either inhibited or ignorant, have aversions, and their parents suffered through various forms of sexual problems. At the time of the commission of the crime they are often frightened and confused. In contrast to most serial killers they generally have knowledge of their intended victims. Disorganized killers are social isolates who live alone, and their crimes are carried out within a short proximity of their home or work.

It is worth noting that to some degree "seepage" occurs between these two categories; that is, while the killer may be of the organized type, he/she may also share some of the characteristics of the disorganized individual, for example, with respect to mutilation of the body or the practice of necrophilia (sexual relations with the dead body). Neither category is absolute, and it is important to remember that since the organized types follow accounts of their crime in the media, they may change their modus operandi to throw police off their trail. In the Atlanta child murders, where Wayne Williams, a black male was convicted of the killings, the media reported that the killer was leaving his bodies nude in the water. The next body to be recovered was fully clothed.

EMERGING TYPOLOGIES AND EXPLANATIONS

A number of researchers some of whom are academics, some involved with law enforcement, and still others whose work bridges both of these worlds have attempted to develop typologies of serial murderers. Arguably typologies are useful not only because they help us to identify the serial killer before they kill as many individuals as they might like to, but because they assist us in making sense of what often appears to be a phenomenon that is senseless. Why would someone want to stalk, torture and kill a random stranger? It is this aspect of the criminal career of many serial murderers that most worries the general public and prompts our interest in scientific understandings of the problem.

Holmes and DeBurger (1988, 55-60) developed an important typology of serial killers that attempts to provide us with an understanding of their acts through an examination of their motivations for murder. Their typology was predicated upon several assumptions which are worth noting:

> i)   The crimes of serial killers are assumed to be psychogenic, that is stimulated by behavioural rewards and penalties. Their "patterns of learning" are related to those they consider "significant others" who play a part in reinforcing the behaviour. (Contrast this to the explanations of Leyton

(1986) who locates motivation within larger political and economic structures).

ii)   Secondly, an "intrinsic locus of motives" is involved which simply translated means that the offender is the only person able to explain what motives were involved as they exist only in his/her mind.

iii)   The reward for killing is realized in psychological "pay-offs" rather than material gain. (Although the acts of "angels of death" may contradict this typology).

The four types they developed were: (1) the visionaries who kill at the prompting of voices asking them to act, whether for good or evil. It is assumed that many of these offenders are suffering from some form of psychosis. David Berkowitz, a.k.a. "The Son of Sam," claimed that voices of an ancient demon that possessed the body of his neighbour Sam Carr's dog commanded him to kill; (2) the mission-oriented type who develop a belief that it is their duty to cleanse the community of a particular type of people whether it is prostitutes (a favourite target of serial killers), the elderly, children, or a specific racial group. Peter Sutcliffe, a.k.a. "The Yorkshire Ripper," chose prostitutes from the red light districts as his victims. Prostitutes, gay persons, and racial minority victims are often viewed as marginally important by police investigators who either bring their own bias to an investigation, or simply do not invest police time in the solving of such cases. There is, arguably, little public pressure asserted to solve cases involving the deaths of prostitutes and other forms of 'deviant' individuals. Serial murderers recognize this concept of "the lesser dead" (Steven Egger, 1992), that is, individuals whose disappearances are not noticed as quickly as that of an average citizen (if at all) and whom the police are less likely to pursue in terms of intense investigative efforts.

The third form of serial killer identified was the "hedonistic type." These individuals have often been referred to as "thrill killers" in popular literature. Finally, there are "power-control oriented" serial perpetrators who find satisfaction when they are in a position of control with regard to their victim. These offenders are sadistic, that is, they derive pleasure from the suffering of their victims, not from the infliction of the suffering as is commonly asserted (Hazelwood, 1992). In concert with the motivational accounts ascribed to rapists who seek dominance over their victims, this form of serial killer wishes to see the victim beg and plead for their life. Robert Berdella, a.k.a. "The Butcher," of Kansas City, during the period 1984 to 1988 had kidnapped six male victims whom he tortured with injections of drugs, electric shocks, and the insertion of various objects into their rectums. After sexually abusing them he killed them and cut up their bodies. The local garbage service unknowingly carted his victims to their graves. It was only because Chris Bryson an intended victim was able to escape, that police became alerted to his crimes. Similarly, there are many examples of cases where the crimes of the serial murderer would have gone undetected but for the escape of a victim, a simple mistake on the part of the perpetrator or routine police work.

Research also instructs us that an important distinction in understanding the serial murderer is the choice of the site for murders. Some serial killers, like Henry Lee Lucas, roam the country killing strangers randomly in one location and then moving on, often hundreds or thousands of miles, until they meet their next victim. While men like Lucas often kill for the sheer pleasure, they also will kill from necessity, i.e, when the need for money or a new car arises. Ted Bundy, one of the better known American serial killers also went hunting for his victims across several states. Bundy killed young women with long hair whom he identified as substitutes for a former girlfriend who had jilted him because he did not have the proper social standing (Leyton, 1986, Rule, 1984). Bundy claimed that an alternate personality took over his body at the time of the killings, a being which he termed "The Entity." Bundy, a charming and manipulative individual, was able to convince young women to assist him to his car with books or a package as his arm was wrapped with bandages. Both the Bundy and the Lucas cases illustrate that serial killers are often convincingly charming at first encounter. Their victims accompany them willingly to a secluded location where the murderer then can release the rage beneath his calm exterior. The mobility of these killers is often astonishing, and an additional factor that frustrates attempts by law enforcement officials to capture them.

A second type of killer is typified by the case of John Wayne Gacey, Jr. Gacey was convicted in the deaths of thirty-three young men who were found buried under concrete in the crawlspace of his home in suburban Chicago or in the surrounding yard area. Gacey lured his victims to the house in a variety of ways, posing sometimes as a police detective, at other times persuading the young man to come to a "party" where drugs and alcohol would be available. Victims were shown Gacey's "handcuff trick"; the trick was they could not get out of the restraints. He then chloroformed them and would torture and sodomize them for hours before strangling his helpless victims. Gacey was a pillar of the community, well respected and active in charity work. He entertained children at hospitals as "Pogo the Clown," drank with the Chicago Black Hawks hockey team, and was involved in Democratic politics. One picture seized in his home featured Gacey with his arm around former first lady

Rosalind Carter.

Jeffrey Dahmer is another representative of this form of serial murderer. Dahmer invited males to his apartment in Milwaukee to drink beer and pose for nude photos in exchange for money. He targeted ethnic minorities as victims believing, obviously quite rightly, that little action would be taken to find them following their disappearance. Dahmer was able to kill thirteen or more victims over several years without being apprehended. He maintained employment in a candy factory for much of this time and was on parole. Dahmer is distinguished from other serial killers who kill at home because although he kept souvenirs of his victims including skulls and body parts, he also cannibalized them, an uncommon form of activity amongst serial killers. Consumption of the victim has been noted in several spectacular cases including that of Albert Fish. Electrocuted at Sing Sing in 1936, Fish who had been born in 1870 was thought by authorities to be responsible for over 400 cases involving the molestation of children. Fish explained that he had been ordered by God "to castrate little boys." He was eventually arrested and convicted in the case of the kidnap and murder of an eleven-year-old girl whom he convinced the parents to let him take to a party. He confessed to three other murders, and his final victim count is believed to number at least seven. He had, after murdering his victims by strangulation, consumed the flesh from their bodies in various soups and stews he prepared.

Ed Gein is perhaps the most well known of the cannibalistic serial murderers not because of the acts he committed which are largely unknown today, but through the movie depictions based upon his life which include *Psycho, The Texas Chainsaw Massacre* and, partially, as the inspiration for Hannibal Lecter in *The Silence of the Lambs* (Ressler, 1992). Gein was born on August 8, 1906 and lived alone with his mother, until her death in 1945, on a farm outside Plainfield, Wisconsin. Following her demise Gein nailed her room shut. Gein was ambiguous about his sexuality and since he could not afford an operation to change his sexual identity he concocted another, far more economical means of "turning female."

Over a four year period he raided the local cemetery removing female corpses and body parts. He fashioned body parts into decorations, lamp shades and waste baskets, and used skullcaps for bowls. He would wear a human scalp and face for his nocturnal dances under the moon, as well as a skinned out "vest" complete with breasts and female genitalia strapped above his own (Newton, 1990:134-135). In 1954 and 1957 Gein's urges could not be satisfied by mere body parts and he killed a living female victim. His last victim, Bernice Worden the owner of a local hardware store, was found headless and hung from the rafters in Gein's larder with the interior organs removed, and thus prepared like a hunting trophy. Gein was found insane and died in Central State Hospital in 1984. There was evidence to suggest that Gein had killed four other women and two males in his criminal career.

Dennis Nilsen, a British serial killer who also selected male victims, shared several characteristics common to both the Dahmer and Gacey cases. All selected male victims and retained the bodies on their premises. Nilsen ostensibly killed "for company" feeling that he was somehow not good enough to retain the companionship of the young men he picked up. After death he dutifully stored their bodies under the floorboards of his flat in London, often retrieving them and propping them up in a chair for a 'conversation.' When they deteriorated beyond a reasonable degree he would chop them up and either dispose of them by incineration in the back garden of his home or boil the flesh off their bones and dispose of the remains down his drains. In the end it was only the clogging of his drain that caused his apprehension and eventual conviction.

PROBLEMS IN POLICE INVESTIGATION OF SERIAL MURDER

The foregoing discussion has provided the reader with an understanding of the modern phenomenon of serial murder including questions of definition and form, typologies and characteristics of such killers, and case histories of some representative case examples. In this section of the chapter my intent is to provide an overview of the shortcomings of police efforts in their attempts to identify and capture serial murderers. Earlier, I alluded to the fact that serial murderers leave behind them a wide range of victims, cutting a wide path of destruction in society. When one considers the number of victims that the serial murder actually kills this is one measure of his victimization of the person. It is common for serial killers to murder more than seven people, and individuals like Bundy and Lucas have victims numbering in the dozens and hundreds. The second type of victim they produce are the immediate family and friends of the victim left either wondering what has become of their loved one who has disappeared until a serial killer confesses, or in many cases, never learning the whereabouts of the mortal remains of the victim. These are the secondary victims of serial murderers. Finally, there is the wider community where fear is engendered, lifestyles are changed and panic can quickly ensue in the wake of reports that a serial killer is on the loose. Again, the seemingly random selection of targets, although women predominate, produces a feeling of intense vulnerability in effected communities.

In the wake of the disappearance of Kristin French and another young woman from St. Catherines, and the subsequent finding of their bodies, a variety of community responses were observed. The condition of their bodies on recovery itself shocked the community. The first girl was found dismembered, encased in cement at the bottom of a body of water. French's body was found abandoned by a roadside, her long hair shorn, the victim of sexual and physical torture. Schools provided psychological counsellors for students afraid of falling prey to the killer. Sales of stun guns to frightened women accounted for a reported 6,000 sales in one month. Similarly, in the wake of the murder of university students in Gainsville Florida in 1991, many students fled the campus afraid to return. Overwhelmingly, the community seeks information on the murders, but as the police officials are the only "official" source of information very little information is made available. As the work of Ericson et al. (1987, 1989) has clearly demonstrated, news reporters depend almost exclusively on such official sources for information.

This unique position of authority provides the first critical problem of policing handling of serial murder cases. Police authorities in serial murder cases have shown a marked reluctance to discuss any relevant information above the basic with the public. The police often justify this stance in terms of the "ongoing nature" of the investigation, an attitude that is meant to convey not only moral authority to the police, but to discredit the questions of others. In practice this means that the secondary victims of serial killers are given very little information on the ongoing investigation as opposed to such victims in non-serial cases. The police are extremely reluctant to make a public admission that a series of serial killings is occurring. While it would be irresponsible to induce public panic in the light of insufficent evidence, two recent cases— one American, the other Canadian—highlight the shortsightedness of this approach.

The Highland Park murders in Detroit, all sharing distinctly similar victims, methods of murder and patterns, are undoubtedly the work of a serial murderer, yet the police have at no time indicated this to be the case. While producing undue public panic is not an acceptable practice, neither is inducing unrealistic feelings of personal security when a killer is stalking victims, and in this case, at a unbelievably accelerated rate. In the past year the killer has accounted for at least eleven known deaths.

While it is conceivable that some of the deaths may be unrelated, this is highly unlikely given our current state of knowledge. A reasonable approach would be to indicate the likelihood of the existence of a serial killer and to provide public warnings to likely victims (in this case black females travelling in the Highland Park district). Similarly, in the St. Catherines cases, despite clear and compelling features of the two murders which indicate the possible existence of a serial killer, the police have made strenuous efforts to deny repeatedly that there was any possibility of a serial killer being on the loose in the district. The further attempted abduction of a woman on the highway by a man in a cream-coloured power car in daylight a few weeks following the discovery of the French girl's body was again not linked into the case by police. Considering the method of abduction, the eyewitness accounts, the condition of the bodies upon recovery, the evidence of mutilation, and the fact that two girls who lived in a small community were abducted by a stranger randomly within a short radius of one another, there is some basis to speculate on the operation of serial killer. The police finally appointed a task force of detectives and has called upon the F.B.I.'s Behavioral Sciences Unit to examine the evidence in their cases to provide profiles of the murderers, as have police in the Highland Park cases. Police in both cases still adamantly deny the operation of a serial killer.

Police reluctance in these matters is prompted not only by their reluctance to share information with a public that they often regard as their enemy (Vincent, 1990), but by concerns that political and public pressures on their inadequacies in the face of a serial killer will soon mount if an admission is made confirming this possibility. Police experience with serial killers, particularly in the Canadian context, is extremely limited and has not been without severe problems, as have investigations in other countries. Serial killers often operate for years without apprehension for police techniques of apprehension and investigation have not been traditionally geared to national investigations, but rather concentrate upon a certain geographic horizon (Egger, 1990). Revealing this type of information makes the police more vulnerable to criticism and increased scrutiny of errors in investigation.

As early as 1984 noted criminologist Steven Egger developed the term "linkage blindness" to describe the lack of co-ordination between police agencies that often characterizes cases involving serial murder. Since he developed that term very little has changed in terms of police co-operation in information sharing where the cases involve unsolved homicides where a suspect(s) cannot be identified within a period of seven or more days. This is key, for in most cases of homicide a suspect is readily apparent whether it is the estranged husband, or the robber who decides murder is necessary to his task. This is not the case in serial murder where motives are not apparent, and there is no relationship between the assailant and his/her victims.

I have already noted that police also have shown a marked tendency towards racist and biased attitudes when dealing with the victims of serial killers. The Dahmer case provides a clear illustration of this problem which resulted in unnecessary deaths. This is a problem not of the individual police officer's attitude but the structural aspects of police socialization which underscore and promote racist and biased attitudes (Vincent, 1990). The officers who responded to neighbours calls when young boy walked naked in a Milwaukee neighbourhood found nothing amiss when they encountered the youngster, blood flowing from his rectum, stumbling disoriented in the street. Fourteen-year-old Konerak Sinthasomphone, a Loatian immigrant who spoke little English, was viewed by the police as a homosexual having a quarrel with his "lover" Jeffrey Dahmer. They obligingly returned the boy to Dahmer's custody. Later that night Dahmer decapitated the boy. The police persisted in their story that the boy was involved in a homosexual lover's quarrel despite telephone calls from several concerned neighbours, after they had left, that the "man" in Dahmer's possession was merely a boy. Two years previously Dahmer had sexually assaulted and been convicted of molesting Konerak's brother (Dvorchak and Holewa, 1991). By permitting both racist and homophobic attitudes to colour their interactions, the officers in this case were later to be the target of intense national criticism when taped conversations of the neighbour's attempts to have the police intervene—which were met with sarcasm, joking and anger at their "intrusion"—were released.

CLIFFORD ROBERT OLSON: "THE ONLY REASON THEY SOLVED THE THING WAS BECAUSE I TOLD THEM."

The case of Clifford Robert Olson is one that is well known to Canadians who are thirty years of age or older. He is one of only a relative handful of serial killers who now reside either in prison or in hospitals for the criminally insane in Canada. Skrapec (1992) interviewed seven serial killers housed in Canadian prisons. The addition of Raymond Legere to this list brings the total to eight known murderers. Additionally, there is evidence of perhaps seven more serial murderers who have not been convicted of their crimes who are currently resident in asylums for the criminally insane. Olson is undoubtedly the most significant serial killer in Canadian history, and has been the subject of two books (Ferry and Inwood, 1982; Mulgrew, 1991) and innumerable newspaper accounts (O'Reilly-Fleming and Eggar, 1993). His case is very well documented, a feature common to well known examples of serial murder, and so provides a useful vehicle for the highlighting of police inadequacies in the area of networking.

Olson was a career criminal, prison informer (Mulgrew, 1991:18) and recidivist who had spent the overwhelming majority of his adult life behind prison walls before his ultimate conviction as a serial killer of children (Shantz, 1990). Throughout his adult life, Olson's short periods of freedom were limited to some 50 months when he was not subjected to institutionalization. He was unable to cope with life outside the carceral network without resort to various forms of violent criminality and petty theft.

In the twenty-four years of his criminal career he had been convicted of 83 offences including armed robbery. Like most serial killers who have spent time in prisons and other institutions, Olson was able to slip through the system. In 1977, for example, charges of sexual assault against several children were not proceeded on by the Crown because he was "already serving time" (Mulgrew, 1991:12). This was a consistent factor in Olson's life as well as that of many other serial killers who eluded prison ironically because they were already in prison on another offence!

In December 1980, the first of Olson's victims, all of whom were children, was discovered in Richmond, British Columbia. Olson chose to murder both female and male victims. In the following eight months a further ten victims would die until the eventual arraignment of Olson on August 21, 1981 in the death of eighteen-year-old Judy Kozma.

The inadequacies of the police investigation began to surface shortly after Olson's arrest, but during the hunt for the killer of children in lower mainland British Columbia, the parents of missing children had become increasingly frustrated and angry with the reluctance of police, (1) to acknowledge the existence of a serial killer, and (2) to share information with them. As children continued to disappear, public fears mounted dramatically, and so did criticisms of the adequacy of the police efforts in the case.

It was not until July 31, 1981 that the Royal Canadian Mounted Police, who are responsible for both provincial (state) and local policing in British Columbia, set up a task force on The Case of the Missing Lower Mainland Children. Police investigators had found only three of the ten bodies of Olson's victims at this point, and these were by accident rather than the result of police efforts. On July 27, 1981 police began surveillance of Olson at 4:45 p.m. about seven hours after he had already sexually assaulted and murdered Terri Lyn Carson, a fifteen-year-old schoolgirl (Ferry and Inwood, 1982:88). On July 28, detective Dennis Tarr from Delta, British Columbia, met with Olson at 9:40 p.m. Olson was taken into custody for a few hours on July 29 after he and two youths picked up two girls and managed to get them inebriated. Police tailing the group feared for the girls' safety. Olson was released after a few hours in custody. On July 30, Tarr wore a bodypack microphone and again met with Olson in the company of two other police officers from the Serious Crimes Unit. Their conversation centred upon rewards for clues leading to the whereabouts of the missing childrens' bodies. Olson left at 11 p.m. to cruise the "killing ground," Highway 7, where he picked up Louise Marie Chartrand, a seventeen-year-old who would be his last victim. Immediately following the murder Olson demonstrated the bravado that is a common feature of serial murderers, that is, the increasing sense of invulnerability they begin to feel as their murderous acts go unsolved and unpunished. He stopped into a local police station to retrieve some belongings left a few months earlier (Ferry and Inwood, 1982:94-98).

The inadequacies of the R.C.M.P. investigation were readily apparent. Four known children had been murdered after their initial meeting on July 15 (Mulrew, 1991:153). Similarly, in the "Ripper" case in England, an independent inquiry found that "major errors of judgement" by the police had likely cost lives. During the course of the investigation, much as in the Olson case, Sutcliffe had been questioned nine times and released. The Sutcliffe case also demonstrated, quite clearly, not only the difficulties but the cost involved in finding serial killers. The investigation took 5 years, and cost some $9 million dollars (Mulgrew, 1991: 153).

By September 21, 1981 Olson faced ten murder counts since he had entered into a "cash for corpses" deal with the police and the government of Canada. Olson's wife received $100,000 in a trust fund, $10,000 for each of the bodies that Olson led the police to Crown Prosecutor John Hall's remarks on the payments underscored the difficulties inherent in police efforts to identify serial murderers, "You are dealing with a crime involving people who are not related in any way by blood, or knowing each other. You do not have any link from an investigative point of view" (Ferry and Inwood, 1982:136).

THE FUTURE OF POLICING OF SERIAL MURDER CASES

The discussion presented thus far demonstrates some of the inadequacies of police efforts to identify and apprehend serial murderers. Many of these difficulties arise not from police incompetence but rather directly from the complex nature of serial murder. At best, such crimes place a severe strain on investigative resources and personnel. However, there are a number of current police practices, some of which have already been explored that directly hinder either apprehension or public safety. Part of this has to do with police reluctance to admit that they are dealing with a rare type of crime with which they may have no experience. Attacking linkage blindness will require that departments and their investigators be more willing to admit their limitations, and seek expert advice both from resources such as the F.B.I and academics who study in this area. Police receive little training in the crime of serial murder in the curriculum of police colleges for its atypical nature means that it is a crime which presumably occurs only rarely in any given police jurisdiction (with some notable exceptions—See Hickey, 1991).

Egger, a former homicide detective and leading expert on serial murder investigation as well as the VICAP (Violent Crime Apprehension Program) a computerized data base system for the collating of data on unsolved homicides in the United States, has summarized six primary areas that must underscore future police efforts in this area:

1. refining definitions of serial murder, still a source of considerable debate within both the academic literature and amongst law enforcement agencies;

2. the development of more sophisticated and exacting crime scene searches and the identification of physical evidence;

3. working to eliminate linkage blindness, i.e., lack of interagency co-operation;

4. analysis of serial murder cases on appeal where there is a possibility of acquittal due to problems with the evidence, investigative procedures, or the infringement of suspect's rights;

5. work on developing serial murder solvability factors;

6. refinement of psychological profiling techniques.

The police must learn to work *with* the public in these cases, instead of developing a defensive stance that they must work *on behalf* of the citizenry unhampered. The value of citizen information is amply demonstrated by the recent Williams case in Detroit, in which two alert citizens came upon the suspect trying to strangle a female in a graveyard (He told the witnesses he was having sex with his intended victim). Rather than accept his explanation they quietly left and flagged down a police cruiser. Williams car was stopped shortly after; the woman was found alive in his trunk. In custody Williams confessed to four murders of young women in the Detroit area over the past year, one incident involving the rape and murder of two teenage sisters at one time, another involving a nine-year-old girl. Williams also admitted his responsibility in a series of sexual assaults on women, many of them recognizing him in television interviews following his arrest and realizing how close to death they had come.

Although serial murder is a relatively rare form of homicide there is evidence to suggest that it may be more common than frequently admitted by police authorities who like to downplay its importance and criticize experts other than the police who comment on the phenomenon (Jenkins, 1993). Consider the problems associated with finding a suspect like Peter Sutcliffe or Clifford Olson, and one can reasonably assert that there is a substantial "dark figure" associated with this form of criminality. There are literally tens of thousands of individuals who go missing in North America each year, many of whom are never seen again. Some undoubtedly wind up as prey for serial killers. It is common for serial killers to have murdered more victims than those for which they are convicted or have confessed to. Ian Brady, the well known Moors Murderer in Britain who, with his paramour Myra Hindley, sexually molested and strangled children, admitted to several new slayings some 22 years following his original convictions. Ted Bundy gave a number of confessions to "clear" cases in the days preceding his execution in the electric chair in Florida. It is known that he killed over 40 women, most of whom he was never convicted for, and in which the remains have not been found due to his habit of disposing of the victims in wooded areas where their bodies would be devoured by wild animals.

The volume of work that must go into solving a serial murder case is almost beyond comprehension. The Yorkshire Ripper case files weighed twenty-four tons by the end of the investigation and had to be moved when they threatened to collapse the building they were stored in (Doney, 1990:102). The British police inquiry which I have already alluded to earlier in this chapter recommended the following changes in police practices based upon the case:

1. the standardization of police procedures to ensure comparability of evidence;

2. computerization of all records for ease of analysis;

3. advanced training for senior police investigators;

4. appointment of an advisory team of experts in the field;

5. use of specialist and scientific support.

The HOLMES (Home Office Large Major Enquiry System) was finally developed after several computer systems were experimented with. The system addresses the substantive problems encountered in serial murder and serial rape investigations. Most pointedly, it ensures that investigating officers have up-to-date information when they interview suspects, a problem that hindered police in the Sutcliffe case (Doney, 1990:100-105). Similar systems have been developed in America (VICAP) and are under development in Canada, but funding priorities to date have severely hindered the development of the system in Canada.

LESSONS

The central priority which will determine the success or failure of efforts in police investigation of serial murders will reside in their ability to communicate across the artificial barriers that have been set up with a variety of communities, including most importantly, the families of victims, other policing agencies, scientific experts, and the general public. Egger (1990:208) has astutely summarized the root of this problem when he states that police agencies must, "put professional competition, jealousies, turf-protecting, case-based investigative assignments and jurisdictional myopia behind them." To do less will allow the serial killer to benefit from these self-imposed limitations, something that they have demonstrated a superior capacity to do in countless cases. Roy Hazelwood (1992), an F.B.I. Agent and noted expert in the area, reports that serial killers are scholars of murder and police techniques. They scour true crime magazines and accounts of crimes learning about police failures and weaknesses. Many read academic and scientific articles in the area and are cogniscent of the latest empirical and theoretical advances in the field. While for many serial killers eluding capture is a game, it is a game that they play to win, at the expense of human suffering and loss of life. Given this, the future of serial murder investigation must not only rectify past mistakes but build upon the many advances made in the apprehension of these heinous individuals. The lesson of the future for serial killers must be that not only are the police capable of efficient and almost instantaneous networking of information, but that they seek the co-operation of the communities they serve to stop serial murderers.

ENDNOTES

* This chapter is printed here by permission of the author.

1. I would like to express my appreciation to Eric Hickey, Candice Skrapec, MaryLou Dietz, R.S. Ratner and especially Steven Egger and James Fox for materials and consultations on some of the ideas presented here.

REFERENCES

Doney, R.H., 1984. "The Aftermath of the Yorkshire Ripper : The Response of the United Kingdom Police Service," in S. Egger, *Serial Murder: An Elusive Phenomenon.* New York: Praeger, 95-113.

Dvorchak, R. and L. Holewa, 1991. *Milwaukee Massacre.* New York: Dell.

Egger, S., 1984. "A Working Definition of Serial Murder and the Reduction of Linkage Blindness." *Journal of Police Science and Administration,* Vol. 12, No.3, 348-357.

_____, 1990. *Serial Murder: An Elusive Phenomenon.* New York: Praeger.

Ericson, R. et al., 1987. *Visualizing Deviance: A Study of News Organizations.* Toronto : University of Toronto Press.

_____, 1989. *Negotiating Control: A Study of News Sources.* Toronto: University of Toronto Press.

_____, 1991. *Representing Order : Crime, Law, and Justice in the News Media.* Toronto: University of Toronto Press.

Ferry, I. and D. Inwood, 1982. *The Olson Murders.* Langley: Cameo.

Hazelwood, R. 1992. "Sadistic Serial Murder." Paper presented at Serial and Mass Murder: Theory, Policy and Research—The First International Conference. University of Windsor, April 4.

Hickey, E. 1991. *Serial Murderers and Their Victims.* Pacific Grove: Brooks.

Holmes, R. and J. DeBurger, 1988. *Serial Murder.* Sage: Newbury Park.

Jackman, T. and T. Cole, 1992. *Rites of Burial.* New York: Pinnacle.

Jenkins, P. 1988. "Serial Murder in the United States, 1900-1940: A Historical Perspective." *Journal of Criminal Justice,* Vol. 17, 377-392.

Jenkins, P. 1993. "New Perspectives on Serial Murder in England." Forthcoming in T. O'Reilly-Fleming and S. Egger (eds.) *Serial and Mass Murder: Theory, Policy and Research.* Toronto: University of Toronto Press, May.

Keppel, R. 1989. *Serial Murder: Future Implications for Police Investigations.* Cincinnati: Anderson.

Levin, J. and J. Fox, 1985. *Mass Murder: America's Growing Menace.* New York: Plenum. (Paperback edition, 1992).

Leyton, E. 1986. *Hunting Humans: The Rise of the Modern Multiple Murderer.* Toronto: Seal.

Manning, P. 1988. *Symbolic Communication: Signifying Calls and the Police Response.* Cambridge: MIT Press.

McMahon, M. and R. Ericson, 1987. "Reforming the Police and Policing Reform" in R. Ratner and J. McMullan, eds. *State Control: Criminal Justice Politics in Canada*. Vancouver: UBC Press, 36-68.

McMahon, M. 1989. "Police Accountability: The Situation of Complaints in Toronto: *Contemporary Crises*, 12: 301-327.

Mulgrew, I. 1991. *Final Payoff*. Toronto: Seal.

Newton, M. 1990. *Hunting Humans:The Encyclopedia of Serial Killers*, Vol. I. New York: Avon.

O'Reilly-Fleming, Thomas, 1992. "Serial Murder: Towards Integrated Theorizing." *The Critical Criminologist*. Forthcoming.

O'Reilly-Fleming, T. and S. Egger (eds.), 1993. *Serial and Mass Murder: Theory, Policy and Research*. Toronto: University of Toronto Press, forthcoming.

Ressler, R. et al. 1986. "Sexual Killers and their Victims" in *Journal of Interpersonal Violence*, Vol.1, No.3, September 1986, 288-308.

Ressler, R. 1992. *Those Who Hunt Monsters*. New York: St. Martin's.

Rule, A, 1980. *The Stranger Beside Me*. New York: Praeger.

Shantz, R. 1990. Lecture on Clifford Olson delivered at The University of British Columbia. (Courtesy, R.S. Ratner).

Vincent, C. 1990. *Police Officer*. Ottawa: Carelton University.

Wilson, C. and Seaman, D. 1989. *Encyclopedia of Modern Murder*. London: Pan.

DEVIANCE
AND
SUBCULTURES

CHAPTER 15
Subterranean Processes in the Maintenance of Power:
An Examination of the Mechanisms Coordinating Police Action[1]

CLIFFORD D. SHEARING

This paper begins with the observation that the legal system in liberal democracies, despite its egalitarian ideals, is used as a resource in political conflict to maintain structures of dominance. It then draws attention to the theoretical requirement to identify the specific mechanisms that provide for this persistent and systematic institutional hypocrisy. Within this theoretical context, the police subculture is identified as a lay social theory which serves to direct working policemen in their selection of candidates for criminalization and in their use of the law to initiate this process. Both the critical features of the police subculture and its relationship to the social structures within which police operate are considered.

One of the most persistent theoretical questions in sociological theory has been how to relate social structure and interaction (c.f. Berger and Luckmann, 1967). This question remains a major concern. Within the context of the conflict perspective, it has been posed as the problem of identifying the processes that provide for the reproduction of power relations (Turk, 1969; Giddens, 1976). In specifying this problem, conflict theorists have identified the role of the state as critical. Quinney, for example, has argued that 'the theoretical problem at this time is that of *linking* the class structure of advanced capitalism to the capitalist state.' (1977:80). This problem implies questions such as, 'how is it that the state does what it is supposed to do', or more concretely, 'what are the mechanisms through which it preserves the hegemony of the dominant classes' (Burawoy, 1978:59).

There is considerable research, especially in the area of criminal justice, that is relevant to these questions. One of the conclusions drawn from it is that law is used as a resource, or weapon, in the preservation of power relations (Bittner, 1967, 1970; Chambliss and Seidman, 1971; Turk, 1976). In support of this, researchers have argued that the egalitarian safeguards built into the law in liberal democracies (via a formal emphasis on universalistic and behavioural, rather than status, criteria) are systematically undermined in practice by law enforcers who in making decisions emphasize extra-legal criteria that identify persons as members of 'problem populations' (Spitzer, 1975; Quinney, 1977). Criminality, it is argued, is an ascribed status applied disproportionately to the least powerful (Turk, 1969).

As a consequence of these arguments, the traditional conception of the law as a guide to law enforcement (Pound, 1942) has been challenged by the more cynical view that the law acts not to direct law enforcement, but to provide an ideological resource that can be used to legitimize political control as a non-political activity based on egalitarian criteria (Carlen, 1976). This raised the question of the coordination of law enforcement, and suggests that whatever the relationships between class structure and law enforcement embedded in the law (Chambliss, 1964; Kolko, 1963; Chambliss and Seidman, 1971; Quinney, 1970, 1974), one must look beyond the law itself if one is to identify the mechanisms that provide for the systematic introduction of extra-legal status considerations in law enforcement (Hopkins, 1975: 615; Turk, 1977: 214-15).

As the 'gatekeepers' of criminal justice (Reiss, 1971), the police have tended to become the focus of much research. However, under the impact of the liberal ideal of 'equal justice,' this research has been inclined to address the problem of inequality produced by patterns of law enforcement. Consequently, the questions most often addressed have been: Are the police biased in their treatment of the public? Do they discriminate? Are they fair? (Skolnick, 1966; Berkley, 1969; Bayley and Mendelsohn, 1968; Chevigny, 1969; Lambert, 1970; Banton, 1973; Rosett and Cressey, 1976). While much has been learned from this research about the correlation between situational factors (such as age, sex, race, socio-economic status, demeanour, complainants' preference and previous record) and law enforcement (Piliavin and Briar, 1965; Reiss and Bordua, 1967; Black, 1968, 1970; Black and Reiss, 1970;

Sullivan and Segal, 1972; Sykes and Clark, 1975), remarkably little progress has been made in accounting for how policemen act together so that their 'joint action' (Blumer, 1969) systematically contributes to the reproduction of relations of subordination and dominance.

To the extent that an answer to this question has been sought, attention has been directed towards the influence exercised by political and senior police authorities (Wilson, 1968; Chevigny, 1969; Davis, 1969; Grosman, 1975). However, although this research has enhanced our understanding of political control of the police, it suggests that this influence is too variable and too related to partisan interests of individuals and political factions to provide a single satisfactory explanation for the systematic, continuous, and pervasive use of status criteria in the maintenance of order.

In considering how to approach the coordination of police activity, the relationship drawn between consensus and conflict theory by David Lockwood (1956) is worth recalling. Lockwood argued that consensus theory, with its focus on explicit political and legal norms, directed attention to the superstructural processes involved in the ideological work of legitimation, while conflict theory, with its Marxian heritage, directed attention to a more substructural level of analysis. This view of the contributions of consensus and conflict theory suggests that if the problem of the coordination of police activity is to be resolved, attention should be directed to the subterranean levels within the police organization and, more generally, within the state. This suggestion finds support in the frequently cited police adage that policing is not done 'by the book' and that the operating principles of police work are learned on the job, and form part of the intuition and common sense that seasoned policemen acquire (Wilson, 1968; Sacks, 1972; Kirkham, 1974; Grosman, 1975; Manning, 1977). It is thus, perhaps, common sense, or 'rules of thumb' (Manning, 1977: 162) that make up the police subculture, to which attention should be directed in searching for the processes coordinating law enforcement practice.

The police subculture has long been a topic of research within the sociology of deviance and a substantial body of literature has been developed (Wexler, 1974). Throughout, one encounters the observation that the police view the public from a we/they perspective. They see themselves, it is argued, as a closely knit group set apart from the public. They believe, it is maintained, that the public view them as a hated and distrusted enemy (Manning, 1971), and they, in turn, reciprocate by regarding the public as their enemy (Westley, 1970; Manning, 1971; Harris, 1973, Wexler, 1974). This perceived enemy relationship, it is suggested, operates to encourage police solidarity, secrecy, and a hostile, sometimes violent, response to the public (Westley, 1953, 1956). In explaining this cluster of beliefs and the responses they encourage, the police subculture has been conceived of as a defense mechanism developed by the police in response to the demands made on them by the public (Buckner, 1973), the public's hostility, and the danger and ambiguities of police work (Reiss and Bordua, 1967; Kirkham, 1974). This conception of the police subculture provides little support for the notion that it may be part of a subterranean process linking police work to the preservation of established power relations. On the contrary, it suggests that far from relating the police to any interest group within society, their subculture sets them apart from all such groups by defining them as an independent body isolated from, and independent of, all others.

Recent research by Shearing (1977), however, calls into question the applicability of the 'public as enemy' metaphor, by arguing that it is applicable only to one of the publics which the police recognize as relevant to their work, and that it is not used by the police with respect to the public at large. In developing this point, Shearing notes that a fundamental distinction is made by the police between people they serve and the troublemakers they control in the course of providing their service—that is, between the people they do things for and those they do things to (Hughes, 1971). It is because this distinction has been largely ignored in the literature on the police subculture that the relevance of this culture, as a mechanism for coordinating police activity which links it to the larger social structure, has been missed.

This paper reviews these findings to show how the police subculture contributes to the maintenance of power within a political and legal structure that defines police action in egalitarian terms. It begins by examining the police view of troublemakers and shows how the police subculture acts as a 'social theory' for coordinating and managing police involvement in class conflict.[2] This discussion raises the issue of the potential effects of the conflict between the police subculture and liberal, democratic ideals. This leads to a consideration of the way in which the police subculture serves to isolate the police from the influence of these ideals. This, in its turn, raises the question of the origin of the police subculture and its relationship to social class.

THE RESEARCH

The tendency in so much literature to gloss over distinctions between different police publics seems, in part, to have been a result of the influence of labelling theory which focussed on police response to troublemakers. One consequence of this was the highlighting of this public as *the* police public. My research, in contrast, took place in a setting in which victims and complaints were as relevant to the police as troublemakers. This setting—the communications centre of a large urban Canadian police department where citizen calls for police assistance were received and responded to—provided an opportunity to examine the police conception of both the people they do thing to and those they serve. Further, as policemen from many other parts of the department were regularly in touch with the centre, it was possible to develop a police view of citizens based on a wide variety of individuals. Research for this study took place over a six-month period in the fall of 1971, and involved the observation of over sixty shifts as well as the tape-recording of several thousand telephone conversations between both policemen in the centre and citizens, and between policemen in the centre and policemen in other parts of the department (see Shearing, 1977 for a detailed description of the research).

POLICE INVOLVEMENT IN CLASS CONFLICT

In contrast to the currently accepted view of the police subculture, my research indicated that the police did not view themselves as enemies of the public at large. In these dealings with citizens, I found that policemen made a fundamental distinction between 'the public' on the one hand, and 'third- and fourth-class citizens,' 'the dregs,' or more expressively, 'the scum,' on the other. This bifurcated concept of citizens related directly to the work of policemen in the centre and those elsewhere in the department. The public consisted of those the police believed they should serve and protect. The scum were very different. They were the people whom the police prosecuted in the course of helping the public. The scum were troublemakers who impelled the public to seek police assistance. In supporting the public, the police controlled the scum.[3]

The scum were viewed by the police as the enemy of the public. Therefore they were, by implication, also the enemy of the police. The scum were supported by the public by public housing subsidies and welfare and by 'ripping them off' through crime.

> That is a pretty run down area as you can hear from old gravel voice. They're at the very bottom of the ladder—third- and fourth-class citizens. When you've worked in that area, you learn that they haven't seen soap for weeks. They and their houses are filthy dirty.

Not only were the scum unclean, but as enemies they threatened the police and the public both physically and morally. They were dangerous.

> In ——, if you get involved in something, you never know whether you'll get out O.K.

> Pick up one garbage can at ——. Imagine getting a station detail to —— you'd be surprised to get out alive.

The scum, the police believed, showed no respect for the authority of the law. They gave no quarter and deserved none. They enraged the police. 'That's the first clown of the night. I'd like to go down and arrest the bum myself. I can't stand those pigs.'

As an enemy, the scum deserved no help from the police—their job was to help the public, not the scum. Any harm the scum did to each other was all to the better, at it assisted the police and the public in their conflict with the scum.

> First Policeman: There was a murder at —— yesterday, you know.

> Second Policeman: That's not a murder, that's a local improvement, but if you called it that you'd have to pay taxes on it.

> First Policeman: They should close down that division and put a fence around it. Everyone there deserves each other.

> Second Policeman: Yeah, you better believe it.

It is the scum who, in an age less embarrassed by class differences and less committed to the ideal of equality, were referred to as the 'dangerous' or 'criminal' classes (Silver, 1967), a 'bastardized race,' a 'class degraded by misery whose vices stand like an invincible obstacle to the generous intensions that wish to combat it' (Foucault, 1977: 276).

This distinction between two classes of citizens with whom policemen come into contact is, Hughes argues, common to many service occupations.

> To understand (service occupations) one must understand the system, including the clients and their wants. People and organizations have problems; they want things done for them—for their bodies and souls, for their social and financial relations, for their cars, houses, bridges, sewage systems; and they want things done to the peo-

ple they consider their competitors or their enemies. (Hughes, 1971: 422).

In distinguishing between clients and competitors and/or enemies, Hughes draws attention to the same sort of relationship as Emerson and Messinger do in their identification of the situation roles of complainants and/or victims and troublemakers. However, unlike Emerson and Messinger, who restricted their analysis to situated roles, Hughes' formulation extends to trans-situational identities. This distinctions is critical to an understanding of the categories of citizens identified by the police subculture. Neither the scum nor the public refer to the situated roles of troublemaker and victim/complainant that emerge in the definition of, and reaction to, particular troubles. Rather, they refer to two relatively stable populations of persons who become involved in trouble. Either the scum or the public could be troublemakers in a particular situation. What distinguishes the scum from the public is that the scum are structurally in conflict with, and are the enemies of, the public. The scum are, to use Katz's (1972) formulation, 'in essence' troublemakers, while the public are 'in essence' their victims.

In distinguishing between the scum and the public as two classes who oppose each other as enemies, the police culture makes available to the police a social theory that they can use in the context of their work to define situations and to construct a course of action in response to them. This theory enables the police to transcend the situated features of encounters by relating them to a broader social context which identified the 'real troublemakers' and 'real victims.'[4] In using this theory as a guide to action, policemen enter, as participants, into the class conflict that the culture describes. As they do, they are able, and encouraged, to use the power of the state, on behalf of the public, to control the scum, thereby preserving not only the dominance of the public vis à vis the scum, but the system of relationships on which the opposition between the two groups depends.[5]

This system of relationships is strikingly similar to that described by Marx in his analysis of capitalism. The scum and the public are categories which are consistent with Marx's notions of the surplus unproductive population and the productive population engaged in capitalistic modes of production. Furthermore, like Marxist theory, the police subculture recognizes that the surplus population, both because it is outside the controls embodied in the economy itself, and because of its parasitic relationship to the productive population, constitutes a threat to the productive classes. The police subculture directs the working policemen to control the surplus population, precisely as Marxist theories argue is the case: 'From arrest to imprisonment...the criminal justice system exists to control the surplus population' (Quinney, 1977:136).

What this analysis adds to the general discussion provided by Marxist and other conflict theorists, is a more specific analysis of the mechanisms that coordinate the activities of those working within criminal justice. Marxism, it has been argued, 'is still grappling with the problem of how to transform a theory into a concrete historical force' (Stewart, 1978:20). In the police subculture, we see how, in a small but systematic way, a conflict theory grounded in an analysis of social class relevant to police work is used as a 'concrete historical force' to reproduce a particular set of relations. This suggests that it is wrong to identify the theory appropriate to advanced capitalism as consensus (Chambliss and Seidman, 1971), and that of revolution as social conflict (Stewart, 1978). Although consensus may be the theory that legitimates criminal justice, our findings suggest that the theory which operates to reproduce order is one that takes class conflict as its major premise. It is at the working level that one finds the 'merger of reason and action' (Stewart, 1978:19), of theory and practice, which conflict theorists refer to. Ironically, however, this merger of conflict theory and action works to reproduce, rather than transcend, capitalist relations.

CLASS CONFLICT AND EGALITARIAN IDEALS

The acknowledgement that capitalist society incorporates two social theories (conflict and consensus) based on opposing premises, each contributing to the maintenance of order, raises the question of the relationship between them. This is particularly relevant in the case of the police who work within a system that is explicitly committed to liberal egalitarian ideals. Within this context the question that arises is: How does the police subculture retain an influence on the motivations of working policemen in an environment in which egalitarian notions are supposed to prevail? In other words: How is it that the conflict theory of the police subculture is able to motivate, and thereby coordinate, individual policemen in the face of the official commitment by the public, political authorities, and the courts to a consensus social theory? How does the police subculture retain its influence over a working policemen given the hierarchical character of the police organization and the frequent attempts by inquiries, commissions, the media, civil liberties groups, and dedicated liberal politicians to bring police practice into line with egalitarian ideals? In order to answer this question, we must examine the beliefs about the public and 'the brass' endorsed by the police subculture.

In contrast to the scum, the public were viewed by the police as allies who they helped and assisted in their conflict with the scum. This alliance, however, was not, in their view, between equals. In fighting the scum and dealing with the trouble they caused, the police viewed themselves as professionals, and contrasted their status and expertise with the helplessness and incompetence of the public. They were, they believed, not only more knowledgeable and experienced than the public, but more objective and impartial. This perceived inequality between police and public proved a chronic source of tension, as it seemed that the public did not always respect professionalism of the law enforcers or acknowledge their own incompetence as laymen.[6]This tension was a primary source of meaning for the set of images the police used to describe the public. Each of these images emphasized the professional distance between the police and the public. Together they identified three major themes which defined the police view of the proper relationship between the public and the police.

In emphasizing their own expertise, the police drew attention to *the helplessness and stupidity of the public*. As one policeman remarked, 'some of them don't have enough brains to pound sand.' The public, they complained, often created problems for themselves that could have been avoided had they had 'an ounce of brains.' The police felt that many of the problems brought to their attention by the public were trivial, and could have been handled by the victims themselves. Noise complaints were frequently used to illustrate this.

> It makes you sick, all you get on weekends are noisy parties. Why don't they go and bang on doors themselves?

> So why did he have to call us? The guy's a neighbour. Why doesn't he go and ask him to shut up his bloody dog himself?

Not only did the public report problems to the police that the police felt they should have been able to resolve themselves, but the police complained they were sometimes so helpless and incompetent that they could not even request police support properly. 'You have to be another Larry Solway sometimes. You have to put words in their mouths just to find out where they live or their phone numbers.'

While the public's stupidity was frequently defined in terms of their inability to prevent and deal with minor problems, it was also seen as arising from naiveté. The police believed that, as a result of the dramatization of the police role in novels, films, and television dramas, the public had developed unreasonable expectations concerning the police capacity to resolve problems. 'Some people think a policeman's uniform will make everything all right. But it only quietens things down for a little while. It really doesn't accomplish anything.'

This naiveté, the police believed, extended beyond a misunderstanding of police resources and even included a definition of 'police trouble.' A principal complaint was that the public simply did not know what an emergency was, and constantly exaggerated trivial incidents by calling them emergencies. For example, they frequently pointed out that what the public defined as an emergency often proved, on closer inspection, to be no more than a noisy party or a minor traffic accident. The conclusion drawn from all this by the police was that you could not rely on the public's judgement about what problems the police should deal with or how this should be done.

While it was the public's helplessness and incompetence that characterized them and their relationship to the police, it was their persistent failure to recognize and accept this that most annoyed the police. This failure was apparent in the public's tendency *to demand help rather than request it,* thus suggesting that the police related to them as servant to master. This failure to recognize the professional status of the police and their ability and authority to respond to trouble angered the police.[7] 'Send out a car immediately. It really bugs me when they say that.' This disrespect was regarded as particularly insulting when the demanding citizen was a low-status person who scarcely qualified as a member of the public.

> The thing that bugs me is getting a call from a person who can barely speak English, but demands a car 'right away'. The two things that they know are 'dollar', and 'send police right away,' and they don't even speak the language. The woman had only called ten minutes ago so I said, 'There are two million people in the city and you are only one of them.'

These views about the public's right to demand police service, like the views about the helplessness and ignorance of the public, served to preserve police autonomy by emphasizing that while the police served the public, they were not to be viewed as the servants of the public. This theme was taken up in a somewhat different form in the police view that members of the public sometimes used the police to *exploit their relationship as allies.* They complained that the public were often not as helpless as they seemed. The public, they believed, sought to use the police to accomplish their own self-serving

SUBTERRANEAN PROCESSES IN THE MAINTENANCE OF POWER

ends. The police became particularly incensed when persons misused their power and status for these reasons. In the police eyes, one of the worst groups of offenders were private alarm companies who 'had the nerve' to ask the police to respond to their alarms for them.

> Alarm companies, they use the police. They get us to do their work for them.

> God damn phoney outfits. They call the owner and he says not to tell the police anything, so our car sits there at the scene waiting and waiting for someone to show.

It was, however, not only the economically powerful who sought to misuse the police—this tendency was seen as much more widespread. Often it was perceived as no more than the result of laziness and a refusal to take responsibility for problems.

> Very often people call about barking dogs because they do not want to get involved themselves. They want to leave it to the police to do something. Complaints about barking dogs just misuse the police. In the vast majority of cases, it is probably quite unnecessary to involve the police, except as a last resort. The thing to do would be to go directly to the dog's owner and ask him to take the dog inside or quiet it down some other way.

In emphasizing their professional status[8] the police culture served to insulate the police from members of the public who might try to influence them, and to encourage the police to rely on their own experience and the collective wisdom of their peers in making their decisions.

Just as the police subculture served to guard against the situated influences arising from the demands of particular complainants and victims, it also served to insulate the police from the more systematic influences directed at them through the chain of command. Interestingly, in this context the autonomy of the working policeman was encouraged by the police culture on the same grounds as it was with respect to the public—by emphasizing the inequality in expertise and 'know-how' between the working policeman and the brass (a term used to refer roughly to all those superiors in the chain of command above the rank of sergeant).

In distinguishing themselves from the brass, police constables recognized that, as policemen, they shared some things with the brass. It is with these similarities that we must begin, because they constitute the backdrop for their differences.

At the most general level, especially when the police were contrasted with the public, the brass were considered to be police. They had shared many of the experiences familiar to ordinary policemen—'they had been there.' They had at one time all been 'front line' policemen. Even now, a major concern of the brass was to protect and enhance the image of the police. Attacks on the police in the press, for example, served to break down the distinction between the brass and working policemen. When newspaper reporters, for example, criticized the brass, policemen would spring vigorously to their defence. 'There's always some nut who wants to get the police into trouble and there's always some reporter who will listen to him.'

Yet the brass, although they had been working policemen, were now 'something quite different.' The concerns of the brass, it was argued, were not only different, but were often competing. When the 'chips were down,' the brass would sacrifice the individual policeman in the name of the 'interests of the force.' Policemen were not reluctant to point out that the 'interests of the force' overlapped with, and were often synonymous with, the 'interests of the brass.'

With promotion out of the ranks, the brass, it was suggested, developed new interests—hey became less concerned about the problems faced by ordinary policemen. What the brass should know, and certainly had known, about the nature of police work, was conveniently forgotten when trouble arose. The brass's concern was not simply 'doing the job,' but rather ensuring that the job was done smoothly and that nothing happened to taint the image of the police in the eyes of the public—a public comprised not so much of people who needed help, but of boards of police commissioners, politicians, reporters, and newspaper editors. This attitude on the part of the brass was lampooned by one policeman after a call from a sergeant for all cars in the division to go in for 'car washes', with the remark: 'We sure have a clean police department. Not an efficient one, but a clean one!'

The brass were accorded an explicitly ideological role and this role was seen as not only different from, but often opposed to, the demands of 'real' police work. This was emphasized by noting that their concern with 'political matters,' resulted in the brass losing touch with 'real police work' and 'real policemen.'

> They don't understand, and they don't care any more. They've been out of it for too long. Most of them have not done real police work

for years. They don't know what police work is any more. They spend their time in their offices. You wonder sometimes. That's why they make all these procedures.

When they get that commission something happens. They don't know you any more. They make new friends when they become officers.

In pointing to the relative ignorance of the brass, the police subculture simultaneously suggested that this ignorance was often more a matter of convenience than anything else. In circumventing brass policy, because you 'can't do it by the book,' working policemen saw themselves as acting with the tacit approval of the brass and their political masters, who subtly and surreptitiously encouraged duplicity and secrecy by rewarding, through advancement into more attractive areas of police work (particularly detective work), performances which ignored 'the book,' but which could be retrospectively reconstructed in accordance with policy and legal procedure (Canada, 1976:116-19).

The apparent ignorance of the brass, together with their tacit approval of 'real police work,' identified a role difference between the brass and working policemen. While the brass were concerned with maintaining an egalitarian image of the police within political and judicial arenas, working policemen were to get on with the job of real policing, or controlling the scum. In providing for this distinction, the police subculture at once encouraged police action which served to reproduce existing power structures, while isolating working policemen from influences which tended to mitigate against this. The police subculture, in contrasting 'real police work' with the brass's concern with legitimizing police work, enabled working policemen to move beyond the common sense view of the law as a set of behaviourally grounded instructions for identifying criminality, to a view of the law as a resource for justifying coercive control of the scum. Good police work, the police subculture made clear, meant participating in the class conflict between public and scum in a way that could be justified retrospectively with reference to legal criteria—that is, to behavioural, universalistic, and egalitarian criteria.

In sum, in answer to the question of how the conflict theory operates in a police subculture dominated by consensus theory, I have shown how a class-based theory of social control is encouraged, along with an institutional hypocrisy that presents police work in egalitarian terms. In short, the police subculture provides for police action based on extra-legal status criteria, while simultaneously allowing for its presentation in terms of legal behavioural criteria.

LINKAGES TO POWER: ORIGINS OF THE POLICE SUBCULTURE

This contrast between the conflict theory of the police subculture and the surrounding ideology raises a final query: Where does the social theory of the police subculture come from, and how does it come to reflect so exactly class structure and class conflict in the face of an ideology that explicitly denies the applicability of status criteria to police work? Although these questions go beyond the scope of this paper, it is possible, from a review of the analysis presented, to suggest the general outline of an answer and the direction to be followed in developing this outline.

The independence of the police subculture, its low visibility, as well as its operation at the 'front line' of policing, is consistent with Foucault's (1977) analysis that social control is no longer imposed from above and outside the fabric of social life by an authority embodied in the person of the sovereign; rather, it is embedded in the very structure of social relations themselves. It is from this structure, rather than from an identifiable political authority, that the social theory of the police subculture arises. The police, by virtue of their occupational position as state agents, participate in the social conflict between the productive and unproductive classes. Their position identifies them as allies of the one and enemies of the other. Within this context the police inevitably come face-to-face with the hostility of the scum. In dealing with this hostility, and in participating in the conflict between the scum and the public, they develop a particular view of the scum and an expertise that sets them apart from the public. In short, a guiding authority emerges which is grounded in the collective experience of working policemen. This authority reflects, in conceptual terms, the social differences and relationships in which it is located. In doing so, it provides a mechanism for transforming structural forces into individual motivations.

The embedded nature of this process gives the police subculture an anonymous and ubiquitous character that 'automatizes and disindividualizes' it (Foucault, 1977:202). It is this feature of modern social control that is reflected in the common sense talk of 'the system.' At first glance, as Foucault notes, this system appears to be 'nothing more than an infra-law' that extends 'the general forms defined by law to the infinitesimal level of individual lives' (1977:222). However, he argues, on closer examination these processes prove to be 'a sort of counter law' which effects 'a suspension of the law that is never total, but is never annulled either,' that maintains 'insuperable asymmetries,' despite the legal definition of 'juridicial subjects according to universal norms,' by means of a 'series of mechanisms for unbalancing power relations definitively and everywhere' (Foucault, 1977:222-3). On even closer inspection, as we have seen, the subterranean structures maintaining the asymmetries of power are revealed not as a 'counter law,' but as one face of the institutional hypocrisy that characterized liberal social control. These structures provide for a process of control through social conflict that by-pass political and legal processes at a macroscopic level. The independence of the political and legal superstructure from 'the system' of control that this provides permits those persons acting to legitimize social control within legal and political spheres to pursue egalitarian ideals energetically and with personal integrity, without undermining the work necessary to reproduce relations of dominance. Similarly, it allows the police, and others in similar positions, to get on with their work as participants in class conflict without undermining the belief in the egalitarian nature of liberal democracy.

It is the relationship between the superstructural and substructural levels of social control that frustrates Marxists committed to a utopian society without class conflict, because 'conquering or gaining access to the state through electoral means cannot lead to socialism since the working class party, when it takes over the government, becomes a prisoner of the very system it attempts to overthrow' (Burawoy, 1978:60). For those of us who do not share this commitment, and who view social conflict in more neutral terms (Turk, 1977), the lesson is simply that the process of social conflict and the stability or change it produces cannot be understood by an analysis that focuses exclusively on political processes and ignores subterranean mechanisms.

ENDNOTES

* This chapter was previously published in *The Canadian Review of Sociology and Anthropology*, Vol. 18 (3). Copyright © 1981 The Canadian Review of Sociology and Anthropology. Reprinted by permission.

1. I would like to thank my colleagues Richard Ericson, John Hagan, Jeff Leon, Dianne MacFarlane, Austin Turk and Livy Visano for their comments on this paper. I am grateful to Wanda Crause for her assistance with the field work.

2. There is no single definition of the police subculture provided in related litera- ture. One definition, and the one we will use here, views the police subculture as embodying the collective 'wisdom' of policemen, passed on from one gener- ation of policemen to another through a process in which it is both embellished and validated. The culture is available to policemen as a guide they can use in going about police work. This definition is consistent with the general definition of culture 'as the "image" of the society, the collective information by which the society attempts to organize itself' (Ball, 1978: 69). This definition equates cul- ture with Mead's concept of the 'generalized other.' The police subculture, as we are using the concept here, thus refers to a device which enables policemen to plan and assess courses of action from the standpoint of other policemen (Blumer, 1969).

3. It has been argued (Cumming, et al. 1967) that 'support' and 'control' constitute latent and manifest aspects of the police role. This view arises out of the ten- dency to regard citizens as all forming part of a single category. These findings indicate that support and control refer to two different role relationships with two different populations.

4. See Kahne and Schwartz (1978) who criticize the Emerson and Messinger for- mulation for its failure to consider the more general social contexts that affect actors' definitions of particular situated roles. As Emerson and Messinger's (1977) analysis demonstrates, if one remains analytically at a situational micro- political level which excludes contextual relationships, decisions about statuses and roles must, of necessity, depend exclusively on an analysis of the activities of those involved. This is precisely the analytical difficulty that labelling theorists like Becker (1973) face in accounting for deviance. It leads them to identify deviance with rule-breaking and thus prevents them from examining how the

claim of rule-breaking is used as a method (or weapon) in responding to deviance defined as a trans-situational 'essence' (see Katz, 1972).

5.   This account of operation of the police subculture permits us to answer some puzzling questions. For example, why is it that working policemen regard some statistically important parts of their job—for instance, domestic disputes and traffic work—as not 'real police work,' and why do the 'crimes' of some—particularly the powerful—'go largely unrecognized and/or unpunished, while the less consequential (for society as a whole) offences of the lower class are given so much punitive attention' (Turk, 1977: 214-215)? What the analysis in the text suggests is that 'real crime' activity is defined by police as any wrong-doing undertaken by the scum against the public. Intra-class conflicts, although they may involve activity that would technically be regarded as criminal, are regarded as 'not really criminal'. Similarly, wrong-doing by the public against the scum is also regarded as 'not really criminal' (Black, 1976).

6.   Hughes (1971) has argued that this tension is found in most service occupations.

7.   This time or disrespect for police authority dominates the literature on police subculture. However, in this literature, as the criminal distinction between the disrespect of the scum as an enemy and the disrespect of the public as an ally is not made, disrespect is generally only considered in the context of the enemy metaphor.

8.   This denial or a servant/employer relationship between the police and the public is related to the legal position the police hold vis à vis the sovereign authority from whom, it is argued, they derive an original authority (Call, 1975-77).

REFERENCES

Ball, Richard A., 1978, "Sociology and General Systems Theory." *The American Sociologist* 12 (1): 65-72.

Banton, Michael P., 1973. *Police Community Relations*. London: Collins.

Bayley, David H. and Harold Mendelsohn, 1968. *Minorities and the Police Confrontation in American*. New York: Free Press.

Becker, Howard S., 1973. *Outsiders: Studies in the Sociology of Deviance*. New York: Free Press.

Berger, Peter L. and Thomas Luckmann, 1967. *The Social Construction of Reality*. New York: Anchor Books.

Berkley, George E., 1969. *The Democratic Policeman*. Boston: Beacon Press.

Bittner, Egon, 1967. "The Police on Skid Row: A Study of Peace Keeping." *American Sociological Review* 32 (6): 699-715.

Black, Donald J., 1968. *Police Encounters and Social Organization: An Observation Study*. Ph.D. Dissertation, Ann Arbor: University of Michigan.

_____, 1970. "Production of Crime Rates." *American Sociological Review* 35 (4-6): 733-48.

_____, 1976. *The Behaviour of Law*. New York: Academic Press.

Black, Donald J. and Albert J. Reiss, 1970. "Police Control of Juveniles." *American Sociological Review* 35 (1): 63-7.

Blumer, H., 1969. *Symbolic Interactionism*. Englewood Cliffs, New Jersey: Prentice Hall.

Buckner, H. Taylor, 1973. "Police Culture." Paper presented at the Canadian Sociological and Anthropological Association Meetings in Toronto (June).

Burawoy, Michael, 1978. "Contemporary Currents in Marxist Theory." *The American Sociologist* 13 (1): 50-64.

Call, Helen N., 1975-7. "The Enigma of a Police Constable's Status." *Victoria University of Wellington Law Review* 8: 148-69.

Canada, 1976. *The Report of the Commission of Inquiry Relating to Public Complaints, Internal Discipline and Grievance Procedure within the Royal Canadian Mounted Police*. Ottawa: Department of Supply and Services.

Carlen, P., 1976. *Magistrates' Justice*. London: Martin Robertson.

Chambliss, William J., 1964. "A Sociological Analysis of the Law of Vagrancy." *Social Problems* 12(1): 67-77.

Chambliss, William J. and Robert B. Seidman, 1971. *Law, Order, and Power*. Don Mills, Ontario: Addison-Wesley Publishing Co.

Chevigny, Paul, 1969. *Police Power: Police Abuses in New York City*. New York: Pantheon Books.

Cumming, Elaine, Ian Cumming, and Laura Edell, 1965. "Policeman as Philosopher, Guide and Friend." *Social Problems* 12(3): 276-86.

Davis, K.D., 1969. *Discretionary Justice*. Baton Rouge, Louisiana: Louisiana State University Press.

Emerson, Robert M. and Sheldon L. Messinger, 1977. "The Micro-Politics of Trouble." *Social Problems* 25(2): 121-34.

Foucault, Michel, 1977. *Discipline and Punish: The Birth of the Prison*. New York: Pantheon Books.

Giddens, Anthony, 1976. *New Rules of the Sociological Method*. London: Hutchinson.

Grosman, Brian A., 1975. *Police Command: Decisions and Discretion*. Toronto: Macmillan of Canada.

Harris, R., 1973. *The Police Academy: An Inside View*. New York: John Wiley.

Hopkins, Andrew, 1975. "On the Sociology of Criminal Law." *Social Problems* 22(5): 608-19.

Hughes, Everett C., 1971. *The Sociological Eye: Selected Papers on Work, Self and the Study of Society*. Chicago and New York: Aldine-Atherton.

Kahne, Merton J. and Charlotte Green Schwartz, 1978. "Negotiating Trouble: The Social Construction and Management of Trouble in a College Psychiatric Context." *Social Problems* 25(5): 461-75.

Katz, Jack, 1972. "Deviance, Charisma and Rule-Defined Behaviour." *Social Problems* 20(2): 186-202.

Kirkham, George L., 1974. "A Professor's Street Lessons." *F.B.I. Law Enforcement Bulletin* 35(3): 14-22.

Kolko, Gabriel, 1963. *The Triumph of Conservatism: A Re-interpretation of American History, 1900-1916*. New York: Free Press of Glencoe.

Lambert, John R., 1970. *Crime, Police and Race Relations: A Study in Birmingham*. London: Oxford University Press.

Lockwood, David, 1956. 'Some Remarks on the 'Social System'." *British Journal of Sociology* 7: 134-46.

Manning, Peter K., 1971. "The Police: Mandate, Strategies and Appearances." In Jack D. Douglas (ed.), *Crime and Justice in American Society*. New York: The Bobbs-Merrill Company, Inc.

————, 1977. *Police Work: The Social Organization of Policing*. Cambridge, Mass.: MIT Press.

Piliavin, I. and S. Briar, 1964. "Police Encounters with Juveniles." *American Journal of Sociology* 70(2): 206-14.

Pound, Roscoe, 1942. *Social Control Through Law*. New Haven: Yale University Press.

Quinney, Richard, 1970. *The Social Reality of Crime*. Boston: Little, Brown and Company.

————, 1974. *Critique of Legal Order: Crime Control in Capitalist Society*. Boston: Little, Brown and Company.

————, 1977. *Class, State and Crime: On the Theory and Practise of Criminal Justice*. New York: David McKay and Company, Inc.

Reiss, Albert J. and David J. Bordua, 1967. "Environment and Organization: A Perspective on the Police." In David J. Bordua (ed.), *The Police: Six Sociological Essays*. New York: John Wiley and Sons, Inc.

Reiss, Albert J. Jr., 1971. *The Police and the Public, New Haven and London*: Yale University Press.

Rossett, Arthur I. and Donald R. Cressey, 1976. *Justice by Consent: Plea Bargains in the American Courthouse*. Philadelphia: Lippincott.

Sacks, H., 1972. "Notes on the Assessment of Moral Character." In D. Sundnow (ed.), *Studies in Social Interaction*. New York: Free Press.

Shearing, Clifford D., 1977. *Real Men, Good Men, Wise Men and Cautious Men*. PH.D. Dissertation, University of Toronto.

Shibutoni, T., 1970. *Human Nature and Collective Behaviour*. Englewood Cliffs: Prentice Hall.

Silver, Allan, 1967. "The Demand for Order in Civil Society: A Review of Some Themes in the History of Urban Crime, Police and Riot." In D.J. Bordua (ed.), *The Police: Six Sociological Essays*. New York: John Wiley and Sons, Inc.

Skolnick, Jerome H., 1966. *Justice Without Trial: Law Enforcement in Democratic Society*. New York: John Wiley and Sons.

Spitzer, Steven, 1975. "Toward a Marxian Theory of Deviance." *Social Problems* 22(5): 638-51.

Stewart, John J., 1978. "Critical Theory and the Critique of Conservative Method." *The American Sociologist* 13(1): 15-22.

Sullivan, Dennis C. and Larry J. Siegel, 1972. "How Police Use Information to Make Decisions: An Application of Decision Game." *Crime and Delinquency*, 18(3): 253-262.

Sykes, Richard E. and John P. Clark, 1975. "A Theory of Deference Exchange in Police-Civilian Encounters." *The American Journal of Sociology* 81(3): 584-600.

Turk, Austin T., 1969. *Criminality and Legal Order*. Chicago: Rand McNally.

_____, 1976. "Law as a Weapon in Social Conflict." *Social Problems* 23(3): 276-91.

_____, 1977. "Class, Conflict, and Criminalization." *Sociological Focus* 10(3): 209-20.

Westley, William A., 1953. "Violence and the Police." *American Journal of Sociology* 59(1): 34-41.

_____, 1956. "Secrecy and the Police." *Social Forces* 34(3): 254-7.

_____, 1970. *Violence and the Police: A Sociological Study of Law, Custom and Morality*. Cambridge, Mass: MIT Press.

Wexler, Mark N., 1974. "Police Culture: A Response to Ambiguous Employment." In C.L. Boydell, C.F. Grindstaff and P.C. Whitehead (eds.), *The Administration of Criminal Justice in Canada*. Toronto: Holt, Rinehart and Winston.

Wilson, James Q., 1968. *Varieties of Police Behaviour; The Management of Law and Order in Eight Communities*. Cambridge, Mass.: Harvard University Press.

CHAPTER 16
A Canadian Metropolitan Police Force:
An Exploratory Case Study Into Application, Training and Advancement Procedures— Subcultural Perspectives

GARY M. O'BIRECK

INTRODUCTION

The primary focus of this inquiry is to provide a forum for the collective voices and individual lived experiences of rank and file police officers in relation to current application, training and advancement procedures within a large Canadian metropolitan police force. The rhetoric of this particular police administration appears to stress partnership, camaraderie and fraternity as its core mentality. Instead, what emerges from this inquiry is a distinct sense of disempowerment, alienation and lack of self-confidence on the part of rank and file officers. It appears that this is in part due to the trivialization and infantilization professional police officers experience at the hands of the administration. This sense of disassociation commences during the hiring process and tends to continue throughout career life.

The subcultural experience of working officers who have proceeded through six separate screening processes enroute to the position of First Class Constable appears to have developed into one which reflects a profound sense of disassociation and disinvolvement. This development is apparently the result of lack of attention and investment paid to rank and file views of police experience and over-scrutinizing of occupational development and behaviour by police administrators. What follows are various descriptions of these screening processes as related to this author by this subject sample.

METHODOLOGY

The data collection period began in December 1991 and continued through February 1992. In total, fourteen police officers were interviewed at social gatherings and during working hours. All respondents were First Class Constables; their tenure on the force ranged from four to eighteen years. A cross-section of rankings was obtained by "snowballing" techniques. Consequently a wide variety of officers was obtained; this selection included: foot patrol, car duty, homicide, drug squad, motorcycle gang squad (biker squad), prostitution, youth bureau and fraud squad. Both uniformed and plain-clothes officers were interviewed in relation to their present occupational positions and strongly encouraged to comment on diverse police roles. Approximately one half of these interviews were tape recorded, but when permission was denied, field notes were recorded both during and immediately after interview sessions.

Police officers tend to be suspicious by nature (Skolnick, 1966:48) both during working hours and while off duty. This is due in part to the unhealthy relationship that has developed in the past between the police and researchers. Since the Civil Rights Movement, most police officers do not appreciate and will not consent to associations and involvements with academic researchers due to unflattering reports and criticisms that have become the result of these associations. In light of this problem, this author was inclined to distance himself from previous research and researchers in order to vault the hurdle of this perception of academic researchers "shafting the police." Therefore, in order to fully deliver the richness of this current ethnographic data this author deliberately avoided traditional bibliographic references. As well, this researcher was forced to work overtime in convincing these subjects that this research would not eventually harm them.

Relentless attempts were made to convince all respondents that all information discussed would be treated in the strictest confidence. All subjects were free to terminate the interviews at any time, especially if the probes were perceived to be restricted, inappropriate or uncomfortable. Each officer was guaranteed total anonymity as names and badge numbers were never consulted or recorded.

Even with these assurances in place respondents initially demonstrated varying degrees of suspicion towards this researcher in the initial stages of interviews. Some officers repeatedly cited the works of Canadian criminologists whom they felt had betrayed the confidence of other officers in the past. Most officers remained wary about allowing an outsider into their occupational and subcultural domain for the express purpose of academic inquiries. However, as the interviews progressed, some of these suspicions abated and data were collected comfortably.

Each interview proceeded from a list of interview questions primarily focussed upon three core areas of interest. First, this investigation was concerned with the subject's view of the organization of their police force from the perspective of their respective location in the work force. Second, both occupational and social aspects of life as a police officer were analysed. Third, the subject's view was studied in order to provide each subject with ample opportunity to express their opinion regarding prospects, trends and problematics the future of policing might entail. While most questions were framed within these three core areas, tangential conversations further revealed a wide variety of additional data pertaining to the general topic of police life.

Admittedly, this relatively small sample may not necessarily be considered representative of the complete attitudes of all police people working within this police department. Interestingly, all respondents were white males since difficulty was encountered by this author in securing interview subjects that were female and of other races. It was discovered that this was due to strong subcultural ties that exist between officers of similar characteristics (i.e., white male officers predominantly associate and form strong bonds with other white officers; female officers and officers of race appear to do likewise). Reasons for this are unclear. Consequently, gaining access to female officers and officers of other races was hindered by this trend. This inability to penetrate all race and gender representatives of this particular police force may limit organizational analysis. However, the general aim of this paper is to contribute to a better understanding of the voices of the police subculture and to open the doors for further research.

APPLICATION PROCEDURES

The basic minimum educational requirement for this metropolitan police force is grade twelve or its equivalent as decided upon by the Board of Education (Employment Services, May 1992). Upon application, each prospective officer is evaluated according to three main criteria: fitness, intelligence and psychology. According to Subject S1, this intensive process is designed to eliminate prospective applicants whom management may find unsuitable or who may present future problems to the force:

S1   It's the same for everybody as far as I know. They want to get rid of as many idiots and morons as possible. You know...these fuckin' wannabees that identify with the man in uniform! I guess that's fair 'cause nobody wants an idiot for a partner.

G.O.   Did you have any problems during your application?

S4   I don't really know! I guess not 'cause they let me in! The tests can be tough, I guess,...especially the psych test...they ask you some pretty weird questions like, 'Do you worship Satan?' and like...uh...'What do you think of your Mother?' It's over 900 questions and a lot of them are asked a lot of times in different ways.

Through the fitness test prospective applicants are tested in all areas of physical fitness to determine if they possess the required physical skills to perform the task of policing society. From the intelligence test, management determines how each applicant may react under conditions of mental pressure often present on the street. Results of the psychological test reveal to the employer the applicant's mental fitness prior to police training. Subject S8 recounts his experience with the "psych" test over seven years ago:

S8   First of all, there's no time limit—that's the good news! (laughs) but there's a lot of questions—about 1000. You do a bit then come back to it 'til it gets done. Strange questions, too, but I guess it's to see if you're a psycho deep down. Everybody can act normal when they want to but this cuts through that...to your real personality. It was a rough one...but I passed so I guess I'm not a psycho! (laughs)

After successfully passing through these three filtering processes another assessment procedure is implemented before an applicant is considered for employment. Applicants are notified that their presence is required at a divisional headquarters at a certain time but never informed about reasons for such an interview. Upon arrival each applicant is placed in a waiting room in the company of approximately 12 other applicants who share similar levels of ignorance. Singularly they are called into another interview room. Subject S9 relates his experience during this filtering process:

S9   I'm really nervous 'cause none of us knew what we were there for, right? Finally my name comes up and I go into this room and this officer starts asking me a bunch of questions about my application—real nice and polite. I answered each question and he went on to the next one.

G.O.   What kind of questions?

S9   Oh...like am I homosexual, or, oh yeah, have I ever taken drugs, that was a big one!

G.O.   Then what happened?

S9   He thanks me and then asks me to go into another room. No one's there so I sit down and wait. Then this other guy comes in and starts asking me the same questions but really gives me a hard time.

G.O.   What do you mean by a hard time?

S9   He won't accept my answers! He questions me, like,...'What do you mean you've never taken drugs? Ever taken aspirin? That's a drug! You lied to me! Do you always lie to your employers?' You know, that sort of thing.

G.O.   What did you do? What did you say back?

S9   Well I was really scared inside, you know, kinda confused because the first guy was very nice. I thought that this was a final check before they hired me, but this guy! So I covered up my confusion and fear, didn't let him see it and I became very calm. I spoke firmly but didn't raise my voice. I told him that any idiot knows that aspirin is not illegal and I thought the other officer meant illegal drugs. So he says 'Oh' and stammers a bit. I don't think he expected me to say that! Then in the same voice I told him that I never take illegal drugs and I never lie and don't take too kindly to people accusing me of lying, doesn't matter who they are.

G.O.   What did he say to that? Any reaction?

S9   He clammed up, really. He mumbled a few things about

not being able to read the other guy's handwriting and then said the interview was over.

This screening process involves what officers referred to as the "good cop/bad cop" routine, a practice credited with being the most efficient method available to management for filtering out inappropriate applicants. Most applicants do not survive this final test. According to Subject S1:

S1   From the dozen or so people in the waiting room only two of us made it through the 'good cop/bad cop' routine. Myself and a girl.

G.O.   Is that pretty well standard as far as you know?

S1   Yeah, the year I applied there were 7500 applications and only 400 of us made it through. All the others were cut out through these tests. They allocate slots for these 400—a certain percentage have to be female and ethnic minority, about 30% each so that leaves less than 200 where I fit in, (white males). That's about standard procedure every year. From there you go to a police doctor who signs a form that says you're fit and you are in.

This five-stage screening process (i.e., initial interview, fitness test, intelligence test, psychological test and the "good cop/bad cop routine") appears to provide the employer with candidates that meet their specific requirements. Throughout this research, the exact composition of these specific requirements could not be established through repeated probings of the administration. It was repeatedly stated that each candidate must possess a grade twelve diploma. No other tests were mentioned. This would imply that the vocation of policing may be available to any citizen. However, assuming that the statistics provided by Subject S1 are approximate and fairly standard, only 5.3% of applicants are actually offered employment as a police officer. Subject S11 believes that this selection process is geared to the basic philosophy of policing that is overwhelmingly militaristic:

S11   It's like the Army, no, I guess a better comparison is the U.S. Marines. They don't just take anyone,...the toughest or the smartest. They take the ones that they think they can mould into supreme fighting machines. I've seen the pattern over the years, the people they take are the ones they can shape into what they want them to be,...cops devoted to the department. Anyone who shows a hint of going against the department or officer brotherhood is axed before they start. Shaping those people would be too difficult. It might not be done at all and then they'd have a loose cannon floating around.

Once successful applicants are decided upon, notification comes swift and sudden. Successful applicants are notified by mail and are granted little time to savour their acceptance. According to Subject S10:

> S10   I got a notice in the mail in my home town of Halifax. That's a funny story! My girlfriend and I were about to take a car trip and the mailman comes to the door with an envelope from the homebase. I figured it was the pink slip, you know, so she bugs me to open it. I don't. We start driving and she's still buggin' me so I finally pull over and open the damn thing! It tells me that I was in but I had to report to Toronto in 24 hours! We turned the car around, packed some stuff and I flew to Toronto. I was in Aylmer the next day.

Further probing of this officer's experience provided plausible reasons accounting for this minimum time frame of notification:

> S10   It's like that for everyone, pretty well. It's about the abrupt change your life takes once you're hired. It really is a big change! Most guys that I know had a vision of what they'd be like as a copper, you know, tough but fair, some Dirty Harry types, whatever. But it's not like that at all. It's very different. They take you out of your familiar surroundings very quickly and don't give you a chance to formulate in your own mind what kind of policemen you're going to be. They want to decide that.

TRAINING

Once the successful applicant has arrived at the police department's operational base, present procedure requires that the first fortnight of training occurs at their own police college. After this basic orientation, the next nine weeks of training take place at the Ontario Police College in Aylmer, Ontario. Following this these students return to the original police college for the last four weeks of training. This is present procedure and not all interview subjects were trained in the same manner or for the same length of time. For instance, Subject S13 has been a police officer for 18 years and recalls his training period:

> S13   I never went to home base college at all. I went straight to Aylmer. I guess all police officers have been through Aylmer.
>
> G.O.   For how long? How long were you a student at Aylmer?
>
> S13   It's nothing like being a student at least not like you are! More like Army boot camp—it's tough—at least it used to be in the 70s. I was there, geeze, about six months I guess, but it felt like six years! They strip you right down to nothin' and build you back up again...
>
> G.O.   It's that brutal, huh?
>
> S13   At least it was for me. They build you up in their image, you know, what a cop is supposed to be like, by the book. They teach you stuff you'll never use.

Evidence from subject interviews, informal discussions and field notes tends to illustrate the combination of immediate notification and conditions within the Ontario Police College as a situation that may be closely aligned to Goffman's (1960) perception of a "total institution." By abruptly removing the successful applicant from civilian life and by immersing him/her in a new world of quasi-military surroundings may contribute towards learning to submit to authority.

Goffman cites three aspects of this submission to authority that seem to apply to this situation:

> First, authority is of the echelon kind. Any member of the staff class has certain rights to discipline any member of the inmate class.... Second, the authority of corrective sanctions is directed to a great multitude of items of conduct of the kind that are constantly coming up for judgement; in brief, authority is directed to matters of dress, deportment, social intercourse, manners and the like.... The

> third feature of authority in total institutions is that misbehaviors in
> one sphere of life are held against one's standing in other spheres...
> (Goffman, 1960:455)

Conversely, Subject S1 completed all of his training without attending Aylmer Police College. Upon notification of acceptance, this officer was required to report to home base college within a 48-hour period from his home town of Ottawa, Ontario.

> S1   When I was hired, Metro was running their own program
>   for a little while. If you go to Aylmer you get taught polic-
>   ing in Ontario; at homebase you get taught policing at
>   homebase. A lot of useless stuff is taught at Aylmer, like
>   the Fence and Skidoo Act—I'll never need that here!
>   Aylmer grads have to be retrained once they get to home-
>   base. It's a waste of time.
>
> G.O. So you went to homebase for one year?
>
> S1   No. From September to the end of January. I guess about
>   5 months.

The data indicated that various training routes were travelled for various lengths of time. Common to all situations was that, upon completion of training, all recruits are sworn in as 4th Class Constables. They are immediately assigned to a division within city jurisdiction and placed on probation for a period of one year. Within their new division each neophyte is placed under the tutelage of a training officer. This is a special rank division of 1st Class Constable awarded to an officer who has endured 10 years on the force and is capable of sharing his experience with new recruits. This rank of Training Constable must be distinguished from the lesser rank of Senior Constable—a status which is awarded only on the merit of 10 years service.

This tutelage is based on the departmental assumption that neophytes, regardless of the quality of their college training, are ignorant of the "correct" method of performing on the street. This view seems to be universal across police departments in North America.

J. Hunt (1985) reports on various police departments in the Mid-Western United States:

> The police phrase, 'It's not done on the street the way it's taught at
> the Academy' underscores the perceived contradiction between the

formal world of the police academy and the informal world of the street. This contradiction permeates the police officer's construction of his world.... (Hunt, 1985:316)

More currently, this similar assessment is echoed by many of the subjects interviewed. According to Subject S12, a 9-year veteran, 4th Class Constables contribute very little to the overall task of policing and at times hinder police functioning.

> S12   4th Class Constables? I just call 'em rookies. They're a fuckin' pain in the ass, really; they don't know how things are really done out there (points to the roadway). The ones that keep their mouths shut and pay attention are okay I guess, but what am I sayin'? I guess I've been on too long, 'cause I was a rookie once too!

Similarly, Subject S1 explains the process and his assessment of the reasoning behind the obligatory placement of a 4th Class Constable with a Training Constable:

> S1   You go to a division and get assigned to a platoon. Then you have to work with a training officer for a coupla weeks to see how you work out. They don't trust you coming from the college because you know nothing! (strong emphasis) You know book learning but you don't know street learning. You are considered dangerous at that point by everyone in the platoon.

Although these requirements explicitly state that only Training Constables are to be responsible for 4th Class Constables, in practice any 1st Class Constable may be assigned the responsibility.

Once assigned a 4th Class Constable's every move is scrutinized while in the mandatory 1-year probationary period. Both management and the police subculture pay attention. From an occupational standpoint, management closely observes the performance of job functions in relation to the assimilation of informal learning. In essence, the neophyte is evaluated in terms of how swiftly formal knowledge is supplanted by practical knowledge of the street and subculture. During this close monitoring process, both formal and informal rule violations may result in the dismissal of a 4th Class Constable.

For the 1-year probation period these officers perform their jobs without the protection of the Police Association. Management seizes upon this opportunity to impose a sixth screening process to ensure that the neophyte is the proper person for the position. Subject S1 explains:

> S1   When I started the probationary period was 18 months, but now it's 1 year. In that time they can fire you with almost no notice. Once you get off probation, they have to go through the Association and they'll go to bat for you.
>
> G.O.   What would the criteria be to fire a 4th Class Constable?
>
> S1   If you pull your gun when you're not supposed to. Get in an accident and it's your fault; get criminal charges laid on you, anything like that. They don't really need a reason, just any screw up where they think you'll be a problem in the future. 4th Class is where they see how you're gonna react on the street—the only real chance to evaluate you. They don't want psychos, or so they say—another filtering process.

While occupational adjustment is evaluated by management's close scrutiny of job performance, the sphere of social adjustment to the subcultural environment inherent in policing is also closely monitored. Values and norms of subcultural life may begin to be instilled during police college and the level at which they manifest themselves during the performance of duty is also monitored by fellow platoon members. Other officers privately assess neophytes and collectively discuss these assessments in order to determine their knowledge and reliability. According to Subject S12, this assessment is a major concern of established officers:

> S12   We check them out pretty closely.
>
> G.O.   How?
>
> S12   We're a pretty tight group and we talk a lot, mostly shop. When a rookie comes in we have to know pretty fast what kind of an officer he'll be—how he'll react in situations. He could be your partner some day and if he's not all there you're gonna wanna know about it ahead of time.
>
> G.O.   Do you check them out on the job, socially, or,

S12   All the way around! You can't really tell what kinda guy he is just by working; we'll take him out for a beer, get him hammered and see what he does—see if he gets lippy. If the guy's gonna be your partner some day you've gotta trust him and to do that you've gotta know him, all about him, his habits—your life could depend on it.

ADVANCEMENT

Progressive movement from the entry position of 4th Class Constable is contingent upon a series of departmental evaluations once the candidate is assigned to a division. Providing that these evaluations are rated average or above average by the department, movement from 4th Class to 3rd Class to 2nd Class and finally to 1st Class each consume one year of a policeman's career. Based on these evaluations, these promotions are automatic and are accompanied by a raise in pay. According to Subject S2, primary evaluations are accomplished by a monthly Policeman Report of Performance (P.R.P.) which states the department's opinion of whether an officer has utilized their time to the best of his ability:

S2   What they call it is justifying your time. These P.R.P.s show what the department feels is important, not what you did, but what they consider important out of all of your activity. A very formal computer printout in accounting format— very black and white—it lists arrests, traffic tickets, hazardous traffic tickets, parking, bylaw tickets. It never used to list occurrences but it does now.

G.O.   What are occurrences?

S2   You go to a call and write up reports about what it was about—about half an hour of my time gone!

This attitude seems to imply that more actual work is performed than is actually recorded in this monthly evaluation. While Subject S2 did not report that this imbalance may contain stress-producing qualities, Subject S6 complained vehemently:

S6   It's a real sore spot for a lot of us.

G.O.   Why is that?

S6   Put it this way: would you want a report card every month?

G.O.   I don't know; it might be beneficial.

S6   Okay, a different way. How many subjects are you taking?

G.O.   3 1/2.

S6   Say you got a report card every month but you only got credit for two subjects, how would you feel?

G.O.   I'd raise hell!

S6   That's what this P.R.P. is all about. It's not about everything we do but what they think is valuable. You get promoted on this basis and other stuff too. They really count a lot.

G.O.   I guess these reports create a lot of stress, huh?

S6   You got that right! As if we don't have enough already. Especially if a guy's up for a promotion 'cause he can be held up if a few P.R.P.s aren't that great.

While this promotion schedule of one rank per year is dependent upon these evaluations and yearly examination, this structure is fixed and cannot be accelerated as may be the case in many other jobs. Extra work, higher quality work, dedication to overtime or any other expression of commitment does not result in accelerated promotion. One small incentive is placed in view for cadets in training at police college. Subject S1 offers an explanation in response to this query:

G.O.   Is there any way to beat the one rank a year deal by making a good arrest or solving an important case, or something of that nature?

S1   No, never. The only advantage is if you're in the top 20% of your graduating class, you get 2 months taken off your promotion to the next rank—10 months in 4th Class. Then it's back to 1 year from that point on.

G.O.   Then a rank a year up to 1st Class Constable?

S1   Yeah and you stay there; that's as high as you can go as a constable. At 10 years you become a Senior Constable, another incentive and a pay raise. It's not really a rank, just a pay raise.

G.O. Every jump is a pay raise?

S1   Yeah.

G.O. A lot?

S1   It jumps a few thousand a year. Standard base pay for a 1st Class is $50,000 or something; it changes all the time. When I started I got $24,000 a year in 1986. Now I'm 1st Class and I made $73,000 this (1991) year. So in 5 years and some I went up $50,000 including my court and plain-clothes pay all thrown in.

Attaining the rank of 1st Class Constable in the homebase appears to be a major milestone since it represents a plateau from which officers may engage in a variety of related assignments. This is demonstrated by the variety of job descriptions within this subject sample of 1st Class Constables. Seniority within this rank is evaluated by both management and the subculture through "years on" the force and the number of different assignments an officer may have participated in (i.e., drug squad, fraud squad, foot patrol, etc.). To this issue, Subject S5 reflects on his eight years on the force:

S5   Getting to 1st Class was a big deal I guess. It's more money but a lot of doors open for you. After a while you get tired of the cars and some guys get tired of the uniform in general. I didn't but I did try the squads for a while. You need a change once in a while.

This milestone may be envisioned as a type of incentive that most officers would aspire to reach. Occupational hardships may become easier for an officer who wishes to expand occupational horizons once four years of service have accrued. However, Subject S1 provides his impression of this ideal by stating statistics that contain a contradictory flavour:

S1   There's not that many people on this force that have that much time on anymore. In my old platoon, the average time on is two years but since they haven't had many new people come in it's probably up to 4 years. I'm just estimating here. A lot of people take off to other forces because they get fed up with homebase, you know, the media, allegations of racism, all that stuff makes our job a lot harder.

If these estimates are somewhat accurate they would imply that many platoons are primarily staffed with 3rd and 2nd Class Constables. This may reflect a more experimental than professional approach to the actual occupation of policing. Subject S1 partly supports this possibility:

> S1   I've been on 5 years and I'm considered a dinosaur. When I joined in 1986 the average time on in our division was 10 years. Now it's 2 or 3 years because we're not getting any new policemen on the job. It's completely different now—different attitudes, different people coming in, I guess a new generation.

These estimates may imply that this particular police force is becoming smaller, younger and less experienced. Perhaps promotional constraints, management scrutiny and outward pressures have resulted in a weakened police force. Perhaps structural changes are indeed warranted.

Past the rank of 1st Class Constable further upward movement can be attained. For 10 years of service the position of Senior Constable is awarded. Should this constable exhibit skill in the training of neophytes, the official rank of Training Constable is awarded.

Should a 1st Class Constable wish to advance toward the management levels the initial step involves the rank of Sergeant. In addition to monthly P.R.P.s, every officer is required to complete a yearly examination in which knowledge of updates on current laws and routine procedures is assessed. A promotional examination is included in this assessment. Success in these three areas is transposed into points. Candidates with the highest point totals are ranked in order for promotional review. New sergeants are taken from this list in rank order as the need arises. This review/evaluation process is repeated every year.

Once promoted from 1st Class Constable to Sergeant the job description and division position changes. Each new sergeant experiences a probationary period of 6 months that resembles the evaluation process imposed upon 4th Class Constables. According to Subject S12, new sergeants are monitored by both the department and the rank and file of which he/she was once a member:

> S12   If you screw up as a sarg. in the first 6 months they can take it away from you. If not you're full-fledged.
>
> G.O.   Is this something that most guys want? To be a sarg.?

S12   It's not the same as moving up in a corporation. It depends on the individual. You get a 15% pay raise but it's a very different job.

G.O.   How so?

S12   A sarg. isn't out arresting people; he supervises the platoon, signs your reports; he'll advise you in a tough situation, same for reports. He makes sure everything that's supposed to be on them is there, then signs it. He might ask you a few questions, then he'll sign it.

G.O.   Sounds like a position of power to me.

S12   Sometimes it is, but I just think it's a different type of job really. Some guys who get promoted to Sergeant let it go to their heads that they're really movin' up in the world (says mockingly).

G.O.   How?

S12   When the guy was still 1st Class he was our buddy but now he's a Sergeant and thinks he's king shit. Or he treats his former buddies like shit. That doesn't happen a lot, but when it does we let him know and it usually stops at some point.

G.O.   How do you let him know?

S12   Shut him out of activity on the shift so he doesn't know what's going on that day. He'll get in deep shit if the brass asks him where we are or what's going on in a certain area and he can't rattle off the info. Then he'll know we're pissed at him and he'll stop being such a snot.

In a supervisory capacity the sergeant is responsible for the constables that constitute a platoon. It should be noted here that at the level of 1st Class Constable, the homebase splits into uniformed and plainclothes officers. Sergeants that supervise uniformed patrols are referred to as sergeants while sergeants in charge of plainclothes squads are referred to as Detectives or Detective Sergeants.

Relationships between sergeants and constables appear to be one of distance in relation to job functioning. Contact is made for parades and report signings but rarely do constables feel the need to consult their sergeant's approval for actions they must take. On the contrary, most American police forces require their constables to contact or seek the presence of their sergeant for many situations encountered during a shift (Rubenstein, 1975:37-40). According to Subject S3, the function of a Canadian sergeant is much different from that of one in the U.S.A.:

S3   I've been all through the States on business and I have friends on American police forces. It's a lot different down there. Our Sergeants at the uniform level are really supervisors. They don't get involved that much.

G.O.   When you were in uniform did you call your sergeant in a tough situation?

S3   No. It's not done here, well, I should say rarely.

G.O.   Why is there such a difference between us and the U.S.?

S3.   They trust us more here. You're looked down upon by everyone if you're calling your sergeant every minute. You could become a laughingstock! Considered a sick puppy very fast if you do that! I think in my 16 1/2 years I might have called my sarg. 2 or 3 times. We don't do it here.

Similarly, Subjects S1 and S2 stand in agreement with S3:

G.O.   If you don't know how to act in a particular situation is that when your sergeant comes in?

S2   Well,

S1   No that's when other people on your shift with more experience come in.

S2   Technically you're right. You could call a supervisor. In twelve years I think I've had to call a supervisor maybe 3 times. He makes more money to make these corporate decisions, so maybe we should call more.

G.O.   That's how it's done in the U.S.

S1   In the States they don't have the level of training that we have so the sergeants don't trust their men as much. They get paid a lot less too. The average Canadian policeman is more qualified to look after himself.

S2   ...and make those decisions! We have to notify our sarges at times but we don't have to clear our moves with him.

S1   They have faith in us! They trust us! If I had to do that I'd feel like a messenger boy, not a policeman. We get paid a lot of money to be our own boss and do a lot of thinking. In the States they're not paid to think! How stringent can their requirements be if they have 20,000 policemen in New York that all make $20,000 a year? You can't even live off that without having a second job or going on the take! No wonder their sergeants can't trust their men!

S2   Absolutely!

Immediately above the rank of Sergeant is the rank of Staff-Sergeant whose responsibilities are expanded to the divisional level. Typically, divisions operate in three overlapping shifts in order to cover a complete 24-hour period each day. Each shift is supervised by a Staff-Sergeant who is responsible for all activity by every officer. Shifts begin with a meeting known as "parade" that is headed up by the Staff-Sergeant. At this time specific details are assigned, current divisional information is announced and platoon inspection may occur at the discretion of the Staff-Sergeant. Some parades are quite formal requiring officers to stand at attention during inspection and direction while others are less formal. Their duration may be between 10 and 20 minutes depending on the Staff-Sergeant. Subject S8 provides information in relation to this difference:

S8   You get the spit and polish types, like the Army or it goes to the other extreme like Hill Street Blues where everyone sits around, everybody talks a bit. Usually he does the talking and we shut up and listen. Depends on the Staff-Sergeant.

G.O.   Which way is better do you think?

S8   I don't like the formal way 'cause it puts me on edge. Before a shift most of the guys wanna be as calm as possible, get the details, any relevant info and hit the streets; there's enough stress from working the streets, we don't need it from him.

After parade the Staff-Sergeant remains at the division as dictated by his supervisory capacity. In the absence of each division's Superintendent or Staff-

Superintendent (who are generally considered to be "the brass" or "the boss" of each division) the Staff-Sergeant is completely responsible for all activity within the division during that shift. Subjects S1 and S2 summarize this structure:

> S1   The Staff-Sergeant is responsible for all of the Sergeants and the platoon. The platoon consists of the constables, the sergeants and one Staff-Sergeant on each shift. Each platoon is supposed to have 36 constables but you never have that many. We're always under strength. Every platoon will have 3 or 4 sergeants and about 30 constables-that make up one shift. So you'll have A platoon relieved by B platoon relieved by C platoon, some overlapping, some on days off, so you cover a 24-hour cycle. In my division we have 5 platoons: A B C D and E which means about 150 or so constables, 18 or 20 sergeants and 5 Staff-Sergeants. But it changes all the time.

> S2   But that's pretty well the standard structure in each division. Mine is roughly the same but I think we're a bit larger in numbers.

It appears that all ranks above the level of Staff-Sergeant are considered by rank and file officers as "Brass." These ranks include Superintendent, Staff-Superintendent, Inspector and Staff-Inspector. The majority of this subject sample referred to these positions as "political positions" and not real police positions. According to Subject S6, this distinction is constructed mentally by most officers:

> S6   I think it is fair to say that all of us feel that anyone above the rank of Staff-Sergeant is not really a policeman. Maybe he was once a policeman, but his job calls for a political mentality. They don't really know what's going on in this city, but they play like they do.

This attitude was prevalent among most subjects but most succinctly stated by Subject S1:

> S1   Above the rank of Staff-Sergeant they aren't really involved with the platoons. They're the Brass at the administration level and responsible for divisions. Staff-Sergeant and down

are the street guys; above that are the politicians because they've got to concern themselves with the public and public interest. Technically they aren't politicians, they are very high-ranking policemen, but in practice they are.

It should be noted that for the most part concern has been shown to the uniform ranks, their structure and organization. All officers must proceed through these ranks in order to reach the level at which specialization is allowed, (i.e. squads). At the level of 1st Class Constable applications may be made to enter these squads depending on qualifications and need. These plainclothes positions are obtained through a process known as "lateraling over." These laterals last for 6 months and are followed by a return to the original platoon. Permanent positions require the officer to commit to the new position for a period of 2 years.

These detective squads are organized in much the same manner as the uniform ranks although actual numbers may vary. Subject S1 summarizes the parallel notion of squad work:

> S1   Each division will have the same number of squads as the uniform street platoons, but in the detective offices—plainclothes—at the same time as the uniforms are patrolling the streets the plainclothes are out as well. All divisions have anti-narcotics, major crime, fraud, warrants, C.I.B. (Criminal Investigation Branch). It all depends on the area of the city the division is in and what it calls for.

CONCLUSION

The findings of this inquiry indicate a recurring theme throughout the hiring, training and advancement procedures which have affected all police officers employed by this Canadian metropolitan police force. While the administration continually stresses openness and professionalism in its rhetoric, in practice, these qualities are rarely applied. As a result, police officers tend to experience a sense of disempowerment and frustration stemming from constant lack of attention paid to the views of their subculture.

The lived experiences of these respondents in both an occupational and social context suggest that this sense of disempowerment originates with the initial application for employment. Apart from a grade twelve diploma, respondents are told very little in relation to personal qualities that may enhance their opportunity of securing employment as a police officer. All potential candidates are relentlessly screened by the administration ostensibly to eliminate potential "psychos." But in essence, it appears that the hidden agenda behind this close scrutiny is related to the malleability of potential candidates.

The respondent's descriptions of additional screening processes appear to buttress this contention. These processes appear to be designed to eliminate prospective employees rather than evaluate potential candidates. The physical fitness and intelligence tests appear to assess physical and mental capabilities against some hidden administrative average when in fact it becomes apparent that candidate elimination is the true motive. The psychological test is another example of these archaic hiring practices. Described as a "confusing and frustratingly-tedious experience" by one respondent, the "psych test" possesses many demeaning qualities that contain the potential for creating serious personal doubts within the consciences of candidates.

Perhaps most humiliating is the continued application of the "good cop/bad cop" routine. Designed as the fifth and last screening process before being hired, this oppressive display of administrative power results in most applicants suffering rejection. Most respondents described this confrontational manoeuvre as being nothing less than the brutal intimidation of both mental and physical capabilities. Do these screening processes co-relate with the rhetoric of camaraderie, partnership and professionalism?

Results from this inquiry indicate that the yearly average of applicants who are offered employment is approximately five percent. The candidates who are hired are then "educated" at police colleges for a period of approximately five months. During this time police professionalism is ostensibly instilled through techniques that appear to resemble militaristic submission to administrative authority. Future police officers are constructed in the image of the administration that emphasizes its hierarchical organizational design.

However, once the neophyte has been assigned to a police division and begins working as a Fourth Class Constable, every occupation and social move is again closely scrutinized during a probationary period of one year. During this time, officers are encouraged to jettison their formal learning in lieu of practical knowledge gained from their working environment, their subculture and senior officers. Both individual and collective judgments are made by both the administration and subcultural members in relation to the swiftness of these procedural changes. Those neophytes who are tardy in terms of adapting to these changes and/or commit rule infractions may be dismissed by the administration with little or no notice. Again, it appears that this final screening process is designed to eliminate potential career police officers instead of providing a shared context of occupational knowledge.

This thread of disempowerment continues through to advancement opportunities available to these police officers. The strict time frame of one rank per year reflects the inflexibility common to militaristic and hierarchical organization. It is widely acknowledged that police officers perform many functions. These include upholding the political and economic system, attending to the task of order maintenance, information sharing and social service as well as law enforcement duties. However, police officers are promoted solely on the basis of a yearly written examination and monthly performance reports. These P.R.P.s succinctly list the activity the administration deems most important to the justification of each officer's time. This report is predominantly concerned with law enforcement duties and ignores the many other facets characteristic of police work. This constraining and restrictive promotional structure and the perceived unfairness of the P.R.P.s contributes to officer demoralization and distancing from an administration that preaches partnership and brotherhood.

What has emerged from the descriptions of the lived experiences of these respondents is an overall sense of frustration, constant erosion of self-confidence and the disassociation of these officers from the administration that controls their career lives. In response to this distancing, many officers leave this metropolitan police force in search of other Canadian police forces or related civilian careers. What does this administration mean by the term police professionalism when it constantly regiments its employees, restricts individual contributions and demonstrates a lack of investment in the body of the rank and file?

REFERENCES

* This chapter is published here by permission of the author.

Emerson, R.M. 1988. *Contemporary Field Research.* Prospect Heights: Waveland.

Goffman, E. 1960. "Characteristics of Total Institutions" in *Identity and Anxiety,* (ed.), M. Stein et al. Glencoe: Free Press.

Hunt, J. 1985. "Police Accounts of Normal Force," *Urban Life,* 13;4 (pgs. 315-341).

Rubenstein, J. 1975. *City Police.* New York: Ballantine.

Skolnick, J.H. 1966. *Justice Without Trial.* New York: John Wiley.

—

ACCOUNTABILITY
AND CONTROL

CHAPTER 17
The Control of Police Behaviour

ALAN GRANT

The Police must be prepared to receive and discuss
communications from the public. Sincere criticism—even
when unfounded—must not be confused with an "attack"
upon the police or an indication of an anti-police attitude.
(*Ouimet Report*[1]).

INTRODUCTION

A great deal has been said and written about the control of police behaviour
and it needs a special reason to justify a further contribution. My excuses for
doing so are twofold, one personal and one of a more general nature.

First, despite all this past activity, there is strong evidence that opposing
sides take totally conflicting positions and very little in the way of a dialogue
has ensued. Police proponents and opponents have tended to talk at each
other rather than to each other.[2] Now I have been a police officer holding all
ranks from Constable to Chief Inspector, have been the recipient of police discipline and, on occasions, an agent in its receipt by others. I have also been
involved in cases where I have been critical of police behaviour and lectured
on law at university where, perforce, I sometimes think I have been critical of
everything! Avoidance of schizophrenia alone would, with that background, be
reason enough to confront the issues.

Second, in my view, the time is now ripe for a re-assessment of the balance between police power and individual liberty. Past means of control may
well have been relevant to past ages, but we must seriously consider whether
our present framework takes account of the vast increase in police power
which has occurred since the foundations of our current restrictions were laid.

Before looking at some of the historical and budgetary factors involved, together with the role of the courts and the "rise in crime" question, let us consider the general state of relations between the police and the public.

POLICE-COMMUNITY RELATIONS

What is the general state of public opinion concerning the police in Canada today? A study by the Centre of Criminology in Toronto in 1970,[3] involved asking nearly 1,000 adults who had lived in Canada for several years:

"How favourable or unfavourable do you feel towards the police?"

No less than 85% of the sample indicated that they were positively disposed towards the police, made up of 42% who were "very favourable" and 43% who were "moderately favourable". On the other hand, only 6% of the sample were negatively disposed towards the police.

A study undertaken in Quebec in 1968 for the Prévost Commission[4] shows that when people living in towns were asked if they were satisfied or dissatisfied with police-public relations, 87% were positively disposed towards the police, made up of 62% who were satisfied and 25% who regarded the situation as "passable", whereas some 12% registered dissatisfaction.

These findings do not seem to be greatly out of line with the findings of a survey undertaken in England for the Royal Commission on the Police (1962) where no less than 83% of those interviewed professed great respect for the police, 16% said that they had mixed feelings and only 1% said they had little nor no respect for them. The Commission concluded that

> ...relations between the police and the public are on the whole very good, and we have no reason to suppose that they have ever, in recent times, been otherwise.[5]

It is not my wish to be seen as oversimplifying individual findings and I recognize that criticisms are often made of such results by social scientists well-versed in the field of the gathering and presentation of statistics. All that said, however, it seems that an onus rests upon those who indicate dissatisfaction with, for example, current police practices in investigating citizen complaints, to attempt to show why this concern is justified in particular when the public at large do not, in general, appear to manifest gross outrage with the present policing system.

One possibility is that citizens may have many misgivings about police practices, but when they subconsciously weigh all of them up against having no police presence at all, they are willing to indicate general satisfaction when a broad question of police-pubic relations is addressed to them. But, even if this is not so, and the apparent general satisfaction were to be taken at its face value, another factor must be considered. The missing factor in most surveys is that little or no account is taken of the actual contacts which the persons questioned have had with the police. It may well be that the police have actual dealings with a segment of the population which is not numerically large, and this becomes even smaller when one counts only those police-citizen contacts which are likely to raise tensions and difficulties. Many citizens in the middle and upper socio-economic groups have little or no contact with the police which has any real potential for conflict. Certainly if one isolates those situations where the police and the citizen have conflicting goals and then seek information from the citizen about police behaviour, the question of "satisfaction" or "dissatisfaction" becomes a more realistic test. The true measure of a satisfied citizen it might be argued, would be the case where his goals have differed from that of the police officer and yet the citizen is able to recognize that, although he may have been thwarted, he was treated with dignity and respect. Such a test would, of course, always uncover some complaints based on unjustified personal bias, but the positive replies would clearly reflect very highly on the police.

A study by the Canadian Civil Liberties Association, which attempted to address itself to a sample which had come into conflict with the police, therefore concentrated on some arrested persons who were being processed through the criminal justice system in Halifax, Montreal, Toronto, Winnipeg and Vancouver during January, 1970. It records, (*inter alia*),

> ...our survey contained some questions about injuries inflicted by police. Of 293 arrested persons who replied to this, 74 or 25.2% complained that they had been hurt by the police.[6]

If we can accept that 25% claimed to have been actually hurt, we can probably assume that others may have been treated in an abusive or obstructive manner short of physical injury. Indeed, of 164 people in custody who requested police to allow them to make a telephone call, 56 or 30% alleged that they were denied this facility.[7]

Thus I am suggesting that the percentage of satisfied clients one ends up with will largely depend upon the clientele to whom one addressed the question "Are you satisfied?" The case for the *status quo* is not made out by an 85% positive reply from a sample who may be largely drawn from those who do not really run much risk of encountering the police in an adversarial setting. At the same time, even in the Civil Liberties study, the police can take credit for the fact that there was a large number of apparently satisfied members of the public who would have been in the best possible position to see the system at its most testing time. Nevertheless, individual complainants are still entitled to proper treatment even if most people are properly treated or do not choose to protect themselves against impropriety. Thus I shall concentrate on seeking ways of improving the negative side of the picture which will, I think, require more than tinkering with current practices. I hope to demonstrate that, in some respects, a new scheme is needed which will have to be practical and effective. What must be avoided is an alternative which amounts to no more than symbolic reassurance to the pubic that all is well.

HISTORY

The early days of modern police organization, notwithstanding the stalwart work done by the Fielding brothers in 18th/19th Century London, are usually regarded as commencing with Sir Robert Peel and the establishment of the Metropolitan Police in 1829 in London, England. History shows that, despite the crying need for some sort of police presence, Peel met agonizing resistance from Parliament in attempting to introduce a Police Act. The reasons were obvious and, to some extent, understandable. First of all, it was innovative and the only thing that terrifies mankind more than a new idea is the appearance on the scene of a man with the ability to see it carried through. Such a man was Peel, but even he knew that a great deal could not be achieved too quickly, because the people, notwithstanding the breakdown in public order then imminent, genuinely and prudently feared the potential power of the "new police" and early budgets were made to reflect that fact. Thus the idea of an organized police force was introduced into society as a lesser of two evils, and society inherited a policing model of modest proportion and little power.

As the police went about their business, cases on the use and extent of police powers came before the courts and 19th-Century *laissez-faire* judges made sure that individual liberty was not sacrificed to the "New-Police" interloper upon the social scene. There was a tendency to liken the police to the ordinary citizen unless some special rule of law or statute so invested him. It is little wonder, then, that there was no corollary need to check and balance the powers of the new police with overly restrictive controlling measures. In the absence of vast and encroaching *de facto* police powers there was little incentive to make the lot of a plaintiff in a civil action for malicious prosecution or false imprisonment an easy one. In the face of a poorly organized, badly-trained constabulary which avoided aggressive encounters with a citizenry that vastly outnumbered it, an impartial machinery to ensure that citizen complaints of police misbehaviour received proper investigation and equitable disposition would also appear to have been superfluous.

Thus, we see the quintessential *laissez-faire* system: a new police whose powers are heavily circumscribed, subjected to only the loosest of active judicial and internal controls. There was nothing wrong with the equation at its inception. It balanced and, consistent with the times for which it was fashioned, it may have functioned well enough. The question of timing, which I mentioned in opening, is highly relevant here. Had the legislature and/or the judiciary set about from the start to hamper the embryo police idea with a confining controlling mechanism, it could not have survived. Rather, the approach was negative—having granted few powers, there was little or no need for reciprocal controlling devices. But is that true of the police machinery today?

It is a truism to state that the police are today much more powerful and efficient than they were in 1829 and the century thereafter. It is true that many of the basic powers of arrest and search are much the same today as heretofore. What has happened is that in numbers, education, equipment and share of society's total budget, the police have rapidly expanded. At the same time they have, in many jurisdictions, occupied the vacuum created by the collapse of the idea of maintaining a large standing army in peacetime. Further, police effectiveness has been strengthened by technology, e.g., the police national computer system known as Canadian Police Information Centre (C.P.I.C.), electronic eavesdropping devices, voice prints, scientific analysis at scenes of crimes, and legislation, e.g., stop-and-frisk laws in the U.S. and some, though not all, aspects of legally authorized "wire tapping" here in Canada.[8] The growth of a private security industry has also relieved the police of many tasks. Private security is a growth industry *par excellence*, which is presently estimated to employ two persons for every public police officer in Ontario.

BUDGETING FOR POLICE SERVICES - PAST AND PRESENT

When one considers that the legal controls upon the police are largely the same now as they were in the nineteenth Century, we are left wondering if the time is not ripe for more controls upon police autonomy, both by means of tort law, and in respect of their self-regulating internal investigation and adjudication role when complaints are made by members of the public against the police.

In order to place present day police power into perspective it is instructive to look at the type of budgeting which existed for the provision of police services at the time when the legal restraints upon police power were being forged in our society and then to compare present-day appropriations for this purpose.

The paucity of financial resources with which early police forces had to contend is well shown by two excerpts from A.K. McDougall's study of policing arrangements in rural Ontario around the 1870s.[9]

Firstly:

> Constables were paid on a fees basis and thus received no support if they failed to administer a judicial process. This meant that a constable had to finance his own travel in search of a culprit and, should he fail to find the culprit, he received no financial assistance from the local governing authorities.

Secondly:

> The chief of the Hamilton Police Force...wrote the Attorney General complaining that when he displaced a constable in pursuit of a culprit into rural Ontario it often took a day to find the local constable who might be "in the bush" logging at the time.

On the other hand, compared with the financial austerity of the past, in 1972 the total police budget for the province of Ontario, including the municipalities, was $229,303,740. This shows more than a 100% increase since as recently as 1967 when it was $110,205,000.[10] Even accepting the diminished purchasing power of the dollar, this seems to indicate a substantial growth rate in real money terms.[11]

In this, the Ontario experience has not differed markedly from that prevailing elsewhere in western democracies. In England, for example,

> [d]uring the fifteen years from 1950 to 1965 the police share of gross national expenditure, although subject to fluctuations, increased substantially. Gross national expenditure rose by 163%, public spending (excluding defence) by 202% and the cost of the police service by 256%.[12]

This growth rate has continued apace so that in 1972 the cost of police services in England and Wales stood at $976,000,000, with an estimated increase of a further 17% on that figure for 1973.[13]

Ontario is therefore playing its part in a general phenomenon: the expenditure of great and increasing amounts, in real money terms, upon the provision of policing services. I do not deplore the expenditure, but I question whether society is well served by allowing this to grow "like Topsy" without apparently stopping to consider whether what is happening is a change not in degree but in substance. Have we moved imperceptibly over a period of 150 years from a society with a weak police force subject to appropriate judicial or administrative controls to a society with a powerful police force subject to a controlling system relevant to a former age?

THE ROLE OF THE CRIMINAL COURTS IN CONTROLLING POLICE BEHAVIOUR

Even accepting the limited nature of the ability of the criminal courts to exert effective control on police behaviour and recognizing the inevitable dichotomy between the "law in the books" and the "law in fact", judicial attitudes towards the police and the prosecutor have emphasized the uncontrolled discretion which they possess. In 1957, in the *Beaver* case,[14] Canada stood poised on the brink of greatly widening the exceptions to the classical doctrine of *mens rea* in criminal cases. This doctrine requires, in the mind of an accused person, full knowledge of all relevant circumstances and, where consequences are a constituent part of an offence, either an intention to bring them about or foresight of the possibility of such consequences. In a three-to-two split decision, the core of this idea was retained in Canada's criminal jurisprudence but the dissent of Fauteux J. is an excellent indication of the extent to which modern courts are willing to grant unstructured discretion to persons in authority. Arguing for a large reduction in the need for classical *mens rea*, Fauteux J. explained "safeguards", which would exist in his new scheme of things, as follows:

> That the enforcement of the provisions of the [then Opium and Narcotic Control] Act may, in exceptional cases, lead to some injustice, is not an impossibility. But, to forestall this result as to such possible cases, there are remedies under the law, such as a stay of proceedings by the Attorney-General or a free pardon under the royal prerogative.[15]

The learned judge might also have added that possibly the police could be relied on not to lay an information in the case of a "technical" breach of the law, or that the judge could, if an information were laid, impose only a nominal penalty where the Crown indicated that this was appropriate. The approach, however, is the same, in effect: "Trust public officials, we, the courts, do not need to control them".

A similar belief underlies the approach of the Supreme Court of Canada in the *Wray* case[16] where it was held that a judge has no discretion to rule out relevant admissible evidence on the ground that it had been obtained in circumstances which tended to bring the administration of justice into disrepute. Thus, whilst a forced confession would be ruled inadmissible, if, as a consequence of it, physical evidence were discovered (in the *Wray* case, a murder weapon), then both the weapon and that part of the confession which led to its finding must be admitted in evidence, no matter what means were used to obtain that result, and the trial judge has no discretion to exclude it.

A further example of this trend is the decision of the same court in *Osborn*,[17] in which three judges disavowed the existence of a right in the courts to control abuse of their own processes and they were prepared to leave to the discretion of the Attorney-General the question of proceeding on another charge based on the same facts where the earlier (and wrongly) selected charge had resulted in an acquittal. Since it was not the same charge, the plea of *autrefois acquit* was not available to the defendant. Does such an approach open the way in Canada to the prosecution depleting the emotional and financial resources of a defendant on a spurious charge, so that the "proper" charge upon the same facts may be brought by the still fresh State against an exhausted opponent? It does not appear as though we can look to judicial control of police and prosecutorial behaviour to provide a potent supervisory device. This is further reinforced by the strong support which, to date, Canadian jurisprudence has given to the idea that the important question to be addressed to evidence in criminal cases is that of relevance not the legality of the manner in which it was obtained. In short, there is no evidence that Canada is contemplating a general rule which would render illegally seized evidence inadmissible.

Thus, for all of the reasons stated so far, I am suggesting that police power today is in danger of outstripping society's mechanisms to control it.

THE RISE IN CRIME AND CONTROL OF THE POLICE

It will be objected that the sixties and early seventies have witnessed a steady increase in crime and that, albeit police forces have been strengthened, they have been unable to reduce crime. There are many reasons for this:

First, there is more property in existence now than ever before. As a percentage of property available to be stolen, have thefts increased? We do not know; that kind of statistic is not available to us unfortunately.

Secondly, as police become better organized, crime reporting techniques improve and part of the *chiffre noir* of previously unreported crime finds its way into the statistics.[18]

Thirdly, the sixties and early seventies saw the growth into adolescence and young adulthood of the huge baby boom of the post-war years and that is the age at which the human animal reaches its zenith in antisocial behaviour. As Stanton Wheeler has noted:

> Certainly it is important theoretically to understand that the rising rate does not appear to be a response to new forces and flaws in mass society, but rather can be explained fairly directly as a function of the age structure of the population.[19]

Finally, just too many crimes are on the statute book anyway. Every arrest for betting and gambling, for example, would be totally unnecessary if society organized off-track betting and casino gaming into a legitimate business and derived revenue from them by taxation.

Thus, to show that crime figures are high and are increasing does not, in my submission, prove that the police are necessarily weak or ineffectual. Neither am I arguing that police strengths and efficiency should not be increased. What I am contending is that we should not increase police power without a commensurate increase in the controlling mechanisms which society makes use of to ensure proper accountability.

CONTROL: EXTERNAL AND INTERNAL

I now turn to the question of how to control the behaviour of police officers in a way which will maximize personal liberty without "handcuffing" the police. In the nineteenth century we may have achieved an acceptable balancing of that most difficult of social equations by having a weak police force subjected only to minimal controls. What must now be faced is that we are rapidly approaching the era of strong, well organized professional police forces and, to maintain equilibrium, we must have controlling mechanisms to match the power of the phenomenon we seek to restrain. Checks have been interposed elsewhere in both the public and private sectors by the introduction of Ombudsmen, Securities Commissions, Labour Relations Boards and Municipal Boards to name just a few. Should not the police receive similar attention?

In this connection, I would suggest a two-pronged policy. First, although it is not the central theme of this paper to investigate applicable tort law, it is felt that, in this field, some changes are needed. I would advocate the removal of the need to prove that the defendant was actuated by malice in a suit for malicious prosecution. Surely it should be enough that the prosecution was launched without reasonable and probable cause. In addition, the Canadian Criminal Code should be amended[20] where it has the effect of requiring that the plaintiff in a civil action for false imprisonment, for example, should prove all of the factors indicating that the defendant police officer had failed to comply with his duty not to arrest under the recent Bail Reform Act. Surely it would be enough to require the plaintiff to adduce some evidence on the issue leaving the defendant to prove the factor which he alleges prevented the duty not to arrest from coming into play. I say nothing on the argument that it may be unconstitutional for the federal government to seek to legislate on the issue, in any event.

Second, there is a need to overhaul police internal discipline systems, which permit the police to be judge and jury in their own cause, in those cases where a citizen makes a complaint against an officer.

It is this second aspect upon which I intend to concentrate as it is the area which numerically affects more citizens and is the one about which many misconceptions are held. As Professor Alan Mewett said recently:[21]

> ...[I]t must be realized that what primarily controls the actions of police officers in this country is not what the civil law says about tort actions or what the criminal law says about their liability or even what an irate judge might say, but rather the internal disciplinary

rules of the force. In many areas a much higher duty is placed upon a police officer than upon a private person. In most cases, the sanction against a police officer for a wrongful act is not a criminal prosecution or a tort action but a disciplinary hearing and its consequent penalties, and this is the true control.

To similar effect, though displaying more scepticism of the effectiveness of the controlling device, Professor Stanley Beck has written:

> In Canada...part time police commissions with a changing makeup of members with no particular expertise are the ostensible controllers. The reality, and it is seen by the public to be the reality, is that the police are self-controlling and that internal administrative discipline, *insofar as it does control*, is the only real control.[22]

Such are the numbers of our police when compared to the total population that, powerful though they undoubtedly are under modern conditions, effective policing must rely on police-public co-operation. One of the best ways to ensure that co-operation is to provide for a disciplinary system which is seen to be fair both by the police and by the citizen. It is often thought that any measure of outside surveillance of police handling of complaints will be opposed en masse by the police themselves. This, I suggest, is not necessarily so. In the past, those within the police who traditionally opposed some public input made strange bedfellows indeed. On the one hand, were the police associations, representing the patrolmen, terrified that "no one but the police could understand police problems" and, on the other, the Chiefs of Police who feared that their power to discipline their own forces would be eroded by any such move. They may have squabbled and fought over many issues but on that one they provided a united front. More recently, however, in England, for example, the idea of agreeing to some form of external review has gained ground amongst police officers. The model currently being investigated is that of *ex post facto* review by an independent lawyer to ensure that due process was accorded to both the complainant and the policeman, but initial investigation and disposition would remain with the police. The U.S. experience, in this respect, seems different in kind and has been marked by activist Patrolmen's Associations seeking injunctive relief in the courts to prevent the operation of schemes intended to implement civilian review of internal police discipline.[23]

The movement, within the police, for some form of external review, where it does exist, probably first gained favour with middle-ranking police officers, that is, the very people who had to administer the present system and who often see it through less rose-tinted spectacles than either the Police Associations, which are heavily oriented towards the patrolman's view, or the Police Chief. Why should that be so?

Clearly it is an uncomfortable undertaking to have to investigate a colleague, especially one who may, in other respects, have proven himself to be a good officer in the past and from whom further proficient work will be expected in the future. In addition, few professional policemen ever built a career out of making cases against other policemen. That is not to say that the police present a monolithic stance towards the public and will never break ranks. On the contrary, an officer is usually a family man with his own interests in job security to protect and this will ensure that 'cover-ups' do not happen as a second-nature defensive reaction. But all this said, it is impossible for the investigating officer to forget that the person under investigation is a police officer, and I think it is misleading to suggest that a complaint against a police officer is investigated in just the same way that an enquiry involving a member of the public is handled.

Now let me turn to those cases where, in my respectful submission, present practice fails to take proper account of the public interest and where there are indications that the system may be too considerate to the policeman suspected of wrong-doing.

Investigations need investigators. Many people who would happily see an outsider sit in judgment in citizen complaint cases, still see the police as the only feasible investigative arm. Whilst the police are used to investigate other police, there will always be a danger that news of the impending enquiry will be 'leaked' to a suspect with the result that things are put right before the investigation begins. This is particularly a problem in police corruption cases, e.g., a man complains that a police officer has threatened to arrest him unless the complainant "pays him off" and a meeting has been arranged to pass over the money. Many such meetings, once surveillance is arranged, never take place. Why? Well, of course, the allegation might have been a malicious one from start to finish: an example of a bad man trying to blacken the name of an effective police officer. But it must be faced that another alternative is that someone inside the organization may have told the police-suspect that he was the subject of an enquiry. I am not suggesting that these cases are numerous. But numbers are not important in this class of case. If it happens at all, it is a serious situation and every effort must be made to guard against it. The conventional wisdom is that police malpractice of the grossest kind is well policed internally whilst in lesser matters the shared morality of the peer-group dampens the ardour to root it out. Some English experiences have shown that a deep public suspicion of "in-force" investigation may be justified even where corruption is suspected. As a general rule, cases investigated by one force member against another in the same force, often come to nothing; the success rate climbs when another force is called in to do the investigation and some noticeable successes have been rung up by investigative reporting teams of *The Times* and *The People* newspapers in the U.K., operating totally outside the police organization. Indeed, a recent case involving the conviction of a Detective Chief Inspector and a Detective Sergeant for conspiracy to pervert the course of justice was particularly noticeable on account of the marked suspicion of the newspaper reporters that an "in-house" investigation would not have been sufficiently penetrating, because the details of the allegations against the officers were not even turned over to the authorities until a very strong case had been established, complete with corroborative tape recordings of the alleged wrong-doings.[24]

Current investigation of complaints made by citizens against police officers in Toronto, for example, exhibit certain departures from normal investigative techniques. That is, a different system is used when police investigate police as opposed to when police investigate citizens. This is explained, in part, by the current practice of requiring a "duty statement" from the officer under enquiry. Following a complaint by a member of the public, the investigating officer will require the officer against whom the complaint has been made to make a statement about the matter in much the same way as he might about any other matter that had arisen in the course of his duty. These statements are made without any warning about their possible later use in evidence and I shall criticize this as unfair to the officer, in another context, later. More important, the demand for them is made without regard to the crucial distinguishing feature that it is the very conduct of the maker of the statement which is called into question by the enquiry.

In one sense, this procedure results in a less penetrating investigation than would otherwise occur. The reason for this is that once the officer has committed his version of the matter to writing, this is normally regarded as the sum total of the contribution from that officer, although, of course, the investigation may proceed elsewhere. The difficulty with this approach is that it tends to leave large holes in the narrative of what really happened during the incident in question. For example, a citizen complains that a particular squad of detectives executed a search warrant at his house and, in doing so, engaged in an orgy of unnecessary damage to his property. In particular one officer, say "the one in the green jacket", is alleged to have been responsible for all of the over-zealous activity. A request will be made to the officers involved for each to make a "duty statement" concerning the part he played in the execution of the search warrant. Typically each reply will assert that the warrant was obtained and the search carried out with a minimum of interference to the comfort and property of the subject of the search. In addition, each statement will probably end with a denial from the officer that he was personally involved in, or that he witnessed anyone else on the squad engaging in, any wanton damage.

The file will typically not identify "the officer in the green jacket". A question to the investigating officer about the identity will, however, receive the standard reply "We know who he is all right, and he's had a telling off from his commander". Now, if normal investigative techniques were followed, the officer conducting the enquiry would have asked each officer what he was wearing on the evening in question and noted each reply. On obtaining an admission from the appropriate officer, a further allegation about this particular part in the raid would have been put to him and his explanation obtained under caution.

Another difficulty which I have with current practice is that the final decision as to the disposition of a citizen-complaint file as "not substantiated", "substantiated in part", "substantiated", "unfounded", or "exonerated" is *de facto* made, in Toronto, by the investigating officer. Admittedly this is then countersigned by the Inspector in charge of the Complaints Bureau and the Deputy Chief (Executive Officer), but so confident are the investigating officers of their judgment based on their own investigation that they often inform the complainant of the result of the investigation before submitting the file for the above counter-signatures. In a sense this emphasizes the point that the key role is played by the investigator. Within a large area of discretion he can investigate a matter so as to find something big, something small, or, like Nelson, "see no ships at all".

But suppose that the complaint is well founded, what do the police do about it? In fact, very few of the complaints against the police made by citizens in Metropolitan Toronto, for example, result in a formal disciplinary trial of the officer involved. Most complaints are held to be unfounded or unsubstantiated, and those which are held to be substantiated in some way, are mostly dealt with by "counselling" i.e., the officer concerned received a word of advice or admonition about his conduct from his Unit Commander or from a staff officer specially appointed to administer such expressions of official disapprobation.

A consideration of the action taken internally by the police on substantiat-ed and partly substantiated complaints by members of the public reveals that, in the whole three year period, 1970-72 inclusive, there was a total of 1,488 complaints of violence, improper conduct or neglect of duty made to the Complaints Bureau against Metropolitan Toronto police officers, of which 304 were substantiated or partly substantiated by police investigation.[25] This means that over a three year period, 20.4% of the citizen complaints which the Toronto Police Complaint Bureau investigated were substantiated either in whole or in part and it is estimated by the officer in charge that 98% of the serious complaints are handled by that office. It is very difficult indeed to track down just how many of those substantiated and partly substantiated com-plaints resulted in an internal discipline trial of the police officer involved. I have been able to trace five such cases in the relevant period together with eight cases where officers resigned to avoid such charges. Thus I can only be sure that in 4.2% of the cases where the Complaint Bureau found the police to be in some way at fault, formal disciplinary action followed or was pre-empted by an officer's resignation. It would be interesting to know the accu-rate percentage of such cases which do result in disciplinary action.

This compared with a total of 140 complaints by members of the public against R.C.M.P. officers in southern Ontario during the same three year peri-od, 12 of which were found, after investigation, to have been substantiated in whole or in part. This in turn, resulted in three discipline charges in service court being laid against the officers involved.[26] Thus the R.C.M.P. investiga-tions returned an 11.6% substantiation rate and a resort to disciplinary trial in 25% of the substantiated cases. R.C.M.P. officers are, of course, governed by the R.C.M.P. Act and Regulations and not by the Police Act (Ontario), but nothing in the form of the legislation would account for such a different result in respect of formal discipline following a substantiated citizen's complaint.

By comparison, the substantiated complaint rate for 1970-72 inclusive was 6.2% in the Metropolitan Police in London, England[27] and 11.3% in all other forces in England and Wales.[28] In England and Wales (excluding London), however, just under 10% of the substantiated complaints resulted in disciplinary charges being laid under the Police Discipline Regulations. No pre-cise figure is yet available for the percentage of substantiated citizen com-plaints which resulted in internal police trials in 1972 in the Metropolitan Police, London, England, but of the 198 officers formally disciplined in that year, no less than 39% of the cases derived from citizen complaints.[29] The English legislation has, to some extent, operated as a model for that pertaining in Ontario and, at least on that basis, the comparison of results would appear to be justified.

The Metropolitan Toronto system seems to be typified by a much higher than normal finding of substantiation of citizen complaints than elsewhere with, possibly, a lower incidence of formal disciplinary proceedings resulting from those findings.

But the police are not slow to take formal disciplinary action when a supervisory police officer lays a charge against another officer, e.g., where a sergeant reports a constable for neglect of duty or a Superintendent reports an Inspector for being absent from his post without good excuse. Almost invariably, in such cases in Toronto, the laying of a charge results in a disciplinary hearing before a Superintendent who is designated by the Chief of Police as the trial officer to carry out his disciplinary functions. It should be noted that these are not cases which originate with a citizen's complaint but relate to internal forces discipline where the initiative to commence action lies with the police themselves.

In the period November 1, 1970 to October 31, 1973 inclusive, 286 discipline charges were laid against 224 Metropolitan Toronto police officers resulting in a yearly average of about 95 discipline charges against 72 officers. There was finding of guild in 88% of the cases going to trial and, in addition, 13 officers chose to resign to avoid proceedings being taken against them.[30] This represents charges laid from all sources, both internal and citizen-complaint cases, but the great bulk of them, as indicated earlier, are purely internal in nature. All discipline charges, however, appear to be on a declining pattern, having moved from 141 four years ago to only 62 in the last twelve-month period.

The pattern seems to be strictly formal discipline action on almost all internally initiated cases and very few examples of disciplinary trials following from substantiated citizen complaints.

This is not the only respect in which a clear distinction is found to exist between intra-police discipline cases and those involving a police-public complaint. An even clearer dichotomy exists in that, in the internal police cases, the decision to proceed to a trial is taken, in Toronto, by the Deputy Chief (Administrative Operations), while in the citizen-police cases, the decision rests with a higher official, the senior Deputy Chief of Police, the force Executive Officer. Now in those police forces where decisions about proceeding to a trial of a disciplinary charge, irrespective of the source of complaint, are taken in the same department, there is at least continuity in approaching the question of sanctioning police misbehaviour. If, however, the decision rests with a completely different man depending upon the source of complaint, it may well be that discrepancies in discipline and prosecution philosophy are occurring simply because different policies are being adopted by different departmental heads. Maybe, however, this is a tacit recognition by the police that control of police behaviour can be effected from two quite different perspectives, depending upon whether the source of the complaint emanates from within the force or from a disgruntled citizen. I shall develop this idea later when I consider reform of the system.

AVOIDANCE BY COMPLAINANTS OF THE INTERNAL COMPLAINT SYSTEM

In theory, the most likely route by which a Metropolitan Toronto Police officer may be called upon to face the possibility of answering a charge of alleged misbehaviour emanating from a citizen under the current system is where a complainant ignores the police machinery completely, lays an information before a Justice of the Peace, and proceeds to trial in the courts.

The following informations were laid in Toronto by private citizens quite outside the official police investigative structure during the years shown:

> 1970   49 informations against 43 officers
> 1971   46 informations against 42 officers
> 1972   85 informations against 74 officers

In practice, however, most of the above informations which relate to allegations of common assault and assault causing bodily harm, are withdrawn or dismissed. Indeed, so far as I am able to ascertain the above cases resulted in only three convictions of police officers at trial and two of those were subsequently reversed on appeal.[31] What may be surprising is the large percentage of people who purposely choose to avoid the official complaint procedures. These figures mean that as many as 25% of the complaints of violence made against Metropolitan Toronto policemen are made directly to the courts and not to the police. The case law often evidences a reluctance on the part of Justices of the Peace to issue summonses where the prospective defendants are police officers purporting to act in the execution of their duty, so that the true number of applications for process of this type may well be much higher.[32] This situation provides some support for the idea that the duty to record public complaints against the police should rest with some body quite independent of the police organizational structure. If one person in four will not go to the police with an allegation of violence, they might be induced to report to a controlling body quite independent of the police, whilst retaining their right to go to court should they so desire.

REFORM OF THE CITIZEN-COMPLAINT SYSTEM

The present system, in my view, works neither totally in favour of the police (as some members of the public suspect), nor in favour of the citizen-complainant (as some police officers suspect). Nothing I have said is intended to be taken as a criticism of individual officers at all levels in the hierarchy who are being asked to perform a task which, no matter what good efforts are made, is ineffective because of defects in the structure as opposed to the men who try to make it work.

T.A. Critchley in his recent work, *A History of Police in England and Wales*[33] says, on the question of complaints against the police:

> It seems unlikely...that any radical change in the arrangements is to
> be expected in the foreseeable future. An entirely acceptable answer
> to the question, "Quis custodiet ipsos custodes?" [Who will watch the
> watchmen?] remains as elusive as when it was first asked in Roman
> times.

That the answer is elusive, I agree, but I sincerely hope that Mr. Critchley has erred on the side of ultra-conservatism when he sees change as unlikely in the foreseeable future.

POSSIBLE MODELS FOR HANDLING CITIZEN-POLICE COMPLAINTS

Let me try to sketch some possible models which could undertake investigation and adjudication of citizen complaints against the police.[34]

1. *The "in-house" model.* Here the duty to record the complaint, to investigate and adjudicate upon it, would be in the hands of the police. This model most closely corresponds to that currently in use in Ontario and In England although, in Ontario, unlike England, there is no express legislative duty upon the police to record complaints against officers by members of the public. It is submitted that the appellate role played by Boards of Police Commissioners, who are not police officers, does not introduce a sufficiently

disinterested factor to remove such systems from the "in-house" category.

2. *The externally supervised "in-house" model*. Here the investigation and adjudication functions follow the "in-house" model but there is an external review factor built in at the end of the process. This reviewing role could be played by an independent lawyer who would have the task of considering the whole conduct of the case to ensure that just and fair treatment was received by either the complainant or both the complainant and the officer about whom the complaint was made. It would be the duty of this independent reviewer, on application of an aggrieved party, to make recommendations to the Solicitor General about further action, if any, which should be taken, either in the instant case, or henceforth, to ensure a proper disposition of the case. A model of this type is currently being studied in England and it has the tentative support of several senior officers associations and of the Police Federation, representing about 100,000 men from Police Constable to Chief Inspector, in England and Wales.

3. *The police investigation with independent adjudication model*. Here investigation of complaints would, as at present, be conducted by the police, but once the investigation was completed the adjudication and disposition would be in the hands of a body independent of the police. This adjudication function might be undertaken by a judge, a lawyer appointed for the purpose or a board upon which the public would be represented by civilian members.

4. *The independent investigation with police adjudication model*. Here the investigation would not be in the hands of the police but would be conducted by investigators employed specially for the purpose and under the control of an Ombudsman or Commissioner of Rights whose duty it would be to report back to the Chief of Police with recommendations for necessary action, leaving final disposition in the hands of the police.

5. *The "truly independent" model*. Here all facets of the complaint, from its initially being recorded until disposition would be kept out of police hands entirely. In effect, the Chief of Police would be notified of the disposition of the complaint by the authority here created and would have no discretion but to comply with the order, although the officer complained of and/or the police force itself would, of course, be represented at the board hearing, by counsel or agents.

Model No. 1 appears to take least account of the public interest and Model no. 5 would be likely to incite greatest police opposition. In a democracy, the number of police employed to keep the peace is very small when considered as a proportion of the total population. Indeed, this approach is only feasible where there is a strong measure of police-public co-operation. It may be that Model No. 1 came to be accepted at a time when the police were not nearly so well organized or powerful as they are now. That a change is needed seems clear, but if the change advocated is to move to the polar opposite in one step, that may, in the long run, be counter-productive. The message from the U.S.A., in the context of their experience with Civilian Review Boards, is clear: "Do not try to impose a change so radical that it will produce a reaction which will prevent the achievement of any reform and help to reinforce the *status quo*". Witness the demise of the "civilian" component in citizen review boards in the U.S.A. From a "high" of four civilians to three police members, in Mayor John Lindsay's original scheme for New York City in 1966, the U.S. is now experiencing a retrenchment in independent civilian review board philosophy. In New York, for example, the "civilians" on the current Review Board are "police civilian employees of at least one year's standing" and in Kansas City the three "civilians" comprise a retired police major, the force chaplain and a sergeant, the last two having been specially retired to take up their duties as "citizens" on the Review Board. If that was the reaction to a modified version of Model No. 3, what might have been experienced in response to a bold sweep to Model No. 5? Even so, the overtly racial and political overtones which have surrounded much of the U.S.A. experience with review boards,[35] might not be as applicable to Canada so that Model 5 must remain a contender for genuine appraisal.

A move towards Model No. 2 seems to achieve very little indeed. An external reviewer coming *ex post facto* upon a file can do little to redress a wrong which occurred at some early stage in the action. In addition, there would have to be some rule against "double jeopardy" limiting the extent of his review since an acquitted officer would have grounds for complaint if, as a result of the external reviewer's work, he found himself facing yet another trial out of the self-same incident which caused him to face one trial and possibly two reviews in the appellate hierarchy.

Any approach to the topic of the model most appropriate to present day Ontario must take account of four particular issues:

(1) the duty to record public complaints against the police;

(2) the investigative stage, together with the decision on further action once the enquiry is completed;

(3) the adjudicative function; and,

(4) the prohibitively narrow nature of all of the above as an approach to the problem.

THE DUTY TO RECORD PUBLIC COMPLAINTS
AGAINST THE POLICE

There should be a clear legislative statement, making it obligatory that public complaints against the police should be recorded and investigated. Reform, in my view, should concentrate on requiring public complaints to be recorded, not by the police, as does s. 49(1) Police Act 1964 (U.K.), but by some independent body of the Commissioner of Rights type. That body would then decide whether an investigation of an individual policeman was necessary following the complaint. If it was, then the case would either be forwarded to the Commissioner of Rights investigative unit or be forwarded to the police for investigation and reporting back of the results to the Commissioner of Rights Office, where a further decision would be made on necessary action. If the complaint was trivial or could be otherwise resolved without resort to a full investigation, the Commissioner of Rights would so classify it.

In this way, whatever the nature of the investigative unit employed on the case, the public would be assured of outside control of the recording of the complaint and of the decision to investigate it.

THE INVESTIGATIVE STAGE

For some critics of the present system, nothing short of the appointment of an independent official with a staff of lawyers and investigators will provide the independence, expertise and professional standards, capable of achieving public confidence.

A recent study at the Center for Studies in Criminal Justice at the University of Chicago looked at the question of an independent agency to investigate public complaints against the police, and highlighted the investigative stage as follows:[36]

> The independence and integrity of the agency are crucial to its ability to contribute to the lessening of police-community tensions. But independence and integrity in this context are easy to define but difficult to assure. A beginning lies in an effort to insulate the investigators from peer group or organizational pressure to favor any particular party. These are the recurring problems which undermine internal investigation by the police department. Removing the investigation function from the police department is the first step in this direction.

Personnel would have to be recruited who had the necessary skill and ability to carry out these investigations. If persons with previous police experience were selected they would have to sever all connections with the police force. The numbers required would not be insignificant. There are no clear figures available for the number of complaints made against all of the police forces in Ontario. It is an amazing fact that the reports submitted annually by the Ontario Provincial Police, the Metropolitan Toronto Police, and the R.C.M.P., for example, do not reveal any information at all about how many complaints were made against their officers, or details of how they were dealt with. Projecting from the available Toronto figures, however, it may well be that in respect of all the police forces in Ontario, not less than 1,000 public complaints are lodged each year against the police and, if the duty to record such matters were in the hands of an agency quite independent of the police, this figure might be expected to grow.[37] This number is not so large, however, that, with some decentralization of investigative units about the province, it could not be handled as a practical proposition. The recruiting and training of the lawyers, investigators, and secretariat would have to be particularly carefully handled as these people would be stepping into a quite new function which, especially in the early stages, would be subject to intense critical appraisal from police and public alike.

Alternatively, if there was no political will to move to a thoroughly independent investigative unit, some element of objectivity could, in my view, be achieved by requiring that public complaints be investigated by police officers from police forces not involved in the complaint, i.e., an Ontario Provincial Police Central Complaints Bureau could be set up to investigate complaints against officers in the municipalities and complaints against Ontario Provincial Police officers could be investigated by a Complaints Unit made up of officers drawn from Metropolitan Toronto and other municipal police forces.

One of the prime areas for reassessment is who makes the decision whether the complaint is substantiated or not and, especially if it is substantiated, what action should be taken upon it. It may well be that remedial action quite outside disciplinary action against an individual officer will be the most positive step which could be taken towards preventing a recurrence of the misbehaviour and I shall expand on this later. But, that said, surely the public is entitled to question the fact that, in police forces generally, few of the cases where investigation shows the police to be in the wrong, actually result in a formal discipline hearing. It certainly means that justice is not seen to be done by the public at large. It may mean that the internal mores of the police are dangerously out of line with those prevailing in the community at large, but I do not think so. It is probably potent evidence of the inappropriateness of the investigative-adjudicative model (with its concentration on punishment of individual officers), to address itself to the causal factors at work. Unfortunately, whilst the whole operation remains in police hands, the public at large will continue to be sceptical of this conclusion. The body making such decisions must, it seems, entail some presence independent of the police, in the case of public complaints.

THE ADJUDICATIVE FUNCTION

One of the most difficult roles which a police officer can be called upon to play is to be designated the trial judge in an internal discipline proceeding where a citizen confronts a police officer with an allegation of misconduct. The appointed officer is conscious that the member of the public may doubt his impartiality and he is under pressure to see that everything is done to ensure that the citizen's complaint is properly ventilated. At the same time he had a duty to see that the officer receives a fair trial. This is not made any easier by the fact that, unless the verdict is the very unusual and draconian one of dismissal from the force, the trial judge and the accused officer will have to go on working together. Make no mistake about internal police discipline trials. They are far from being a whitewash operation. I regard it as no evidence of forensic acumen that I won the cases I prosecuted, nor do I feel disgrace to confide that I lost the ones I defended, though I doubt that such a limited experience has any statistical significance. But much like the painstaking investigator, the police judge in a citizen-police confrontation is always tainted with the obvious fact that he cannot be seen, by the outsider, to be totally indifferent between the complainant and the police officer.

It is tempting to say that the task of judging such cases should be passed over to the judiciary since the organization already exists and the avoidance of a new bureaucratic invention in a period of governmental over-kill might be a virtue in itself. This temptation should, in my view, be resisted. I defer, not to those who clamour that judges always believe the police in preference to the public, but to one of the arguments which, to my mind, likewise disqualifies the senior police officer, namely: the possibility of a continuing relationship. It would be uncomfortable to both the judiciary and the police to be engaged in a "gamekeeper-poacher" relationship in the field of police discipline whilst contemporaneously fulfilling their respective functions in the administration of criminal justice.

An initiative which should be pursued is the concept of the tripartite arbitral tribunal, i.e., in the event that a complaint from a member of the public against a police officer cannot be resolved in any other way, then both the citizen-complainant and the police officer would be allowed to appoint his own representative to a hearing board under the chairmanship of an independent person agreeable to both parties. It would be the duty of the Commissioner of Rights to maintain panels of suitable people who would be willing to act in these capacities and to pay all of the expenses involved in such a hearing.

The main objections to this approach might be that it is top-heavy and would be too cumbersome to be practicable and that the two appointees would always support the side which appointed them, thus leaving the Chairman with a casting vote so that the split decision might exacerbate rather than resolve the conflict.

In answer to the first point, it should be remembered that very few citizen-complaint cases, indeed, end up as a full blown disciplinary hearing. In the section below in which I develop alternatives to the largely predominant investigative-adjudicative model of the present time, it will be suggested that many alternatives to the formal hearing exist and have not been satisfactorily explored to date, let alone implemented.

In regard to the second point, certain experience in the U.S.A. in connection with representation on citizen review boards suggests that blindly partisan voting has been surprisingly absent.[38] In addition, some fact situations really are capable of quite different interpretations by perfectly objective commentators, and to conceal this fact within a specious cloak of unanimity or sole adjudicator's statement of the facts, is to ignore the obvious and invite criticism for over-simplicity.

BEYOND THE INVESTIGATIVE-ADJUDICATIVE MODEL

One of the most depressing facts about the use of an investigative-adjudicative model as a control mechanism for police misbehaviour is that it is often irrelevant and, on occasion, positively harmful. The current system is geared to finding an individual culprit who often, at the conclusion, is seen to receive no visible punishment. Emphasis is placed on wilful or negligent wrong-doing or thoughtlessness on the part of individual officers where the problem may well be of a more generalized nature. For example, a crop of careless accidents with firearms on the part of police officers may excite one of four responses:

(a)   charge the officer involved under the discipline code with negligently discharging his firearm;

(b)   check the circumstances under which firearms are issued to members of the force and ensure that training in safe handling is not only taught initially, but is also the subject of constant refresher courses; in addition, review of force policy on the use of firearms on duty may well be indicated;

(c)   do both; or,

(d)   do nothing.

Our current system often sets out to achieve (a) and ends up by doing (d).

Patterns of police behaviour or misbehaviour may, indeed, be more important in the long run than a minute investigation and adjudication assigning specific blame in a particular case. In many instances, as Professor Paul Weiler has noted,

> ...[P]olice disregard for the demands of legality, the Rule of Law, is not a matter of individual deviation or wrong-doing. Rather, it is an organizational and occupational phenomenon which manifests itself in patterns of behaviour of the normal officer.[39]

Indeed, the assignment of blame and infliction of punishment on an individual officer is often not at all what an individual complainant wants, and could well be the reason why the police statistics show such a low level of trials following from substantiated complaints. If the decision as to further action, following investigation, were removed from police responsibility, this fact, where appropriate, could be more clearly established without the very real fear, sometimes felt at present, that where a complainant says that he seeks no further action, it is merely the result of the police having used undue influence to assist a colleague in trouble.

The Commissioner of Rights could be required specifically to monitor particular patterns of police behaviour across the Province, or in a particular city, which might reflect bad recruiting, training, or procedural techniques[40] and could send details to the Solicitor General's Department, the Provincial and local police authorities, and to the Chief of Police, seeking co-operation in trying to ensure remedial action. A recurring problem, cured in one area and continuing in another could be further pursued by general adoption of the remedial action found in practice to be most effective. At present, something of this pattern-aspect is discerned at police headquarters but there is little public confidence that it is sufficiently pursued and moreover there can be only limited province-wide over-view. Society has much to gain from a system which would place broad policy direction before Chiefs of Police and reduce the degree of agonizing over the individual case which presently occurs, though I do not seek to underestimate the unhappiness which such a case can visit on a member of the public or a police officer.

The existence of a Commissioner of Rights would not affect the investigation of crime and internal police discipline which should remain in the hands of police, if the matter is uncovered in the normal course of police investigation. If, however, a member of the public feels that, from whatever cause, the police are not investigating a crime or proceeding against another police officer with due dispatch, an office should exist, outside the police organization, to which complaint might be made. The Commissioner of Rights would be required to place annual reports before the Legislature and, to ensure political neutrality, the appointment should be made by agreement between the Provincial Prime Minister and leaders of the opposition parties.

It might be objected that all of this would reduce the traditional role of the Chief of Police as the official responsible for the maintenance of discipline in his force.[41] This criticism, in my view, fails to recognize the much broader context in which discipline should be seen. If the Chief is seen as the fount of authority from which all individual punishments are meted out to individual men for individual acts of misbehaviour, then it truly means that his authority is diminished, though only in citizen-complaint cases. But if the Chief is seen as having the good of the community as his principal concern, he must view the behaviour problem within a whole range of organizational and administrative problems, no one of which can be successfully solved by mistaking the symptom for the disease. An enlightened Chief of Police would welcome the opportunity to allow more of his men to engage in law enforcement activities, either by relieving them from the investigatory role entirely or, if police are still to be so employed, by reducing the number of investigations since the Office of the Commissioner of Rights would be able to filter out the trivial and inappropriate matters. The reports from the Commissioner of Rights would assist the Chief of Police to observe the patterns of behaviour which emerge in his personnel, and to plan counter-measures at a level which would significantly affect more than the fate of the one individual defaulter.

REFORM OF THE INTERNAL DISCIPLINE SYSTEM

The purely internal investigation and adjudication system which, in my scheme, would remain with the police, is, itself, in need of some overhaul and certain current practices should be reviewed and amended. I shall give some examples of what I mean, most of which go to explode any public misconception that the police, at all times, "look after their own".

When an officer is suspected of committing an offence against the internal discipline system, his senior officer will demand a "duty statement" from him, as I explained earlier. If the officer declines to make a statement in these circumstances, he commits a disciplinary offence, namely, failing to obey a lawful order. If he complies, he has been compelled, without any caution, possibly to incriminate himself. In Toronto, for example, there is a purely verbal administrative direction that such statements should not be used at a disciplinary trial of an officer. Surely this is not a sufficient safeguard since, presumably, other police chiefs may not give such a direction, and such a crucial trial issue should not be left to the unstructured discretion of a particular Chief Officer. Much to be preferred, would be a procedure which abandoned the concept of the demand for a duty statement and replaced it with the caution and question and answer technique of the normal investigation. This should be the subject of specific legislation.

A further defect in internal procedure is that a disciplinary offence can be termed a major or a minor infraction of the discipline code at the discretion of the police officer who approved the laying of a charge against the accused policeman.[42] This again is a question of unstructured discretion. If the infraction is prosecuted as a major offence then the punishments available in the case of a finding of guilt can range all the way up to dismissal from the force. If the same factual situation is, in the judgment of the officer who approves the laying of the charge, to be termed a minor infraction then the maximum penalty which may be imposed is a monetary one only.

We are all familiar with the idea of summary and indictable offences in the field of criminal procedure and I suppose a rough analogy to that framework might be drawn to the police discipline idea of the 'major' and 'minor' infraction. In my view, however, the analogy breaks down at its most vital point since, in a criminal prosecution on indictment, an accused may choose to have preliminary enquiry by which he obtains discovery of the prosecution's case. However, in the case of a major infraction of the police discipline code, an accused has no such preliminary enquiry, neither does he even receive copies of the statements of the witnesses to be called against him. The result is that, in such a disciplinary trial, the police officer stands the risk of being dismissed from the force, yet only hears the evidence against him for the first time as it is spoken by the witnesses called by the prosecution. How can effective cross-examination be achieved in such a case? I am told by apologists for the present system that it is not necessary to furnish copies of the statements of prosecution witnesses to the defence since the defendant officer receives a form long before his trial which informs him of the nature of the discipline offence alleged against him and gives him particulars of it.[43] I personally fail to see how one or two short sentences can properly be regarded as adequate discovery in the case of a man on trial for his very livelihood. The statements of the prosecution witnesses are all available to the authorities long before trial; it would seem to be a matter of no great difficulty to supply the accused officer with copies of them, at least in the case of a major offence. If, as a *quid pro quo*, the prosecution demanded discovery of the defence case, then I would say so be it, but I have some sympathy for these who would counter that, in such a case, the presumption of innocence puts the accuser to the proof of his allegation and that nothing should therefore be demanded by way of disclosure by the defence.

Another hazard to due process in internal discipline results from the fact that in Ontario, today, more than 56% of the police forces have nine or fewer members in them,[44] and the Police Act and Regulations are really aimed at much larger forces. In some of these smaller forces the police chief may have to investigate a matter of internal discipline, give the evidence against the officer, then adjudicate on the question of his guilt or innocence and impose the penalty. The Police Act would allow the first instance trial to be before the Board of Police Commissioners in the case of a major (but not a minor) offence,[45] although it is not obligatory to do so, and some Chiefs of Police who request such a step are told by their Commissioners, "Deal with it yourself, we'll hear it if the officer chooses to appeal". This could be cured by requiring investigation or adjudication by members of another police force.

The greatest breach of good faith in the police service between commanders and men, however, consists in a totally informal sanctioning system whereby, on being confronted by a unit commander with a defalcation which is admitted, a junior officer "agrees" to the summary imposition of a sanction such as a forfeiture of a rest day or reduction in outstanding holidays. Clearly in such a case the position of a Unit Commander relative to a patrolman is such that no true 'agreement' to the sanction exists. It is summary justice at its worst. Now I do not wish to see "due process" erected into a system of such hidebound formality that no senior officer would ever be able, informally, to castigate a junior officer for misbehaviour. Where I do draw the line, however, is that such informal disciplining should never involve a sanction being applied which deprives a defaulter directly of money or money's worth (e.g., leisure time). Quite apart from the fact that a fatigued officer who has been guilty of rudeness or abuse to a member of the public will be a potentially more rude officer if deprived of his day off, no informal sanctioning should result in more than a record being kept that the officer was cautioned together with details of the impugned conduct. This might, then, be supporting evidence of any later allegation of "persistent misbehaviour" against the officer.

Apart from the danger of doing injustice in the particular case, society runs a great risk in expecting fidelity to the principles of due process of law from a body of men who do not see themselves as recipients of such safe-guards. In all of these examples, it is clear that officers could feel that they are not the recipients of a fair, open-handed system. What must never be forgot-ten is that we demand of these self-same officers that they should act courte-ously towards the public, use tact and forbearance if provoked, never take advantage of the weakness or ignorance of others and, above all, be careful to avoid threats or inducements to persons suspected of crime. Respect for the dignity of man is a reciprocal principle. It will be better practised by those who are its beneficiaries.[46]

But not all aspects of the internal discipline system favour the force admin-istrator to the detriment of the officer against whom a disciplinary charge has been made. A policeman in Ontario is entitled to instruct legal counsel to defend him on an internal discipline charge.[47] When the defence is legally represented and the police case is put by a presenting officer without legal qualifications, the balance of advantage can move towards the defence. For example, a charge is laid against an officer for wilfully or negligently damaging police property, contrary to the discipline regulations. Before the officer enters his plea, his legal counsel interjects with a pre-trial motion claiming that the charge is null and void on the grounds of duplicity. How is the trial judge (in Metropolitan Toronto, a Superintendent) to rule on this? What assistance is he to receive from the presenting officer who, perfectly understandably, may never have heard of "duplicity", let alone understand the counter-arguments which could be made to the defence submission. Whilst not wishing to make the internal discipline vehicle too cumbersome, it seems only fair to the police force proceeding with the charge that if the defence is legally represented then so too must the presentation of the police case be handled by a lawyer. In short, I advocate that the regulation which would allow the police to be legally represented,[48] be made mandatory in those cases where the defence has counsel. This suggestion, of course, levels up the adversaries, but places the trial judge in an even greater limbo of legal jargon. My suggestion for over-coming this would be to require any legal and jurisdictional arguments to be reserved as they arise and without interruption to the trial. These could be answered by a County Court Judge, leaving the appointed police-officer-judge to try the facts. The County Court Judge playing this role would not be involved in the "gamekeeper-poacher" relationship with the police which I criticized earlier, since only "dry questions of law" would be addressed to him and he would not be called on to adjudicate upon the facts of the case or to render any final resolution of it. Introducing a little more legalism into the internal trial system would not necessarily be a bad thing. Some very important questions of principle in these trials have never been satisfactorily answered. For example, to this day no section of the Police Act, or of the Regulations made under it, and no decision of the courts, is available to tell the trial judge whether, in an internal discipline case, the standard of proof which must be achieved for the prosecution to succeed, is that of proof "beyond a reasonable doubt" or only proof "on a balance of probabilities".

That all is not well with the internal police discipline trial has been eloquently put by Sydney Brown, the President of Metropolitan Toronto, and Ontario, Police Officers Associations. Mr. Brown, after unrivalled experience in defending officers in such cases, addressed the following remarks to the Board of Police Commissioners of Metropolitan Toronto, following the hearing of an appeal:

> I would like to say to the Board that, regardless of what your decision might be in this case, a thorough study should and must be made by the Commission, of the trial procedures used during disciplinary proceedings. The present system leaves a great deal to be desired. The saying that 'Justice must not only be done, but must have appeared to be done'...do[es] not necessarily always apply to Department discipline trials.

On that subject I am happy to leave the last word to Mr. Brown.

CONCLUSION

In attempting to balance out de facto police power and individual civil liberty, I have suggested that changes are required in tort law and in internal discipline procedures, both at investigation and trial. But most of all I have been at pains to suggest the adoption of a new model for dealing with complaints made against the police by members of the public. In this field I have endeavoured to show that the road to reform should first be taken by adopting a model which would emphasize the importance of some office outside the police structure to record the complaint, to supervise the investigation of it and to make the decision on appropriate further action. If that further action should take the form of a disciplinary trial I have suggested that a board of three comprising an independent chairman plus an appointee of both sides to the dispute could best reflect the delicate balance which must be sought in facing this crucial social issue. In addition, I have tried to emphasize that reform must concentrate much more on the identification of causal factors and on remedies therefore and less on apportioning blame, after-the-fact, in individual cases.

That, then, is my civil liberty issue for the seventies, namely "Who will watch the watchmen?" Juvenal posed the vexed question and Mr. Critchley echoed it. I am conscious of having struggled with it but even more so of having failed to resolve it in any final way. I should regard this exercise as a modest achievement if I have succeeded in making even a minor contribution towards its resolution at some time in the future.

ENDNOTES

*   This chapter is published here by permission of the author.

1.   Canada. *Report of the Canadian Committee on Correction,* Ottawa; Queen's Printer, 1969, 42.

2.   This phenomenon has been noted by several commentators: Peter G. Barton, "Civilian Review Boards and the Handling of Complaints Against the Police", (1970) 20 *U. Toronto L.J.* 448; The President's Commission on Law Enforcement and the Administration of justice, *Task Force Report: The Police,* Washington: U.S. Gov't Print. Off., 1967, 193; Herman Goldstein, "Administrative Problems in Controlling the Exercise of Police Authority", (1967) 58 *J. Crim. L.C. & P. S.* 160.

3.   M.C. Courtis and I, Dussuyer, *Attitudes to Crime and the Police in Toronto,* University of Toronto, Centre of Criminology, 1970, 94.

4.   Jose M. Rico et Guy Tardif, *La Société Face au Crime, Annexe 2,* Montréal: La Commission d'Enquête sur l'Administration de la Justice en matiere criminelle et pénale, 1968, 73.

5.   Cmnd. 1728, 103, para. 338.

6.   Canadian Civil Liberties Education Trust. *Due Process Safeguards and Canadian Criminal Justice,* Toronto: Canadian Civil Liberties Education Trust, 1971, 30.

7.   *Ibid.* 25, 26.

8.   I have in mind the fact that the legislature has, for the first time, expressly provided for the admission of illegally obtained evidence which has previously always relied on judicial authority, e.g., *A-G. Québec V. Bégin* [1955] S.C.R. 593; 5 D.L.R. 394; 112 C.C.C. 209; 21 C.R. 217.

9.   A.K. McDougall, *Law and Politics: The Case of Police Independence in Ontario,* a paper presented to the Canadian Political Science Association, 1971, unpublished, 13, 14.

10.   Letter to the author dated Oct. 5, 1973, from Elmer D. Bell, Q.C., Chairman, Ontario Police Commission.

11.   If the main reason for such increases is better salaries reflecting higher job status, then I see nothing wrong with a social equation which requires that such status and public accountability be directly proportional to each other. This theory places doctors and lawyers in a category requiring more public accountability, too, and I, for one, would not seek to deny it.

12. J.P. Martin and Gail Wilson, *The Police: A Study in Manpower,* London: Heinemann, 1969.

13. *Report of H.M. Chief Inspector of Constabulary for the year 1972,* London: H.M.S.O., 1973, 7.

14. *Beaver v. The Queen* [1957] S.C.R. 531; 118 C.C.C. 129; 26 C.R. 193.

15. *Ibid.,* 554, 118 C.C.C., 151; 26 C.R., 271.

16. *Regina v. Wray* [1971] S.C.R. 272; (1970) 11 D.L.R. (3d) 673; 11 C.R.N.S. 235; [1970] 4 C.C.C. 1.

17. *Regina v. Osborn* [1971] S.C.R. 184; 15 D.L.R. (3d) 85; 1 C.C.C (2d) 482; (1970) 12 C.R.N.S. 1.

18. Stanton Wheeler, "Criminal Statistics: A Reformulation of the Problem", in Abraham S. Goldstein and Joseph Goldstein eds., *Crime, Law, and Society,* New York: The Free Press, 1971, 131, 137.

19. *Ibid.,* 142.

20. R.S.C. 1970, c. C-34, s. 450 (3) (b), as am. by R.S.C. 1970, c. 2 (2d Supp.), s. 5. For a critical analysis of tort law as it applies to certain aspects of police behaviour see Paul C. Weiler, "The Control of Police Arrest Practices: Reflections of a Tort Lawyer", in Allen M. Linden ed., *Studies in Canadian Tort Law,* Toronto: Butterworths, 1968, 416.

21. Alan Mewett, *Private Policing in Canada,* Address to the Workshop on Private Policing and Security in Canada, University of Toronto Centre of Criminology, Oct. 1973, unpublished, 6.

22. Stanley M. Beck, "Electronic Surveillance and the Administration of Criminal Justice", (1968) 46 *Can. Bar Rev.* 643, 677 (emphasis added).

23. See, *e.g.,* Barton, *supra,* note 2, 458, 459.

24. *The Observer* newspaper march 5, 1972. "...The court was told by a defence counsel that *The Times* would not put the enquiry in the hands of the police 'because the police could not be trusted to enquire into the dirty laundry in their own house'...." *Regina v. Robson and Harris,* Central Criminal Court, England, February 1972, before Sebag Shaw J.

25. Details abstracted in part from the quarterly returns of work submitted by the Inspector in charge of the Metropolitan Toronto Police Complaints Bureau to Chief Harold Adamson, copies of which were kindly made available to the author during his study.

26. Letter to the author, Dec. 7, 1973, from Assistant Commissioner E.R. Lysyk, Commanding Officer, 'O' Division (Southern Ontario) R.C.M.P.

27. In 1970 it was 5.8%, *Report of the Commissioner of Police of the Metropolis for the year 1970, 1971, Cmnd. 4680, 26.*
In 1971 it was 6.9%, Report of the Commissioner of Police of the Metropolis for the year 1971, *1972, Cmnd. 4986, 34.*
In 1972 it was 6.1%, Report of the Commissioner of Police of the Metropolis for the year 1972, *1973, Cmnd. 5331, 28.*

28. In 1970 it was 12%, *Report of H.M. Chief Inspector of Constabulary,* London: H.M.S.O., 1971, 73.
In 1971 it was 11%, *Report of H.M. Chief Inspector of Constabulary,* London: H.M.S.O., 1972, 72.
In 1972 it was 11%, *Report of H.M. Chief Inspector of Constabulary,* London: H.M.S.O., 1973, 73.

29. Letter to the author, Jan. 8, 1974, from Deputy Asst. Commissioner, New Scotland Yard, London.

30. In 1969-70 there were 141 charges laid against 94 officers.
In 1970-71 there were 133 charges laid against 98 officers.
In 1971-72 there were 91 charges laid against 73 officers.
In 1972-73 there were 62 charges laid against 53 officers.
(Information abstracted from returns submitted by the Inspector in charge of Trial Preparation, Metropolitan Toronto Police Force, and kindly made available to the author by Chief of Police Harold Adamson.)

31. Letter to the author, Sept. 10, 1973, from Inspector W. Myers, Officer in Charge of the Complaint Bureau, Metropolitan Police Force. (I am unable to ascertain the extent to which the low "success-rate" is due to plea-bargaining deals whereby the withdrawal of the allegation against the officer is part and parcel of any agreed disposition of outstanding charges against accused persons. Certainly it seems a fact that many of the civilian complainants have already been arrested before they lay their informations against the police).

32. *Glover v. MacKay* (1961) 34 C.R. 360; (1962) 131 C.C.C. 183; (1961-62) 4 *Crim. L.Q.* 468, sub nom. Re Glover and MacKay. *Regina v. Jones, ex p. Cohen,* [1970] 2 C.C.C. 374 (B.C. S.C.). *Evans v. Pesce* (1969), 70 W.W.R. 321; (1969-70), 8 C.R.N.S. 201; [1970] 3 C.C.C. 61, *sub nom. Regina v. Coughlan, ex p. Evans.*

33. T.A. Critchley, *A History of Police in England and Wales,* 2d ed., Montclair, N.J.: Patterson Smith, 1972, 324.

34. For an excellent study of three possible models for citizen review of alleged police misconduct see Wayne A. Kerstetter, *Citizen Review of Police Misconduct,* Chicago: University of Chicago Law School, Center for Studies in Criminal Justice, ca. 1970.

35. Barton, *supra,* note 2, 461, n. 98.

36. Kerstetter, *supra,* note 34, at 24.

37. Approximately 5000 officers produce nearly 500 complaints per annum in Metropolitan Toronto; 13,700 officers (all provincial and municipal police officers, including Metropolitan Toronto) might, therefore, be expected to produce 1,370 complaints per annum. That this is a very rough estimate and subject to many objections is true, but in the absence of detailed figures from each Chief of Police in the Province it is the only estimate I can produce. *Even if every other proposal in this paper is rejected, police forces should be required, as a very minimum, to report statistics on the number of citizen complaints made against them each year, together with details of the action taken thereon and the results.*

38. Algernon D. Black, *The People and the Police,* New York: McGraw-Hill. 1968, 221-2. In no case was the 1966 New York City board divided along civilian-police lines.

39. Paul C. Weiler, "'Who Shall Watch the Watchman?' Reflections on Some Recent Literature About the Police", (1968-69) 11 *Crim. L.Q.* 420, 426.

40. See D.J. Watchorn, "Abuse of Police Powers: Reasons, Effect and Control", (1966) 24 *U.T. Faculty L. R.* 48, 53, 54, 56 and 57 where recruiting, training, promotion, supervisory structures pertaining in the Metropolitan Police Force are criticized.

41. *Ibid.,* 65.

42. R.R.O. 1970, Reg. 680, s. 5 (11), made under the Police Act, R.S.O. 1970, c. 351.

43. *Ibid.* s. 5 (8).

44. Letter to the author, Oct. 5, 1973, from Elmer D. Bell, Q.C., Chairman, Ontario Police Commission.

45. R.R.O. 1970, Reg. 680, s. 17 (6).

46. H.W. Arthurs, "And Who Will Watch the Watchman?", (1966-67) 9 *Crim, L.Q.* 122, 123-4; "[W]e can hardly expect policemen to treat citizens with dignity and propriety if they live under an administrative regime which disregards their own basic rights."

47.   R.R.O. 1970, Reg. 680, s. 13(3).

48.   *Ibid.*, s. 13(1).

CHAPTER 18
The Role of Police Boards and Commissions as Institutions of Municipal Police Governance

PHILIP C. STENNING

INTRODUCTION

Research and writing on control of the police has tended for the most part to concentrate on those aspects of the internal administration, management and reward structures within police forces which are thought to encourage (or at least not discourage) proper police practices. In this essay, some aspects of the structures of external control over police forces are examined within the Canadian context. Until very recently, extremely little research of significance has focused on the various structures which have been established to provide for the government of police forces, the relationships between the police themselves (especially the chief) and these governing authorities, and the influence of politics on their operations. By examining the historical and modern development of one type of police governing authority in Canada, this essay takes a first tentative step in filling this gap in existing knowledge about police accountability and control, and in identifying some important issues for further study.

Policing in Canada in undertaken by a variety of public, quasi-public and private bodies operating under widely divergent mandates.[1] Thus, existing public police forces here include a federal police force (the Royal Canadian Mounted Police) operating under a federal legislative mandate;[2] two provincial police forces (the Ontario Provincial Police force and the Quebec Police Force/Sûreté du Québec), each operating under provincial statutes;[3] a large number of municipal police forces, most of which operate under a combination of provincial statutes and municipal by-laws;[4] and a host of special-purpose police forces (e.g., harbour and railway police), each operating under specific federal or provincial statutory mandates.[5] To further complicate matters, the federal police force provides police services, under contract, to eight of the ten provinces, and to a large number of municipalities in those same eight provinces, and the Ontario Provincial Police force provides such services on a similar basis to a number of municipalities in that province.

The concerns of this essay are limited to the operation of *municipal police forces*—that is, those police forces established by municipalities under the authority of provincial legislation and/or municipal by-laws. More particularly, the essay focuses on the evolution, status and role of a particular kind of special-purpose body—known colloquially as a local police board or commission[6]—which has been adopted by a number of these municipal jurisdictions as the governing authority for their municipal police forces. The essay will also touch on the role of the provincial police commissions which have been established in seven of the ten provinces, but only to the extent that this role impinges on the government of municipal police forces. The essay will not concern itself, however, with the particular issues which arise over the government of municipal police services which are provided not through an autonomous municipal police force, but by an external police force (e.g., the RCMP or the OPP) under contract with a municipality.

Although the focus of the essay will be on police boards established to govern municipal police forces, it will be readily apparent that many of the issues and principles that arise out of a discussion of the status and role of such boards have implications of a much more general nature relating to the governance and control of policing in a democratic society. The purpose of this essay is to draw out these more general issues and principles and illustrate their application and significance in the context of the governance of municipal police forces in Canada.

The essay begins with a brief description of the historical origins of modern municipal police forces in Canada, emphasizing the traditional connection between the police and the lower judiciary. The essay then describes the development of modern municipal police boards, and discusses some possible explanations for the original adoption of this mode of police governance. This discussion focuses particularly on two dominant themes—the shift from judicial to non-judicial control of the police, and the struggle between provincial and municipal governments for domination over the structure of municipal police governance. There follows a description of the current variety of municipal police boards found in Canadian jurisdictions, and of their mandate and the functions they perform. Four significant influences on the role of municipal police boards in governing their forces—the notion of police independence, the concept of police professionalism, the rise of police unionism, and the modern resurgence of provincial influence over municipal institutions—are then described and discussed. The essay next considers the matter of the accountability of police boards themselves, and describes some recent controversies which this issue has generated in the Province of Ontario. This discussion, as well as the essay's conclusions, focuses particularly on the issue of the role of politics in the government of municipal police forces, and the different positions which have been propounded on this controversial issue. The extent to which this debate has been coloured by the historical association between the police and the judiciary is also considered.

THE ORIGINS OF MUNICIPAL POLICE FORCES IN CANADA

At the time of Confederation in 1867, policing systems were already well established in many parts of Canada. Kelly and Kelly (1976:1) note that the first "policeman" in the colonies which later became Canada appeared on the streets of Quebec City in 1751. During these early days, in both Upper and Lower Canada, and later on the West coast and in the Maritimes, the power to appoint constables resided exclusively in judicial officers, usually called justices of the peace. These early constables, then, although they performed a variety of protective functions, such as watching for fires and patrolling the streets at night (the so-called "night watch"), were in essence officers of the law whose primary function was to perform the administrative tasks (such as the serving of writs and summonses, and the making of arrests) which were necessary to the effective performance of the judicial process. In fact, until quite late in the nineteenth century, their remuneration (for those who were remunerated) was usually determined in accordance with a well-established tariff associated with the performance of these administrative tasks. Thus, a constable would receive so much money for each summons served, each arrest effected, and so forth (McDougall, 1971b:15-16).

With the great industrial development and urbanization of the late eighteenth and nineteenth centuries, the basic community structures within which the early constables were able to work to maintain order and preserve the peace began to break down. In particular, the increased mobility of the population (itself spurred by the rising demands for labour to service new industrial enterprise, and facilitated by the development of more sophisticated transportation technologies) meant that communities themselves, particularly urban ones, no longer had the capacity for self-policing on which the early system of constabulary had relied so heavily for support. Under these circumstances, it became increasingly evident, both in England and in Canada, that a new system of policing would be required to cope with the problem of maintaining order in these new urban environments. In Quebec, the authorities initially resorted to the militia for this purpose (Barot and Berard, 1972), a tactic which was perhaps understandable in light of the recent conquest of that territory by the British. Elsewhere in the country, however, and in Quebec as well once civilian government was re-established, the traditions of local responsibility for, and control over, policing were not to be so easily swept aside,[7] and the authorities sought to adapt the old system of constabulary to meet new demands. At first, therefore, the power of appointing the new urban constables, and of thereby creating the first modern municipal police forces in the larger urban centres, remained with judicial officers such as the justices of the peace and the newly established "police magistrates." In some instances, grand juries were given such powers of appointment.[8]

This assignment of responsibility for the municipal police to the lower judiciary was a clear reflection of the prevailing practice with respect to the government of the police in England at the time (Critchley, 1978), and is understandable not only by reference to the history of the police in the mother country, but also in the context of the absence, at the time, of any structure of locally elected municipal government. It is important to understand, furthermore, that while today we think of justices of the peace and magistrates as purely judicial officers, this was not the case in the eighteenth and early nineteenth centuries. Justices of the peace in particular, at that time, were charged with a whole range of functions and responsibilities, which included not only, or even primarily, judicial functions, but also administrative functions of local government (see Moir, 1969). The fact that the responsibility for the government of municipal police forces originated with the judiciary in Canada, however, is of cardinal importance in understanding subsequent developments with respect to the government of these forces.

The nineteenth century saw the emergence, both in England and in Canada, of local municipal government, and with it some highly significant transformations in the arrangements for the government of municipal police forces. After the failure of the reformers to achieve the election, rather than appointment by the central authorities, of justices of the peace in Upper Canada, one of the first steps toward responsible elected local government was the creation, during the 1830s, of five-member elected boards with local government powers in the province's towns (Aitchison, 1949). These boards were called boards of police[9]—a nomenclature that is indicative of the fact that the term "police" originally had a much broader meaning than is normally ascribed to it today. As the editor of *The New Municipal Manual for Upper Canada* noted in 1859, referring to the power of municipalities in Upper Canada at that time to "establish, regulate and maintain a police":

> The word "police" is generally applied to the internal regulations of cities and towns, whereby the individuals of any City or Town, like members of a well governed family, are bound to conform their general behaviour to the rules of propriety, good neighbourhood, and good manners, and to be decent, industrious and inoffensive in their respective situations...; but the word, as here used, has a still more restricted meaning, for it is intended to apply to those paid men who in every City and Town are appointed to execute police laws, and who in many respects correspond with Constables of Rural Municipalities. [Harrison, 1859: 158]

While the justices of the peace retained control of the police in the smaller towns and rural areas, the incorporation of the cities and larger towns of Upper Canada during the 1830s and 1840s saw this control pass to the newly established mayors and their elected local councils. These newly elected officials were granted authority and powers that would astonish their modern counterparts, including not only the administrative, but in some cases also the judicial powers that had formerly been exercised by the justices of the peace. The Act incorporating the City of Toronto in 1834,[10] for instance, gave to the city council the authority "to regulate the police of the said City," and imposed on it the duty to "from time to time, employ so many Constables for the said City as to them may seem necessary and proper, and pay them such sum per annum for their services as to the said Common Council shall appear just." Such constables were "bound to obey the orders of the Mayor and Alderman, or any or either of them, in enforcing the laws of this Province, and the ordinances of the said City." Another section of the Act provided that:

> The Mayor and Alderman, or any one or more of them shall have full power and authority to take up, arrest or order to be taken up or

arrested, all or any rogues, vagabonds, drunkards and disorderly persons, and as the said Mayor or Alderman, or any two of them, shall
see cause, to order all or any such rogues, vagabonds, drunkards and
disorderly persons to be committed to any workhouse that may
hereafter be erected, or else to any House of Correction, there to
receive such punishment, not exceeding one month's imprisonment,
or the common stocks, as the said Mayor and Alderman, or any two
of them, shall think fit.

In addition to these substantial powers, the Act provided that the mayor,
assisted by the aldermen or any one of them, were constituted as a court of
record called "the Mayor's Court of the City of Toronto," having "the like
powers and...the same jurisdiction over crimes and misdemeanours arising
within the City...which the courts of General Quarter Sessions of the Peace
[i.e., the justices of the peace] within this Province now or hereafter shall have
by law."[11]

From these provisions it will be apparent that as a result of the efforts of
the nineteenth-century municipal reformers in Upper Canada, not only the
executive and administrative powers of the justices of the peace (including
their control over municipal police forces), but also their judicial powers, were
transferred without discrimination into the hands of the new local politicians.
The fact that control over municipal police forces was transferred to elected
municipal politicians not as a discrete policy decision, but as part of a wholesale transfer of local government power from justices of the peace to locally
elected politicians, and that this local government power included virtually the
whole administration of justice (including the lower courts), is critical to an
understanding of subsequent developments with respect to the government of
municipal police forces. For clearly, at a time when even judicial authority over
the disposition of criminal cases was viewed as appropriately placed in the
hands of elected local politicians, there could be no doubt that control of the
police was just as properly placed in the hands of these same politicians. The
seeds of doubt on this matter only began to arise with the emergence, later in
the nineteenth century, of the notion that certain aspects of the administration
of justice (and most particularly judicial functions) were not only not appropriate to be left in the hands of locally elected politicians, but were not even
appropriately subject to the control of elected politicians at all, be they locally
or centrally elected.

By 1849, with the passage of the Baldwin Act,[12] the power to establish,
maintain and regulate a municipal police force had been granted by statute to

the elected council of every city and town in Upper Canada, and during the succeeding 130 years this power was extended to include the councils of townships and villages as well as, more recently, regions in Ontario. Furthermore, provincial legislation gradually changed this from an option to a mandatory requirement for the cities and larger municipalities.[13]

While Upper Canada (later Ontario) has been chosen as an example to illustrate the origins of municipal police forces, a similar history can be traced in each of the other jurisdictions of Canada. The essential feature of this history is that of the gradual transfer of control over municipal police forces from judicial officers to locally elected municipal councils. The timing of this transfer of control varied enormously from one jurisdiction to another. Control of the City of Charlottetown Police force, for instance, did not finally pass from the city's magistrate to the police magistrate to the police committee of the city council until 1941,[14] more than a hundred years after many city and town councils in Upper Canada first gained control of their municipal police forces. In every jurisdiction in Canada, however, this transfer of control over municipal police forces has occurred.

The transfer of control of municipal police forces from the hands of judicial officers to those of locally elected politicians involves two important dimensions. Since the judicial officers involved had always been persons appointed by the provincial, rather than the local, authorities, the transfer represents not only a shift in control from an appointed judicial officer to a body of elected politicians, but also a shift in control from a provincially appointed authority to a locally elected authority. It is these two aspects of the shift in control—the shift from judicial to non-judicial control, and the shift from central to local control—which have been at the heart of the long controversy over the control of municipal police forces.

THE ORIGINS OF LOCAL MUNICIPAL POLICE BOARDS

Within a very short time after the earliest manifestations of this radical shift in the control of municipal police forces in Upper Canada from the justices of the peace to the new municipal councils, a significant reaction to it occurred. Just nine years after the passage of the famous Baldwin Act of 1849, the legislature of Upper Canada enacted the Municipal Institutions of Upper Canada Act.[15] From the point of view of the control of municipal police forces, this statute initiated a radical reversal of the policies effected through the reform legislation of the preceding 30 years. For while the right

of city and town councils to establish, regulate and maintain their own municipal police forces was preserved, it was, in the case of cities but not of other
municipalities, made subject to the requirement for the creation of boards of
commissioners of police. Section 374 of the Act provided for these police
boards in the following terms:

> 374. In every City there is hereby constituted a Board of
> Commissioners of Police, and such Board shall consist of the Mayor,
> Recorder and Police Magistrate, or if there is no Recorder or Police
> Magistrate, or if the offices of Recorder and Police Magistrate are
> filled by the same person, the Council of the City shall appoint a
> person resident therein to be a member of the Board, or two per-
> sons so resident to be members thereof, as the case may require.

The earliest legislative provision for the creation of a local police board illustrates the kind of flexibility that has been built into so many of its successors in
other jurisdictions in order to strike some kind of compromise between municipal and provincial interests in the governance of municipal police forces. Both
the recorder and the police magistrate were judicial officers who were appointed by, and held office during the pleasure of, the Crown (i.e., the province).
They were both *ex officio* justices of the peace. The recorder's salary was
fixed by the provincial government, and was paid out of the same fund as that
of county judges. The police magistrate's salary, however, was fixed and paid
by the municipal council. The recorder had to be a barrister of not less than
five years' standing.

The flexibility in the composition of the boards established by the Act,
however, derived from section 352 of the Act, which provided that:

> 352. A Recorder or a Police Magistrate shall not in the first instance
> be appointed for any Municipality, until the Council thereof commu-
> nicates to the Governor its opinion that such an officer is required.

In theory, therefore, if a city council decided that it did not need a recorder or
a police magistrate, it could have a police board consisting of the mayor and
two residents of the city appointed by the council. Thus, at the city council's
option, the composition of the police board could vary from, on the one hand,
the mayor and two judicial officers appointed by the province, to, on the other
hand, the mayor and two other persons appointed by council. Alternatively, it
could be composed of the mayor, one judicial appointee of the province, and

one person appointed by the council. There seems to have been no requirement that appointees of council should not also be members of council, so in
theory a board could consist of the mayor and two other members of council.

It is not clear whether these theoretical options envisaged by the Act were
reflected in practice, but it seems likely that most, if not all, of the five cities in
Upper Canada at that time would have had both a recorder[16] and a police
magistrate, and therefore a police board composed of the mayor and two
provincial judicial appointees.

The significance of the concept of this police board, however, lay as much
in the nature of its status and authority, as in its composition. The members of
the police force were appointed by the board and held office at the pleasure of
the board. Although the size of the police force remained within the discretion
of the city council, it nevertheless had to be "not less in number than the
Board reports to be absolutely required." The board, as well as thus determining the minimum size of the force, was required to, "from time to time, as
they may deem expedient, make such regulations for the government of the
force, and for preventing neglect or abuse, and for rendering the Force efficient in the discharge of all its duties." Most importantly, the constables
appointed to the force were required by the Act to "obey all the lawful directions, and be subject to the government of the Board." The salaries of members of the force were to be fixed and paid by the council, but the council was
required to pay for "all such offices, watch-houses, watch-boxes, arms, accoutrements, clothing and other necessities as the Board may from time to time
deem requisite and require for the accommodation and use of the force."

The scheme of this legislation makes it quite clear that it was intended that
the board should have a considerable degree of autonomy and independence
from the dictates of the municipal council, no matter what its composition
may be. The powers and functions of the board were not powers and functions delegated by the council, but statutory powers and functions conferred
directly on the board itself. From this it is clear that even if the board were
composed of three members of the council (i.e., the mayor and two aldermen
appointed to it by council), it could not in any sense be considered a committee of council. Indeed, it is precisely this notional independence from the local
council which constitutes one of the major characteristics of many of the modern, as well as of the original, police boards in Canada. While this notional
independence existed irrespective of the actual composition of the board, it
will be readily apparent that the extent to which such notional independence
was translated into real independence in practice almost certainly hinged very
much on the actual composition of the board.

Two important aspects of the compromise which this early conception of a police board represents should be emphasized here. In the first place, it represents a compromise between provincial and municipal control of municipal policing and police policy, since a majority of the members of the board could be, and in most cases probably were, provincially appointed. In this context, it is important to bear in mind that since Confederation, municipalities have never had any constitutionally defined sphere of jurisdiction. For, while the legislative jurisdiction of the federal and provincial legislatures is defined constitutionally by the British North America Act[17] (principally by sections 91 and 92 of the Act), all municipal authority is delegated constitutionally by the provincial legislatures. The significance of this constitutional arrangement, of course, lies in the fact that the municipalities have no constitutional claim to any jurisdiction over any municipal service, including policing. This means that the extent of municipal control over municipal policing is legally and constitutionally, if not politically, entirely at the discretion of the provincial legislature. Indeed, even the definition of policing as a municipal service is constitutionally within the exclusive jurisdiction of the provincial legislatures.

The second important aspect of the police boards envisaged by Ontario's early legislation is the compromise it represents between judicial and elected political control over municipal policing and police policy. The significance of this compromise in the context of Upper Canada in 1858 is by no means clear, and, more particularly, must be recognized as potentially quite different from the significance of the inclusion of members of the judiciary on municipal police boards in the present era. This is because, in the intervening years, the status and role of the lower judiciary have undergone major changes. As has been noted earlier, the notion of the political independence of the judiciary (especially the lower judiciary) which is so familiar to us today, but which, in the case of the lower judiciary, has doubtfully been totally realized even today in all jurisdictions in Canada (see, e.g., Alberta, Board of Review, 1975: 7-8), was apparently unknown in the Upper Canada of the mid-nineteenth century.

Similarly, the notion that the functions of the lower judiciary should be confined principally or exclusively to judicial duties was virtually unheard of at this time. Under these circumstances, the transfer of control over municipal police forces in the cities from the municipal council to a board composed of a majority of lower judicial officers should probably most accurately be interpreted as little more than a transfer of control from local back to provincial authorities. With the changing status of the lower judiciary during the ensuing 120 years, however, the significance of this compromise has come increasingly to be interpreted in terms of a transfer of control from political to non-political

authorities (see, e.g., Edwards, 1980: 72). Clearly such an interpretation suggests quite different issues about the nature of municipal policing and of the
municipal police function than are raised by the interpretation which emphasizes the municipal-provincial dimensions of the compromise. For it suggests
that at the heart of the compromise lies a conception of the municipal police
function as being not simply another municipal service over which municipal
and provincial governments may struggle for control, but as a judicial or quasi-
judicial function over which the influence of elected politicians of any kind
should be reduced or eliminated altogether. This ambiguity over the role of the
judiciary as members of police boards lies at the heart of the controversies
which have surrounded such boards ever since their inception as institutions of
municipal police governance in Canada over 120 years ago.

THE ORIGINAL JUSTIFICATIONS FOR POLICE BOARDS

Adequate research has not yet been completed to explain the radical
reversal of policy which the inclusion of the requirement for police boards in
the 1858 Act seems to reflect. Some speculation on this question can be
made, however. In the first place, it is clear that the idea for the creation of
such boards derived not from England (still the colonial power), but from the
United States. In England, with the exception of the Metropolitan London
force, which was under the control of the Home Secretary, control over
municipal police forces had been given to local municipal councils without
reservation by the Municipal Corporations Act of 1835. The "watch committees" which this statute required municipalities to set up to govern their municipal police forces were composed entirely of members of the elected municipal
councils. The composition of these watch committees remained unchanged
until 1964, when the new English Police Act of that year required their membership to consist of two-thirds municipal councillors and one-third local magistrates (Critchley, 1978).

According to Fosdick (1969:77), the idea of a "board of police" as an
institution of municipal police governance first emerged in an ordinance proposed (but never passed) in New York in 1844. The board proposed by this
ordinance was to be composed of seven senior officers, including the superintendent, of the New York City police department, and was to be charged with
"general administrative functions." This idea was taken up and put into effect
for the City of Philadelphia in 1850, but later in the same year the composition of this board was changed so that it consisted of the marshal of police and

the presidents of the respective town boards of the communities within the police district. Three years later, a "board of police commissioners" was established to govern the New York City police force, which was clearly the model on which the police boards required under the 1858 Upper Canada statute were based. The New York board consisted of the mayor, the recorder and the city judge. According to Fosdick:

> Apart from the fact that the chief of police was selected by the mayor with the boards' approval, the board had full powers of appointment and dismissal of all members of the force and was charged with general administrative duties. [1969:78)

Noting that "the origin of this novel experiment, particularly in its relation to police organization, cannot be exactly determined," Fosdick explains the change (which, he says, "came into instant and widespread favor") in the following terms:

> The office of mayor had not yet been associated with broad executive powers, and appointments, as well as administrative responsibilities, were lodged in the common council. The decade just referred to [i.e., 1845-55], however, witnessed the waning influence of the council as an administrative body. This change was undoubtedly due in part to the rising democratic sentiment which brought with it a pronounced distrust of the legislative departments of the government, both state and local. It was due, too, to the growing complexity of municipal functions and the increasing difficulties of supervision through committees of council. [1969:76-77]

Fosdick also noted that, in creating the police board in 1853, "the legislature had hoped to eliminate the political favoritism and ward control which prior to that time had dominated the [police] department." This hope, he added, was justified only in part, mainly because "the recorder and the city judge, serving *ex officio*, took little interest in the affairs of the force, and control was gradually assumed by the mayor" (1969:80-81).

To what extent similar considerations led to the adoption of the provisions of 1858 in Upper Canada can only be guessed at, at the present time. McDougall (1971a) has asserted that the 1858 provisions were enacted with the intention of "removing the police from politics." Referring to the period immediately prior to the introduction of these measures, he wrote that, by the 1830's cities and towns were authorized to appoint full-time police forces if they wished. Members of these forces were still appointed annually and their selection was based on patronage. The political character of appointees proved nothing short of disastrous when riots and religious rivalry shattered the peace of the community, since the faction in control of the municipal government was not above using the police as a partisan force. [1971a:11-12]

Although McDougall cites no specific source for this last allegation, there seems little reason to believe that it is not accurate (cf. Quebec, 1855: 15). The notion that this early police board could "remove the police from politics," however, is not without problems. In the first place, within the context of Upper Canada in 1858, there seems little enough reason to believe that the recorder and police magistrate who were to form the majority of the membership of such boards were in fact, or even in theory, any less "political" than the members of the municipal councils which they replaced, although undoubtedly they reflected different political interests (i.e., central rather than local interests). In the second place, it seems strange that a measure the intention of which was to "remove the police from politics" would nevertheless provide that the mayor should have, *ex officio*, a seat on the police governing authority, and that the council should have power to fix the size (subject to a minimum) and salaries of the force. Nor would the flexibility built into the provision governing the composition of the governing authority, whereby it could consist of three members of the council, seem to be compatible with an unequivocal intention to "remove the police from politics."

Finally, the fact that the requirement for a police board was not extended to towns which maintained their own police forces gives pause again to question the true motivations behind the creation of this institution. One would have thought that if the sole motivation had been to "remove the police from politics," there would have been little justification for not insisting that any municipality which maintained a municipal police force should have a police board. Yet to this day there are only two jurisdictions in the country which have legislated such a requirement.[18] Part of the reason for this may have been the small size of many municipal forces (sometimes no more than one constable). In such circumstances it might be thought somewhat ridiculous to insist that one policeman should be governed by a board consisting of three persons. Nevertheless, this does not in itself seem to be an adequate explanation of the distinction which such legislation has consistently made between large and smaller municipalities.

A much more plausible explanation for the creation of police boards would seem to be the desire of the central (provincial) authorities to remove the municipal police forces out of the control of local political interests and back into the sphere of their own political influence. In this context, the creation of police boards as institutions of government of municipal police forces may be seen not so much as a measure to "remove the police from politics," as an attempt to move the control over municipal police forces from one sphere of political interests toward another. Clearly, it would always be very much in the interests of the proponents of such a change to create the impression that the new governing authority is in some way demonstrably less "political" than its predecessor. In this context, the preference of the advocates of police boards for having the majority of their membership comprised of members of the judiciary seems readily explicable, and the provision whereby such boards could still, in certain circumstances, be composed entirely of locally elected politicians becomes understandable as a necessary concession to the contemporary realities of the struggle for power over municipal institutions between municipal and provincial authorities (Aitchison, 1949).

The notion that characterizations of municipal police forces and their governing authorities as autonomous "non-political" institutions may be little more than a strategy invoked to justify their removal from one sphere of political interests to another is not a new one. In his penetrating study of municipal police forces in the United States, Fogelson (1977) has amassed a great deal of evidence in support of his claim that the move toward municipal police autonomy from local government, and consequent changes in the structure of municipal police government, in that country were no more nor less than a means whereby control over these forces could be shifted from lower- and lower-middle-class immigrants to upper-and upper-middle-class native-born Americans. Similarly, Critchley (1978), in his classic study of the British police, has demonstrated quite clearly how the struggle for power over local forces between the justices of the peace and the locally elected municipal councils in the nineteenth century can most convincingly be understood in terms of a struggle between two quite clearly identifiable political factions (representing the landed aristocracy and the new middle-class bourgeoisie respectively) for control over these forces.

Whether the apparently sudden political *volte face* of the 1858 Act in Upper Canada can be understood in terms of an analysis such as this remains to be demonstrated. As an analytical framework, however, it would seem far from implausible, and should not too readily be discarded in favour of the more commonly heard explanation of the measure as representing an attempt to "remove the police from politics." The notion of the "independence" of municipal police forces and of their governing authorities, however, is one which requires further elaboration and which will be considered in more detail later in this essay. For the moment, the 122-year history of municipal police boards in Canada, and their current status, must be briefly described.

THE HISTORY OF POLICE BOARDS IN CANADA

Police boards are not unique in Ontario, although historically that has been, and remains today, the province in which they are most commonly found. The model for a police board which the Act of 1858 established in Upper Canada has, with a few important exceptions, remained substantially unchanged in Ontario. With the advent of Confederation in 1867, the place of recorders on such boards was taken by the new, federally appointed, county court judges.[19] Despite their federal appointment as judges, however, the power to appoint them as members of police boards remained with the provincial authorities. In 1936, the power of municipal councils to fill vacancies in the membership of police boards resulting from vacancies in either or both of the judicial offices concerned (i.e., county court judge and magistrate) was removed,[20] thus guaranteeing without exception both the judicial character, and the provincial control over the appointment, of the majority of the members of police boards. For a short period (1946-58) Crown attorneys (also provincial appointees) could be appointed as members of police boards instead of magistrates,[21] but in 1958 this requirement that the third member of such a board was to be either a magistrate or a Crown attorney was abolished, and instead the third member was now to be "such person as the Lieutenant-Governor in Council may designate."[22] From this time on it became the practice to appoint lawyers or businessmen, so that the tradition of the majority of board members being judicial officers ended. In 1979, the Ontario government finally succumbed to long-standing pressures from a variety of sources (including the judiciary themselves)[23] and removed the requirement that at least one member of a police board had to be a county or district court judge,[24] thus signalling the end of the legal requirement for judicial representation on most police boards in Ontario. Despite this legislative change, however, the present provincial solicitor general has publicly stated his intention to continue to appoint members of the lower judiciary to membership of police boards whenever this is possible.[25]

With the regionalization of police forces in the province, beginning with the creation of the Metropolitan Toronto Police Force in 1956, provision was made for five-member regional police boards.[26] Like the municipal police boards, the regional boards consist of a majority of members appointed by the provincial authorities. One of these, however, must still be a county or district court judge, and in Metropolitan Toronto another must also be a provincial judge.[27] These regional police boards in Ontario, and the Charlottetown board in P.E.I., are now the only police boards in Canada whose membership in required by law to include at least one (and in the case of Toronto, two) members of the judiciary.

In the other provinces the institution of police boards has historically been received with considerably less enthusiasm than in Ontario. Although it is not intended to review in detail here the experience which each of these jurisdictions has had with police boards, a very brief summary will give some idea of the rate at which this institution spread in Canada after its initial introduction in Upper Canada in 1858.

The first province to adopt the concept of a police board after Ontario was Manitoba. The charters of the cities of Brandon and Winnipeg, both enacted in 1882, permitted, but did not require, the establishment of police boards as the governing authority for their respective police forces.[28] The establishment of such a board was made mandatory for the city of Winnipeg four years later,[29] but such a requirement was not imposed on the city of Brandon until 1949.[30] Police boards have not been created for any other municipalities in this province.

The charters of the cities of Vancouver and New Westminster, enacted in 1886 and 1888 respectively, each required the establishment of a municipal police board.[31] In 1893 this requirement was extended to every city and town in the province,[32] but three years later the requirement was lifted in the case of towns.[33] Police boards of one form or another have existed in British Columbia ever since, and it is now the only jurisdiction which legally requires every municipality which maintains its own municipal police force to have a police board.[34]

In 1907 and 1908 respectively, police boards were established for the cities of Moncton[35] and Fredericton,[36] and in 1961 legislation was enacted permitting the council of the city of St. John to establish a police board for the government of its police force.[37] These are the only municipal police forces in New Brunswick that have ever been subject to the governance of police boards.[38] In 1908 police boards were made optional for cities in Saskatchewan,[39] but in 1915 this provision was amended to require all cities in the province to establish police boards.[40] Legislation establishing a police board for the City of Charlottetown was enacted in 1938, and this remains the only police board in Prince Edward Island.[41]

The concept of a police board was not introduced generally into Alberta until 1951, when such boards were made optional for the province's city police forces.[42] In 1968, this option was extended to include any municipality having its own police force,[43] and in 1971 police boards were made mandatory for the governance of police forces in the larger municipalities.[44] At the present time all 11 municipal police forces in the province are governed by police boards.

With the exception of the Public Security Council of the Montreal Urban Community, which was established in 1969 to oversee the creation of (and subsequently to govern) the city's new unified police department,[45] police boards have been unknown in the Province of Quebec, which has the largest number of municipal police forces of any province (196 at the last count). With the exception of the Montreal force, each of these forces is governed directly by the local council.

Police boards were unknown in Nova Scotia until 1974 when the province's new Police Act, enacted in the face of considerable opposition, required the establishment of police boards for the government of police forces in the larger municipalities, and made them optional for the smaller ones.[46] Currently all 25 municipal police forces in the province are governed by police boards. There has never been any police board in the Province of Newfoundland.

It will be apparent from this brief historical summary that any realistic assessment of police boards in Canada must bear in mind that some provinces have had long experience with this institution, while for others it represents a new and unfamiliar form of police government. Historically, the majority of the experience with municipal police boards in Canada has occurred in Ontario and the western provinces. In Quebec and the eastern provinces, with some exceptions, this institution has been virtually unknown until very recently. There appears to be no obvious explanation for this fact.

THE CURRENT VARIETY OF POLICE BOARDS IN CANADA

The composition of police boards in Ontario has been described in some detail not only because they were first introduced there, but also because at present the majority of police boards in Canada are to be found in Ontario, and because that province's police boards have been the subject of the most persistent controversy in recent years. It should not be imagined, however, that the police boards in Ontario are, or ever have been, in any sense typical of all police boards in Canada. In fact, nothing could be further from the truth, and the most striking finding which emerges from a review of the history of police boards in Canada is the amazing variety of forms in which this institution has manifested itself. Indeed, almost the only things these various police boards have in common are the fact that they have all played some role in the government of municipal police forces, and that they all have had at least a notionally separate identity from that of their local municipal councils.

In terms of their composition alone, it is possible to identify no fewer than 38 different models of police boards during the institution's 122-year history in Canada, ranging from boards whose members were all appointed by the provincial authorities,[47] through boards whose members were all chosen by and/or from among the members of the local council,[48] to boards whose members were chosen through direct public election to office.[49] Composition, however, has been by no means the only source of variety among Canadian police boards. Other important dimensions of variety have included their size, status, degree of autonomy, authority, powers and functions.

Obviously this great variety poses some problems for theoretical analysis, since it is arguable that police boards do not represent a sufficiently homogeneous category for such analysis. In this essay it is clearly not possible to describe the whole range of variety which this institution has manifested over the years.[50] Some, but by no means all, of this variety may be illustrated, however, through an examination of those police boards which exist at the present time in Canada. But before entering upon such a review, some contextual statistics are required.

There are currently approximately 450 municipal police forces in existence in Canada, almost three-quarters of which are to be found in the provinces of Ontario (128) and Quebec (196). These forces range from forces of one or two members in some rural municipalities, to forces of over 5,000 members in the metropolitan areas. The fact that there is thus no such thing as a "typical" municipal police force in Canada goes a long way toward explaining why there is also no such thing as a "typical" police board.

The majority of municipal police forces in Canada are not now, nor have they ever been, governed by police boards. Rather, they are subject to the direct control of their local municipal councils, or committees thereof. The majority of municipal policemen, however, do now belong to police forces that are governed by police boards. This is explained by the fact that a few large metropolitan police forces, which are subject to the governance of police boards, account for the great majority of municipal policemen in the country (Canada, Statistics Canada, 1978).

At the present time there are approximately 130 police boards in existence in Canada, more than half of which are in the Province of Ontario (71). The police forces governed by these boards thus represent less than one-third of all the municipal police forces in the country. It has already been noted that the establishment of a police board for the governance of a municipal police force in any given jurisdiction may be either a local option or a mandatory statutory requirement. While the exact number of the existing police boards which are optional rather than mandatory was not ascertained during the research undertaken for this essay it must be noted that this number is not insignificant. In Ontario, for instance, 34 of the 71 police boards currently in existence are optional boards.[51]

The significance of whether a board is optional or mandatory lies, of course, in the implications this has for the status of the board. If a board is a mandatory board it will by definition have some guaranteed legal autonomy vis-à-vis the local municipal council, whatever its composition. An optional board, however, may or may not have such autonomy depending on the nature of the option. While in some jurisdictions the dissolution of optional boards, once established, is.subject to the consent of the responsible provincial minister (usually the attorney general),[52] in other it is not.[53] Obviously, where a police board's very continued existence is within the discretion of some external authority such as a municipal council or a provincial government minister, however, any autonomy which might be claimed for it may be regarded as fundamentally undermined.

The significance of a police board is related, of course, not only to the size of the police force that it governs, but to the size of the budget that it administers. While by no means all police boards in Canada have complete control over their forces' budgets, once approved by the local council, in most cases they do, and such budgets are often of very sizeable proportions indeed. The budget for the Metropolitan Toronto Police Force, for instance, which once approved by the Metropolitan Toronto Council, is administered exclusively by the Metropolitan Toronto police board, stood in 1980 at an unprecedented $202 million, and represented the largest single item (almost 13 per cent) of Metropolitan Toronto's operating budget. Over 80 per cent of this police budget is paid out of funds raised through local taxation, the remainder being supplied through a provincial grant. When it is appreciated that the Metropolitan Toronto police board is comprised of five persons, a majority of whom are appointed by the provincial authorities and are not locally elected office-holders, and that the board enjoys complete autonomy vis-à-vis the Metropolitan Toronto Council, the potential for controversy over this institution can be readily understood. Indeed, a review of the history of police boards in Canada leaves little doubt that the issue of control over the municipal police budget has been the greatest source of controversy over this institution.

With this contextual information in mind, some of the essential features of the variety among existing police boards in Canada can be described.[54]

SIZE OF BOARDS

Most existing police boards consist of three or five members. The great majority of the boards in Ontario (61 out of 71), all boards in Saskatchewan, and the boards in Fredericton and Charlottetown are three-member boards. In addition, in Alberta, where municipalities have the option of establishing boards of three or five members, many have opted for three-member boards. The option for three-member or larger boards also exists in Nova Scotia, but research for this essay did not reveal whether any municipalities there have chosen the smaller boards. All 12 boards in British Columbia are five-member boards, as are the two boards in Manitoba, and the ten regional boards (including Metropolitan Toronto) in Ontario. Some of the Alberta boards are also five-member boards (e.g., Calgary and Edmonton), although again research did not reveal how many. Larger boards exist in Montreal (with a seven-member board) and in Nova Scotia (where legislation permits municipalities to create boards of any size, provided they consist of a minimum of three members). In Halifax, for instance, the board currently consists of 12 members (the entire city council plus one nominee of the provincial attorney general).

COMPOSITION OF BOARDS

The composition of existing police boards varies greatly. Members of all boards acquire their positions either *ex officio* or through appointment by either provincial authorities or municipal councils. The variations in the composition of police boards may thus be considered in terms of the two dimensions of (1) how membership is acquired and (2) who acquires membership. The mayor or other head of the municipal council is an *ex officio* member of the board in all jurisdictions in British Columbia and Saskatchewan, as well as in Fredericton, Charlottetown, Brandon (Manitoba), and in all jurisdictions in Ontario (including Metropolitan Toronto) except the nine regional jurisdictions. Provincial authorities in British Columbia and Ontario have the power of appointment of the majority of members of all police boards in those jurisdictions, but in all other cases control over the selection of the majority of the members of boards is in the hands of municipal authorities. The only police boards with respect to whose membership provincial authorities have no control at all are those in Alberta, Saskatchewan and Winnipeg.

In Ontario, British Columbia, Alberta and Fredericton the law provides that the majority of members of a police board must be persons who are not members of the municipal council. In all the other jurisdictions members of council form the majority on police boards. As was noted earlier, the only existing police boards which include members of the judiciary in their membership are those in Ontario and Charlottetown.

From the foregoing, it will be apparent that the categories of persons who are eligible for appointment to police boards are: (1) members of the municipal council, (2) members of the lower judiciary, and (3) other unspecified persons. In some cases, these other unspecified persons are required to be residents (e.g., in Brandon, Manitoba), ratepayers (e.g., in Fredericton), or electors (e.g., in Winnipeg) of the municipality concerned.

As to the actual membership of existing police boards, preliminary research suggests that the majority of members of police boards are drawn from the ranks of civic politicians, lawyers, businessmen, school principals and teachers. Other "professional" people (e.g., doctors, psychiatrists, chartered accountants) are also found on some boards, as are social and community workers in small numbers, and on two of the ten urban boards studied, former military officers, and "housewives" were also members. The labour movement, women and persons under 35 years of age seem to be particularly underrepresented, as are ethnic minorities. As previously noted, at least one member of every board in Ontario is a member of the judiciary, but elsewhere this is rare or non-existent. It is very uncommon for members of boards to be ex-policemen. There are instances in which persons sit as members of more than one police board; this, however, is rare. More comprehensive research is required to substantiate these preliminary findings.

THE POLITICAL CHARACTER OF BOARDS

Most of those persons interviewed on the subject of the composition of boards during the research in preparation of this essay seemed to be agreed that appointments to police boards tend to be "political" in the sense that those who exercise the power of appointment are free to exercise their political judgement in the choice of appointees, subject, of course, to the statutory requirements with respect to qualification for appointment (e.g., that the appointee is or is not a member of the municipal council, or is a judge, or is a resident of the municipality, etc). This is not to say that all such appointments are made strictly on the basis of partisan political loyalties. It is recognized, however, that sound political judgment may often commend appointment of actual or potential opponents, or persons with no declared political affiliations. The commonly heard characterization of police boards as "non-political"— a characterization often employed by those who wish to contrast police boards with other "political" police governing authorities (e.g., municipal councils)— seems to be derived not so much from the nature of individual appointments to boards, as from the fact that in some jurisdictions (e.g., Ontario, British Columbia, Nova Scotia and New Brunswick) police boards are required to be composed of members appointed by more than one appointing authority, and in some jurisdictions (British Columbia, Alberta, Ontario and New Brunswick) a certain number of appointees must be persons who do not hold municipal political office. This characterization, however, if it is intended to refer to anything other than the fact that some boards have as a majority of their members persons who are not at the time elected politicians, is one which, to the author's knowledge, has never been either clearly enunciated or empirically substantiated.

TENURE OF OFFICE OF BOARD MEMBERS

The term of office of members of police boards varies greatly, and to some extent depends on the source of appointment. Persons who are appointed in their capacity as civic politicians, of course, may serve only as long as they retain their seats on council, although in many instances such appointments are made on an annual basis. Re-appointments for successive terms are not uncommon, however. Other appointees are frequently appointed for longer terms, usually of two or three years, and re-appointments of such persons are not uncommon either. In some jurisdictions, appointment to, and retention of, membership of boards is dependent on residence within the community concerned. The British Columbia Police Act is unique in providing for a maximum period (six years) of membership of a police board. The legislation governing police boards reveals no other provisions guaranteeing the tenure of members of boards, and it would appear that members of police boards all serve "at pleasure."

PART-TIME, SHORT-TERM NATURE
OF BOARD MEMBERSHIP—IMPLICATIONS

With the exception of the chairman of the Metropolitan Toronto Board, all chairmen and members of police boards serve on a part-time basis. In many jurisdictions, members of police boards serve without remuneration. This is the case even with respect to members of some of the boards serving major cities in Canada.

The part-time nature of almost all, and the short-term nature of a great many, appointments to municipal police boards probably represent their two most important characteristics, with respect to the implications they have for the role and status of police boards. They exert a strong inhibiting influence not only on the ability of board members to develop expertise with respect to their functions as board members, but on the ability of police boards to engage in long-term policy planning and development for the forces under their jurisdiction. They also contribute in large measure to a heavy dependence of police boards on chiefs of police for information, expertise and the development of long-term planning. Indeed next to the "political/non-political" argument, these implications seem to be those which are most often cited in favour of police boards whose membership is not dependent on the members holding elected political office.

The problems generated by part-time and short-term membership of police boards, however, are not limited to those members who hold elected office, although, as noted above, appointed members seem generally to serve for longer terms. Most members of police boards have quite substantial commitments and responsibilities beyond those they owe to their function as board members. Opinions vary substantially on the extent to which this may impair their contribution to the work of police boards. Those who hold the view that it does, however, frequently cite it as a reason why heads of municipal councils should not be chairmen of police boards. Those who support the idea of mayors being chairmen of boards, on the other hand, will often, while conceding that mayors sometimes are unable to devote adequate attention to police board business, argue that the mayor is the most appropriate person to represent the interests of the municipality that should be prominently reflected in the governance of the police force.

The part-time nature of boards inevitably means that they do not shoulder the main burden of the administration of the police forces under their jurisdiction, but function more in a supervisory capacity. As a result, the day-to-day administration of the police force, as well as the initiation of policy development and planning, resides in many cases solely with the chief of police and his staff. The fact that most police boards do not have any separate staff, apart perhaps from the services of an administrative secretary and a stenographer, further contributes to this division of responsibilities.[55]

Most police boards meet formally on an average of once a month, although some of the boards in larger urban areas meet more frequently.[56] A board which actively engages in contract negotiations with its police personnel, as some boards do, will often have to meet more frequently for the purpose of such negotiations. Regular meetings of police boards, however, generally last from two to four hours. Most police board members, therefore, are not expected to devote more than a day a month to this responsibility. Despite this, a number of board members interviewed in different cities during the study referred to problems of absenteeism of members at meetings. These problems were most frequently associated with board members who were also members of municipal councils and had to attend to competing civic responsibilities. One chief of police interviewed during the study, however, explained some of the absenteeism in another way. Politician members of police boards, he suggested, tend to handle "crunch issues" by absenting themselves.[57]

CHAIRMANSHIP OF BOARDS

Another very important implication of the part-time, short-term nature of appointments to municipal boards is the significance of the role of the chairman of the board. Often, as a result, the chairman becomes, by default, by far the most active and influential member of the board.

The chairmen of most municipal police boards tend to be either mayors or other heads of municipal councils, or lawyers. Judges are chairmen of a minority of police boards in Ontario (14 out of 71). Except in British Columbia (where the mayor is *ex officio* chairman of the board) and Montreal (where the chairman of the MUC Public Security Council is appointed as such by the lieutenant governor in council) chairmen of boards are normally elected as such by the board members annually.[58]

THE MANDATES OF MODERN POLICE BOARDS

The statutory mandates of police boards in Canada vary considerably. They do, however, share the common features of being vaguely defined by legislation. In this connection, an interesting comparison may be made with the quite specific legislative definitions, which are to be found, of the mandates of the more recently established provincial police commissions, of which more will be said below. The provisions of the Ontario Police Act may be considered as a case in point, the only sense in which the Ontario legislation is atypical in this regard being that the definition of the mandate of police boards in Ontario is somewhat *less* vague than in other provincial Police Acts.

Section 41 of the Ontario Police Act defines the mandate of the Ontario Police Commission (the provincial body) in terms of 14 specific functions which are enumerated in the section. By comparison, the mandate of a municipal police board is defined in sections 14 to 17. Section 14 gives a board the power to determine the size of the force, and the accommodation, equipment, and so forth, which it requires. Section 15 gives a board the authority to appoint the members of the force, and section 16 allows it to make by-laws, not inconsistent with provincial regulations enacted under the Act, "for the government of the police force, for preventing neglect or abuse, and for rendering it efficient in the discharge of its duties." Finally, section 17 provides that a board "is responsible for the policing and maintenance of law and order in the municipality," and that "the members of the police force are subject to the government of the board and shall obey its lawful directions." The Ontario Police Act gives no indication of what may or may not be a "lawful direction" for the purposes of this section, and a review of pertinent judicial decisions yields no guidance on this matter beyond the bald assertion that "neither the board nor a municipality not having a board can lawfully give directions to any member of a police force prescribing the duties of his office."[59] Since duties of police constables in Ontario are more or less specifically enumerated in section 55 of the Act, this judicial interpretation of section 17 is of little value in discerning the mandate which is contemplated for police boards under that section. It will be apparent that the language in which this mandate is expressed is almost identical to that of the original Upper Canada statute of 1858 (see above, at 168).

In many jurisdictions, the role of the police board which is provided for in the relevant provincial statutes is much less specific than this. The statutes governing police boards in Nova Scotia and Winnipeg, for instance, give to the relevant municipal councils almost complete freedom to define, by by-law, the role of these boards.[60] As a result, the mandate of the police board in Winnipeg has undergone radical changes at the hands of the city's municipal council in recent years.[61]

The result of such provisions is that the degree to which responsibility for, and control over, municipal police forces is shared between police boards and their municipal councils varies greatly from one jurisdiction to another. In terms of extremes, one could say that boards in Ontario have more than the lion's share at present (municipal councils there do not even have ultimate control over the size of the police budget),[62] while those of Winnipeg and Fredericton are effectively limited to that of holding hearings into public complaints against members of their police forces, and (in the case of the Winnipeg board) hearing appeals from disciplinary decisions of the police chief and "advising" him on community relations and crime prevention policies.[63]

Adequate empirical research into the role of police boards in the governance of Canada's municipal police forces has not yet been undertaken. A preliminary review of the operations of police boards in ten of Canada's major cities, however, reveals the following range of functions.

PREPARATION AND CONTROL OF THE POLICE FORCE BUDGET

Although control of the budget of a police force would seem to be a vital function for anybody charged with the government of a police force, by no means all police boards in Canada have this responsibility. In those cases (the majority) where police boards are involved in the preparation of the budget, the final approval of the budget generally lies with the municipal council, and the board must accept any limitations which may be placed upon it by council. In Ontario and British Columbia, however, the provincial police commissions are given final authority to resolve disputes between a municipality and its police board over the budget.[64] Control of the budget, of course, carries with it a great deal of power, including the authority for determining the size of the force and the provision of equipment, accommodation and facilities.

COLLECTIVE BARGAINING

In a great many jurisdictions, the board plays no role in collective bargaining other than that of providing those responsible (usually civic officials, such as city managers, personnel directors, finance commissioners, etc.) with information they may require for this task. It will be readily apparent that the role of those boards which have no control over the police budget or over the collective bargaining process is already substantially circumscribed by comparison with those boards which have control in both of these areas.

PROMULGATION OF RULES AND REGULATIONS

The rules and regulations promulgated by boards, along with the collective agreements and the chief's standing and daily or weekly orders, constitute the principal administrative documents governing the operations of municipal police forces. Such rules and regulations, which almost all boards have author-ity to promulgate, cover such matters as the duties of various ranks in the administration of the force; police procedures such as the handling of lost and found items; the treatment of persons in custody; the care of equipment and its use; reporting procedures; the maintenance of police records and access to them; relations of members of the force with the media and other persons seeking information about police matters; the offering of rewards; the treat-ment of informants; the conditions under which officers may perform special pay duties, and so forth.[65] They may also deal with other personnel under the board's jurisdiction, for example, auxiliary policemen, parking control officers, by-law enforcement officers, school crossing guards.

SUPERVISION OVER RECRUITMENT, HIRING, PROMOTIONS, SUSPENSIONS AND DISMISSALS

In most, but by no means all, jurisdictions the police board has final authority over these matters. In some jurisdictions, however, the appointment of the chief of police must be either made by (e.g., in Nova Scotia), or ratified by (e.g., in Alberta), the municipal council.

GENERAL POLICY DIRECTION OR APPROVAL

A few boards—but definitely a minority—are highly active in the initiation and direction of police policy, some even striking committees (sometimes including appointed community representatives) or hiring consultants to devel-op policy and make recommendations in particular areas. The majority of police boards, however, seem to rely almost exclusively on the chief of police to generate policy issues and proposals for the board's approval. Interviews with board members and chiefs of police in ten major Canadian cities generat-ed the following list of examples of topics with respect to which boards played some role in policy formulation:

- meeting the policing needs of particular areas of a city
- recovery of stolen articles from pawn and second-hand dealers
- preventing suicides in police cells
- security measures for apartment and other buildings
- assistance to other police departments
- recruitment from other police departments
- treatment of ethnic minority groups
- installation and use of communication systems
- dissemination of accident reports
- support of force members taking educational courses in com-munity colleges, universities, and so forth

- setting of departmental goals and objectives
- whether routine police presence should be maintained at a hospital
- the placing of shotguns in police vehicles
- the hiring of experts to perform psychological testing of recruits
- the establishment of a tactical unit
- the establishment of a domestic crisis intervention unit
- hot pursuit by police vehicles
- dealing with the problems of prostitution
- treatment of juveniles

PUBLIC AND COMMUNITY RELATIONS

This is seen by many police boards as one of their major functions. It is accomplished in a variety of ways, including attendance at public meetings; speeches to community groups, schools, and so forth; attendance at municipal council and committee meetings; promotion of "police week"; the award of citations to members of the public who have assisted the police; and receiving and responding to deputations and representations from citizen groups on matters of concern to the police.

INTERNAL DISCIPLINARY MATTERS AND PUBLIC COMPLAINTS

Almost all police boards have supervisory and appellate jurisdiction with respect to the disposition by the police chief of internal disciplinary matters and public complaints against the police. In many cases, boards also have original powers of investigation and inquiry with respect to such matters. Frequently, however, such powers are subject to provincial regulations governing procedures in such matters. The great potential for conflict between these responsibilities and the other functions of boards has led to much serious questioning of the appropriateness of the exercise of such powers by them.[66] Concern is particularly expressed about the difficulty of creating the appearance of impartiality in the exercise of such powers, when boards may be so involved in the supervision of the administration of their forces through their other responsibilities. The fact that such concerns are frequently expressed by members of boards themselves[67] contributes to the probability that reforms in this area may be not far off.

MISCELLANEOUS FUNCTIONS

Police boards also perform a variety of other miscellaneous functions. These include such matters as the review of reports by the chief of police on matters connected with the administration of the police force, and on crime within the force's jurisdiction; consideration of requests for information on policing matters from municipal councils and other civic authorities (e.g., a transit commission), providing such information, and sometimes consulting with such bodies; hearing grievances of force members pursuant to the terms of a collective agreement; review of reports on the use of firearms by police force members involving death or injury to a third party, and making reports thereon to the provincial police commission; the award of merit marks and commendations to police force members for outstanding service.

In addition to these functions, police boards in some of the larger cities of Canada have quite extensive responsibilities with respect to the licensing of persons carrying on various businesses within the jurisdiction of the board. Such businesses include taxicab, newspaper vending, second-hand goods dealing, fruit and vegetable vending businesses, door-to-door salesmen and a host of other concerns.[68]

While the list of functions just described may seem to constitute an impressive mandate for police boards, it must be stressed that many police boards do not enjoy all of these powers and responsibilities, and a good many enjoy only a few of them. Furthermore, the mere fact that a police board enjoys a particular mandate is no indication of the extent to which a board will exercise that mandate in practice. Again, adequate empirical research into the actual work of police boards is sadly lacking, but preliminary studies in this area suggest that in practice most police boards (and there are notable exceptions) play a very passive and minimal role in the governance of their police forces, even when they enjoy a theoretically expansive mandate in this regard. Some of the factors which may account for this have already been identified in this paper. They include the short-term, part-time nature of most police board membership, the perceived lack of the requisite expertise on the part of police board members, the absence of clear definitions of police board mandates, and the lack of adequate staff and support services to allow police boards to take a vigorous, independent approach to their mandate. All of these factors encourage a situation in which police boards develop a heavy reliance on their chiefs of police and the forces themselves for the information and the support services necessary for the exercise of their responsibilities. The result in many cases seems to be that police boards come to be little more than rubber-stamp agencies of approval and public relations for the policies and procedures adopted by their chiefs of police.

Four other important factors, however, have to be considered in any attempt to account for such emasculation of the role of police boards in governing their police forces. These are the notion of police independence, the notion of police professionalism, the rise of police unionism, and the growing influence of provincial agencies—especially provincial police commissions—in the control of municipal police services.

THE NOTION OF POLICE INDEPENDENCE

After reviewing the historical common law status of the constable in England, Marshall (1965:33) commented:

> In the twentieth century there has been contrived out of the common law position a novel and surprising thesis, which is sometimes now to be heard intoned as if it were a thing of antiquity with its roots alongside Magna Carta.

Marshall was referring to the thesis of police independence. A leading English constitutional lawyer, in a brief to the Royal Commission on the Police, described the notion of police independence as "obscure," and concluded that "there can...be little ground in law for the assumption that the discretion exercised by a chief constable is peculiar to himself" (Great Britain, Royal Commission on the Police, 1962b: App. 2, at 33). Nevertheless, the notion of the independence of the police has attracted a substantial degree of support from the courts in England[69] and Canada,[70] as well as from a variety of commentators, including the English Royal Commission on the Police[71] and, most recently, the English Royal Commission on Criminal Procedure.[72]

Space does not permit a detailed account here of the content and origins of this notion of police independence. Statements of the concept of police independence vary greatly,[73] but one of the more extreme (and most often quoted) versions of the concept is that offered by Lord Denning in the English case of R. v. *Metropolitan Police Commissioner ex parte Blackburn.* Referring to the constitutional status of the Commissioner of the Metropolitan London Police, he said:

> I have no hesitation, however, in holding that, like every constable in the land, he should be, and is, independent of the executive. He is not subject to the orders of the Secretary of State, save that under the Police Act 1964 the Secretary of State can call on him to give a

report, or to retire in the interests of efficiency. I hold it to be the duty of the Commissioner of Police, as it is of every chief constable, to enforce the law of the land. He must take steps so to post his men that crimes may be detected; and that honest citizens may go about their affairs in peace. He must decide whether or not suspected persons are to be prosecuted; and, if need be, bring the prosecution or see that it is brought; but in all these things he is not the servant of anyone, save of the law itself. No Minister of the Crown can tell him that he must, or must not, keep observation on this place or that; or that he must, or must not, prosecute this man or that one. Nor can any police authority tell him so. The responsibility for law enforcement lies on him. He is answerable to the law and to the law alone....

Although the chief officers of police are answerable to the law, there are many fields in which they have a discretion with which the law will not interfere. For instance, it is for the Commissioner of Police, or the chief constable, as the case may be, to decide in any particular case whether enquiries should be pursued, or whether an arrest should be made, or a prosecution brought. It must be for him to decide on the disposition of his force and the concentration of his resources on any particular crime or area. No court can or should give him direction on such matters. He can also make policy decisions and give effect to them, as, for instance, was often done when prosecutions were not brought for attempted suicide; but there are some policy decisions with which, I think, the courts in a case can, if necessary, interfere. Suppose a chief constable were to issue a directive to his men that no person should be prosecuted for stealing any goods less than £100 in value. I should have thought that the court could countermand it. He would be failing in his duty to enforce the law.[74]

Until very recently, the applicability of the notion of police independence to police forces in Canada has received little attention, either by the courts or by commentators. Rather, on the basis of a few decisions of the Canadian courts in which the concept has been given more or less passing recognition,[75] its applicability in Canada seems to have been assumed. Court decisions governing the civil liability of municipalities and provincial governments for the actions of municipal police officers have been cited to justify an immunity for the police from the normal processes of democratic accountability and control.[76] Marshall (1965:45), however, has concluded that "no such immunity and no general constitutional autonomy can be inferred from the much-handled civil liability cases."

Given the terms of modern police legislation in Canada, along with the fact that most of the Canadian cases which are relied upon in support of the notion of police independence were decided prior to the enactment of these legislative provisions, the applicability of this concept in Canada today remains highly questionable, and a thorough analysis of this question is long overdue. The likelihood of judicial review of this matter, however, has recently been greatly enhanced by the Quebec Court of Appeal's decision in the case of *Bisaillon v. Keable and the A.G. of Quebec*.[77] In that case, Mr. Justice Turgeon, with whose opinions on this matter the other two members of the court concurred, thoroughly reviewed the legislation governing the police in Quebec, and concluded that the notion of police independence, as it has been expounded by the English courts, is not applicable in the Province of Quebec. This is the first reported case in which any superior court in Canada has so explicitly rejected the application of the English jurisprudence on this matter. The fact that Mr. Justice Turgeon chose not to refer to any of the extant Canadian case law on the subject, however, as well as the fact that the judgment is being appealed to the Supreme Court of Canada, ensures that judicial consideration of this matter in Canada is by no means at an end yet.

Even assuming the validity (not to mention the desirability) of the concept of police independence and its applicability in Canada, however, two things are quite clear. First, the concept itself has exerted a considerable influence on the relationship of police boards to the forces that they govern, encouraging a posture of substantial restraint, and a tendency to favour a limited interpretation of their mandate, by the former,[78] and a good measure of hostility toward attempts to impose democratic control on the police, by the latter.[79] Secondly, the precise implications of the notion of police independence for the relationship of a police board to its police force are the subject of substantial disagreement among police chiefs and police board members alike across Canada. This disagreement ranges from those who believe that the chief of police of a municipal police force is, in consequence of his independent status, not subject to any directions from his police board with respect to law enforcement policy or operations, and that a board has no right of access to police-held information pertaining to such matters, to those who believe that a board is entitled to issue instructions to its chief of police on any matter pertaining to the operations of the police force, and that, as one police board chairman put it, "there is nothing in that department which I am entitled to be privy to."[80]

THE NOTION OF POLICE PROFESSIONALISM

McDougall (1971a) has described in fascinating detail, for Ontario, the historical emergence of the notion of police professionalism and its relationship to the notion of police independence and to the ongoing struggle between provincial and municipal authorities for control over municipal policing. His analysis leaves little doubt that the development of the notion of police professionalism tends to favour central rather than local interests in this struggle. Fogelson (1977) has illustrated a similar tendency with respect to city police forces in the United States, as has Critchley (1978) in relation to the development of municipal policing in England. The implications of the development of the notion of police professionalism for the role of police boards in Canada, however, has not been systematically studied. Nevertheless, there can be little doubt that, along with the notion of police independence, the notion of police professionalism has had its influence in encouraging restraint and passivity on the part of police boards in their governance of municipal police forces. No better illustration of this influence could be found than the following description, published recently by the Ontario Police Commission, of the proper relationship between a police board and its chief of police:

> The primary rule is that the Chief of Police is charged with the responsibility for the control of the conduct of his men, particularly as it relates to the wide discretionary power which they exercise. Boards of Commissioners of Police represent civilian control of the force much the same as national governments represent civilian control of the Military Forces of the nation. National governments rarely have the technical knowledge to command armies, and must rely heavily on the expertise provided by the "general staff". Likewise, Boards of Commissioners of Police, by the very nature of their composition, must rely heavily upon their Chief of Police for the expertise required to operate the police force. They must spell out general policy through regulation and direction, but in the administration of the Force, they must rely upon the Chief of Police, otherwise the Board is assuming the prerogative of the Chief, and is, in effect, becoming the Office of the Chief, for which the Board has neither the time nor the expertise. [Ontario Police Commission, 1978: 116]

During interviews conducted while the research for this essay was being prepared, the influence of police professionalism on the police board/police chief relationship was constantly reiterated. One police chief commented, for instance, that the investigative techniques used by the members of his force are the chief's responsibility and that he does not normally inform his police board about them. These are, he urged, "professional matters with respect to which members of the police commission are amateurs." For the police board to attempt to give instructions with respect to what investigative techniques should be used would, in his view, be inappropriate, and would be comparable to "a hospital board telling a doctor how to operate."[81]

THE RISE OF POLICE UNIONISM

Closely associated with the trend toward police professionalism, although doubtfully consistent with such a concept, has been the significant development of structures of collective bargaining for the police. Although full-fledged police unionism is in many jurisdictions both prohibited by law and considered undesirable by the police themselves (cf. Reiner, 1978), this is by no means the case in all jurisdictions, and police unions now flourish in a number of Canada's major cities. The principal significance of these developments for the role of police boards is the extent to which matters of a non-economic nature that were once thought to be within the exclusive prerogative of the police chief and his governing authority have now been recognized as falling within the scope of collective bargaining and related arbitration processes. For many police boards, and especially those which do not have responsibility for collective bargaining, this trend has effectively resulted in significant loss of jurisdiction. Decisions that have major implications for the allocation of resources (e.g., the organization of the shift system, the issue of whether patrols should be manned by one or two officers, etc.) are increasingly being made not by chiefs in consultation with their police boards, as was previously the case, but by municipal labour negotiators, arbitrators and the courts (see, e.g., Arthurs, 1971; Swan, 1980). Furthermore, the fact that police associations and unions are organized on a provincial as well as a municipal basis has encouraged a tendency toward centralization in the definition and resolution of specific issues which further erodes the practical autonomy of individual police boards in their relations with their police forces. This, in turn, has been a major factor in the resurgence of provincial influence over the governance of municipal police forces, to which we turn next.

THE RESURGENCE OF PROVINCIAL INFLUENCE

During the last 35 years, post-war Canada has witnessed major overhauls of provincial legislation governing municipal policing, beginning with the enactment of the Ontario Police Act in 1946.[82] Invariably, such overhauls have involved a significant increase in the influence and control of provincial authorities with respect to municipal police forces. Standardization in the form of provincial regulations, uniform discipline codes and procedures for handling public complaints against the police, and the provision of systems of inspection and monitoring of municipal policing services by provincial agencies have characterized this period. The only provinces which have not yet completely revamped their policing legislation in this way are Manitoba and Newfoundland.

The principal vehicles of this growing provincial influence over municipal policing in recent years have been the new provincial police commissions. First introduced in Ontario in 1962, such commissions now exist in seven provinces,[83] and somewhat similar mechanisms of provincial authority are to be found in an eighth (Alberta).[84] Prince Edward Island and Newfoundland do not at present have such commissions, although the former province has enacted legislation, which is not yet in force, to establish one.[85]

Consisting usually of three or five members, often serving on a part-time basis, provincial police commissions play a role which, for the most part, consists in the provision of advisory services and technical and support services (e.g., co-ordinated criminal intelligence services to combat organized crime) to local authorities and municipal police forces. In some cases they run provincial police training facilities to which municipal police forces have access. While in no case does any provincial police commission have direct responsibility for the government of municipal police forces, in many cases such commissions are endowed with substantial powers to inspect local forces, to monitor the adequacy of municipal policing services, and to hold public inquiries into various aspects of municipal police services. Most provincial police commissions also have appellate jurisdiction with respect to the disposition, by municipal police chiefs and/or police boards, of internal disciplinary charges and public complaints against municipal policemen.

While most provincial police commissions are currently quite small organizations, some (notably those in Ontario, Quebec and British Columbia) are not. The Ontario Police Commission, for instance, currently has a staff of approximately 50 persons (not including the staff of 70 at the Ontario Police College, for which the commission is responsible), and in 1979-80 had an operating budget in excess of $7 million, of which just under half related to the commission's head office, the remainder being for the operation of the Ontario Police College.[86]

The precise impact of the growing influence of provincial authorities on the role of municipal police boards is difficult to gauge accurately. There is no doubt, however, that it has been substantial. The way it is perceived by some municipal police board members is amply illustrated by the following comments contained in a letter to the author from the chairman of the police board of a medium-sized Canadian city:

> While a degree of autonomy still remains in the hands of local
> Boards, this has been substantially eroded over the past few years,
> on the one hand through the development of the [provincial] Police
> Commission through mandatory and uniform practices regulations,
> and on the other hand by the steadily encroaching influence of
> police unions on administrative matters. Since the principal authority
> of the Boards is now to develop and control budgets on behalf of the
> individual municipalities, there may not be the same current need for
> the Board to be independent of the Municipal Councils. The need
> for Provincially-appointed Board Members is no longer as significant
> or important as the [provincial] Police Commission assumes an ever-
> enlarging role in the development of policy and standards for police
> departments throughout the Province. The principal concern in this
> regard, however, is that the [provincial] Police Commission is totally
> lacking in municipal representation on the one hand while heavily
> influenced and advised by the police unions on the other hand.

Another medium through which provincial authorities are able to exert a growing influence over municipal police policies is that of their ultimate control over prosecutions. To a limited extent, this relationship is entrenched in legislation. Section 59 of the Ontario Police Act, for instance, provides that a local Crown attorney (who is responsible to the provincial attorney general, and not to local authorities) may call in the provincial police force to handle problems arising even in an area which is under the jurisdiction of a municipal police force and its police board, and charge the cost of such services to the municipality. Furthermore, section 12 of the Ontario Crown Attorneys Act[87] empowers Crown attorneys to cause charges "to be further investigated, and additional evidence to be collected"—a provision which seems to envisage some degree of control by Crown attorneys over investigations by municipal police forces.[88] In New Brunswick, the provincial Ministry of Justice has adopted formal policies whereby the laying of criminal charges, applications for search warrants and applications for wiretapping orders by the police are subject to strict supervision and control by provincial Crown prosecutors (Gregory, 1979: 14-15). As was noted earlier, however, police boards are at present virtually unknown in this province, and New Brunswick appears to be unique in its adoption of such comprehensive policies of supervision of the actions of municipal police forces. Nevertheless, the New Brunswick experience serves to illustrate what a powerful source of control the provincial control over prosecutions can be.

PUBLIC ACCOUNTABILITY OF POLICE BOARDS

Since police boards are mostly statutory bodies which are notionally independent vis-à-vis both municipal and provincial authorities, the question of their public accountability is inherently problematic. With few exceptions, police boards are not required to report to any representative body.[89] Nor, in strict legal terms, are most of them subject to direction from anyone. Furthermore, the majority of the meetings of most police boards are held in private, as sanctioned by law,[90] and in most cases the rules and regulations promulgated by such boards, despite the fact that they have the force of laws, are not public documents. In at least one court decision, these and other documents relating to the operations of a police board have been held to be legally immune from public scrutiny.[91]

Under these circumstances, public accountability of such boards, such as it is, tends to be accomplished through indirect rather than direct means. Such indirect means include the lack of guaranteed tenure of board members, the ultimate control over the police budget by municipal councils or provincial police commissions, and the powers of supervision, monitoring, and inquiry vested in provincial police commissions and provincial prosecutorial authorities already described.[92]

It will be apparent that many, and in some cases most, of these indirect means of achieving public accountability of police boards are at the disposal of provincial rather than municipal authorities. It is the combination of this absence of direct local accountability of police boards with the fact that the substantial funds which they administer are either mostly or entirely raised through local taxation, which has given rise to most of the recent controversy over the legitimacy of such boards as institutions of municipal police governance.

RECENT DEVELOPMENTS—AN INSTITUTION UNDER ATTACK

The history of police boards in Canada is marked by persistent controversy, and in recent years this controversy has shown no signs of abating. In Ontario during the 1970s three separate local government review commissions, appointed by the provincial government, independently recommended the abolition of police boards as they currently exist in the province, and advocated the return of control over municipal police services to elected municipal councils.[93] A fourth recommended no substantial change in existing arrangements.[94] Of these four commissions, the Robarts Commission on Metropolitan Toronto and the Waterloo Region Review Commission were the most thorough in examining the question of the governance of municipal police forces.

The Robarts Commission stressed "the importance of policing to the local community both as a service on its own and in its interrelationships with other local services," as well as "the principle of fiscal accountability, which holds that the spender of public funds should be responsible for raising them." The commission argued that the present arrangements for governance of the police force "have made it virtually impossible for either the public or its local elected representative to make an informed assessment of the policies of the police commission and to evaluate the management and operation of the police force" (Ontario, Royal Commission on Metropolitan Toronto, 1977: vol 2, at 276). Commenting on the commonly heard view that some municipal services need to be "protected from politics," the commission suggested that "this attitude ultimately reduces to a view of politics as a sinister process and municipal councils as unworthy of confidence." The commission rejected this attitude, saying that it felt that "the public holds a more positive view of politics as a healthy resolution of community issues through the democratic process. Municipal politics are no exception." The commission argued that "if it is contended that some local public services must be 'protected from politics,' then it is up to the proponents of that view to demonstrate why some services are needful of this protection, while others are not." Without explicitly saying so, the commission went on to imply that no such argument could be convincingly made (1977:vol. 2, at 105).

The Waterloo Region Review Commission reiterated many of the arguments put forwarded by the Robarts Commission, but was more blunt on the subject of the claim that police boards are non-political bodies. In an interim report, *Police Governance in Waterloo Region*, which constitutes a unique contribution to Canadian literature on this subject, the commission argued that the "values and beliefs" of a position which "places great emphasis on the need for keeping an emotional public from influencing police policy directly...are, or should be, unacceptable in a democratic scheme of government." The empirical evidence in the region, the commission urged, shows not only that "skillful political behaviour and continuous political processes" are required for "the effective resolution of police issues, often in relation to other public issues," but that the recent absence of it has, in the long run, ill served the community and the police (Ontario, Waterloo Region Review Commission, 1978:100). In its final report the following year, the commission criticized the argument that a "non-political" board is needed for the governance of municipal police forces. Comparing this with the possibility of governance by a representative regional council, the commission observed:

> The arguments for "keeping politics out of the police" are largely fraudulent. No matter how this system is structured, the police governing body must ultimately be responsible to the public—that is accountability and that is politics. The present system where the Provincial Government, elected through a party system, appoints the majority of police commissioners is every bit as "political" and more potentially dangerous than a situation in which a government composed of twenty-four separately elected individuals with at least three different political stripes and seven different factions appoints the police governing body. Recent allegations of impropriety against provincially appointed police commissioners in York and Halton suggest that no structure is immune from such accusations.[95]
> [Ontario, Waterloo Region Review Commission, 1979:156]

In its interim report, the commission also attacked the notion that the concept of police independence makes the police "simply not manageable to the extent that other municipal departments are." The commission asserted that it is "somewhat spurious" to suggest that the legally independent character of the individual policeman's authority in law enforcement "is itself a major problem in management of the police force." The commission commented that:

> The broadest areas of police activity is designed to prevent the breaking of law. This includes the way the force is organized and the amount of patrol duty itself. This is not legally subject to the discretion of the individual policeman as is his behaviour on patrol. Hence,

the police are eminently "manageable" by the police governing authority. [Ontario, Waterloo Region Review Commission, 1978: 91]

To the argument that municipal policing must conform to provincial rather than local standards and policies with respect to law enforcement and the administration of justice, the commission countered that this fact, by itself, cannot justify the removal of governance of municipal police forces from the local elected municipal council, any more than it can justify it in the case of other municipally controlled municipal services which share a similar need for provincial (e.g., education), or even federal (e.g., welfare) input. Such necessary provincial influence, the commission argued, can be accomplished in more direct ways than through provincial control of the police governing authority. One such way, the commission suggested, would be to expand, where necessary, the supervisory powers of the provincial police commission (Ontario, Waterloo Region Review Commission, 1978:95).

In addition to these review commission reports, police boards in Ontario have come under criticism recently from a variety of other sources. Two major commissions of inquiry into the Metropolitan Toronto Police Force have recommended the removal from the police board of certain of their responsibilities with respect to the disposition of public complaints against the force (see Maloney, 1975; Ontario Royal Commission into Metropolitan Toronto Police Practices, 1976), and a bill to put their recommendations into effect is currently before the Ontario legislature.[96] More recently, mounting confrontations between the Toronto police and certain minority groups in that city have led to an unprecedented public censure of the police board by city council,[97] and further calls for the return of control over the force to municipal authorities.

Ontario is not the only jurisdiction, however, that has recently experienced controversy over the institution of the police board. In Winnipeg, as a result of a dispute between the city's police board and city administrators, the city council took action in 1978 to strip the board of most of its major functions in governing the police force, and placed these responsibilities in the hands of city administrators responsible to the city council.[98] In New Brunswick, an attempt by the provincial government to introduce legislation in 1973 which would have required municipal police forces in the province to be governed by police boards rather than by local municipal councils,[99] as at present, met with what one document summarizing reaction to the proposal at the time described as "almost universal opposition," and was subsequently withdrawn as a result. The bill which was introduced in its place, and finally passed in 1977, provided that such boards would be optional only.[100] This legislative provision was only proclaimed in force in December 1980, so it remains to be seen whether any municipalities in that province will opt for this form of municipal police governance.

CONCLUSIONS

Police boards have had an uncertain and controversial history as institutions of municipal police governance, and continue today to be the subject of a good deal of quite highly charged debate in some quarters. As an institution they epitomize fundamental differences not only over the nature of the police function, but also over the appropriate means of ensuring the accountability of this function in a democratic society. The defenders of police boards stress the judicial (or at least quasi-judicial) nature of the police function, and point to the original judicial responsibility for the police. This "judicial location" of the police, as McDougall (1971a:31) has described it, is said to require the removal of direct political supervision for its preservation, and police boards, it is argued, fulfil this need for "non-political" governance of the police. Many advocates of police boards, citing what is claimed to be a historic independence of the law enforcement function, and the growing "professionalism" of modern police personnel, go further to argue for a restricted role in governing the police even for such a "non-political" governing authority, contending that a substantial portion of police activity should be subject only to supervision by the courts rather than by any governing authority. An extreme statement of this view may be found in the now-famous reply of Prime Minister Trudeau, in 1977, to the journalist who asked him: "Just how ignorant does a minister have to be before...some responsibility is applied to the advisers who seem to have kept him ignorant?" Trudeau is reported to have responded:

> The policy of this government...has been that they, indeed—the politicians who happen to form the Government—should be kept in ignorance of the day-to-day operations of the police force and even of the security force....That is our position. It is not one of pleading ignorance to defend the Government. It is one of keeping the Government's nose out of the operations of the police force, at whatever level of government. On the criminal law side, the protections we have against abuse are not with the Government, they are with the courts.[101]

The courts, in their turn, have on occasion pushed this line of reasoning still further to suggest that there may be areas of police discretion in which even they should not interfere.[102] And in the heat of the debate, those who favour the institution of the police board will invariably recall the "bad old days" when policemen were so obviously the willing henchmen of the most blatantly self-serving factions engaged in the crassest political partisanship (Fogelson, 1977; Tardif, 1974).

Yet the detractors of police boards can find much to criticize in such justifications. Their critique ranges from the moderate to the extreme, but despite this it usually shares the same starting point—that the municipal police function is more essentially a municipal service than a judicial or quasi-judicial function, and that its comparability and relationship to other municipal services is of greater significance (in terms of how it should be governed) than any unique "judicial" characteristics it may have.

The moderates, while conceding that the police function includes some quasi-judicial elements which need to be protected from partisan control, argue that such requirements can be met within the framework of normal democratic processes for the control and accountability of municipal services, as they are in the case of many other municipal employees whose role includes a law enforcement function (e.g., building inspectors). Any need for the imposition of standards (be they provincial or federal in scope) which transcend the local jurisdiction can be accomplished, they argue, through directly increasing the authority of relevant provincial or federal agencies, without the need to remove the governance of municipal police entirely from responsible municipal authorities. And they question why, in the case of other services the control of which has been assumed or retained by provincial authorities because of their perceived linkage to the administration of justice (e.g., prosecutorial functions, maintenance and administration of the courts, etc.), the provinces have also assumed the cost of such services, whereas by far the lion's share of municipal police services continues to be paid for out of locally raised funds. They point to the growing sophistication of municipal government, and to the absence of any very clear evidence that modern municipal police forces which are currently directly or primarily governed by municipal authorities are demonstrably inferior to those which are governed by police boards.

More radical critics, however, will challenge the whole notion of municipal policing as a "non-political" function which needs to be protected from the normal political processes of democratic control. In doing so, they will point to the ambiguity of the historical evidence for this position, and particularly to the doubtful nature of the claim that the historical control of the police by the lower judiciary is any real indication of their essentially "judicial" character. The law, they will argue, is itself essentially "political," in the sense that it favours some interests over others. Under these circumstances, they continue, it is simply naive and misleading to suggest that law enforcement (or any other police function) can be essentially a non-political function (see, e.g., Fogelson, 1977:111-12.) They will point to the doubtful historical origins of the notion of police independence in this regard, and to its uncritical acceptance as applicable to contemporary Canadian municipal policing. The notion that the supposed independence of the police requires their governance to be "removed from politics" is, they will claim, no more nor less than a superficially attractive item of packaging for what has always in reality been an attempt to shift an essentially political control of the police from local to central (provincial) authorities. In this connection they will point to the inconsistency of the requirements for police boards (only certain municipalities are required to have them), to the lack of any clearly non-political criteria of eligibility for police board membership, and to the lack of any clear empirical evidence that the members of such boards and their governance of police forces are in fact any less "political" than those of other, more locally controlled, police governing authorities.[103]

Some will go further and argue that the notions of police independence and of police professionalism, and the postures of restraint and passivity which they engender on the part of police governing authorities, are in reality no more than strategies to legitimize the denial of real conflicts in society in order to ensure that the municipal police function is operated for the benefit of certain elite political interests, at the expense of others (see, e.g., Brodgen, 1977).

The advocates of police boards will often respond to such arguments by drawing a distinction between the partisan and the non-partisan interpretation of the term "politics." The purpose of the institution of the police board, they argue, is to protect the police from politics in the partisan sense of the term, and not from politics in a more general sense (see, e.g., Edwards, 1980:70). The response of the critics to such a distinction tends to take two forms, a practical one and a theoretical one. On the practical level, critics point out that even if the validity of the distinction is assumed, there is still an absence of any clear evidence that police board members in their governance of municipal police forces are any less partisan than municipal councils which govern police forces. In particular, they point to the fact that the powers of appointment of members of police boards are always in the hands of partisan politicians, and that legislation governing the composition of such boards not only includes few, if any, prohibitions on partisan appointments, but also typically provides that police board members hold office "at the pleasure" of those politicians who are responsible for their appointment. Furthermore, they point out that in its need to be protected from crass, self-serving political partisanship the police service is essentially no different from a host of other municipal services, and that in this sense all municipal services should be dedicated to the service of the general public interest rather than personal or partisan interests of those who are responsible for their government. Taken to its logical conclusion, they would claim, this argument in favour of police boards would deny legitimacy to almost all forms of direct municipal government by locally elected representatives.

Others, however, would go further to suggest that the theoretical distinction between partisan and non-partisan politics, while superficially attractive, is in reality an unworkable one. The very question as to what is or is not a partisan political decision, they point out, is itself likely to present itself as a political question which will often engender substantial partisan political disagreement. While from an academic point of view this may not be a necessary conclusion, in practical terms it will always be, because the only forum in which the question of whether a police governing authority has acted from partisan motives is in practice resolved in an institution (Parliament, a provincial legislature, a municipal council, or even a government itself) which is entirely committed to the resolution of all political question through the medium of partisan politics. Indeed, proponents of this view argue that partisan politics are a fundamental condition of our current democratic political system, in which the definition of actions or policies as being "in the public interest" depends entirely on the ability of their partisan proponents to convince a majority of the partisan elected representatives that this is the case.[104]

Yet over their 122-year history, and throughout the period in which such debates over their legitimacy as institutions of municipal police governance have raged, police boards in Canada have displayed a bewildering diversity of form and function which seems to defy the simple application to them of such ideological labels. In form, they have ranged (and continue to range) from the highly representative to the highly bureaucratic, and in function they range from those which are highly active in the shaping and supervision over the implementation of police policy, to those which appear to be little more than agencies of almost rubber-stamp approval and public relations for the policy and operational initiatives of highly autonomous chiefs of police. They range from those which place a high priority on their public accountability (or at least on the appearance of public accountability), to those which are perhaps best epitomized by the remark made to the author by one police board chairman to the effect that his board actively discourages public participation in its meetings because its members are of the view that the municipal council is the proper forum for "that sort of thing."

At the present time, however, only the most superficial and tenuous empirical evidence is available on the actual role played by police boards in the governance of Canada's municipal police forces. Indeed, the sparsity of the literature on this subject prompts legitimate questions as to why legal as well as political science scholars have devoted so little attention to the control and accountability of municipal policing, given its considerable political and constitutional significance. That, however, would be subject-matter for an essay which others would undoubtedly be more qualified to write.

For the moment, it seems that in our understanding of the institution of police boards in Canada, we have advanced little from the insights of Fosdick, who in 1920 wrote of the American experience with such boards, that "in the kaleidoscopic variations and adaptations which followed upon the adoption of the board plan of control, it is difficult to trace the line of police development" (1969:80). Fosdick's difficulties in this regard did not dissuade him from a blunt and negative assessment of the American experience with police boards. In Canada, 60 years later, however, much work remains to be done before truly informed judgments can be made about the role of police boards and commissions as institutions of municipal police governance.

ENDNOTES

*This essay is based on research commissioned by the Commission of Inquiry into Certain Activities of the Royal Canadian Mounted Police (the McDonald Inquiry), and completed in 1979. The author wishes to express his gratitude to the commission for its support of this research, as well as to the numerous persons and organizations across Canada who so willingly and extensively co-operated in this research. The views expressed in this essay are those of the author, and do not necessarily reflect those of the commission or of others who participated in the research on which it is based. This essay was presented as a paper at the 52nd Annual Meeting of the Canadian Political Science Association, Université du Québec à Montréal, June 4, 1980.

This chapter was previously published in *Police Deviance in Canada*, C.D. Shearing and E. Mann (eds.). Copyright © 1981, C.D. Shearing and E. Mann. Reprinted by permission of C.D. Shearing, University of Toronto, Centre of Criminology.

1.   For a brief summary of these, see Freedman and Stenning (1977, chap. 2); Kelly and Kelly (1976, part 2).

2.   R.C.M.P. Act, R.S.C. 1970, c. R-9.

3.   Ontario Police Act, R.S.O. 1970, c. 351, Part IV; Quebec Police Act, S.Q. 1968, c. 17, Division III.

4.   The relevant provincial statutes are listed in note 54, below.

5.   E.g., National Harbours Board Act, R.S.C. 1970, c. N-8, section 5; Railway Act, R.S.C. 1970, c. R-2, sections 400-406; Ontario Northland Transportation Commission Act, R.S.O. 1970, c. 326, section 24(6); British Columbia Railway Act, R.S.B.C. 1960, c. 329.

6.   Municipal police governing authorities described in this essay are variously named in different jurisdictions. While in most jurisdictions they are called boards of commissioners of police, in some they are called police commissions. Furthermore, whatever their official designation, they are frequently referred to colloquially as either "police boards" or "police commissions." In order to avoid confusion in this essay the term police board or board will be used throughout to refer to such municipal police boards or commissions. The adoption of this terminology is not intended in any way to derogate from the official nomenclature of municipal police governing authorities in some jurisdictions, but is merely for the purpose of minimizing the reader's possible confusion between these

institutions and the provincial police commissions to which reference is also made in the essay.

7. In 1855, commissioners in Quebec appointed "to investigate and report upon the best means of re-organizing the militia of Canada and upon an improved system of police," recommended that all municipal police forces in Quebec be replaced by members of a newly created provincial police force organized along military lines: see Quebec (1855: 15-20). This recommendation was not implemented, however, and the Quebec Provincial Police Force, which was established in 1870 (by S.Q. 1970, c. 24) was not given anything like such hegemony as the commissioners had recommended.

8. See, e.g., section 15 of Nova Scotia's Townships and Officers Act, Rev. Statutes 1864 (3rd Ser.), c. 47.

9. The first such board was established by An Act to Establish a Police in the Town of Brockville, 2nd Wm. IV, c. 17 (1832).

10. Statutes of Upper Canada, 4th Wm. IV, c. 23 (1834). See in particular sections 22, 57, 65, 74, 77, 78.

11. Vestiges of powers such as this are still to be found today, e.g., in section 2 of the Criminal Code, R.S.C. 1970, c. C-34, which provides that the term "peace officer" includes a "mayor, warden, reeve," etc. Section 212 of Ontario's Municipal Act, R.S.O. 1970, c. 284, still endows mayors with the authority to "call out the posse comitatus to enforce the law within the municipality."

12. The Upper Canada Municipal Corporations Act, 12 Vict., c. 81 (1849).

13. The relevant provisions are: 1873, c. 48, section 333; 1874, c. 16, section 10; 1936, c. 35; 1938, c. 23, section 4; 1943, c. 16, section 7; 1947, c. 77, section 5; 1960, c. 84, section 1; and 1965, c. 99, section 2.

14. City of Charlottetown Incorporation Amendment Act, 1941, c. 24, Section 4.

15. 1858, c. 99. See in particular sections 347-53 and 369-80.

16. Section 348 of the Act, however, clearly provided for the possibility that a city might not have a recorder.

17. 1867, 30-31 Vict., c. 3 (U.K.); reproduced, as amended, in R.S.C. 1970, App. II, No. 5.

18. British Columbia Police Act, 1974, c. 64, sections 19-21, and Alberta Police Act, 1973, c. 44, section 18.

19. Law Reform Act, 1868-69, c. 6, section 15.

20. This was effected through the reform of the magistracy including the abolition of the "police magistrate" as a locally optional office: see Magistrates Act, 1936, c. 35.

21. Police Act, 1946, c. 72, section 6(2).

22. Police Amendment Act, 1958, c. 79, section 1.

23. See *Toronto Globe and Mail*, May 8, 1979, "Judges to continue on police

bodies."

24.   Police Amendment Act, 1979, c. 74.

25.   R. Roy McMurtry, letter to the editor, *Toronto Globe and Mail*, July 23, 1979.

26.   There are currently ten regional police forces (including Metropolitan Toronto) in Ontario.

27.   Municipality of Metropolitan Toronto Act, R.S.O. 1970, c. 295, section 177.

28.   City of Brandon Incorporation Act, 1882, c. 35, sections 119-31; City of Winnipeg Incorporation Act, 1882, c. 36, sections 121-32.

29.   Municipal Institutions Act, 1886, c. 52, sections 352-75.

30.   Brandon Charter Amendment Act, 1949, c. 79, section 3.

31.   Vancouver City Incorporation Act, 1886, c. 32, sections 171-84A; New Westminster City Incorporation Act, 1888, c. 42, sections 165-75.

32.   Municipal Act Amendment Act, 1893, c. 30, section 63.

33.   Municipal Clauses Act, 1896, c. 37, section 217.

34.   See British Columbia Police Act, 1974, c. 64, sections 19-21.

35.   City of Moncton Police Commission Act, 1907, c. 97 (repealed by the City of Moncton Incorporation Act, 1946, c. 101, sections 113-26 which transferred control of the city's police force back to the city council).

36.   City of Fredericton Police Commission Act, 1908, c. 42.

37.   Saint John City Police Commission Act, 1960-61, c. 133. Apparently no board has ever been established pursuant to this statute, and the city police force is still governed by the city council.

38.   The Marysville Police Commission Act, 1971, c. 82, also provided for the creation of a police board for that municipality, but the municipality became a part of Fredericton shortly thereafter. New Brunswick's new Police Act, 1977, c. P-9.2, provides for optional police boards for municipalities having their own police forces. These provisions were proclaimed in force in December 1980.

39.   Cities Act, 1908, c. 16, section 79.

40.   Cities Act, 1915, c. 16, section 92.

41.   City of Charlottetown Incorporation Amendment Act, 1938, c. 29, section 2. The new P.E.I. Police Act, 1977, c. 28, Part V, provides for the establishment of police boards in the province's municipalities; the Act, however, has not yet been proclaimed in force.

42.   City Act, 1951, c. 9, sections 81-91. Provisions for a police board for the city of Calgary, however, were enacted in 1934 in section 309 of the Calgary Charter, 1893, c. 33, as amended by 1934, c. 72, section 9.

43.   Municipal Government Act, 1968, c. 68, sections 94-101.

44.   Police Act, 1971, c. 85, sections 9-23.

45.   Montreal Urban Community Act, 1969, c. 84, sections 196-241. See now the Public Security Council of the M.U.C. Act, 1977, c. 71.

46.   Police Act, 1974, c. 9, sections 19-21.

47.   E.g., the Fredericton Police Commission from 1908-11: see Fredericton Police Commission Act, 1908, c. 42.

48.   E.g., existing police boards in Alberta: see Alberta Police Act, 1973, c. 44, sections 23-27. Also the Vancouver and New Westminster police boards from 1888-1906 and 1890-1900 respectively: see note 31, above. Also police boards in Saskatchewan from 1908-15: see note 39, above.

49.   E.g., the police boards in some British Columbia municipalities (other than Vancouver) from 1917-57: see Municipal Act Amendment Act, 1917, c. 45, section 61.

50.   A more detailed description of this variety will be found in Stenning (1981: part 1, chap. 1).

51.   Information supplied to the author by the Ontario Police Commission.

52.   See, e.g., section 11 of the Ontario Police Act, R.S.O. 1970, c. 351.

53.   See, e.g., sections 462-71 of the City of Winnipeg Act, 1971, c. 105.

54.   The following is a list of the relevant provincial statutes governing existing and proposed police boards in Canada: B.C., Police Act, 1974, c. 64, sections 19-21; Alberta, Police Act, 1973, c. 44, sections 23-27; Saskatchewan, Police Act, R.S.S. 1978, c. P-15, sections 27-36; Manitoba, Brandon Charter Amendment Act, 1949, c. 79, section 3, and City of Winnipeg Act, 1971, c. 105, sections 462-72; Ontario, Police Act, R.S.O. 1970, c. 351, sections 8-17; Quebec, Public Security Council of the M.U.C. Act, 1977, c. 71; New Brunswick, Police Act, 1977, c. P-9.2, sections 7-9, and Fredericton Police Commission Act, 1908, c. 42, as amended; Nova Scotia, Police Act, 1974, c. 9, sections 19-21; P.E.I., Police Act, 1977, c. 28, Part V. Ten statutes providing for regional governments in Ontario (including Metropolitan Toronto) also provide for police boards for these regions, but are too numerous to be listed here.

55.   The Metropolitan Toronto Board, however, which administers the largest municipal police force in Canada (5,384 policemen and 1,126 other employee in 1979), has a separate staff of seven, consisting of an executive secretary, a secretary, an assistant secretary, two clerks, a liaison officer (who investigates minor matters for the board), and a civilian labour relations officer. The board however, can call on the ad hoc assistance of any member of the force.

56.   The Toronto and Regina boards, for instance, meet once every two weeks. The Public Security Council in Montreal meets every week.

57.   As an example of such a "crunch issue," he cited the decision as to whether his force's patrol cars should be equipped with shotguns.

58.   In Ontario, however, and possibly in other jurisdictions too, it sometimes hap-

pens that a person is appointed to a board by the provincial authorities on the clear understanding that that person will be elected chairman. The only way in which such an understanding can be ultimately enforced, of course, is through the power which the provincial authorities have over the appointment of the majority of members of the board. Another practice which has occurred on at least two occasions in Ontario is that of the provincial authorities appointing a person to be a judge for the express purpose of immediately appointing him to membership of a police board.

59.   *Re a Reference under the Constitutional Questions Act,* [1957] O.R. 28 at 30 (Ontario Court of Appeal).

60.   Nova Scotia Police Act, 1974, c. 9, section 20; City of Winnipeg Act, 1971, c. 105, section 465.

61.   A brief account of these changes will be found in Stenning (1981: part 1, at 33-34, and part 3, at 74-78).

62.   In the event of a dispute between a police board and a municipal council over a municipal police force budget, section 14(3) of the Ontario Police Act, R.S.O. 1970, c. 351, gives authority to resolve such dispute to the Ontario Police Commission. This power, however, was only first formally exercised in 1981, in a dispute concerning the budget of the Niagara Regional Police force. A similar provision is to be found in section 23 of the British Columbia Police Act, 1974, c. 64.

63.   See City of Winnipeg By-Law No. 2150/78, section 7. Recently, however, there have been recommendations to re-establish the Winnipeg Police Commission with a much broader mandate: see Ross (1980: 40-42).

64.   See note 62, above.

65.   This is an illustrative, rather than an exhaustive, list. Police board rules and regulations are not normally public documents, and during the research in preparation for this essay, the author neither sought nor was offered access to such documents in most instances.

66.   See, e.g., Maloney (1975).

67.   See, e.g., *Toronto Globe and Mail,* September 12, 1979, "Godfrey joins Sewell, backs review of complaints over police."

68.   See, e.g., sections 377-86 of Ontario's Municipal Act, R.S.O. 1970, c. 284.

69.   E.g., *Glasbrook Bros. v. Glamorgan County Council et al.,* [1925] A.C. 270; *Fisher v. Oldham Corporation,* [1930] All E.R. Rep. 96; A.-G. *for New South Wales v. Perpetual Trustee Co.,* [1955] 1 All E.R. 846; *R. v. Metropolitan Police Commissioner ex parte Blackburn,* [1968] 1 All E.R. 763.

70.   E.g., *Nettleton v. Prescott* (1908), 16 O.L.R. 538; *Bruton v. Regina Policemen's Association* (1945), 3 D.L.R. 437; *R. v. Labour Relations Board ex parte Fredericton* (1955), 38 M.P.R. 26; *Myers v. Hoffman,* [1955] O.R. 965; *The King v. Labour Relations Board (N.S.)* (1951), 4 D.L.R. 227; *Re*

St. Catharine's Police Association and Board of Police Commissioners for the City of St. Catharine's (1974), 1 O.R. 430; Re Nicholson and Haldimand-Norfolk Regional Board of Commissioners of Police (1979), 88 D.L.R. (3d) 671.

71.   Great Britain, Royal Commission on the Police (1962a: chap. 4).

72.   See Great Britain, Royal Commission on Criminal Procedure (1981: 2-4).

73.   See, e.g., Anderson (1929); Marshall (1965); Cull (1975); Plehwe (1974); Mitchell (1962); Gillance and Khan (1975); Leigh (1975); Milte and Weber (1977); Edwards (1980).

74.   [1968] 1 All E.R. 763 at 769.

75.   See note 70, above.

76.   Examples of the uncritical acceptance of the applicability of the English notion of police independence to the Canadian situation abound: see e.g., Ontario, Task Force on Policing in Ontario (1974: 15); Canada, Canadian Committee on Corrections (1969: 45); Kelly and Kelly (1976: 201-2).

77.   (1981), 17 C.R. (3d) 193.

78.   See, e.g., Toronto Globe and Mail, January 19, 1973, "30% abused bail law last year, Bick says."

79.   See. e.g., Toronto Globe and Mail, January 25, 1973, "Political control of commission would hinder police, chief says."

80.   Interview with the author, July 1979.

81.   Interview with the author, July 1979.

82.   1946, c. 72.

83.   Quebec in 1968, Manitoba and Alberta in 1971 (the Alberta Police Commission was disbanded two years later, however), British Columbia in 1974, Saskatchewan in 1975, Nova Scotia in 1976, New Brunswick in 1978.

84.   The functions of the Alberta Commission, disbanded in 1973, are now essentially performed by a Director of Law Enforcement (who is a member of the provincial solicitor general's department) and a Law Enforcement Appeal Board: see Alberta Police Act, 1973, c. 44, sections 4-17.

85.   Police Act, 1977, c. 28, Part I.

86.   A more thorough description of provincial police commissions will be found in Stenning (1981: part 2).

87.   R.S.O. 1970, c. 101.

88.   This, at least, is clearly the way it has been interpreted by provincial attorneys general: see, e.g., Bales (1973).

89.   Edmonton City By-Law No. 4188, section 12, however, imposes reporting requirements (to the city council) on the Edmonton police board. Some provincial Police Acts also require boards to report certain information to provincial

police commissions.

90. See. e.g., section 10(3) of the Ontario Police Act, R.S.O. 1970, c. 351.

91. *Re McAuliffe and Metropolitan Toronto Board of Commissioners of Police* (1976), 9 O.R. (2d) 583.

92. A notable example of how these various indirect pressures may come to bear on a municipal police board is the recent series of events surrounding Chief Brown and the Waterloo Regional Police Force. A description of these events will be found in the court decision in *Re Brown and Waterloo Regional Police Commissioners Board and Ontario Police Commission* (1979), 13 C.R. (3d) 46, and in Stenning (1981: part 2, at 80-88).

93. See Ontario, Ottawa-Carleton Review Commission (1976); Ontario, Royal Commission on Metropolitan Toronto (1977); Ontario, Waterloo Region Review Commission (1979).

94. See Ontario, Hamilton-Wentworth Review Commission (1978).

95. With respect to these allegations, see *Toronto Globe and Mail,* February 6, 1978, "Investigator's Status on Police Board Probed, " and ibid., December 6, 1978, "Ex-Halton Police Commissioner Won't be Charged, Officials Say."

96. Bill No. 68 (1981).

97. See *Toronto Globe and Mail,* September 18, 1979, "Council Censures Police Commission." In May 1980 the executive of Metropolitan Toronto Council voted in support of a proposal that the Toronto board should be enlarged from five to seven members, the majority of whom should be appointed by the Metropolitan Toronto Council: see *Toronto Globe and Mail,* May 28, 1980, "Metro to Seek Majority on Police Board."

98. For an account of this dispute, see Stenning (1981: part 3, at 74-78).

99. 1973, Bill No. 43. See also 1975, Bill No. 89.

100. Police Act, 1977, c. P-9.2, sections 7-9.

101. See *Toronto Globe and Mail,* December 12, 1977, "Trudeau: Keep Politicians Ignorant of Police Actions," and the critique of Trudeau's statement by Edwards (1980: 94-97).

102. See, e.g., the passage from Lord Denning's judgment in *R. v. Metropolitan Police Commissioner ex parte Blackburn,* [1968] 1 All E.R. 763 at 769, quoted above at 187-88.

103. Edwards (1980: 72), however, has argued that in the debate over police boards the onus is on their detractors to produce evidence that police boards display "subservience to the will of the Provincial Executive."

104. The so-called "Nicholson Affair," which involved the resignation of the Commissioner of the RCMP in 1959, may be viewed as a classic illustration of this point: see, Canada, House of Commons Debates, March 16, 1959, at 1959-66 and 2005-7. The incident is discussed in Stenning (1981: part 3, at 35-39).

REFERENCES

Aitchison, J.H. 1949. "The Municipal Corporations Act of 1849." *Canadian Historical Review* 30: 107-22.

Alberta, Board of Review. 1975. *Administration of Justice in the Provincial Courts of Alberta: Report No. 2.* Edmonton.

Anderson, J. 1929. "The Police." *Public Administration* 7: 192.

Arthurs, H.W. 1971. *Collective Bargaining by Public Employees in Canada: Five Models*, chap. 4: "The Formal Public Sector Model: Collective Bargaining by Police Forces in Ontario." Ann Arbor: Institute of Labour and Industrial Relations, Wayne State University-University of Michigan.

Bales, D. 1973. "Address to the Association of Municipal Police Governing Authorities." *Crown's Newsletter* (June 1973): 1-7.

Barot, D., and N. Bérard. 1972. *Etude Historico-Juridique: Organisation et pouvoirs de la police.* Montréal: Centre International de Criminologie Comparée, Université de Montréal.

Brogden, M. 1977. "A Police Authority—The Denial of Conflict." *Sociological Review* 25: 325-49.

Canada, Canadian Committee on Corrections. 1969. *Toward Unity: Criminal Justice and Corrections* (the Ouiment Report). Ottawa: Queen's Printer.

Canada, Statistics Canada. 1978. *Police Administration Statistics 1977.* Ottawa: Statistics Canada.

Critchley, T. A. 1975. *A History of Police in England and Wales.* London: Constable.

Cull, H.A. 1978. "The Enigma of a Police Constable's Status." *Victoria University of Wellington Law Review* 8: 148-69.

Edwards, J.Ll.J. 1980. *Ministerial Responsibility for National Security.* Ottawa: Department of Supply and Services Canada.

Fogelson, R.M. 1977. *Big-City Police.* Cambridge, Mass.: Harvard University Press.

Fosdick, R.B. 1969. *American Police Systems.* Montclair, N.J.: Patterson Smith.

Freedman, D.J., and P.C. Stenning. 1977. *Private Security, Police and the Law in Canada.* Toronto: Centre of Criminology, University of Toronto.

Gillance, K., and A.N. Khan 1975. "The Constitutional Independence of a Police Constable in the Exercise of the Powers of his Office." *Police Journal* 48: 55-62.

Great Britain, Royal Commission on the Police. 1962a. *Final Report.* London: HMSO.

_____, 1962b. *Appendix II to the Minutes of Evidence*. London: HMSO.

Great Britain, Royal Commission on Criminal Procedure. 1981. *The Investigation and Prosecution of Criminal Offences in England and Wales: The Law and Procedure* (Cmnd. 8092-1). London: HMSO.

Gregory, G.F. 1979. "Police Power and the Role of the Provincial Minister of Justice." *Chitty's Law Journal* 27: 13-18.

Harrison, R.A. (ed.) 1859. *The New Municipal Manual*. Toronto: Maclear and Co.

Kelly, W., and N. Kelly. 1976. *Policing in Canada*. Toronto: Macmillan/Maclean-Hunter.

Leigh, L.H. 1975. *Police Powers in England and Wales*. London: Butterworths.

Maloney, A. 1975. *The Metropolitan Toronto Review of Citizen-Police Complaint Procedure*. A Report of the Metropolitan Toronto Board of Commissioners of Police, May 12, 1975.

Marshall, G. 1965. *Police and Government*. London: Methuen and Co.

McDougall, A.K. 1971a. "Law and Politics: The Case of Police Independence in Ontario." Paper presented to 43rd Annual Meeting of Canadian Political Science Association, June 1971 (unpublished).

_____, 1971b. "Policing in Ontario: The Occupational Dimension to Provincial-Municipal Relations." Doctoral thesis, University of Toronto, 1971.

Milte, K.L., and T.A. Weber. 1977. *Police in Australia*. Sydney: Butterworths.

Mitchell, J.D.B. 1962. "The Constitutional Position of the Police in Scotland." *Juridical Review* 7 ns: 1-20.

Moir, E. 1969. *The Justice of the Peace*. Harmondsworth, U.K.: Penguin Books.

Ontario, Hamilton-Wentworth Review Commission. 1978. *Report*. Toronto: Queen's Printer.

Ontario, Ottawa-Carleton Review Commission. 1976. *Report*. Toronto: Queen's Printer.

Ontario Police Commission 1978. *Report on an Inquiry into Police Practices of the Waterloo Regional Police Force*. Toronto: Ontario Police Commission.

Ontario, Royal Commission into Metropolitan Toronto Police Practices. 1976. *Report* (the Morand Report). Toronto.

Ontario Royal Commission on Metropolitan Toronto 1977. Report (the Robarts Report). Vol. 2: *Detailed Findings and Recommendations*. Toronto: Queen's Printer.

Ontario, Task Force on Policing in Ontario. 1974. Report, *The Police Are the Public and the Public Are the Police*. Toronto, 1974.

Ontario, Waterloo Region Review Commission. 1978. *Police Governance in Waterloo Region*. Toronto: Queen's Printer.

_____, 1979. *Report.* Toronto: Queen's Printer.

Plehwe, R. 1974. "Police and Government: the Commissioner of Police for the Metropolis." *Public Law:* 316-35.

Quebec, Commissioners appointed to Investigate and Report upon the Best Means of Re-organizaing the Militia of Canada, and Upon an Improved System of Police. 1855. *Report.* Quebec: Derbishire and Desbarrats.

Reiner, Robert. 1978. *The Blue Coated Worker.* Cambridge: Cambridge University Press.

Ross, P.S., and Partners. 1980. *A Review of the Operating Efficiency and Effectiveness of the Winnipeg Police Department: Final Report.* Edmonton: P.S. Ross and Partners.

Stenning, Philip C. 1981. *Police Commissions and Boards in Canada.* Toronto: Centre of Criminology, University of Toronto.

Swan, K. 1980. "Interest Arbitration of Non-Economic Issues in Police Bargaining" in B.M. Downie, and R.L. Jackson (eds.) *Conflict and Co-Operation in Police Labour Relations.* Ottawa: Department of Supply and Services Canada.

Tardif, G. 1974. *Police et Politique au Québec.* Montréal: éditions de L'Aurore.

PROTECTING PROFIT

CHAPTER 19
Taking Care Of Labor:
The Police
in American Politics

BRUCE C. JOHNSON

American police have been the object of much social science scrutiny during
the last fifteen years, for reasons which should be obvious to all. One of the
most promising recent developments within this field has been the program-
matic declaration of a "new" criminology which labels itself as critical, radical,
Marxist.[1] Many of the preoccupations and claims of this school of thought are
not new to social science generally, having long ago found a place in sociology
and in legal scholarship. Still, this scholarly insurgency is a welcome step
toward maturity for criminology, a discipline too long abjectly subservient to
the criminal justice agencies which it studies.

The chief strengths of the new criminology are its critical distance from
the legal order and its determination to build a systemic analysis of criminal
justice functioning. The new criminology recognizes that the state and its
agencies are not neutral arbiters of social and economic disputes, much less
the embodiment of the public interest and the public will. The legal order is
rather a servant to power, the guarantor of society's class and status
inequities. Particular instances of such inequities in the United States are well-
known. In policepatrol activities, plea bargaining, access to legal counsel, jury
composition and more, criminal justice serves as an affliction upon the poor,
the non-white and the outcast. The new criminology's second strength is that
it seeks to integrate these various specialized findings into a coherent structural
analysis of the legal order as a whole.

Despite these assets, the new criminology remains to date a flawed enterprise. It claims Karl Marx as a mentor, but produces work which Marx would
have found wanting. The new criminology is neither historical nor dialectical.[2]
This reproach has nothing to do with a condemnation of heresies from the
faith. It is rather a matter of apprehending what remains valuable in Marx's

work, of grasping those intellectual guidelines which have been absorbed by the best social scholarship of the last century. Marxist or not. The new criminology has some distance to travel in this regard.

Social life is historically conditioned and imbedded; all particular concatenations of social institutions and processes are the product of specific historical forces. This means that one must build a time dimension into social analysis. Timeless social science propositions are intrinsically incomplete, be they cast in terms of intersubjective understandings among small groups of people or universally valid social laws. Understanding these things, Marx made the notion of historical development, in its continuities and discontinuities alike, central to his work.

The notion of the dialectic, stripped of mystification, comes down to something like the following. Societies and social institutions always exhibit contradictions, the simultaneous existence of stabilizing and disruptive elements. Further, specific institutions serve progressive roles in some situations and regressive roles in others. This means that stable social structures must be studied with reference to the elements which undermine them, and social change with reference to its constraints. No social system is perfectly integrated, and propositions which suggest so (e.g., the law serves the ruling class) are as likely to mislead as illuminate.

This essay, then, is rooted in a sympathetic critique of the new criminology. The critical approach to the criminal justice system comes alive only when it is historical and sensitive to social contradictions. The police are a natural center of attention in criminal justice studies, for they are the system's gatekeepers. It is police activities which provide the prosecutorial, judicial and correctional apparatuses with involuntary clients to process. The police are the only criminal justice functionaries with which most citizens ever interact. For the American case in particular, local public police are far more important than their state or federal counterparts. Most penal code provisions in the U.S. are state (not federal) enactments; criminal jurisdiction is mostly delegated to local (not state) authorities.

Further, no comprehensive analysis of the American legal order can afford to ignore the nation's vast private police apparatus. We cannot rest with that narrow definition of police which includes only public employees with police powers, so-called sworn personnel. A wider definition, including anyone doing security-related work, is more appropriate. This latter demarcation draws in not only private police (museum attendants, bouncers, private investigators and more), but also government guards (in prisons, parks, toll bridges, and other settings). One careful, though necessarily incomplete count, indicated that there were some 805,000 police in the United States in 1969.[3] Of these, 324,000 were local sworn personnel and 71,000 were state and federal sworn personnel; 120,000 were government guards and 290,000 were private police.

The American legal order is characterized by profound contradictions, internal cleavages which were astonishing in the past and which even today remain prominent. If criminal justice and police work in the United States constitute a system, it is not a unitary one. It is rather an apparatus whose multiple parts serve different masters. The new criminology's polemic claim that American law serves capitalist elites makes sense for courts, extra-local public police and private police (though even here, significant variability exists). These agencies, so to speak, have taken care of business. However, local public police (the most important single component of our criminal justice system) have "*taken care of labor.*" Today and over time, local public police have been accessible to the viewpoints and preoccupations of the American working class; many of their activities have served and do serve to defend or extend the (modest) social privileges of this class. This recognition is the key which unlocks American police work, past and present.

In both England and America, the modern criminal justice system was inaugurated during the second quarter of the nineteenth century. The hallmark of this transformation and initial modernization was the creation of the police as a separately administered and paid component of the criminal justice system. The London police were organized in 1929. Allan Silver and others have argued that a central impetus of this event was the sense of threat to the social order which two social phenomena had aroused in respectable sections of English society.[4] The first was a diffuse and apparently expanding criminality. The second was the political agitations of the "dangerous classes." Roger Lane's analysis of the early history of the Boston police indicates that American police forces had origins very similar to these.[5]

The police debut, then, was similarly timed and motivated in the two societies. Thereafter, however, developments began to diverge rather sharply. Normative violence and civil strife declined markedly in England, while they have remained prominent features of American life to this day. During the first third of the nineteenth century, there was a considerable amount of violent working class protest in England.[6] That violence ran its course soon after Robert Peel founded the London police. The passing of collective violence from the English scene was accompanied by a steady growth in what Silver calls the "moral assent" offered to police by the general population. In the United States, by contrast, a policeman's command has always been more likely to inspire fear than respect.

Numerous American social scientists have found in these well-known contrasts a basis for Anglophilia. Edward Shils and others have characterized English society as socially integrated, cohesive and happy. Yet it can be persuasively argued that political civility and social deference are but surface features of English life.[7] Looking deeper, we see that class conflict continued to develop in England throughout the nineteenth century and into the present one.[8] Similarly, Shils misleads when he locates the disorderliness of American life in a series of general cultural failings.[9] It is more to the point to look to the concrete historical development of American politics. Over time, diverse dispossessed segments of American society have failed in their strenuous attempts to build progressive movements, radical or reformist. Consequently, these non-elites have been reduced to destructive and conservatizing conflicts among themselves.[10]

Significant aspects of these larger developments can be illuminated by scrutiny of American police work. The United States is almost unique among advanced industrial nations in its persistent extension of the penal code (and thus, of police work) into areas of obvious normative disagreement. Various social groups in America, alert to the power of the legal sanction, have agitated for the inclusion of almost any kind of behavior which they find objectionable in the penal code. This agitation has met with considerable success. One classic example is the criminalization of various activities associated with labor organizing; another is the criminalization of nonvictim behaviors, such as public drinking, consensual sexual activities and drug use. In regard to early police participation in class and status conflicts, the case of Boston is instructive.

The Boston police force was organized as a group of fulltime professionals in 1837, after three major riots. Two of these three were anti-Irish nativist outbursts. Crime and political unrest continued to be serious problems in Boston at least through 1870. Lane sees this social dislocation as associated in one way or another with the massive Irish influx into Boston. The Irish gained steadily in political power in Boston after the Civil War. Lane closes his narrative in 1885; by that time, Irish-Americans were a substantial component of the Boston police force. We may consider that the Irish moved to join the police force in order to protect their own community.

Even before the Irish entered the Boston police force in large numbers, the respectable elements of Boston society (abolitionists, prohibitionists and large property holders) were profoundly disturbed by their police department. Lane explains this discontent by noting that American police exhibited much more "organic involvement" in the community which they policed than did

English police. English policemen were denied the vote (as were most ordinary Englishmen of that time). Further, English police were closely supervised in their choice of residence and off-duty employment, and were bureaucratically responsible to Parliament rather than to local authorities.

Much less central control was exerted over the Boston police of the time. As a consequence, officers often stood by while mobs attacked abolitionists, typically declined to enforce the wide variety of vice laws on the books, and otherwise offended middle class proprieties. Respectable Bostonians made a concerted effort during the 1860's to imitate the English pattern of control. Specifically, they sought to transfer direction of the Boston police from the city to the state. Similar efforts were made in numerous other American cities during this period. In many cities, these efforts succeeded for a time, though they were strenuously resisted by political forces based in lower status sectors of the white community. In New York City, for instance, two competing police departments fought one another during 1857.

The problematic success of these early control efforts is illustrated by the fact that late in the nineteenth century, another wave of police reform efforts occurred in American cities.[11] The manifest concern of most of these reform efforts, early and late, was police corruption (e.g., toleration of vice and participation in election fraud). These reform efforts, however, were not simply episodes of selfless and high-minded civic upgrading. Very often, they involved Republican efforts to discredit Democratic party machines. Further, direct protection of business was occasionally involved. Lane notes that when state control over the Boston police was finally achieved in 1885, the new police commissioners had the police assume the locally unpopular function of protecting during strikes.

The social basis for this community involvement by urban American police during the nineteenth century may be briefly noted. From 1840 onward, the United States was industrializing rapidly. Immigrants, who provided the essential manpower base for this economic development, flooded into American cities. Immigrants also became the basic manpower source for urban police departments at this time. Further, police officers tended to be recruited from a special subset of the immigrant population. The Irish were a very substantial fraction of many urban police departments by the late nineteenth century. The second great influx of police officers came from the Italian community.

The police forces of the urban North maintained their ethnic character over time. Many of them continued to be closely intermeshed with local political machines and with the Catholic Church. Both of these latter institutions tended to be Irish-dominated. Police officers of the time were dependent upon these institutions, especially the political machines, for their jobs. Each new election raised the possibility of massive manpower turnover in a given police department. The frankly political character of police departments in this era was such that in 1868, Allan Pinkerton, the founder of the famed private detective agency, turned down an opportunity to become head of the New York Police Department. His reason for doing so was that:

> political influence would only prevent the operation of the depart-
> ment in the manner in which I would want to conduct it, making
> necessary changes for the interest of efficiency.[12]

The frustrations experienced by George Walling, who actually was head of the NYPD during this period, suggest that Pinkerton knew whereof he spoke.[13]

Control of local public police forces was a deep and persistent political problem for higher status whites in the urban North throughout the last half of the nineteenth century. The community involvement of the police was a thorn in the side of middle-class and upper-class elements of these cities. One of their responses, as noted, was to seek to remove control of police departments from the local setting. By and large, this strategy was fruitless. Even in those instances where extralocal control was formally imposed, the results were far from satisfactory from the standpoint of the *haute bourgeoisie*. Since administrative ineffectiveness was deeply rooted in these municipal police departments, even the establishment of formal control was but the beginning of the task of reform.

At this juncture, a fateful choice was made by the respectable elements in American cities, and by business elements in particular. These elements turned away from local police departments. They began to place their reliance upon police forces of their own creation, private ones. One cannot speak here of a coordinated extra-local decision of a class-conscious sort. Big business in particular did not develop a substantial class consciousness in America until the Progressive era.[14] Private police were an experiment, a thrust into the unknown whose significance varied by locality. Nonetheless, private police grew steadily in importance as the nineteenth century wore on. What began as a tentative experiment evolved into a central feature of American law enforcement.

The emergence of private police is a development of enormous importance for this period of American urban history. This development profoundly undermined the American legal order and the public order generally. It underscored the political untouchability and irresponsibility of big business in America.[15] One later consequence was the disproportionate violence of

American labor history. In effect elites in America withheld their "moral assent" from the social and political order to the same substantial degree as did many elements of the mass of American citizens.

Private police were not the only strategic alternative available to American business interests at this time. Even if one concedes that from their own standpoint, there was a substantial need for policing and a substantial unavailability of local police departments, at least one obvious alternative to private police existed. A national police force could have been created. Canada and Australia, which faced a similar array of police problems, turned very early in their histories to such centralized public police forces. For instance, the Royal Canadian Mounted Police was established in 1873, at the very outset of industrialization in that country. In the United States, the Federal Bureau of Investigation was not even created until 1908 and did not assume important duties until the 1920's. Thus did the well-known decentralization of political power and authority in the United States serve to undermine the public order generally.

The first large private police force in the United States was the Pinkerton Detective Agency.[16] Its initial expansion during the 1850's was subsidized by the railroad industry. By 1870, Pinkerton's was the leading American police organization. The later notoriety of Pinkerton's in strike-breaking has obscured the major role which this private agency played in law enforcement during the nineteenth century. Much of the initial modernization of American police work was carried out by Pinkerton's. Pinkerton's was the first to fully develop the detective as an occupational role, and the first to use fingerprints as a tool for identification. Pinkerton's was far more effective in apprehending criminals than were local police departments. There were two reasons for this, beyond its unquestioned loyalty to business interests. It had superior investigative competence and mobility across all jurisdictional boundaries.

Befitting its corporate clientele, Pinkerton's specialized in the investigation of major property crimes. These included bank, train and jewel robberies, and insurance fraud. Prior to the Civil War, bankers and other victims of such crimes usually sought no more than recovery of the stolen goods. Pinkerton's set out to change this norm. It convinced these industries that legal prosecution of thieves was a more useful goal than mere recovery of the loot. The idea was that making legal prosecution more certain would reduce the incidence of robbery. The means to legal prosecution was the organization of protective associations staffed (of course) by Pinkerton's. Eventually, Pinkerton's came to guard thousands of banks and jewelry stores.

The formative decades of modern American police work roughly include the half-century following 1830. These years saw substantial community involvement on the part of the local public police, and the consequent emergence of large-scale private police organizations. During the middle period of American police history (roughly 1880-1930), the strains inherent in the existence of this dual police apparatus revealed themselves ever more clearly. My analysis of this latter period will focus upon labor conflict, since it was this era's pre-eminent police problem. Historians agree that the United States has had "the bloodiest and most violent labor history of any industrial nation in the world."[17] Most of the violence surrounding American labor history was instigated by elites, business or governmental. The repression of the *Industrial Workers of the World* is perhaps the outstanding episode of elite violence in the industrial sphere, though there are many competitors for this dubious distinction. Most worker violence in the United States, and there has not been much of it, has been a desperate response to elite violence. What distinguishes American labor history in a comparative framework is not simply violence, but the extraordinary duration and intensity of employer repression of labor organization.

The first year of massive labor organizing activity in the United States was 1877. Throughout the six decades or so following this date, employers made the legal order a central instrument of their anti-labor actions. Labor strikes were legalized in England in 1824, and in many other European countries during the 1860's.[18] In the United States, strikes were not legalized until 1935. In other words, strikes were legalized very early in industrialization in Europe, and very late in the United States. The same is true of other activities associated with labor organizing, such as joining a union and picketing. Until the New Deal reforms took hold, labor organizing in the United States was a police problem by definition.

The American legal order institutionalized those libertarian features celebrated in high school civics texts only recently. One usually understands the legal order as counterposed to violence, though not to force. This is not true of American law during the six decades in question. During this period, American courts were heavily involved (through the use of the injunction and other devices) in sanctioning and legitimating elite violence, giving it the color of legality. Police participation in this grim drama varied markedly according to the three major divisions: public police, local and extralocal, and private police.

Private police were prominent in the repression of labor organizing. When the courts accepted the private apparatus as a legitimate source of criminal cases in labor disputes, they opened a very wide gate indeed. For instance, it was Pinkerton operatives who obtained the evidence necessary to bring to trial the leaders of the Molly Maguires in the Ohio Valley during the 1870's and the leaders of the Mafia in the South during the first decade of the twentieth century. Both the Mollys and this early Mafia were ethnically-based labor organizations (Irish and Italian, respectively). Local public police were unavailable for the duties which Pinkerton's undertook in these two instances, for reasons explained above.

By Horan's count, Pinkerton's helped to break seventy-seven strikes between 1869 and 1892. Two of the most important of these were the 1888 strike of the Chicago, Burlington, and Quincy Railroad and the 1892 Homestead (Pa.) steel strike. These strike-breaking activities made Pinkerton's bitterly and widely hated. For instance, the 1892 Populist Party platform was composed at a time when agrarian protestors were seeking labor allies; in it, Pinkerton's was condemned by name.

After 1892, the private police role in strike-breaking as such tapered off, partly due to the pressure of public opinion. But this specific decline bespoke no general exit of private police from labor conflict. During the first third of the twentieth century, private police activities against labor organizations tended to be carried out on a smaller scale than earlier, but they remained exceptionally significant as instruments of repression. Among the most important of these smaller-scale activities was industrial espionage. Labor spying, carried out on a massive scale during this period, enabled employers to penetrate and destroy many nascent labor organizations by exposing potential union leaders. This spying was backed up by a massive blacklisting apparatus in many industries.

Beyond industrial espionage, private police were involved during the Progressive era in numerous extravagant trials of labor leaders. Pinkerton's set up two infamous legal prosecutions of radicals in the West. These were the trials following the 1905 Steunenberg murder in Idaho and the 1916 Preparedness Day bombing in San Francisco. Both episodes were widely regarded at the time as frameups; subsequent historical research has confirmed this view. Further, the Burns Detective Agency (a Pinkerton competitor) was involved in two other legal prosecutions of moderate labor leaders during this period.[19] The first was the campaign against the *Union Labor Party* leadership in San Francisco between 1906 and 1912. The second was the prosecution of the *Los Angeles Times* bombing of 1910.

The fact that private police were little used for large-scale anti-labor operations after 1892 does not mean that such operations ceased after this period. The void left by the departure of the private police was taken up by state and federal police organizations. The initial impetus for the formation of many state police forces in the United States was repression of the labor movement. William Preston has dissected the remarkable process by which corporate interests and private police managed during the first third of this century to pass the anti-labor torch to federal government agencies such as the Bureau of Immigration and the U.S. Army.[20] During the nationwide 1919 steel strike, most of the large scale antilabor action was carried out by state police and federal marshalls, though the private police had some role. The larger point is that, when massive coercive resources were sought during labor conflict, employers consistently bypassed local public police forces throughout the half-century under consideration.

The specific role which local public police played during industrial conflicts varied according to the political and cultural setting. The most dramatic episodes of local public police support for labor occurred in medium-sized industrial cities of the Midwest and East. Herbert Gutman's work has brought to light numerous episodes wherein police deputized strikers, arrested strike-breakers, and the like.[21] Gutman argues that in such towns, industrializing elites were often seen as an intrusive and alien force. During labor disputes in this setting, all local social elements (including the middle class) tended to unite behind the workers. The typical employer response in these situations was to bring in private police or state police.

The other end of the spectrum is represented by company towns in the West. Local public police could hardly avoid acquiescing to employers in these settings, since the latter often entirely financed the town government in question. This did not give such employers a free hand, however, for the workers situated in company towns (miners, lumberjacks) exhibited extraordinary solidarity and toughness in their organizing efforts. Consequently, even in their own preserves, employers faced with labor agitation frequently resorted to private police or state police.

During labor conflict in large industrial cities, the behavior of local public police tended to fall between the extremes just discussed. Only one such episode will be examined here, the Pullman strike of 1894. This strike was one of the most important in American history. It destroyed the *American Railway Union*, the first strong and effective mass labor organization to emerge in the United States. Pullman was a company town near Chicago. The strike itself was basically centered in Chicago, though it had regional and national dimensions for a time. This strike provides a significant case study in the process of corporate decision-making with regard to coercive resources in urban strike situations.[22]

The Pullman strike substantially disrupted Chicago life, especially during the period when the boycott of all trains was being pressed by the ARU. Nonetheless, public sympathy for the strikers persisted. This posture was shared by the Chicago police. They actively supported strikers' relief committees. They sought to interfere with an inflammatory anti-strike publicity campaign carried out by newspapers, as by harassing newsboys. Finally, these local police failed on numerous occasions to prevent railroad property from being damaged by protestors.

The political unreliability of local public police was well-known to the railroad interests at the outset of the strike. Their first response was to mobilize private police. When the strike escalated past the control capabilities of these forces, the railroads moved to bring extra-local public forces into the conflict. Illinois Governor Altgeld hesitated for a time, wrestling with his pro-labor sympathies, but eventually state militia were sent in. President Cleveland had no such ambivalence, and dispatched federal troops at the first opportunity. Of the thirteen people killed and fifty-three seriously wounded during the strike in Chicago, none were harmed by local police. State troops and federal marshalls carried out the bulk of this violence.

The American economy's industrializing period lasted around eight decades (c. 1840-1920). Throughout this time, the working class in the urban North possessed substantial local political strength, including considerable influence over local public police. In consequence, business and other middle class elements in these cities came to rely upon alternative apparatuses of social control. Much of the serious work which these elites wanted done, in prevention and investigation of crime and in containment of labor insurgency, was carried out by private police. In the larger labor disputes, state and federal police resources were also mobilized.

As the United States reached industrial maturity early in this century, the social composition and political structure of the urban North began to undergo considerable change. These changes had an impact, both accidentally and by design, upon urban police work. The two inter-war decades (1918-1941) represent an era of transition into today's troubled urban policing situation. Most of the received structure of police work survived into today's cities, but not without certain crucial shifts of emphasis.

During the inter-war period, the private police apparatus underwent a relative decline in importance. Much of the growth of the FBI, for instance, occurred at private police expense. Just after World War I, the FBI was given jurisdiction over bank and train robberies, thereby eliminating a major and lucrative source of private police business. This transfer of law enforcement functions was reproduced on the symbolic plane as well. Up through World War I, the role of national police spokesman had been played by heads of the Pinkerton Agency. Allan Pinkerton, and his sons, wrote popular books on the horrors of crime and political subversion, and gave keynote speeches at police conventions. In 1924, J. Edgar Hoover succeeded William Burns (another famous private detective) as head of the FBI. Thereafter, it was Hoover who wrote the eyecatching books and gave the speeches.

Private police continued to play a major role in labor conflict right up to the point of permanent legalization of labor organizing in 1935. Labor spying was a vital weapon in the great union busting campaigns of the 1920's. Nationally, union membership fell one-third between 1920 and 1929, most of that loss having been enforced by 1923. In 1929, when union membership across the country was 3.4 million, there were an estimated 200,000 labor spies at work.[23] Given this remarkable 17:1 ration, union members assembled in a meeting anywhere in the country could usually be certain that someone in their midst was an employer agent. When the New Deal reforms took hold in the late 1920's, this particular variety of police work was not assumed by public police, but simply passed into history.

Today, most private police do the work in which they found their historic origins: the detection and sanctioning of crimes against business enterprises. They patrol industrial and commercial premises, seeking to prevent shoplifting and employee pilferage. They investigate sophisticated crimes such as embezzlement, insurance fraud and thefts of insurance data. The American private police apparatus is today large and efficient enough that crimes against corporations are in all likelihood policed more effectively than are those crimes against individuals to which public police attend. It is only the crimes of corporations (e.g., advertising fraud, negligent manufacture of unsafe products, antitrust violations) which go entirely unpoliced in America.

Despite their relative circumscription over the course of this century, private police remain today a major bulwark of American social stratification. The American private police apparatus is probably much larger, relative to public police, than are its counterparts in other advanced industrial nations. Further, public regulation of private police, whether by administrative agencies or courts, is almost non-existent in the United States today. Finally, public and private police in modern America often cooperate in ways which increase the power of both, while undermining civil liberties. The fact that private police remain almost unresearched is an indictment of contemporary social science.

During the 1920's and 1930's, the public police apparatus in America was considerably expanded in size, in organizational effectiveness and in the range of functions it was called upon to perform. The emergence of the FBI was but a part of this story, for the crucial task was reform of local public police. This latter effort was spearheaded by a burst of policy-oriented social science.[24] Raymond Fosdick wrote influential books on American and European police systems. In 1922, Fosdick and other notables (e.g., Felix Frankfurter, Roscoe Pound) collaborated in the famous Cleveland survey, a work which spawned imitators in other states. August Vollmer and the Wickersham Commission were other well-known spokesmen for local police reform in this era. The 1920's also saw, perhaps coincidentally, the first serious move by appellate courts in the United States to apply legal controls to police behavior.

The inter-war drive to reform local police departments was a direct descendant of the failed efforts of the 1860's and 1890's. Like those first two reform efforts, this third great effort was elite-instigated and led. A large part of its purpose was the enhancement of the political reliability of local police from the elite standpoint. The inter-war effort was far more energetic and sophisticated than the earlier ones had been. This later drive did not confine itself to matters of formal control or police corruption, but directed itself to a thoroughgoing administrative transformation of local police departments.

The inter-war police reform drive further gained strength from the fact that it was not an isolated effort, but part of a larger movement to reform municipal government generally. Beginning in the Progressive era, various kinds of rationalization and centralization of urban government were undertaken in dozens of American cities.[25] In smaller cities, city manager and city commission forms became widespread. In larger cities, political machines were hobbled or destroyed by the introduction of civil service bureaucracies. Though "nonpartisanship" was the rhetorical watchword of these reforms, their substantive import was otherwise. The municipal reform drive was led by business interests, manufacturing and commercial, and by emergent professional groups (e.g., engineers, lawyers). One of its crucial goals was to wrest political control of cities from the hands of the working class and the older middle class.

Municipal reform was, from the standpoint of its promulgators, a fairly successful movement. The formal changes sought were institutionalized in most American cities by the close of World War II. The social foundations of the older urban political forms have also been undercut over time. Specifically, ethnic institutions in American communities have been in decline, as assimilation proceeded apace. The upshot has been that urban government is today perceived by lower status whites as remote from them and unresponsive to their needs. Testimony to this process may be found in comparison of two well-known studies of Italian-American neighborhoods in Boston.[26] William Whyte's ethnography of the North End during the late 1930's depicts a community closely and productively involved in city politics. Herbert Gans' ethnography of the adjacent West End during the late 1950's depicts a community frustrated and alienated by city politics.

The political effectiveness of white ethnics has generally declined over the course of the last century. This conclusion, however, should not blind us to counter-indications. The municipal reform movement had some definite weak spots. Its most conspicuous failure in Northern cities was a crucial one: local public police departments. During the inter-war period itself, the administrative reform of urban police departments was halting, almost non-existent. Fosdick et al. could see this well enough. A good deal of the frustration of these particular reformers was rooted in an important historical accident: the existence from 1920 to 1933 of Prohibition. The outlawing of liquor consumption seems ridiculous to "hyphenate Americans," including Irish and Italians. The bootlegging industry which organized crime created in response to Prohibition found willing accomplices in local public police. The corruption of local police which attended Prohibition maintained, and even solidified, their ties with the community they policed, especially those of an ethnic sort.

Prohibition, of course, was repealed soon enough. This fact, however, leaves us with an important anomaly. As a general movement, municipal reform in the North was relatively complete and being consolidated by the end of World War II. Police reformers, by contrast, have had very limited success right up to the present day. Enormous efforts to rationalize and professionalize America's local public police departments have been made over the last three decades.[27] This movement improved police training, tightened organizational controls over police officers, lowered police discretion, and more. However, the very prolongation of this effort to modernize urban police departments is an important indication of its relative ineffectiveness. Another such indication is the fact that this movement has made no headway at all in numerous larger cities (e.g., New York, Boston, San Francisco). Finally, when the administrative controls over urban police work which reformers had so painstakingly constructed were tested during the 1960's, they fell to pieces. This latter conclusion will be further explained toward the end of this paper, since a full understanding of its import requires an explication of the nature of urban police work in our time.

The contemporary sociological literature on the police has taken note of the weaknesses of the police modernization movement, of the special difficulties attending its implementation. The roots of these weaknesses and difficulties are partly found, as this literature suggest, in the existence of a hardy and insular police occupational subculture. This explanation, however, is hardly sufficient in itself. The essential clue to the large truth lies in the fact that the content of the police subculture is largely ethnic and working class in character. The crucial social basis for the relative freedom from top-down administrative control enjoyed by urban police today is the close and cooperative relationship which the police have with the white working class community. The police are one of the few elements of urban government for which the lower status sector of the white community retains a positive regard today. The two groups share many social sentiments and preoccupations.

Social scientists studying American police today have been led away from exploring this police/working class symbiosis because of their lack of an historical and comparative perspective. For instance, contemporary studies have shown that American police are socially isolated. Relative to workers in other occupations, police have a much stronger sense of separateness from those outside their occupational group and a lower degree of off-duty interaction with such others. And if the police are socially isolated, are they not also politically isolated? The flaw in this common-sense inference is shown by the English case. Even though English police are socially isolated from the respectable elements in English society, they are politically responsive to that sector. To whom, then, are American police normatively responsive? The whole history of local public police in America suggests that the essential constituency of today's urban police is the working class. To recognize the possibility, even probability, of such a connection is not, of course, to demonstrate its existence. To this latter task, I now turn.

The American labor movement today is well-known to be one of the most conservative in the world, and there is little evidence that American labor unions are drastically out of step with the social sentiments of the American working class generally. American labor has not always had this character, but was forced into it as the result of specific historic struggles. By the 1930's, it is clear in retrospect, the American working class had shot its bolt in its attempt to play a genuinely progressive role in American politics. Since that time, American labor has accommodated itself to a subservient role and has mounted no serious challenge to business domination of American life. During the late 19th and early 20th century, American labor entertained much higher hopes and expectations regarding its role in American life than present realities suggest. Only a part of the historic process through which American workers retreated from these dreams has been treated in this paper—namely, the repression of labor organizing and the eclipse of urban political machines.[28]

The historic exhaustion of the American working class did not eliminate it as a factor in urban politics. Rather, it ensured that the working class role there would be a defensive one. If workers could not advance as a group, they could at least seek to consolidate what they had and to avoid further retrenchment. The defensive politics of American workers in our day has come to express itself most significantly in the race issue. As immigration from Europe to American cities ended around World War I, blacks began to migrate out of the South in great numbers. Their arrival in the North interjected a dramatic new factor into American urban life. The racial question today pervades urban politics. It is the crux of police politics in particular, due in fair measure to the influence over police possessed by the working class.

The relationship between the white working class community and the black one in Northern cities was a troubled one from the beginning. The first great wave of black migration northward occurred during and after World War I. This era was punctuated by numerous riots during which lower status whites rampaged in the black community, killing, burning and looting. The second great wave of black migration northward occurred before and during World War II. Again, numerous riots occurred. Their character was similar to that of the earlier riots, except that in the later riots blacks did not hesitate to fight back. During all of these riots, the behavior of local public police left no doubt that their earnest sympathies were with the white rioters.[29]

While riots are extreme social phenomena, they are not unrevealing or merely bizarre. For one thing, they are almost always seen by the participants therein as legitimate and useful forms of protest. The race rioting visited upon American cities during the two World Wars is strong evidence that white workers (and local public police) saw the establishment and enlargement of the black presence in Northern cities as a threat to their social interests. This same constellation of interests has become imbedded in routine police work in the urban North during the last three decades. In the past, American workers sought to make local public police a progressive political resource, as by resisting repression of labor organizing. Today, the quest is to make them a reactionary political resource, as by enforcing black social subordination.

From the tumult of recent years in Northern cities, three basic political stances toward the police have emerged. The urban social group most deeply opposed to the police is the black community. The urban social group most strenuously supportive of the police is lower status whites, and the white working class more particularly. Higher status whites tend to fall in the middle of this spectrum, being variously skeptical, ambivalent or unconcerned about the police. Materials corroborating this broad overview abound in the scholarly and popular literature on the police problem.

That blacks distrust and hate the police (and the police, blacks) can hardly be doubted. This attitudinal abyss has been documented by dozens of studies, by researches undertaken from the most diverse theoretical, methodological and ideological postures. Further, it is the black community which has most persistently struggled in recent years to create avenues for redress of grievances against the police. In those localities where proposals for civilian-controlled complaint review boards or for decentralized ("community") control of police have come forward, the critical impetus and support has been found in the black community. The black-led efforts to influence police behavior have thus far come to very little. This indicates, not a lack of black concern, but the strength of police resistance. Police invulnerability to pressure from this quarter is partly rooted in the general organizational autonomy of police departments. More importantly, however, the police turn out to have considerable political and cultural resources at their disposal in the urban arena. These resources have been crystallized around such potent abstractions as "law and order" and the "crime wave."

Such social support for the police is basically located in the white working class; pro-police sentiment is far less prominent in the middle and upper class sectors of the white community. This bifurcation of white opinion was shown in the famous civilian review board referendum in New York City in 1966.[30] Working class voters overwhelmingly took a pro-police position in this election; the higher status sector of the white community was evenly split. The major correlate of middle-and upper-class white support for the police on this occasion was a Catholic background. Working class Jews, normally liberal, voted pro-police. The lower middle class was also pro-police, but the heart of police support was among white workers.

This constellation of current social sentiment regarding police in urban America is well-known. Rarely, however, is it taken seriously, as a possible clue to something larger. Typically, social scientists have sought to discount these attitude configurations. (Blacks don't "really" hate the police. White workers aren't "really" racist). This is a mistake, for the attitudes reflect genuine social interests. The black and the white working class communities both have a considerable direct stake in the social organization and social impact of contemporary urban police work. For higher status whites, what local police do is of but indirect and secondary concern. Basically, the political structure of modern police work damages the black community while serving the white working class one. An examination of police work itself, what police do and the social consequences thereof, will show how this works.

The black ghetto is a central concern of contemporary urban police departments. Blacks are greatly over-arrested in proportion to their numbers in the population. This disproportion is such that in any of the dozens of cities where blacks make up over one-fifth of the population, it is likely that the majority of police cars in service at any one time will be operating in the ghetto. And this heavy patrol is carried out with a special attitude. "From the front seat of a moving patrol car, street life in a typical Negro ghetto is perceived as an uninterrupted sequence of suspicious scenes."[31] The same is not true of police patrol in white neighborhoods. Thus, the fact of police preoccupation with the ghetto is not problematic. It is only the meaning of this preoccupation which must be discovered.

The police themselves claim that they work in the ghetto because that is where crime is socially located. Most criminologists agree that blacks commit more crime than whites, even though this proposition is impossible to prove or disprove. No random sample of all crimes, along with race-of-suspect information, could ever be assembled; the available indirect indicators are highly contaminated. This issue is an academic red herring which mainly serves to reify existing police biases. Criminologists have studiously ignored the fact that the crime rate is vastly lower in today's black-dominated cities than it was in the white-dominated cities of a half-century or a century ago.[32]

To the limited extent that police work consists of fighting crime, police are led into the ghetto only by being highly selective in which crimes they attend to. Because the black community is a poor one, it makes sense to suppose that blacks commit a disproportionate share of personal violence crime and of the "blue collar" variety of property crime. The most significant type of property crime, however, is white collar; blacks have little opportunity to commit such crimes and the police ignore them. Further, police devote substantial attention in the ghetto to non-victim crime. This moralistic intervention into ghetto life serves no compelling public purpose. Its perniciousness is compounded by the fact that police ignore those prostitutes, drug dealers, gamblers, etc. who possess higher social status and/or a white skin.

If fighting crime is what the police are doing in the ghetto, why do law-abiding blacks fail to welcome the police there? There is apparently no shortage of black criminal victims, yet most of them fear the police as much as they do criminals. More generally, why does the black community complain bitterly and persistently about inadequate police protection, even as the police saturate the ghetto? These are but apparent paradoxes. Their resolution can be found in the fact that the police and the black community have divergent and conflicting normative priorities.[33] The preoccupations which the police bring to their routine work in the ghetto are not those of the black public which they allegedly serve.

A good many police man-hours are spent in trivial and benign activities to which almost no citizen objects. Examples here include directing traffic and transporting pregnant or injured persons to the hospital. When, however, one considers significant police activities (those which may produce arrests), important normative contrasts between policing in the white and the black communities become obvious. Most of the significant policing of whites involves potential normative conflicts which are but rarely actualized. Two major examples may be given. Police often keep tabs (as through licensing) on hotels, bars, pawn shops, massage parlors and the like. Entrepreneurs operating on the edge of the law usually regard police attention merely as a cost of doing business. Police often help manage the daily life of winos and other inhabitants of skid-row. These inhabitants have few resources with which to avoid or resist police attention. These regularly policed whites, both entrepreneurs and fallen alcoholics, find themselves able on the whole to passively acquiesce in the situation.

The black reaction to police attention is quite another matter. Police patrol in the black community is so heavy and so indiscriminate that it is actively resented and normatively resisted by most blacks.[34] Being stopped or dispersed by police without obvious basis is a routine part of life in the black community, especially for adolescent males. While searching for imaginary trouble, police help to create the real thing. By the same token, when the police encounter real trouble in the ghetto, they often escalate it. The family disturbance, that classic occasion for police intervention in ghetto life, is often inflamed rather than cooled off by police arrival on the scene.

Black irritation with the police is a consequence not only of heavy police patrol, but also of the way that patrol is carried out. Police have a special concern to demand respect from citizens, to make it clear that they are in control of all police/citizen encounters. Further, police often bring a law enforcement mentality to bear upon situations which are only remotely criminal, and rely excessively upon arrest as a method for handling such situations. Finally, the abrasiveness of police operations in the ghetto has been heightened in recent years by the new police doctrine of aggressive patrol. Headquarters often establishes explicit production quotas for field interrogation reports, while leaving the more sensitive question of arrest quotas to informal policy.

The upshot of all this is that police make an enormous number of unnecessary arrests of urban blacks. Even though the average police officer makes only one or two arrests a week, the cumulative effect of police patrol is staggering. Careful study in one large northern city showed that some fifty per cent of the black males there had been arrested by age 18, compared to some twenty per cent of the white males.[35] A necessarily provisional study of national statistics indicated that the lifetime probability of arrest for urban black males was over ninety per cent.[36] Traffic violations were ignored in both studies.

Arrest visits a variety of personal costs upon the arrestee. At the outset, a day or two is spent behind bars and money disappears into the hands of bailbondsmen and lawyers. Eventual adjudication as guilty mandates further penalties. However, case attrition in American criminal justice processing is so high that it is the social, rather than the legal, consequences of arrest which count. I refer to legal stigma, the long-term life chances penalties visited upon persons who possess arrest records.[37]

Arrest record information is used widely by employers, lenders and insurers in the United States today. Applicants for jobs, credit or insurance are often asked directly about their arrest records. Because it is expected that such applicants will lie about this aspect of their life, independent checking is common. The organizational key to such checking is America's private police apparatus. Arrest record information held by public police is routinely available to private police, though not to other private parties. The emergence, in recent decades, of computer-based private dossier systems has made it more difficult for arrested persons to escape the social consequences of a criminal record.

Some aspects of legal stigma may be desirable social practice. For instance, many will find it easy to justify screening convicted embezzlers away from money-handling jobs. However, the basic thrust of legal stigma in America is more disturbing. Persons with arrests, but no convictions, are often stigmatized, even though they are legally innocent. (In England, unlike the United States, police do not keep records on persons merely arrested.[38]) Further, legal stigma in the United States is often operative in menial and nonsensitive jobs. For instance, the city of Los Angeles will not hire as a custodian anyone arrested for burglary or theft.

Possession of an arrest record is not an insurmountable barrier to employment or other social desiderata. Some employers do not inquire about the job applicant's arrest record. Most of those who do so inquire turn away only those with the most serious police records. However, it is precisely the discretionary character of legal stigma which makes it hit arrested blacks harder than it does arrested whites. The police records of blacks tend to have more entries and more convictions for more serious charges than the police records of whites. Even though a minority of all those arrested in the United States are black, it is likely that a substantial majority of the legally stigmatized are black.

The phenomenon of legal stigma reminds us that arbitrary damage to the life chances of most blacks is a central consequence of urban American police work today. Further, police have regularly sought to interfere with change-oriented varieties of black politics. During the civil rights era, police attempted to hamper or prevent the formation of reformist political organizations in the black community. They also savagely repressed organized black militancy, as for instance the Black Panther Party and the Lost-Found Nation of Islam (Black Muslims). In sum, the core of the police role in the black communities of the urban North today is enforcement of black ghettoization. Police work in the ghetto does not serve merely, or even primarily, to control its criminal elements. (Recall that blacks regard the police as deficient in this function.) Police work in the ghetto rather serves to control the black ghetto as a whole.

Police work, it should be stressed, is not the linchpin of black poverty and social subordination in urban America. Many public institutions play a similar anti-black role: schools, welfare, urban renewal, and so on.[39] The activities of these various urban institutions reflect and maintain a variety of white interests—political, status and economic. Black subordination endures in America because it is based on far more than vicious feelings, misunderstandings and similar irrationalities. For instance, it has been estimated that as of 1960 the several varieties of discrimination present in the labor market produced a yearly income gain of $250—for the average white member of the labor force and a corresponding loss of $2100—for each non-white member of the labor force.[40] The distribution of other social desiderata is less quantifiable, but the same principle holds: blacks lose and whites gain.

It is this rational underpinning which makes race such a stubborn problem for America. At the same time, racial domination is neither the sole nor the decisive form of inequality in American society. The black sector of the American population has been too small, especially over the last century, to sustain such a claim. If racial discrimination benefitted all whites equally, it would benefit none of them very much. Racial privilege is differentially salient for different sectors of the white community.

The question of where the stable material benefits of racial discrimination gravitate to within white society has been much debated in recent years.[41] Some have sought to see in the corporate economy, the five or six hundred largest firms in the nation, racism's crucial beneficiary. This is a false trail. Some of these firms operate "runaway" plants in the South, and some of them are linked to the ghetto through financial credit chains. These, however, are marginal phenomena. Corporate America does not profit crucially and centrally from domestic racial discrimination. These largest firms have bigger fish to fry; their class privileges far outweigh their racial privileges.

Middle-sized business interests of many kinds profit rather obviously from the ghettoization of blacks. Blacks are important consumers for those real estate interests and merchants operating in and around the ghetto. Blacks are also an important source of cheap labor for many service industries. These latter include hotels, restaurants, laundry services and hospitals. The dependence on the perpetuation of black subordination is much more central for these firms than it is for the corporate economy. This is why the large corporations can be pushed toward a liberal position on the race issue, while middle-sized businesses cannot.

The major group outside of the business community which benefits from the perpetuation of the black ghetto is the white working class, along with part of the lower middle class. These lower status whites, unlike higher status ones, are in competition with blacks for numerous specific desiderata in urban America. These include opportunities in employment, housing and education. Lower status whites see racial privilege as vital to their life chances. Though the increment in job opportunities and the like which subordination of blacks offers these whites is relatively modest, it is of considerable significance in a stagnating economy.

The major direct beneficiaries of the ghettoization of the black community are, in a word, merchants and workers. Of these two racist complexes, it is the working class one which is most importantly sustained by police work. The legal stigma system helps lower status whites retain differential access to the modest social opportunities which are up for grabs in the lower echelons of urban life. While legal stigma is neither the only nor the primary means by which such differential access is institutionalized, it is the key to the contemporary politics of police work. Legal stigma is the rational kernel within the mystical shell—that is, the concrete phenomenon which gives warrant to both black opposition to the police and working class support for them.

Much of the underside of contemporary urban police work remained invisible until the 1960's, when the black political awakening spread from South to North. At this time, reform of local public police became a major black political preoccupation. Police successfully resisted reform proposals in city after city, even thought the changes under consideration were rather mild and limited. The outcome was surprising, for in most Northern cities blacks could count on the support of liberals from the higher status sector of the white communi-

ty. This latter group had access to most of the command posts of urban governance, yet the police could not be moved. The legacy of the municipal reform
movement was to no avail, and the depth of police independence and autonomy stood revealed.

In recent years, American police have begun gambling for higher stakes.
The most dramatic evidence of this has been several dozen police strikes. The
most significant of these to date occurred in New York in 1971 (six days),
Baltimore in 1974 (four days) and San Francisco in 1975 (three days).
American cities struck by their police forces have uniformly been quiet for the
duration. Police strikes in overseas cities (e.g., Montreal 1969, Stockholm
1970, Lima 1975) have been attended by immediate and dramatic upsurges
in crime and rioting. American cities in particular can do without their police
forces temporarily because the slack is taken up by this country's massive private police apparatus.

Strikes are but the most visible manifestation of a more general police
revolt in America.[42] Police have engaged in ticket slowdowns or ticket bliz-
zards. They have picketed and marched. They have court-watched, to help
purge liberal judges. They have run for office, or campaigned for others so
running. They have lobbied, at local and state levels. These diverse confrontations have mostly been with civilian authorities, though activist police have not
hesitated to move against high police officials who failed to keep pace with the
rank and file mood. Jerome Skolnick has argued that the police revolt is a
frank bid for independent political power, a major challenge to higher authority.

Numerous mayors of American big cities have complained publically that
they do not control their police departments. The mayors with such troubles
have mostly been liberal ones, such as Lindsay, Cavanaugh, White and Stokes
(of New York, Detroit, Boston, and Cleveland, respectively). These and other
urban politicians, influenced by corporate leaders, have found that the present
configurations of urban police work increase racial tension in their cities. This
seems to be the ultimate source of their interest in police reforms. For the
police, their revolt has become a defense of the established way of policing the
black ghetto, the assertion of their right to continue to do so without outside
interference.

While the police seek independent power, their revolt remains closely correlated with the social sentiments of lower status whites. It is these sentiments
which the police mobilize when resisting civilian review boards and parallel
reforms. The police are a prominent positive symbol for such whites, one of
the few government agencies in which they have confidence. Today, as in the

past, local public police remain an improbable outpost within the American legal order and its private appendages—namely, a bastion of white working class sentiment.

The police/working class alliance is under pressure from two sides today. Higher status whites are continuing their efforts to "professionalize" and otherwise re-direct police behavior. This sector is also hedging its bets, by supporting a concomitant expansion of the private police. Blacks, deeply damaged as a community by the present structure of police work, are searching resolutely for means to free themselves of its burden.

Naturally, radical social scientists, inside of the new criminology and out of it, will seek to have a hand in shaping that future. The many issues which this commitment raises can hardly be fully aired, much less resolved, in a few pages. Still, the topic is important enough that a few remarks on it are appropriate in closing.

To begin with, a great many concrete changes in the contemporary functioning of the criminal justice system are needed. Any list of such progressive changes would include, in the American context, the repeal of statutes which create non-victim crime, the development of effective grievance procedures for victims of police misconduct, the destratification of the panels from which juries are chosen, and the development of due process safeguards in the parole and probation systems. Radicals often dismiss the effort to institute changes of this sort as liberal reformism. This is short-sighted, for ours is a retrograde political era. For the foreseeable future, the real alternative to incremental reforms is likely to be, not revolution, but no reform at all. Even the small changes just listed are not going to come easily. Support for them can be justified on the simple ground that they would improve the life chances of many of the criminal justice system's victims.

The scholarly and intellectual questions underlying even the simplest reforms in criminal justice are far from trivial. It often takes a good deal of serious social research to uncover the workings even of injustices whose existence seems manifest and obvious. More generally it takes a discerning eye to see the most strategic points of intervention into criminal justice functioning. For instance, contrast community control of police and the dismantling of the legal stigma system. While implementing either of these changes would be a major step forward in the United States, the latter would be far easier to achieve. Legal stigma could be challenged without directly confronting the politically well-entrenched police, and this challenge could evoke and develop existing norms (e.g., right to privacy and to due process). Neither advantage obtains in the effort to institute community control of police, and yet this latter cause has attracted far more radical interest.

Beyond the question of short-term reforms, much larger dreams and tasks also loom. Radicals envisage an equalitarian society, and mean their intellectual work to hasten the transformations in that direction. Unfortunately, a good deal of the radical social science which has recently emerged in the United States is unlikely to be adequate to these high hopes.[43] The new criminology, in particular, needs to undertake some changes if it is to fulfill its promise.

New criminologists have sought to differentiate their work from established criminology by labeling the latter as either liberal or conservative. This tactic is unlikely to bear much fruit. Scholarship does not always come in neat ideological packages, and ideology is not an infallible test of intellectual quality in any case. The real need is not to learn to view crime and deviance from a left-wing perspective. It is rather to learn to see them as part of a much wider institutional nexus. This nexus includes, at the least, politics, stratification, social change and (for America) race relations. Some conventional work on criminal justice has already achieved this wider vision; such work should be adapted to radical analysis, not rejected out of hand.

One essential task of any radical social science is the demystification of presently prevailing social arrangements. New criminologists have chosen a simple device for this ends, the declaration of dissenting value judgements. They curse the present and commit themselves to work for a better world. In itself, however, this is a superficial and arbitrary way to demystify present realities, for a worse future is as easy to imagine as a better one. Standing out for a socialist or other desirable future does not break new ground, but only offers the possibility of doing so. A grounded demystification of the present is only possible when humane values are informed by a penetrating intellectual strategy. Such a strategy has to place central emphasis upon serious historical work.

New criminologists often declare it their intention to view social phenomena historically. However, few of them have acted on this pledge. The few pieces of work in the new criminology which have dealt with the past have tended to be historical only in a weak sense. They have either been antiquarian analyses of the remote origins of present institutions or a mere rummaging through the past for examples of repression, racism and other horrors. The real promise of historical work is to be found in the much stronger notion of historical *development*, the linking of past and present in specific concrete ways. Work of this kind demystifies the present in a general way by showing us that all social arrangements come into being through open-ended indeterminate processes. Further, if such work is any good, it can demystify the present in a specific way by revealing its major contradictions. Once the malleable elements of present social arrangements are sorted out from the intractable ones, points of leverage for progressive social change can be specified.

The lessons offered by good historical analyses are not likely to be simple ones. For instance, in the American case, ethnic solidarity has been a double-edged feature of our national life, having both progressive and regressive implications. The same is true of political decentralization. Nonetheless, the analysis of historical development remains indispensable to radical social science. It is the only intellectual wedge with which we can split the present open and ensure its passage into history.

ENDNOTES

* This chapter was previously published in *Theory and Society* Vol. 3, pages 89-117. Copyright © 1976 Klewer Academic Publishers. Reprinted by permission of Klewer Academic Publishers.

1.   American representatives of this school include Anthony Platt and Lynn Cooper, eds., *Policing America*, (Englewood Cliffs, 1974); Richard Quinney, ed., *Criminal Justice in America* (Boston, 1974); and Charles Reasons, ed., *The Criminologist* (Pacific Palisades, 1974). English representatives of this school include Ian and Laurie Taylor, eds., *Politics and Deviance* (Harmondsworth 1973); Ian Taylor *et al.*, *The New Criminology*, (London, 1973); and Ian Taylor *et al.*, eds., *Critical Criminology* (London, 1975).

2.   This criticism applies with fragmentary exceptions, to all of the works cited above. See the close of this paper for further comments.

3.   James Kakalik and Sorrel Wildhorn, *Private Police in the United States: Findings and Recommendations* (Santa Monica, RAND Corporation Report R-869/DOJ, 1971), pp.10-12. This report is the first of a five volume set.

4.   Allan Silver, "The Demand for Order in Civil Society," in David Bordna, ed., *The Police* (New York, 1967), pp. 1-24; Egon Bittner, *The Functions of the Police in Modern Society* (Chevy Chase: National Institute of Mental Health, 1970), Chapter 3.

5.   Roger Lane, *Policing the City* (Cambridge, 1967); Roger Lane, "Urbanization and Criminal Violence in the 19th Century," in Hugh Graham and Ted Gurr, eds., *Violence in America* (Washington, 1969), Chapter 12.

6.   E.P. Thompson, *The Making of the English Working Class*, (New York, 1966); Ben Roberts, "On the Origin and Resolution of English Working Class Protest," in Graham and Gurr, *Violence in America*, Chapter 7.

7.   See *e.g.*, Birnbaum's critique of Shils and Young. Edward Shils and Michael Young, "The Meaning of the Coronation," *Sociological Review, I*, (1953) pp. 63-81; and Norman Birnbaum, "Monarchs and Sociologists," *Sociological Review, 3* (1955) pp. 5-23.

8.   *Cf.* Nigel Young, "Prometheans or Troglodytes?" *Berkeley Journal of Sociology*, 12, (1967), pp. 1-43.

9.   See. *e.g.*, Edward Shils, *The Torment of Secrecy*, (Glencoe, III. 1956).

10. *Cf.* Bruce Johnson, "The Democratic Mirage," *Berkeley Journal of Sociology*, 13, (1968), pp. 104-143.

11. The Lexow Committee investigations in New York in 1894 are but the best known of numerous such efforts. See New York State Senate, *Report and Proceedings of the Senate Committee Appointed to Investigate the Police Department of the City of New York*, (New York, reprint edition, 1971). Originally issued 1895.

12. James Horan, *The Pinkertons* (New York, 1967) p. 181.

13. George Walling, *Recollections of a New York Chief of Police* (Montclair, reprint edition, 1972). Originally published 1888.

14. *Cf.* Robert Wiebe, *The Search for Order.* (New York, 1967); James Weinstein, *The Corporate Ideal in the Liberal State,* (Boston, 1968).

15. *Cf.* Louis Hartz, *The Liberal Tradition in America,* (New York, 1955), pp. 219-224.

16. Unless otherwise noted, the discussion below of the Pinkerton Agency is drawn from Horan, *Pinkertons.*

17. Philip Taft and Philip Ross, "American Labor Violence," In Graham and Gurr, *Violence in America,* Chapter 8. *Cf.* Irving Bernstein, *The Lean Years,* (Baltimore, 1960), pp. 204-206; and G.D.H. Cole, and Raymond Postgate, *The British People* (London, 1961), pp. 481-482.

18. Charles Tilly, "Collective Violence in European Perspective," in Graham and Gurr, *Violence in America,* Chapter 1.

19. Walton Bean, *Boss Ruef's San Francisco,* (Berkeley, 1968); Weinstein, *Corporate Ideal,* pp.173-178.

20. William Preston, *Aliens and Dissenters,* (New York, 1963).

21. Herbert Gutman, "The Worker's Search for Power," in H. Wayne Morgan, ed., *The Gilded Age,* (Syracuse, 1963) Chapter 3; Herbert Gutman, "Class, Status, and Community Power in Nineteenth-Century American Industrial Cities," in Frederic Jaher, ed., *The Age of Industrialism in America* (New York, 1968), Chapter 8.

22. See Almont Lindsey, *The Pullman Strike,* (Chicago, 1964) esp. Chapters 9, 10, 13; Stanley Buder, *Pullman,* (New York, 1967), esp. Chapters 13-15.

23. Bernstein, *Lean Years,* pp. 84, 149.

24. Raymond Fosdick, *European Police Systems* (Montclair, 1969), originally published 1915; Raymond Fosdick, *American Police Systems* (Montclair, 1969), originally published 1920; Raymond Fosdick, *et al., Criminal Justice in Cleveland,* (Montclair, 1968), originally published 1922; August Vollmer, *The Police and Modern Society* (Montclair, 1971), originally published 1936; National Commission on Law Observance and Enforcement; George Wickersham, Chairman *Wickersham Commission Reports* (Montclair, 1968) originally published 1931; The Wickersham Commission reports were fifteen in number, published in fourteen volumes with various titles.

25.   Samuel Hays, "The Politics of Reform in Municipal Government in the Progressive Era," *Pacific Northwest Quarterly, 55,* 1964; pp. 157-169; Weinstein, *Corporate Ideal,* Chapter 4.

26.   William Whyte, *Street Corner Society* (Chicago, 1943); Herbert Gans, *The Urban Villagers* (New York, 1962).

27.   *Cf.* James Wilson, "The Police and their Problems: A Theory," *Public Policy, 12,* 1963, pp. 189-216.

28.   For a fuller analysis, see Johnson, "Democratic Mirage."

29.   Gary Marx, "Civil Disorder and the Agents of Social Control," in Reasons, *Criminologist,* pp. 290-321.

30.   Edward Rogowsky, *et al.,* "Police: The Civilian Review Board Controversy," in Jewel Bellush and Stephen David, eds., *Race and Politics in New York City,* (New York, 1971), Chapter 3.

31.   Carl Werthman, and Irving Piliavin, "Gang Members and the Police," in Bordua, *Police,* pp. 56-98.

32.   Today's "soaring" crime rate exists only on paper. It is an artifact of the increased citizen disposition to report crime and the increased honesty of police record-keeping. For the historical evidence, see Lane, "Urbanization and Criminal Violence," and Theodore Ferdinand, "The Criminal Patterns of Boston Since 1849," *American Journal of Sociology,* 73:1 1967, pp. 84-99.

33.   Albert Reiss, Jr. and Donald Black have argued that the black arrest rate is higher than the white because police respond to the expressed desires of (arrest-minded) black complainants. This suggestion is disconfirmed by their own data. When one controls for complainant preference (or suspect deference) in their tables, the black arrest rate remains higher. See Donald Black and Albert Reiss, Jr., "Police Control of Juveniles," *American Sociological Review* 35:1 (1970), pp.63-77; Reiss' *The Police and the Public* (New Haven, 1971) is the best single overview we have of modern American police work. Nonetheless, this book's general thesis (that citizens control police by choosing when to call them into action) is deeply misleading vis-à-vis the black community. Reiss errs in giving all police/citizen encounters (trivial and important) equal analytic weight. He also obfuscates the issue of which citizens police are responding to, partly by understating the significance of non-victim arrests. Black hatred of the police needs to be explained, not explained away.

34.   National Advisory Commission on Civil Disorders, *Report,* (New York, 1968), Chapter 11; Werthman and Piliavin, "Gang Members;" Ronald Sullivan, "Violence, Like Charity, Begins at Home," *New York Times Magazine* (November 24, 1968.)

35.   National Commission on the Causes and Prevention of Violence, *To Establish Justice, to Insure Domestic Tranquility* (New York, 1970), pp. 20, 47.

36.   The comparable figure for urban white males in this study was 58%. This latter

statistic may seem to remove much of the force from my claim (below) that legal stigma is a racial issue. However, the black/white divergence in *socially costly* arrest-proneness is far greater than these two percentages indicate. This is because arrests for chronic drunkenness constitute almost half of all white arrests but only about one-sixth of all black arrests. Such arrests do not appreciably diminish life chances, as these latter have already been profoundly constricted by the time a man arrives on skid-row; Ronald Christensen, "Projected Percentage of U.S. Population with Criminal Arrest and Conviction Records," in President's Commission on Law Enforcement and Administration of Justice, *Task Force Report: Science and Technology* (Washington, 1967), Appendix J.

37.   *Cf.* Bruce Johnson, "Discretionary Justice and Racial Domination," Unpublished Ph.D. dissertation, Department of Sociology, University of California at Berkeley, (1973), Chapters 7-8.

38.   James Rule, *Private Lives and Public Surveillance* (New York, 1974), Chapter 2.

39.   *Cf.* Robert Blauner, *Racial Oppression in America* (New York, 1972).

40.   *Ibid.*, pp. 24-27.

41.   *Cf.* Michael Tanzer, *The Sick Society,* (New York, 1968), Chapter 4; William Tabb, *The Political Economy of the Black Ghetto,* (New York, 1970), esp. Chapters 3, 4, 6; Jeffrey Prager, "White Racial Privilege and Social Change," *Berkeley Journal of Sociology, 17,* (1972-1973); pp. 117-150, Jan Dizard and David Wellman, "I Love Ralph Bunche, but I Can't Eat Him for Lunch," *Leviathan, 1:4,* (1969), pp. 46-52.

42.   *Cf.* William Bopp, ed., *The Police Rebellion,* (Springfield, 1971); Jerome Skolnick, *The Politics of Protest,* (Washington, 1969), Chapter 7.

43.   *Cf.* Eugene Genovese, *In Red and Black,* (New York, 1971), Chapter 1.

CHAPTER 20
Private Security:
Implications for
Social Control

CLIFFORD D. SHEARING
PHILIP C. STENNING

Private security has become a pervasive feature of modern North American policing, both because of its rapid growth since 1960 and because it has invaded the traditional domain of the public police. Because this development has been viewed as an addendum to the criminal justice system, its significance for social control has not been recognized. This paper traces the development of private security in Canada and the United States since 1960, examines the reasons for its present pervasiveness, and explores its essential features: it is non-specialized, victim-oriented, and relies on organizational resources as sanctions. We conclude that private security is having a major impact on the nature of social control.

One of the most striking features of social control in North America is the pervasive presence of private security, which embraces a wide variety of services from security guards to computer fraud investigators, from home burglar alarms to sophisticated industrial and commercial surveillance systems, from anti-bugging devices to anti-terrorist "executive protection" courses. Private security offers protection for both persons and property which is often more comprehensive than that provided by public police forces. Internal security— so-called "in-house security"—has traditionally been provided by "corporate entities" (Coleman, 1974) such as profit-making corporations, and public institutions such as schools. Since the early 1960s there has been an enormous growth in "contract security," which provides police services on a fee-for-service basis to anyone willing to pay.

Private security is not a new phenomenon. Self-help and the sale of protection as a commodity have a long history (Becker, 1974; Radzinowicz, 1956). Even after the state sought to monopolize public protection through the establishment of public police forces in the 19th century, private interests continued to provide additional protection for themselves through private security (Spitzer and Scull, 1977). What is new about modern private security is its pervasiveness and the extent to which its activities have expanded into public, rather than purely private, places. In urban environments at least, private security is now ubiquitous and is likely to be encountered by city dwellers at home (especially if they live in an apartment building or on a condominium estate), at work, when shopping or banking, when using public transit, or when going to a sports stadium, university, or hospital. In this paper we consider the extent and nature of modern private security in Canada and the United States and its implications for social control. In doing so, we draw on the findings of research which we and our colleagues have undertaken since the early 1970s in Canada. This has included a series of studies of the legal context within which private security operates (Freedman and Stenning, 1977; Stenning, 1981; Stenning and Cornish, 1975; Stenning and Shearing, 1979); a major survey of the contract security industry—guard and investigative agencies—in the province of Ontario during 1976, which involved interviews with security agency executives and the administration of a questionnaire to their employees (Shearing, et al., 1980); a similar, but less extensive, survey of "in-house" security organizations in Ontario in 1974 (Jeffries, 1977); an examination of the available national statistics on the size and growth of private security in Canada between 1961 and 1971 (Farnell and Shearing, 1977); and three related studies of police, client, and public perceptions of private security, focusing primarily on the province of Ontario, using both interviews and questionnaires during 1982.

Most studies of formal social control within sociology have focused on systems of state control. They view law, justice, and the maintenance of public order as having been virtual state monopolies since early in the 19th century. Even those studies focusing on private forms have typically examined those instances in which state functions have been contracted out to private organizations (Scull, 1977), thus implicitly reinforcing the notion of a state monopoly over such functions (Cohen, 1979).[1]

The few sociologists who have studied the modern development of private security (Becker, 1974; Bunyan, 1977; Kakalik and Wildhorn, 1977) have, with few exceptions (Spitzer and Scull, 1977), broadly followed this tradition and have treated private security as little more than a private adjunct to the public criminal justice system. They assume that private security is essentially a private form of public policing, and that it can be understood in the same way as the public police.

We argue that this approach to understanding private security is inadequate because it fails to account for some of the most important differences between private security and public police and, more importantly, between the contexts within which each operates. The context in which private security functions is not public law and the criminal justice system, but what Henry (1978:123) has called "private justice." We follow the view of legal pluralists who maintain that "in any given society there will be as many legal systems as there are functioning social units" (Pospisil, 1967:24).

We begin by examining the size and growth of private security in Canada and the United States. Then we look at changes in the urban environment which have been associated with the involvement of private security in maintaining public order. Finally we consider various features of private security: who supports it, its authority, its organizational features, and its relationship to the public police.

THE SIZE AND GROWTH OF PRIVATE SECURITY[2]

While private security has probably existed in one form or another in North America since the continent was first settled by Europeans, little is known about its practice prior to the mid-19th century. Older accounts contain no reliable information about the size and growth of private security (Horan, 1967; Johnson, 1976; Lipson, 1975.) It was not until 1969 that the first major study of contract security was undertaken in the United States (Kakalik and Wildhorn, 1971), and not until these researchers revised their findings in 1977, in the light of 1970 census data, that a reasonably complete picture of size and growth trends became available. For Canada, the available statistical information is even less adequate.

Table 1 provides a summary of the statistics available for the United States and Canada respectively. We emphasize, however, that because of definitional difficulties and unreliable record-keeping practices, these figures are at best approximate. Table 1 shows that in the United States in 1960, private security almost equalled the public police in number. By 1970, both sectors had experienced substantial growth, with public police outdistancing private security. The early 1970s show a significant slowdown in the growth of public police, but a continued escalation in the growth of private security, especially in the contract security sector; by 1975, private security outnumbered public police.

Table 1
Public Police and Private Security Personnel, in Thousands (Rounded)

	Police		Security					Ratio of Police to Security	Ratio of In-house to Contract
		% Increase	In-house	% Increase	Contract	% Increase	Total	% Increase	
United States									
1960[a]	258		192		30		222		1.2:1	6:1
		51		15		103		27		
1970[a]	390		220		61		281		1.4:1	3.5:1
		5		18		187		55		
1975[b]	411		260		175		435		0.9:1	1.5:1
Canada									
1971[c]	40		25		11.5		36.5		1.1:1	2.2:1
		30		14		65		32		
1975[d]	51		29		19		48		1.1:1	1.5:1

Sources:

a. *Adapted from table 2.11 "Security Employment Trends by Type of Employer" (Kakalik and Wildhorn, 1977:43).*

b. *Police strength figure derived from U.S. Department of Justice, Federal Bureau of Investigation (1976:26). Private security figures, which are estimates only, adapted from Predicasts, Inc. (1974:26).*

c. *Adapted from Farnell and Shearing (1977).*

d. *Adapted from Friendly (1980).*

Between 1960 and 1975 the ratio of in-house to contract security diminished from 6:1 to 1.5:1, indicating a major restructuring of the organization of private security.[3]

Directly comparable data on the growth of private security in Canada from 1960 to 1970 are not available.[4] Census data suggest, however, that growth rates within the contract security sector may have been as high as 700 percent (Farnell and Shearing, 1977:113). By 1971, however, there were almost as many private security as public police in Canada, but in-house personnel still outnumbered contract security by more than 2 to 1. Within the next four years, both public police and private security personnel continued to increase, at approximately the same rate (30 percent). Within private security, however, contract security increased 65 percent, a rate almost five times that of the rate of growth of in-house security.

While reliable national statistics since 1975 are not available, statistics for the province of Ontario (which have in the past proved a good indicator of national trends) indicate a levelling off of contract security growth during the latter half of the 1970s. Overall, contract security in Ontario appears to have increased 90 percent from 1971 to 1980, while the growth rate of public police during the same period was 29 percent (Waldie et al., 1982:8). Assuming that there has been no absolute numerical decline in in-house security, this almost certainly means that in Ontario (and probably the rest of Canada) private security now outnumbers the public police. Furthermore, contract security alone now rivals the public police numerically. In Ontario, by 1980, there were three contract security personnel for every four public police officers—15,000 contract security, and just under 20,000 public police officers (Waldie, et al., 1982:9).

These findings indicate that in Canada and the United States the public police have for some time shared the task of policing with private organizations, and that private security probably now outnumber public police in both countries. The major change has been the rapid growth, since the early 1960s, of policing provided on a contract basis, for profit, by private enterprise (Spitzer and Scull, 1977). This has established private security as a readily available alternative to public police for those with the means to afford it, and has made private security a much more visible contributor to policing than it has been hitherto. The result has been an unobtrusive but significant restructuring of our institutions for the maintenance of order, and a substantial erosion by the private sector of the state's assumed monopoly over policing and, by implication, justice.

MASS PRIVATE PROPERTY

To understand the locus of private security it is necessary to examine the changes that have taken place, particularly since the early 1950s, in the organization of private property and public space. In North America many public activities now take place within huge, privately owned facilities, which we call "mass private property." Examples include shopping centers with hundreds of individual retail establishments, enormous residential estates with hundreds, if not thousands, of housing units, equally large office, recreational, industrial, and manufacturing complexes, and many university campuses. While evidence of these developments surrounds every city dweller, there is little data on how much public space in urban areas is under private control (Bourne and Harper, 1974:213; Lorimer, 1972:21). However, the available data do indicate an enormous increase in mass private property.

Spurr (1975:18) surveyed 60 major companies producing new urban residential accommodation in 24 Canadian metropolitan centers:

> Forty-seven firms hold 119,192 acres (186 square miles) of land, including 34 firms which each own more than one square mile.... Forty-two firms hold 95,174 apartment units including 13 firms with 123 apartment buildings. Twenty-nine firms have 223 office and other commercial buildings, while 23 firms have nearly 26,000,000 square feet of commercial space. While these commercial and apartment figures may appear large, the survey is particularly incomplete in these areas. Finally, twenty-seven firms have 185 shopping centres and sixteen firms own 38 hotels.

Gertler and Crowley (1977:289) used data collected by Punter (1974) to study four townships within 40 miles of Toronto, from 1954 to 1971. They identified

> ...two striking changes in the ownership patterns. Absentee ownership by individuals increased from less than 5 per cent of total area to about 20 per cent; and corporate ownership of the land which was negligible in 1954 increased to more than 20 per cent in 1971, with increases occurring particularly in the investment-developer category.

Martin (1975:21), in a study of the north-east Toronto fringe, found that corporations represented 22 percent of all buyers and 16 percent of all sellers. He argued that these transactions represented "the nucleus of land dealer activities in the study area between 1968 and 1974" (1975:27). Gertler and Crowley (1977:290) comment on these findings:

> Land development has changed from an activity carried out by a large number of small builder/developers in the 1950s to a process in the seventies which is increasingly shaped by large public companies. These firms are vertically integrated, that is, organized to handle the entire development package from land assembly to planning and design, construction, property management, and marketing.

The modern development of mass private property has meant that more and more public life now takes place on property which is privately owned. Yet the policing needs of such privately owned public places have not been met by the public police for two reasons. First, the routine "beat" of the public police has traditionally been confined to publicly owned property such as streets and parks (Stinchcombe, 1963). Therefore, even when they have had the resources to police privately owned public places—and typically they have not—they have been philosophically disinclined to do so. Second, those who own and control mass private property have commonly preferred to retain and exercise their traditional right to preserve order on their own property and to maintain control over the policing of it, rather than calling upon the public police to perform this function.

Because more and more public places are now located on private property, the protection of property—which lies at the heart of private security's function—has increasingly come to include the maintenance of public order, a matter which was, hitherto, regarded as the more or less exclusive prerogative of the public police. With the growth of mass private property, private security has been steadily encroaching upon the traditional beat of the public police. In so doing, it has brought areas of public life that were formerly under state control under the control of private corporations.

LEGITIMATION OF PRIVATE SECURITY AUTHORITY

The close association between private security and private property provides its most important source of social legitimation as an alternative to systems of public justice, and helps to explain why its development has proceeded with so little opposition. Because the development of modern institutions of public justice (during the early 19th century) necessarily involved the conferring of exceptional authority, such as police powers, on public officials, it has required legislative action and all the public debate which that engenders (Baldwin and Kinsey, 1980). By contrast, the development of private security has required virtually no legislation and has generated little public interest. This is because the authority of private security derives not so much from exceptional powers as from the ordinary powers and privileges of private property owners to control access to, use of, and conduct on, their property. While modern private security guards enjoy few or no exceptional law enforcement powers, their status as agents of property allows them to exercise a degree of legal authority which in practice far exceeds that of their counterparts in the public police. They may insist that persons submit to random searches of their property or persons as a condition of entry to, or exit from, the premises. They may even require clients to surrender their property while remaining on the premises, and during this time they may lawfully keep them under more or less constant visual or electronic surveillance. Before allowing clients to use the premises (or property such as a credit card) they may insist that clients provide detailed information about themselves, and authorize them to seek personal information from others with whom they have dealings. Private security may use such information for almost any purpose, and even pass it one, or sell it, to others.

In theory, the public can avoid the exercise of such private security authority by declining to use the facilities, as either customers or employees. In practice, however, realistic alternatives are often not available; for example, airport security applies to all airlines. This is a function of both the modern trend toward mass private property, and the fact that more and more public places are now situated on private property. Between them, these trends result in a situation in which the choices available to consumers are often severely limited. Employees and customers alike must submit to the authority of property owners and their agents as a condition of use. Thus, because private security is so pervasive, and because it is found in so many services and facilities essential to modern living (employment, credit, accommodation, education, health, transportation), it is practically impossible to avoid.

The fact that private security derives so much of its legitimacy from the institution of private property involves a profound historical irony. In the United States and Canada, state power has historically been perceived as posing the greatest threat to individual liberty. The legal institutions of private property and privacy arguably evolved as a means of guaranteeing individuals a measure of security against external intrusions, especially intrusions by the state (Reich, 1964; Stinchcombe, 1963). These institutions defined an area of privacy to which the state was denied access without consent, other than in exceptional circumstances. On private property, therefore, the authority of the property owner was recognized as being paramount—a philosophy most clearly reflected in the adage, "a man's home is his castle."

The validity of this notion, however, requires a reasonable congruence between private property and private places: a man's home was his castle, not because it was private property as such, but because it was a private place. However, as more and more private property has become, in effect, public, this congruence has been eroded. The emergence of mass private property, in fact, has given to private corporations a sphere of independence and authority which in practice has been far greater than that enjoyed by individual citizens and which has rivaled that of the state. The legal authority originally conceded to private property owners has increasingly become the authority for massive and continuous intrusions upon the privacy of citizens (as customers and employees) by those who own and control the mass private property on which so much public life takes place. Nevertheless, the traditional association between the institution of private property and the protection of liberty has historically been such a powerful source of legitimacy that, despite these important changes in the nature of private property, the exercise of private security authority is rarely questioned or challenged.

What little resistance has occurred has been mainly in the workplace, and has taken one or both of two forms—one an "underground" movement, and the other a more open and organized phenomenon. The underground movement is apparent in a "hidden economy" (Henry, 1978) of systematic pilfering, unofficial "perks," "padding" of claims for sickness benefits and other forms of compensation, as means of circumventing the formal structures and procedures established to protect corporate assets and profits. While such resistance sometimes occurs on a grand scale, it is mostly informal and individualistic.

Labor unions have posed a more formal and openly organized challenge to the unrestricted exercise of private security authority. They have fought private security processes and procedures through industrial action, collective bargaining, and arbitration. For example, in our research we have encountered collective agreements containing clauses specifying in detail the occasions on which employees may be searched, the procedures to be used in such searches, and the processes to be followed in the event that employees come under suspicion (Stenning and Shearing, 1979:179). Indeed, the growing body of so-called "arbitral jurisprudence" suggests there may be a trend toward a greater degree of accountability within private justice in the industrial and commercial sectors, just as the growing body of administrative law suggests a similar trend in the public domain (Arthurs, 1979).

To regard such developments simply as resistance to the growth of private security, however, is obviously overly simplistic, since in an important way they serve to institutionalize and legitimate it. When private security has been negotiated rather than imposed, its legitimacy is enhanced, co-opting the unions in the process. Furthermore, as private security procedures become more formalized and institutionalized they are often abandoned in favour of newer, less formal, and more flexible ones. An example of this is the replacement of formal arbitration by informal on-site mediation processes. Other researchers have noted similar reactions in the fields of administrative and labor law (Arthurs, 1980; Zack, 1978).

THE NATURE OF PRIVATE SECURITY

Three characteristics of private security reveal its essential nature: (1) its non-specialized character; (2) its client-defined mandate; and (3) the character of the sanctions it employs. We discuss each of these in turn.

NON-SPECIALIZED CHARACTER

The criminal justice system is divided into many specialized divisions and employs people in distinct roles, such as police, prosecutors, defence counsel, judiciary, and correctional officers. In contrast, we have found that private security is often integrated with other organizational functions, as the following example illustrates.

One of the companies which we studied operated a chain of retail outlets selling fashionable clothing for teenagers and young adults. Officials of the company emphasized that security was one of their principal concerns, because the company operated in a competitive market with slender profit margins. The company tried to improve its competitive position by reducing its losses, and boasted that it had one of the lowest loss-to-sales ratios in the industry. In accounting for this, officials pointed to the success of their security measures. Yet the company employed only one specialized security officer; security was not organizationally separated into discrete occupational roles. Rather, officials attributed responsibility for security to every employee. Moreover, employees typically did not undertake security activities distinct from their other occupational activities. Security functions were regarded as most effective when they were embedded in other functions. For example, officials believed that good sales strategies made good security strategies: if sales persons were properly attentive to customers, they would not only advance sales but simultaneously limit opportunities for theft. The security function was thus seen as embedded in the sales function.

What, then, is the role of specialized persons such as security guards? Our survey of contract security guards indicated that, while they frequently engaged in such specialized security functions as controlling access to commercial facilities (26 percent), they were employed mainly to supervise the performance of security functions by non-specialized personnel (Shearing, et al., 1980). Thus 48 percent reported that the problem most frequently encountered was the carelessness of other employees. An important element of the security function, therefore, was to check on employees after hours, to see whether they had kept up with their security responsibilities by seeing whether doors had been left unlocked or valuable goods or confidential papers had been left in the open. When they discovered such failings, security guards would inform the employees' supervisor, using strategies such as the one described by Luzon (1978:41):

> In support of the project drive for theft reduction, Atlantic Richfield security instituted an evening patrol, still in effect. For each risk found, the patrolling officer fills out and leaves a courteous form, called a "snowflake," which gives the particular insecure condition found, such as personal valuable property left out, unlocked doors, and valuable portable calculators on desks. A duplicate of each snowflake is filed by floor and location, and habitual violators are interviewed. As a last resort, compliance is sought through the violator's department manager.

This feature of private security is reminiscent of the pre-industrial, feudal policing system in Britain known as "frankpledge," in which policing was the responsibility of all community members, was integrated with their other functions, and was supervised by a small number of specialized security persons— sheriffs and constables—designated to ensure that community members were exercising their security responsibilities properly (Critchley, 1978). This non-specialized character of private security, however, creates particular difficulties in numerically comparing private security with public police and in attempting to measure the extent of the shift in policing from public to private hands.

CLIENT-DEFINED MANDATE

The mandate and objectives of private security, we found, were typically defined in terms of the particular interests and objectives of those who employed them. Table 2 presents results from our study of contract security in Ontario, which show that the employers of private security are most commonly private industrial and commercial corporations.

Table 2

Classification of Five Largest Clients

| | \multicolumn{6}{c}{Type of Contract Security Agency} | | | | | |
| Client | \multicolumn{2}{c}{Guard (N = 19)} | \multicolumn{2}{c}{Investigator (N = 26)} | \multicolumn{2}{c}{G. & I. (N = 47)} |
	%[a]	Rank	%[a]	Rank	%[a]	Rank
Industrial	42	1	31	5	70	1
Lawyers	5	c	92	1	28	c
Construction	32	2	b		55	2
Shopping Mall	21	5	35	4	36	4
Offices	32	2	b		45	3
Hospitals	10	c	b		30	5
Education	32	2	b		21	c
Insurance	b		69	2	17	c
Citizens	5	c	54	3	19	c
Government	21	5	15	c	28	c

Notes:

a. As a result of multiple responses, percentages do not total 100.

b. Client type not mentioned.

c. Client type mentioned but not ranked within first five.

Source:

Adapted from Shearing et al., (1980).

Furthermore, we found that contract security agencies, in their advertising, appeared to assume that their major audience was made up of executives of private corporations, and that they typically promoted their services on the basis that they would increase profits by reducing losses (Shearing, et al., 1980:163). While we do not have exactly comparable data revealing the distribution of in-house security, there is every reason to believe that here too private industrial and commercial corporations are the major users.

Private security is most typically a form of "policing for profit" (Spitzer and Scull, 1977:27)—that is, policing which is tailored to the profit-making objectives and its corporate clients. In those cases in which the principal objective of the clients is not the making of profit (e.g., where the client's principal objective is to provide health services, education, or entertainment) it will be that objective which will shape and determine the mandate and activities of private security.

This client orientation has important implications for the nature of policing undertaken by private security, and serves to distinguish it from public policing. In the criminal justice system, the state is nominally impartial and individuals are judged in terms of crimes against the public interest. By contrast, private security defined problems in purely instrumental terms; behavior is judged not according to whether it offends some externally defined moral standards, but whether it threatens the interests (whatever they may be) of the client. This establishes a definition of social order which is both more extensive and more limited than that defined by the state; more extensive because it is concerned with matters such as absenteeism or breaches of confidentiality (Gorrill, 1974:98) which may threaten the interests of the client but are not violations of the law; more limited because it is not normally concerned with violations of the law—such as some victimless crimes—which are not perceived as threatening the interests of the client.

In this sense, policing by private security is essentially victim-controlled policing. Corporate victims can maintain order without having to rely exclusively, or even primarily, on the criminal justice system. By establishing their own private security organizations directed to maintaining their own definitions of social order, corporate landlords and entrepreneurs not only ensure that their interests as potential victims are given priority in policing, but also avoid "the difficulty of proving matters in a formal system of justice arising from the extension of individual rights" (Reiss, forthcoming). With private security, conflict remains the property of victims (Christie, 1977). As one of the security managers we interviewed put it:

> See those *Criminal Codes*? I got a whole set of them, updated every year. I've never used one. I could fire the whole set in the garbage, all of them. Security is prevention; you look at the entire operation and you see the natural choke points to apply the rules and regulations. The police, they don't understand the operations of a business. They don't come on the property unless we invite them.

Just as social order enforced by private security is defined in terms of the interests of the client, so are the resources which are allocated for enforcement and the means which are employed. Thus, a retail organization which sells clothes will usually not install surveillance systems in changing rooms; this is not because such systems are ineffective in catching thieves, but because they might deter too many honest shoppers. The inevitable result of such instrumental policing is, of course, that a certain amount of known or suspected deviance will often be tolerated because the costs or the means of controlling it would threaten the interests of the client more than the deviance itself. There is little room for retribution within this instrumental approach. Social control exists solely to reduce threats to the interests of the client and the focus of attention shifts from discovering and blaming wrongdoers to eliminating sources of such threats in the future. This shifts the emphasis of social control from a judicial to a police function, and from detection to prevention. As one steel company security director expressed it:

> The name of the game is steel. We don't want to be robbed blind, but we aren't interested in hammering people.... I'm not responsible for enforcing the *Criminal Code*, my basic responsibility is to reduce theft, minimize disruption to the orderly operation of the plant.

In our study of contract security we found that both security guards and private investigators focused attention primarily on identifying and rectifying security loopholes rather than on apprehending or punishing individuals who actually stole goods (Shearing et al., 1980:178). This focus generates a new class of "offenders"—those who create opportunities for threats against the interests of the client. For example, a major Canadian bank launched an internal investigation into the loss of several thousands of dollars from one of its branches. The emphasis of the investigation was not on identifying the thief, but on discovering what breach of security had allowed the loss to occur and who was responsible for this breach, so that steps could be taken to reduce the risk of it recurring. The police were not involved in the investigation, despite the obvious suspicions of theft, and its results were the tightening up of security rules within the branch and the disciplining of the head teller who had breached them (*Freeborn v. Canadian Imperial Bank of Commerce*, 1981).

Even when a traditional offender is caught by private security, the client's best interest will often dictate a course of action other than invoking the criminal justice system. In 1982 in Calgary, Alberta, a bank succeeded in tracking down someone who had stolen over $14,000 from its automatic tellers.

Instead of calling the police, the bank tried to persuade the offender to sign for the amount as a loan. Only when he refused to agree to this resolution of the matter was the case turned over to the police (*Globe and Mail*, 1982).

THE CHARACTER OF SANCTIONS

The fact that private security emphasizes loss prevention rather than retribution does not mean that sanctions are never employed. When they are invoked, however, they usually draw on private and corporate power, rather than state power.

The sanctions available within the criminal justice system rest ultimately on the state's access to physical force, over which it has a legal monopoly (Bittner, 1970). Private security's use of force is legally limited to cases in which they act as agents of the state, using citizen powers of arrest, detention, and search (Stenning and Shearing, 1979). This does not mean that private security lacks powerful sanctions; on the contrary, as the agents of private authorities they have available a range of sanctions which are in many respects more potent than those of the criminal justice system, and which they perceive as being far more effective (Scott and McPherson, 1971:272; Shearing et al., 1980:232). One of the corporate security executives whom we interviewed said:

> [In a court] a different degree of proof is required; if the judge decides that there is insufficient evidence, you might be reinstated, because of some *legal* reason; in the disciplining process, I can get rid of you. If he's charged, we may have to continue him with benefits. To charge a person is a very serious thing, a very complicated process. We have to ask ourselves, do we just want to get rid of him, or do we want to throw the book at him? Maybe he's not a crook, he's just a dope.

As this example illustrates, foremost among the sanctions available to private security is the ability of corporations to restrict access to private property and to deny the resources which such access provides. Thus, private security can deny persons access to recreational and shopping facilities, housing, employment, and credit.

The essentially economic character of private security's sanctions does not mean that physical force has no bearing on what happens. When organizations want a legally imposed resolution to their problem, they can involve the police or initiate a civil suit. In drawing upon state power to support their legal rights to control access to property, organizations effectively expand the range of sanctions available to them.

PRIVATE SECURITY AND THE CRIMINAL JUSTICE SYSTEM

While many writers have suggested that private security is a mere adjunct to the criminal justice system—the so-called "junior partner" theory (Kakalik and Wildhorn, 1977)—our research suggests that many of those who control private security view the relationship quite differently. They saw the criminal justice system as an adjunct to their own private systems, and reported invoking the former only when the latter were incapable of resolving problems in a way which suited their interests.

Nevertheless, private security executives as well as senior public police officers preferred in public statements to characterize private security as the "junior partner" of the criminal justice system. For private security, this characterization minimized public fears that private security was "taking over" and that "private armies" were being created. It also carried the welcome implication that private security shared in the legitimacy and accepted status of the public police. The "junior partner" theory was attractive to the public police because it downplayed suggestions that they were losing their dominant role, while allowing them to take advantage of the inter dependence of the private and public security systems.

The "junior partner" theory significantly distorts the relationship between the public police and private security in at least three ways. First, the theory implies that private security is concerned only with minor cases, thereby freeing the public police to deal with more serious matters (Harrington, 1982). Yet this proved to be *not* true for property "crime"; in fact, the reverse was probably the case. Private security routinely dealt with almost all employee theft, even those cases involving hundreds of thousands of dollars. Security directors told us that they typically reported only relatively petty cases of theft to the public police and one Canadian automative manufacturer reported that it was their policy never to refer employee theft to the public police. Even serious assaults, such as employee fights involving personal injury, were sometimes handled internally. Furthermore, while most serious personal injuries resulting from crimes were reported to the police, most so-called "industrial accidents" were dealt with internally (Carson, 1981).

A second, unfounded implication of the "junior partner" theory is that the public police direct the operations of private security. While the public police sometimes attempt such direction by establishing crime prevention squads and acting as consultants, private security personnel often mocked what they saw as presumptuous police officials who set themselves up as "crime prevention experts." Furthermore, because private security are usually the first to encounter a problem, they effectively direct the police by determining what will and what will not be brought to their attention (Black, 1980:52; Feuerverger and Shearing, 1982). On those occasions where the public police and private security work together—for example, police fraud squads with bank security personnel—it cannot be assumed that the public police play the leading role, either in terms of investigative expertise or in terms of direction of the investigation.

Third, private security is by no means a "junior partner" to the public police in the resources it draws upon, such as mechanical hardware or information systems. Private security not only frequently has access to sophisticated weapons and electronic surveillance systems, but is well equipped with standard security hardware including patrol cars and armored vehicles (Hougan, 1978; Scott and McPherson, 1971).

What, then, is the relationship between the public police and private security? Our research left little doubt that it was a co-operative one, based principally on the exchange of information and services. This was facilitated by the movement of personnel from public police to private security (Shearing et al., 1980:195). This movement was particularly prevalent at the management level. Thirty-eight percent of the contract security executives we interviewed (Shearing et al., 1980:118) and 32 percent of the in-house executives (Jeffries, 1977:38) were ex-police officers. Furthermore, many organizations reported relying on ex-police officers to gain access, through the "old boy network," to confidential police information. This was particularly common within private investigation agencies (Ontario Royal Commission, 1980:166). A private investigator summed up the exchange of information between private investigators and the public police this way:

> There are approximately a hundred private investigators in Toronto who can literally get any information they want whether it is from the Police Department, Workmen's Compensation records, O.H.I.P. [Ontario Health Insurance Plan] insurance records, or whatever. In the space of a ten-minute telephone conversation I can get what it would take me perhaps three weeks to discover. With experience and contacts, a well-established investigator can provide a better quality of information and can do so at a much lower cost to his client even though his hourly rates might be twice as much as a new investigator might charge.

The extent of this cooperation with the public police was summed up by the director of security we interviewed at a large commercial shopping mall in Toronto. After noting how easy it was for him to obtain the support of the local public police, he described his relationship with them as "one big police force." Yet there was no doubt in his mind that it was *he* who effectively controlled this force, through his control over access to the private property under his jurisdiction.

SUMMARY AND CONCLUSIONS

Private organizations, and in particular large corporations, have since 1960, and probably earlier, exercised direct power over policing the public through systems of private security. The growth of mass private property has facilitated an ongoing privatization of social control characterized by non-specialized security. As a result, North America is experiencing a "new feudalism": huge tracts of property and associated public spaces are controlled—and policed—by private corporations. To undertake this responsibility, these corporations have developed an extensive security apparatus, of which uniformed security personnel are only the supervisory tip of the iceberg.

The shift from public to private systems of policing has brought with it a shift in the character of social control. First, private security defines deviance in instrumental rather than moral terms: protecting corporate interests becomes more important than fighting crime, and sanctions are applied more often against those who create opportunities for loss rather than those who capitalize on the opportunity—the traditional offenders. Thus, the reach of social control has been extended. Second, in the private realm, policing has largely disappeared from view as it has become integrated with other organizational functions and goals, at both the conceptual and behavioral levels. With private security, control is not an external force acting on individuals; now it operates from within the fabric of social interaction, and members of the communities in which it operates are simultaneously watchers and the watched. They are the bearers of their own control. Third, this integration is expressed in the sanctioning system, in which private security draws upon organizational resources to enforce compliance. Together these three features of private security create a form of social control that Foucault (1977) has termed discipline: control is at once pervasive and minute; it takes the form of small, seemingly insignificant observations and remedies that take place everywhere (Melossi, 1979:91; Shearing and Stenning, 1982).

Is private security here to stay? We think this depends less on the fiscal resources of the state, as some writers have suggested (Kakalik and Wildhorn, 1977), and more on the future structure of property ownership and the law related to it. There is little reason to believe that mass private property will not continue to develop, thereby permitting corporations to secure control over "relationships that were once exclusively in the public realm" (Spitzer and Scull, 1977:25). Thus, we believe private security will continue to develop as an increasingly significant feature of North American social life.

To the extent that control over policing is an essential component of sovereignty (Gerth and Mills, 1958:78), the development of modern private security raises the possibility of sovereignty shifting from the state directly to private corporations in both their national and, more significantly, their international guises. This in turn raises questions about the limitations of state control over private security and the validity of claims that the state is becoming more dominant in capitalistic societies (Boehringer, 1982; Cohen, 1979). Indeed, the evidence of direct control by capital over important aspects of policing points to the necessity of a thorough re-examination of conventional theoretical statements—be they instrumentalist or structural (Beirne, 1979)—about the relationship between the state and capital under modern capitalism.

ENDNOTES

* This is a revised version of a paper presented at the 33rd annual meeting of the American Society of Criminology in Washington, D.C., November, 1981. The authors thank John Gilmore and the anonymous *Social Problems* reviewers for their comments. Correspondence to: Centre of Criminology, University of Toronto, 8th Floor, John Robarts Library, 130 St. George Street, Toronto, Ontario M5S 1A1, Canada.

1.   An exception to this is the research on dispute resolution, especially that done by anthropologists (Nader, 1980; Pospisil, 1978; Snyder, 1981).

2.   For a more detailed analysis of current statistics on the size and growth of private security see Shearing and Stenning (1981:198).

3.   Reliable data for the United States since 1975 are not yet available.

4.   Although 1961 and 1971 census data are available they cannot be compared to establish growth rates due to changes in category definitions (Farnell and Shearing, 1977:39).

REFERENCES

Arthurs, Harry W. 1979. "Rethinking administrative law: A slightly dicey business." *Osgoode Hall Law Journal* 17(1):1-45.

_____, 1980. "Jonah and the whale: The appearance, disappearance, and reappearance of administrative law." *University of Toronto Law Journal* 30:225-239.

Baldwin, Robert, and Richard Kinsey. 1980. "Behind the politics of police powers." *British Journal of Law and Society* 7(2):242-265.

Becker, Theodore M. 1974. "The place of private police in society. An area of research for the social sciences." *Social Problems* 21(3):438-453.

Beirne, Piers. 1979. "Empiricism and the critique of Marxism on law and crime." *Social Problems* 26(4):273-385.

Bittner, Egon. 1970. *The Functions of the Police in Modern Society.* Chevy Chase, Maryland: National Institute of Mental Health, Centre for Studies in Crime and Delinquency.

Black, Donald. 1980. *The Manners and Customs of the Police.* New York: Academic Press.

Boehringer, Gill. 1982. "The strong state and the surveillance society: Changing modes of control." Paper presented at the Australian and New Zealand Association for the Advancement of Science Congress, Macquarie University, New South Wales, Australia, May.

Bourne, Larry S., and Peter D. Harper. 1974. "Trends in future urban land use." Pp. 213-236 in Larry S. Bourne, Ross D. MacKinnon, Jay Siegel, and James W. Simmons (eds.), *Urban Futures for Central Canada: Perspectives on Forecasting Urban Growth and Form.* Toronto: University of Toronto Press.

Bunyan, Tony. 1977. *The History and Practice of Political Police in Britain.* London: Quartet Books.

Carson, W. G. 1981. *The Other Price of Britain's Oil: Safety and Control in the North Sea.* Oxford: Martin Robertson.

Christie, Nils. 1977. "Conflicts as property." *British Journal of Criminology* 17(1):1-15.

Cohen, Stanley. 1979. "The punitive city: Notes on the dispersal of social control." *Contemporary Crisis* 3(4):339-364.

Coleman, James. 1974. *Power and the Structure of Society.* New York: Norton.

Critchley, Thomas A. 1978. *A History of Police in England and Wales:* 900-1966. London: Constable.

Farnell, Margaret B., and Clifford D. Shearing. 1977. *Private Security: An Examination of Canadian Statistics, 1961-1971.* Toronto: Centre of Criminology, University of Toronto.

Feuerverger, Andrey, and Clifford D. Shearing. 1982. "An Analysis of the Prosecution of Shoplifters." *Criminology* 20(2):273-289.

Foucault, Michel. 1977. *Discipline and Punish: The Birth of the Prison.* New York: Pantheon Books.

Freedman, David J., and Philip C. Stenning. 1977. *Private Security, Police, and the Law in Canada.* Toronto: Centre of Criminology, University of Toronto.

Friendly, John Ashley. 1980. "Harbinger." Unpublished paper. Osgoode Hall Law School, Toronto.

Gerth, Hans H., and C. Wright Mills (eds.). 1958. *From Max Weber: Essays in Sociology.* New York: Oxford University Press.

Gertler, Leonard O., and Ronald W. Crowley. 1977. *Changing Canadian Cities: The Next Twenty-Five Years.* Toronto: McClelland and Stewart.

Globe and Mail (Toronto). 1982. "Bank scolded over theft." October 16:11.

Gorrill, B. E.. 1974. Effective Personnel Security Procedures. Homewood, Illinois: Dow Jones-Irwin.

Harrington, Christine B. 1982. "Delegalization reform movements: A historical analysis." Pp. 35-71 in Richard L. Abel (ed.), *The Politics of Informal Justice.* Volume 2. New York: Academic Press.

Henry, Stuart. 1978. The Hidden Economy: *The Context and Control of Borderline Crime.* London: Martin Robertson.

Horan, James D. 1967. *The Pinkertons: The Detective Dynasty that Made History.* New York: Crown Publishers.

Hougan, Jim. 1978. *Spooks: The Haunting of America: The Private Use of Secret Agents.* New York: Bantam.

Jeffries, Fern. 1977. *Private Policing: An Examination of In-House Security Operations.* Toronto: Centre of Criminology, University of Toronto.

Johnson, Bruce C. 1976. "Taking care of labor: The police in American politics." *Theory and Society* 3(1):89-117.

Kakalik, James S., and Sorrel Wildhorn. 1971. *Private Policing in the United States.* Five volumes. Santa Monica, Calif.: Rand Corporation.

_____, 1977. *The Private Police: Security and Danger.* New York: Crone Russak.

Lipson, Milton. 1975. *On Guard: The Business of Private Security.* New York: Quandrangle/New York Times Book Co.

Lorimer, James. 1972. *A Citizen's Guide to City Politics.* Toronto: James Lewis and Samuel.

Luzon, Jack. 1978. "Corporate headquarters security." *The Police Chief* 45(6):39-42.

Martin, Larry R. G. 1975. "Structure, conduct, and performance of land dealers and land developers in the land industry." Mimeographed. School of Urban and Regional Planning, University of Waterloo.

Melossi, Dario. 1979. "Institutions of control and the capitalist organization of work." Pp. 90-99 in Bob Fine, Richard Kinsey, John Lea, Sol Picciotto, and Jock Young (eds.), *Capitalism and the Rule of Law: From Deviance Theory to Marxism.* London: Hutchinson.

Nader, Laura. 1980. *No Access to Law: Alternatives to the American Judicial System.* New York: Academic Press.

Ontario Royal Commission of Inquiry into the Confidentiality of Health Records in Ontario. 1980. *Report of the Commission of Inquiry into the Confidentiality of Health Information.* Volume 1. Toronto: Queen's Printer.

Pospisil, Leopold. 1967. "Legal levels and the multiplicity of legal systems in human societies." *Journal of Conflict Resolution* 11(1):2-26.

_____, 1978. *The Ethnology of Law:* Menlo Park, Ca.: Cummings.

Predicasts, Inc. 1974. *Private Security Systems.* Cleveland, Ohio: Predicasts Inc.

Punter, John V. 1974. *The Impact of Ex-Urban Development on Land and Landscapes in the Toronto Central Region, 1954-1971.* Ottawa: Central Mortgage and Housing Corporation.

Radzinowicz, Leon A. 1956. *A History of English Law and Its Administration from 1750: The Clash Between Private Initiatives and Public Interest in the Enforcement of the Law.* Volume 2. London: Stevens and Sons, Ltd.

Reich, Charles A. 1964. "The new property." *Yale Law Journal* 73(5):733-787.

Reiss, Albert J. forth. "Selecting strategies of control over organizational life." In Keith Hawkins and John Thomas (eds.), *Enforcing Regulation.* Boston: Kluwer-Nijhoff.

Scott, Thomas M., and Marlys McPherson. 1971. "The development of the private sector of the criminal justice system." *Law and Society Review* 6(2):267-288.

Scull, Andrew T. 1977. *Decarceration: Community Treatment and the Deviant—A Radical View.* Englewood Cliffs, N.J.: Prentice Hall.

Shearing, Clifford D., and Philip C. Stenning. 1981. "Private security: Its growth and implications." Pp. 193-245 in Michael Tonry and Norval Morris (eds.), *Crime and Justice—An Annual Review of Research.* Volume 3. Chicago: University of Chicago Press.

_____, 1982. "Snowflakes or good pinches? Private security's contribution to modern policing." Pp. 96-105 in Rita Donelan (ed.), *The Maintenance of Order in Society*. Ottawa: Canadian Police College.

Shearing, Clifford D., Margaret Farnell, and Philip C. Stenning. 1980. *Contract Security in Ontario*. Toronto: Centre of Criminology, University of Toronto.

Snyder, Francis G. 1981. "Anthropology, dispute processes, and law: A critical introduction." *British Journal of Law and Society* 8(2):141-180.

Spitzer, Stephen, and Andrew T. Scull. 1977. "Privatization and capitalist development: The case of the private police." *Social Problems* 25(1):18-29.

Spurr, Peter. 1975. "Urban land monopoly." *City Magazine* (Toronto) 1:17-31.

Stenning, Philip C. 1981. *Postal Security and Mail Opening: A Review of the Law*. Toronto: Centre of Criminology, University of Toronto.

Stenning, Philip C., and Mary F. Cornish. 1975. *The Legal Regulation and Control of Private Policing in Canada*. Toronto: Centre of Criminology, University of Toronto.

Stenning, Philip C., and Clifford D. Shearing. 1979. "Search and seizure: Powers of private security personnel." Study paper prepared for the Law Reform Commission of Canada. Ministry of Supply and Services Canada, Ottawa.

Stinchcombe, Arthur L. 1963. "Institutions of privacy in the determination of police administrative practice." *American Journal of Sociology* 69:150-160.

U.S. Department of Justice, Federal Bureau of Investigation. 1976. *Uniform Crime Reports for the United States: 1975*. Washington, D.C.: U.S. Government Printing Office.

Waldie, Brennan, and Associates. 1982. "Beyond the law: The strikebreaking industry in Ontario—Report to the Director, District 6, United Steelworkers of America." Mimeographed. United Steel Workers of America, Toronto.

Zack, Arnold M. 1978. "Suggested new approaches to grievance arbitration." Pp.105-117 in *Arbitration, 1977, Proceedings of the 30th annual meeting of the National Academy of Arbitrators*. Washington, D.C.: Bureau of National Affairs, Inc.

Case Cited

Freeborn v. Canadian Imperial Bank of Commerce, 5(9) Arbitration Services Reporter 1 (Baum), 1981.

CHAPTER 21
Privatization and Capitalist Development:
The Case of the Private Police

STEVEN SPITZER
ANDREW T. SCULL

This paper investigates some of the relationships between private policing and the development of capitalist economic systems. We argue that the emergence and transformation of profit-oriented police services must be understood as part of a larger movement toward the extension of capitalist control over the labor process and the rationalization of productive activity. Three distinctive stages in the privatization of policing are discussed—policing as piece-work, policing in the industrial age, and policing under corporate capitalism—with special attention to how these arrangements reveal the priorities and reflect the limitations of capitalist development. The shifting balance between public and private "crime control" is also explored as part of the changing relationship between policing and the political economy of our society.

Within the last decade there is growing evidence to suggest that the involvement of private enterprise in the public services sector has expanded at an unprecedented pace. Services and responsibilities which were once monopolized by the state—such as education, health care, welfare, and crime control—have been transferred in varying degrees and through a variety of arrangements to profit-making agencies and organizations. This development, described in one commentary as "creeping capitalism" (Forbes, 1970), has appeared in many forms.

One of the most interesting components of this trend toward privatization is the burgeoning of the private police industry.[1] It is generally assumed, for example, that private police now outnumber their counterparts in public service. According to one industry estimate (Forbes, 1970), two out of three law enforcement officers in the nation are actually on private payrolls. The most comprehensive study on the subject (Kakalik and Wildhorn, 1971:6) concludes that

> the private security industry has been growing at a recession-resistant rate of ten to fifteen percent annually over the last few years...In 1969 over 510,000 persons were employed in public police protection at all government levels. Depending on the source, estimates of the total number of private officers (guards, investigators, etc.) vary between 350,000 and 800,000.

The provision of private police services has progressively assumed the character of a modern industry—an industry dominated by major corporations like Pinkerton's, Burns, Walter Kidde and Co., and Wackenhut. The revenues of these corporations, the "big four" of the "rent-a-cop" industry, "more than tripled between 1963 and 1969, rising from $93 million to $312 million, and nearly doubled in the next five years" (Klare, 1975:487). The two largest corporations, Pinkerton's and Burns, have grown at a phenomenal rate.

> In 1960, Burns International Security Services was billing $29 million a year. In 1975, Burns—which now has eighty-five offices across the United States—reported revenues of over $181 million....Pinkerton's—has 40,000 guards who earned the company over $200 million last year, triple its revenues of 1965 *(New York Times Magazine*, 1976:21).

These figures show a rapid expansion in private policing that

> has come by way of the nationally based, heavily capitalized firms that are able to utilize equipment and methods usually not available to public police agencies. The expansion has also come from increased use of security personnel employed by firms engaged in commercial or industrial activity (Scott and McPherson, 1971:285).

What is perhaps most intriguing about this movement toward privatization is the way it parallels the rise of policing for profit in earlier historical periods. Prior to the eighteenth century, crime control in English-speaking societies was generally a community affair. Enforcement of the law was either achieved collectively through the medieval institutions of the "hue and cry" and *possee comitatus* (Pollock and Maitland, 1968), or through unpaid, rotating service by all citizens in the offices of watchman and constable (cf. Critchley, 1972; Fosdick, 1972). But as these communities were transformed from a series of relatively homogeneous and tightly integrated groupings into a differentiated and loosely articulated society, the informal and voluntary system of social control became increasingly suspect (Spitzer and Scull, 1977). Personal needs and interests began to take the place of "public spirit" as the mainspring of social control. By the eighteenth century the system had reached a point where the architects of legal control were beginning to ask

> private individuals for no higher motive than self-interest, and were confident that they could, by a system of incentives and deterrents— rewards and punishments, bribes and threats—so exploit human greed and fear that there would be no need to look for anything so nebulous and unrealistic as public spirit (Pringle, 1958:212).

POLICING AS PIECE-WORK

The origins of private policing during this era are to be found, curiously enough, in the office of the constable. Although this office traditionally "rested on the principle of unpaid performance of duty by members of the community as their turn came round" (Tobias, 1975:106), it gradually acquired pecuniary characteristics, as citizens who "disliked having to assume for a whole year an unpaid, arduous office which might entail enforcing unpopular laws" (Hart, 1951:24) chose to pay deputies to perform these disagreeable services in their place. Once in office the deputies soon found that profits could also be gained from selling protective and investigative services, or demanding rewards and fees in return for recovered goods. Deputies often "made such a profitable trade of their offices that many were prepared to serve for nothing" (Radzinowicz, 1956:278).

The reluctance of public authorities to support a salaried force, along with the growing opportunities for enterprising constables, combined to promote the appearance of specialists in police services. The pattern was first established in England where

> an officer who had risen high enough in his profession to become personally known could aspire to more than occupational remuneration for petty services. The next step in his career would be to obtain

> a number of well paid special employments consisting of permanent
> or temporary duties, for which he might be hired by any one willing
> and able to pay (Radzinowicz, 1956:261).

In America the situation was much the same. In a study of the early New York police, Richardson (1970:30) observed that during the first decades of the nineteenth century officers were more "private entrepreneurs than public servants." According to Wilson (1973:589), detectives in nineteenth century Boston also served essentially private interests. Since the main concern of the victim was restitution, they "functioned then as personal-injury lawyers operate today, on a contingency basis, hoping to get a large part, perhaps half, of the proceeds."

Much of the policing in England and America during the eighteenth and first half of the nineteenth century thus took on the character of a contractual arrangement negotiated between clients or victims who sought protective, investigative, or enforcement services, and independent agents who were willing to supply such services in return for a fee, reward, or share of recovered goods. Under this system, the buyer and seller of police services were brought together in the market-place as autonomous agents, with the latter maintaining considerable control over the conditions of labor. Much like the "putting-out" system in manufacturing (the precursor of modern factory production), the production of policing was highly decentralized and those who supplied police services retained considerable discretion over how much policing was done and the methods for achieving results. The method of payment-by-results or piece-rates, central to these managements, offered a way of organizing law enforcement in the absence of centralized administration and wage controls.

The major flaw in this form of private control, and an apparent reason for its decline, can be found in the contradictions of the piece-rate system itself. In an economy where the work force had not yet been habituated to the conditions of industrial labor

> while the employer could raise the piece rates with a view toward
> encouraging diligence, he usually found that this actually reduced
> output. The worker, who had a fairly rigid conception of what he felt
> to be a decent standard of living, preferred leisure to income after a
> certain point, and the higher his wages, the less he had to do to
> reach that point (Landes, 1972:58-59).

This trend was especially found in the production of policing where the employer had little, if any, knowledge of or influence over the productive process. Moreover, since exertions were rewarded by results alone, the system actually encouraged many of the activities it was ostensibly established to control. In the words of one critic, these arrangements led to an increase in crime "fostered and cultivated by the very persons set to watch over and prevent it" (*London Times*, 1817 cited in Radzinowicz, 1956:338). An instructive example of these abuses in New York is provided by Richardson (1970:30-31):

> The police reports published in the newspapers in these years are filled with accounts of instances in which the property was returned, with financial rewards for the police officer, but in which the criminal was not brought to justice....The officer received a larger fee or reward for recovering the stolen property than he would have received for bringing the criminal in...Often the arrangement was consummated even before the robbery or burglary took place. An officer would be privy to a crime, and after its commission would endeavor to recover the stolen property in return for a liberal reward. Part of the reward would then go to the thief as his share.

It should be clear from this example why private policing, at least in the form that it took in the eighteenth and early nineteenth centuries, was destined to fail. But while we may easily understand the reasons behind the search for an alternative method of policing the metropolis, we cannot as readily explain why the alternative was a publicly supported and highly centralized force of "preventive police" (Colquhoun, 1806). The adoption of such a force is especially puzzling in light of the long-standing opposition to centralized domestic controls in Anglo-American societies—an opposition which defined this type of policing as "a system of tyranny; an organised army of spies and informers, for the destruction of public liberty, and the disturbance of all private happiness" (Thompson, 1963:82).

To explain why the "experiment" in public policing became the dominant modality of urban law enforcement in the nineteenth and twentieth centuries we need to look beyond the problem of predatory crime. It is certainly true that the "new police" promised a more detached and professional approach to the regulation of property crime than their entrepreneurial counterparts. But the ultimate justification and *raison d'etre* of such a force was tied to their role as "keepers of the peace" rather than retrievers of property.

Unlike their pre-industrial predecessors, market societies were extremely allergic to collective disorder (cf. Polyani, 1944; Silver, 1967; Spitzer and Scull, 1977). In both England and America the establishment of municipal police systems was intimately linked to mounting threats to public order.

> In message after message the mayors of Boston, New York and
> Philadelphia called attention to the need of a new system. This need
> was emphasized by the increasing disorder of the times and evident
> inability of existing police forces [made up of untrained and generally
> inept watchmen] to cope with it. Beginning in 1835 a series of mob
> riots swept the country (Fosdick, 1972:65).

In Baltimore, Philadelphia, New York and Boston alone, there were at least
thirty-five major riots during the period 1830-1860 (Brown, 1969:40-41).
These disturbances called into question the very preconditions of rational calculation and predictable exchange and, in so doing, gave decisive impetus to
the search for an effective means of insuring domestic tranquility. This search
culminated in the development of the first centralized systems of policing in
the United States between 1845 and 1858. "The emergence of a municipal
police force...," was therefore, "not so much the result of mounting crime
rates as of growing levels of civil disorder" (Wilson, 1973:589). A method had
to be found of securing public order, and that method, at least in urban areas,
was to be the newly constituted public police.

By the end of the Civil War the urban market in private policing was
eclipsed by bureaucratically organized, salary-based and tax supported policing. Nevertheless, policing for profit was far from extinct. An entirely different
form of private enforcement was to reemerge during the last quarter of the
nineteenth century.

PRIVATE POLICING IN THE INDUSTRIAL AGE

Nascent capitalism was primarily concerned with establishing a secure
environment for exchange and commerce in the metropolis. But as industrial
development accelerated in the post-bellum period, and as the locus of production shifted toward segregated industrial areas, threats to economic development changed in degree and kind. In American, the end of the nineteenth
and beginning of the twentieth centuries witnessed the birth of large-scale primary industry (coal, steel, oil, railroads). These industries, which were to
become the backbone of future capitalist development (Kirkland, 1961;
Cochran and Miller, 1961), brought together vast numbers of unskilled laborers within geographically circumscribed areas—the company towns. Once
these areas were established, attempts were made to encapsulate and regulate
much of the worker's existence through company control over housing, religion, recreation, family relationships, and medical care. A central feature of

this experiment in "welfare capitalism" (Brandes, 1976) was the paternalistic relationship between industrial entrepreneurs and the working class.

In contrast to the anonymity and impersonality of the city, these industrial towns functioned in terms of direct, personal relationships between social classes. Social authority was personal and conformity was rooted in the traditions of pre-industrial society. This variety of "paternalistic domination" proved workable in industrial towns because the working class in these areas, unlike their urban counterparts, "often clung to an older ('agrarian') set of values" and "judged the economic and social behavior of local industrialists by these older and more humane values" (Gutman, 1963:43). As long as prosperity reigned the "closed town" could function as an analogue of the feudal manor. However, once the "captains of industry" were faced with economic crises which forced cuts in production they:

> found that certain aspects of the social structure and ideology in small industrial towns hindered their freedom of action. It proved relatively easy for them to announce a wage cut or to refuse publicly to negotiate with a local trade union, but it often proved quite difficult to enforce such decisions easily and quickly. In instance after instance, and for reasons that varied from region to region, employers reached outside of their local environment to help assert their local authority (Gutman, 1963:45-46).

The growth of labor militancy—there were nearly 23,000 strikes between 1880 and 1900 alone (Brandes, 1976:1)—when combined with the unreliable and sometimes hostile reactions of local enforcement officials, did much to promote the search for extra-local controls over the working class. Beginning in the 1870s, private police began to fill this demand with the Pinkertons (Horan, 1967) playing the most significant role. By 1892, the Pinkertons had been instrumental in breaking seventy-seven strikes, and although their overt activities tapered off after that time, they (along with the Burns Detective Agency) remained active in industrial espionage for the next several decades. According to Johnson (1976:97), "labor spying, carried out on a massive scale during this period, enabled employers to penetrate and destroy many nascent labor organizations by exposing potential union leaders." In fact, up until the 1930s,[2] the private police proved an essential ingredient in industrial capitalism's struggle against working class militancy and the operation of what one industrialist called "the 'big stick' system" (Brandes, 1976:2).

Perhaps the most palpable reasons for the decline of private policing in the 1920s and 1930s were (1) "the remarkable process by which corporate interests and private police managed during the first third of this century to pass the anti-labor torch to federal government agencies such as the Bureau of Immigration and the U.S. Army" (Johnson, 1976:98; see also Millis, 1956 and Preston, 1963); (2) the creation of the Federal Bureau of Investigation as a national police agency; and (3) the growing willingness of unions, unlike their nineteenth century predecessors, to play by the "rules of the game" (Moffett, 1971). But a closer examination suggests that this decline was more fundamentally influenced by the changing structure of the capitalist economy and changes in the organizational form of capitalist enterprise.

Martin Sklar (1969:15-16) reports that

> in 1870, 77 percent of the gainfully employed persons in the United States were 'engaged in transforming the resources of nature into objects of usable form through manufacturing, mining, and agriculture,' in 1930 only 52 percent were so engaged....During the 1920s 'the trend of actual employment in manufacturing industry was downward for the first time in our history'.

This shift was important because it signaled a move of the locus of economic development away from extractive industries and those involved in the production and transportation of capital goods, toward enterprises engaged in the production of consumer goods, the provision of services, consumer-financing, installment selling, market research and advertising. As labor was freed from its dependence on primary industrial processes and channeled into administrative, marketing, and promotional tasks, and as transportation improvements removed proximity as a condition of employment,[3] the economic foundations of the company town were seriously undermined. At about the same time (1920's-30's), corporate activity was geographically dispersed and decentralized (Chandler, 1962). The locally-based, paternalistic structures of the Gilded Age gave way to the diversified and impersonal corporation. Because "the corporation as a form severs the direct link between capital and its individual owners" (Braverman, 1974:258), control over the work force became less and less dependent on the wealth and capabilities of individual capitalists. By the beginning of the 20th century the "captains of industry" were being replaced by a professionalized managerial class and "as corporations became larger and larger, their managements became so distant that they lost all contact with their employees" (Brandes, 1976:14). Taken together, these changes destroyed the structural supports for the paternalism upon which welfare capitalism had been built.

As the basis for and feasibility of private control were eroded, many of the costs which once fell upon private capitalists were absorbed by the state. In the maintenance of public order, "socialization" had been made possible by the expansion in size, organizational effectiveness, and functional responsibilities of local police (Johnson, 1976:101), as well as the far-reaching reforms of municipal police departments during the 1920's and 1930's (cf. Carte and Carte, 1975). At this juncture, public enforcement proved more attractive than private arrangements from the point of view of both legitimacy and costs. When the functions once delegated to private police were turned over to the state, the dominant class could ideologically separate the enforcement of "constitutional" authority from its own social ascendence. Once the separation had been achieved, it was easier to claim that the social order was preserved by the "rule of law and not men." Since the law could be defined as impersonal, external, and given, rather than the arbitrary creation of particular men, it was a far more effective basis for "legitimate" order-maintenance than the directives of private employers.

Moreover, when the yoke of dependency and contrived monopoly surviving in company towns was broken, it was no longer in the interest of individual businessmen to pay for the costs of maintaining civil order. On the one hand, the geographic areas requiring pacification had become too extensive, and the number and diversity of actors whose interests and activities had to be coordinated were too great for privately organized enforcement. On the other hand, the diffusion of economic activity discouraged private solutions to the problem of public order because of the "free rider problem" of collective goods (cf. Olson, 1965; Buchanan, 1968). Under conditions of high labor mobility, "open towns," and fluid markets, the first businessman to underwrite the costs of preserving order would be at a competitive disadvantage. He would be forced to face increased costs of production while other capitalists could benefit from domestic tranquility at no cost to themselves. In other words, if a collective good like public order (or other transferable benefits like education, welfare, or health care) were to be provided privately in an "open society," those who did not contribute but reaped the rewards would get a "free ride." "The more social life becomes a dense and close network of interlocked activities in which people are totally interdependent," and "the more atomized they become" (Braverman, 1974:277), the more difficult it becomes for any one entrepreneur to exclude another from the benefits of social stability. Hence, as order became more and more a "public commodity" in the first half of the twentieth century, there were fewer incentives for individual capitalists to provide for peace-keeping at their own expense. And as private policing withdrew from the public arena, tax-supported enforcement came to assume more and more of these regulatory tasks.

PRIVATE POLICING UNDER CORPORATE CAPITALISM

In segregated industrial areas the tasks of maintaining order and protecting profits were essentially the same. Under welfare capitalism private police
protected profits by breaking strikes and disrupting labor organization. This
type of order-maintenance was vital to profit protection because it enabled
industrialists to achieve a monopoly over the pricing of what was considered,
at least at that time, a decisive cost of production—the cost of labor. But as
the twentieth century unfolded and the corporation became the dominant economic force in capitalist society, several important changes occurred. These
changes met a growing division of responsibility between the functions of
order-maintenance and profit protection. The former occupied more of the
time and resources of public authorities, while the latter increasingly provided
a basis for the expansion of the private police industry.

The task of maintaining order[4] has become far more generalized and
complex as the problems of social regulation and coordination engendered by
industrial development have outstripped the capacities of traditional social
institutions. More and more of the resources of the public sector, once devoted to productive investment, must now be diverted to cope with the corrosive
effects of capitalist growth (O'Connor, 1973). Particularly significant in this
regard is the burgeoning demand for "human services" and "dirty work"
(Rainwater, 1967)—a burden falling to an ever increasing extent upon the
public police.

Although the official purpose of public policing is crime control, investigations have revealed that (1) the overwhelming majority of calls for police assistance are service rather than crime related (Bercal, 1970), (2) most of the
increase in police budgets over the last century can be "explained away" as a
function of population growth, inflation, urbanization, and motor vehicle
increase (Bordua and Haurek, 1970), and (3) eight out of ten incidents handled by patrols in a number of urban police departments were regarded by the
police themselves as non-criminal matters (Reiss, 1971:73). The overload of
citizen demands for service such as "sick runs" and dispute management, coupled with the growing responsibilities of traffic control and "social sanitation"
(cf. Cumming et al., 1965; Bittner, 1967), leaves a relatively small proportion
of time and resources available to those who face low-visibility threats to their
property and profits. This pattern is especially found true when control of

these threats requires highly specific enforcement and investigative capabilities.

The ability of public policing to provide direct services to private enterprise has also diminished because of the fiscal crisis besetting the entire public service sector. This crisis is attributable in part to the labor-intensive character of public services. Welfare, education, health care, crime control are plagued by a high proportion of wage to capital costs. Rand reports, for example, that "in large municipal police departments, personnel costs account for 90% to 95% of the total" (Kakalik and Wildhorn, 1971:48). It is well known that productivity in labor-intensive organizations rises considerably slower than in their capital-intensive counterparts, with the result that greater levels of expenditure on police budgets are required simply to maintain the same level of service in real terms (cf. Gough, 1975). When this fact is considered in connection with the recent growth of unionization in policing (Grimes, 1975) and other public services, we may better understand why public police are hard put to provide the kind of sophisticated and expensive services that modern corporations require.

Within the private sector we find that as corporations have integrated, diversified, and attempted to "rationalize" (Kolko, 1963) their activities, the protection of profit has become a far more complicated and "public" process that it was under "laissez-faire" capitalism. While the nineteenth century firm was primarily concerned with lowering the cost of the labor supply, modern corporations have concentrated on (1) making more efficient use of labor power through "scientific management" (Braverman, 1974) and (2) extending control over many factors of production, distribution and consumption external to earlier forms of business enterprise.[5] This latter process—the *internalization* of what were previously unpredictable, disruptive, and potentially costly factors under a single, centralized, and highly rationalized system of administration—is crucial to the interpretation of modern forms of private policing for several reasons.

As corporations have expanded their range of operations through vertical and horizontal integration, what was once outside the boundaries of business activity is now within the corporate domain. It is now in the interest of large corporations to consider and manipulate relationships once assumed to exist exclusively within the public realm. The nineteenth-century entrepreneur had to depend on others to supply investment capital, raw materials, storage facilities, transportation and distribution networks. He had a geographically limited physical plant producing for specific markets, and his work force was relatively interchangeable and untrained. Because the modern corporation often maintains direct interest in and control over sources of investment, supply, storage, transportation, as well as the marketing of its products and the training of its work force, it has both the capability and the incentive to regulate, coordinate, and protect activities external to the nineteenth-century firm. Thus, as physical plants expand, the problems of security multiply. As payrolls and financial transactions increase in size and frequency, the problems of financial security grow. As corporate control extends beyond production to distribution and transportation, and as networks of distribution increase in terms of volume, distance and complexity, problems of pilferage, transportation security, and embezzlement increase. As employees are paid more and entrusted with more information, and as their work requires more sophisticated skills and longer periods of training, it becomes more and more desirable to investigate their backgrounds, moral character, and private activities. As research and development becomes an in-house capability, the opportunities for industrial espionage broaden.

The process of internalization thus creates a market for a whole new range of investigative and protective services. Not surprisingly, a recent Rand study of private policing (Kakalik and Wildhorn, 1971:62-63) reported that of all the markets of private police services, "industrial markets have grown the fastest, almost tripling between 1958 and 1968; they now comprise more than half the total." Corporations are now willing to pay for investigations of

> inventory losses, pilferage,...falsification of records,...low employee morale, willful neglect of machinery, waste of time and materials, thefts of tools, unreported absenteeism, supervisory incompetence..., pre-employment...and personal security checks, including polygraph examinations; financial responsibility investigations; electronic sweeps for hidden listening devices; surveillance of business and residential premises,...investigation of potential contest winners for compliance with contest rules; fingerprint and document analysis and shopping tests of all kinds to determine the honesty of employees and dealers (Klare, 1975:488-489).

In sum, how corporations have developed and changed in recent times has caused a growth in demand for specialized security services and equipment— services and equipment sold in larger and larger amounts by the private police industry.

To complete our comparison, we may summarize the advantages of private policing from the point of view of corporations purchasing the services and utilizing the equipment of private agencies. First, private policing is much more effective in achieving restitution than public law enforcement. In cases where compensation is more important than revenge and public handling is likely to be embarrassing or damaging, private arrangements offer advantages. Since private police have the privilege, but not the obligation, to arrest and detain offenders, they can deal with many transgressions extra-legally, minimizing the risks and costs of public processing while maximizing the probability of restitution. Second, private policing is far more flexible and efficient than public enforcement because it can be more readily adjusted to changing levels of consumer demand.

> The prerogative of private agencies to hire and dismiss personnel, as well as employing people for temporary and part-time assignments, in response to varying demands is not possible in public agencies operating under civil service regulations (Scott and McPherson, 1971:278).

As corporate needs change, private police services can be adapted in ways that are beyond the capabilities of unionized and bureaucratically ossified public systems.

In addition to these virtues, private agencies can benefit from aspects of public policing and pass on those benefits without requiring clients to pay for them. Police operating under private auspices can frequently borrow the halo and symbols of authority (uniform, gun, badge, accessories) associated with public enforcement and increase their effectiveness as enforcement agents. Private police may also benefit from exchanges of information obtained at taxpayers expense when the fruits of public investigation are made available to private firms. In other instances, public police agencies actually provide a valuable manpower resource to private firms through the cross-employment of retired officers and the wide-spread practice of "moonlighting" (Kakalik and Wildhorn, 1971:105-132).

Finally, private agencies are able to use much more sophisticated, scientifically advanced, technical equipment than most local law enforcement agencies can afford.

> To the extent that large, nationally capitalized firms are better able to purchase, maintain, and utilize the most highly sophisticated technical equipment under fewer constraints and with greater impunity than virtually all urban public police systems, they can provide better security and investigative service to those willing and able to pay (Scott and McPherson, 1971:281).

CONCLUSION

The purpose of this analysis has been to explore some of the relationships between the development of private policing and the political economy of capitalist society. We have argued that the privatization of policing must be understood in relation to the organization of society on a market basis. We have also attempted to demonstrate how socialization and privatization are integrally embedded in the unfolding of capitalist economic systems, and how both represent historically specific responses to the changing problems and priorities of such systems.

Policing for profit made its initial appearance during the transition from a mercantile to a capitalist economic system. Accordingly, one of the earliest "commodifications" of policing took the form of an unregulated market in police services where the "merchant" and the "consumer" met in the marketplace as autonomous agents. Because this system could not organize police labor on a rational basis and integrate control services within a coherent administrative framework, it proved relatively unstable and short-lived. In a similar sense, the private policing of the industrializing period was built upon the traditions and assumptions of an earlier age. When the paternalism which had survived in company towns proved incompatible with the exigencies of capitalist development, the "big stick system" was sacrificed in favor of more sophisticated labor controls and more rationalized methods of management. It became clear in this context that if private policing was to justify itself as worthy of capitalist investment it would have to offer more than force and intimidation alone.

In the modern era, the human problems generated in the wake of capitalist development, coupled with the deepening fiscal crisis of the state on the one hand and the extension of corporate hegemony on the other, have set the stage for the recrudescence of policing for profit. However contemporary varieties of private policing bear little resemblance to their eighteenth- and nineteenth-century ancestors. They reflect, rather, the pattern of economic concentration and principles of management characteristic of monopoly capital (Baran and Sweezy, 1966). For the most part, the private policing of today is organized as a corporate undertaking; and its major customers are large-scale organizations who invest in policing for the same reasons they make other investments: to guarantee profits and secure an environment for uninterrupted growth.

ENDNOTES

*Revised and expanded version of a paper presented at the 72nd Annual Meeting of the American Sociological Association, September, 1977.

1. The growth of the "rent-a-cop" industry may be distinguished from other varieties of privatization on the grounds that most private policing is supported by "private" rather than "public" expenditures (i.e., corporate revenues rather than tax-generated budgets). However, as we will argue, such distinctions are less and less defensible as changes in the economic structures of capitalist societies have blurred the boundaries between the public and private sector. As private organizations (i.e., corporations) expand their ability to "tax" the public, either directly through state subsidies or indirectly through administered prices (cf. O'Connor, 1974), the source of funding becomes a less reliable differentia between private and public activity.

2. Horan (1967:507) reports that in 1936 thirty percent of the Pinkerton's business was made up of industrial services which "offered to the employer confidential information...as to the degree of unrest in a plant, the presence of outside agitators and organizers, and the general run for what was called labor espionage." After a series of legislative hearings and a condemning resolution by the House of Representatives, Pinkerton's dropped its industrial services and in 1938 "the firm's income dipped to $1,224,661, the lowest it had been since 1921" (Horan, 1967:510).

3. Brandes (1976:141), for example, claims that "the popularity of inexpensive automobiles ended the need for company towns."

4. The task of "maintaining order" clearly goes far beyond the control of collective violence. Analysts of contemporary policing have stressed the fact that many of the central functions of police work involve a type of "peace-keeping" (Bittner, 1967) which focuses more on the resolution of disputes "over what is 'right' or 'seemly' conduct or over who is to blame for conduct that is agreed to be wrong or unseemly" (Wilson, 1968:16), than the strict enforcement of the law.

5. The attempt to achieve a "monopoly by exclusion" so characteristic of closed towns reflects the limitations and instability of nineteenth-century firms. In contrast to this pattern, modern corporations have adopted a strategy of "monopoly by penetration."

REFERENCES

Baran, P.A. and P.M. Baran. 1966. *Monopoly Capital*. New York: Monthly Review Press.

Bercal, T.E. 1970. "Calls for police assistance," Pp. 267-277 in H. Hahn (ed.), *Police in Urban Society*. Beverly Hills: Sage Publications.

Bittner, E. 1967. "Police on skid row: a study of peace-keeping." *American Sociological Review* 32 ((October): 699-715.

Bordua, D.J. and E.W. Haurek. 1970. "The police budget's lot: components of the increase of local police expenditures, 1902-1960." Pp. 57-70 in H. Hahn (ed.), *Police in Urban Society*. Beverly Hills: Sage Publications.

Brandes, S.D. 1976. *American Welfare Capitalism*. Chicago: University of Chicago Press.

Braverman, H. 1974. *Labor and Monopoly Capital*. New York: Monthly Review Press.

Brown, R.M. 1969. "Historical patterns of violence in America." Pp. 35-64 in H.D. Graham and T.R. Gurr (eds.) *Violence in America: Historical and Comparative Perspectives*. Washington: Government Printing Office.

Buchanan, J.M. 1968. *The Demand and Supply of Public Goods*. Chicago: Rand McNally.

Carte, G.E. and E.H. Carte. 1975. *Police Reform in the United States*. Berkeley: University of California Press.

Chandler, A.D. 1962. *Strategy and Structure: Chapters in the History of the American Industrial Enterprise*. Cambridge, Mass.: The M.I.T. Press.

Cochran, T.C. and W. Miller. 1961. *A Social History of Industrial America*. New York: Harper and Row Publishers.

Colquhoun, P. 1806. *A Treatise on the Police of the Metropolis*. Montclair: Patterson Smith.

Critchley, T.A. 1972. *A History of Police in England and Wales*. Montclair: Patterson Smith.

Cumming, E., Cumming and L. Edell. 1965. "Policeman as philosopher, guide and friend." *Social Problems* 12 (Winter): 276-286.

Forbes. 1970. "Creeping capitalism." 106 (September): 22-28.

Fosdick, R.B. 1972. *American Police Systems*. Montclair: Patterson Smith. (Originally published in 1920).

Gough, I. 1975. "State expenditure in advanced capitalism." *New Left Review* 92 (July/August): 53-92.

Grimes, J.A. 1975. "The police, the union and the productivity imperative." Pp. 47-85 in J.L. Wolfle and J.F. Heapy (eds.) *Readings on Productivity in Policing.* Washington: The Police Foundation.

Gutman, H.G.. 1963. "The worker's search for power." Pp. 38-68 in H.W. Morgan (ed.) *The Gilded Age: A Reappraisal.* Syracuse: Syracuse University Press.

Hart, J.M. 1951. *The British Police.* London: George Allen and Unwin.

Horan, J.D. 1967. *The Pinkertons.* New York: Crown Publishers, Inc.

Johnson, B.C. 1976. "Taking care of labor: the police in American politics." *Theory and Society* 3 (Spring): 89-117.

Kakalik, J.S. and S. Wildhorn. 1971. *The Private Police Industry: its Nature and Extent.* Vol.II. RAND Corporation study for the National Institute of Law Enforcement and Criminal Justice. Washington: Government Printing Office.

Kirkland, E.C. 1961. *Industry Comes of Age.* Chicago: Quadrangle Books.

Klare, M.T. 1975. "Rent-a-cop: the boom in private police." *The Nation* 221 (November): 486-491.

Kolko, G. 1963. *The Triumph of Conservatism.* Chicago: Quandrangle Books.

Landes, D.S. 1969. *The Unbound Prometheus: Technological Change and Industrial Development in Western Europe from 1750 to the Present.* Cambridge, England: Cambridge University Press.

Millis, W. 1956. *Arms and Men.* New York: Capricorn Books.

Moffett, J.T. 1971. "Bureaucracy and social control: a study of the progressive regimentation of the western social order." Unpublished Ph.D. dissertation, Columbia University.

New York Times Magazine. 1976. "In guards we trust." September 19, 1976: 20-41.

O'Connor, J. 1973. *The Fiscal Crisis of the State.* New York: St. Martin's Press..

_____1974. *The Corporations and the State.* New York: Harper and Row, Publishers.

Olson, M. 1965. *The Logic of Collective Action: Public Goods and the Theory of Groups.* Cambridge, Mass.: Harvard University Press.

Pollock, F. and W. Maitland. 1968. *The History of English Law.* Vol. II. Cambridge, England: Cambridge University Press.

Polyani, K. 1944. *The Great Transformation.* Boston: Beacon.

Preston, W. 1963. *Aliens and Dissenters.* New York: Harper and Row, Publishers.

Pringle, P. 1958. *The Thief-Takers.* London: Museum Press.

Radzinowicz, L. 1956. *A History of English Criminal Law and Its Administration from 1750.* Vol. II. London: Stevens and Sons Limited.

Reiss, A.J., 1971. *The Police and the Public.* New Haven: Yale University Press.

Richardson, J.I., 1970. *The New York Police: Colonial Times to 1901.* New York: Oxford University Press.

Scott, T.M and M. McPherson, 1971. "The Development of the Private Sector of the Criminal Justice System," 6 (Nov.): 267-288.

Silver, A., 1967. "The Demand for Order in Civil Society: A Review of Some Themes in the History of Urban Crime, Police and Riot." Pp. 1-24 in D. Bordua (ed.) *The Police.* New York: John Wiley and Sons, Inc.

Sklar, M.J., 1969. "On the Proletarian Revolution and the End of Political-Economic Society." *Radical America.* 3 (May-June): 1-41.

Spitzer, S. and A.T. Scull, 1977. "Social Control in Historical Perspective: From Private to Public Responses to Crime," Pp. 281-302 in D.F. Greenberg (ed.) *Corrections and Punishment: Structure, Function and Process.* Beverly Hills: Sage Publications.

Thompson, E.P., 1963. *The Making of the English Working Class.* New York: Vintage Books.

Tobias, J.J., 1975. "Police and Public in the United Kingdom," Pp. 95-113 in G.L. Mosse (ed.) *Police Forces in History.* Beverly Hills: Sage Publications.

Wilson, J.Q., 1968. *Varieties of Police Behavior: The Management of Law and Order in Eight Communities.* New York: Atheneum.

_____, 1973. "The Dilemma of the Urban Police." Pp. 586-595 in A.B. Callow Jr. (ed.) *American Urban History.* Second Edition. New York: Oxford University Press.

CHAPTER 22
Policing
Corporate Collusion

DONALD W. SCOTT

This is a documentary study of the origin and investigation of all criminal prosecutions of collusive trade agreements filed by the Antitrust Division, U.S. Department of Justice from 1946 through 1970. The methodology seeks to reconstruct these cases from previously classifed investigative files of the division. Observations include the sources of organizational intelligence, investigative methods, and encounters among antitrust victims, offenders, and officials. Most cases originate with complainants and informants outside the agency, but most evidence is obtained with the cooperation of offenders, who usually receive immunity or leniency in return. The conclusions suggest that public exposure of trade conspiracies serves as a deterrent despite weak penalties.

INTRODUCTION

Free competition among buyers and sellers in open markets yields the most efficient allocation of resources, restrains the prices of goods and services, and spurs innovation and progress. Marginal utility, or how much a consumer is willing to spend, is theoretically the determinant of value. Although these logical predictions are derived from an abstract model that bears questionable resemblance to its institutional counterpart, even planned economies have come to acknowledge the superiority of market mechanisms over centralized planning to adjust supply with demand. The benefits of free competition, however, are subject to subversion when rivals become sufficiently organized to restrict production or set prices. For the past century, the laws of competition, known as the antitrust laws, have prohibited such arrangements and have virtually eliminated formal cartels from our economy (Posner, 1976). The major premise underlying the antitrust laws is that competition, not combination, shall determine who will enter and survive in the marketplace.

This study traces the origin and investigation of all criminal prosecutions of trade conspiracies filed by the federal government over a 25-year period following the Second World War.[1] The study describes the sources used to detect violations, the methods of investigation, and the nature of evidence in prosecutions of criminal collusion. The relations among victims, offenders, and officials form the organizational basis of trade enforcement. The data are drawn from staff memorandums and other documents contained in the investigative files of the Antitrust Division of the U.S. Department of Justice. The analysis focuses on the organization of intelligence, which determines those relationships that enter the legal system and sets the parameters of official discretion .

Decisions by the Antitrust Division tend to constitute informal precedents, which are relatively consistent and subject to administrative and judicial review. The decision to prosecute represents a significant commitment of personnel, other resources, and reputation. Each case designated for prosecution requires greater adherence to procedural norms, higher standards of evidence, and greater legal and investigative resources than comparable administrative proceedings against corporate illegality. This is reflected in the small number of cases brought by the Antitrust Division. Such cases are selective prosecutions that are intended to exert some deterrent effect on the larger corporate sector. The population of criminal prosecutions filed from 1946 through 1970 constitutes the parameters of this study. The important question of why these cases were selected for prosecution and others dropped or settled informally is beyond the scope of this work. This study is based on the chronology of those cases chosen for prosecution, which absorb most of the agency's time and effort.

THE NATURE OF COLLUSION

Price-fixing and other forms of collusion among sellers who operate in the same market, such as restraints on production, bid-rigging, and market, territory, and customer allocation, are prosecuted as criminal conspiracies under the provisions of the Sherman Act of 1890. Collusion among competitors is better defined, its detection and prosecution less expensive, and the economic effects of its prohibition more beneficial than other types of antitrust enforcement. Collusive agreements are illegal per se. Investigators need only demonstrate the existence of an agreement to prove its illegality, and courts are relieved of weighing complex economic arguments and evidence for which they have limited expertise (Scherer, 1980:509-513). Once it is established that there is a trade restraint with the power to suppress competition or otherwise injure the public, the courts have not recognized evidence of good intentions or beneficial results as an acceptable defense (Neale, 1970: 434-440).

To prosecute a collusive violation successfully, the government must discover some behavioral pattern that cannot be understood as the pursuit of individual self-interest, along with evidence of explicit contacts among those suspected of collusion. The behavior and communication among suspected conspirators are investigated rather than the nature and structure of the companies and their markets. Communication among rivals prior to concerted action is a necessary, but not sufficient, condition of conspiracy. To sustain criminal charges, prosecutors must prove that competitors communicated among themselves and reached a common understanding or actual agreement about how to divide business or orchestrate a price increase. Uniform price changes or market division may arouse suspicion, but only the nature and content of the communications that precede uniform behavior can distinguish competition from conspiracy.

Although clear moral turpitude is often lacking in antitrust offenses, collusion is a concealable violation and often shrouded in clandestine and fraudulent activities that imply criminal knowledge and intent. Corporate officers are seldom indicted, however, if the only evidence against them is knowledge of collusive activity. Criminal charges can be filed against corporate officials who authorize criminal acts,[2] but it is usually necessary to prove their physical presence in specific locations where an agreement was reached. The doctrine of strict liability has been largely repudiated within antitrust law.[3]

After an evolution toward an increasing willingness to infer illegal collusion from circumstantial evidence, the legal definition of collusion as interpreted by the courts has narrowed considerably during recent years.[4] Following an exhaustive investigation of "shared monopolies," which failed to produce a single case (Taylor, 1981), the U.S. Department of Justice (1978) has concluded that parallel or interdependent behavior that is the result of purely tacit understandings is not currently illegal.

BUSINESS ORGANIZATION AND ENVIRONMENT

Antitrust enforcement has influenced the direction rather than the extent of industrial combination. Although there is little monopoly (Nutter and Einhorn, 1969), in several manufacturing markets (e.g., computers, telephones, buses and locomotives, camera film, and copiers) one firm is clearly dominant (Scherer, 1980; Shepherd, 1970). The typical market structure is oligopolistic—a market is divided among a number of large firms that face varying competition from smaller rivals (Gross, 1980:69; Scherer, 1980:67; Worcester, 1967). The concentration of markets in a few firms facilitates communication and the ability to reach and maintain agreements. The prevalence of oligopoly provides the conditions necessary for social behavior to emerge and develop within markets (Phillips, 1962:235-240).

EXTENT OF COLLUSION

There is little agreement among economists regarding the extent of actual collusion. The "Harvard" school views informal collusion and effective market control as inherent within concentrated markets (Bain, 1956; Kaysen and Turner, 1959; Shepherd, 1975). High fixed costs and long periods of research and development require that investment decisions be based on long-range planning, which presumes organizational stability and some control over the environment (Shonfield, 1965:221-236). The incentives for investment and innovation are thus transferred from the competitive market to large industrial bureaucracies (Schumpeter, 1942:87-106). Economic domination is maintained through barriers to entry, product innovation and differentiation, heavy advertising, and tacit collusion.

The rival "Chicago" branch of neoclassical economics believes the market mechanism is still operative. The natural forces of divergent self-interests, the threat of potential entry, and ubiquitous incentives to "cheat" on agreements discourage or undermine collusion, especially if such agreements are legally prohibited. Even concentrated industries may be highly competitive (McGee, 1970). If oligopolistic behavior is highly coordinated, explicit agreement and communication probably exist and, although covert, can be investigated through conventional means (Stigler, 1964).

EXTENT OF INDUSTRIAL CONCENTRATION

Aggregate concentration is expressed as the proportion of sales, assets, employment, or value-added controlled by the largest corporations within general industrial sectors. Communications, utilities, transportation, manufacturing, and banking are controlled by a few large firms; agriculture, real estate, construction, and service industries tend to be less concentrated (Scherer, 1980:46). There was a significant upsurge in industrial concentration as a result of the failure of many small businesses during the Great Depression, but concentration declined when small companies increased their proportion of industrial sales during the World War II mobilization and the strong postwar economy. As the prosperity receded, however, the share of industrial assets owned by the largest 100 firms increased from 40% in 1947 to 47% in 1955 and, after a period of stability, then rose more modestly during the late 1960s (Scherer, 1980:69). The degree of aggregate concentration among the largest 100 firms increased about 10 points during the 25 years covered in this study, but most of that increase occurred in the early postwar years, when the level of concentration was unusually low. Despite this increase, the widespread fear that our economic destiny will be dictated by a few large companies appears to be exaggerated.[5]

OWNERSHIP AND CONTROL

Ownership is separated from control in the large, publicly held corporation (Berle and Means, 1932; Dahrendorf, 1959; Galbraith, 1967). By virtue of its commercial and technical expertise, management controls corporate resources and policies, and managerial interests are often viewed as in conflict with those of owners. Managers pursue organizational stability and growth rather than maximization of profit (Marris, 1964). They are also seen as diverting profits from stockholders through excess privileges, staff, expense accounts, and employee benefits, which impose artificial costs on owners (Williamson, 1970).

The distinction between owners and managers may be overdrawn, however (Larner, 1970; Nichols, 1969; Zeitlin, 1974). Managers hold large quantities of stock in their own companies. Indeed, most large companies maintain stock-option plans, which allow senior executives to acquire company shares at prices below market value. Deferred earnings are then linked with the performance of the company's stock. Other forms of compensation, such as year-end bonuses, are also associated with company profits, which ensures that managers derive a significant part of their income from their ownership interests (Unseem, 1984:30).

Significant departures from profit-oriented behavior would likely lower stock valuation and make the corporation vulnerable to a takeover. Competitive and financial threats to managerial tenure clearly exist, especially during periods of merger activity (Marris, 1964:47-48). Expansion with consistent profitability, on the other hand, increases corporate assets as well as the market value of its stocks, thereby serving managerial autonomy as well as the financial interests of large stockholders (Marris, 1964:61-78).

Contrary to the predictions of managerial theory, the large corporation has become more dependent on external financing, which raises questions

about its control over capital reserves and possible influence by financial institutions. There is evidence of a reverse pattern of corporate ownership, with
institutional investors displacing individuals as the major stockholders
(Unseem, 1984:37). Officers and directors of large financial institutions are
heavily represented on the board of directors of most leading corporations
(Goldsmith, 1973; U.S. Congress, 1968).[6] Financial institutions may regulate
debt or influence investment policy, but they probably do not interfere with
managerial decisions unless their investments are jeopardized.

DIVERSIFICATION AND THE MULTIDIVISIONAL FIRM

Although the level of aggregrate concentration has increased somewhat,
there is little indication of growing concentration in most markets. The explanation of these seemingly inconsistent trends lies in the diversification of large
firms. While competition and the saturation of demand eventually erode the
profitabilty of a single market, a firm expanding by diversification may be able
to grow continuously (Marris, 1964:175–182). This enables the modern corporation to control its own demand by creating new markets for its goods and
services.

Diversification, however, creates problems of its own in regard to managing the complexities of divergent corporate activities. The organizational
response to this complexity was the development and proliferation of the mul-
tidivisional corporate structure, which separates authority into administration
and policymaking (Chandler, 1962).

Most large corporations have decentralized operating divisions that roughly conform to related product markets. Operational autonomy is delegated to a
divisional manager, who is responsible for price and output decisions.
Accounting, financial, and planning functions are centralized at the corporate
headquarters (Chandler, 1962). Financial controls, like cost accounting and
profit responsibility centers, are used to coordinate the various components of
the capitalist firm to maximize its overall economic position.

The decentralization of price and output decisions increases the opportunities for collusion within large corporations, especially those that operate in a
number of different markets. Senior executives may not really know the
degree of illegality within their own companies. Subordinates may restrict
information concerning problems or illegitimate activities. Moreover, organizational methods of monitoring managerial performance through objective indicators weaken direct administrative control and may generate hierarchical
pressures that encourage the adoption of expedient means to achieve managerial goals (Smith, 1961).

THE ORGANIZATION OF ENFORCEMENT

THE ADVERSARY AGENCY

Criminal jurisdiction over the antitrust laws is vested with the Antitrust Division of the U.S. Department of Justice. The division operates within the federal law enforcement and court systems. It derives much of its investigative authority from the grand jury, and much of its investigative resources from the Federal Bureau of Investigation (FBI). The division shares some parallel responsibilities with the Federal Trade Commission (FTC), primarily in merger enforcement. It has sole criminal jurisdiction over trade violations, and it is responsible for prosecuting most incidents of collusion (Katzmann, 1980; Posner, 1969, 1970).[7]

Unlike an administrative agency in which investigative and adjudicative functions are combined, the Antitrust Division is a prosecutorial agency, which means it must litigate its actions before courts of law. Officials view themselves obligated to assume an adversary position (Weaver, 1977). They are not forced to take a comprehensive view of the merits or consequences of their cases nor to weigh explanations of adversaries. That is the responsibility of the courts, which decide whether a violation has occurred and administer appropriate sanctions to those found guilty. This connection to the courts insulates the agency from congressional criticism and helps avoid excessive compromise with business interests.

THE INVESTIGATION OF COMPLAINTS

Most investigations of collusion originate with complaints from the private business sector, but the Antitrust Division appears to have considerable discretion over those that evolve into official actions. Only a limited number of investigations can go forward at a time, and a greater number of complaints are received than can be adequately investigated. Most complainants do not allege any real violation of the law or never respond when written for further information (Weaver, 1977:60-62).

Initial contacts with complainants are usually informal, but subsequent communications must be officially authorized. The decision to open a formal investigation often depends on the quality of the evidence provided by the complainant. Most preliminary investigations do not uncover any evidence of illegality (Weaver, 1977:100). Other investigations are closed if there is insufficient commerce, lack of federal jurisdiction, or a voluntary cessation of illegality. Some are deemed private matters or are referred to the FTC. Informal settlements are most often reached when small businesses are the focus of the investigation (Weaver, 1977:81-85).

THE DECISION TO PROSECUTE

Although investigations are initiated and carried on at the staff level, the decision to continue or expand an investigation is based on the circulation of evidentiary memorandums among the various levels of authority. Section and field office chiefs are involved at the initial stages of an investigation, and they generally support staff requests to continue or close an inquiry. These must be approved in turn by the Director of Operations, a senior career attorney, whose principal concerns are the quality of evidence, the amount of interstate commerce, the size of the involved parties, and a general concern for the reputation of the agency (Weaver, 1977:102-103). Until 1974, the Attorney General had to give final approval for filing a case or convening a grand jury investigation. This hierarchical review process exerts a conservative influence on the number and types of cases filed.

DECRIMINALIZATION OF TRADE ENFORCEMENT

The organizational structure of the division can lend direction and purpose to antitrust enforcement. Thurman Arnold was the "moral entrepreneur" who institutionalized the policy of antitrust in the late 1930s. Arnold favored publicity and moral condemnation as instruments of corporate control. Some 30 years later, Donald Turner initiated a reverse trend toward decriminalizing trade violations by major corporations. Turner attempted to create an economically coherent enforcement program administered by a policy planning office, which reviewed the economic effects of proposed cases. Many criminal cases lacked economic significance, and Turner doubted their deterrent value. He believed civil intervention was a more rational instrument for influencing economic behavior. Large firms tend to be involved in more open violations, like mergers and contractual restraints on patents or distribution, which are usually regarded as civil matters, and Turner directed his enforcement efforts toward those areas (Green et al., 1972:89; Weaver, 1977:130-136). In 1962, Congress expanded the agency's civil authority by granting it administrative subpoena power, thereby reducing its dependence on the grand jury for investigative purposes.

DATA AND METHODOLOGY

Direct observation of the social control of corporate illegality is not possible because of the multiplicity of actors and the geographical and temporal dispersion of organizational encounters (Shapiro, 1984:195-196). Corporate illegality and its social control may be better viewed as ongoing relationships or as serial or interrelated encounters rather than as discrete events with clear boundaries in time and space. An advantage of studying law enforcement within bureaucratic settings is the formal nature of official discretion. Public bureaucracies tend to record all contacts with outsiders, and official decisions must be justified in writing to superiors before they are authorized. Archival residues in the form of written documents chart official decisions and activities.

The methodology entailed reconstructing antitrust cases from the archival record of the Antitrust Division. Previously classified materials were requested over a 2-year period under the Freedom of Information Act (FOIA). The principal data were drawn from staff memorandums and other documents contained in the investigative files of the division. An inductive rather than deductive coding strategy was used to gather as much information as possible with little theoretical specification.

In a criminal proceeding, the final fact memorandum is ordinarily written after all grand jury testimony has been heard, but those memorandums were unavailable for the research because of the secrecy surrounding grand jury investigations. The FOIA exempts grand jury records from mandatory release and permits no discretionary release.[8] The secrecy surrounding grand jury investigations was the most serious obstacle to the research and to its empirical findings.

Requests for grand jury authority from the attorney general, postindictment bills of particulars, and presentencing memorandums were the major documents used to trace criminal investigations. The nature and scope of the investigation preceding the grand jury can be comprehensive, and the memorandums requesting grand jury authority were usually written after the major facts of the case were already known. The official prosecution is the unit of analysis. Official prosecutions are those investigations that result in complaints or indictments filed in federal court. The extent to which alternatives to litigation were used by the agency cannot be determined with these data.

Attempts to define a sampling frame for the population of investigations would encounter several difficulties. While the number of attorneys in the division remained constant at about 300 during the 25-year period, the number of investigations fluctuated widely; there were almost four times as many investigations in the last years as in most other years. About 30% of formal investigations became cases during the first 17 years included in the study, but the proportion fell to about 10% during the last 8 years. The dramatic increase in investigations is due to changes in recordkeeping and enforcement responsibilities rather than productivity increases. There has been progressive differentiation within the agency's system of classifying investigations. Related investigations, which would be placed in a general industry file during the first part of the period, were given separate approval and their own file number in the later years. The extreme inflation in the number of investigations can also be attributed to the growing importance of merger enforcement in the mid-1960s. Merger investigations can rely on civil discovery to gather evidence, and because the initial investigations are shorter and require fewer resources, many more can be conducted.

A final research boundary is the time frame that covers a 25-year period from the postwar era—1946 through 1970. The beginning year signaled the return of antitrust enforcement, which had been suspended during the war, and the closing year minimized the need for access to sensitive and unavailable materials. The final population consisted of 347 cases. Files were completely missing for 21 cases (6%) of the total. This gap reflects the reluctance of the FOIA office to search for missing files and the practice of government attorneys to use old files in current investigations. A smaller number of files are presumably lost.

ANALYSIS

PATTERNS OF ENFORCEMENT

Criminal collusion is a corporate offense. Corporations were named as defendants in 305 of 347 cases, or in 88% of all criminal indictments filed from 1946 through 1970 under Section 1 of the Sherman Act. In half of all the indictments, there were corporate defendants only—no individuals were named. Price-fixing was the most common criminal charge, cited in 250 (72%) of the indictments or in one-third of all antitrust cases filed during these years.

The most striking characteristic of collusion is its continuing nature. The average duration of criminal price-fixing, the most discrete, conduct-oriented antitrust offense, spanned 7 years, often ending only when the conspirators learned of the investigation. Even though price-fixing is relatively easy to investigate and prosecute, the average price-fixing case required 21 months to investigate and 23 months to litigate.

About half of all price-fixing involves regional or local conspiracies. Again, because the violations are relatively easy to detect and prosecute, price-fixing investigations tend to cluster around division field offices. The Washington, D.C. office, which employs the vast majority of staff, concentrates on civil matters. There may be substantial undetected collusion in localities not closely monitored.

The number of criminal indictments and their economic significance, as measured by the mean sales of corporate defendants and the mean annual commerce involved, fluctuated substantially over the period (see Table 1). A few patterns can be noted, however. About 40% of all antitrust cases filed during the period were criminal, but a greater percentage of criminal cases were filed during the early postwar years. After the early 1960s, erratic but declining trends are evident in the number of indictments, the amount of commerce affected, and the average sales of corporate defendants.

The number of criminal cases and their economic significance crested about 1960, when the notorious electrical equipment conspiracies were prosecuted, and fell until the end the decade. From 1946-1950, 44% of trade cases were criminal, from 1951-1955, 46% were criminal, and from 1956-1960, 48% were criminal. From 1961-1965, criminal prosecutions fell to 35% of all cases, and from 1966-1970, only one-fourth of antitrust cases were criminal. Criminal enforcement became more selective and focused on narrower spheres of economic activity. Although the post-Watergate era brought a resurgence in criminal indictments and an increased use of incarceration (Eckert, 1980), it is unlikely that those changes represent reversals of the trend toward decriminalization of corporate collusion.[9] The probability of confrontations between government and business similar to those between the Kennedy administration and steel companies appears remote at the present time.

Sixty-nine percent of all criminal cases were settled by *nolo contendere* pleas. The government opposed the plea in about half of the cases, but much of this opposition was largely ceremonial and was routinely ignored by the court. *Nolo* pleas seal the government's evidence documenting the offense and protect offenders from damage suits.[10] In 15% of the cases, the government was able to obtain guilty pleas or convictions. In 14% of the cases, the defendants obtained dismissals or acquittals.

The stigma of indictment, the costs of a defense, and the risk of treble damage suits are credible sanctions, but the only real punishments imposed by the courts during these years were fines. Fines were inconsequential before 1955, when the maximum penalty was raised from $5,000 to $50,000. The amount of the fine imposed was related to the number of corporations indicted (r = .33), their overall sales (r = .13), and sales within the relevant market (r = .27).

Sanctions other than fines were imposed in about 10% of criminal cases, or in about 20% of those cases that named individuals. Of 1,351 individual defendants, 125 (9.2%) received suspended prison sentences and 95 (7%) were given probationary terms. The average term of probation was 14.5 months, with a range of 6 months to 3 years. Thirty-six defendants in 12 cases served time in prison, with a mean of 149 days and a range from 24 hours to 1 year. Most sentences were imposed in the service and construction industries and involved labor combinations or racketeering. Businessmen were actually incarcerated for simple price-fixing in only three cases, which involved the manufacturers of hand tools, electrical equipment, and plumbing fixtures.

During the period, 30% of those corporations charged with criminal collusion were small firms with less than $1 million in annual sales, 36% were firms with $1-$10 million in sales, and the remaining one-third were firms with over $10 million in sales. Although large firms were not routine targets of criminal prosecutions, defendants with sales over $100 million (n = 240) slightly outnumbered firms with $10-$100 million in sales (n = 235), and, given their relative numbers in industry populations, large firms appear more likely than intermediate-sized firms to be implicated in criminal violations. Given the range of activities of the large multiproduct firm, the probability of indictment does not appear very large, and it diminished over the years.

Table 1
Criminal Indictments, Mean Annual Sales of Defendants, and Annual Commerce in Relevant Markets, 1946-1970

Year	Criminal Indictments, N	All Cases, N	Criminal Cases, N	Criminal Cases, %	Corporate Defendants, N	Mean Sales, $M years	Mean Commerce, $M Years
1946	10	10	31	32	41	133.6	158.8
1947	9	9	25	36	53	268.9	498.2
1948	24	22	39	56	131	63.4	75.0
1949	15	15	30	50	107	5.4	148.0
1950	18	17	41	41	88	14.2	35.2
1951	13	13	38	34	49	8.0	13.0
1952	12	11	27	41	49	1.2	25.0
1953	14	12	17	71	30	4.0	18.5
1954	8	8	33	24	36	20.0	17.8
1955	20	18	33	55	94	124.5	41.5
1956	18	13	32	41	58	493.4	14.4
1957	24	24	42	57	131	110.6	75.1
1958	20	18	40	45	56	137.9	148.0
1959	35	20	40	50	114	241.1	59.2
1960	40	19	42	45	110	571.2	93.1
1961	22	18	45	40	77	806.5	69.0
1962	34	26	53	49	144	227.2	49.6
1963	13	10	28	36	58	289.3	63.4
1964	14	11	41	27	53	366.6	141.5
1965	8	7	27	26	67	593.7	132.8
1966	19	12	29	41	66	53.1	36.3
1967	13	10	30	33	61	56.8	53.3
1968	16	16	47	34	84	32.4	9.3
1969	1	1	38	3	1	8.9	9.0
1970	10	10	51	30	33	23.8	30.7
Means	17.2	13.9	35.6	39	70.3	195.4	67.5

NOTE: *The official number of cases represented by the adjusted counts contains 431 indictments and 207 civil complaints. The adjusted totals represent the effort to eliminate "double-counting" present in the official numbers. About half of all criminal indictments were accompanied by parallel civil complaints. These are considered criminal cases because the criminal charges are those that are litigated and most parallel civil suits against collusion seek no substantive relief. Different indictments were sometimes filed against conspiracies delineated along narrow product lines involving the same or mostly overlapping membership. These were usually treated as a single proceeding. This method and the resulting totals are similar to those of Posner (1970). 1966 dollars.*

Large firms were more likely to become involved in conspiracies operating in peripheral than in their primary markets, especially in those markets that were shared with smaller rivals, a "competitive fringe." The average annual sales for corporate defendants were $195 million, with $67 million annual sales in the affected market. The average number of indicted conspirators was 4.7 when defendants' annual sales averaged less than $100 million, and 5.4 when defendants' mean sales were more than $100 million. Large firms were involved with as many conspirators as smaller firms.

Criminal collusion is either less visible or less prevalent in concentrated industries. Explicit collusion may be unnecessary when concentration is high, because organization, mutual interdependence, and communication provide alternative means of managing uncertainty. Although intervention against large firms in concentrated industries was rare, investigations were more common. Many inquiries that led to the prosecution of narrow violations or local conspiracies began as broader investigations of large manufacturers. The proportion of resources spent investigating large firms is not reflected in official cases, but it may have exerted some deterrent effect on their behavior.

ECONOMIC DISTRIBUTION OF CORPORATE OFFENDERS

Organizations engaged in industrial production tend to be larger than those businesses that supply their raw materials or distribute their output. Manufacturing markets are more concentrated and large firms make highly visible suspects. Manufacturing firms were named as defendants in 201 cases, or 58% of the total. Some of those cases involved producer goods, like chemicals (n = 13 or 3.7%), industrial machinery (n = 37 or 10.7%), and primary metals (n = 13 or 3.7%). However, three times the proportion of civil cases were filed in basic industrial sectors as criminal cases.

About half of the prosecutions involved local manufacturing, retailing, and service markets not ordinarily regarded as concentrated. Typical manufacturing industries involved in criminal proceedings included local food processing (n = 53 or 15.3%), especially bread and milk products, and building materials (n = 15 or 4.4%). Oil refiners were prosecuted more often in asphalt than in petroleum markets.

Illegal trade agreements were found in virtually every construction trade (n = 22 or 6.3%), including general contractors, electricians, plumbers, plasterers, and road contractors. Twenty percent (n = 68) of the cases charging criminal collusion fell in the retail or wholesale sectors. Those cases included almost every product line, from groceries to office furniture to sporting goods, but more (n = 11) involved the sale of liquor and beer than other merchandise. Local service industries, like trucking, linen supplies, and vending, have been routine targets of government probes, and a large number of antitrust cases were filed against such businesses.

THE DISCOVERY OF COLLUSION

The principal means of detecting criminal collusion was through complaints from competitors or from institutional and industrial buyers who believed themselves victimized. Competitors initiated 97 (28%) of those cases charging criminal collusion (see Table 2). Sixty-one (17.7%) of these conspiracies were discovered from complaints from private buyers, and public buyers initiated a similar proportion. Eighty-three percent of the discoveries of criminal collusion were initiated by outsiders.

Detection was classified as proactive in 60 cases or in 17.2% of the criminal actions. In contrast to criminal organizations, public corporations are highly visible and their activities widely reported in the public and business media. Eleven price-fixing conspiracies were discovered in suspicious advertisements or activities reported in the press. Grand jury investigations led to over half of the proactive detections. Six percent of criminal conspiracies (n = 21) were discovered in incriminating documents, including correspondence, internal memorandums, price lists, and sales reports. In 12 other cases (3.4%), disclosure came through subpoenaed testimony. Most of these disclosures came from officials of large firms who were exposed to a variety of collusive settings. Because of the continuing nature of collusion, recollections under oath sometimes revealed old conspiracies that were still operating.

DEFECTORS AND INFORMANTS

Price-fixing is usually a covert violation, and informants were a major source of intelligence; they accounted for 14% of the detections. Elaborate conspiracies in the electrical equipment, steel, plumbing fixture, and paper industries remained hidden from the government throughout recurrent investigations until insiders unveiled elaborately concealed arrangements. Most informants were individual defectors or disgruntled employees who reported the conspiracy to authorities while their companies remained involved in the illegal activity. Not surprisingly, former officials, many of whom were "disgruntled," outnumbered current employees 28 to 13 as principal sources of intelligence in price-fixing cases. In five instances, informants directly involved in the conspiracy provided unsolicited information that incriminated their companies. About 70% of informants came from current or former sales management positions, 20% from sales staff, and the remainder from other corporate positions. Several informants expressed the complaint that collusive agreements closed off potential customers or business opportunities, which impaired their performance and jeopardized their success.

Table 2
Criminal Collusion: Source of Investigation

	N	%
Internal Detection		
Staff Interview	6	1.7
Staff File Search	4	1.1
FBI Investigation	3	.9
Subpoenaed Document	21	6.0
Subpoenaed Testimony	12	3.5
Newspapers or Trade Publications	11	3.2
Private Antitrust Litigation	2	.6
Internal Detection, Other	1	.3
	60	17.3
Public Complainants		
Military	14	4.0
Department of State	2	.6
U.S. Forest Service	2	.6
Tennessee Valley Authority	8	2.3
Other Federal Agencies	10	2.9
State Officials	5	1.4
Local Officials	13	3.7
School Board	4	1.1
Voluntary Associations	2	.6
	60	17.3

Table 2 (continued)

Private Complainants		
Supplier	9	2.6
Competitor	97	28.0
Buyer, Producer	22	6.3
Buyer, Retail	13	3.7
Buyer, Wholesale	11	3.2
Buyer, Other	15	4.3
Current Official/Participant in Crime	5	1.4
Current Official/Nonparticipant	8	2.3
Former Corporate Employee or Official	28	8.1
Trade Association Official	5	1.4
Anonymous Informant	2	.6
Individual Consumer	1	.3
	216	62.2
Missing Cases	11	3.2
Total	347	100.0

COMPETITORS AS INSIDE SOURCES

The most direct victims of price-fixing are buyers, but the most useful intelligence regarding trade conspiracies comes from competitors. Competitors are closer to the violation, are able to offer better evidence of conspiracy, and generally provide the government with access to the private business world. Most were defectors from the conspiracy, but in only 11 cases (11% of competitor-initiated prosecutions) was the original complainant indicted. The vast majority were perceived more as victims than offenders or traded information for immunity. Public or industrial buyers were influential complainants, but they could rarely offer direct evidence of collusion because they were usually not parties to the conspiracy. Competitors were able to describe specific meetings, identify those in attendance, and perhaps offer documentary evidence, ranging from tape recordings to handwritten notes, to support their allegations.

The role of the competitor-complainant was primarily limited to intelligence. The victim exerted very little influence over the outcome of an investigation. With the exception of a few racketeering investigations, smaller competitors were responsible for exposing trade conspiracies. Most complaints of price-fixing and collusion came from private firms that had marginal positions in the market and little social or economic influence in their relations with larger rivals. Antitrust officials were deliberately suspicious of their motives and considered most allegations too personal and biased. Antitrust officials did not help or advise private victims, nor were victims apprised or consulted regarding the progress of an investigation. Private complainants were told to seek the advice of private legal counsel. Private enforcement operates as an incentive to settle with antitrust officials. The threat of public indictment and damage suits gave government officials substantial leverage in corporate affairs.

INTERAGENCY REFERRALS AND COMPLAINTS

About one-fourth (n = 89) of all complainants were referred to the Antitrust Division by other public agencies. Most referrals came from components of the federal justice system rather than the regulatory agencies that monitor corporate behavior. U.S. attorneys' offices accounted for 6% (n = 22) of all cases and the FBI for 4% (n = 15). The Criminal Division of the Justice Department uncovered four incidents of price-fixing. Congressional referrals accounted for 7% (n = 27) of the total, and there were six additional cases in which Congress was the principal complainant. The FTC discovered 11 incidents of collusion. Most of these referrals were accompanied by some background investigation, which made the initiation of a formal inquiry more likely. Public corporations are subject to a wide range of reporting requirements by regulatory, tax, and census agencies, but such agencies showed little interest in antitrust action. The Internal Revenue Service referred only one incident of collusion to the Antitrust Division that led to an indictment, and the Securities and Exchange Commission did not refer any. One apparent explanation for this lack of cooperation appears to be that administrative agencies prefer to proceed independently because each has its own distinctive enforcement apparatus, authority, and mandate. Moreover, competition is the antithesis of regulation, and the division has adversary relations with most administrative agencies.

COLLUSION IN PUBLIC PROCUREMENT

Collusion interferes with the objectives of and victimizes most of those agencies whose primary responsibility is procurement. The incidence, detection, and prosecution of price-fixing were more likely to occur in transactions with public institutions, such as governments, utilities, schools, and hospitals, than with private buyers. About one-fourth of all price-fixing prosecutions involved collusive sales to public organizations.

Thirteen cases of criminal price-fixing involved municipal purchases of products, like water equipment, fire engines, street lights, and pipe. Fifteen cases involved school purchases of milk, books, pencils, shelving, and athletic equipment. Twelve cases involved sales to utilities and 5 involved transactions with hospitals. At the federal level, the military accounted for 14 cases. These involved collusion in consumer goods (e.g., beer, milk, and moving services) rather than strategic product markets. Perhaps most surprising, the General Services Administration, the major purchaser of office equipment for the federal government, had no apparent role or interest in detecting or policing collusion in government procurement.

The vulnerability of public procurement to bid-rigging is related to the way public contracts are awarded. Alchian (1977:267) argues that the effort to eliminate favoritism and corruption through the sealed bid denies public officials the freedom to bargain and negotiate contracts because they are required to accept the lowest bid. Stigler suggests the sealed bid also serves as a device to police an agreement. If deviance from cartel agreements can be concealed, it is in the interest of sellers to cheat. By announcing the winning bid, deviations from agreements are identified and subject to economic retaliation (Stigler, 1964:46). Public demand may be "inelastic," that is, governments tend to purchase the same quantity of goods regardless of price, while raising prices restricts private demand. The size and infrequency ("lumpiness") of institutional orders make the loss of a single public contract a threat to firms heavily dependent on government purchases, and there is substantial incentive to ensure predictable sales through allocation schemes.

Purchasing officials were usually unaware of collusion, but some fostered its existence through indolence or occasional corruption. Although purchasers were more likely complainants in allocation schemes, competitors sometimes alleged that collusion existed between government officials and favored sellers. Allegations of conspiracy usually concerned rigid specifications of public purchases that restricted the eligibility of bidders. Allocation schemes are inherently exclusionary, and competitors who receive little of the allocated business are likely complainants. Of the 15 price conspiracies involving sales to schools, 5 came from competitors, and 3 of 5 cases of price-fixing in hospital purchases were initiated by competitors.

If collusion occurs, public officials can become influential complainants with access to legal remedies. Private buyers rarely resort to litigation because of the high cost and the availability of alternatives. Government agencies are more likely to seek legal action because they do not bear its cost, and the Antitrust Division has an obligation to investigate a public complaint. When a bidding cartel allocates business, the remaining parties have to submit fictitious bids that are higher than that submitted by the designated winner. The need to maintain the appearance of competition through this deception gives the bidding cartel a fraudulent character more flagrant than that found in most collusion, and criminal intent is easier to prove.

THE INVESTIGATION OF COLLUSION

The detection of criminal collusion is usually through complainants or informants, but most evidence substantiating the violation is obtained through grand jury subpoenas and grants of immunity from prosecution. Testimony given in return for immunity by principals or ringleaders in the conspiracy was the government's principal evidence in 60% of the prosecutions, and in 30% it was "confessional," that is, testimony from those most culpable. When a major figure in the conspiracy testified before the grand jury, the practice was to give immunity to the remaining individuals. As a result, half of all indictments failed to name any individual defendants.

Federal officials used grand jury subpoena authority to gain entry into those areas of organizational life in which criminal violations were suspected. Corporations do not have the same constitutional privileges against self-incrimination as individuals, and corporate affairs are accessible for inspection through the subpoena process. Subpoenas *duces tecum,* which require the production of documents, do not confer the same immunity as subpoenas *ad testificandum,* which compel testimony. Both subpoenas were used extensively. Testimonial evidence was more critical in proving the existence of a violation.

ENCOUNTERS WITH SUSPECTED OFFENDERS

If the role of the complainant diminished when a case entered the legal system, the role of the offender loomed larger. This was because of the nature of the offense, and because influential corporations were more likely to be offenders than complainants. Most street crimes have victims or witnesses who can reconstruct the event through personal testimony. Most victims of collusion do not witness the offense and can offer only suspicions or circumstantial rather than direct evidence. Evidence is in the files of an offender and in the testimony of its officials.

Voluntary requests for information from suspects or targets of an investigation were not very effective in eliciting cooperation. Two-thirds of those who were approached prior to the grand jury withheld documents, denied access to company records or employees, or were otherwise uncooperative. Before 1963, grand jury authority was the only means of compelling cooperation from those suspected of collusion, and refusals to cooperate increased the probability of indictment. Subpoenas also served to protect the testimony of reluctant informants from disclosure. The first official notice received by most suspects or targets of a criminal investigation was a subpoena.

Most contacts with suspects were mediated by defense attorneys. The early entry of defense counsel represents an attempt to avoid indictment, control access to clients and information, and restrict disclosure (Mann, 1985). The subpoena *duces tecum* relies on the integrity of the corporate secretary, who is served with the subpoena to deliver the documents, and company counsel, who selects the documents that comply with the order. This screening process controls the nature and content of the submissions.

Most attorneys maintained ceremonial compliance with government demands, but the good faith inherent in the subpoena process was subject to apparent abuse. Withholding or suppressing documents was routinely alleged in government memorandums, and investigators had to piece together cases from partial returns. Missing key documents might be identified in submissions from other parties, but the typical government response was to make subsequent demands for compliance rather than to request contempt charges.

Antitrust investigations are governed by reciprocal norms of civility, and a recurrent lack of cooperation rarely led to the kinds of confrontations that often result when citizens defy official authority. Government attorneys experienced threats of career damage, aspersions on character, insults, refusals, and much evasion. But no instance was discovered in which an investigator was even verbally threatened with physical violence. Government investigators were under no apparent physical jeopardy even in probes involving organized crime or violence.

DOCUMENTARY EVIDENCE

Corporate offenders are torn between the criminal need to erase any documentary traces of collusive activity and the bureaucratic need to preserve organizational records (Barnett, 1982). In almost 40% of the cases the principal evidence was documentary. Incriminating letters to competitors were the most common documents cited (n = 23 or 7%), followed by correspondence with buyers and internal memorandums (n = 16 or about 5% each). Four percent (n = 13) of prosecutions relied on written minutes of trade association meetings. A few cases hinged on evidence provided by price lists or catalogs. Company reports or organizational charts were used to identify possible subjects to be interviewed. Hotel records, telephone bills, or expense accounts were used to specify the incidents of conspiracy and to confront witnesses before the grand jury. Much of this evidence was circumstantial rather than probative.

With the related developments of routine document destruction programs and heightened sensitivity concerning any discussion of prices or threats, documentary evidence became less important over the years covered in the study. "Hot documents" tend to produce leads rather than admissible evidence of collusion. Business executives have learned to be more cautious about what they put in writing.

Although the fear of document destruction was a common reason cited by the Antitrust Division for requesting grand jury authority, there were relatively few documented incidents (21 or 6% of the total) of deliberate destruction of evidence by those under investigation. The lack of serious penalties for those incidents of obstruction that were proven, was perhaps the most critical limitation of governmental investigative authority.

The Antitrust Division was sometimes unable to persuade the Criminal Division to prosecute its most compelling cases. During the 25 years covered here, 21 instances of document destruction were recommended for prosecution in at least one staff memorandum, several of these were investigated by the FBI, half were referred to the Criminal Division, and 2 cases were filed. In the one successful prosecution, two individuals pleaded guilty. Modest fines and "lengthy verbal reprimands" were imposed by the court. The response by the Criminal Division and the courts to the obstruction charges may have exerted a "chilling effect" on the Antitrust Division's willingness to recommend incidents of contempt for prosecution.

TESTIMONIAL EVIDENCE

The government places even greater reliance on subpoenaed testimony to prove organizational crimes. The gist of conspiracy is agreement, and establishing this subjective state often requires testimony from those individuals who were present. In 60% of criminal proceedings, the primary evidence was testimonial. In 20% of the cases, principal conspirators provided testimony in return for immunity. It may be difficult to assess the relative culpability of the various members of a conspiracy in advance of the actual testimonial evidence, and some ringleaders were given immunity inadvertently before the full facts of the conspiracy were known. Other principals may be granted immunity because they offered early cooperation, or because they possessed the most comprehensive knowledge of the conspiracy's activities. About 30% of the cases were built on the testimony of subordinates against superiors.

Many original complainants offered eyewitness testimony of collusion, but the government still conferred immunity on more active members of the conspiracy. This practice appears to be due to the reluctance of prosecutors to rely on the testimony of single individuals, especially when the character and motives of informants were suspect. The value of most informants was to provide the government with their version of events, which was then refuted or corroborated by those responsible for the violations.

If asked specific questions, corporate officials were sufficiently candid to avoid perjury charges; actual perjury charges were rare. Fourteen formal recommendations for perjury charges were made in division memorandums, 6 of those were referred to the Criminal Division for prosecution, 3 cases were filed, and 1 conviction resulted. The Criminal Division declined prosecution of most referrals because the testimony was thought to be more evasive or hostile than deliberately false. False testimony was described as possible lapses of memory. Thus, the agency was denied ultimate compulsory authority, but this compromise was imposed on the division from the outside.

Because of the reluctance of the Criminal Division to accept perjury cases, most individuals suspected of lying were recalled before the grand jury in an effort to obtain admissions of false prior statements under threat of prosecution. Because of grand jury secrecy, it is not known how well this procedure worked. Even if witnesses persisted in their deception, however, prosecutors were more likely to resort to the sanction of indictment or a more severe sentencing recommendation than to charge perjury.

Although obstructive behavior increased the probability of indictment, those who destroyed documents or committed perjury ran little risk of significant sanctions. Fines, the only likely sanction during this period, were not significantly different for defendants who had obstructed an investigation than for defendants who had cooperated. Since there was no effective mechanism to compel cooperation or even penalize false statements and obstructive behavior, the Antitrust Division was at a serious disadvantage.

The allegiance of corporate officials to suspect organizations substantially weakened once an investigation was under way, however. Most business collusion disintegrated on discovery and conspirators routinely offered to incriminate their companies and associates. Since the government was unable to sanction those who engaged in clearly subversive activity, the agency granted concessions to those who did cooperate. The compromise of its reputed prosecutorial mode was the agency's adaptation to this enforcement dilemma.

CONCLUSION

There is substantial normative concern among most economists that economic efficiency should be the only goal of antitrust enforcement (Bork, 1978; Elzinga and Breit, 1976; Posner, 1976). Critics claim antitrust agencies are mired in disputes among competitors and enforce a policy of competition they do not understand. Other public policies, like mediating organizational conflict, protecting freedom of entry and contract, promoting economic diversity, and restricting concentrated economic power may interfere with consumer welfare.

Consumers are a disparate group, however, and they experience diffuse and indirect victimization. The interests of individual stockholders are guarded by institutional investors and managerial stockholdings, but consumers have no comparable institutional protection. Increasing social distance and diminished accountability between producers and consumers remove individual consumers from those transactions that provoke government intervention. Losses from price-fixing may be passed along to the consumer by intermediaries who suffer no direct injury and may be integrated into the conspiracy. Courts have held claimants who have suffered remote or incidental injury to be outside the permitted universe of plaintiffs. To bring a private suit, there must be a direct relationship of exchange or rivalry with an offender (Areeda and Turner, 1978:183-198). When victimization is diffuse, offenders unknown, injury slight, and evidence weak, cases are rarely if ever initiated.

A PROACTIVE AGENDA

In the late 1970s, an attempt was made to alter the enforcement agenda of the Antitrust Division by modifying its process of case selection. A massive "shared monopoly" probe was launched using detailed economic indicators. Over 300 concentrated industries were examined for indications of collusion. Eighty industries were investigated for tacit collusion in pricing or other conduct. Some of those investigations lasted over 3 years before being terminated. No case was filed and the departing assistant attorney general was quoted as saying that shared monopolies were "less of a problem" than he first thought (Taylor, 1981). The failure to discover pervasive collusion does not conclusively demonstrate its absence, but the argument that collusion in concentrated markets is easy to effectuate through informal understandings and implicit agreements has come under severe theoretical and empirical criticism (Goldschmid et al., 1974). The paucity of conspiracy charges in concentrated industries may be because such arrangements are relatively rare within those sectors of the economy.

DATERENCE AND SEVERITY

If increased crime results when rewards outweigh possible costs, as economic logic suggests, the actual amount of undetected illegal collusion should be enormous. Deterrence depends on the certainty, swiftness, and severity of punishment, and antitrust enforcement lacks credibility in all these dimensions.[11] Given the limited resources available for enforcement, the reliance on reactive sources of intelligence, and the tremendous breadth of the modern economy, the probability of detection must be incredibly low. Because of the protracted nature of antitrust investigations and prosecutions, the probability of punishment is even lower. Penalties against those who refuse cooperation or even actively obstruct an investigation are rare, and the consequences of conviction are not severe. In fact, the actual criminal penalties imposed have been more of a nuisance than a threat.

To make antitrust enforcement less of a "charade," Congress attached felony penalties to the 1974 revisions of the Sherman Act to make the punishment fit the crime. There is considerable evidence, however, that increasing the severity of sanctions limits the number of prosecutions and the probability of conviction (Wilson,1977:194-204). Increasing the severity of punishment reduces the role of other elements of deterrence, including certainty, swiftness, and equity. For white-collar offenses, certainty, or the probability of detection, may be a more critical deterrent than a sentence because those persons may be particularly responsive to stigma and the shame of public condemnation (Fisse and Braithwaite, 1984).

Although incarceration is apparently more common since 1974, the increased penalization of antitrust violations has had several unanticipated consequences. Gallo et al. (1985) concluded the effects of the new felony sanctions were to reduce the number of cases, discourage plea bargaining, increase acquittals, and lower the overall significance of the criminal enforcement effort. Increased criminal penalties have also weakened the deterrent threat of private litigation. Prosecutions in the paper industry during the 1970s, for example, were followed by some private litigation, but the felony cases filed against highway and electrical contractors in the 1980s generated few private suits (Kauper and Snyder, 1988:358). Beginning in 1978, the Antitrust Division's attention shifted away from major price-fixing complaints to narrower bid-rigging actions involving state government contracts.

Policing collusion poses similar problems as policing other forms of "victimless crime," like political corruption or drug dealing, but enforcement problems have been addressed much differently. Whereas extensive use of undercover investigators, "sting" operations, and electronic surveillance has become commonplace, antitrust suspects have been afforded a much greater degree of trust than conventional criminals. This is despite the substantial suspicion and some evidence that this trust was routinely abused. Dilatory and obstructive behavior were masked by deference and civility, and the government used summonses rather than arrest authority and served subpoenas rather than executing search warrants. There were no known attempts to eavesdrop on boardrooms or install wiretaps on corporate telephones.

The major objections to a more coercive enforcement posture inhere within the nature of antitrust violations and the society in which they occur. Our society is characterized by a relatively high degree of institutional integration and consensus between business and government. Any major change in policing business would require increased government authority and institutional chasms that appear unlikely to develop.

CLOSING COMMENTS

A punitive enforcement policy toward business may be unnecessary because corporations seem amenable to social control. The general deterrent value of criminal prosecutions cannot be reduced to the actual parties and penalties. This study has attempted to show that organizations are susceptible to close scrutiny through the revelations of their documents and officials. The stigma of indictment, the costs of conducting a defense, and the threat of multiple damage suits have all been credible sanctions and have given the

Antitrust Division considerable leverage in the inspection and control of corporate behavior. The most severe corporate sanctions may be detection and exposure, and the post-Watergate escalation of penalties has impaired the agency's overall performance.

The Antitrust Division possesses relatively few proactive methods of investigation to monitor or inspect organizational environments, and victimization plays an essential role in detecting criminal collusion. Complainants and informants provide access to violations shielded by organizational labyrinths and private authority. This study suggests that economic purposes cannot easily be divorced from the behavioral foundation of trade enforcement. The growing trend to isolate the Antitrust Division from competitive conflict threatens the intelligence that permits rational intervention in the first place and promises sterility of purpose in future confrontations between business and government.

ENDNOTES

* This research was supported by Grants 78-NI-AX-0048 and 75-NI-99-0127 from the Law Enforcement Assistance Administration, U.S. Department of Justice. The views and conclusions expressed are those of the author and do not necessarily represent the official position or policies of the U.S. Department of Justice. The author would like to express his gratitude to Leo Neshkes and Robert Huber for access to and assistance in the data collection. I wish to thank Albert Reiss, Jr., Kathleen Daly, and an anonymous reviewer for their helpful comments on an earlier draft.

1. This analysis is limited to criminal prosecutions under Section 1 of the Sherman Act, which provides that "every contract, combination, in the form of a trust or otherwise, or conspiracy, in restraint of trade or commerce among the several States, or with foreign nations, is deemed illegal" (15 U.S.C. 1). During the period covered by this study, a violation of the Sherman Act was a misdemeanor. In 1974, Congress passed the Antitrust Procedures and Penalties Act (88 Stat. 1706), which raised Sherman Act violations to felony status. The maximum individual fine was raised to $500,000 and the maximum corporate fine to $1 million. Individuals convicted under the new provisions may be imprisoned for 3 years.

2. Officials who authorize but do not personally commit criminal acts may be indicted under Section 14 of the Clayton Act (38 Stat. 730). This provision has seldom been used.

3. Felony charges have increased the level of evidence necessary to convict executives of criminal collusion. In *U.S. v. United States Gypsum Co.*, (438 U.S. 422), the Supreme Court held for the first time that intent is an element of a criminal antitrust offense. *Mens rea* need not be proven, but "knowledge of the probable consequences" of criminal acts must be demonstrated (Kerwin, 1980:322).

4. *United States v. General Motors Corp. and Ford Motor Co.*, (1970-1979 Transfer Binders) Trade Reg. Rep. (CCH) para. 45072 (Case No. 47-140) (E.D. Mich. May 1, 1972). The major automakers were acquitted on charges that they conspired to fix prices through public announcements ("price signaling") in auto fleet sales. See White (1975).

5. The data on aggregate concentration are limited to the most concentrated segment of the economy—the ownership of manufacturing assets. Employment is

much less concentrated in large manufacturing corporations than value-added and sales, which are less concentrated than total assets (Scherer, 1980:46). Large corporations tend to be more capital intensive than smaller businesses. The numerator of concentration statistics includes nonmanufacturing and foreign assets held by large corporations, but the denominator contains only domestic manufacturing assets, thus overstating the degree of concentrated ownership (Scherer, 1980:49-50). There has also been considerable turnover in the membership of the largest firms, and there are different leading firms when the percentage of sales or value-added is used rather than assets (Scherer, 1980:54-56). Finally, increased imports from foreign suppliers provide evidence of continuing competition and diminished validity of concentration ratios as measures of competition.

6. The Patman Report found that directors of 49 large banks had 768 positions with 286 of the 500 largest manufacturing corporations. In 66 of those companies, a bank interlock was supported with at least 5% ownership interest in the common stock of the corporation (U.S. Congress, 1968:91). The growth of corporate ownership by banks and investment companies accelerated at the end of the period considered in this study. The share of all outstanding corporate shares owned by financial institutions was 23% for 1958 and 24% in 1968. By 1972, the proportion had climbed to 30%, and by 1977, banks, investment and insurance companies, and trust funds controlled almost 40% of all common stock in U.S. corporations (Scherer, 1980:52-53; Unseem, 1984:37). It is unlikely that banks exert much influence on business conduct, but the presence of such influential stockholders may be partly responsible for the recent crackdown on insider trading and other securities violations.

7. The FTC filed about one case per year alleging horizontal collusion during the 1960s (Posner, 1970: 408).

8. Exemption 3 of the Freedom of Information Act (5 U.S.C. 552(b)(3), as amended by Section 5(b) of the Government in the Sunshine Act (90 Stat. 1241)) "requires that the matters be withheld from the public in such a manner as to leave no discretion." This includes all "matters occurring before the grand jury." Federal grand juries are created by, report to, and are discharged by U.S. district courts and judicial records are exempt from the Freedom of Information Act, which applies to Executive Branch records only. Rule 6(c), Federal Rules of Criminal Procedure (Title 18, U.S.C.), provides for the secrecy of grand jury proceedings and punishment for contempt of court for unauthorized disclosure.

9. Of 83 criminal cases instituted in 1980, 62 involved local or family businesses in the roadbuilding industry (Clabault and Block, 1981:687). Gallo et al. (1985) found that the government inflated the number of prosecutions by filing separate indictments against each instance of bid-rigging charged to a single conspiracy. If the case count is adjusted, the actual number of criminal cases sharply declined after the change to felony status took effect. Since the felony change, dismissals have increased and the economic significance of criminal cases has fallen (Gallo et al., 1985).

10.   Section 5(a) of the Clayton Act (15 *U.S.C.* Sec. 16(a)) provides that in a govern-
       ment case a final judgment that a defendant has violated the antitrust laws shall
       be *prima facie"* evidence of a violation. Protection from treble damage suits is
       afforded by the proviso exception to Section 5(a), which states the *prima facie*
       effect of final judgments or decrees cannot apply to a defendant who pleads
       nolo contendere.

11.   The first systematic test for a deterrent effect in antitrust prosecutions concluded
       that criminal prosecutions in the bread industry led to significant reductions in
       price levels, both in cities where cases had been filed and in adjacent cities as
       well (Block et al., 1981). Although incarcerations and fines were weaker influ-
       ences than treble damage suits, government prosecutions have been an impor-
       tant antecedent to successful private litigation (Kauper and Snyder, 1988).

REFERENCES

Alchian, Armen A. 1977. *Economic Forces at Work.* Indianapolis, Ind.: Liberty Press.

Areeda, Phillip and Donald F. Turner. 1978. *Antitrust Law.* Boston: Little, Brown.

Bain, Joe S. 1956. *Barriers to New Competition.* Cambridge, Mass.: Harvard University Press.

Barnett, Harold C. 1982. "The production of corporate crime in corporate capitalism". In Peter Wickman and Timothy Dailey (eds.), *White-Collar and Economic Crime.* Lexington, Mass.: D.C. Heath.

Berle, Adolph, Jr. and Gardiner C. Means. 1932. *The Modern Corporation and Private Property.* New York: Harcourt, Brace, and World.

Berry, Charles H. 1975. *Corporate Growth and Diversification.* Princeton, N.J.: Princeton University Press.

Block, Michael K., Frederick C. Nold, and Joseph G. Sidak. 1981. "The deterrent effect of antitrust enforcement." *Journal of Political Economy* 89:429-445.

Bork, Robert H. 1978. *The Antitrust Paradox: A Policy at War with Itself.* New York: Basic Books.

Breit, William and Kenneth G. Elzinga. 1986. *Antitrust Penalty Reform.* Washington, D.C.: American Enterprise Institute.

Caves, Richard. 1972. *American Industry: Structure, Conduct, Performance.* Englewood Cliffs, N.J.: Prentice-Hall.

Chandler, Alfred. 1962. *Strategy and Structure.* Cambridge, Mass.: MIT Press.

Clabault, James and Michael Block. 1981. *Sherman Act Indictments 1955-1980.* New York: Federal Legal Publications.

Dahrendorf, Ralf. 1959. *Class and Class Conflict in Industrial Society.* Stanford, Calif.: Stanford University Press.

Eckert, David. 1980. "Sherman Act sentencing: An empirical study, 1971-1979". *Journal of Criminal Law and Criminology* 71:244-254.

Elzinga, Kenneth G. and William Breit. 1976. *The Antitrust Penalties.* New Haven, Conn.: Yale University Press.

Fisse, Brent and John Braithwaite. 1984. *The Impact of Publicity on Corporate Offenders.* Albany: State University of New York Press.

Galbraith, John K. 1967. *The New Industrial State.* New York: Houghton Mifflin.

Gallo, Joseph C., Joseph L. Craycraft, and Steven C. Bush. 1985. "Guess who came to dinner: An empirical study of federal antitrust enforcement for the period 1953-1984." *Review of Industrial Organization* II:106-130.

Goldschmid, Harvey, H. Michael Mann, J. Fred Watson (eds.). 1974. *Industrial Concentration: The New Learning.* Boston: Little, Brown.

Goldsmith, Raymond. 1973. *Institutional Investors and Corporate Stock.* New York: National Bureau of Economic Research.

Gort, Michael. 1962. *Diversification and Integration in American Industry.* Princeton, N.J.: Princeton University Press.

Green, Mark, Beverly Moore, and Bruce Wasserstein. 1972. *The Closed Enterprise System.* New York: Grossman.

Gross, Edward. 1980. "Organization structure and organizational crime." In Gilbert Geis and Ezra Stotland (eds.), *White-Collar Crime: Theory and Research.* Beverly Hills, Calif.: Sage.

Hay, George and Daniel Kelley. 1974. "An empirical study of price-fixing conspiracies." *Journal of Law and Economics* 17 :13-38.

Katzmann, Robert. 1980. *Regulatory Bureaucracy: The Federal Trade Commission and Antitrust Policy.* Cambridge, Mass.: MIT Press.

Kauper Thomas E. and Edward A. Snyder. 1988. "Private antitrust cases that follow on government cases." In Laurence J. White (ed.), *Private Antitrust Litigation: New Evidence, New Learning.* Cambridge, Mass.: MIT Press.

Kaysen, Carl and Donald F. Turner. 1959. *Antitrust Policy: An Economic and Legal Analysis.* Cambridge, Mass.: Harvard University Press.

Kerwin, Thomas A. 1980. "Antitrust violations." *American Criminal Law Review* 18:321-336.

Larner, Robert J. 1970. *Management Control and the Large Corporation.* Cambridge, Mass.: Harvard University Press.

Mann, Kenneth. 1985. *Defending White-Collar Crime: A Portrait of Attorneys at Work.* New Haven, Conn.: Yale University Press.

Marris, Robin. 1964. *The Economic Theory of Managerial Capitalism.* London: Macmillan.

McGee, John S. 1970. *In Defense of Industrial Concentration.* New York: Praeger.

Neale, A.D. 1970. *The Antitrust Laws of the United States.* Cambridge: The University Press.

Nichols, W.A.T. 1969. *Ownership, Control and Ideology.* London: Allen & Unwin.

Nutter, G. Warren and Henry Adler Einhorn. 1969. *Enterprise Monopoly in the United States, 1899-1958.* New York: Columbia University Press.

Phillips, Almarin. 1962. *Market Structure, Organization, and Performance.* Cambridge, Mass.: Harvard University Press.

Posner, Richard A. 1969. "The Federal Trade Commission." *University of Chicago Law Review* 37:47-89.

_____, 1970. "A statistical study of antitrust enforcement." *Journal of Law and Economics* 13:365-419.

_____, 1976. *Antitrust Law: An Economic Perspective.* Chicago: University of Chicago Press.

_____, 1979. "The Chicago School of antitrust analysis." *University of Pennsylvania Law Review* 127:925-948.

Reiss, Albert J., Jr. and Albert Biderman. 1980. *Data Sources on White-Collar Law-Breaking.* Washington, D.C.: National Institute of Justice.

Scherer, F.M.. 1980. *Industrial Market Structure and Economic Performance.* Chicago: Rand McNally .

Schumpeter, Joseph. 1942. *Capitalism, Socialism, and Democracy.* New York: Harper and Row.

Shapiro, Susan. 1984. *Wayward Capitalists: Target of the Securities and Exchange Commission.* New Haven, Conn.: Yale University Press.

Shepherd, William G. 1970. *Market Power and Economic Welfare.* New York: Random House.

_____, 1975. *The Treatment of Market Power.* New York: Columbia University Press.

Shonfield, Andrew. 1965. *Modern Capitalism.* London: Oxford University Press.

Smith, Richard Austin. 1961. "The incredible electrical conspiracy." *Fortune* 63:132-137, 161-164.

Stigler, George. 1964. "A theory of oligopoly." *Journal of Political Economy* 72:44-61.

Taylor, Robert. 1981. "Touted search by Justice Department fails to find a solid case of shared monopoly." *The Wall Street Journal,* January 16:121

U.S. Congress, House. 1968. *Commercial Banks and Their Trust Activities: Emerging Influence on the American Economy.* House Committee on Banking and Currency, Domestic Finance Subcommittee, 90th Cong., 2nd Sess., Washington, D.C.: Government Printing Office.

U.S. Department of Justice, Antitrust Division. 1978. "A Section 1 Approach to Shared Monopoly Prosecutions: Facilitative Devices." *Memorandum,* May 26.

Unseem, Michael. 1984. *The Inner Circle.* New York: Oxford University Press.

Weaver, Suzanne. 1977. *Decision to Prosecute: Organization and Public Policy in the Antitrust Division.* Cambridge, Mass.: MIT Press.

White, Lawrence J. 1975. "A legal attack on oligopoly pricing: The Automobile Fleet Sales case." *Journal of Economic Issues* 9:271-283.

Williamson, Oliver E. 1970. *Corporate Control and Business Behavior.* Englewood Cliffs, N.J.: Prentice-Hall.

Wilson, James Q. 1977. *Thinking About Crime.* New York: Vintage Books.

Worcester, Dean A., Jr. 1967. *Monopoly, Big Business and Welfare in the Postwar United States.* Seattle: University of Washington Press.

Zeitlin, Maurice. 1974. "Corporate ownership and control: The large corporation and the capitalist class." *American Journal of Sociology* 70:1073-1119.

CHAPTER 23
Inclusionary Strategies

WILLEM DeLINT

What remains unexplored is the way in which punishment is involved in the production of wider and more fundamental social meanings, which go beyond the immediacies of condemnation and speak of other subjects and other symbols.... Penality communicates meaning not just about crime and power but also about power, authority, legitimacy, normality, morality, personhood, social relations, and a host of other tangential matters. Penal signs and symbols are one part of an authoritative, institutional discourse which seeks to organize our moral and political understanding and to educate our sentiments and sensibilities.... Penality is thus a cultural text—or perhaps better—a cultural performance—which communicates with a variety of social audiences and conveys an extended range of meanings"[1]

This paper will explore recent scholarly work on sanctions that pertain to corporate wrongdoing, which is defined here, with a modification to Clinard & Yeager's[2] definition, as any act committed by corporations or persons acting on behalf of a corporation which contravenes and is punishable under administrative, civil, or criminal law.[3] Writing on the subject of corporate sanctions has explored the topic in terms of models or strategies of social control.[4] These are variously defined as, for instance, compliance/deterrence,[5] co-operation/criminalization[6] or accommodation/stringency.[7] They all, however, refer to the "severity" of the sanctions,[8] the use or disuse—it might be better to say proximity—of the criminal law as an enforcement weapon.[9] This paper will contribute to the debate on the differential application of sanctioning strategies by highlighting the various background considerations which play into the choices made.

I want to argue here that the choice of regulatory or enforcement strategy is one which both influences and is influenced by political and moral[10] considerations. Underlying ideologies about the proper role of law and the state inform sensibilities which are in turn generated from present sanctioning strategies. If the charge is made that corporations are inherently crimogenic[11] then one is forced to find ways of reducing corporate power.[12] Indeed, the critical or Marxist fringe of the scholarly debate on corporate sanctions is in large measure devoted to the study of corporate crime in order to carry forward a particular redistributive agenda.[13] If, on the other hand, it is argued that corporations and individuals acting on their behalf are essentially non-culpable wealth producers whose control, to be effective, should respond to their peculiar properties and conditions, then ones panacea will fit that claim, will focus on the effectiveness of strategies to prevent or reduce violations, whatever their nature.

Discussions about regulation or deregulation, about applying criminal sanctions to the corporation *and* its executors or administrative fines to the corporation alone are generated in part from divergent assumptions about the place of the state in society. There are those with socialist political affirmations on one extreme, and those with *laissez faire* or libertarian democratic assumptions favouring minimal state interference in the market on the other.[14] In the political climate of the 1980s, proposed remedies had become subject to scrutiny according to their utility and practicability, their cost-effectiveness. Conversely, proposals which have been authored with non-normative[15] intentions, which have stretched the parameters of extant practice and have been intended by their authors as ways of affording greater control over corporate activities, have been adopted by "the political economy of regulation and enforcement" to achieve those normative objectives.[16] In this way the overcriminalization of corporate wrongdoing may be seen to have led to underenforcement.[17]

Part of the complaint launched by critics of compliance or co-operative sanctions is that the control strategies these offer are not sensitive enough to redistributive exigencies. At bottom, the criticism is launched at power distribution. Thus, the issue in social control has often been characterized in terms of who is included and excluded from the process, how the process is used to include or exclude, and how social marginalization and its justificatory sensibilities are, in part, one consequence of this selection. In support of this viewpoint, I will compare the treatment of corporate violators under co-operative regulation to the ordering of people at a shopping mall. To go back to the observations of David Garland at the head of this paper, the disparate treatment of corporations by regulatory agencies and non-shoppers by mall security itself informs and constitutes social meanings and sensibilities which, in turn, call upon divergent enforcement approaches.

REGULATION AND CRIMINALIZATION

Roger Cotterrell and Brian Bercusson write that the law has two faces, one negative and one positive. The law's negative face, which is currently its "official face," is presented as "cumbersome, intrusive, and even potentially destructive in social and economic life, except as an absolutely necessary regulatory minimum by which basic order is maintained."[18] Law's positive face, on the other hand, which is currently "unofficial," is a powerful "and indispensable directive instrument of government policy, actively used on an extensive scale to reshape social and economic conditions and even popular attitudes."[19] This positive face is reflected, for instance, in the law's facilitation of property rights: most of the time unseen, it provides the reassurance that ownership carries various rights securing it. Thus the law has very powerful ideological functions; its positive and negative "faces" are used diversely to influence and shape opinion, not only via its capacity to reward and sanction behaviour, but also in its perpetuation of particular ideologies about the law itself.[20]

There are a number of "supporting ideologies" which contribute to the presentation of the law as an instrument of last choice with regard to means by which economic or power redistribution may be obtained.[21] As will be discussed, law (especially criminal law) is often depicted as a crude and ineffectual instrument of equalization. However,

> The ideology of law's incompatibility with substantial egalitarian policies is not based on specific experiences of regulatory failure alone. It is grounded more fundamentally in what may be termed "supporting ideologies" of property, liberty, the minimal state, and the rule of law.[22]

The founding assumptions of the liberal frame serve to juxtapose the individual and the state. The individual is seen as a "residual character"—what is left over once the state is defined. And, as Shearing and Stenning[23] argue, this allows corporations to be considered as legal persons, as individuals with all the rights which attach to that entity. Although the social reality of the corporation as a "politico-legal entity,"[24] with vast resources and with authority to order[25] and punish, is much like the state itself, and sometimes greater, in its ability to exercise will, the liberal democratic precepts which have facilitated the growth of corporate empires are in turn subverted against individual autonomy and freedom, leaving them to stand unprotected.

A consensus interpretation of the justification for the use of the criminal law highlights a general consensus on the moral nature of the act outlawed: it offends widely shared sensibilities and requires a punitive response. A conflict interpretation, on the other hand, highlights the use of law as an instrument to forge a "true" consensus. Ironically, the consensus perspective sees regulatory infractions as representative of "incompetence" or "random error," and not generally as demonstrating or requiring a response reflective and affirmative of a moral position; people are seen as constrained from doing right. Conflict theorists, ironically again, highlight how the use of ideologies obscures embedded moral choices. These reflect systematic distributions of sanctions and rewards in favour of a dominant class. The contradictions within those ideologies are exposed to highlight that regressed choice. Thus the justification of the decision to regulate polluters on grounds of economic expediency —a regrettable but inescapable evil, a *mala prohibita*—is juxtaposed with the decision to punish vagrants: although representative of a putatively equally regrettable and inescapable evil, it is termed a *mala en se* and the use of a punitive enforcement strategy is justified on those grounds.

Indeed, the question of which kind of sanction ought to apply to behaviour—whether, for instance, it ought to be considered to be a breach of a widely held value and be criminalized or whether it ought to be considered a technical violation and fall under regulatory sanction—does not wish away a moral choice, always embedded in the style of enforcement and penality, whether deterrent or compliance-based, preventative or reactive. If, as Foucault argues, discipline is embedded and dispersed throughout the micro-relations which constitute society, then the choice of sanction, the choice of ordering modes—whether punitive or preventative—cannot be split on the basis of being moral or non-moral: they both generate and reflect moral choices. The justification both of criminal justice ordering and ordering by regulatory statutes is on the basis of subjectively experienced loss.

Thus, the sensibilities about whether to regulate or punish behaviour is rooted to justifications backed by supporting ideologies such as free enterprise and the minimalist state. It is enabled by the discourse of punishment and regulation itself—a discourse which, like administrative and criminal law, legitimates its own inclusions and exclusions.[26] However, it is that very justificatory ideology which may need the greatest reform. If, as has been argued widely, the liberal democratic protections of property and the legal characterization of

the individual have afforded the large corporation a position of virtually unmiti-
gated power and authority, then sanctioning strategies which play them
according to the adversarial myth of equal combatants are wrongheaded: they
are unlikely to yield a broadly-defined justice, and will certainly be ill-equipped
to encourage a redistributive agenda.

Indeed, in the arena of corporate regulatory strategy today there are
numerous doubts expressed about the ability or propriety of state-regulation.
These doubts are consistent with the emergence of the new right and its sup-
ply-side economic policies and interests in reducing the growth of government.
In keeping with Cotterrel's negative face of the law, the absolute regulatory
minimum is articulated: the state has little business in the boardrooms of the
nation. The cost and the justifications for government intervention in the market is scrutinized and questioned.[27] This position is expressed most avidly in
scholarly works on economic theory or administrative science,[28] but is not
restricted to those disciplines. Yet, these doubts or oppositions to state regulation are intended more for their rhetorical and symbolic value, for at the same
time that *standards* and *regulations* on pharmaceutical companies are
deemed by advocates of the minimalist state to be too interfering, intensive
and *criminal justice* prosecution of the (unlicensed) drug trade is vigorously
demanded, despite the expense.[29] Put another way, corporations rely more
heavily on state regulation by dint of the barriers to competition of, for example, trade restrictions than does the prostitute selling his wares on the street.
This differential application of ideology alerts us to the possibility that affirmations other than the "protection of the individual" are being reproduced.

On the other side of the ledger, it is a common inconsistency among criminologists on the left to urge for penalties on corporations which stress and
assume the sort of responsibility and culpability rarely attributed (by them) to
those persons convicted of various "street" crimes. What is curious about this
is the dexterity with which the concept of individual responsibility is turned this
way and that.

THE DEBATE TODAY

In the current debate about what sanctions ought to pertain to corporate
wrongdoing, conflict scholars advocate the use of coercive and criminal sanctions for their symbolic and moral value, and for their value as redistributive
agents. On the other hand, a more conciliatory approach favours "softer"
sanctioning strategies which pay heed to perceived utilitarian exigencies and

the requirements of the current regulatory climate.

However, the debate about modes of enforcement does not of itself imply leftists on one side and liberals and conservatives on the other. As Peter Manning says, these "rule-enforcement systems" are neither mutually exclusive nor applicable only to types of penalties, they also "cut across forms of law," and "given institutions or agencies."[30] They can also be seen as *positive*, that is, enabling. Thus they are not simply summed up as taxes, duties, conditions, or penalties, but as a form of state assistance. While industry may see regulation as another cost, this cost is often an insulation against the vicissitudes of public opinion, lobbyists, and activists. The mode of enforcement thus attaches to a political or moral affirmation about desired states and ultimate ends, and ought to be seen in the context of the regulation of behaviour as a whole, that is, comparatively.

Edwin Sutherland made the observation almost half a century ago that the differential application of the law to large corporations was, in part, a consequence of the "status of businessmen...and the relatively unorganized resentment of the public against white collar crime."[31] He also compared this differential treatment as consistent with the practice of benefit of clergy, which was the medieval English equivalent of "benefit of business or profession."[32] Thus a conflict perspective draws out how protections from punishment are more readily obtained in environments likely to be dominated by members of the dominant class, and how there is historical continuity of differential punishment based on class, and class associations.[33] It also emphasizes the redistributive function of the law. I now want to look at the two divergent perspectives on regulation to examine how the conflict perspective on corporate crime is being assailed.

THE INCLUSORY MODEL &
THE ARGUMENT AGAINST CRIMINALIZATION

> Cooperation/Compliance/Accommodation
> In certain aspects of punishment, as elsewhere in modern society, technical relations have tended to displace moral ones, therapies have replaced judgments, and the social sciences have occupied a space that used to be definitively moral and religious.[34]

The inclusory model of sanctioning is one by which enforcers seek to find ways of keeping transgressors or would-be transgressors *in*: in business, in action, within law. The operating assumption is thus one of moral relativity rather than one of moral absolutes. Deviations are normalized, are negotiable, are standardized. The attitude is familial: the door is kept open, knowledge and information are shared freely, and bargaining for standards of behaviour is ongoing. The criminal law is seen as an ultimate failure, a breakdown of communication, negotiation, commitment to process.

Maintaining an in-group does not imply that corporate wrongdoing be removed from the jurisdiction of the criminal law. Rather, the criminal law is seen as a last resort to which the matter is referred after intermediary measures have failed to produce a settlement which satisfies both regulator and regulated. Thus, although the tendency is away from criminal sanctions, the proposals advocated by writers under this general heading do not think away the criminal law as a final arbiter should these intermediary measures fail, and should the offence be beyond the pale. Nevertheless, the scale that measures how bad is too bad is both *weighted* more favourably from the point of view of corporate actors and is *determined* by a process which is bound to be more deferential to the concerns of those actors and their representatives. Thus this approach is essentially inclusory: it seeks to include both the police/regulator and the potential corporate violator in a process of negotiation about both standards of conduct and the applicable sanctions. By the same token, it seeks to avoid the "excesses" of a more rigid regulatory enforcement (policing) where there are no exceptions and there is very little discretion exercised.[35] It seeks to avoid also the impracticalities of tighter criminalization. The authority of these inclusory approaches often rests on the appeal to more efficient social control,[36] and the moral or symbolic considerations of criminalization become tertiary to considerations of prevention and efficient control.

Compliance strategy seeks, as Manning says, "conformity with a condition or state specified in rules" and aims at "preventing harm."[37] It often does not make due process in the legal sense available. The aim is to facilitate an ongoing condition or order which meets given standards, which standards and penalties are often negotiable. High standards of co-operation guarantee the level of information exchange necessary for the facilitation of control. Thus it is inclusory.

One variation on the compliance model of regulation is advanced by Scholz. According to this strategy, both regulators and regulated adhere to co-operation because it minimizes costs to the regulatory agency, and sanctions to the regulated corporation. However, when one player defects from the co-operative model, the other player must immediately follow suit: "if the defector is a firm, the regulatory agency should instantly abandon persuasion/education and move to a deterrence strategy through appropriate legal mechanisms (If it is the regulatory agency that abandons the co-operative mode, the firm should immediately, according to this model, adopt avoidance/evasion strategies)."[38]

This model is not atypical of compliance models generally in that ultimate recourse to the criminal law is often implicit or explicit,[39] strategies are geared to elicit high information turnover, regulator/regulated interdependence, and a mode of enforcement justified on efficiency, on its ability to exact results: the maintenance of a safety standard.

Along with libertarian or growth-promoting rhetoric, the strongest argument used to support more inclusory enforcement strategies is the efficiency argument. And, indeed, some studies support the contention that regulators restricted to the laying of administrative penalties both produce more and bigger penalties. In a study comparing firms regulated by the Worker's Compensation Board to those regulated by Waste Management Branch of the Ministry of the Environment, Richard Brown and Murray Rankin found evidence to suggest that "the administrative process is much more likely than the criminal justice system to punish offenders whose transgressions create a risk of harm that never materializes."[40] They found that the administrative process produced more and larger penalties, and suggested that the reasons for the relative inefficiency of the Waste Management Branch are related to the view of harm of judges and prosecutors and the reluctance to apply criminal stigma in the absence of positive culpability. However, in the sense that, as Reiss argues, the production of penalties is a mark of *failure* for compliance systems whereas it marks *success* for deterrence systems,[41] a comparison on the basis of penalties assessed may not be appropriate.[42]

Perhaps more damning to the efficacy of compliance strategies is work, such as that by Keith Hawkins, which documents its shortcomings in practice. In *Environment and Enforcement*, Hawkins writes of how moral and political ambivalence and pressures are fixtures of the environment in which the regulatory inspector operates. In effect, the compliance strategy perpetuates a status quo in which regulatory rule-breaking is seen by inspectors as "commonplace and routine," and in which a game of "bargaining and bluffing" sets flexible violation thresholds.[43] The regulatory agency's political position between pro-business publics on one hand and enforcement activists on the other encouraged the occasional prosecution—prosecutors lacked training in prosecution and were ignorant of legal process[44]— of cases about which little or no moral ambivalence was experienced: "By prosecuting the clearly morally blameworthy cases the Water Authorities were placing the behaviour complained of in a framework which was familiar and comprehensible to all, even the most pro-business advocate."[45]

The very susceptibility—by design—of compliance strategies leads, as it does in proactive policing environments, to the corruptibility or co-optation of enforcement agents by the often more powerful regulated bodies. But whereas at a street policing level, the police can usually rely on strong or at least consistent public moral support reflected, in large measure, by the resources supplied them, the regulatory official, by contrast, is disadvantaged by equivocal support both financially, morally, and politically.[46] This imbalance leads not only to regulatory agents being lured to join the "other side" for usually greater wages—agent or agency capture— but also to a far greater number of prosecutions against smaller, more vulnerable companies[47] when it is big businesses which are reported to commit more violations.[48] Thus, the compliance strategy, to work, may require the development of means to redress the power imbalance particularly between the large corporation and the regulatory agency. Such means, however, appear to be antithetical to libertarian and growth-promoting rhetoric which so strongly favours inclusionary tactics.

The inclusory predilections of regulators also create uncertainty about the use of criminal sanctions.[49] It does so, partly, because the ideology which is favourable to a less punitive approach to corporate crime is one which is consistent with the belief in the basic goodness of profit-making—that corporate or individual profit-making will eventually benefit the community at large. This belief is quite pervasive, and has been noted among judges,[50] prosecutors,[51] and the regulators themselves.[52] Thus, as Calavita and Pontell[53] report, the recent savings and loan crisis is in large measure a consequence of the ideology of deregulation. They point out that under emerging finance-capitalism—as opposed to industrial capitalism—capital gains are "at best irrelevant to the welfare of the general population. Unlike the production of goods and services, 'fiddling with' money produced few new jobs and no consumer goods. Policies based on outdated assumptions about the intrinsically beneficial nature of entrepreneurial activity tend to exacerbate the situation."[54] They further point out that the "casino economy"—finance capitalism—is founded on illusions which it is against the state's—and the regulator's—interest to unmask.

A final point about the pitfalls of inclusory regulation relates to the utilitarian ethos or econometric analyses by which standards and sanctions are produced and justified. Particularly with regard to environmental and health and safety regulation, this approach tends to "harden" "soft" variables such as the corruption of a natural landscape or the moral outrage felt at bid-riggers who artificially inflate the price of flour the federal government buys to send to starving populations in the third world.[55] Where regulators and regulated bargain on the value of such "costs," a moral relativity is produced with the defining upper hand often going to the more powerful bargainer. In negotiations with the big corporation, an inclusory consent-oriented process grants considerably more leverage to the corporation and its executors in bargaining with regulators than it does to the vagrant or street criminal "bargaining" with the police. This is a consequence of relative power, of the pre-defined weights placed on the interests affected.[56] "Indeed, regulatory control is fundamentally influenced by the way agency officials *interpret* the conflict between the protective issue, which led to the law, and pressures for economic efficiency which arise in particular cases."[57]

The problems with inclusory models may be vitiated somewhat if the regulatory agency's bargaining position is strengthened, but it seems that this can only be accomplished by providing it with the widest range of options, including, as Snider says, the "symbolism and the universalism of the criminal law."[58] Thus "pure" inclusivity is, at best, a misguided regulatory ideal.

THE EXCLUSORY MODEL &
THE ARGUMENT FAVOURING CRIMINALIZATION

> Deterrence/Stringency
> The professionalization of the punitive process has, in the twentieth century, reached a point where penal professionals have been able to redefine the social meaning of punishment...Once penalties ceased to be executed in public, or in ways which sought to express public sentiments, the direct expression of outrage or emotion was increasingly cordoned off—limited to the public galleries of the courtroom or the letters columns of the press. (Garland: 184-185)

Under an exclusory model of enforcement, the wrongdoer or potential wrongdoer is individualized as an adversary, and enforcement officials are therefore symbolically distanced from the act and actor. Sanctioning or deterrent systems are used to express moral distancing; as opposed to the notion of a moral relativity espoused by compliance or inclusionary models, where there is an invocation of moral absolutes. And the criminal law is favoured as a means of finesse, a moral distance. It provides a means by which certain acts and people are symbolically turned out or expelled. Thus, certain acts are seen to require from law enforcement personnel a hard and fast application of sanctions. Both in the streets and in the suites, the regulatory agent or police officer is oriented to a punitive enforcement once a violation has occurred. Additionally, once a transgressor had been isolated, she or he is made known to the coercive reserves of the policing agency. Shows of force or its threat will serve as a persistent reminder to others that matters of ordering are being regularly and vigorously pursued.

Two arguments for the imposition of criminal sanctions against both the corporation itself and those who represent its "guiding mind and will,"[59] are expressed in the current critical or conflict-based writing on corporate regulation. They are, firstly, that state agents and agencies need more power to reduce their relative powerlessness vis à vis the corporate wrongdoers they handle. Equal justice, it is argued, favours the imprisonment and heavy penalization of corporations and corporate actors for the symbolic and democratizing message the criminal law can carry. The will of the people is not reflected in the process or the content of much of the legislation aimed at corporate regulation. That legislation reflects the interests of the dominant class. Conflict theorists argue strenuously about the relative harm of corporate illegalities, which is viewed to be much greater than that of petty street criminals,[60] but which are rarely prosecuted because of the interests at stake. Thus, the conflict position rejects the position that inclusory strategies can exact better control on corporations: that strategy is seen, rather, as doomed to allow the more powerful interests a vehicle expressly suited to the expression and perpetuation of those interests. Those powerful interests need to be, it is argued, if not excluded entirely from the sanction-determination process, at least have their representation diminutized, made secondary to democratizing interests.

This is related to the second argument, which is that the criminal law can exact systematic changes in that it can produce attitudes and sentiments about acts and behaviours. The use of the criminal law to jail corporate executives can produce or augment—crystallize—a general consciousness about those acts, affirming them to be morally repugnant. As Glasbeek says, "it is the stigmatization of behaviour that makes it possible to question its general utility and acceptability."[61]

The first argument calls into question the ideologies which back up the role that regulators are to take. The contradictions in the notion of the minimalist state are made explicit. For instance, barriers to competition, such as those of protectionism, are seen as illustrative of the contradictions of market self-regulation: those that have a share of the market use regulation to maintain power, and it is the law itself which is used by corporations to introduce stability into otherwise unpredictable environments.[62] Indeed, as Gross comments, government interference is often criticized by corporate executives in spite of the fact "that they could hardly operate one hour without (the law's) interference."[63] Thus, the partial truths of the ideology are generalized at convenient times to claim immunities. As Garland states, "the key to understanding criminal law is to appreciate the ways in which particular interests are interwoven with general ones...the same law which protects everyone at one level, also legalizes the basis whereby one class exploits another."[64]

Regulators fall prey to this ideological thinking and interpret corporate wrongdoing as a regrettable yet intractable side-effect of useful citizenship, of exuberance, of healthy appetites for growth. A regulatory strategy may be disabling of the safeguards that may be constructed around regulators' own unique interpretation of corporate wrongdoing; it may enable invasion and reconstruction via regulator/regulated interactions. At issue here is the image of the corporation: How is it to be constructed? As basically law-abiding and therefore amenable to "soft," controls? or fundamentally crimogenic and requiring "hard" and stringent control strategies?

The second argument, then, refers to the use of penal strategies to produce sensibilities and redistribution. The criminalization of drugs and penalization of drug users are not simply reactive, they are productive of sensibilities about drug use as well. And so the tremendous expenditures on policing the drug war, which is defended in moral terms, is, in part, a definitional battle about the inclusions and exclusions of law's moral territory. The degree of public hostility to the drug menace is pointed to (and fabricated) in support of heavy criminal penalization. But will compliance-favouring writers call forth public opinion about price-fixing to allow outrage about *that* to inform *regulatory* strategy?[65] The argument about negotiated versus stringently applied penalties is thus not simply an argument about the relative merits of exacting an efficient *activity tax* versus expressing social disapproval, but is about the inclusions and exclusions in the narrative of penality. Where may moral arguments be justifiably applied, where are they disallowed, or reduced to a cost of business?

And what are they used for? If, as Garland says, the expressive element of punishment is being ushered out of public forums, then who is served when moral attributions are allocated in the office of a bureaucrat? Who may be that bureaucrat? The conflict theorist sees the presumed consensus applied differentially to justify ongoing inequities in the distribution of power and wealth. They seek to channel outrage on corporations which conservative writers will have channelled on the street. By in this way "equalizing" its applicability, penality might perform a redistributive function.

As Glasbeek and Orland have said, it is necessary to distinguish between acts which are truly immoral and acts which are violations of the law, acts which are, as Conklin's executive terms them, "illegal but not criminal." There is no doubt, that there are innumerable difficulties in attaching culpability to corporations *and* the person or persons who constitute its "guiding mind and will." However, a great many solutions have been offered—from licensing schemes which attach accountability,[66] to federal chartering,[67] to making controlling shareholders responsible.[68] All of these seek to remove the insulation which attaches the corporation and which makes it a modern-day sanctuary from criminal prosecution.

All of this is not to say that adopting a more rigid and exclusory strategy, one which explicitly restricts opportunities for bargaining and negotiation about standards and penalties,[69] and one which attempts to insulate the regulatory agency from the direct pressures of the regulated industry and lobby groups, is not problematic. As has been often stated, such a strategy may indeed lead to an information shortfall or "counter-productive backlash,"[70] or even to fewer prosecutions.[71] However, it is to stress alertness to the uses made of knowledge. Hawkins sums his discussion of the nature of corporate illegalities by stating, "One consequence of a more punitive enforcement strategy might well be to unbalance this relationship and lead to business withdrawing their cooperation to some degree which in turn might perversely lead to an increase in the incidence of the events and problems which the regulatory agency is trying to contro.l. Compare such a statement to, "One consequence of jailing drug users is that it might lead to an inbalance in the relationship that our police have with their subculture and lead to its withdrawing its cooperation. This might, perversely, lead to an increase in..etc. etc." Certainly, this comparison underlines the fact that present practice does not enable our thinking around illicit drug use as subject to inclusory enforcement strategies. But I want to emphasize that the discourse helps to disable thinking about this phenomenon as a shared problem which cannot be overcome by shutting people out and locking doors. The discourse itself, when casting about for justifications, latches onto current practices and ideologies.

To sum up then, the current debate about enforcement strategies is at odds on fundamentals. On one extreme, there is the moral component of a bevy of behaviours, both diffuse and isolated, both without identifiable victims and with immense death tolls. On the other, there are petty violations and sanctioning programmes designed to prevent and normalize behaviour. On the one hand, there is a redistributive agenda, and on the other, a furtherance of the status quo, a typically *liberal* legitimation of extant practice. On the one extreme, there are strategies for keeping doors and dialogues open, and on the other, justifications for excluding, for expelling the evil from the community.

The final portion of this paper will look briefly at the shopping mall as a penal site—a site where a sanctioning strategy is exercised. This will be used as a point of comparison to set in relief the differences in sensibilities which pertain in the the arena of corporate regulation. The compelling argument which assumes the necessity of thinking about violators as "amoral," as prone-to-mistakes-but-not-culpable, is not one which finds much sway at the mall. There, the common sense assumption is the necessity of exclusory means and ends. This has to do, certainly, with basic differences between these two sites, but the mode of penality—as we have seen with regard to corporate sanctions—is based in large measure on ideologies and their usages in differentiating the morally repugnant from the accidental transgression. In a capitalist society, one may expect certain systematic differences between regulation at a site of production and at a site of consumption. Those differences can be expected to facilitate productive and consumptive necessities, to include harmonious conditions and to exclude disharmonious ones.

Penal Sensibilities and Redistribution
In penality the instrumental *is* symbolic and the social act of punishment, however mundane, is at the same time an expression of cultural meaning."[72] Institutions of punishment, "give their authority to a particular form of accountability...(sanctioning) a particular form of moral offering and a specific conception of morality" Punishment creates a "regime of truth." [73]

I want to devote the remainder of the paper to exploring the idea that forms of punishment assume and generate different kinds of discipline. It can be argued that the opinions expressed by inclusory strategy proponents assume that corporations do not need to be disciplined, while advocates of exclusory enforcement want to use the mode of punishment as a means of exacting some measure of societal change. The debate about sanctioning strategies for corporate wrongdoing is informed by the recognition that the mode of punishment is seen to carry a great deal of weight as a producer of sensibilities: putting a corporate executive in prison has a symbolic value which informs public opinion about the character not only of the corporate executive so punished, but about corporate executives generally.[74] Similarly, popular opinions about young Black men are informed by the barrage of television reportage of young Black men being placed in jail.

While in the regulatory arena the compliance sanction tends to normalize[75] *actions* of the violators, at the mall it normalizes the *process* by which transgressors are excluded. Additionally, while in the regulatory arena the normative regulatory strategy is inclusory, it is exclusory at the mall. Finally, the tendency at both sites is to regress the moral evaluation, to make enforcement not an expressive exercise of moral condemnation, but to make it instrumental.

A compliance strategy is preferred at the shopping mall because it is preventative and proactive; and the strategy is enforced via private police because this offers more control over the means of prevention and over sanctioning options and outcomes. Private property rights are sufficiently wide and known to the public to enable that option, thus offering a basis for exclusion and expulsion. Moreover, like it is with public police, the power differential between the private police and the public they handle is sufficiently great not to require more coercive persuasion.[76] Property owners don't want to use public police primarily because that entails the unpredictability of the criminal justice system. Thus, whereas sanctioning processes available to private police working for the mall are enabled by Trespass to Property legislation and determined in large measures by the policies of the mall, public reactive policing is unpredictable, governed by a wider range of citizen rights and police duties, and leaves the mall owner a narrower range of options with regard to outcome and recovery. Private policing allows the mall owners to retain control over the sanctioning process, allows them to embed, normalize and routinize it.

Secondly, whereas compliance strategies of corporate regulation afford inclusory enforcement, compliance strategy via private policing allows for exclusory sanctions. It is exercised by the use of the "ban." A ban is simply the right to deny access to private property exercised by the mall owner via the enforcement mechanism. The ban is legitimated on property rights[77] and is exercised very inclusively.[78] This is legitimated on the basis of the liberal democratic view of order-maintenance. Mall owners constitute—through inclusory and exclusory definitions—their own legitimate order.[79] Both the process and the penalty is delivered with little room for negotiating or bargaining.

Pfol says that personalization combined with event-orientation "produces the appearance that troublesome persons rather than troublesome social structures are at fault."[80] Clearly, this linkage between order and the troublesome person is central to the style of order-maintenance of institutions such as the shopping mall: disorder is individualized and human; order is impersonal environment management; and opportunity for human innovation and experimentation is purposely reduced: the resulting order has the look of a totalitarian regime. The mall is a Hobbesian world where reason is expressed in the threat of coercive authority and non-consumptive passions are disciplined and excluded.

In contrast, the mechanistic model, the Hobbesian model, as recent writing concludes, is not descriptive of a financial market.[81] Control in the corporate halls recognizes the value of human innovation and experimentation: it is a negotiated order in which human passions are seen as necessary and consistent with the social value of capital production (this accounts for the difference between penalties for wrongdoing which are favourable to the corporation as opposed to unfavourable to it: white collar vs corporate crime (Orland; Wheeler: Hagan). Ordering does not reflect the exteriority, the individualization, and the sanctioning of prosecutorial justice but rather the interiority, contextualization, and informality of the compliance strategy. Sometimes, that ordering is so minimal it hardly exists.[82] Order-maintenance of corporations under compliance is supple and negotiated. So much so, that the rules, like free enterprise itself, sometimes become a "practical anarchy."[83]

Finally, as it is in the corporate arena, the order which compliance strategy attempts to facilitate at the mall is instrumental. The strategy is to regress moral decisions and take them out of the playing field where they may produce unpredictable consequences. The badges and the uniforms are thus significative of a moral decision made in a boardroom, as a means of tilting the balance of persuasion and foreclosing possible outcomes. As Richard Ericson says, "Morality is built into the classifications that members use for conducting their routine business. The very act of classification, including disputes about misclassification, involves questions of right and wrong and is therefore loaded with moral content."[84]

At the mall, and in the corporate halls, the discourse of profit and loss is emphatically moral:[85] it seeks hegemony over legitimate justifications, commentaries. It excludes and trains. It reflects an affirmative choice about order, it facilitates the evaluation of personal or corporate financial gain as more important than anything else, including deprivations to (conflicting and dangerous) competing liberties. The language of the amusement park or mall owner which denudes actions of their moral evaluations is an attempt to delimit the parameters of debate such that essential, radical categories of freedoms, liberties, and rights are pushed outside of legitimate argument. The rejection of the very idea of moral reform does not alter the morally reforming quality not only of their particular manifestation of order, but also of the very real deprivations of liberty they exert both at an individual and at a societal level (by identifying and punishing certain individuals and justifying the deprivation as consistent with a particular version of social necessity). Amusement park and mall owners actively engage in the construction and affirmation of certain identifiable moral choices: and they do so by exercising a punitive choice: the private "right" to exclude. The physical realities of shopping malls and amusement parks, complete with their modes of control, represent, to borrow Joseph Gusfield's terms, non-neutral facts constructed by power.[86]

But where compliance is used in the mall to facilitate the determination and exclusion of non-normative behaviour, that strategy is used in the regulatory environment to normalize and include even morally questionable conduct. Why? I believe that the answer lies in problemizing the mode of consumption and highlighting the fact that the liberal state has been continually reconstituted against a self-defined backdrop of *laissez faire* accumulation. This context of the utility of growth has always militated against the application of moral penalties in the productive sphere. Indeed, it is logical that a society which has an economy which depends on private entrepreneurship will offer protections and inducements (inclusionary strategies) rather than vulnerabilities and moral censure (exclusionary strategies) to whomever are perceived as the wealth-creators.

Thus the mode of penality can be seen to be influenced by economic exigencies. The protection of the institution of private property, of the current mode of production, and of high consumption levels, is to some degree determinant of the style and emphasis of order maintenance. This is the familiar and compelling argument of revisionist Marxist thinking on policing: mode of production is seen as related to changes in order-maintenance styles.[87] In this respect the security guards at the mall are chiefly accountable to the client and the client's interest not only in the protection of property and staff and the maintenance of a "well-ordered" environment, but to popular definitions of the experience of shopping. Economic exigencies also both shape and are shaped by a culture of images or life styles, the shape and shaping of which is itself endlessly reflexive.

While sanctioning in the productive (or private) sphere is inclusory, sanctioning in the public sphere of consumption is exclusory. Because high levels of consumption are integral to our economics, the arenas of consumption must be ordered to facilitate high turnover: shopping must be made to seem enjoyable. This ordering entails disciplining the public to a particular prioritizing of values whereby possibilities of consumption are enhanced and constraints on consumption reduced. In the soft mediation of advertising, this is accomplished by defining or constituting the consumer along dimensions which do not even suggest the possibility of non-compliance. But in the physical settings and "town square"-like dimensions of the shopping mall, compliance is ensured with the ordering of space and management of traffic to and from the stores. For the most part, compliance is accomplished because there are few who offer and assert competing definitions to the order of the mall as defined by its ownership, a privately-defined order so licensed by the state, which already assumes profit-taking as the mall's essential function in a capitalist economy.

Ordering at the mall centres around removing the barriers to consumption, which includes the activities of non-consumers, and around excluding competing claims—such as presented by pamphleteers—for the use of the site. Finally, the non-shopper must be excluded, he is the threatening reminder of the existence of the marginalized, the other, the non-player person. Indeed, it is the existence of the non-shopper and those persons who would shape the order of the shopping mall around alternate axes, such as that of community centre or town square, which most tests the seemingly instrumental definition of order and the attendant inclusionary strategy used in its facilitation.

Property rights, once used to defend individual liberties are already being invoked to curtail them. Policing, ever adaptive to the exigencies of capital requirements, appears to continue to be facilitative of the emergent ordering agendas of the minimalist state struggling with the effects of growing marginalization and disparity. Surveillance, and the enmeshing or embedding of discipline, although ideologically antithetical to the liberal-democratic state, is gaining a legitimacy in the ordering of public private property (and in community-policed neighbourhoods), where sacrifices to civil liberties and police accountability are willingly exchanged for security and order.

CONCLUSION

There is, then, a real danger to those very freedoms which the liberal democratic ideology would protect. Our classifications of things, our uses of penal strategies, their exclusions and inclusions, offer possibilities of marginalizing and expelling not only ideas but flesh and blood people. This we can see in practice at the shopping mall, where the right to exclude and banish is interpreted as consistent with the right to property. Equally, however, sanctioning strategies can facilitate the inclusion, the normalization, of otherwise repugnant behaviour. In the case of rootless multinational corporations and of many smaller ones, the sanctioning profile bartered out between regulatory agency and corporate officials has the effect of shaping expectations such that it becomes the black and white character of rule-breaking behaviour itself which is pushed to the margins of sensibility. Here, violations are not the justification of exclusion, but the stakes of inclusion: part of the package of arrangements of doing business.

ENDNOTES

1.   David Garland, *Punishment and Modern Society*. Chicago: University of Chicago Press. 1990. pp. 252-253.

2.   Marshall Clinard & Peter Yeager, *Corporate Crime*. New York: The Free Press. 1980. p.16.

3.   This is not inconsistent with the definitions of John Conklin, *Illegal But Not Criminal*. Englewood Cliffs: Prentice Hall. 1977, at p. 13.; Laureen Snider, "Cooperative Models and Corporate Crime: Panacea or Cop-Out?," in *Crime & Delinquency*, Vol 36, No. 3, July, 1990, at p. 374 or; James Coleman, *The Criminal Elite*. New York: St. Martin's Press. 1985, at p. 8.

4.   Social control will be regarded here as organized behaviour informed by a given procedural strategy which is dedicated to the ordering of the activities or behaviours of groups or individuals.

5.   Albert Reiss, Jr., "Selecting Strategies of Social Control Over Organizational Life," in K. Hawkins & J. Thomas (eds.), *Enforcing Regulation*. Boston: Kluwer-Nijhoff. 1984.

6.   Laureen Snider's conceptualization in "Cooperative Models and Corporate Crime."

7.   Robert Kagan, *Regulatory Justice*. New York: Russell Sage. 1978.

8.   Snider, p. 373. This is not to attempt to exhaust the dichotomous varieties. Michael CLark provides yet another with criminal prosecution versus administrative action. In "Prosecutorial and Administrative Strategies to Control Business Crime: Private and Public Roles," in Shearing and Stenning (eds.). *Private Policing*. Newbury Park: Sage 1987

9.   Attempts have been made to break away from this dichotomous interpretation of corporate sanctioning. Attempts have also bee made to forge alternatives to regulation. An example of the latter is Michael Baram's, *Alternatives to Regulation*. Lexington: Lexington Books. 1982. This work is in line with the deregulatory agenda of the Reagan government. A detailed analysis of this deregulation and its political economy is provided by Richard Harris and Sidney Milkis, *The Politics of Regulatory Change*. New York: Oxford University Press. 1989.

10.   An evaluation of right and wrong; a choice between alternatives based on ethical considerations.

11.   A claim made by Stephen Box, Edward Gross, and Diane Vaughan, among others.

12. One of the more recent depictions of the corporation offers three characterizations, that of "amoral calculator," "political citizen," and "organizationally incompetent" (Robert Kagan and John Scholz, "The Criminology of the Corporation and Regulatory Enforcement Strategies,m," in *Enforcing Regulation*.

13. E.g., Stephen Box, H. J. Glasbeek, Edward Gross.

14. Having said this, I want to stress the caveat that erroneous assumptions can be made about reading a researcher's political agenda from policy advocacy, which advocacy is often more complex and rounded than a brief synopsis may allow for.

15. The term "normative" has been applied to regulatory practice to refer to those policies and policy proposals which meet a "reasonableness" standard (e.g., Hawkins), which standard is derived from a cost-benefit analysis (economic costs versus social benefits) in which industry and the general public (often through lobby groups) may make submissions as to either. Under Reagan in the United States of the 1980s, however, the "reasonable" balance has favoured industry and reduced expenditures on regulatory protections.

16. I am referring here to some of the work in the early 1980s by compliance model proponents. As Laureen Snider writes, the political uses of the promotion by scholars of the co-operative model cannot be ignored: "At particular ideological junctures, ideas are seized upon, popularized, and thereby transformed into instruments that increase the power of the dominant class" ("Cooperative Models and Corporate Crime," p. 382). "When Yeager (1986) said that calling corporate misbehaviour criminal was resorting to an unnecessary 'linguistic flag,' he was forgetting all that we know about the political economy of regulation and enforcement. Obscuring the link between corporate crime and traditional crime may have a profound and deleterious impact on the already weak structure of regulation" (p. 383).

17. For example, Leonard Orland cites a litany of "trivial" regulatory statutes which carry jail term penalties. This has the effect of conflating acts which conform to a reasonable person standard of culpability with those that do not, and should therefore be divested of the criminal stigma. Underenforcement is the result, in part, of the common-sense determination by regulators not to pursue—or not to pursue the maximum—prosecutions in the face of this lack of distinction. See Leonard Orland, "Reflections on Corporate Crime: Law in Search of Theory and Scholarship," *American Criminal Law Review*. 17: 1980.

18. Roger Cotterrell & Brian Bercusson, "Introduction: Las, Democracy and Social Justice", *Journal of Law & Society* . No. 1, Spring 1988. , p. 5.

19. *Ibid.*, p. 6.

20. *Ibid.*, p. 7.

21. *Ibid.*, p. 8.

22. *Ibid.*, p. 9.

23. Clifford Shearing & Philip Stenning, "Reframing Policing," in *Private Policing*, at pp. 14-15.

24. *Ibid.* p. 14.

25. Order means the disposition of things (or people, or concepts) according to a procedural, moral, hierarchical norm. See, Richard Ericson, *Representing Order*. Toronto: University of Toronto Press. 1991, p. 5.

26. H. J. Glasbeek, "Why Corporate Deviance is not Treated as a Crime—The Need to Make Profits a Dirty Word," in *Osgoode Hall Law Journal*. 1984. At pp. 427-428.

27. Harris and Milkis, 1989, p. 17.

28. E.g., Michael Baram, *Alternatives to Regulation*.

29. In a recent article on the opinions of prosecutors, it was found that while prosecutors had "no philosophical or conceptual objections" to using the criminal law on corporate offenders, the resources were not available to deal with that problem, as they are spent on drug crimes. As one prosecutor said: "For 8 years or so all our State's Attorney shouted was 'gangs and drugs, gangs and drugs.' So after 8 years of that approach the problem is 10 times worse, and it has hurt every other area of prosecution...You bring in a white-collar executive to the bar of justice, and the judge looking at all of this, goes, 'What, what is this?'." In Michael Benson, Francis Cullen, and William Maakested, "Local Prosecutors and Corporate Crime," *Crime and Delinquency*. Vol. 36, No. 3, July 1990, at p. 361.

30. Peter Manning, "Ironies of Compliance," in *Private Policing.*

31. Edwin Sutherland, *White Collar Crime*. New York: Holt, Rhinehart, and Winston., p. 47.

32. Edwin Sutherland, *On Analyzing Crime*. Karl Schuessler (ed.) Chicago: University of Chicago Press. 1973. p. 57.

33. Examined and argued in the works of the Marxist revisionist school, e.g., Michael Ignatieff, Douglas Hay, George Rusche and Otto Kircheimer.

34. Garland, p. 187.

35. This, for example, was the complaint launched against the EPA of the 1970s. Described by former director of Water Criteria and Standards, Joseph Krevac, as "shock troops committed to stringent environmental regulation" (Personal interview with Harris and Milkis, in Harris and Milkis, p. 231.)

36. Snider makes this point. She says: "Criminal law is rejected by cooperative models not because it is too punitive or controls too heavily, but because it controls too little. Criminalization models are punitive only in theory, only in the law books, because laws are not enforced." (p. 381). An example of the "compliance school" as Tombs and Pearce controversially call it is Robert Kagan and Eugene Bardach's *Going By the Book: The Problem of Regulatory*

Unreasonableness. Philadelphia: Temple University Press. The book's subtitle is sufficiently explanatory, and the book is concerned with the development of more efficient regulatory policy. As Keith Hawkins acknowledges in "Compliance Strategy, Prosecution, and Aunt Sally" in *The British Journal of Criminology.* Vol 30, No. 4, Autumn 1990, this book is "explicitly normative."

37. Manning, p. 297.

38. Snider, p. 379.

39. It may otherwise be called a hybrid scheme, by which both administrative and criminal sanctions may apply, depending upon whether a consensual solution is reached. It is also consistent with the traditional or otherwise called *normative* approach to the place of the criminal law, which until the regulatory boom of the 1970's, always stood at some distance as a measure of last resort.

40. Richard Brown & Murray Rankin, "Persuasion, Penalties, and Prosecution: Administrative v. Criminal Sanctions," in Martin Friedland, (ed.) *Securing Compliance.* p. 340. This example is not to suggest that administrative penalties cannot use a deterrent or exclusory strategy, but only to point to the difference, which is often cited, between strictly rigidly punitive enforcement strategies and those which offer to facilitate bargaining and negotiation. The latter is characteristic of agencies with recourse to administrative, rather than criminal penalties.

41. Reiss, p. 25.

42. Shapiro makes the broader charge that criminal prosecution is evidence of *regulatory failure.* In Snider, p. 376.

43. Hawkins, *Enforcing Regulation.* Biston: Kluwer-Nijhoft. 1984.

44. *Ibid.* Hawkins discusses the lack of awareness of the powers which officers had in relation to prosecution in general, and the severity of available fines in particular.

45. *Ibid.*

46. For example, Coleman comments that enforcement in the U.S. petroleum industry is marked by a susceptibility of enforcement agents to "periodic waves of public indignation," and the reluctance to initiate antitrust cases without "prior political approval," 1985, p. 188.

47. E.g., Hawkins, *Environment and Enforcement.* Oxford: Clarendon. 1984.

48. It also exacerbates the moral ambivalence felt by the agents. Clinard & Yeager, 1980, report that larger businesses commit disproportionately more violations.

49. Keith Hawkins and John Thomas, "The Enforcement Process in Regulatory Bureaucracies," in *Enforcing Regulation.* p. 5.

50. For example, Kenneth Mann, Stanton Wheeler, and Austin Sarat, "Sentencing the White Collar Offender," in *American Criminal Law Review, 17,* 1980.

51. *Ibid.*

52.   *Ibid.*

53.   Kitty Calavita & Henry Pontell, "'Heads I Win, Tails You Lose': Deregulation, Crime, and Crisis in the Savings and Loan Industry," *Crime & Delinquency*, Vol. 36, No. 3, July 1990.

54.   *Ibid.*, p. 337.

55.   A now famous example is the Ford Pinto case. The decision to go ahead and market the Pinto was made after it was discovered to be potentially hazardous to drive: "The decision, the grand jury found, was predicated on a cost-benefit analysis. Officials at Ford allegedly predicted the number of severe burn injuries and deaths that would result from the defect, and estimated that the cost of repairing the car would exceed aniticpated court settlements.
      "The use of human life in calculations of corporate profits is by no means unique to the Ford Motor Company." Swigert & Farrell, "Corporate Homicide: Definitional Processes in the Creation of Deviance." *Law & Society Review.* 1980-81.

56.   Snider makes the point that the limits to negotiation are set by "a) the enabling legislation and precedents; b) the power of the targeted groups; c) and the subjective and objective relevance of structural variables (such as the interests affected, national policies, and the like)." "Obviously," she continues, "this process grants more leverage to the corporate executive than to the armed robber," Snider, p. 383.

57.   Hawkins & Thomas, p. 6. Italics added.

58.   Snider, p. 385.

59.   As Glasbeek describes it, this is a "jurisprudential minefield." Nevertheless, the problem of identifying culpability is not intractable: it requires to have put in place licensing schemes, accountability procedures. See Glasbeek for a full discussion and presented solutions to the problems of assigning liability to the corporation.

60.   Previously rated anywhere from four to ten times as costly, e.g.: Conklin, pp. 2-6; Coleman, pp. 5-7; Box, pp. 23-34. Both in terms of numbers killed and injured and in terms of economic costs, corporate crime is routinely measured as far higher than the costs to society of street crime. The economic costs are even higher in the United States since the savings and loan debacle. That scandal will cost the American tax payers an esimated $500 billion. (L.J. Davis, "Chronicle of a Debacle Foretold," *Harpers*, September 1990.)

61.   Glasbeek, p. 429.

62.   Gross, "Organization Structure and Organization Crime."

63.   Gross, p. 67.

64.   Garland, p. 117.

65.   The normative debate over sanctions that applies to the suite is the opposite of what is used to justify sanctions which apply to street crimes. The reasonable or

normative model, to borrow Hawkins description, which pertains to corporate sanctions is concerned with efficiency and cost-effectiveness. That concern is often cited to back "soft," informal, and inclusory sanctioning strategies, rather than strict liability criminal sanctions. At the street level, conversely, utility arguments *dissuade* law enactment which is offender-enabling. Partly, this is a result of the nature of the perceived threat, partly this a function of the point of view of the perceiver, and her affirmations about the just role of enforcement, which is class-defined: defined by the power imbalance between enforcer and enforcee, which on the street is usually the inverse of what is it in the suite.

66.   E.g., Braithwaite, 1984.

67.   E.g., Clinard & Yeager; Ralph Nader, *Unsafe at Any Speed.* New York: Grossman. 1965.

68.   E.g., Glasbeek.

69.   This is central to agencies such as as the SEC. Type of penalty is institutionalized in certain agencies, such as the SEC, through formal agreements, such as consent decrees (Hawkins & Thomas, p. 15).

70.   As has happened, as Hawkins reports, with the U.S. Occupational Safety and Health Administration and the Environmental Protection Agency. However, as Harris and Milkis argue, this backlash is politically motivated; attributing it to the switch to a punitive strategy is to place too much causal emphasis on strategy mode and not enough on political motivations. See generally, Harris and Milkis.

71.   The deterrent value of one stiff sentence by the court may be worth 500?

72.   Garland, p. 255.

73.   *Ibid.*, p. 265.

74.   For example, the Ford Pinto case had enormous impact on sensibilities. It drew immense press not only because it was a landmark case, but also because it reflected a definitional contest with tremendous ramifications for business. Thus the corporation put much more effort into its defense on the criminal charge than it did on civil law suits and regulatory actions. And the more was *articulated* about the possible criminality of the corporation, the more public sentiment against the corporation increased, and the more political and regulatory activities were set in motion. Glasbeek cites Swigert & Farrell, "Corporate Homicide: Definitional Processes in the Creation of Deviance." *Law & Society Review, 15*, 1980-81.

75.   That is, to make them appear normative. Foucault uses the term "normalize" to denote the corrective function of penality. I take *that* term to encompass an implicit moral program: there is a normative standard which the individual is being *corrected* to follow.

76.   Richard Ericson, *Representing Order.*

77.   *Harrison v. Carswell* (25 C.C.C. (2nd) 186) makes it clear that "the right of the owner to control his property, and access to it, appears to be recognized by our

law as paramount" (Shearing & Stenning, 1979: 21).

78. For example, in Ontario Raj Anand reported to Ian Scott for the Task Force considering amendments to Ontario's Trespass to Property Act that the provinces "Trespass to Property Act had potential to be used and was—not often, but occasionally—being used, as a means of discriminating against young people and those who looked or acted differently." In Ian Scott, "Statement to the Legislature," June 1, 1988, p. 1. Indeed, as Reiss, "The Legitimacy of Intrusion into Private Space", in *Private Policing*, points out, shopping mall owners have sought relief in the U.S. courts to evict people who distribute politically related pamphlets on the premises. The courts have ruled that constitutional guarantees of free speech were intended "to govern the rights of citizens with respect to their government, not the rights of private individuals against private individuals, at p. 40, citing *New York Times*. In Ontario the proposed amendments to the TPSA were vigorously fought by mall owners. They sent a petition to the legislature and actively lobbied against amendments which would reduce their right to exclude. Those amendments are in the "Statement to the Legislature."

79. However they also extend ownership itself: because these geographical locations are *"public* private places" (Stenning and Shearing), at least as interpreted by the public, the constitution of the well-ordered mall as a privately-controlled and patrolled domain is an encroachment on our conception of public space. In this way it represents a species of public capture: the capture of state-defended space. This contrasts with agency-capture, a phenomenon of the capture of public interests (represented by a regulatory agency) by a private organization (the regulated organization).

80. In Ericson, 1990, p. 8-9.

81. Philip Stenning, Clifford Shearing, Susan Addario & Mary Condon, "Controlling Interests: Two Conceptions of Order in Regulating a Financial Market," in *Securing Compliance: Seven Case Studies.* Martin Friedland (ed.). Toronto: University of Toronto Press. 1990.

82. John Braithwaite cites one researcher, "You can stand and piss in the batch and turn around and shake the FDA inspectors hand." Braithwaite, *Corporate Crime in the Pharmaceutical Industry.* London: Routledge & Kegan Paul. 1984. Braithwaite says that transnationals are able to use "(regulatory) system against (regulatory) non-system" (p. 270). He describes how none of the pharmaceutical executives he talked to were able to lay their hands on a copy of the regulations.

83. So described by Braithwaite. *Ibid.*, p. 270.

84. Ericson, 1990, p. 7.

85. I am referring, albeit somewhat indirectly, to Clifford Shearing and Philip Stenning, "From the Panopticon to Disney World: The Development of Discipline," in Tony Doob, *Perspectives in Criminal Law.*

86.   Joseph Gusfield, "Constructing the Ownership of Social Problems: Fun and Profit in the Welfare State," in *Social Problems*. Vol. 36, No. 5. 1989.

87.   For example, S. Spitzer, and A. Scull, "Privatization and Capitalist Development: The Case of the Private Police," in *Social Problems*. 1977.

PROSPECTS

AND

PARADOXES

CHAPTER 24
Policing and
Aboriginal Justice*

JIM HARDING

As the systemic discrimination against Aboriginal people in Canada has become more apparent, the call for reform in policing—the front end of the criminal justice system—has intensified. Past reforms—including cross-cultural training, legal education of Aboriginal people. and 'indigenization' of policing—have clearly not had sufficient effect. Tribal policing, in itself, cannot address the systemic discrimation operating with the massive urbanization of Aboriginal people. An independent complaints system and constitutional reforms that enable "legal pluralism" and Aboriginal self-government are probably required to create the context for adequately reforming policing in Canada.

OVERCOMING DENIAL

Since the 1960's, we have witnessed a change from widespread denial of systemic discrimination in policing of Aboriginal people to the pondering of fundamental alternatives to the traditional organization and role of peace officers as law enforcers. To say this is not to scapegoat police forces, since in some ways they are reflections of the larger society. The same negative stereotypes of Aboriginal people existing within police forces have been found in other strata as well (Hylton, 1979,1980). In a general sense, then, the RCMP Assistant Commissioner is right that:

* Reproduced by permission of the *Canadian Journal of Criminology*, Vol. 33(3-4), pages 363-383. Copyright © by the Canadian Criminal Justice Association.

> ...it should not be surprising that we have racial intolerance within
> the force because, as products of a larger Canadian society, we enter
> its ranks with all the usual bias, prejudice, and racism baggage that
> this society generates (Head, 1989:25).

If police forces truly wish to professionalize in the best sense then, this will
not be taken as an excuse for the shortcoming. Rather, it will act as a challenge to change and possibly advance beyond other sectors of Canadian society. Because some people who plan to be doctors hold vestiges of pre-medical
myths about the body is no excuse for graduating medical students who would
constitute a risk to their patients. Racism in policing is no less a risk to the targeted citizenry than would be a surgeon's stereotypes of body functioning to a
patient on an operating table.

Nor is this mirroring of racism within policing necessarily any greater than
within other parts of the criminal justice system. Racial as well as class and
gender discrimination within the Canadian legal process has been documented
by several people (Comack, 1990; Samuelson and Schissel, 1991). As was
written in one of Prairie Justice Research's major research reports on
Aboriginal justice:

> It is not difficult to illustrate the extent to which both the substantive
> law and the law enforcement system discriminate against the poor of
> whom Indigenous people make up a disproportionately large group
> (Havemann,Couse, Foster and Matonovitch, 1985:20).

The fact that it took the $7,000,000 Commission of Inquiry into the
wrongful conviction of Donald Marshall to confirm this to a broader, somewhat skeptical, public only shows how deep the denial of systemic discrimination has been.

WHY FOCUS ON POLICE

There remains a strategic reason for putting extra attention on overcom-
ing racism within Canadian policing. As the front-end of the criminal justice
system, discriminatory discretion in policing shapes everything that follows. If
any significant change is to be made in the steady trend to overincarcerate
Aboriginal people, something must change in policing itself. Furthermore,
policing is the most powerful part of the criminal justice system, utilizing about
two-thirds of the funds used for criminal justice in Canada in the 1970s, when
charges of racism against police in Canada first became pronounced.

There is another related reason for focussing on policing. Research in the mid-80s suggested that the deployment of both police and police budgets was greater on a per capita basis in the hinterland areas of Canada where aboriginal people are in greater numbers. This was particularly the case for the North, where police per 100,000 were more than twice the Canadian average (4.9 to 2.2 in 1980), and where policing expenditures were 171% to 244% higher than the Canadian average. Also, with the highest incarceration rate of Aboriginal people in Canada, Saskatchewan had the highest per capita rate of police (2.8) (Havemann et al., 1985:23-24). Other research suggests that the growth of private and public police in the North came with the expansion of corporate development which was itself dislocating to Aboriginal communities (Harding, 1978; Schriml, 1985).

Research on private policing raises another dimension. Though Stenning focuses on urban private policing of mass corporate property, his analysis raises pertinent questions about accountability and Aboriginal justice. He notes that:

> Agreeing that what they do is not 'real policing' is... a naturally attractive public position for private policing spokespeople to adopt, since it allows them to get on with what they are doing without attracting the unwanted public scrutiny and constraints which are being applied with increasing intensity to the public police (1989: 181).

He reiterates that "If agreeing that they do not do 'real policing' turns out to be an effective way of avoiding these kinds of accountability and constraints, one can hardly be surprised to find them doing so" (1989:183).

Stenning sees private policing as an alternative, less criminalizing model for public policing to consider. But we also have to recognize that private police are part of the social control system which separates most Aboriginal (and other poor strata) from the dominant, corporate society. Aboriginal youth are already in greater conflict with private police, as seen in some urban shopping malls. This, in part, is because their high unemployment and relative impoverishment makes them less attractive for profitable consumerism. As urbanization and demographics converge, this could prove to be a source of systemic discrimination that is more invisible than is the public policing which is presently being scrutinized by various judicial inquiries. From this perspective, private policing shouldn't be confused with community-based policing alternatives.

A variety of studies confirm that:

> ...in the hinterland there is a greater chance of contact between
> Indigenous peoples and police officials, given the higher ratio of
> police to general population and the role of the police as 'gatekeep-
> ers' to the criminal justice system (Havemann et al., 1985:25).

And the exact same structural predisposition to arrest and incarceration exists
for Aboriginal people migrating to the more intensely policed inner-city areas.

The extent of denial of such systemic discrimination should not be over-
looked. Such denial was quite typical among researchers looking at the
increasing incarceration of Aboriginal people in the 1960s. In the influential
Indians and the Law (1967), the Canadian Corrections Association wrote:

> The constant surveillance sometimes required by the Indian and Métis
> people can, under these circumstances, harden into open dislike on
> the part of the police.... It is obvious that the Indian people, particu-
> larly in the cities, tend to draw police attention to themselves, since
> their dress, personal hygiene, physical characteristics and location in
> run-down areas make them conspicuous. This undoubtedly results in
> more arrests (1967:36-37).

Such "reasoning" reflects ethnocentrism at best, and racism at worst.
Such seemingly white supremacist thinking was not that uncommon at the
time. In an inquiry in the N.W.T. (Morrow, 1968:22-23), a denial of racial discrimination was cloaked by its acceptance of rationalizations for such discrimination. Nor was there any mainstream political encouragement to question the
ethnocentric or racist notions that helped cloak the systemic discrimination
against Aboriginal people. We only have to remember that it was in 1969 that
Jean Chrétien, then Minister of Indian Affairs in Trudeau's government, introduced the White Paper which rejected all Aboriginal rights and declared an
assimilationist policy for Aboriginal people.

REFORM AS TECH-FIX

There are no short cuts if policing is to respond to the growing pressures
for Aboriginal justice in Canada. It is quite enlightening to look back with a
critical eye at the way reforms in policing, which were to take Aboriginal people into account, were first conceptualized in the 1970s.

There have been four main approaches to reforming policing to redress
the problems being faced by Aboriginal people in the criminal justice system.

The first two, an emphasis on cross-cultural training programs for police forces, and legal education for Aboriginal people, both assumed that enhanced attitudes and information would help correct injustices. The last two, often confusedly linked together as "indigenization of policing" included the creation of native constable and tribal policing programs. Native constable programs have been the preferred strategy over the last 15 years. Pressure, however, continues to grow for the transfer of more policing to autonomous tribal programs.

It is important to recognize how policy and program-related research usually reinforces underlying political and ideological assumptions. If the assimilation of Aboriginal people is desired, then certain approaches to research, policy, and program will tend to follow. Since fundamental Aboriginal rights were not widely accepted within Canadian politics or the dominant society in the 1970s, when the first stab at police reform was taken, it is not too surprising that the approaches tended to contradict fundamental Aboriginal justice.

All the above four approaches, especially the grouping of tribal policing along with Native constable programs, tended to assume and pronounce that the problem was one of correcting the use of police discretionary powers. None of them, not even a narrowly conceived tribunal policing, complemented the notion or demands for self-government among Aboriginal people.

CROSS-CULTURALISM

Cross-culturalism training was embraced as some sort of panacea which would not require any fundamental rethinking of policing, or for that matter, anything else. It was usually envisioned in terms of the dominant culture, not in terms of two historically distinct cultures. One criminological analysis of cross-culturalism stated:

> The criminal justice system exists to preserve the basic values of our culture. If properly understood, those of the native are not basically different. Insofar as the current cultural manifestations of the two value systems appear in conflict, these must be resolved based on the core values underlying both (James, 1979:461-462).

French social historian Michel Foucault would have a field day with this analysis, for the criminologist continues:

> Perhaps it is the fact that the prison represents the ultimate failure to succeed in the dominant society that forces some natives to face the

option of becoming successful natives, better able to face with pride the challenge of surviving in today's world (1979:457).

No one will deny that the prison plays a role in disciplining Aboriginal (and minority groups) to live within the dominant society. But that hardly suggests or, for that matter, promotes any underlying harmony of cultures. From such a perspective you do not have to do much guessing which normative system will be the integrating and, hence, dominating one.

The cross-cultural approach to reforming policing sometimes gets explicitly linked to the notion of multi-culturalism which emerged in Canada in the late 1970s. This did no more to affirm Aboriginal culture than the kind of neo-colonialist perspective reflected above. This reduction of Aboriginal culture to the notion of multi-culturalism was all too common:

> ...while some countries have tried to assimilate minority groups so that there is only one set of values and traditions, in Canada we have traditionally fostered and encouraged ethnic pluralism (Hylton, 1981: 9-10).

A somewhat similar treatment is offered by Linden who deals with Aboriginal people as part of a changing ethnic and racial structure in Canada, and concludes:

> The effects of racism combined with the social and economic deprivation which faces some minority groups can lead to over-involvement in crime...some parts of the country may face more crimes as the minority population increases unless these underlying problems are dealt with (1989: 119).

Though this notion of ethnic pluralism sounds great, it obscures the fundamental difference between Aboriginal and immigrant peoples. In reducing both to multi-culturalism, it totally ignores the problems of self-determination peculiar to colonized peoples.

Furthermore, without a workable system of legal pluralism such as suggested by the Canadian Bar Association (Jackson, 1988), cultural pluralism is rather meaningless when it comes to issues of policing and criminal justice. There remains a vast amount of conceptual, policy, and political confusion in our country as presently pulled between bilingualism and multi-culturalism. It might be more accurate and helpful to talk of the need for multi-nationalism, not to be confused with the corporate version. Certainly until the two founding nations of Canada (1867) agree to a responsible social contract with the Aboriginal nations, or first peoples, the confusion will persist.

The same underlying problems exist with the thrust for legal education for Aboriginal people. It is noteworthy, however, that the Native courtworkers program in Saskatchewan—one of the few programs that might have provided concrete legal information to Aboriginal people at risk of incarceration—was cut early in the term of the present Conservative government. Backlogs and fees in legal aid have just further exacerbated the situation. Without effective legal counsel and legal education for Aboriginal people, particularly youth at risk of incarceration, it is unlikely that cross-cultural awareness would make much difference.

NATIVE CONSTABLES

A neocolonial and/or multi-cultural view of policing reforms predominated in the Native constable programs launched in the 1970s. Though it acknowledged the need to bring policing closer to the community, the Indian Affairs Task Force on Policing on Reserves (Department of Indian Affairs and Northern Development, 1973) saw problems of Aboriginal people as those of a minority group (1973:5-6). And, though it considered two options for indigenizing policing (the so-called options 3(a) and 3(b)), it rejected the first option of autonomous Aboriginal police forces, as advocated by Indian groups in Saskatchewan and New Brunswick, purportedly due to a lack of police experience in Aboriginal communities. Instead it embraced Option 3(b), or the Native Special Constable program.

It is worth considering why it took until the mid-70s for "indigenization of policing" to be taken seriously as an option in Canada. Though lip-service was given to this as a step towards more Aboriginal self-government, it seems clear that the need for a more effective social control system was the paramount consideration. Certainly, this was the case in the United states, where one review of the use of Indian police concluded:

> It provided that they should be employed also 'for the purposes of civilization of the Indians which eventually was to inspire some of the most interesting, if debatable, duties of the Indian police (Hagan, 1966:69).

Like cross-cultural training, Native constable programs were primarily concerned with making policing more effective. They were not fundamentally concerned with reducing incarceration rates of Aboriginal people, though the supporters of the program would likely prefer this to happen. If it didn't, however, the program would not be seen to have failed. Social control, not self-determination, was the main concern.

Though the federal government adopted option 3(b), most Aboriginal authors remained critical of the program. A summary of the critique by Brass (1979) stated:

> ...special constables are recruited from the 'affluent' elements in the band population, not the traditional or poor families, and yet it is mostly these latter groups of Indigenous peoples who are in conflict with the law... peer pressure to identify with while fellow officers is likely to occur and thus defeat the purpose of the special constable program... the 'special' status with lower pay and entry qualifications will promote a double standard and reinforce cultural relativism and stereotyping (Havemann et al., 1985:33-34).

It is not too surprising that:

> most studies done by or for Indigenous organizations approve of autonomous policing while those done by or for government agencies appear to prefer policing by special constables (Havemann et al., 1985:37).

One Ontario evaluation of Option 3 (b) found a definite increase in reported crime, and hence an increased involvement of Aboriginal people within the criminal justice system (Harris, 1977). This is not necessarily to suggest that any more conflict existed with the involvement of the special Native constables. It is quite likely that these Native police were intervening in real problems in Aboriginal communities. But the outcome was more criminalization of Aboriginal people, and not necessarily the strengthening of the community to address these problems. A higher proportion of arrests in Aboriginal communities appears to be for assaults, and a lower proportion for property crimes. As such, special constables may just be furthering the systemic discrimination which already has Aboriginal people doing more time for less serious offenses than the norm.

Nevertheless, government evaluations tended to encourage continuation of the special constable programs. As Justice Kirby of Alberta remarked:

> Not only does it afford an opportunity for Indians to assume greater

responsibility in law enforcement on reserves, it can also be a means of solving the problem of communications between Indians and the RCMP (1978:28).

It should come as no big surprise that very few Aboriginal people were consulted in this or other government inquiries of the time. Furthermore, you don't have to be cynical to see that the criteria of success are self-serving for the police.

Meanwhile, an Aboriginal evaluation of the same Alberta special constable program by Native Counselling Services came to a very difficult conclusion:

> ...Option 3b cannot now be regarded as a viable program for most reserves. Although it was conceptually solid and there was potential for its constructive development, the program has become politically defunct. The current trend is clearly towards autonomous Indian policing (1980:25).

TRIBAL POLICING

Support for tribal policing has clearly increased as the limitations of these piece-meal approaches to police reform have become more apparent. An alternative to crime-control policing is essential if overincarceration is to be averted while community-based problems are addressed in a preventive manner. This unified approach is not realistic for policing which is controlled by authorities outside the emerging processes of Aboriginal self-government.

There are now several tribal policing programs which allow more in-depth consideration of a fundamental alternative to traditional policing. These include the Dakota Ojibway Tribal Council (DOTC) in Manitoba, the Amerindian Police Force in Quebec, the Louis Bull Police Force in Alberta, the Aboriginal Peace Keeper Force in British Columbia, and The Mohawk Police Keeper Force in Ontario. All of these involve, to some extent or another, the devolution of traditional policing. They all involve the creation of Aboriginal police who are as much human service and community development workers, and play a role as conflict resolvers, as they are classical peace officers. From the start the DOTC program describes its reserve police officer as "...part social worker, taxi driver, alcohol worker, ambulance driver, peace keeper and dog catcher" (Singer and Moyer, 1981:20).

As Havemann et al. wrote: "...policing issues have lesser significance if social problems are dealt with by methods other than the criminal justice system" (1985:45). What is needed in most Aboriginal communities is more help to local people, and not criminalization of the underlying social, economic, and political problems. Mediation is much more crucial than prosecution.

We know that this objective is not always met, nor is it easy to meet. Increases in reported crime can occur with tribal policing, in part because the Aboriginal community lacks the infrastructure and resources to directly deal with the problems criminalized. As such, the tribal police face the same dilemma as federal and municipal police. By consequence they too contribute to the net-widening process that community policing and community corrections has sometimes been found to create.

Part of this net-widening likely results from the emphasis on law enforcement in police training. But it is also necessary to consider the part played by the growing role of social class within Aboriginal communities. An evaluation of the RCMP Native Special Constable program found that officers were recruited from upper socio-economic and educational levels of the reserve population. This may also be occurring with tribal policing. Even if tribal programs have more direct community accountability, the dilemma remains that Aboriginal people are increasingly stratified in terms of both poverty and economic and political power. And this will shape the kinds of interests which influence policing priorities and methods.

Granted the opportunity exists within Aboriginal communities to establish a broader-based network of community accountability than is typical or very realistic in the rest of society. This potential, reflected in the growing use of elders, clearly grows with a resurrection and revitalization of Aboriginal cultural approaches to conflict-resolution. However, this depends greatly on a political and constitutional resolution of outstanding historical grievances. And even if the role of stratification can be downplayed in Aboriginal policing in Aboriginal communities, the issues cannot be ignored in the urban areas. It is the steady urbanization of Aboriginal people that constitutes the greatest challenge to the viability and effectiveness of tribal policing.

URBAN POLICING

With the highest per capita Aboriginal population of any province, it is not surprising that Saskatchewan's cities also have the highest per capita Aboriginal population. The extent of urbanization in the last few decades is rather astonishing, akin to the pattern seen in some third world countries.

Since the mid-60s the registered Indian population in Saskatchewan has more than doubled to 68,000. Combined with Métis and non-Status Indians, the total Aboriginal population is now about 170,000. With the existing birthrate, it is likely there will be one-quarter of a million Aboriginal people in the province by 2000, which would amount to about 25% of the total population.

With present trends, the vast majority of Aboriginal people will live in urban areas. At present it is estimated that 50% or more of all Aboriginal people live in cities and towns. Approximately 35,000 people of Aboriginal background live in Regina alone. The population of the city of Prince Albert could be 75% Aboriginal by 2000 according to one researcher (Elliot, 1989:12-14).

Because the birth rate of Aboriginal people remains higher than the Canadian rate, there will be an overall increase in young Aboriginal people. With the Canadian population aging, there remains the possibility of enhanced generation conflict between young, relatively poor Aboriginal youth and an older, mainstream population. As Elliot has written:

> High unemployment, low education levels, a political will for nationalism, unsettled land claims and a weak and inconsistent aboriginal political leadership will probably be the key factors leading to aboriginal youth discontent (1989:8).

Though generational differences would contribute to any tension or conflict, there is always the chance that the differences would be interpreted in terms of racism, which would just further aggravate the problems.

Furthermore, the breakdown of the Aboriginal extended family in rural and northern areas may be even more exaggerated in urban areas. It was estimated in 1981 that one-third of all Aboriginal families were headed by a single parent and 90% of these single-parent homes lived below the poverty line. Two-thirds of two-parent Aboriginal families were also thought to live below the poverty line (Elliot, 1989:14). Urban poverty, like rural poverty and family breakdown, will continue to contribute to the well known vicious circle. It becomes a vicious cycle of social problem, conflict with the law, penalty, retribution, social problem" (Elliot, 1989:17).

Urbanization and heightened disadvantage and conflict may already be reflected in a shift in urban criminalization rates for Aboriginal people. Elliot argues that incarceration of Aboriginal people used to be fairly evenly split between rural and reserve areas, on the one hand, and urban centres, on the other. Now she says "...the breakdown is 15% reserve based and 85% off-reserve, predominantly urban based, which points to a near epidemic of aboriginal justice and crime issues in the urban area" (1989:18). Clearly, there is need for research to explore and confirm this trend. It could have devastating implications for the attempt to address the overincarceration of Aboriginal peoples through a parallel Aboriginal justice system.

At the same time, it must be recognized that the high rate of criminalization of urban Aboriginal people, particularly youth, reflects the systemic discrimination and outright racism which persists in many police forces. It is no accident that the largest grouping of recommendations from the Marshall Commission (37 of 82) had to do with policing. These highlight the need to "improve the professionalism among municipal police departments", to consider whether to "regionalize municipal policing", to establish "minimum policing standards", "to ensure the independence" of the process of handling Citizen complaints, and for municipal forces to "develop official policies on racial discrimination". (Royal Commission on the Donald Marshall Jr. Prosecution, 1989:16-17) All of these relate to making policing more accountable.

This line of reasoning has some direct implications for other jurisdictions especially on the Prairies—where contact between police and Aboriginal people is even higher than in Nova Scotia. If we are to reduce and ultimately prevent the kind of racism and wrongful conviction reflected in the Marshall case, public accountability will have to be strengthened in all police forces across Canada. And it is well known that resistance to a fully independent process of citizen complaints persists within many police forces. One can only hope that there is no longer an outright rejection of the notion, as was reflected in a police conference on police accountability in the early 1980s in Saskatchewan (Harding, 1981:9-10).

An underlying resentment towards police and the criminal justice system clearly persists among Aboriginal people. Elliot says Aboriginal people

> ...see police services as perpetuators of oppression and insensitive to cultural etiquette and social values. Concerns...centre around policing styles, intimidation in policing and court process...(Specific complaints include)...police assaults, the need for an unbiased complaints mechanism, how police handle themselves when searching a home or vehicle...how people are handled in the cell blocks....(1989: 16-17).

In Regina there are some signs of improvements since the late 1970's and early 1980s. In that period, a short-lived and financially insecure Race Relations Committee was not designed nor resourced to address the underlying reasons for serious maltreatment of some Aboriginal people by the police.

The matter came to a head with the City's Inquiry into its use of police dogs (Couse, Geller, Harding and Havemann, 1982). Our discussion of this Inquiry and its findings noted that:

> The Review found that the use of dogs in Canada is most common west of the Lakehead, precisely in these urban areas in which the urban migration of Indigenous people has occurred. The use of dogs also began when this migration was on the rise (Harding and Matonovitch, 1985:147).

Some people at the time referred to Regina as the Apartheid city of Canada.

Since the Inquiry, the blatant and discriminatory use of police dogs has receded. In the last few years, however, there has been one death of a distressed Aboriginal youth in the midst of a SWAT team action (by suicide, according to an inquest), and another death of an Aboriginal adult while under police arrest (police officers were charged and acquitted). These events—along with the provincial judicial inquiries underway—have helped refocus the attention of the media on perceptions and problems of racism within the city and police (Appleby, Cemetig and York, 1990).

It is not surprising that Aboriginal organizations are beginning to think seriously about the problems of survival let alone self-government in an urban era. The Federation of Saskatchewan Indian Nations (FSIN) is considering extending its mandate to the cities where over one-half of Treaty Indians already reside. Indian-controlled programs and services in the cities are now on the political agenda. At the same time, differences among Aboriginal political organizations—themselves partly rooted in colonial distinctions and jurisdictional disputes—make consolidated services and programs to meet the immense needs of urban Aboriginal people highly problematic. There are now four major different Aboriginal organizations in Saskatchewan: one of Treaty Indians (FSIN), one for Métis (Métis Society), another not excluding Non-Status Indians (Assembly of Aboriginal Peoples), and an Aboriginal Women's Council.

All these groups face serious contradictions rooted in history, conditions, and policy. How, for example, do Treaty Indian groups establish administrative centres in cities when the federal government which directly pays for many of the services of Treaty Indians no longer considers them federal wards after one year off the reserve? Formal but largely meaningless self-government could end up being granted when resources to an urbanized Aboriginal people are drying up.

Unless Aboriginal rights are acknowledged in the Canadian constitution and substantial resources are ensured, the prospects for most urban Aboriginal people do not look good, going into the next century. It could be said that the alternative to substantive self-determination could be urban ghettoization. At just the time that policing is becoming more sensitized to the need for new approaches on reserves and in other rural areas, urban trends are converging in such a way that without social justice for Aboriginal people the likelihood is that the criminal justice system and a law and order politics will continue to dominate.

THE POLICE RESPONSE

Canadian police forces are clearly caught between the apparent lack of political will on the part of the federal government to resolve a social contract with Aboriginal people (Kly, 1991) and the powerlessness, impoverishment, and strife persisting within many aboriginal communities and families. (This is a variation of the predicament whereby police often see themselves as the filling in the social sandwich.) Though there is some sensitivity among police forces to the desires for both Aboriginal self-determination and self-government, there also remains a deep ambivalence towards the kind of legal pluralism which would be required to enable this to occur.

Some senior federal police officials seem more astutely aware of the need for changes in policing. RCMP Commissioner Inskster has recently stated:

> I think that providing a policing service for the native community in this country is the single largest challenge of police officers in this country today. It is my hope that, while we have not always given that community the highest priority, we can turn that around (Head, 1989:15).

In his Directional Statement for 1989 he indicated:

> We must all consider a new policing approach for aboriginal people. Our emphasis must be policing of native people rather than for native people. We must have imagination to truly understand their culture and problems so that we can adjust our approach to provide a service that is fair and sensitive to their needs (Head, 1989:14).

A recent speech by the Assistant RCMP Commissioner (also Director of Aboriginal Policing Services) shows both an underlying sympathy, but also ambivalence towards Aboriginal justice. Certainly Assistant Commissioner Head recognizes that Aboriginal people:

> ...have been held out of the mainstream since we began our inter-
> pretation of the Treaties and very simply they are seeking their place
> in the larger society (1989: 13)...(For him the)...number one priority
> between Canada's aboriginal people and elected governments would
> quite frankly be an early settlement of outstanding land claims.

He has expressed some urgency about this, saying "I am afraid that if those land claim settlements are not soon reached the frustrations will boil over into the streets and roadways" (1989: 33). A similar warning has come from George Erasmus, President of the Assembly of First Nations:

> The Oka crisis and confrontation between warriors and the Quebec
> police and Canadian army in the summer of 1990 clearly shows
> how right both men were.

With all this apparent concern for better cross-cultural relations and land settlements, ambivalence remains about an Aboriginal-controlled parallel justice system. It can even be argued that cultural sensitivity may, in part, be seen as necessary for institutional survival, for the Assistant RCMP Commissioner stated:

> We will either adapt and change or we will be out of the policing
> business as we know it, for there are many tribal groups who are
> looking for alternative methods. The opportunity for us is now and
> the time is relatively short (1989:19).

As pressure for Aboriginal justice grows from revelations from various judicial inquiries, the RCMP seems intent on integrating the remaining consta-bles of Aboriginal background into the regular forces. According to Assistant RCMP Commissioner Head's statistics, there are already more Native consta-bles in the regular RCMP, than operating under the Special Constable pro-gram started in the 1970s. (He indicates about 180 are in regular service com-pared to 165 in the latter program. Furthermore there are another 55 Special Constables employed under provincial contracts.) RCMP policy now seems to be that:

> The Special Constable program served us well until 1989 but it is
> now time to move on to eliminate the stigma of the "Special
> Constable" category and to look at affirmative action in its full con-

text (Head, 1989:18).

For me the most telling statement by Assistant Commissioner Head was when he said, referring to Aboriginal people coming into the RCMP: "We want them to understand us because we want them to become part of us" (1989:34).

This policing model is not one inclined towards a parallel Aboriginal justice system, though some views exist that could still encourage moving in that direction. Assistant Commissioner Head perceptively comments that:

> ...where we have municipal contracts with towns and cities, we sit with the police committees in developing goals, objectives and strategies. Surely the native communities, where we police, should have the same opportunity (1989:22).

But this is not intended to reinforce Aboriginal-controlled community-based policing so much as to say that native communities deserve the same treatment as "other" municipalities.

TOWARDS LEGAL PLURALISM

Very little is presently being written which considers the issues of policing and Aboriginal people in their full political context. Yet, without a fully political resolution to the problems arising from colonialism, Aboriginal justice is not possible. The question that everyone working within the criminal justice system must ask is whether the moves towards a parallel justice system present any way to prevent the kind of future urban conflict and aggravated racism projected above.

One way that this may happen is through the courts, through *Charter of Rights* challenges. As Cohen has stated:

> Proposals previously dismissed out of hand for such novel initiatives (as) the creation of alternative court systems are now receiving a respectful audience. However, significant attention has not yet been paid to the equality dimensions of the nostrums that have been proposed (1989:40).

One concern is that formal equality, i.e., using the same justice system, may take precedence over substantive equality—which recognized the need for alternatives due to differential treatment and need—in Supreme Court decisions. Certainly this kind of judgment has become typical of the Supreme

Court since the Charter (Mandel, 1989). However,

> ...questions involving the adequacy of the delivery of police and
> court services in aboriginal communities in Canada may be brought
> before the courts in Canada for early consideration. If they are, it is
> quite possible that these issues will find their way onto the legislative
> agenda as well (Cohen, 1989:62).

The Canadian Bar Association report on Aboriginal Justice also raises the constitutional issues about equality before the law. It states:

> ...one of the principal reasons for considering aboriginal justice sys-
> tems is that the existing criminal justice system has created a condi-
> tion of disadvantage, particularly in terms of the number of native
> people in Canada's prisons (Jackson, 1988:49).

But to achieve an Aboriginal justice system we must learn from the past attempts at cultural as well as legal domination of Aboriginal people. Jackson advances the notion of legal pluralism:

> The idea of native justice systems requires us to address the place
> that legal pluralism should play in Canada, particularly in the context
> of criminal law (1988:46).

We can, perhaps, even turn colonialism on its head. He notes that the first basis for an "Aboriginal" court was created in Section 107 of the Indian Act in 1881, by which the Indian agent also became a justice of the peace. Obviously,

> The creation of Section 107 Indian Act justices of the peace did not
> spring from the federal government's concern to maintain the dis-
> tinctiveness of Indian societies and communities within a pluralist
> Canada; quite the reverse (1988:36) ...(He continues) ...Given the
> repressive antecedents of Section 107 courts and their association
> with the power and authority of Indian agents, they hardly appear to
> be an appropriate model for justice mechanisms which further native
> self-determination. However, if Indian communities wish to pursue
> the early implementation of some form of tribal court system, the
> enabling provisions of section 107 may be of some significance
> (1988:37-38).

The Marshall Inquiry has followed this legal argument by recommending a parallel justice system based on this precedent in the Indian Act. However, there are several questions that should be raised about this legal strategy. For one thing this "parallel" system would not extend beyond reserves covered by the Indian Act. And we have seen what accelerating urbanization is doing to undercut the viability of the reserve system as a basis for self-government. Furthermore, this "parallel" system would only apply to status Indians, and so would not only exclude other groups of southern Aboriginal people but also the vast majority of those in the NWT, including all Inuit. The applicability of such a system, as a basis for community-based alternatives to incarceration, would therefore be greatly restricted, especially in view of the high overall rate of incarceration of urban Aboriginal people.

Then there is the added fact that a parallel indigenous criminal justice system could still constitute a form of cultural oppression for some Aboriginal people as Jackson notes:

> ...in Dene and Inuit communities, the designation of an individual with unilateral powers of decision-making over others runs counter to deeply held concepts of egalitarianism and social structures which are built upon complex diffusion rather than concentration of authority (1988:41).

When the limited view of a parallel justice system such as recommended by the Marshall Commission is scrutinized, it reveals many of the same shortcomings we noted about police reforms in the 1970's. Jackson himself comments that:

> In Saskatchewan, where native justices of the peace were introduced in the 1970's and operated for several years, the system was bedevilled by the lack of adequate training for justices, little or no support staff, inadequate facilities for holding hearings and a lack of consensus among native communities on the appropriateness of a native justice of the peace holding court on the reserve in which he was residing (1988:41-42).

This sounds much like the limitations noted above for the Special Constable program.

Limited or not, it is clearly time to begin to make changes that will enable Aboriginal people to take control of their lives in fundamental ways. And this must occur in the criminal justice system. As Jackson himself concludes:

> The task of accommodating aboriginal justice systems with individual

rights is a necessary part of the recognition of legal pluralism in the particular context of the criminal justice system. It should not be beyond our legal imagination to reach such an accommodation. The tension between collective and individual rights in the criminal justice system is not new.... It is not unrealistic to anticipate that models of aboriginal justice systems can be worked out in a Canadian context which, cognizant of the experience of other jurisdictions, can reflect the accumulated wisdom of both aboriginal law and the common law (1988:51).

There is presently a political opening to begin such changes. Opportunities for change in the pursuit of fundamental justice do not occur that frequently. Encouraging the creating of processes and resources for Aboriginal justice is in the fundamental interest of Canadians, and perhaps more so, of those who work within the criminal justice system. As the front end of that system, the police—especially urban police—have much to gain. We can only hope that more policing officials will provide positive leadership on this in the coming years.

To not move in this positive, transformational direction will be to guarantee further Okas. We eagerly await the perspective and recommendations of the Manitoba Aboriginal Justice inquiry in this regard.

REFERENCES

Appleby, Timothy, Miro Cemetig, and Geoffrey York. 1990. "Policing the Prairies, Part 1-3." Toronto: *The Globe and Mail,* April 20-21, p. A1.

Brass Oliver, J. 1979. "Crees and Crime: A Cross-Cultural Study." Regina: University of Regina, mimeographed.

Canadian Corrections Association. 1967. *Indians and the Law.* Ottawa, Ontario: Canadian Corrections Association.

Cohen, Stanley A. 1989. "Human rights and criminal justice in the 1990s." In Donald J. Loree (ed.), *Future Issues in Policing and Symposium Proceedings.* Canada: Ministry of Supply and Services.

Comack, Elizabeth (ed.). 1990. "Race, class, gender and justice." Vancouver: *The Journal of Human Justice.* Vol.1, No.2. Spring.

Couse, Keith, Gloria Geller, Jim Harding, and Paul Havemann. 1982. Brief submitted to the Public Hearing for the Review of the City of Regina Police Canine Unit Regina, Sask.: School of Human Justice, University of Regina.

Department of Indian Affairs and Northern Development. 1973. *Report of the Task Force: Policing on Reserves.* Ottawa, Ont.: Indian and Northern Affairs.

Elliot, Maxine. 1989. *Policing in the 1990s: Environmental Issues for the Prairies.* Regina: Mebas Consulting Ltd.

Hagan, William T. 1966. *Indian Police and Judges: Experiments in Acculturation and Control.* New Haven Conn.: Yale University Press.

Harding, Jim. 1978. "Development, underdevelopment and alcohol disabilities in Northern Saskatchewan." *Alternatives* 7: 4.

Harding, Jim. 1981. "Policing the Police: Conference Defends Self-Control Method." *Briarpatch* 10 (10): 9-10.

Harding, Jim and Rae Matonovitch. 1985. *Self-Study of Justice Research About Indigenous People: 1981-1984.* Regina: Prairie Justice Research, University of Regina.

Harris, R .E. 1977. "Evaluation of the Indian Policing Program." Ontario Provincial Police, Planning and Research Branch

Havemann, Paul, Keith Couse, Lori Foster, and Rae Matonovitch. 1985. *Law and Order for Canada's Indigenous People.* Regina: Prairie Justice Research, University of Regina.

Head, R.H.D. 1989. A speech to the Canadian Association of Chiefs of Police and Federal Corrections Services. Banff, Alta.: R.C.M.P., mimeographed, Nov. 10.

Hylton, John, Rae Matonovich, James Varro, Bijal Thakven, and Dave Broad. 1979. *Public Attitudes About Crime and Police in Regina*. Regina: Prairie Justice, University of Regina.

Hylton, John and Rae Matonovich. 1980. *Public Attitudes About Crime and the Police in Moose Jaw*. Regina, Sask.: Prairie Justice Research, University of Regina.

Hylton, John. 1981. "Policing in a Multicultural Society: Some Implications for Police Educators." Presented at Eight Annual Police Educators Conference, Thunder Bay, Ont.: May 18-22.

Jackson, Michael. 1988. "Locking up Natives in Canada." A Report of the Committee of the Canadian Bar Association on Imprisonment and Release.

James, J.L.T. 1979. "Towards a cultural understanding of the Native offender." *Canadian Journal of Criminology* 21(4): 453-462.

Kirby, W.J.C. (Chairman). 1978. "Native People in the Administration of Justice in the Provincial Court of Alberta." Edmonton: Alberta Board of Review, Provincial Court, Report No. 4.

Kly, Yussuf. 1991. "Native people and the criminal justice system: Racism in an international context." In L Samuelson and B. Schissel (eds.), *Criminal Justice's Sentencing Issues and Reforms*. Saskatoon, Sask.: Social Research Unit, University of Saskatchewan.

Linden, Rick. 1989. "Demographic change and the future of policing." In Donald J. Loree (ed.), *Future Issues in Policing and Symposium Proceedings*. Canada: Ministry of Supply and Services.

Mandel, Michael. 1989. *The Charter of Rights and Legalization of Politics in Canada*. Toronto: Wall and Thompson.

Morrow, William G. 1968. *Inquiry Re: Administration of Justice in the Hay River Area of the North West Territories*. Ottawa, Ont.: The Privy Council.

Native Counselling Services of Alberta. 1980. *Policing on Reserves: A Review of Current Programs and Alternatives*. Edmonton: Native Counselling Services of Alberta.

Royal Commission on the Donald Marshall, Jr., Prosecution. 1989. "Digest of Findings and recommendations." Province of Nova Scotia.

Samuelson, L and B. Schissel (eds.). 1991. *Proceedings: Criminal Justice: Sentencing Issues and Reforms*. Saskatoon: Social Research Unit, University of Saskatchewan.

Schriml, Ron. 1985. "Public and private policing: The accountability debate." In Jim Harding (ed.), *The Politics of Social Policy: The Blakeney Years in Saskatchewan*, unpublished.

Singer, Charter and Sharon Moyer. 1981. *The Dakota-Objibway Tribal Council Police Program: An Evaluation, 1979-1981.* Ottawa, Ont: Ministry of Solicitor General, Research Division.

Stenning, Philip C. 1989. "Private police and public police: Toward a redefinition of the police role." In Donald J.Loree (ed.), *Future Issues in Policing and Symposium Proceedings.* Canada: Ministry of Supply and Services.

CHAPTER 25
Race Relations and Policing

DAN MCINTYRE

Considerable attention has been given in Canada in recent years to the treatment of racial minorities by overwhelmingly white-dominated police forces. A number of incidents of conflict between racial minorities and the police have been highlighted by the media, and the causes of concern have been documented and confirmed in a number of government reports: in Toronto by such reports as *Now Is Not Too Late* (1977) chaired by Walter Pitman, and the *Report to the Civic Authorities of Metropolitan Toronto and its Citizens* (1979) by Cardinal G. Emmett Carter. In Ontario, the most recent report is that of the *Race Relations and Policing Task Force* (1989). Elsewhere in Canada in the criminal justice system, racism has been documented by the *Royal Commission on the Donald Marshall Jr. Prosecution* (1986), and the most recent report emanating from the *Halifax Race Riots* (1991), the *Harper Commission* (1991) in Manitoba, and the *Rolf* and *Cawsey* reviews of the criminal justice system in Alberta (1991).

The "symbolic reassurance" of these task forces and official reports in and of themselves might be regarded as important and successful in the immediate political sense. However, even if all the recommendations of these reports were implemented, if we don't at the same time address the wider economic, social and political aspects of racial inequality it is safe to predict that the state of police-race relations will continue to be an uneasy and volatile relationship for some time to come. If one were to succeed in eliminating the wider racial inequalities in our society, it would of course be much easier to attain a much healthier police-race relations climate.

Changing expectations and definitions of policing, demographic changes, the changing nature of crime, the economic situation, and many other factors are forcing a recognition of the need to link issues of policing within a wider community social framework. The notion of community-based policing has become no longer simply a nice philosophy. Rather than a luxurious ideal, circumstances have created the imperative to implement community-based policing as the only method and practice that will allow policing to cope and respond effectively to the challenges of the twenty-first century.

Recent incidents and all the government reports have certainly heightened the awareness and concern of decision-makers within the policing community of the realities of a racially diverse population and its impact on the way policing is carried out. Yet what are the practical, hands-on, results-oriented initiatives that can be undertaken by the police that will have a measurable impact on improved relations with the minority communities? Beyond ad-hoc, temporary responses, this article suggests that the groundwork is being laid for permanent, integrated strategies that will fundamentally alter the way in which policing services will be provided in the future.

Within this framework it is clear that police race relations is moving from a reactive, incident driven process to an agenda that focuses on a relationship that is based on cooperation and true partnership.

A MINORITY PERSPECTIVE

The dramatic revelations and condemnation of the inherently unfair and racist practices of the criminal justice system, including police practices, are coming to public attention across the country. Royal Commissions and public inquiries are regularly calling into question the credibility of police to effectively provide fair and just services in their contacts with Aboriginal people and racial minorities, in particular members of the Black community.

At the outset, it is important that the reader understands that this writer does not profess to be an expert in the field of race relations and policing nor would I necessarily recognize one if I met such a person. The perspective that I bring to this subject is based on a lifelong residency in Canada as a member of the Black community, and several years of work in the race relations and human rights field.

Recently I have had a remarkable opportunity to work on race relations and policing issues in Ontario with an exceptionally talented and committed group of people, including police and community leaders.

This chapter represents a"minority" perspective on race relations and policing.

Racism is not exclusively a "policing problem." It is a problem which has existed and does exist in all of our institutions and relations since the European explorers first came into contact with the First Nations of this land. The legacy of exploitation and genocide of the Aboriginal people in this country is at long last being acknowledged by non-native Canadians.

We also know that others have been victims of racism—subjected to slavery, economic exploitation and discrimination, exclusion and expulsion. Some, because of physical characteristics distinct from those of European descent, continue to be victims of discrimination in employment, housing, education, access to services and decision-making structures. They are victims of discrimination regardless of how long they have been Canadians, and how well they speak the language and understand or adopt the customs. We are collectively referred to as racial minorities.

Having recognized that all institutions must change does not diminish the duty of the institution of policing to ensure that its house is clean, and not "lily white."

Demographic changes, as reflected by the majority of newcomers to Canada who are from Asia, Africa, the Caribbean, and Latin America, will continue to put pressure on police services to change the complexion of the police personnel as well as the way services are delivered to these communities.

The emerging strength and voices of the Aboriginal communities, as they assert their rights to self-government and empowerment, present a new challenge to the traditional ways that police have addressed the native people.

With respect to the Aboriginal communities, we have seen shocking evidence of racism as represented in the *Nova Scotia Royal Commission on the Donald Marshall Jr. Prosecution (1990), Policing and the Blood Reserve* (Alberta, 1990), and the *Aboriginal Justice Inquiry of Manitoba* (1991). The last study not only concluded that the "justice system has failed Manitoba's Aboriginal people on a massive scale" but has called for an Aboriginally controlled justice system including police services. Concerning policing and racial minorities, in addition to the Donald Marshall Jr. Commission which addressed the issues of racism and the criminal justice system related to Black Nova Scotians, there have been several reports in Ontario including:

- The report of the late Arthur Maloney to the Metropolitan Toronto Police (1975);

- The *Royal Commission into Metropolitan Toronto Police Practices* conducted by the Honourable Mr. Justice Donald R.

Morand (1976);

- The report by Walter Pitman, *Now is Not Too Late* conducted for the Municipality of Metropolitan Toronto (1977);

- The *Report to the Civic Authorities of Metropolitan Toronto Council and its Citizens,* by Cardinal G. Emmett Carter, former Archbishop of Toronto (1979);

- The *Report of the Task Force on the Racial and Ethnic Implications of Police Hiring, Training, Promotion and Career Development,* chaired by Dr. Reva Gerstein for the Ontario Ministry of Solicitor General (1980); and,

- The *Report of the Race Relations and Policing Task Force,* appointed by the Ontario Solicitor General and chaired by Clare Lewis, Police Complaints Commissioner (1989).

While the various reports prior to the Lewis Task Force provided useful recommendations, it was the Lewis Task Force that provided a comprehensive "blueprint" for change. It has been that report which has guided the work of the Ontario Ministry of Solicitor General in its race relations and policing change strategy.

In addition to the numerous reports in Ontario, there was a similar study by a task force chaired by J. Bellemare, *Investigation into Relations Between Police Forces, Visible and Other Ethnic Minorities* (Montreal, 1988).

All of these task forces and reports were responses to high-profile incidents involving Aboriginal people and racial minorities, and in many instances, incidents which have implicated the police in the serious injury or death of members of the Aboriginal or Black communities.

Notwithstanding the studies, the incidents continue with alarming frequency, as this excerpt from a column on Montreal by André Picard in *The Globe and Mail* (November 8, 1991), so poignantly illustrates:

> Why they (human rights activists) ask, do police so fear visible minorities?.... Why, when non-whites are alleged to have been involved in crimes, do police assume they will act violently?" The pertinence of such questions and the need for answers was underscored last Friday when witnesses—in laudable Crime Prevention Week style—complained that a black youth was being subjected to racial taunts by three white men. Police who arrived on the scene ignored the men but pulled a gun on the boy and took him into custody. Had he run or struggled, he could easily have become another statistic. "The question I'm asking myself...is what's behind this, how is it that this officer's first reaction was to go toward a black?" said MUC Police Chief Alain St. Germain.

Less than a week after that column appeared, yet another Black youth in Toronto was shot (in the head), allegedly by a Metro Toronto police officer as the youth was fleeing a crime scene involving a warehouse break-in *(Toronto Star,* November 10, 1991). The newspaper reported that investigators of the shooting did not believe that the fleeing suspects were armed.

WHAT IS MEANT BY INSTITUTIONALIZED OR SYSTEMIC RACISM?

In the midst of these charges of racism are a number of bewildered, angry, and defensive police officers who feel that they are the victims of injustice. They hotly deny any wrongdoing or racist practices. There are also police officers who admit that the institution as a reflection of Canadian society is de facto racist. It is racist, not necessarily because of ill will, but because the racism is built in (or "systemic") to policing. The examples of how that racism is reflected in policing have been well documented elsewhere. However, one need only to review the employment practices of police services to get but one indication of the problem.

The challenge to bring about positive changes to policing starts with a recognition and a common understanding of the issues. While there has been some progress in this area, unfortunately when there is any suggestion that racism is an issue we have been conditioned in Canada to deny its existence, or to dismiss it as an isolated incident or aberration. This rationalization might be described as the "rotten apple" syndrome. In other words, it is recognized that in any large workforce there will be the occasional bad apple who is racist.

While indeed there are the hardcore racists in any large segment of Canadian society, the concept of institutionalized racism does not denote any particular motive or explicit ideology about the superiority of one racial group over another. Rather it refers to such institutional customs and procedures such as the "old boy's" network of hiring in which only Whites hear about the jobs, or are encouraged to apply, or get coaching on how to get selected.

It's the assumption (unconscious or otherwise), that if someone is of a different race, especially Aboriginal or Black, then they are to be viewed as a threat.

It's the conviction that turbans should not be allowed as part of the police uniform to accommodate Sikh officers. Such a position does not recognize that this denies an employment opportunity to a significant group of

Canadians because of their religion. In other words in the name of tradition, notwithstanding that it is inherently racist, police should only accommodate those of predominantly European and Christian background.

Whether intentional or not the outcome, as documented time and again, points to unequal, unfair and sometimes tragic consequences.

Consequently, there continues to be a need to raise the level of debate and understanding so that there is a degree of commitment to address racism as an institutionalized part of Canadian society. There needs to be an understanding that even if all the "rotten apples" were removed, we would still have a profound problem because the same old assumptions, practices and policies would remain intact

FAIRNESS AND EQUALITY: CONFLICTING VIEWS

As part of that debate there is and will continue to be a perspective shared by many police officers that current moves to address the institutionalized racism in policing will result in lower standards, which will jeopardize the safety of officers. Much of the present focus on race relations and policing is viewed as a result of pandering to minority extremists by politicians who should be kept at arm's length.

Perspectives from many in the minority and Aboriginal communities differ significantly from that view. There is a strong belief that police as well as other parts of the justice system do not in fact dispense justice. Therefore, special measures to improve the representation and service provided to address inequities and tensions between minorities and police are urgently needed. In summary, new initiatives are needed to enhance community confidence and empowerment, proportional representation and justice.

One perspective is that race relations initiatives are moving too far, too fast. The other is that there has been too little, too late.

CURRENT TRENDS

I would agree that too little has been done in the area of race relations. However, it is not too late and there are positive developments in policing. That obviously does not mean that the changes can take place soon enough to turn around an institution overnight. Unfortunately the inequities and perhaps tragedies will remain with us for some time to come but hopefully at a reduced rate. There is no question that change is inevitable in policing. And it will continue at an ever accelerating rate for the next while. Some view this change as a serious threat to the integrity of policing, while others see it as an opportunity to improve it. Some of those positive signs of change which can have an impact on improving race relations and policing include:

- The concept of community policing which embraces the principles of community partnership and empowerment;

- Employment equity to improve the representation of racial minorities and Aboriginal people in police services;

- New developments in training for police personnel to improve the service to minority and Aboriginal communities;

- First Nations policing agreements and services are being established in different parts of the country in recognition of the principles of self-government and that non Aboriginal police services have been inadequate;

- Civilian review and investigation mechanisms are being established in some jurisdictions to address the concern that these procedures must be at arm's length from the police to have any credibility with the public;

- The federal government recently announced the establishment of a Centre for Race Relations and Policing to provide support and information to police services to enhance their services to the racial minority and Aboriginal communities;

- The Municipality of Metro Toronto is currently doing a comprehensive race relations audit on the Metro Toronto Police Service, which is a first in the country and should provide valuable experience in addressing the accountability issue.

There is arguably no other sector in the public domain which is doing so much to address the race relations issues in Canada. That is the good news. The flip side to that assertion is the paucity of work that is being done in other sectors. In addition, there is an almost complete absence of evaluation or accountability for the work that is in process including policing. While policing is doing more than others in race relations, almost none of it is being audited or evaluated. Also, the race relations initiatives are for the most part ad hoc and disjointed. There is a general lack of a coherent and comprehensive change strategy in place to address the various employment, training, and service issues in race relations in an integrated way. For example, it is not of much use to put into place a race relations training program unless the police department at all levels is ready and supportive of the changes that the training requires of the police service.

At the risk of being chauvinistic, there is at least one exception to the above. While still very much in its infancy, that is the Ontario policing scene. Currently there is a comprehensive change strategy to address the issues raised by the Lewis *Task Force Report on Race Relations and Policing*. The strategy includes employment equity legislation, integration of race relations content in police training, development of police/community relations models through a grants program, and the development of a model race relations policy and guidelines. All of these initiatives are moving forward in a holistic and integrated fashion. There is also a new Police Services Act which addresses a number of race relations issues including community policing, civilian complaints review and civilian investigation of police action, which result in serious injury or death. This ensures that there is a legislative base to much of the race relations development.

LEADERSHIP AND ACCOUNTABILITY

Ensuring that these changes to improve policing in terms of race relations actually occur requires leadership. There is a need for leadership with the requisite commitment to bring about the change. There is a need for the strategic, financial and human resource skills to create an environment conducive to change, and the tenacity to follow it through over the long haul.

This leadership must be reflected in the top echelons in the organization including the chief and the police boards. Also, that leadership must be demonstrated by the police unions and associations.

One veteran police official commented, in reference to the need for police services to develop a comprehensive strategic plan on race relations, that most police chiefs do not develop strategic plans for anything so this is a foreign concept for which they are ill prepared.

Whether that comment is valid or not, unless the leadership and the mechanisms to monitor progress are in place, the change process will be characterized by tremendous resistance including misinformation, backlash and sabotage. The change may still occur but it will be largely cosmetic and ineffective. It is under these circumstances that minority and Aboriginal communities, especially the youth, throw their hands up in despair and the "too little too late" perception becomes reality.

CONCLUSION

There have been a number of developments across the country to address the very real problems of institutionalized racism and racial tensions between police and minorities. The extent to which these initiatives are effective is still uncertain. However, we have come some distance in acknowledging the problem.

The challenges ahead of us are to place these race relations initiatives and others in the context of a comprehensive strategic plan. This plan must include short and long term initiatives, a financial plan, accountability mechanisms, monitoring and evaluation processes, and provision for rewards and sanctions.

It does not mean the development of special measures if or when there are surplus resources. It means using current resources in a different way. When that is understood and achieved, then we will have truly turned the corner in addressing the critical issue of institutionalized racism in policing.

* Dan McIntyre, "Race Relations and Policing: A Minority Perspective," is reprinted from *Currents*, Vol. 7, No. 4, published by Urban Alliance on Race Relations. Reprinted by permission of Urban Alliance on Race Relations.

CHAPTER 26
Job Stress and Burnout Of New Police Officers

MIMI H. SILBERT

A large and steadily growing body of literature attests to the importance and continuous negative impact of job stress on workers.[1] Within the general area of job stress, a special interest has been granted to policing and some of the idiosyncratic sources of stress police officers encounter.[2] Indeed, much of the literature seems to suggest not only that job stress is currently common among all workers, but that it may in fact be "the paramount problem facing policemen today."[3] While police work does include the physical stress of working at a job of general inactivity punctuated by periods of extreme physical danger and high physical activity, the most serious and dangerous sources of stress in police work are the psychological problems police officers face on the job.

Police work can be viewed as combining two elements, both of which research has indicated cause the most significant stress to workers: (1) work with people and (2) work within a bureaucratic organization.

WORK WITH PEOPLE

When professionals work with people over long periods of time in situations that are emotionally demanding, they often pay the heavy psychological price of burnout. Not only are police officers often required to make decisions that have major consequences for the lives and property of others; but they also work in those areas of the city in which they must deal consistently with the pain, the crime, and the poverty and despair of the city's people. Furthermore, the immediacy of time in which they must make these life-affecting decisions creates situations of such emotional intensity that the negative impact upon the worker can be debilitating.

WORK WITHIN A BUREAUCRACY

Large, complex bureaucratic organizations are notoriously slow and unresponsive. Work literature depicts the nature of the bureaucratic organizations as generally self-serving rather than being oriented to serve the purposes for which they were established. Bureaucracies are hierarchical and slow in providing appreciation and recognition for effort. Therefore, work in such organizations is found to be extremely frustrating and a high generator of stress.

Stress from both these aspects of police work can affect the individual in different ways. Job stress can affect an individual's performance on the job, his or her personality, and his or her health. Indeed, the cumulative effects of stress can be so destructive as to become, in effect, a Sisyphian rock for the worker, wherein work becomes simply carrying on a futile, uphill battle.

METHODOLOGY

This report presents the findings of a study conducted on 267 police officers who have been in the San Francisco Police Department from one to five years. The survey instrument was pretested, distributed, and then completed anonymously over a one-week period during on-duty time, supervised by a specially trained sergeant available to answer questions. The questionnaire measured stress by four separate indices:

> 1.   Stress is discussed in terms of 40 features which describe the individual's work as well as his/her life outside of work. Included among the *Life and Work Features* are several questions which measure the relationship between work and family life, and whether or not the demands of work are in conflict with those of life outside of work.
>
> 2.   Stress is measured by 21 symptoms which cluster together to determine the worker's tedium and *Burnout* from the job, as well as several questions related to job, life, and self-satisfaction.
>
> 3.   The third cluster of stress measures are those related to physical condition and a series of physical symptoms which have been found to be related to stress. Along with these *Stress Symptoms* are direct questions of whether or not police work creates stress for the subject, both at work and at home.
>
> 4.   Finally, the discussion of job stress concludes with a series of items which have been cited in the literature as *Sources of Stress* unique to police officers.

Two hundred sixty-seven (267) police officers (89 percent of all officers on the force from one to five years) completed the survey. Of these, 81 percent were male and 19 percent were female; 67 percent were white, 14 percent were black, 9 percent were Asian, 8 percent were Latin, and 2 percent were other races. The mean age was 28. The mean height was 5' 10"; the mean weight was 172 pounds.

At the time of joining the department, 61 percent had never been married, 28 percent were married and had never been divorced or widowed, 6 percent were divorced, 3 percent were separated, 2 percent had remarried after a divorce, and 1 percent were widowed. Current marital status shows that an additional 18 percent have married for the first time, 6 percent have divorced, 5 percent have remarried after a divorce, 1 percent have separated, and none have been widowed. Those with children have an average of 2.1 children.

The mean last grade completed in school was 14.4, two years of college plus. When asked to describe their financial situation, 40 percent rated themselves as "managing to get by," 45 percent rated themselves from slightly to highly secure financially, and 15 percent rated themselves slightly to highly insecure financially.

RESULTS

Findings of this study corroborate the theory that job stress may indeed be the paramount problem facing police officers today. The vast majority of the officers sampled stated that being a police officer creates stress for them at work; and almost half of the officers sampled stated that being a police officer creates stress for them at home. Considering the fact that the officers surveyed have been on the job only one to five years, these were extremely disturbing results.

LIFE AND WORK FEATURES

The data from this index show a prevalence of negative features in the work environment and a dramatic absence of positive features for the officers surveyed. The officers were stressed by a great number of administrative hassles such as paperwork and red tape, the physical danger of the job, combined with inadequate tangible rewards and appreciation for their performance. Despite the fact that the majority of officers stated that their lives outside of work were significantly more important to them than their work, when there is a conflict between work and family, it is most often the family that is compromised. More than three-fourths of the officers surveyed stated that such a conflict exists for them. Conflict between life and work has been found in all the research on stress to have extremely negative effects; and indeed in this study, it was found to be positively correlated with burnout. When asked directly how work affects family life, the mean response was a slightly negative effect.

Comparison of these data between police and two other samples—724 human service professionals from around the country and 205 professionals from various occupations in the San Francisco Bay Area—indicated that the police officers were more highly stressed by their jobs, reported receiving significantly fewer tangible rewards for their performance, and significantly less appreciation and recognition for their work than the other samples. When asked how they felt about their work in general, police officers reported feeling less satisfied with their work than did the other two samples.

BURNOUT

This cluster of physical, emotional, and mental exhaustion reactions was more affected by physical components than by emotional ones in this sample. The highest contributors to the officers' burnout score were being tired, feeling anxious, and being physically exhausted. The lowest contributors were feeling worthless, feeling hopeless, and feeling rejected.

When the average burnout score reported by San Francisco police officers was compared with previous studies of over 4,000 men and women, it was found that the San Francisco police officers experienced less burnout than the majority of the other samples studied. Without discounting the possibility that these results may in part be reflecting socially desirable response biases, as well as a sample biased by time on the force, the data suggest that, although more highly stressed, police tend to be less burned out emotionally by the stressful nature of their work than do other professionals.

It is interesting to note that the sample identical to San Francisco police in mean burnout score is a group of 109 Israeli business managers. When these Israeli managers were compared with similar samples of American managers, it was found that the Israelis had lower burnout scores because they had more social support to protect them from work stress, and they used more active, outer-directed coping strategies aimed at the source of their stress. It is hypothesized here that the San Francisco police officers can be compared to the Israeli sample in using coping strategies that are more action and outward-oriented rather than passive, and the fact that they rely on a great deal of social support which they receive from other officers. These factors seem to be significant in reducing the adverse effects of burnout.

The highest symptoms of stress among officers sampled were headaches, being fidgety or tense, backaches, being nervous or shaky inside, stomach aches, and loss of appetite on duty; and problems with falling or staying asleep, headaches, backaches, and nightmares, off duty.

SOURCES OF STRESS IN POLICE WORK

The findings here indicate that the highest stressor for officers is poor pay. This one stressor was rated significantly higher than any of the others. The next three were disruption of schedule with court appearances, court's leniency with offenders, and interference of the court's decisions with police work. Stressors considered by the officers to impose the least amount of stress of those noted were middle and top management policies.

A review of all the stress indices points to a trend showing that the women surveyed are slightly more stressed by police work than the men surveyed. A pattern emerges in the data on life and work features suggesting that women had more positive features in their lives outside of work than did men, while men had those features more than women in their work. The same pattern emerges with regard to the negative features. Women had more negative features than men in their work, while men had more negative features than women in their lives outside of work. The policewomen's average burnout score was slightly higher than that of policemen.

An examination of the 21 symptoms associated with burnout and tedium showed that women experienced 11 of these stress symptoms compared with only four such symptoms experienced by men. Additionally, women felt more jittery, more physically exhausted, and more irritated than men. They had significantly more headaches and backaches, both on and off the job. They also experiences more stomach aches and sleeping problems off duty. In support of this pattern of women being more highly stressed than men is the fact that the women showed a statistically significant higher intention to leave the police force than did men if offered another job at similar pay.

It is hypothesized that the extra stress reported by women is related to the additional burden they experiences as a result of some of the negative attitudes which they encounter daily from their co-workers.[4] The lack of social support in the policewomen's work is evident in the fact that they describe their relationships with co-workers in less positive terms than do policemen and report less sharing of duties at work than men. Since social support has been shown to be extremely important in reducing the negative features of the job, the lesser amount of social support which exists for women in the department would seem to account for a significant portion of the extra stress reported by the women sampled.

Although a racial breakdown was conducted on all the stress indices and antecedents, few significant race differences emerged. The one consistent pattern in the results showed that black officers reported the lowest stress as a result of policing frustrations, while Latin officers reported the highest stress, followed by the Asian officers. When stress is measured by life and work features, work was characterized by the prevalence of negative features and the absence of positive features compared to life outside of work for all five races. A significant difference was found regarding conflicting demands outside of work, with the highest conflict being reported by whites. Of the 21 symptoms associated with burnout, the only one which showed a statistically significant race difference was physical exhaustion, with Asian officers reporting these symptoms most often.

Pearson correlation coefficients between environmental features and various indices of stress on the one hand, and height on the other hand, show a consistent pattern in which the taller officers report more positive environmental features and less stress than do shorter officers. Additionally, taller officers show lower scores in burnout, higher work satisfaction, and significantly less intention to leave the police force if offered another job at the same pay, than shorter officers. Taller officers reported being in better physical condition, both when they entered the academy and at the present time, and reported having fewer headaches and backaches on duty, and fewer headaches and fewer problems falling asleep off duty than shorter officers. Taller officers were generally less bothered than shorter officers by the sources of stress in police work; the only item which bothered taller officers more than shorter officers was court interference with their work.

The pattern emerging from the data on stress as measured by time on the force supports the stages described in the literature. The results reflect a process of routinization officers go through as a way of coping with stress on the job which suggests that although they are currently coping with the stresses, the stresses are slowly taking a toll both on the physical side of the person as well as on the job, and can ultimately have serious negative consequences on both.

The pattern emerging from the life and work data shows that officers who have been on the force longer take their work less seriously and have learned to make their lives outside of work more important for them than those in the department a shorter time. Officers with greater time on the force reported a slightly higher life satisfaction and experienced lower work satisfaction than officers with less time on the force. Those with more time on the force tended to spend slightly fewer hours per week in physical conditioning and sports activities than did officers with less time on the force. Although the officers with greater time reported 13 of the 20 sources of stress in police work as less stressful than those with less time on the force, they were more stressed by such serious items as poor pay, poor equipment, poor career development opportunities, poor supervision, and adverse local government decisions. Of statistical significance as well as significance in interpreting the theory of stress, officers on the job longer reported that they were doing their best on the job less often than those with shorter time in the department. They also showed a higher tendency to leave the job if offered another one at the same pay.

CONCLUSION

The results of the study, then, are alarming. The amount of stress experienced by officers is significant, and even more significant when it is noted that the longer the officers stay on the job, the less work satisfaction they have. Although, as a way of compensation, they have learned to focus on their lives outside of work and have learned to protect themselves by not taking difficult issues involved in their work too seriously, they begin to take less physical care of themselves, give their best to their job less often, and begin to think more of leaving it. *

ENDNOTES

* This study was undertaken in October 1980 by Mimi H. Silbert, Ph.D., for the San Francisco Police Department in her capacity as its Training Consultant. The author thanks Research Assistants Ayala Pines, Carol Kizziah, and Karen Brown Davison for their assistance. The opinions expressed in this report are those of the researchers and do not necessarily reflect the points of view of the San Francisco Police Department.

Mimi Silbert, "Job Stree and Burnout of New Police Officers" is taken from *The Police Chief*, Vol. XLIX, No. 6, published by the International Association of Chiefs of Police. Reprinted by permission of the International Association of Chiefs of Police.

1. See, for example, Appley & Trumbull, 1967; Cox, 1978; Lazarus, 1976; McGrath, 1976; McLean, 1974.

2. See, for example, Ahearn, 1972; French, 1975; Kroes, 1976; Kroes & Hurrell, 1975; Kroes, Margolis, & Hurrell, 1975; Maslach & Jackson, 1979; Reiser, 1974, 1976.

3. Kroes, 1976.

4. Silbert (1980), in a report on male attitudes toward women on patrol in the San Francisco Police Department, found that policemen hold predominantly negative attitudes toward women on patrol.

CHAPTER 27
Misogyny, Law and The Police: Policing Violence Against Women

R. NEUGEBAUER

In the past few decades the phenomenon of wife assault has come under considerable public scrutiny. The Women's Movement brought to public awareness the fact that wife assault continues to be the most hidden crime. Furthermore, scholarly and community interests have focused on the inadequacies of the criminal justice system to protect women from their husbands' violence. Both misogyny and racism loom large within the legal system. This paper critically examines the police response to the victimization of women. In addition, the experience of women of colour is explored as the outcome of both racism and misogyny. The argument herein presented is premised on a feminist perspective which views wife assault and its attendant neglect by the police and the entire legal system as logical manifestations of a misogynist society.

HISTORICAL AND THEORETICAL OVERVIEW

A feminist perspective views wife assault as a consequence of inequality of power and status between men and women. This violence is a fundamental expression of the historical processes of misogyny which pervade all social institutions including the family. Moreover, misogyny and violence against women are legally legitimated through the legal system.

Dobash and Dobash 1979:43-45) maintain that wife assault is the manifestation of the patriarchal structure of the family and of society as a whole. Patriarchy is embedded in both structure and ideology. The structural aspect of patriarchy is evident in the hierarchical organization of social institutions and relations which relegate men to positions of power and privilege and women to subservience. This hierarchy in concert with the authority of those in power is dependent on collective acceptance, and is sustained and legitimated through ideology. In brief, the patriarchal ideology ensures the acceptance of dominance by men, and subservience by women. The patriarchal ideology legitimates inequality by making it appear moral, natural, sacred and just. The family, the educational system, social institutions, the law and even the media sustain such an ideology (Neugebauer, 1990). Socialization into an acceptance of this patriarchal order and its inherent inequalities permit such inequities to go virtually unchallenged.

Regrettably, the family is the cornerstone of a patriarchal society. Moreover, since its order is perceived as moral and its hierarchy seen as sacred, it has remained safe from outside scrutiny. This patriarchal order is demanded and thus reinforced by law, religion, and societal agencies and institutions. Under patriarchy, the rights of husbands to control, dominate, and even beat their wives are sustained. The status of women under patriarchy has been that of property of men (Beverley, 1992). Hence, historically men could legally do whatever they pleased with women. Since the Roman period husbands had the legal right to control their wives using whatever means of control they wished, including physical force. In turn, women had the legal responsibility to obey their husbands. Later, Judaeo-Christian law reinforced this patriarchal order. The biblical laws of marriage and the prescriptions of conjugal duties historically had stressed the inferiority and subjection of women to their husbands' authority and control. Religious scriptures provided a moral ideology that made the subjection of women appear natural and just.

During Medieval times the Jewish, Christian, and Muslim doctrines openly encouraged men to beat their wives. Husbands could kill their wives for adultery without threat of legal sanctions since husbands had complete authority over their wives. Likewise the Renaissance period provided men with the same rights. Even during the 18th and 19th centuries men were still given the legal right to beat their wives. It was not until the 20th century that wife assault was declared illegal throughout all of Europe and North America (Martin, 1976).

With legal reform appearing quite recently it is not surprising that our contemporary legal system condones wife assault. Hence, even though wife assault is illegal and thus a crime, the actual behaviour of law enforcement personnel condones and legitimates such behaviour. This phenomenon is directly linked to the perceived sanctity of marriage. Violence against women is also

linked to the marriage contract. Marriage was originally formulated as a property arrangement—an exchange of property whereby women were bought
and sold as property in exchange for goods. Even before marriage was formalized into legal contract, the practice of bride capture, the earliest form of
consummating a marriage was highly acclaimed. The act of bride capture or
rape staked a man's claim on a woman as his property.

In sum, marriage and the family have been given immunity from the
scrutiny of the criminal justice system. The distinction between public property and private property is central to the understanding of this phenomenon.
Since criminal law is concerned with maintaining public order, what a man
does on his own private property, to his private property (his wife) is beyond
the interest and intervention of the legal system.

The law perceives and treats women in the manner that advances the
interests of men. The law and the administration of justice reflect the interests
of men. Moreover, the state coercively and authoritatively sustains the existing
social order in the interests of men through its legitimizing norms and ideologies, and through its actions and policies. As such, violence against women is
merely an affirmation of the existing misogynist social order. The responses
of the criminal justice system further legitimate this social order (Neugebauer,
1987).

THE LEGAL AND POLICE RESPONSE TO WIFE ASSAULT

Although the common law concept of "spousal immunity" which prevents a wife from laying charges against her husband have been abolished,
notions of marital unity prevail in the response of the legal system to wife
assault. The law continues to recognize legal unity between a husband and a
wife with respect to certain rights, duties, and obligations arising from the marriage. Consequently, the actions of law enforcement personnel legitimate violence against wives. Male-dominated agents of the state—police, prosecution,
and judiciary—deny the existence, prevalence, and seriousness of wife assault.
Wife assault continues to be perceived as a private matter between a husband
and wife. The depth of the legal system's tolerance of wife assault is
expressed by the use of convenient labels such as "domestic disturbance,"
"domestic," and "family squabble."

While the response to assaults between non-family members usually results
in successful police intervention, the police response to wife assault has been
ineffective. Much criticism about police intervention has been made. Poor

police response is a consequence of their attitudes toward women and wife assault, and of police department policy directives.

Most police departments in Canada and the United States exercise a policy of non-arrest (Eisenberg and Micklow, 1977; Buzawa and Buzawa, 1985; Burris and Jaffe, 1983). As a result of these directives, police rarely make arrests and only do so in rare cases such as when there is a direct threat to their own authority and safety, use of a weapon, or critical injury (Buzawa and Buzawa, 1985; Berk and Loseke, 1981; Bell, 1984; Bell 1985a, b, c; Homant and Kennedy, 1982).

Like the police, prosecutors and judges express the conviction that wife assault is not a crime and that the courts should not intervene in "family problems." Prosecuting attorneys exercise considerable discretion in deciding whether to proceed with a criminal charge. Unfortunately, most criminal charges of wife assault are routinely dropped in exchange for promises of proper conduct or reconciliation. The prosecution and judiciary also dispose of cases by delaying the preliminary hearing for several weeks. These procedural delays are designed to subtly coerce the victim to voluntarily withdraw the complaint and reconcile with her spouse. To further complicate matters for the victim, prosecution is difficult due to the fact that often there are no witnesses present. Children are rarely required to testify, and extended family members who are aware of and who have even witnessed assaults refuse to come forward to assist in the protection of the victim.

Furthermore, judges routinely dismiss cases of wife assault. The attitudes and actions of judges toward violence against women and victims of wife assault are important in influencing the behaviour of police officers and prosecutors since they typically do not follow through with sentencing, and their opinions are held in highest regard. Hence, the perceptions and actions of police officers have been enforced and encouraged by the judiciary.

The weak arrest and sentencing practices that keep women powerless prisoners of their violent spouses can be understood in the context of the laws affecting the family. The arrest and prosecution of violent offenders is a powerful societal tool for dealing with wife assault. A strict enforcement of the law may deter wife beaters. When violent offenders are not punished for their crimes, society validates their behaviour. The failure to arrest and prosecute wife beaters presents the impression that the justice system and thus, by implication, society views such behaviour as legitimate.

RESEARCH FINDINGS

This research explores the police response to wife assault. The data are based on research findings of a report conducted in 1991 (Neugebauer, 1991). The research is based on in-depth interviews with 40 battered women and 12 shelter workers in Ontario.

According to both shelter workers and battered women, the police response to violence against women is ineffective. Shelter workers maintain that police departments discourage police officers from making arrests even when a policy directive was in place to do so. Consequently, police officers were reluctant to press charges. Police intervention typically resulted in more conciliation and mediation. Police officers typically attempted to discourage women from pressing charges.

As reorted by shelter workers and wives, police officers believe that it is legitimate for men to beat their wives and blame the victim for provoking the attack. Moreover, police officers tend to openly side with the assailants in the abuse of their wives. In fact, the interaction between assailants and police officers has been described as instances of male bonding. Likewise, a common report of victims was the tendency of police officers to interact primarily with the offender, a finding also noted by Homant and Kennedy (1982). Police officers tended to speak to offenders privately, while talking to victims in the presence of the victimizer. The following comments typify such a phenomenon:

> ".....He (the police officer) sympathetically invited him for a friendly drive in the cruiser, while I stood there bruised and crying..." (Cynthia, age 35).

> "The officer took him politely into the other room patting him on the shoulder as if I had done something wrong....he harshly asked me in front of my husband what the problem was...Couldn't he see my bruises for himself..." (Stephanie, age 28).

Respondents indicated that police rarely made an arrest, and only did so in the presence of severe wounds, or when the offender directly threatened the officer. Victims of wife assault prefer police officers to act like law enforcement officers and make arrests as they would if the assault had been between strangers. Doing so would also remove the fear of retaliation from the victim as dealing with the offence would be the responsibility of the police and the legal system. Women also believe that husbands would actually be less likely to beat them again if police would lay charges. A most distressing factor reported by shelter workers and victims alike, was the treatment and definition of victimization as a "family problem" and not as a crime. Repeated attempts by police officers to encourage the woman to "kiss and make up," "to forgive and forget," and reminders of "sacred" marriage vows such as "till death do we part" were cited by most women. Moreover, additional pleas regarding family unity, and staying together for the sake of the children were reported:

> "the police officer said that if I leave my husband the children will suffer" (Zanina, age 30).

> "They asked why I would consider ruining my child's life over a silly argument" (Maria, age 32).

Many victims and shelter workers complained that police officers used sexist terminology in reference to their situation. Terms like "bitch" and "whore" were noted by most women. Moreover, questions and insinuations regarding their provocation of violence were particularly unnerving. One woman noted, following repeated episodes of violence:

> "They asked what I did to make my husband do this to me, and suggested that I was probably withdrawing sex from my husband..." (Ruth, age 45).

Women also noted disbelief among police officers that their husbands actually beat them. Both shelter workers and victims reported comments and questions such as "Did he really beat you?", "I don't see any open wounds," and "Just take a tranquillizer and you'll feel better in the morning."

Overall, the police response to the violence reinforced a woman's decision to remain in a violent relationship. Moreover, much recidivism and cumulatively more serious assaults were noted. Often the same police officers would return to the home following another assault, yet shockingly, would do little to prevent further violence.

Shelter workers noted that police officers claimed that "they cannot lay charges," that they don't want to because "it would involve too much work," or that " women will eventually drop the charges." Shelter workers also reported that in the rare cases that charges were laid it was due to a personal interest, or because the damage was so severe that it could not be ignored. They also noted that the presence of a female officer paired with a male officer did not make a difference in the treatment that women receive, and in fact female officers tended to defer to their male counterparts:

> "Women police officers with male partners don't act much different-
> ly.... The male officers do most of the talking, while the female offi-
> cers just stood there" (Rabia, shelter worker, age 26).

> "Most female officers subordinate themselves to their male part-
> ners...they usually hesitate to say or do anything contrary to them"
> (Lily, shelter worker, age 40).

In contrast however, there appears to be a notable difference in response to
violence against women when female officers are alone or are paired with
another female officer. Respondents maintained that female officers were
quite sympathetic and supportive of the plight of battered women and were
more likely to follow suit with an arrest. A few sympathetic and supportive
male officers were reported. These officers appeared to be positively moved
by the small size of the woman, but at the same time experienced discomfort
by their sympathy for the woman:

> "The police who care are unusual but seem embarrassed to care and
> are not thought of too highly by their fellow officers" (Bonnie, shel-
> ter worker, age 33).

WOMEN OF COLOUR: DOUBLE INJUSTICE

In addition to misogynist attitudes, in the case of assaulted women of
colour or immigrant women, police reinforce racist attitudes. Class, race, and
language barriers accentuate the problems experienced by some battered
women.

Immigrant women are in especially critical situations. Often police from
their own background would respond to the call as "culturally sensitive" inter-
preters/mediators. The attempt to provide assistance would typically backfire
on the woman as these officers supported the husband whose version of the
events would contradict that of the victim. Immigrant women were also more
vulnerable due to threats of deportation by their husbands —of themselves and
their children. Husbands reportedly threatened not to sponsor the children if
they were still in another country. Regrettably, wives are unaware of their own
immigration status.

Furthermore, officers who share the culture of the respondents seem to
engage in greater male bonding given their shared gender and cultural background. This was especially true if the husband was a police officer in another
country. Similarity of background usually did little to assist the woman, and in

fact did more harm than good. Several women commented on being asked to uncover their clothing to display their wounds, but when they did so they were chastised by the officer since showing skin within certain cultures was forbidden.

In situations where white officers were called to the homes of non-white victims explicit forms of racism prevailed. Both racist and misogynist terms were used against the women. For example, racial slurs such as "turbans," "spooks," "nigger," and "blackie" were used. One shelter worker summed it up as follows:

> "They (the police) use racial slurs not even realizing that they are racial slurs.... Slurs within the police force have become normalized" (Bonnie, shelter worker, age 33).

An interesting phenomenon was also reported among women of colour—the tendency of white officers to beat up their husbands. As one woman stated:

> "We would like police officers to arrest our husbands, not necessarily kill them" (Sally, age 28).

DISCUSSION

Misogyny and racism which pervade all social institutions including the family are sustained by the legal system. Moreover, because the family has been treated as a special case, immune from judgment by law enforcement agencies, wives are not protected by the law as ordinary citizens are. Moreover, the neglect of the legal system of violence against women and women of colour is a reflection of the larger male-dominated, racist society of which it is a part. The administration of justice in violence against women reflects the interest of men who are more powerful than women, and who are after all the law makers, the judges, the prosecutors, the police officers and the offenders. Misogyny is reflected in the immunity of wife beaters from the law. By refraining from arresting wife beaters, the police legitimate violence against women.

Furthermore, the failure of police to deal adequately with wife assault is due in part to their discretionary powers, and that of other criminal justice agencies. Due to such discretionary powers, the legal system has exercised a selective enforcement of the law.

Laws governing assaults against women have been under enforced. This under enforcement of the law renders women vulnerable and at risk to further assaults, some of which have been fatal. Part of the solution to this problem would be for police departments to adopt strict policies and practices of mandatory arrest in wife assault cases. However, the implementation of these policies and practices requires strict legislative directives from the government, as it appears that simple policy changes have left too much room for discretionary action. Simply changing police behaviour is not sufficient without prosecution and judicial behaviourial changes. Strict legislation emphasizing the prosecution of wife beaters must also be developed.

Moreover, the trend toward the use of domestic crisis intervention programs with their emphasis on mediation and referral reflects the archaic tradition of treating violence against wives as a private family matter as opposed to serious criminal activity. Such "solutions" merely reflect patriarchal views of women as property of men and legitimate such behaviour. The failure of domestic crisis intervention teams to end recidivism is a testimony to this fact. Hence, one viable solution to repeated violence against women lies in legislative changes. Since it is the legal system which sets standards of behaviour, it is the legal system which must reflect an intolerance of violence against women.

However, the ultimate solution to violence against women involves changes in societal attitudes toward and treatment of women. For it is profeminist attitudes which must ultimately direct such legislative changes. Wife assault reflects the devaluation of women as human beings. It reflects the historical treatment of women as the property of men. Yet, a legal system which does not recognize the seriousness of the act only serves to legitimate the authority of men to subordinate women through assault.

The primary solution to wife assault also involves remedying structural inequalities that keep women prisoners of their violent husbands—it lies in the empowerment of women. Many abused women remain in their marriage because they see no alternative to their present means of subsistence. Women in our society are socialized to be dependent—financially and psychologically—on men for survival. The task of a liberal democratic society should be to socialize women to be financially independent and self-directing. But, it should also provide them with the opportunities necessary for independence. Abused women would be less likely to remain in violent situations if they had viable alternatives outside of marriage. Most importantly, the presence of supportive extended families would lend further protection to women in violent relationships. A harshly negative reaction to wife assault and to assailants on the part of the family—the cornerstone of patriarchal societies—would act as a significant agent of social control.

CONCLUSION: SETTING THE STAGE
FOR FURTHER DEVELOPMENTS

A central theme of this paper is that the policing of wife assault warrants careful scrutiny. The "feminization" of wife assault relegates this social problem to a more trivial domain. Consciousness-raising is a major mechanism for social change that undoubtedly will have an impact on the more substantive legal concerns. The oppressive conditions and consequences of wife assault must firmly be addressed. The inappropriate response of police officers to assaulted women—the treatment of victims as criminals—for example the necessity of women leaving their homes while their husbands the offenders are allowed to remain in the home must be reversed.

A remedy that is currently being advanced by feminists and generally dismissed in law concerns the empowerment of women. Working closely with victims of assault and investigating the realities of a powerless predicament will serve to shatter myths that have been well propagated. Further research which validates and seriously acknowledges the complaints of victims will certainly inspire a moral, economic, and political commitment to supportive remedies. In the area of criminal law the practice of encouraging "stand in" may facilitate a genuine desire for legal change. In other words, women as victims ought to have the benefits of enlisting the support of organizations, research centres, and enlightened representatives to "stand in" for them during the criminal process. The wider mobilization of interests and expertise undoubtedly would render the trial process more just. Such an innovative practice is currently being advanced in Charter litigation cases. Traditional practices of dealing with the victim as an individualized casualty deplete of organizational resources enhances the vulnerability of women to unequal protection.

This paper which is grounded in the experiences of women seeks to generate further directions for resolving problems that have been readily glossed over by the practices of legal agents.

Sociology requires a vigilant approach in unravelling the seemingly complex contours of legal responses. The blending of sociologies of law, family, and women in an effort to yield meaningful inquiries about violence against women is a fertile ground for the subordination of women. This paper highlights the need for empowerment of women. This goal will gradually be accomplished with the consciousness of both women and men who are demonstrating a genuine commitment in removing the historically and structurally entrenched blinkers.

The law has been selected as a meaningful focus of inquiry primarily because it reflects prevailing social values which are both racist and misogynist. More importantly, law is the ultimate and legitimate recourse to which all are entitled by virtue of citizenry. Regrettably, this "enabling" mechanism has, according to the behaviour of its enforcers, remained inaccessible and laden with conflict. In conjunction with the research presented, this undertaking demonstrates that incremental progress to date has been dubious at best. A redirection in priorities which bridges the gap between rhetoric and practice is long overdue.

REFERENCES

Bell, D.J. 1984. "The Police Response to Domestic Violence: An Replication Study." *Police Studies,* 7: 136-144.

Bell, D.J. 1985a. "Domestic Violence: Victimization, Police Intervention, and Disposition," *Journal of Criminal Justice,* 13: 525-534.

Bell, D.J. 1985b. "The Police Response to Domestic Violence: A Multi-year Study." *Police Studies,* 8: 58-64.

Bell, D. J. 1985c. "A Multi-year Study of Ohio Urban, Suburban, and Rural Police Dispositions of Domestic Disputes." *Victimology,* 10(1-4): 301-310.

Berk, S.F. and D.R. Loseke. 1981. "Handling Family Violence: Situational Determinants of Police Arrest in Domestic Disturbances." *Law and Society Review,* 13(2): 317-346.

Beverley, R. 1992. "Where Are Our Sisters: Mobilizing a Feminist Revolution." Unpublished paper, panel discussion, University of Toronto, (June 16).

Burris, C.A. and P. Jaffe. 1983. "Wife Abuse as a Crime: The Impact of Police Laying Charges." *Canadian Journal of Criminology,* 25: 309-318.

Buzawa, E.S. and C. Buzawa. 1985. "Legislative Trends in the Criminal Justice Response to Domestic Violence." In Lincoln and M. Straus (eds.) *Crime and the Family.* Springfield: Charles C. Thomas, 134-147.

Dobash, R.E. and R.P. Dobash. 1979. "Love, Honour and Obey: Institutional Ideologies and the Struggle for Battered Women." *Contemporary Crisis,* 1: 403-415.

Eisenberg, S.E. and P.L. Micklow. 1977. "The Assaulted Wife: 'Catch 22' Revisited." *Women's Rights Law Reporter,* 3(3-4): 138-161.

Homant, R.J. and D.B. Kennedy. 1982. "Police Perceptions of Spouse Abuse: A Comparison of Male and Female Officers." *Journal of Criminal Justice,* 13: 29-47.

Martin, D. 1976. *Battered Wives.* San Francisco, C.A.: Glide.

Neugebauer, R. 1987. "Wife Assault: The Limitations of Legal Responses." Annual Conference of the American Society of Criminology, Montreal, November.

Neugebauer, R. 1990. "The Social Context of Wife Assault." Paper presented at Responding to Victims of Violence: A Cultural Perspective—A Two-day Training Workshop for Service Providers. Council on Race Relations and Policing, May 7-8.

Neugebauer, R. 1991. *Wife Assault, Sexism and Police Response.* Report. Equity Research and Management, Toronto.

CHAPTER 28
Some Important Challenges

ANDRÉ NORMANDEAU
BARRY LEIGHTON

There are some issues that will pose a particular challenge to police departments in the years to come. First there are Canada's aboriginal people. One key issue is whether they police themselves on the reserve or whether existing police services become more sensitive to their particular situation.

Canada is also experiencing changes in terms of its ethnic and racial composition. Police services will need to be more sensitive to different cultures and recruit more visible minorities to reflect Canada's changing population.

The international movement in victim rights has been under way for over a decade. Police personnel must exercise caution to avoid victimizing victims a second time when victims come forward about an offence. This form of secondary victimization, in which victims are often made to feel that they are blameworthy for the offence, has been particularly common with respect to victims of sexual assault and domestic violence.

The international drug traffic also poses numerous challenges. Society must decide whether the emphasis, in terms of prevention, should be on suppressing the traffic itself or on curtailing demand. Police services must be prepared to interact with other agencies both in Canada and abroad.

A final issue to be discussed in this chapter is the impact of the *Canadian Charter of Rights and Freedoms* on policing in Canada. Although police departments might view some of the provisions of the Charter as a hindrance to law enforcement, they can also view it as a challenge to successfully pursue their objectives while protecting the civil liberties of Canadians. Just as they see themselves, at least partly, as enforcers of the law, police officers and other personnel can see themselves as protectors of the Charter.

POLICING AND ABORIGINALS

The aboriginal population of Canada is comprised of four main groups: status Indians; non-status Indians; Metis; and Inuit. In the 1986 Census, 711,120 individuals reported some aboriginal ancestry including: 263,230 status Indians; 23,465 Inuit; and 415,030 other. Approximately two-thirds of the status Indians live on 2,200 reserves, organized into 604 Bands, with most reserves located in rural and isolated areas. While there are a number of rural Metis communities, most Metis and non-status Indians reside in semi-urban and urban areas.

One cannot speak of a single aboriginal community. The aboriginal people of Canada exhibit considerable diversity in terms of such matters as culture, spirituality, religion, custom, language, socio-economic and political development. At the same time, there are shared problems in such areas as poverty, unemployment, under employment, substance abuse, limited economic resources, under funded social services, and meagre recreational facilities.

It is apparent that the public's view of the treatment of aboriginals is changing. An Angus Reid poll conducted in October 1987 found that 51% of Canadians surveyed believed that aboriginal people were not treated fairly by the courts and justice system, while 39% disagreed, with some 10% undecided. A similar poll in February 1990, showed that 57% agreed that "native people in Canada are treated unfairly by our courts and justice system", with 29% disagreeing.

The report of the Nova Scotia Royal Commission on the Donald Marshall, Jr. prosecution (1990) stated that the criminal justice system failed Donald Marshall, Jr. in part at least because he was a native. Two other judicial inquiries have heard recently allegations of racism, discrimination and insensitivity:

a)   policing and the Blood Reserve (Alberta, 1990); and

b)   policing and the cases of J.J. Harper and H.B. Osborne (Manitoba, 1990).

These incidents have occurred in the context of a consistent pattern of over-representation of aboriginals in Canada's correctional institutions. Aboriginal people constitute approximately 3% of the total Canadian population. In 1987-88, 11% of the admissions to federal correctional facilities were self-identified as aboriginals. In the western jurisdiction, the percentage of aboriginal admissions to provincial correctional facilities range from a low of 19% in British Columbia to a high of 66% in Saskatchewan.

On the basis of current understanding of the broader issue, there would appear to be three types of problems relating to the administration of justice in general, and policing in particular; namely:

1) equity of treatment (i.e., the extent to which the component parts of the criminal justice system treat aboriginals justly and fairly in accordance with the fundamental principles underlying our criminal justice system);

2) equality of service (i.e., access to justice services, including policing by aboriginal communities, that corresponds to acceptable norms and standards);

3) over-representation (i.e., the disproportionate representation of aboriginals in the correctional system).

It is clear that improved policing services for aboriginals can, and should address the equity of treatment and the equality of service problems. Aboriginal people have a right to expect fair, just and impartial treatment, and the appropriate protection afforded by policing and law enforcement services. It is arguable whether improved policing services will significantly affect the overrepresentation problem, if this problem is primarily attributable to factors external to the criminal justice system such as poverty, unemployment and the health of the social/institutional support arrangements in aboriginal communities.

Having identified the key problems related to the administration of justice and aboriginal people, and situated policing within the context of these problems, it remains to discuss the implications of current pressures and governmental policies on the development of policing arrangements for aboriginal people over the next decade.

Essentially, there are two parts to the issue of policing arrangements for aboriginal people, the first relating to the off-reserve situation and the second relating to the on-reserve situation.

There are ten urban centres in Canada where the aboriginal population consists of 5,000+. In addition, there are a number of smaller urban centres where the aboriginal population, largely non-status Indians and Metis, account for a significant proportion of the local population. In this circumstance, the issues connected to policing for the aboriginal population are not dissimilar to other segments of the non-white population. Such initiatives as enhanced recruitment, cross-cultural training, and the development of consultative and advisory bodies show promise in providing a more effective policing service, one that is more accepted by and responsive to the aboriginal community.

The on-reserve Indian communities and other aboriginal communities that are entitled to pursue community self-government negotiations present a different range of issues and associated options. Programs to improve the policing services provided to Indian communities began in earnest in the early 1970's. Currently, under a variety of policing arrangements there are approximately some 700 Indian officers employed in a "policing" or "para-policing" role on Indian reserves. On a per capita basis, this represents a ratio of one officer per 370 persons on reserves. In certain respects, this ratio compares favourably with the national average of approximately 1 police officer per 488 persons. It is understood, however, that police workload on Indian reserves is appreciably higher than the national average.

There are a number of broad policy issues to be addressed concerning policing arrangements for Indian communities over the next decade including:

- the establishment of appropriate legislation;
- the management and control of policing; and
- funding arrangements.

Given the current thrust of governmental policy, the following optional policing arrangements will likely be made available to Indian communities over the next decade:

1) An Indian Government Administered Police Service

   This policing arrangement would see Indian governments having "local" government type responsibilities for administering the police service. The police service itself would likely be largely composed of Indian officers.

   This policing arrangement could be organized on a band, regional, or provincial/territorial basis and range in size from an individual officer to a moderate sized police service depending on the size of the Indian community and the nature of the self-government proposal.

2) An Indian Contingent Within an Existing Police Service

   a) Under this arrangement, Indian police officers would be employed within an existing police service (i.e., the RCMP, OPP, QPP or a municipal police service where they are adjacent to the reserve) with dedicated responsibilities to police Indian communities.

This arrangement would likely see Indian governments having somewhat less than local government type responsibilities for administering the police service, although Indian input could be provided through the establishment of advisory/consultative bodies under appropriate terms of reference.

b) In certain circumstances (i.e., larger reserves or in an arrangement incorporating several small reserves) contractual arrangements, similar to those entered into by some municipalities for the RCMP or OPP could be made available. Such a contractual arrangement could be cast as a "developmental policing arrangement" which could evolve over time into an Indian government administered police service once the appropriate level of expertise and experience has been acquired.

3) Development Policing Arrangement

Under this arrangement, the responsibility for the administration of the policing service would move over time from joint (i.e., Indian and non-Indian) administration to an Indian government administered police service.

Similarly the composition of the police service would move over time to a body of Indian police officers.

4) Enhancement of Non-Indian Policing Services

The arrangements outlined above would not be practical for many of the smaller communities. In such cases, enhanced policing arrangements could be provided through the establishment of police consultative/advisory bodies, and arrangements provided in agreements to enforce laws enacted under self-government.

These developments will require policy decisions related to a range of service delivery issues including:

- mechanisms to ensure police accountability and independence;
- cost shared arrangements and mechanisms of financial accountability;
- accessibility to optional policing arrangements that take into account matters relating to police effectiveness and efficiency;
- quality and level of service matters;
- role and jurisdiction of Indian police officers;
- mechanisms of cooperation and support;

- employment equity and affirmation action programs; and
- implementation considerations.

If community policing is to become the basic police philosophy for the end of this century, policing for Aboriginals is surely moving ahead in this perspective and context.

POLICING AND MULTICULTURALISM

DOES A MULTICULTURAL AND MULTIRACIAL CANADA WARRANT SPECIAL INITIATIVES IN POLICING?

Canadian society is rapidly becoming more racially, culturally and religiously diverse. How will Canadians perceive and react to this increased diversity?

A recent Environics poll concluded that 17% of Canadians were bigots—a disturbing snapshot. Even more disturbing was another finding from the same poll stating that about half the population was becoming increasingly concerned about the growing number of visible minority Canadians in this country. The implication was that a very large number of Canadians were uncomfortable, or even distressed, with the prospect that the population of Canada was changing in a way that they did not like.

Surprise is often the emotion used to describe our reaction to this seemingly intolerant reaction of our fellow citizens. Should we be surprised?... probably not. We should be disturbed and concerned and perhaps appalled. The controversy that raged over changes to the RCMP uniform demonstrated quite clearly the feelings of many Canadians toward changes associated with full acceptance of a multicultural and multiracial society. The 1989 Annual Report of the Canadian Human Rights Commission stated that, "...the demons of racist and cultural prejudice have never been either officially or unofficially exorcized from Canadian Society".

Recognition of Canada's officially espoused and truly diverse nature has been slow in coming and, as yet, has left many living outside large urban centres unaware. As recognition of our diversity grows, as it will, how will Canadians react and what will be the implications for policing as one of the most, if not the most, critically placed services to the public?

The Canadian Human Rights Commission, in its 1989 Annual Report, suggests that, within the next two decades, 20% of the populations in major Canadian cities will consist of non-white minorities. This reference is included in a section of the report entitled Opportunities for Racism. Logic would tell us that, if a certain percentage of the population are racial bigots, an increase in the number of visible minority Canadians will increase the opportunities for racism. How this intolerance will manifest itself is open to interpretation.

Interpreting the poll results cited above, one commentator suggested that there was little that could change the attitude of hard-core bigots, rather we could only hope to control their behaviour. More importantly, preventative action was recommended to keep the large population that is uncomfortable, but not yet bigoted, in their reaction to racial and cultural diversity, from becoming increasingly intolerant.

This has substantial implications for police, now and in the future, institutionally and individually; in the ways in which policing authorities deal with themselves and the public. Even with the most optimistic view, it is safe to say that police, individually and institutionally, will be called upon to deal with the obvious and subtle, external and internal manifestations of prejudicial behaviour.

It achieves little to speculate on how far behind or ahead of the general public police are in addressing these implications. A lot of isolated efforts at police training and recruitment have born fruit in the last several years. But the Marshall, Bellemare and Lewis reports, numerous other enquiries, conferences and consultations have shown clearly how much more needs to be done; and how much policing authorities can learn from each others' experience.

A multicultural and multiracial Canada requires special initiatives in policing, not because a current crisis has suddenly come upon us, but rather because, consciously or not, so little has been done in the past. To provide effective policing services to all Canadians, we need to redress the inadequacies so poignantly cited in referenced enquiry reports. We need to do well the things that we would need to do anyway, but ensure that we do them well within a multicultural context.

Effective policing in any society, including one that is multi-racial and multi-cultural must be receptive, responsive and representative of the community it serves. Receptive to learning more about the special nature and changing circumstances affecting the community, and by extension its police. Responsive to the individual and collective needs of the community. Representative of the community in terms of the people who provide the policing services and the broader societal values of equity and justice and fairness.

Community policing is, in effect, a preventative approach to policing that builds a relationship between the community and the police. It prepares them to anticipate and deal effectively with problems when they do arise. Better community-based policing contributes to increased interaction, understanding and tolerance—contributes to stronger relationships and to racial harmony.

Effective community liaison is not only something that you do, but something that you achieve on a day to day and continuing basis. The only way to achieve success is to have the right tools. The only way to determine the extent of achievement is to ask the community.

Most often cited as the essential tools are recruitment, training, internal discipline, public accountability, and, as an essential ingredient to all, institutional will. As with most social issues each of these elements comes with its own set of questions and concerns.

RECRUITMENT - IS REPRESENTATION IMPORTANT?

Representation of visible minority persons on Canadian police forces is much below levels of representation in the general population, especially in large urban settings. Experience tells us that recruitment of under-represented groups is difficult. It has also been stated there are no guarantees that visible minority personnel will be more effective in doing the job or substantially influencing institutional change.

One response to these challenges is that representation is important for equity reasons. Secondly, gradual success is being experienced in recruitment and more innovative programs are being developed to interest young people in policing before they make other career choices. Thirdly, an organizational philosophy that includes a will to change has to exist before substantial change can take place.

One fundamental way to initiate and sustain that change is to ensure that the police force genuinely reflects the interests and faces of the population it serves. It would seem difficult to provide effective policing services to, and draw recruits from, a community that cannot see its membership represented among the police. Representativeness can best be pursued, supported and sustained if it applies to all aspects of police organizations—officers, civilians, boards and commissions.

WILL EMPLOYMENT EQUITY LOWER STANDARDS, AFFECT MORALE, RECEIVE SUPPORT FROM POLICE ASSOCIATIONS, WORK BEST IF COMPULSORY?

The answers to the questions are:
No, probably, yes and hard to say are the short responses. Effective

employment equity programs would require all recruits to meet identified standards while removing systemic barriers to recruitment of qualified candidates from under-represented groups. Recent consultations have noted that there is a limited understanding of employment equity among police executives and commensurate levels of concern among police officers about perceived "reverse discrimination". Employment equity includes targets and goals for representation, not quotas.

The concept and implementation of employment equity programs will affect police morale and resist the support of some police associations and individual officers at least as long as it is misunderstood and misinterpreted. The sooner we support informed dialogue and understanding, the easier it will be to make progress under favourable conditions. Police officers need to understand that they will be affected, but not victimized by employment equity.

The efficacy and enforcement of compulsory employment equity is an item of hot debate. As with so many issues the relative support among individuals for the manner and speed with which objectives are achieved is largely proportionate to the perceived effect that said change will have upon their status. In other words, this is an issue that requires judgement, leadership and follow-up to ensure that real progress is made and accepted.

DOES CROSS CULTURAL TRAINING MAKE POLICE MORE EFFECTIVE?

There is widespread agreement that cross-cultural training of police is essential to enhance awareness, reduce frustration and improve the safety of police officers. All major enquiries into police-race relations have recommended the establishment and/or improvement of cross-cultural training and many police academies and organizations have introduced programs of one type or another.

The answer to the effectiveness question is probably as varied as the number of programs under way. An inventory and evaluation of cross cultural training is under development and should provide some insight into key components of effective training. Knowledge also is spreading about some of the basic methodology associated with creating awareness without reinforcing negative stereotypes.

The need to place cross-cultural training in the context of ongoing practical application supports the idea of including cross-cultural elements within all modules and levels of police training.

The demand from diverse sectors for current and effective training and recruitment tools and information has fostered cooperative action on the development of a Canadian Police-Race Relations Centre to be located at the

Canadian Police College in Ottawa. With adequate support, the Centre will offer a variety of services to key sectors to advance relations between police and ethno-cultural and visible minority groups.

How Can Progress Be Measured?

The effectiveness of combined training and recruitment efforts will be exemplified in the public conduct of police personnel. Externally, the true indicators of success will be community satisfaction, or lack thereof, as measured through official public complaints and less formal barometers of public opinion. To be an accurate reflection of public sentiment, complaint procedures must be impartial and easy to access.

Within police organizations, institutional commitment and progress will be measured by the achievement of recruitment and training objectives, the number of complaints received and satisfactorily resolved and the exercise of internal discipline. The most effective way to convey a corporate philosophy is leadership by example. The acceptable code of corporate conduct will be determined and maintained by the penalties applied to misconduct. Police executives and supervisors must not tolerate a corporate culture that ignores or even sanctions racially motivated intolerance or misconduct. If police organizations are truly reflective of the society in which they operate, most members will be persuaded with strong leadership to adapt and respond to the needs of a changing community. We may only be able to control the behaviour of others through the exercise of sufficient discipline when required.

Why Not Test and Select Recruits That Are Unbiased?

There is potential to improve selection techniques to screen out undesirable recruits. However selection means such as psychological testing should not be viewed as a panacea that will remove the need for one or all of cross-cultural training, internal discipline, effective community liaison and institutional change. Simply reducing the odds of hiring "bad attitudes" will not guarantee cultural sensitivity or effective police relations with all communities. Nor will it necessarily mitigate community reaction when a serious incident occurs.

For How Long Will Special Initiatives Be Required?

The question implies that the current emphasis on police-race relations is a passing phenomenon that will one day disappear and we will drop this issue and go back to "mainstream" policing. The point made, it could also imply that, with time, social change and sufficient effort, recruitment, cross cultural understanding and institutional change will lead to effective community-based policing in a multicultural Canada. What is now special will have become a regular part of providing good police services to all Canadians.

POLICING AND VICTIMS

THE VICTIM AND THE CRIMINAL JUSTICE SYSTEM

In response to calls from victim groups and advocates, a federal/provincial Task Force on Justice for Victims of Crime was established in 1981 to study the situation and to make recommendations to improve the criminal justice system's response to victims. As part of its response, the federal government, in 1984 and again in 1987, sought and obtained approval from Cabinet to continue its "victims' initiative". The initiative contained several key focuses including a social service component and a criminal justice component. Provincial governments have also responded through the formation of structures and agencies to address the needs of victims, and have established numerous programs and supported local initiatives. The federal and provincial governments are continuing to work closely to improve the criminal justice system response to the needs of victims.

Victimologists in the United States and Canada had been saying for some time that the victim was being twice victimized, once by the offender and again by the criminal justice system. This view was supported by the findings of the Task Force and by early research and demonstration studies to determine the needs experienced by victims of crime. These studies were conducted early in the initiative by the Ministry of the Solicitor General as part of their efforts to understand better the plight of victims and to contribute to a more sensitive criminal justice system.

THE CHANGING ROLE OF THE POLICE

The studies also showed clearly that the police had a very important role in addressing several key needs of victims. The police are, in fact, at the forefront of the criminal justice system's response to crime. We have come to expect them to prevent crime in our society, to uphold the law, to protect us as individuals from crime, and to remove the perpetrators from our midst. At the scene of a crime, the police are, more often than not, the first sign of authority, having been called there by the victims themselves or perhaps by a witness to the event. They are often the first of society's agencies to deal with the victim and are increasingly being expected to provide them with primary services.

Until the reintroduction and general acceptance of community policing, the police were not comfortable with and were generally ill prepared to deal with their recently defined responsibility to victims, preferring to see themselves as "law enforcement officers" and as members of a police "force" as opposed to a police "service". There have, however, been remarkable changes over the last several years. A recent survey of police services revealed, for example, that well over 50% provided specialized services to victims of crime, virtually all police personnel now receive sensitization training to make them aware of the unique circumstances of crime victims and many receive specialized training in the provision of services. Indeed, several of the larger police services in Canada have created specialized units to address the needs of specific victims as, for example, victims of spousal assault. Increasingly, protocols are being developed to assist police in providing the most appropriate services to victims.

The acceptance of the additional responsibilities police are being asked to shoulder is clearly exemplified by the recent passing, in Ontario, of the *Police Services Act* to replace the *Police Act*. This Bill stresses the value of police *service* and embodies the declaration of "respect and sensitivity for victims of crime".

It has been suggested that the police are in a unique position to provide victims with the primary services they require. As mentioned above, the police are often the first authority figures a victim sees after the incident. The nature of that first police-victim interaction is extremely important in determining how the victim will come to terms with the incident. It has been shown, for example, that very basic reactions experienced by victims of crime include those of abandonment, of fear, of isolation, of guilt, of a loss of self-worth. Appropriate intervention by the police goes a long way to minimizing these feelings and to showing the victim that society does care and that the criminal justice system will treat them with respect, with understanding, and with sensitivity.

The police are ideally suited to serve as an information and referral service at a time when the victim needs this most. While court based victim services provide invaluable assistance at a later stage in the criminal justice process, significant benefits to the victim can be realized at the time of entry into the system. This contribution by the police becomes even more significant when one considers that victims have needs the addressing of which require a multi-disciplinary approach.

A Focus on Priority Victims

Currently, there are three primary areas of victimization considered priority areas for criminal justice intervention. These are family violence, elder abuse and the abuse of children.

Family Violence

While it is widely accepted that, in order to reduce and ultimately prevent family violence, it is critical to change the underlying attitudes, values, behaviours and social structures that contribute to and perpetuate violent and abusive interpersonal relationships, it is also accepted that the police must play a key role in intervening, in protecting victims from further abuse, and in providing primary services to victims. That police are succeeding in their efforts to provide appropriate services to victims of spousal assault, a recent study in Toronto showed that victims were satisfied with the way in which the police handled the situation and with the overall demeanour of the police.

Abuse of Elderly People

The policing implications of elder abuse are also becoming increasingly recognized. Indeed, the RCMP launched, in 1989, a special initiative to address the problem through education programs and the provision of specialized services to elderly Canadians. A recent study indicated that social agencies and seniors believe that police can play a major role in alleviating seniors' biggest fear of being injured and dying alone. "But many seniors want something much less dramatic from police...a kind word, a nod of recognition, some respect, some kindness...a return to the old community beat cop...." Police are responding, though the study also stresses that there is still a debate on the most appropriate methods of addressing the needs of elderly victims of crime.

Youth at Risk

Recent studies in the area of missing children in Canada showed clearly that a major problem facing police is the preponderance of young Canadians running away from home and ending up on the streets. These children are often running away from family violence and physical or sexual abuse and are in danger of being further victimized by criminal elements to which they will be exposed on the street. Returning some of these children to the homes or institutions from which they have fled is perhaps the worst action that can be taken. How to deal appropriately with these young victims, how to salvage the rest of their lives is an increasingly important question facing police services.

THE FUTURE

The trend toward accepting their role in dealing with victims of crime, toward accepting the need to work with social and non-governmental agencies, toward accepting their increasingly relevant role as agents of social change is one that must continue if police services are to fulfil their responsibilities and to contribute to improving the situation for unfortunate victims of criminal activity. Some of the more readily defined directions for the future can be outlined in terms of the envisioned policing response to family violence. The term "family violence" is used in this context to encompass a variety of criminal and antisocial behaviour, including spousal abuse, physical and sexual abuse of children, and the abuse, neglect and exploitation of elderly people.

PUBLIC AWARENESS AND EDUCATION

Making Canadians aware of the extent, nature, causes and consequences of family violence is an important first step to the long-term prevention of the problem.

In keeping with the philosophy and practice of community-based policing, the police today play a central role in crime prevention and the promotion of community awareness and action to combat crime problems at the local level. As such, the police have a unique opportunity and responsibility to undertake and to participate in activities designed to educate and thereby increase public awareness about family violence and the related issues of elder abuse, children/youth at risk, such as child sexual abuse, parental and stranger abductions, runaways, and street youth.

Linguistic and cultural differences, inaccurate perceptions and other access issues discourage and prevent individual victims and communities from deriving full benefit from programs to prevent family violence and assist victims. People living in rural and remote areas of Canada have relatively limited resources to address the problem and police personnel represent a comparably accessible reservoir of expertise and a catalyst for coordinated community approaches.

EDUCATION AND TRAINING OF PROFESSIONALS AND VOLUNTEERS

There has been a strong need expressed by both governmental and non-governmental sectors for increased and ongoing education and training to better prepare front-line workers, including criminal justice personnel, to deal with family violence situations.

Enhanced police awareness, understanding and sensitivity to the dynamics of family violence will provide police officers with the knowledge and skills necessary for effective protection and intervention approaches to victims, offenders and families experiencing domestic violence. Improved understanding and sensitivity of police is particularly important when investigating and intervening in cases of violence and abuse where ethno-cultural or disability factors are present.

Similarly, education and training opportunities for correctional staff working with offenders in institutional settings as well as those responsible for the release and management of offenders within the community is seen as a priority. This is particularly important given the finding that offenders are often victims as well as perpetrators of family violence.

INFORMATION COLLECTION, DISSEMINATION AND EXCHANGE

At the present time, policy makers and front-line workers lack the comprehensive data on family violence needed to assess and improve the criminal justice and social service response to these crimes. It is essential that complete and accurate information on individual cases as well as overall trends and patterns in family violence be collected, analyzed and used as a basis for measuring the extent and nature of the problem and designing more effective prevention, protection, intervention and treatment strategies.

More complete utilization by criminal justice agencies of advanced technology and expert and automated systems will permit them to derive full benefit from current information systems and resources. Information exchange is also essential to ensure coordinated multi-disciplinary approaches to addressing the problem of family violence.

INTERVENTION AND TREATMENT

The research and programming emphasis has been on identifying and addressing the needs of Canada's urban population. While victims in urban and rural settings face very similar situations regarding their victimization, the service networks available to them are very different. In urban centres there often exist an array of social service, voluntary, and criminal justice agencies offering differing responses to the needs of victims. The major need in these situations is for an interdisciplinary approach well coordinated with the use of effective protocols.

Individuals living in rural and remote areas as well as socially isolated groups require programs and intervention models that are tailored to their specific needs. Conventional urban models are doomed to fail as they do not take into account the unique needs of these particular groups. In rural settings there are often very few services to which victims can be referred and the police often provide the primary, if not the only, services to victims of crime. The victims' expectations of the police are very different from those in urban centres, and the police role is expanded considerably. Policing, law enforcement and corrections strategies must take this into account.

With limited resources and limited access to social services in rural and remote communities, it means police personnel often represent a relatively accessible reservoir of help and expertise. Enhancing the ability of small town and rural police forces to effectively intervene in domestic violence situations will not only improve policing services to these populations but will also improve the overall response to family violence in these communities.

RESEARCH, EVALUATION AND STATISTICS

A strong knowledge base, founded on sound research, is needed to support and guide the development of new approaches to family violence. By continuing to conduct qualitative and quantitative studies and by critically evaluating our efforts and experiences in the area of prevention, protection, intervention and treatment, this information base will be strengthened.

The need to understand more fully and to document the effectiveness and implications of existing programs, services and policies regarding family violence is widely accepted. In order to continue to improve the response of the criminal justice system in general, and policing, law enforcement and corrections strategies in particular, it is critical to know what works, what does not work and exactly what should be changed.

THE CHARGING POLICY

The issue of the implementation of a charging policy regarding spousal assault demonstrates clearly one of the key avenues for the evolution of the policing role in regard to victims of crime. While there is little standardization in the implementation or application of charging policies in Canada, virtually all police agencies are encouraged to lay charges of assault in cases where there is reasonable and probable grounds that an assault took place. The police are, in other words, encouraged to remove this onus from the victim.

It is important to note that the charging policy, like many other such directives, is the result of decisions taken by policy makers and legislators who are not directly involved in police work. The decisions, however, have a tremendous impact on police work and on the evolving role of the police regarding victims. A challenge for police, legislators, and social service administrators is to collaborate in the development of such policies to ensure appropriate and coordinated strategies that capitalize on the strong contributions to be made by each of the agencies involved in addressing the needs of victims of crime in Canada.

POLICING AND DRUGS

INTRODUCTION

Traditionally, the police and the public have shared a common unrealistic expectation that with sufficient enforcement resources illicit drug supplies can be eradicated and hence the drug problems solved. Canadian society may gradually be moving away from this simplistic notion of the capabilities of law enforcement. 'Supply reduction' initiatives alone *will not* eliminate drug abuse. Supply reduction enforcement strategies to control drugs are marginal activities that can have only a limited impact on this illicit activity and even less impact on the drug using behaviour of the population.

Over the years, resources made available to the RCMP, provincial and municipal police forces, Customs, and other law enforcement agencies have been used to attempt to stop the supply of drugs from reaching the public— either by stopping it at the border or through street level enforcement to catch distributors. While large seizures are frequently being made by the police, the drugs keep coming into the country. There is now a general recognition that as long as a market exists for drugs, drugs will continue to arrive in sufficient amounts to be accessible to even the naive school child. Drug law enforcement in Canada has not succeeded in making drugs harder to obtain, nor in raising the prices or lowering the purity—all indications that the policing strategies that aim at "elimination" of the drug problem are not having a direct impact. The street price of drugs is actually decreasing and the purity is increasing.

POLICING AND THE NATIONAL DRUG STRATEGY

In May 1987 the National Drug Strategy (NDS) was launched in Canada and allocated a total of $210 million, over five years, to the drug abuse problem. Of these funds, 30% were allocated to law enforcement and interdiction initiatives with the larger percentage (70%) aimed at 'demand reduction' activities including drug awareness, prevention, treatment, and research. These figures are in direct contrast to the U.S. drug strategy that allocated 70% of the funds to enforcement and 30% to demand reduction initiatives.

The Drug Strategy adopted two main philosophies. First, a balance ought to be maintained between supply reduction initiatives and demand reduction initiatives. Prior to the National Drug Strategy a disproportionate amount of resources had been allocated to the enforcement side of drug abuse. Second, combatting drug abuse necessitates a wide range of 'partnerships' among diverse organizations, levels of government, community organizations and the police, who must work together.

A focus on demand reduction initiatives implies different "players" than a more strictly law enforcement approach would include. A successful strategy must incorporate the efforts of all organizations and individuals who are interested in working together to combat the drug abuse problem. The strategy therefore speaks of "partnerships".

In some cases these partnerships had not existed before. For example, it has been essential for the RCMP, and provincial and municipal police officers to work closely with the provincial addictions agencies across Canada and also with National Health and Welfare. The credibility and expertise of the police makes them valued participants in the coordinated effort against drug abuse. However, few officials at Health and Welfare had considered there to be an important role for the police in the area of drug prevention and working with the police community was for these health professionals largely a new experience. Through a gradual process of interactions on both sides, these new partners are more trusting of each other's expertise.

In addition to the need to recognize the *new* partners, there was the additional need to encourage former partners to work in a more truly collaborative manner. For example, various police forces must work together on specific cases but in the area of drug prevention and enforcement more is required. For an effective strategy, the police were asked to share their prevention resources and expertise in the development of additional materials. Likewise, federal government departments such as the Department of the Solicitor General, Customs, Justice, and National Health and Welfare, had worked together on numerous initiatives in the past, but the National Drug Strategy involves continued, more structured interaction.

Specific aspects of drug abuse fall under the mandates of diverse departments. Hence, in some situations, more than one department saw itself as having main responsibility. Even where the key players were clear, the involvement of "new" players into an area, traditionally the domain of one specific department, created debate and occasionally disagreement. It became clear that the issue of drug abuse is no less susceptible to problems of jurisdiction than any other area of joint endeavour. It is important to manage this potential for disunity in trying to attain cooperation and coordination of effort. This was an important issue for the original National Drug Strategy to recognize and is a continuing essential aspect of the involvement of the police in this field.

DRUG DEMAND REDUCTION POLICING

The strategy therefore places an emphasis on the ability of the police to participate on the 'demand reduction' side of the strategy in addition to their more traditional enforcement role. To some extent this new role merely emphasizes the integration of community-based policing strategies into the larger approach to drug reduction in Canada. Working in communities, with community members, for community initiated objectives is a recognized essential aspect of Canadian police work. Drug awareness/prevention work illustrates this community-based approach.

School administrators, principals and teachers have been inviting the police into the schools to talk on a range of topics from road safety, fire safety, to crime prevention. Now, across Canada, at the invitation of the schools, police departments in most areas have a special unit of officers who assume as one of their main responsibilities the task of giving presentations to youth.

While the RCMP, municipal and provincial police forces had been active in responding to requests for drug prevention presentations from schools, parent groups, work places and community organizations, little coordination of effort had been applied to the activities. While no one would maintain that the police should be primarily educators, what is recognized is that the police have both *credibility and experience* that can be used as a major strength against drug abuse. Coupled with this "new" role for the police is the fact that policy-makers, educators and parents have come to view the schools as the site providing the greatest potential for children's health education intervention.

In working with the Canadian Association of Chiefs of Police, municipal, provincial police forces and the RCMP, Solicitor General officials determined that what was needed was not necessarily more school presentations, because some of the police forces were already responding to as many invitations from the schools as man-power would allow. Rather, the police asked for more guidelines as to what kind of messages ought to be given, and requested that more resources be made available to assist in the teaching effort.

Educators have emphasized that merely "informing" children/youth about potential health problems is not enough. Ways have to be found to mould or change attitudes. The greatest barrier of all is seen to be negative peer pressure. The police messages can therefore no longer simply be "don't take drugs because it is against the Law". Rather, the messages have to be much more sophisticated to encourage the youth to arrive at the decision that drugs just might not be the clever or "in thing"—even when friends attempt to encourage others to participate.

Officials had to turn to experts in these fields and to encourage the police to recognize the available specialists. In addition to addictions expertise, educational expertise was required. Therefore each "partner" had to bring to the prevention effort his/her own particular skills. The educators bringing their knowledge of how kids learn, the addictions experts bringing their knowledge of drug use and addictions, and the police bringing their credibility and street policing experience.

It was next essential to determine what were the actual needs of the police—what were the skills that the police already had, and what resources were required. To accomplish this a workshop was held with support from the Canadian Association of Chiefs of Police. Representatives from the provincial addictions agencies, school boards and the police community participated.

At this workshop it was decided that police needed an accredited drug prevention training program that would encourage a uniformity of *tone* of message in the schools across the country. It was recognized that many of the police jurisdictions had their own materials and would continue to use various programs but that the "tone" ought to be similar and compatible with the messages given by National Health and Welfare and school educators.

It was also felt that an accredited training program would serve symbolically to emphasize to the Police Chiefs the importance of drug prevention officers and the need for police management to recognize this expertise by choosing the best officers for this police responsibility and not use these positions as either rewards or as punishments within departments.

A committee was formed to work with the Canadian Police College officials to discuss the format of the course. The Commissioner of the RCMP intervened personally to ensure that this course would become a priority and after soliciting recommendations from across Canada, a pilot course was offered in January 1989. Over 60 police forces representing municipal, provincial and federal policing, have participated in this Drug Abuse Prevention Training Officers' Course.

In addition to this training course, the police perceived a need for assistance with the actual material that was to be presented to youth in schools. With the assistance of the Addiction Research Foundation in Ontario, a booklet of lesson plans titled "Kids and Cops", was made available for presentation by the police to grade six students. Over 20,000 copies of this booklet of lesson plans has now been distributed in English and French and has been seen to be useful to the police.

Likewise, the Federal government assisted the Nova Scotia Commission on Drug Dependency to produce lesson plans, titled "Police Assisting Community Education" (PACE), for the police to use in presentations aimed at grades 5, 6, 7, 8, and 9. A training component specific to PACE is an essential aspect of this program and courses have been offered in French and in English at the Canadian Police College and regionally across Canada.

The Canadian Association of Chiefs of Police proposed that a video be produced to serve as an additional resource for the police. The federal government funded the production and distribution of a video titled "Choose". Together with two additional videos, "Choose" was made available to all police forces for use in classrooms.

Therefore the "package" intended to enhance the ability of the police to work as drug prevention officers now includes an accredited drug prevention training course, lesson plans, videos, and any additional resources available within each jurisdiction.

During this same period the RCMP have expanded their drug awareness program and have been extremely active with:

- community-based initiatives in each of the divisions across Canada and drug prevention activities specific to native communities and workplace prevention;

- drug displays in malls and at special events; telephone video disc display with messages from role models for youth;

- high profile personalities involved in speaking against drugs i.e., Olympic swimmer Carolyn Waldo, international fashion model Monica Schnarre, National Hockey League stars together on a "Be Yourself.." poster;

- publications including:
  - *Is Your Child a Drug User*
  - *Drugs in the Workplace*
  - Pride/RCMP *Manual for Parents*
  - "Selected Reference Notes for Drug Awareness Officers"
  - *Five Facts About Drugs*

While these activities must all continue, there is a need now to focus on the "harder to reach" youth who are not necessarily in schools, or who do not have either French or English as a first language. Posters, radio and television public service announcements and publications have been produced by the RCMP in Inuit, various native dialects, Spanish, Swedish and Finnish.

Initiatives are now being developed to target other groups plus the more "at risk" youth that police may have additional problems in relating to. Focus groups are taking place across Canada to pull together community members representing a wide range of communities including the Chinese, Vietnamese, Italian, Asian, Spanish, South American and black communities. The aim is to use these meetings to identify resource needs to assist the police to work more effectively with each of these communities for drug awareness and prevention rather than enforcement.

SUPPLY REDUCTION POLICING

Supply reduction initiatives were not ignored in the National Strategy but did not dominate. Drug law enforcement has traditionally epitomized the notion of street warfare rather than street interaction and 'buy and bust' policing strategies were as sophisticated as many of the operations became. The National Drug Strategy emphasized the need to target the upper-echelon of the drug trafficking hierarchy in addition to the lower level street busts.

"Taking the Profit from Crime" and controlling money laundering have become a national, as well as an international, law enforcement focus. Canada's *Proceeds of Crime* legislation, drafted as part of the drug strategy, was proclaimed in January 1989. The 'Proceeds of Crime' approach recognizes that street enforcement tends to target the lower levels of drug trafficking organizations and arrests made at this level do not harm the larger organization. The philosophy has become to take the profits away from the criminal enterprise and in that way put the entire operation, rather than specific individuals, out of business.

These complex financial investigations are usually extremely resource intensive and require a commitment by police management over a long time and sufficient financial resources to see the investigations through to a conclusion. However, increasing policing resources may have an impact on other functions. The criminal justice system must be viewed as a "linked" process in that increases in resources to one segment of the process will put strain on other stages. For example, increasing police investigators may be counterproductive without adequate street level traditional drug enforcement officers to provide information 'up' to the investigators. Likewise, increasing police resources will necessitate an increase in prosecutors. In order to secure the necessary authorizations the police are having to work closely with the Crown council very early in these investigations rather than bringing them in at the end when they are ready to contemplate charges.

Just as demand-reduction policing involved a new range of partners or a different working relationship between the police and other agencies, likewise proceeds of crime investigations must involve a greater appreciation of diverse expertise. Hence, creating a distinct, elitist unit to handle these upper-echelon investigations must not be allowed to cause a split within police departments and between the police and the communities with a resulting barrier to the flow of information between street officers and the financial investigating officers. "Partners" must include forensic accountants, national or international computerized informational systems, intelligence analysts, and the police officers involved in diverse policing strategies who can contribute information to feed into these 'proceeds' investigations.

The argument behind a focus on the proceeds of crime or the upper echelon criminals is based on a sound theory. However, it must not ignore the realities of police work—police reliance on street information, use of informants, knowledge of the community and the need for frequent interaction with the institutions who are being used by launderers or directly by enterprise criminals to legitimize the illicit proceeds. Therefore even this form of policing must not be divorced from the communities which will provide the essential information from which to build police cases.

Therefore on both the demand and the supply reduction side of drug abuse reduction, few areas within the police mandate illustrate the pull towards community-based policing as clearly as the innovative strategies that are becoming a part of drug enforcement in Canada—while also illustrating some of the tensions found in departments that are realizing the impact that this shift may have on their departments. The assertion that enforcement strategies alone are not and can not work to eliminate drug abuse has been hard for some police departments to accept. However, the eventual acceptance of this fact has led to the valuable alternative policing strategies that may now be having some impact on the drug problem in Canada.

POLICING AND THE CHARTER

The future for police in terms of the measures that can be employed in investigating offences and gathering evidence to support prosecutions is unsettled, if not unsettling. Even more uncertain is the future for the measures required to detect or discover crime as opposed to detecting or discovering persons believed to have committed crimes which have been officially noticed. Where the yardstick for comparison are those practices, procedures and measures which are currently available, the future will provide the police either with less or perhaps worse, with powers coupled with so many restrictions and incidental complex duties and responsibilities that their utility may be neutralised.

Commonly referred to as 'police powers'—an unfortunate phrase which contributes inevitably to the tendency to reduce or confine them—these activities cover a wide range from the innocuous to the deadly. Over the course of the last 20 years most if not all of these measures have, in one way or another, been placed under official scrutiny. Change, of course, is the inevitable product of this scrutiny. There is no prospect that this intense scrutiny will cease. Perhaps this is as it should be. Nevertheless, if the question relates to what the police will be able to do in the future the answer lies in looking at what has happened in the past. We should expect more of the same.

The blue prints for these changes—past and future—can be easily found: the 1969 Ouimet Report (Canadian Committee on Corrections), working papers and reports of the Law Reform Commission of Canada (1970-1990) and most significantly, the enactment of the *Charter of Rights and Freedoms* (1982). Legislative reforms, judicial decisions and institutional responses have followed.

Very few discrete 'powers' have been outright abolished or eliminated. The one which would likely come to mind is the 'writ of assistance', the general warrant authorizing its holder to enter premises at will to search for drugs and other contraband. Abolished legislatively (and, strictly thereafter albeit symbolically, judicially), it was meant to be replaced, in part at least, by the 'telewarrant' procedure, designed to enable the issuing of a judicial warrant quickly by telephone or other means of communication.

In some respects what was done was a simple balancing of relevant interests with a view to achieving an equilibrium more in tune with today's climate. There is no question that the writ of assistance had the potential for abuse. Furthermore, should there be an abuse, there was no effective remedial procedure. On the other hand, adequate means were needed to cope with the situations that writs of assistance were being used to combat —rapidly developing and highly transient drug deals. Hence, an attempt was made to replace the objectional writ with an expeditious procedure to obtain a judicial warrant while maintaining the appropriate safeguards.

This has also been the approach of the courts when considering the validity of challenged police practices and procedures. As was stated in *R. v. Beare; R. v. Higgins*, [1988] 2 S.C.R 387 a recent Supreme Court of Canada decision challenging legislation permitting fingerprinting suspects prior to conviction "...these procedures have been permitted because of the felt need in the community to arm the police with adequate and reasonable powers for the investigation of crime". While the court rejected the challenge and validated the legislation, it went on to note that it did not "authorize their unconstitutional retention" referring to the rather common practice of retaining fingerprints of persons who ultimately were not convicted.

This is a good example of judicial legislation. Though the courts are more limited then the legislator in being able to mandate the manner in which policing activities are to be carried out, they do have the ability to control matters by providing views as to what may or may not be acceptable. Pre-Charter cases dealing with access to information used to obtain search warrants (*A.-G. N.S. v. MacIntyre,* [1982] 1 S.C.R 175) and search warrants directed at lawyers (*Descoteaux v. Mierzwinski and A.-G. Que.,* [1982] 1 S.C.R. 860) amply demonstrate this ability. Cases based on *Charter* issues are of course even more apt to be informed with judicial opinions as to how the police must conduct their business.

The field of electronic surveillance or the interception of private communications is ideally suited for perspectives on how the modern legislator and judge approach policing practices. Out of a legitimate concern for personal privacy and with an appreciation for the level of intrusiveness made possible by advances in technology, along with a due recognition of the difficulties needed in getting at secret crime or at sophisticated criminal enterprises, Parliament enacted a complex code to control and regulate the interception of private communications.

Both the legislative and judicial responses to this sensitive area illustrate the police predicament. The elaborate scheme enacted in 1973 as a result of recommendations made in the Ouimet Report made it possible for police to obtain authorizations to intercept private communications. While making it possible, it did not make it easy.

Applications had to be made through specially designated lawyers to senior judges in respect to a limited number of offences and only when conventional investigative methods were not of use. Authorizations were limited in a number of respects and subject to a variety of conditions. Strict record keeping was required and a variety of notifications and reports were mandated. The consequence of error, at least as regards to criminal investigations, was the inadmissibility of relevant evidence. As a consequence the focus of many criminal prosecutions involving electronic surveillance shifted from what the accused did to how the police conducted the investigation. This foreshadowed what has now become routine in many criminal trials involving the exercise of other police practices and procedures.

Notwithstanding the legislative attempt to balance matters, through carefully controlling the basis upon which the interception of private communications could be lawfully made, the scheme has not gone without criticism. The Law Reform Commission of Canada in its Working Paper 47 acknowledged this attempt to balance. It noted that "implicit in the legislation are the principles of restraint, respect for privacy, definition of the powers of the police and judicial review". Nevertheless, the paper went on to severely criticize the scheme, making over 75 recommendations for change.

Though a number of the recommendations were meant to facilitate and streamline matters, most were meant to tighten up procedures or further circumscribe the basis upon which interceptions should occur. The view of the Law Reform Commission (LRC) was that electronic eavesdropping was being used too frequently; then their proposals seemed to be to discourage further the use of this measure by making it more difficult to employ it. In this they may have succeeded: in 1985, the year preceding the paper, 603 federal authorizations were granted; in 1988, there were 303.

While there has been no legislative reaction, there has been significant judicial response. Two areas in particular have been radically, altered. The first relates to the abandonment of the secrecy requirement. The requirement to keep material filed on the application secret, by keeping it in a sealed packet in the custody of the court was initially interpreted to be needed to encourage full disclosure by police when making an application for an authorization. Charter based litigation on the right to make full answer and defence has effectively opened all packets with the consequence that the process of using intercepted evidence has been further complicated. Worse, the use of electronic surveillance has been discouraged in situations where the risk of disclosure of confidential sources and methods can not be taken.

The second area of judicial intervention is in the area of participant monitoring. Parliament consciously decided not to require an authorization for surreptitious recording of conversations where one of the parties consented. The Supreme Court of Canada thinks otherwise.

Recently, in *R v. Duarte* (1990) the Court found that it would be 'anomalous' to consider participant surveillance as 'reasonable' in the context of s. 8 of the *Charter*. This is because it "leaves to the sole discretion of the police all the conditions under which conversations are intercepted". This compares unfavourably to the stringent scheme for controlling interceptions generally, providing as it does "numerous safeguards designed to prevent the possibility that the police view recourse to electronic surveillance as a humdrum and routine administrative matter". The solution is to require obtaining an authorization. It is not an untypical judicial solution. The practice in question is not prohibited; instead it is confined through the judicially imposed procedures with a view to removing police discretion and ensuring that the police do not see the procedure as "a humdrum and routine matter".

The future of policing practices and procedures will also be shaped by a much greater emphasis on institutional rules. Standing orders and internal operating procedures will provide more detail then has hitherto been the case at least as regards to the intrusive and complex areas. Most Canadian police agencies have regulations controlling the use of deadly force which impose limits well within what is legally available. Those that do not, soon will. The same goes for closely related areas such as vehicle pursuit procedures.

In the short-term, clearly defined, sensible policies, will forestall legislative or judicial regulation. Particularly, if the policies are complemented with effective training programmes and adequate review and accountability mechanisms. Nevertheless, sooner or later desired police behaviour will be reflected in the law, whether it be through legislation or as a consequence of judicial decision. Perhaps the value of extensive internal rules will lie in their use in pointing the legislator or the judge to the sensible solution.

Indeed, a critical issue for the future will be the ability to convincingly justify the need for challenged practices. One should read the two Supreme Court cases mentioned above. Much more notice was taken of the policing side of the equation in the fingerprint case then in the participant surveillance case. The fact that the Canadian Association of Chiefs of Police intervened in the fingerprint case may have had some bearing. It may be the reason why the court seemed to have a better sense of the importance of the policing issues at play in that case. In any event, an avowed principle of the courts is that society wishes to arm the police with adequate and reasonable powers. There are claims being made regularly that current policing practices are excessive and unreasonable. It would seem that these claims have to be met head on with legally acceptable refutations.

It may be tempting to conclude that the future of policing powers looks somewhat bleak. This should be resisted in favour of a much more positive approach. In many ways what Canadian society is doing in this important area is not much different than what it is doing in many other critical areas.

Parliament and the Courts are responding to changing times and conditions and are attempting to come to grips with a variety of conflicting forces in a complex world.

Though it is unfortunate that in doing so, the traditional confidence that Canadians have had in their police has been put in issue and equally unfortunate that the arena for discussing the limits of the policing authority of the State is the criminal trial, the fact is that we are engaged in an exercise in re-striking the balance between the measures needed to effectively maintain the safety and security of all citizens and the acceptance by these same citizens of the consequential impairment on their basic liberties.

For the police community, cynicism and discouragement need not be the consequence. They are in a position to take a more active role in explaining why changes in challenged areas ought to be resisted. Furthermore they can also show leadership by demonstrating a readiness to contribute to finding acceptable alternatives to undesirable practices in order to ensure that any redefined balance is sensible.

In order to assist society in its responsibility to provide the police with the right tools to do the job, society must be accurately informed about the nature of the job. This is particularly important when measures that offend some sen-sibilities are needed. Eavesdropping, paying informers, using trickery and other 'unsporting' means, may be the only realistic approach to discovering particular types of criminal activity. Decision makers must realize the implica-tions of curtailing or circumscribing such measures.

Similarly, decision makers must be provided with the dollar cost and resource implications when consideration is being given to particular legislative solutions. Finally, the question of converting the criminal trial from a determi-nation of guilt or innocence of an accused person to a trial of the criminal jus-tice system must be squarely faced.

---

* A Normandeau and B. Leighton, "Some Important Challenges," is reprinted from *A Vision of the future of Policing in Canada: Policing Challenge 2000.* Reproduced with permission of the Minister of Supply and Services Canada, 1992 and the Solicitor General Canada.